797,885 Books
are available to read at

www.ForgottenBooks.com

Forgotten Books' App
Available for mobile, tablet & eReader

ISBN 978-1-330-22409-0
PIBN 10057030

This book is a reproduction of an important historical work. Forgotten Books uses state-of-the-art technology to digitally reconstruct the work, preserving the original format whilst repairing imperfections present in the aged copy. In rare cases, an imperfection in the original, such as a blemish or missing page, may be replicated in our edition. We do, however, repair the vast majority of imperfections successfully; any imperfections that remain are intentionally left to preserve the state of such historical works.

Forgotten Books is a registered trademark of FB &c Ltd.
Copyright © 2015 FB &c Ltd.
FB &c Ltd, Dalton House, 60 Windsor Avenue, London, SW19 2RR.
Company number 08720141. Registered in England and Wales.

For support please visit www.forgottenbooks.com

1 MONTH OF FREE READING

at
www.ForgottenBooks.com

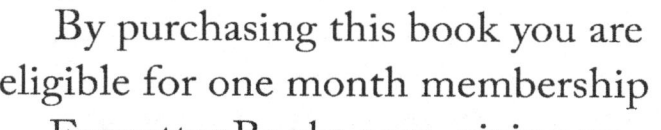

By purchasing this book you are eligible for one month membership to ForgottenBooks.com, giving you unlimited access to our entire collection of over 700,000 titles via our web site and mobile apps.

To claim your free month visit:
www.forgottenbooks.com/free57030

* Offer is valid for 45 days from date of purchase. Terms and conditions apply.

English
Français
Deutsche
Italiano
Español
Português

www.forgottenbooks.com

Mythology Photography **Fiction**
Fishing Christianity **Art** Cooking
Essays Buddhism Freemasonry
Medicine **Biology** Music **Ancient Egypt** Evolution Carpentry Physics
Dance Geology **Mathematics** Fitness
Shakespeare **Folklore** Yoga Marketing
Confidence Immortality Biographies
Poetry **Psychology** Witchcraft
Electronics Chemistry History **Law**
Accounting **Philosophy** Anthropology
Alchemy Drama Quantum Mechanics
Atheism Sexual Health **Ancient History**
Entrepreneurship Languages Sport
Paleontology Needlework Islam
Metaphysics Investment Archaeology
Parenting Statistics Criminology
Motivational

HISTORY OF PAGANISM IN CALEDONIA,

WITH AN

EXAMINATION INTO THE INFLUENCE OF ASIATIC PHILOSOPHY,

AND

THE GRADUAL DEVELOPMENT OF CHRISTIANITY

IN PICTAVIA.

BY

THOMAS A. WISE, M.D.,

F.R.S.E., F.R.A.S., F.S.A. Scot., &c.

LONDON:
TRÜBNER & CO., LUDGATE HILL.

1884.

THE LIBRARY
BRIGHAM YOUNG UNIVERSITY
PROVO, UTAH

"May He who has implanted in our hearts a craving after the discovery of truth, and given us our reasoning faculties to the end that we should use them for the discovery, sanctify our efforts, and bless them in their results."

The Prince Consort.

"The study of antiquity is the study of Ancient History; and the proper business of an antiquary is to collect what is dispersed, to examine controverted points, to settle what is doubtful, and, by the authority of monuments and Histories, to throw light upon the manners, art, language, policy, and religion of past ages."

Borlase's Antiquities of Cornwall.

"Who knows, but some future critic in antiquity, from the very symbols and hieroglyphics now exhibited, may discover still stronger circumstances, to convince the enemies of the Scots, that their nation is not quite destitute of all vouchers of Historical fact, notwithstanding that they have had the misfortune more than once to be barbarously and ungenerously plundered of their records and archives."

Gordon's Itinerarium Septentrionale, page 160.

PREFACE.

THE identity of idea and design which reveals itself in the ancient paganism of Asiatic nations, as well as the similarity of the symbols of the stone monuments of Asia with several of those on the sculptured stones of ancient Pictavia, indicate a line of enquiry by which it is believed that the obscurity resting over the earliest monuments and history of Western Europe may, in a certain degree, be removed. With the assistance of our present knowledge of Eastern customs and usages, which has been much extended in modern times, the interest of these peculiar symbols is increased, as they appear in the North-east of Scotland, carefully delineated on the circles of Celtic boulders, usually called Druidical.[1]

Researches into the history of primitive races prove that they sometimes have an imperfect idea of a Supreme Divinity; as in the cases of some of the Hill tribes of Hindustan, the Esquimaux, and the aborigines of New South Wales, who have neither idols nor temples, while other races believe in beings wiser and more powerful than themselves as the immediate source of what they either love or fear. These are supposed to send the devastating tempests, the thunderstorms, and destructive diseases, as small-pox, cholera, and fever, which they in consequence dread and worship together with the sun and other sources of permanent good to mankind. These gods are represented by symbols of material form, or Fetishes endowed with the power of doing good and evil: and the priest, or Fetisher, being proxy to all these divinities, and believed to be acquainted with the thoughts and actions of men, rewarded or

---

[1] I use the word Druid in the following work as a useful term without conveying the theoretical nature, which has been so long attached to the name.

PREFACE.

punished each individual according as he made or did not make propitiation by sacrifice, the spiritual part being offered to their god, the idol sprinkled with the blood of the victims, and the flesh eaten by the worshippers.

Such rude races were neither able to comprehend, nor was their language capable of expressing, abstract ideas to argue from effects to causes; nor from the creation, to infer the existence of the Creator. It is, therefore, remarkable to find a race so primitive as the Pictavian, carefully symbolising on their monuments the idea of an immaterial God.

The descendants of the Aryan races believed that the sun, the origin of light, heat, and vegetation, was the proper emblem of the Deity; hence the prevalence of sun-worship, which was a mode of adoring the attributes of the Supreme Power as most emphatically revealed to man in the beneficent action of that luminary.

The object of this work is to describe those monuments in Pictavia which contain heathen symbols, such as we find nowhere else out of Asia, in evidence of the conclusion to which we have come, of an early direct communication between the extreme East and the extreme West of the world, the region of sunrise and the region of sunset, the band of connection being the existence of sun-worship.

    Thornton,
        Beulah Hill,
            Upper Norwood, S.E.

CONTENTS.

PREFACE.—GENERAL INTRODUCTION.

BOOK I.

SOCIAL CHARACTER OF THE INHABITANTS OF CALEDONIA.

CHAPTER I.	CHAPTER II.
SOCIAL CHARACTER OF THE INHABITANTS OF CALEDONIA DURING THE MEGALITHIC AGE.	DOMESTIC MANNERS AND CUSTOMS OF THE INHABITANTS OF CALEDONIA DURING THE MEGALITHIC AGE.
PAGE	PAGE

SECTION I.—Personal Character - - - 1
  (a) *Cleanliness of Body,* 2; (b) *Dress and Ornaments,* 3.
	SECTION I.—Dwelling Places - - - - 9
	  (a) *Huts,* 9; (b) *Caves or Weems,* 10; (c) *Lake Dwellings or Crannoges,* 13; (d) *Refuse Heaps,* 14.

SECTION II.—Social Grades - - - - 4 (a) *The Slaves,* 4; (b) *The Common People,* 5; (c) *The Tempster,* 5; (d) *The Thane or Chieftain,* 6; (e) *Druids or Ministers,* 7.	SECTION II.—Household Furniture - - - 14 SECTION III.—Hunting and Fishing - - - 15

	PAGE
SECTION IV.—Canoes and Coracles	16
SECTION V.—Agriculture, Barter, and Trade	17
SECTION VI.—British Carriages and Cars	18
SECTION VII.—Food and Drink	19
(a) *Food*, 19; (b) *Drinks*, 19; *Celtic Urns*, 21.	
SECTION VIII.—Celtic Weapons	21
SECTION IX.—Celtic Forts	22
(a) *Fortified Villages*, 22; (b) *Primitive Celtic Forts*, 22; (c) *Earthern Forts in Ireland and England*, 22; (d) *Primitive Stone Forts*, 23; (e) *Hill Forts built with Mortar*, 27.	

	PAGE
SECTION IV.—Wrought and Compound Circles of Stones in Asia	38
(a) *Culna*, 39; (b) *Depaldinna*, 39.	
SECTION V.—The Gigantic or Compound Circles of Stones in Europe-	40
(a) *Snago*, 40; (b) *Glendallock*, 40; (c) *Crichie*, 41; (d) *Huntly Tumulus*, 42; (e) *Stonehenge*, 43; (f) *Callernish*, 46; (g) *Maes Howe*, 47.	

CHAPTER III.

PRIMITIVE SYMBOLIC STONE MONUMENTS IN ASIA AND EUROPE, WITH AND WITHOUT INSCRIPTIONS: DESCRIPTIONS AND USES.

	PAGE
SECTION I.—Primitive Symbolic Monoliths	28
(a) *As Symbol of the Deity*, 29; (b) *Boundary Stones*, 32; (c) *Charter and Coronation Stones*, 32.	
SECTION II.—The Obelisks and Pyramids of Egypt	34
SECTION III.—Circles of Erect Stones and Wheels	35
(a) *Circles as Symbols of the Sun-God*, 37; (b) *For the Administration of Justice*, 37; (c) *For Sepulchral and Memorial Purposes*, 38.	

CHAPTER IV.

PRIMITIVE MONUMENTS WITH ARCHAIC MARKINGS IN ASIA AND EUROPE.

	PAGE
SECTION I.—Primitive Markings	49
(a) *Chalk Lines*, 49; (b) *Scores or Tallies*, 49; (c) *Clog Almanac*, 50.	
SECTION II.—Primitive Measures and Cups	50
(a) *Forms and Situations*, 50; (b) *Their Uses*, 51; *Landmarks*, 52; *Commemorating Events*, 55; *Cups*, 57; *Monumental and Burial Uses*, 58; (c) *Ages of Cups*, 59.	
SECTION III.—Sacred Shells, and Rock Basins or Depressions	59
SECTION IV.—Hole Stones	61
(a) *Small Holes*, 61; (b) *Large Holes*, 64.	
SECTION V.—Footprints on Stones and Rocks	66
(a) *Fanciful*, 66; (b) *Real*, 68.	
SECTION VI.—Oghams, Runes, &c.	69
(a) *Ogham Characters*, 71; (b) *Runic*, 73; (c) *Romanesque*, 73.	

CHAPTER V.

EARLY CELTIC ARCHITECTURE AND PILLAR TOWERS.

SECTION I.—Cyclopean Buildings - - - 74
   (a) *Block Buildings*, 74; (b) *Flag-stone Erections*, 75; *Oratories*, 76.
SECTION II.—Round Towers or Brochs   77
SECTION III.—Pillar Towers in Asia and Britain   79

CHAPTER VI.

LAWS AND INSTITUTIONS OF CELTIC RACES.

SECTION I.—Patriarchal Religion and Social Polity - - - - - 87
SECTION II.—High Places and Mounds   88
SECTION III.—Legal Monuments - - - 90
   (a) *Monoliths, Pillars*, 90; (b) *Circles for Legal Purposes*, 90; (c) *Altars*, 91; (d) *Rocking Stones*, 91.

CHAPTER VII.

NATURE WORSHIP AMONG THE PRIMITIVE RACES OF ASIA AND EUROPE.

SECTION I.—Primitive Paganism among the Rude Turanian Races of Asia - 93
SECTION II.—The Worship of the Aryan and Early Celtic Races - - - 94
   (a) *Sun Worship*, 94; *The Moon*, 101; *The Stars*, 102; (b) *Worship of the Elements*, 102; (c) *Serpent Worship*, 105; *The Dragon*, 110; (d) *Horse Worship*, 111.

CHAPTER VIII.

RELIGIOUS SYMBOLS AND IDEAS AMONG PRIMITIVE RACES IN ASIA AND EUROPE.

SECTION I.—Monolithic Symbols of the Deity - 115
   (a) *Simple Erect Boulder*, 115; (b) *Boundary Pillar*, 115; (c) *Sepulchral Monuments*, 116.
SECTION II.—Sun Symbols of the Deity in Circles, Discs, and Wheels - 116
SECTION III.—Primitive Pagan Crosses - - 117
SECTION IV.—Early Religious Polytheistic Ideas, particularly in Asia - - - 118
   (a) *Sacred Deities*, 119; (b) *Sacred Persons*, 121; (c) *Effigies of Sacred Persons*, 123.
SECTION V.—Means of Marking the Period for Holding the Great Celtic Festival 123
   (a) *Cup-dial*, 123; (b) *The Cairn Leath Broch*, 124; (c) *The Lindores Standing Stone*, 125.

CHAPTER IX.

CELTIC USAGES AFTER DEATH IN ASIA AND EUROPE.

SECTION I.—Disposal of the Dead - - - 128
   (a) *Burial*, 128; (b) *Cremation*, 130; (c) *Burial-Places and Funeral Rites*, 131; (d) *Mourning*, 131; (e) *Embalming and Entombing*, 131; (f) *Exposure of the Dead*, 133.
SECTION II.—Sepulchral Monuments   133
   (a) *Pillar Stones*, 133; (b) *Muts and Pyramids*, 134; (c) *Kistvaens*, 134; (d) *Cromlechs*, 135.
SECTION III.—Cairns, Tumuli, Mounds or Barrows - - 138

CONTENTS.

BOOK II.

BUDDHISM: ITS HISTORY AND TENETS.

CHAPTER I.
BUDDHISM.
                                PAGE

SECTION I.—The Rise, Spread, and Decline of Buddhism in Hindustan, with its Extension to other Lands -   143

SECTION II.—Buddhist Priests, their Character, Ritual, and Missionary Modes - 151

CHAPTER II.
TENETS, ORGANIZATION AND SYMBOLS OF BUDDHISM.
                                PAGE

SECTION I.—The Buddhist Triratna -   156
(a) *Buddha, the Supreme Intelligence*, 157; (b) *the Dharma, the Law of Teaching*, 158; (c) *The Sangha, or Sacred Brotherhood*, 159.

SECTION II.—Buddhist Circles and Wheels, Prayer-wheels, and Wheels of Transmigration - - - 161
(a) *Sacred Circle, representing the Sun-God*, 161; (b) *Wheels*, 162; (c) *Wheel of the Law*, 163; (d) *Prayer Wheels*, 163; (e) *Wheel of Transmigration*, 164.

SECTION III.—The Dorge Symbol - - 165
Mundane Triad.—The Dorge, 165.

CHAPTER III.
SYMBOLS OF BUDDHISM IN PICTLAND.
                                PAGE

SECTION I.—Symbols of the Sacred Triad -   168
(a) *Circles*, 169; (b) *The Dorge, or Spectacle Ornament*, 170; *The Looking Glass and Comb*, 175; *The Horse-Shoe*, 175; *The Third Member of the Mundane Triad*, 175; *The Altar*, 176.

CHAPTER IV.
SACRED PLACES AND MONUMENTS.
                                PAGE

SECTION I.—Caves   179

SECTION II.—Elevations, Mounds, Hills, and Groves - - - 179

SECTION III.—Monasteries (Vahara) - - 180

SECTION IV.—Pillar Towers, or Towers of Deliverance - - 180
Pagan Pillar Towers in Ireland, 180; *Varieties of Towers*, 182

SECTION V.—Pillars of Victory - - 183

SECTION VI.—Inscriptions on Pillars or Lâts - 183

CHAPTER V.
SACRED BUDDHIST ORGANIC SYMBOLS ON THE SCULPTURED STONES OF PICTLAND.
                                PAGE

SECTION I.—Sacred Animals - 185
Monkeys, 185; *Serpents*, 185; *The Celestial Elephant*, 185; *Horse Worship*, 187; *Dog*, 188; *Centaur*, 188; *The Sacred Bull*, 189; *The Sow and the Boar*, 190; *The Stag*, 190; *The Lion*, 190; *Camel and Dromedary*, 191; *Birds*, 191; *Fish*, 191.

SECTION II.—Sacred Trees   192
(a) *Lotus Flower*, 196.

BOOK III.

HISTORY OF CHRISTIANITY IN PICTLAND.

INTRODUCTION.

CHAPTER I.

PAGAN SYMBOLS OF THE DEITY ADOPTED BY PRIMITIVE CHRISTIANS.

	PAGE
SECTION I.—Primitive Circles Incised, and in Bas-Relief	207
SECTION II.—Symbolical Christian Monoliths	207
SECTION III.—The Christian Pillar Towers of Ireland and Scotland	208
(a) Pagan Towers: General Description: History, and uses, and transition from Book II., page 180, 201; (b) Modern Varieties in Ireland and Scotland, 211.	

CHAPTER II.

FORM OF THE ANCIENT INCISED AND BAS-RELIEF GREEK AND LATIN CROSSES IN THE BRITISH ISLANDS.

	PAGE
SECTION I.—Primitive Incised Crosses	214
SECTION II.—Primitive Bas-Relief Crosses— The Maiden Stone	217
SECTION III.—Primitive Varieties of Crosses in the British Islands	221
SECTION IV.—Varieties of Crosses in the British Islands	221
(a) In Ireland; (b) In Isle of Man.	

CHAPTER III.

USES OF THE CHRISTIAN CROSSES IN PICTLAND: PREACHING CROSSES, AS WELL AS PRAYER AND MEMORIAL CROSSES.

	PAGE
SECTION I.—Prayer and Preaching Crosses	222
SECTION II.—Boundary Crosses	228
SECTION III.—Memorial Crosses	229

CHAPTER IV.

CHRISTIAN SYMBOLS, WITH ORNAMENTS AND ANIMALS ON THE CROSSES.

	PAGE
SECTION I.—Varieties of Symbols upon the obverse and reverse of Crosses	231
SECTION II.—Asiatic and British Animals upon the reverse of Crosses	234
SECTION III.—Ornaments on Christian Crosses	235

CHAPTER V.

PROCESSIONS AND ÆGIS, OR SACRED SHIELDS.

	PAGE
SECTION I.—Developed Processions	238
SECTION II.—The Ægis, or Sacred Shield	242
(a) *The Deity*, 242; (b) *Symbols*, 244; (c) *Angels*, 244.	

CHAPTER VI.

CHRISTIAN COMMUNITIES, RITUAL, AND CHURCHES.

	PAGE
SECTION I.—Ancient Churches	247
(a) *Earthern Churches*, 247; (b) *Stone Churches*, 248.	
SECTION II.—The Primitive Christian Communities in Caledonia	249
SECTION III.—Ritual and Vestments	251
SECTION IV.—Separation of the Greek and Roman Churches	252
SECTION V.—The influence of St. Palladius on the History of Christianity in Pictland	252
SECTION VI.—Final dispersion of the Pictavian Christians under the name of Culdees	256

LIST OF ILLUSTRATIONS.

N.B.—The head and tail pieces to chapters have been designed and engraved especially for this work.

FRONTISPIECE.—The Maiden Stone, Aberdeenshire.
PLATE OPPOSITE PAGE 237.—Various Ornaments on Stone Ornaments.

FIG.		FIG.	
1.	Celtic Tunic.	39.	Cup Stone on the Grampians.
2.	,, Slaves.	40.	,, Belmont, Perthshire.
3.	, Plebs.	41.	Cup Stones.
4.	,, ,,	42.	,,
5.	,, Tempster.	43.	
6.	Scottish Thane.	44.	,, sculptured
7.	,, ,,	45.	,,
8.	,, ,,	46.	,, ,,
9.	Scottish Chieftain.	47.	,, ,,
10.	Celtic Hut.	48.	Obelisk at Dingwall.
11.	,, Weem.	49.	,, ,,
12.	British Canoe.	50.	Cross near Inverussie.
13.	,, ,,	51.	Altar Stone near Balmoral.
14.	,, Coracle.	52.	Cairn at Glen Urquhart.
15.	,, Car.	53.	Stones at ,,
16.	,, Fortified Village.	54.	,, ,,
17.	,, ,, Camp.	55.	Basin Rocks, Galway.
18.	Monolith at Plumen.	56.	,, ,, ,,
19.	,, with Cross on top.	57.	Hole Stone, Edderton, Ross-shire.
20.	Eastern Obelisk.	58.	,, ,, Kilmakedar, Kerry.
21.	,, ,,	59.	,
22.	,, ,,	60.	,,
23.	Pyramids of Egypt.	61.	,,
24.	Stone Circles at Darmacotta.	62.	,, ,, Aberlemno, Forfarshire.
25.	Khotub.	63.	,, ,, ,,
26.	Pillar Tower at Gowar.	64.	,, ,, in Cornwall.
27.	Temple at Culna.	65.	Men-an-tol.
28.	Depaldinna at Darmacotta.	66.	Stone Footprints, Shetland.
29.	Sculpture on ditto.	67.	Block Buildings, Duncinnan Hill.
30.	Monument at Crechie.	68.	Oratory at Gallerus.
31.	Huntley Tumulus—plan of	69.	Pillar Tower, Asia.
32.	,, ,, sculpture on.	70.	,, ,, ,,
33.	,, ,, general plan.	71.	,, ,, ,,
34.	Stone Semicircle at Lackin.	72.	,, ,, ,,
35.	Stonehenge—ground plan.	73.	Buddhist Pillar Tower on Coin.
36.	,, general view.	74.	,, Pillar Tower.
37.	Tope at Sánchi.	75.	Pillar Tower, Drumcliff.
38.	Stone Circle. Callernish.	76.	,, ,, Seeling.

LIST OF ILLUSTRATIONS.

FIG.
77. Pagan Altar, Rostellan.
78. Nepaulese Tope.
79. Figure of the Elements
80. ,, ,, Typhon.
81. Serpents on Farnell Stone.
82. St. George, Python-slayer.
83. Horse Worship.
84. White Horse, Berkshire.
85. Horse, Inverury.
86. ,, Glammis.
87. ,, Meigle.
88. White Horse, Banffshire.
89. Stone Circles, Knockando.
90. Crux Ansata.
91. Maltese Crosses.
92. ,, ,,
93. Swastica Cross, Isle of Wight.
94. Cup Dial at Fodderty.
95. Diagram, Cairn Leath Broch.
96. Lindores Standing Stone.
97. Symbols of the Elements.
98. Cromlech.
99. Cromlech at Raidrogg.
100. Buddhist Priest.
101. Rock Symbols at Anworth.
102. Buddhist Wheel.
103. Sacred Wheels, variety of.
104. ,, ,,
105.
106. ,, ,,
107. ,, ,,
108. Wheel and Triad.
108*. Buddhist Priest with Dorge.
109. Dorges.
110. ,,
111. Temple Dorges.
112. ,, ,,
113. Buddha.
114. Sacred Triad.
115. Sacred Elephant.
116. Incised Stone at Kinnellar.
117. ,, ,, Rothienorman.
118. ,, ,, from Western Highlands.
119. Triad Symbol, Strathpeffer.
120. Spectacle Ornament.
121. The Keillor Stone.

FIG.
122. The Dyce Stone.
123. Altar Stone.
124. Sculptured Stones, Corgah.
125. Pillar Tower, Duncliffe.
126. Buddhist Trumpets.
127. Pillar Tower, Cloyne.
128. ,, ,, Ardmore.
129. ,, ,, Keneith.
130. Elephants' Heads, Benares.
131. Sacred Horse on early British Coins.
132. ,, ,, ,,
133. ,, ,,
134. Symbolical Sculpture.
135. The Centaur.
136. ,, armed.
137. Tree Worship.
138. Procession on Eassie Obelisk.
139. Abernethy Pillar Tower.
140. Brechin Pillar Tower.
141. ,, ,, ,, interior.
142. Stone Cross.
143. Buddhist Symbols, and Latin Cross.
144. Cross at Deir.
145. ,, Rossie, front.
146. ,, ,, back.
147. ,, Meigle, small.
148. ,, ,, large.
149. ,, ,, procession upon.
150. ,, ,, "The twa Chappies."
151. ,, Golspie.
152. ,, ,, Buddhist Symbols upon.
153. ,, Meigle.
154. Equestrian Procession on Meigle Cross.
155. ,, ,, ,, Obelisk at Hilton Cadbolt.
156. ,, ,, ,, Obelisk at Fowles.
157. ,, ,, ,, ,, Aberlemno.
158. Priests Sculptured on St. Vigean's Cross.
159. Ægis on Pillar Stone.
160. Sacred Stones, Deity.
161. ,, ,, Trinity.
162. Wheel Ornament.
163. ,,
164. Serpent Symbols.
165. Guardian Angel.
166. Cross at Dunfallandy.

GENERAL INTRODUCTION.

SO little authentic is known of the ancient inhabitants of the British Islands, and particularly of Scotland, that in consequence, the interest naturally felt in the investigation of their manners and customs cannot be directly gratified. Unlike the ancient races of the East, they have left no records of their internal wars, religious revolutions, and heroic deeds. The connection or identity, however, of the different families of the wide-spread Celtic races, both in Asia and in Europe, enables us (by the examination of their history as contained in ancient records, and as marked on their monuments), to note the peculiarities derived from internal and local influences, compared with the facts marking stages of advancement in different countries; and, moreover, explains the similarity in form, purpose, and art-workmanship of the primitive monuments in these countries. To illustrate this identity, it will be necessary to notice the habits and customs of the Asiatics, and to compare them with those of various ancient nations. We shall then find, that both classic and Christian authors have observed, and travellers have proved, that between the Asiatic and European nations, there existed a connection earlier and much more intimate than is generally supposed. A marked resemblance will also be found between the monuments and peculiar burial customs of the ancient inhabitants of Hindústan, and those of the British Islands.

The conviction of the close connection of former Asiatic races with the Pictavians, has become stronger as our knowledge of Eastern antiquities and learning has been rendered more intimate, by the researches of Wilson, James Prinsep, Hodgson, Laidlay, Cunningham, Turnour, Kitto, Ferguson, and Thomas. These writers have made us familiar with ancient Buddhist philosophy, and this has been increased and rendered more complete by the researches of Max Müller and others, particularly by those of Eugene Burnoup, who has greatly elucidated the subject by his mastery of the Sanscrit, Pali, and Thibetan languages, and by his acquaintance with the Buddhist authorities of the north and south of India. This knowledge of their sacred books, enabled him to explain the opinions and usages of the Buddhists, and their varied customs in different countries, and to illustrate the modifications in religious symbols among different and distant races.

We have now, also, accurate delineations of Celtic and Buddhist remains in Asia and Europe, and in particular of a large series of monuments of great artistic beauty, in that portion of the north-eastern part of Scotland, which, at an early period, formed the kingdom of Pictland, remarkable for the bravery and religious fervour of its inhabitants. Over the nature and history of these monuments, much obscurity still lingers, but our knowledge of the archæology of both this country and of the countries of the East is rapidly increasing; and an attempt is now made, to remove some of this darkness by a comparison of the meaning of the sculptures, with the religious opinions and philosophy of the Buddhists; and by arranging the monuments, with their peculiar designs and religious symbols, in chronological groups, and explaining their uses.

It cannot be supposed that the ornate sculptured stones in Pictland, with their representation of Eastern animals, were the work of native artists, at a time when we know that the natives of Caledonia were so low in the social scale, as to be living in caves and huts, and so defective in knowledge, as to understand nothing of the opinions, manners, or customs of foreign nations. In order to discover these artists, we must extend our view beyond the narrow bounds of these Islands, and enquire whether strangers—such as the followers of Buddha, and, in after times, the enlightened as well as zealous Christian Missionaries, having points of resemblance—might not have erected these stone pillars and sacred crosses, during their visits to Caledonia for the purpose of propagating their faith. One of our aims will be to explain the nature and probable uses of these monuments, and the meaning of the symbols sculptured on them, and some of them may with a considerable degree of confidence, be explained by an Eastern interpretation.

The primitive antiquities of a people are the unfailing teachers of remote history. They are the symbols of races that at one time existed in the countries in which they are found, whether in Asia or Europe, though we must always expect to find them modified in different localities, by peculiarities of climate, by mixture of races, or by the advancement of civilisation. Investigations connected with them will always lead to an advance of knowledge.

The present work is, then, intended to collect the scattered passages preserved in ancient authors, who had opportunities of acquiring information regarding the ethnology of the ancient inhabitants of Caledonia; to examine their megalithic and other antiquities; to compare these memorials with those of the same race in different ages and countries wherever there seems to be any connection in habits and customs; and by the assistance derived from these, to attempt the unfolding and explanation of the history of the Pagan and the early Christian communities of Pictland. The ancient history of any country generally reveals a mixture of races: such mixture having taken place at different periods, and the inhabitants being often drawn from distant countries. The proofs of this are more or less strong according to the manners and customs, the intelligence, and development of the people. In some cases we have only the evidence of character and peculiar habits; in other cases we have the more certain indications of similarity in language and of identity of religious monuments. On our own shores this mixture appears to have taken place at such an early period, that in dealing with it we are without any assistance from history or even from tradition. But the little we do know of the early population, shows us traces of their connection with the ancient inhabitants of Hindústan in the physical conformation of the race; in the similarity of customs and observances; and in the decided and extensive affinity of the Celtic and Sanscrit languages,[1] as well as in the ancient monuments of these distant races,—such as obelisks, circles of stones and pillar stones, cromlechs, kistvaens, barrows, and cairns.[2] The similarity of the stone monuments of Asia to those of the ancient kingdom of Pictland, indicates a line of inquiry by following which it is believed that the obscurity resting over the earliest monuments and history of Western Europe may, in a certain degree, be removed.

When we are informed that all the works of creation were pronounced "very good"—being harmonious and beautiful—and that all things animate and inanimate were created perfect; and when we know that they still continue to be a constant source of wonder and admiration, is it possible for us to believe that man—the greatest and noblest work of the Almighty—formed in the very image of God—was made imperfect? The image of God, impressed on him, brought beauty and majesty and perfection not only to his physical form, but, through his soul, influenced his actions. Happiness reigned on earth as in heaven—"the morning stars sang together, and all the sons of God shouted for joy." Thus perfect man was endowed with knowledge and judgment, with language for communicating his thoughts, invention to supply his necessary wants, and fervour for worshipping and praising that bountiful Maker who created and preserved him. The fall of man, with the rapid corruption of the race ensued, and, finally, the dispersion of the tribes took place.[3]

Of the Turanian or primitive races in Asia and Europe, little is known. They varied very much according to the character of the country that they inhabited, and their connection with other nations; but the close resemblance of the language and customs among the different tribes is very striking, and the monumental remains in Asia are identical with those all along the route by which these primitive tribes were pushed forward to the north and west of Europe. Ever pressed on by the conquering Celts, they have never been able to develop their intellectual qualities, and have remained unmixed with other races in those sterile countries to which they have been driven, and where they are quickly diminishing in number before disease, and the new habits and customs introduced by the superior race. They can still be studied in Asia at the present day, and from such study and from the remains they have left, we may infer various points connected with them.

---

(1) Prichard's Celtic Nations, pp. 20–22.
(2) Worsæ Primitive Antiquities of Denmark, by Thoms, p. 132, *et seq.* Newbolt, Asiatic Society, July, 1846. Transactions of the Royal Society of Edinburgh, vol. xxx. p. 255.
(3) Genesis, xi, 8.

The Turanians were gradually displaced by a fresh people, destined to rise to the very highest eminence, whose mission it was to spread useful and industrial arts over all the world, to produce that unity that had long been lost, and to bring about such reverence for the works of God as would make man a wiser, humbler, and more devout servant of his Creator. This new and remarkable race—the Aryans—came originally from the North-west of Asia,[1] and occupied at an early period Persia and the North of Hindústan. From this they spread slowly southward, subjugating the Turanians and driving them forward to Central India, where they still linger as the Gonds, Bhels, Santals, &c., and perhaps as the fisherman race of the Kanwarthas-rajas. Some of the races thus subjugated remained as degraded as ever, but others were, under favourable circumstances, and by intermarriages, improved in character, religion, and government.

The Aryans brought with them much of the original learning of mankind—"the wisdom of the elder and better times." They believed in one God, whose greatness no intellect could measure, and whose attributes no language could adequately express, whose presence was everywhere, and who ruled over all creation. They considered the sun as his suitable symbol, fire as his emblem, the heavens as his home, the earth as something he had created. They reverenced the moon, the stars, and the elements,[2] but the pure Aryans never regarded or worshipped them as gods. Though they afterwards adopted a symbolical worship, this was rather that they might inculcate duty in the regulation and government of the spiritual wants of the community, piety towards God and charity towards one another, than a necessity of their religion. They, in fact, required no temple for such a deity as theirs, and no ceremonial for such a worship. It was purely domestic, and prayer was the act of the individual, standing in presence of an Omniscient Being in the midst of His marvellous works. It was alone required of each that he should acknowledge the greatness of God, his own insignificance, and consequently his absolute trust and faith in the beneficence and justice of the Divine Being, and that these should strengthen him to live pure and free from sin, so as to deserve happiness. There were merely a few formulæ to mark the modes of worship: sacred hymns and texts, the recital of which might remind them of their duties. Superstition was prevented by their eager and ardent aspiration towards a purity and goodness, which the finite mind of man could never actually attain.

The Aryans had such an innate passion for self-government that the patriarchal power was strictly limited, and there was even a tendency towards republicanism. Every town had a municipality, every village a system of government, and these in India have survived the changes and revolutions of fifty centuries. They have remained the same under Hindú, Buddhist, and Moslem rulers, and unchanged and unchangeable in the midst of despotism and of anarchy, they have preserved the country from

---

(1) Probably from the regions of the Upper Oxus, now forming part of the dominions of the Khan of Bokhara.

(2) *Kaivan* (Saturn) was the spleen of the Great Being; *Burjis* (Jupiter), his liver; *Behren* (Mars), his gall; *Nahid* (Venus), his stomach; *Tir* (Mercury), his brain, &c. The air was his breath; the earth, the place on which he stepped; the thunder, his vow; the lightning, his laugh; the rain, his tears.

sinking into a state of savage rudeness. The municipalities and self-governing guilds are to be found wherever the Aryan race exists in Europe, and it was the Teutonic guilds that checked and ultimately supplanted the feudal despotism of the Celts. Thus constantly accustomed to government carried on by individuals sharing equally a common power and acting in harmony, the Aryan was trained to govern himself and to respect the independence of his neighbours, and so fitted for a share in the government of the State. He was elevated into an independent reasoning being, animated by self-respect, by love of truth, by a desire to control his passions, and to command the respect and esteem of his fellow-men. The institution of caste seems to be at variance with this principle of self-government, but as it originally existed among them, it was intended simply as a recognition of the inevitable accident of birth, and as a means of fostering high feeling, by restraining men from unworthy acts of self-aggrandisement; and although in Europe, in consequence of the mixture of races, the theory has been lost, the practice in reality still remains, and seems a natural distinction among freemen.

With a noble language, and from a very early period, an alphabet much more complete than the Semitic, they entered, much earlier than any other nation, into questions of grammar, logic, and philosophy, while their whole history constitutes an essay on the polity of mankind. Their poetry assumed a didatic rather than a lyric form, and among them the Epos first rose to eminence, and the drama was elevated above a mere spectacle. They endeavoured to portray vividly events that possibly never did happen among men, but which might have happened, and thus they contrast strongly with the Semites, who delighted in wild fancies that could only exist in the brain of their author; in short, their literature consisted of works of history and philosophy rather than of those of creative power and imagination. This same tendency for the practical, accounts as well, for their deficiency in the fine arts, as for their earnest and successful cultivation of the useful arts and sciences. They were distinguished in Commerce (with its attendant arts of ship-building and road-making), in Manufactures, in Agriculture, and in all that tends to accumulate wealth, and to advance material prosperity. They fully appreciated the beauty of scientific truth, and the harmony of the laws of nature, and developed them into that system of Buddhism whose excellence, beauty, and truth must by and by be considered.

While one branch of the Aryan race pressed westward and became the ancestors of the leading nations of Europe, another—the eastern branch—descended into the fertile plains of Hindústan[1] where they rapidly increased in riches and power, and became the progenitors of the modern Hindús. They extended slowly southwards, and at the Christian era had conquered *Maharashta*, which Ptolemy calls Ariski, whence they advanced to the extreme south of Ceylon and into part of the Indian

---

(1) They occupied Arya-Vorta (the land of the Aryans) or Hindústan (the land of the Hindús). The word Hindú is not Sanscrit. It designates that branch of the Aryans that passed east across the river "Scindha," the western boundary of India; and as the letters S and H are convertible in the Zend or ancient Persian language, the name of the river explains the appellation given to those who passed it. The term Hindú was first used by Herodotus and the Greeks, and was adopted by the more modern inhabitants of Hindústan.

Archipelago. They were early distinguished for their intellectual endowments, for sacred as well as traditional history inform us that the Magi of the East, who distinguished themselves by their skill and learning, and still more by their subsequent migrations, were of this race and nation. The same people were regarded proverbially as being possessed of "the wisdom of the East" [1] which may in some measure explain the first mention made of a social community "as journeying from the East." [2] Their productions are refined by natural genius and delicacy of touch, and stereotyped by hereditary castes.[3] From them Abraham probably obtained his knowledge, as we are told, that Terah, his father, "dwelt on the other side of the flood" (the river Euphrates), and served other gods, and their worship was mixed up with what would be considered as idolatrous ceremonies. The learned Mr. Orme states that "India was inhabited from the earliest antiquity by a people who had no resemblance, either in their figure or manner, to any of the nations contiguous to them;" and Sir William Jones observes, "however degenerate the Hindús may now appear, at some early day they were splendid in arts and arms, happy in government, wise in legislation, and eminent in knowledge." "In medicine," writes the distinguished Professor Wilson, "as in astronomy and metaphysics, the Hindús once kept pace with the most enlightened nations of the world; and they attained as thorough a proficiency in medicine and surgery as any people whose acquirements are recorded, and as, indeed, was practicable, before anatomy was made known to us by the discoveries of modern enquirers." [4] Sir Chas. Fellows has clearly shown that many of the arts, in which the Greeks attained eminence, were known to and introduced into Lycia, by a still more ancient people from some eastern country, probably from Hindústan.[5]

The repute of the Asiatics for knowledge and wisdom induced at an early period the Egyptians, and at a later period the Greek sages, to visit India. On the return of the latter to their own country, they propagated the Hindú philosophy, and the knowledge thus early acquired was supposed by their descendants to be of native growth or derived from the ancient Egyptians, rather than from the distant and little known Eastern people. This learning was at first handed down orally, and afterwards it is possible that the primitive Hindús may have used symbols or hieroglyphics, as an assistance to memory and to give authority to their maxims regarding grammar, ethics and medicine; but all their knowledge that has come down to us is contained in books written in Sanscrit. This language, Max Müller tells us, approaches nearest the primitive type in its originality, its purity, and in the abundance of its forms. Modern philology has shown that it lies at the root of all the languages of one great branch of the human race, and it has thus proved of great service to the historian in enabling him to record the pedigrees of nations. It is found to connect the Zend (the ancient Persian language), the Armenian, the Greek, the Latin, the German, the Sclavonian, and the Celtic tongues. "The Sanscrit language," writes Sir William Jones, "whatever be its antiquity, is of wonderful structure; more perfect than the

---

(1) 1 Kings iv. 30.   (2) Gen. xi. 2.   (3) Gen. xxxvii. 26.
(4) Works, vol. iii. p. 269.   (5) Athenæum, 1846, p. 1047.

Greek, more copious than the Latin, and more exquisitely refined than either; yet bearing to both of them the strongest affinity in roots and verbs, and in the forms of grammar. This resemblance is so strong, that no philosopher could examine all the three without believing them to be sprung from one common source which, perhaps, no longer exists."[1] Frederick Von Schlegel, some twenty years later, in his "Languages and Philosophy of the Indians," had no doubt that the Sanscrit was not only related to Greek, Latin, and German, but was the very ancestor from which their descent was to be traced;[2] or, as Max Müller puts it, "the first derivation from the primitive Aryan speech." The grammatical works of Panini, and his Hindú successors, are the most complete that ever were employed in arranging the elements of speech.[3] This majestic and richly inflected Sanscrit is still viewed by the Hindús as their national language, written in the "devanagri" character, or divine alphabet, (so called from its supposed origin from the gods), and in it the oldest works in Indian literature are composed, embracing memorials of ancient theology, poetry, science, and philosophy, that have exerted an influence over the most distinguished nations of antiquity, and to which Europe is indebted for the rudiments of her learning. Sir William Jones declares that the Hindú geometry, arithmetic, and astronomy, "surpassed that of Ptolemy; their music, that of Archimedes; their theology, that of Plato; and their logic, that of Aristotle." Creuzer says, "S'il est une Contrée sur la terre qui puisse réclamer à juste titre l'honneur d'avoir été le berçeau de l'espèce humaine, ou au moins le théâtre d'une civilization primitive, dont les developpements successifs auraient portés dans tout l'ancien monde, et peut-être au-délà, le bienfait des lumières—cette seconde vie de l'humanité—cette contrée assurément c'est l'Inde."[4] "It might be easier," writes the Hon. Mountstuart Elphinstone,[5] "to compare them (the Hindús) with the Greeks, as painted by Homer, who was nearly contemporary with the completion of the code of Manu;[6] and however inferior in spirit and energy, as well as in elegance, to that heroic race, yet, on contrasting their laws and forms of administration, the state of the arts of life, and the general spirit of order and obedience to the laws, the Eastern nation seems clearly to have been in the more advanced stage of society. Their internal institutions were less rude; their conduct to their enemies more humane; their general learning was much more considerable; and in the knowledge of the being and nature of God, the Hindús were already in possession of a light which was but faintly perceived, even by the loftiest intellects, in the best days of Athens. The Brahmins, as the dispensers of religion, of the laws, and of medicine, exhibited a superiority of intelligence, which is in vain looked for in other ancient nations, except among the Greeks. Under the native government, the Hindú literature was carefully cherished by the princes and opulent individuals, who thus increased their temporal power and religious influence; and such encouragement operated powerfully as an incentive to study and literary exertion. It was the endeavour of the influential class, and one

---

(1) Asiatic Researches, vol. i, p. 422. (2) Philo. of Language, Lect. III, page 399. (3) Goldstüker's Panini.
(4) Creuzer's Religions de l'Antiquité Tom i., p. 133. (5) Elphinstone's History of India, vol. i, p. 94.
(6) The Code of Manu is stated by Prof. Monier Williams, in his "Hindúism," chap. v, page 54, to be perhaps the oldest and most sacred Sanscrit Work after the Veda and its Sranta-sûtrus. It is in other respects one of the most remarkable books that the whole world can offer, and some of its moral precepts are worthy of Christianity itself. It may be assigned in its present form to about the fifth century B.C.

of their proudest objects, to cherish these learned Brahmins, many of whom devoted their whole lives to intellectual cultivation; more particularly to education and poetry, to medicine and religion; by the former preparing the intellect of the rising generation, and immortalising in verse the grandeur of their patrons; by the latter explaining the treatment of the body in health and disease, and the means of insuring happiness to the individual after death.

The study of the heavenly bodies was considered by the Hindú sages as the noblest to which they could devote themselves, whether to view the order, economy, and regularity of their movements, or to contemplate the sun "as a giant running his course," travelling unseen through the realms of night, returning in the morning to shed his benefits over the world, and at last, at the end of the year, reaching the point from which he set out. The distribution of the stars into groups or constellations in the compass of the visible heavens, extending on each side of the ecliptic, appears to have been made in the earliest ages of the world, and, though it is highly probable that the zodiacs of all nations are derived from a common source, yet Sir William Jones supposed that the Indian division of the zodiac was not borrowed from the Greeks and Arabs, as it had been known in India from time immemorial.[1] A remarkable example of the attention the Hindú Brahmins paid to accurate observation in science, is seen in their recording astronomical facts from which they drew conclusions, without forming theories. They do not even give a description of celestial phenomena, being satisfied with calculating the changes in the heavens. The diurnal revolution of the earth on its axis, the number of the days of the week, and the division of the ecliptic into twenty-seven mansions or constellations (B.C. 1442),[2] were known to them, and they had accurate notions regarding the precession of the equinoxes. An intimate knowledge of astronomy is proved from the remarkable Vedic calendar (Jyotisham) of the Hindús which gives the position of the solstitial points; carrying us back to the year B.C. 1181, according to the calculations of the able Archdeacon Pratt; and to 1168, according to that of the Rev. R. Main.[3] It is, however, possible that the Hindús may, at a later time, have improved, in some respects, their astronomy from the knowledge possessed by the Greeks of Alexandria, as suggested by the able and accurate Colebrook.[4]

The remarks of the ancient Hindús in the Aitareya Brahmanan Sattrass, prove that many correct astronomical observations were recorded so early as the twelfth century B.C.; which led Professor Haug to assign the composition of the bulk of the Brahmanas to the years 1400—1200 B.C.[5]

At this early and enlightened period, the Ketaya princes were prudent, liberal, and skilful in political transactions; their Turanian subjects were industrious and frugal;[6] the Brahmins exercised

---
(1) Asiatic Researches vol. ii, p. 289.   (2) Bailey's History of Astronomy.
(3) Jour: Asiatic Soc. of Bengal for 1862, p. 49-50; see also Max Müller, pref. Rig-Veda vol. iv, p. 85.
(4) Asiatic Researches, vol. ix.   (5) Artareya Brahmanan of the Rig-Veda, vol. i. Jut. p. 47.
(6) The remains of the magnificent temples in the south and west of Hindústan belonged to the developed Turanian, rather than to the Aryan race, who supposed no temples were worthy of the great Deity, who accepted the prayers and humiliation of men, unadorned with gold or silver, or the lustre of precious stones.

spiritual influence; and besides cultivating the arts and sciences, with the success we have just seen, they administered the laws.[1] All the civilisation was based on the sacred books, which were supposed to have been received direct from the Deity to assuage the sufferings and misery of mankind, and whose mysteries, though inscrutable, were bound to be believed by the faithful. But herein lay elements of mischief. Conscious of their superior intelligence, and disinclined to travel, they came to regard their own rich country as favoured by the special protection of their deities, to deem it sinful to look beyond it, and to despise the productions and learning of strangers. The activity of intellect became, in consequence, deadened; each age was a mere reproduction of the past, and the Eastern branch of the Aryans sank into a condition of apathy and torpor, that contrasts strongly with the career of progress that has waited on the Western branch—the founders of the leading nations of modern Europe.

We have seen that, while one branch of the Aryans overspread Hindústan, another passed westward, no doubt, displacing in their progress, aboriginal savage tribes, of which we know almost nothing. They seem to have pressed forward in a succession of waves, each advancing further than the one that preceded it, till, in the course of their migrations, they had succeeded in making themselves masters of almost the whole of Europe. Though modified in their appearance and character, by change in the surroundings by which they were affected, and to some extent, also, by mixture with the tribes conquered or driven out, they retained much that leaves no doubt of their Eastern origin. The early monuments of Europe, whether in the form of circles of stones, of sepulchral mounds, of cromlechs or of barrows, are the same as those of India. The early languages are closely connected; the early mythologies are the same.[2] Both peoples believed in the god, Hu, the Buddha of the East; in the tradition of the flood; in the sacredness of the oak; in sacred pillars; and in transmigration of souls, and other doctrines of a like nature. To express some of their tenets, both made use of the triad and other similar symbols.[3] Both were domineered over by a caste of priests, who arrogated to themselves the first rank among the people.

Attached to personal leaders, they broke up into various tribes that took different names in different districts. Those in Continental Europe, in the countries opposite the shores of Britain, were the Belgae, the Celts, and the Germani; and, as might be expected, these must have migrated into Britain at a very early period, for the first glimpses that history gives of our country shews us that its

---

(1) The work known as The Institutes of Manu, bears date 962 B.C.

(2) Pliny, the younger, remarks on the resemblance between the religious ceremonies of the Britons and those of the Persians. Nat. Hist. xxx, 51.

(3) This explains a number of the peculiar symbols on the obelisks in Pictland, and also the occurrence on these pillars of sculptures of Asiatic animals. With the exception of a few in Strathspey and Strathclyde, one on a rock in Galloway and two in Northumberland, all the obelisks, with the peculiar symbols and the Asiatic animals, numbering more than one hundred, are found only in Pictland. See Burton's Hist. of Scotland, vol. i, p. 139.; Wilson's Prehistoric Ann. of Scotland, p. 536; Chalmer's Sculptured Stones of Forfarshire; Stewart's Sculptured Stones of Scotland; Prof. Stuart-Robinson's Character of the Picts; King's Book of Wales, Quarterly Rev. No. 209, July, 1873.

inhabitants were of the same tribes as those on the neighbouring shores; and from incidental notices, we may infer that their relations with their continental brethren were of a very close kind. Cæsar[1] notices the resemblance that existed between the two countries in religion, manners and customs, and he also mentions that Divitiacus, one of the most powerful men in Gaul, had possessions in Britain, and that the younger Druids used to pass across to Gaul to perfect themselves in their studies. Tacitus concludes from their religion and from their appearance—large limbed and red haired—that the Caledonians were of German extraction.[2] The condition of Britain under the Romans is too well known to need more than passing notice. In the South the Roman power was, from the time of Agricola down to the date of the final withdrawal of the Legions, firmly established, but in the North the case was far otherwise, and the Northern Celts can still boast of having preserved their independence. Though Agricola pushed his victorious arms as far as the chain of forts extending between the Firths of Forth and Clyde, yet the hold of the country between this wall and the one extending from the Solway to the Tyne was precarious, and the rebellions of the tribes between the walls—the fierce and brave Meatae—and the incursions of the tribes to the north of the *Vallum Antonini*—known collectively as the Caledonii—were so numerous and destructive that the Roman general was induced to purchase peace with the former people. To their ignorant minds this was a mere proof of weakness, and afforded protection to the Romans only as long as their enemies found it convenient to respect the agreement. When a favourable opportunity occurred, they immediately re-commenced their predatory incursions with greater ferocity than before. An application was at last made to the Roman Emperor for assistance, and Severus, old, infirm, and labouring under a painful disease, hurried to Britain late in the year 208. In a short time he concentrated his forces and advanced against the enemy. The Caledonian chiefs sent envoys begging for peace, but Severus distrusting them, sent them back without giving any reply; and having established his headquarters at York (Eboracum), he began operations at the beginning of the year 209. He speedily crushed all resistance between the walls, but no sooner had he advanced beyond the wall of Antonius, between the Forth and the Clyde, than his army was harassed by bodies of the enemy, who were constantly cutting off stragglers and foraging parties. But though the aged Emperor, unchangeable in his determination, amid the attacks of the enemy, the severity of the climate, the density of the forests and the dangers of marshes, pushed steadily forward (carried most of the way in a litter), and after sacrificing some fifty thousand men, at last reached the Moray Firth, yet his labour was in vain, for the territory in the North, held by the Romans, was never more than the space actually covered by their army at any given moment, and the successor of Severus was glad even to withdraw within the wall of Hadrian. The Druids were the priest caste, and seem to have regulated social and legal matters, but unfortunately the remarks of the Roman authors regarding them, though sufficient to indicate their peculiar and dignified manners and great intellectual acquirements, are very scanty and inadequate as regards their doctrines. Indeed, the Roman estimate of them was harsh and unfair in consequence of the patriotism that induced these men to organize revolts and inculcate resistance

---

(1) Cæsar De Bello Gallico iv., 2; Tacitus agrees 811 (?); Gibbon's History, vol. viii. and vol. iv., p. 291.
(2) Tac. Agr. chap. ii. See also Labueron Orig. Celt. Nouv. Dict.

to the invaders, and finally caused Claudius to proscribe the caste, and to take every opportunity of destroying their establishments and sacred groves. They were, in the early part of the first century, in the zenith of their glory and power. Presiding at courts and councils, and held everywhere in the highest esteem, they enjoyed almost absolute authority over their countrymen [1]—an authority maintained and enforced by the natural attachment of the tribes to their ancient faith, as well as by the power they themselves possessed of excommunicating and interdicting from public worship all obnoxious members of the community.[2] They met together every year to decide disputes, and to consider points of public advantage.[3] This assembly was presided over by the Chief or Arch-Druid, who was appointed by the Druids themselves, and had despotic authority over all the other members of the order. They were distinguished by their dress—on ordinary occasions a long flowing robe, or when engaged in religious rites, a white vestment—by the white wand that they carried as a badge of office, and by their wearing their hair short, and their beards long, while the other classes of Celts had their hair long and their beards short, except the moustache on the upper lip. The knowledge we possess of their learning —whether secular or sacred—is very scanty, but they seem to have had some acquaintance with geometry, geography, astrology, medicine, and physics, and to have taught the doctrines of the spirituality of God, and the immortality of the soul with its transmigration from one body into another.

1. They were divided into Bards or poets, Vates or prophets, and Druids proper. The Bards were either chronologers *(prwardh)*, who sang the praises of great men, or heralds *(teolur)*, or satirical poets *(cherur)*.

2. The second class of Druids were philosophers, or prophets *(vates, vacerri)*, who studied nature and her laws, by which they predicted future events.

3. The Druids proper[4] were the interpreters of religion, they attended the sick, presided at the administration of justice, settled public and private controversies, were invested with the power of life and death, and regulated the education of the young. They were priests, physicians, magistrates, and teachers, and in their office resembled the priests of Egypt, the Magi of Persia, and the Brahmins of India; while the fact of the religion and philosophy of all these being so similar, is a convincing proof of their having sprung from a common source. Aristotle states it as his conviction that philosophy passed from the Indo-Celts into Greece, and not, as was originally supposed, from Greece to the Celts.[5] The Druids appear to have devoted much of their time to the education of the young,

---

(1) Cæs. de Bell. Gal. Lib. VI. ch. xiii.

(2) Quibus est interdictum, ii numero impiorum ac sceleratorum habentur; iis omnes decedunt, aditum sermonemque defugiunt, ne quid ex contagione incommodi accepiant, neque iis patentibus jus redditur, neque honos ullus communicator. *Ibid.*

(3) Cæsar, *Ibid.*

(4). Studia liberalium doctrinarum inchoata per Bardos, Tavates et Druides! *Am*: *Marcellinus. Druid*, plural *Druidon*, from the old Celtic word *trows* or *banivid*, a doctor of the truth and faith; or from the British word *derw*; or the Greek word *drus*, an oak, from the sacred character of this tree, and from the residence of the Druids among the groves.

(5). Ap. Laert. De. Vet. Philos. i.

who were brought from great distances in order to obtain the benefit of their instruction, and they were at an early period so celebrated for their schools, that the Gallic chiefs sent their sons to receive instruction from them. One of these training Colleges was at Anglesea, others were at the Isle of Man, and at Iona, in all of which remains of their religious monuments are still to be found. The priests had a partiality for these islands, as typifying their own solitary position amid the ocean of lesser humanity, and they, no doubt, also appreciated the safe refuge as well as the retirement which these afforded them.

For the few historical notices we possess of the Caledonian people we are indebted to the Romans, but their accounts must be accepted with reserve, as their historians had but little opportunity of knowing the real character and customs of a people whom they despised as barbarous, and knew principally by their vigorous defence of their country from invasion and subjugation. Though known collectively to the Romans as Caledonii, they no doubt consisted of a number of separate tribes drawn probably into union for the first time by the great danger of the Roman invasion. If this were so, the lesson that union is strength was not lost on them, for we find all the tribes north of the Firths of Forth and Clyde united into the kingdom of Pictland—a country that possessed a considerable degree of civilization and remained a free State till A.D. 838, when it was conquered by the people of the south-west under Kenneth II., and became part of the United Kingdom of Scotland. It was during the Roman occupation that Christianity was first gradually introduced into Britain under the management of its earlier teachers, displacing that system in which the beliefs of the Celtic races all over the north and west had latterly been embodied, viz., Druidism. Thus the Druids laid the foundation of the edifice of which the philosophy of the East and the tenets of Christianity afterwards constituted the superstructure.

HISTORY OF PAGANISM IN CALEDONIA.

BOOK I.

History of Paganism in Caledonia.

CHAPTER I.

SOCIAL CHARACTER OF THE INHABITANTS OF CALEDONIA DURING THE MEGALITHIC AGE.

Section I.—Personal Character.

ÆSAR and other ancient authors say so little of the character of the Ancient Britons, that we must consult the habits and antiquarian remains of their neighbours the Gauls, as well as other primitive nations, whom they resembled, in order to draw conclusions from the comparison.

The Celtic races are branches of the Aryan family of nations, who migrated from Central Asia, and were at one time spread over Europe and the British Islands. These, mixing with the native races, the friendly indigenous inhabitants of Gaul, and the Scandinavian sea-rovers, gave birth to a body of hardy, brave, and industrious descendants, such as we afterwards meet with on the soil of Pictland; and this explains the difference in the physical character of the Britons, which varied considerably—*habitus corporum varii*, as Tacitus says—according to diversities of origin, locality, and other conditions. As regards figure, they were, in general, middle-sized in stature, with small heads and extremities, like those of primitive races; although, according to Strabo and Diodorus Siculus, the Celtic inhabitants of Britain were sometimes large and strong in person, blonde in complexion, with blue and quick eyes. They were brave and irritable; and, when excited, always ready to strike. They were simple in character, being without malice, craft, or subtilty, fond of war, and prodigal of life. In battle they often attacked the enemy without due consideration, and without order, and would sacrifice their lives rather than yield or retreat. They were open to conviction, and ready to learn. According to Ammianus Marcellinus, their women were beautiful, though rude, with blue eyes and fair skins, strong, brave, and voluptuous. When enraged, their necks swelled, their teeth gnashed, and they threw about their arms with a machine-like action and violence. The Caledonians, or Northern Celts, resembled the Southern. They were sometimes distinguished for their great height; some skeletons of them found in stone coffins being more than seven feet long.[1]

The Celts retained the characteristic features of the Indo-Germanic race. The Celtic Gauls, the Celtic Cimmerians (Greeks), the Cimbri, Cimbrians, or Kimris (Latins), according to Cæsar, were all of the same family, although *different names were given to them* according to the country they chanced to inhabit. Their identity is proved by the similarity of their physiognomies, their religious beliefs,[2] their language, as well as their manners and customs. The Germans of Cæsar, Tacitus and Pliny are the Scythians of Herodotus, and were supposed to have issued from the eastern extremities of the earth, which were covered with large forests. Cæsar concludes that the Caledonians were of German extraction from their habit of body.

The skulls of the Britons are of a short round aboriginal form with prominent parietal protuberances, and show a narrowness of forehead as compared with the occiput, agreeing to the brachy-cephalic crania of Professor Ritzius.[3] The race lived by hunting and fishing, were clothed in the skins of animals, and used stone instruments.

Diodorus speaks of the Britons who lived near the Lands End in Cornwall as peaceable and fond of the Phœnicians, with whom they carried on an advantageous traffic.[4] Strabo states that the Britons were taller and slighter in person than the Gauls; and Tacitus that the Caledonians had red hair and large limbs. The Celtic invaders from the East who succeeded these had a more lengthened oval head than the primitive race, and a larger anterior skull, with a more prominent occipital region. These were the *dolicho-cephalic* cranii of Prof. Ritzius.[5]

Like all rude races inhabiting a healthy climate, the Caledonians were naturally lazy, and averse to exertion, even though the consequence of their indolence might be the cramping of that liberty they loved so much. But for an evident gain and a congenial object, they would work long and strenuously, on a very scanty supply of food, and walk long distances without giving way to, or even feeling, fatigue.

(*a.*) *Cleanliness of the Body.*—Rude races are noted for their aversion to personal cleanliness. The Britons, instead of washing the body with water, which the ancient tribes seldom did, used fumigations of hemp-seed, accompanied with dry rubbing. The women used a paste, compounded of cedar and frankincense, ground upon a rough stone and soaked in water. With this they anointed their bodies and faces, and next day when they removed it, their skins looked clean, shining, and soft.[6] According to some authors it was this practice which gave rise to the name "Pict," since to satisfy their wild fancy, and astonish and frighten their enemies, the Picts were in the habit of tracing, by painting or tatooing, grotesque figures over their bodies.[7]

The Hindus believed in the importance of cleanliness, as well as of other personal duties, and attended to food and drink, clothing, sleeping and waking, as religious observances, which they were careful to enjoin in their religious precepts. In a hot country like India, the natives, however, found much benefit from smearing the exposed surface of the body with an oleaginous substance, which kept the skin soft, cool, and perspiring. In certain countries of Asia, where the temperature is low, and the wind dry, a black greasy pigment was applied to protect the skin; this custom is still followed by the rude hill tribes of Asia.[8]

---

(1) Stat. Account of Scotland, vol. ix, p. 51, 52.
(2) Proximi Gallis, et similes sunt. Eorum sacra deprehendas, superstitionum persuasione. Tacit. Agric., ch. ix.
(3) Crania Britannica, ch. ii, 15. Prof. Nilsson : Report of British Association for 1847.
(4) Latham's Ethnology of British Islands, p. 42, 1852. (5) Cran. Brit., p. 17.
(6) Herod. ch. 73, 75. (7) Sculptured Stones of Scotland, (Spalding Club), vol. i, pl. 71.
(8) Hooker's Journey in the Himalaya Mountains, vol i, p. 228.

(b.) Dress and Ornaments.—The women wore a profusion of hair, and the men, besides allowing the hair of the head and the moustache to grow long, wore warm woollen clothing during the cold season. Except a few, who wore sandals, the majority went barefooted. Cæsar and Pliny allege that the Celts of Britain stained their skins with the juice of the woad plant, in all probability to harden and defend the skin against the influence of the weather, as in cold countries people sometimes smear their bodies with a mixture of mud and water to protect them from cold. It was among the higher classes of ancient Britons especially that the custom was resorted to of tatooing the body with various figures, and colouring them with the woad or other paints ; and it would seem that it was because they stripped on entering battle, either for lightness of movement or to scare the enemy, that the Romans were led to suppose that they went always naked. The Highlanders followed this practice in war, when they threw away their plaids and short coats, and fought in their shirts.[1] When Dion states that the British dwelt in tents, naked and without buskins, the remark applies probably to the condition of some of the lowest classes.

At the time of the Roman invasion, as Herodian informs us, " the greater part of the Island of Britain was frequently flooded by the rivers and tides; and these constant inundations made the country full of lakes and marshes. Across these the inhabitants sometimes swam, or waded through them up to the middle, regardless of mud and dirt. As they always went about naked, being ignorant of the use of clothes,[2] they covered their necks and bellies with fine plates of iron, which they looked upon as a decoration and a sign of wealth, and were proud of as other barbarians were of ornaments of gold. They likewise stained their skins with pictures of various kinds of animals, which was one principal reason why they wore no clothes, because they were loth to hide the paintings on their bodies." This is an exaggeration. It is probably due to the fact that the inhabitants of Britain were only met with in the field in summer, and as they lay dead with their faces to their enemies. Then it is probable that before engaging with the enemy they threw aside their usual upper clothing that they might have greater freedom of movement in the use of their weapons. Dion Cassius,[3] who lived at the time of the Severus expedition, states that "the Caledonii and the Meatæ are the two chief British tribes, the latter dwelling near the boundary wall, which joins the Clyde and the Forth, and the former living beyond them in the northern mountains of Scotland. These Caledonians inhabited a rugged mountainous district, with desert plains, full of marshes."

The primitive inhabitants of Britain wore the skins of deer, wild bulls, foxes, hares, and also those of the smaller fur-clad animals, prepared with more or less skill. Not until a comparatively late period did they begin, at least the better class, to wear lighter clothing during the summer season, and in winter they wore long coats of home-woven wool or made of the skins and hides of animals, which they prepared by stretching them upon boards to dry, and then sewing them together with animal sinews or vegetable fibres. From the remains of their clothing which have been found in bogs, it is evident they knew the means of rendering leather supple and durable, although the method has been lost.[4] The sandals made to protect the feet were probably also of leather. Their dress consisted of Gaulish trousers, called "braccæ." Over this they had a cloak and blanket to protect the body from the inclemency of the weather. In the warmer months of the year the Celtic inhabitants wore knitted woollen garments, portions of which have been deposited in different museums. In Dunrobin Museum there is a fine specimen of this knitting, which was found in a peat moss, along with perforated bronze needles, bone pins, and other implements used in the manufacture of these fabrics.

Dress of the Britons before the Roman Invasion.—Chieftains. The men wore a close coat or covering for the body, called by Dion a tunic, checkered with various colours in divisions. It was open before, and had long

---

(1) Whitaker's History of Manchester, vol. i, p. 300. In the Battle of Killiekrankie, "Dundee gave the word to advance : the Highlanders dropped their plaids. The few who were so luxurious as to wear rude socks of untanned hide spurned them away. The whole advanced."—*Macaulay's History of England*, vol. iii, p. 300.

(2) Gildas complains bitterly of their want of decency.

(3) Pinkerton's Enquiry into the Early History of Scotland.

(4) See Keller's Lake Dwellings.

loose sleeves to the wrist. Below, pantaloons were worn, called by the Irish *brigis*, and by the Romans *bracae* or *braccae*, or breeches; and over the shoulders was thrown the mantle or cloak, called by the Romans *sagum*, from a Celtic word *saic*, signifying skin or hide, which was the original cloak of the country. Diodorus tells us that it was of one uniform colour, generally blue or black, the prevailing tint in the checkered trousers, the tunic being red, to prevent their enemies seeing their wounds. Their heads were generally bare, or, if covered, they wore a cap, that derived its name from the cot or hut of the Britons, which was of a similar form.

They wore shoes, which reached to the ankles, made of raw cow-hide, with the hair turned inwards. Even within the last few years shoes so constructed were worn in Ireland, of cow-hide drawn together by a string over the foot, while a leather string fastened beneath the heel inside and passing over the instep tightened the shoe like a purse. They were of untanned leather.

Fig. 1.

Dress of Females during Roman Period.—The females wore a British *gwn*-gown, which descended from the neck to the middle of the thigh, girt about with a girdle, with the sleeves reaching to the elbows. Beneath this a longer dress was worn, which reached to the ankles, after the Roman fashion. They wore shoes sometimes; these were of a costly character, and of purple leather. The articles used for fastening on the dress were bone and bronze pins, and buckles of bronze. Combs, either of wood or bone, have been found in graves with bronze articles.

Ornaments.—The Celtic ornaments may be divided into Primitive and Artistic. The former consisted of bones, horn, teeth, and shells, disks of earthenware or stone, which were perforated, and strung together by a cord of vegetable fibre, or a thong of skin, to form necklaces. Rings of jet, brass, amber, and even gold, are sometimes met with in England and Scotland. Glass beads are of more modern invention. They are sometimes called adder or serpent-beads. Gold was often used for ornaments, such as armlets, torques, rings, and serpent ornaments. We sometimes meet with bronze pins, hair-pins, tweezers, &c. In barrows were found silver ornaments of a later period, as in Norrie's Law, in Fifeshire, coins and pellets of gold, ornamented slightly with combs of wood and horn.

The upper class wore a profusion of gold bracelets (*armillæ*) on the arms and wrists, torques, or twisted collars of gold round the neck, and sometimes breast-plates, and rings on the middle finger. Such articles formed their chief wealth. Ornaments of amber, glass, and jet beads and amulets were worn by the ancient Britons.

The dress of the Scandinavian people, their weapons, and manner of living, their respect for the female sex, and their religious worship, were almost identical with the British, only modified by their peculiar character. The ignorant warriors of Scythia despised learning, and their ambition, in that direction, was limited to the wish to have their deeds recorded in song by their bards, and handed down by tradition. Agreeably to their ancient religious notions, they raised the great conqueror Sigga, of Denmark, Sweden, and Norway, to whom they owed the salutary laws under which they lived, to the rank of deity, and declared that he was to be worshipped with prayer and sacrifice, by valour in battle, and by respect for the distinction between right and wrong.

Section II.—Social Grades.

According to Strabo, the Celtic nation was divided into three, or perhaps four, classes; but a more useful division is that into Slaves (servi), common people (plebs), and elders (temsters); thanes, with chieftains, kings, as they appear on the sculptured stones of Scotland, and Druids and ministers.

(a.) Slaves.—Among rude races the lower classes were slaves or serfs. Of these some were hereditary, and were regarded as animals, a part of the proprietor's "goods," with which he could do as he pleased; and this

HISTORY OF PAGANISM IN CALEDONIA.

bondage could only be removed by the money they might save, although that was considered by right their master's, seeing they were his slaves. The Christian religion did not alter their political condition, and they are represented on the sculptured stones of Pictavia discharging their usual manual occupations. They were naked, and were considered to be without arms (*Fig.* 2), went barefoot, and wore only a woollen blouse or mantle, which covered the body, to which in winter were added the skins of animals. On the sculptured stones they are represented performing such acts as that of killing an animal, leading one to sacrifice with uncovered head or driving a cow, or a cart on a platform containing a sacred tree. Another class of slaves were prisoners of war, and they were often treated in a much harsher manner.

Fig. 2.

(*b.*) The *Common people* (plebs) formed the second class. These were more independent, being subject to

Fig. 3.

Fig. 4.

their chiefs, and in towns under their own magistrates. They were tributary to the state, and had to give their services in the time of war, as well as on other emergencies.

(*c.*) The *Tempster* was the trustee of the civil rights of the clan, and, on being installed in his civil function, received a wand as the symbol of his office. This office consisted in holding the lands in trust for the clan, to whom they belonged in common. By virtue of this trust the whole of these lands were treated as his, agreeably to the constitution of a patriarchate. His chief duty was to defend and maintain the rights of the community to the lands, against every attempted encroachment or alienation. "Hence they say, as erst I told you, that they reserve their titles, tenures and seigniories, whole and sound to themselves." It thus appears that the aboriginal inhabitants of Scotland and Ireland had, by their patriarchal laws, entailed their lands on their whole posterity, and that by forms the most clear, public and solemn, so as to render all misrepresentation or misapprehension respecting the inviolability of land tenures in the country impossible:—by which they make good a claim to rank above the enactments of the feudal code, and the law of primogeniture, as established in England at the present day. These Briton or Celtic laws, says Spenser, constitute a body of regulations, which though they are unwritten, and delivered only by tradition from one generation to another, are not unfrequently conceived in the interest, and intended to enforce the principles, of equity.

Fig, 5.

(d.) The Scotch Thane, or Chieftain, was the administrator of the King's royal rents, and his descendants retained the title after they had ceased to exercise the office, the land having become their own, and the King simply drawing a fixed "reddendo." There were country courts, where local gatherings took place, to decide on local affairs, and to settle differences; at least, we think we may conclude that there were such, when the excellent Cosmo Innes, although he declares he cannot tell, acknowledges "that there are indications of such assemblies," and believes that there were such among the Celts;[1] and, while he remarks that they left no code or chronicle—nothing but the circles of gray stones on the heath—in record of their national customs,

Fig. 6.

Fig. 7.

their manners and forms of proceedings, he adds, in a note, "that it will be curious if the circular monuments, formerly called Druids' circles, were places where the old Celtic people met for deliberation and for administering their common affairs, for judgment-giving, as well as for burial, for religious rites and ceremonies, and for solemn contracts; in short, fulfilling the idea and original purpose of a church."[2] We have no records of a date so ancient, but we have the evidence connected with the history of the race of other countries to assist us in filling up a gap here and there in the antiquities which still remain.

The feudal system is supposed to have been first introduced into Scotland by Malcolm Canmore, and by it the king came to be considered not only the fountain of honour and power, but also the rightful owner and inheritor of the land. Thus invested, the kings exerted themselves to put down the patriarchal system; but this met with strong opposition on the part of the people, and was the chief cause of the constant broils which for a long period embittered the reigns of the Scottish sovereigns. Charters of land were at first chiefly made to foreigners, and were freely offered to such as were in a position to assert and make good their title to a grant. From the difficulty of enforcing these claims in the Highlands, they were often allowed to lie dormant, and so the people of the districts included in the grant continued for ages after to hold their lands on the old tenure, and to pay their *calpa* to the hereditary chiefs, under whose banners they still fought in war time.

The chieftain was the head of the tribe or collection of families sprung from a common stock. His figure is a very conspicuous one in the equestrian processions, as delineated on the sculptured stones of Scotland. He is the largest figure in the group and rides first, mounted on the largest horse, with his hunting dogs by his side, and his protecting angel preceding him. On the St. Andrew's stone the chief is represented at his full height, vanquishing the largest lion and wearing the largest size Assyrian [3] wig. *(Fig. 9.)*

On the death of the chief the heads of the clan assembled to choose a successor. They did not necessarily select from the sons, or from the immediate family of the deceased, but the nearest to him in blood, who happened

---
(1) Cosmo Innes's Lectures on Scotch Legal Antiquities, p. 97.   (2) See Note *Loc. Cit.* p. 98.   (3) Sculpt. Stones, vol i, plate 55.

to be the eldest, worthiest, and most warlike of the *kin* or *sept*. Not fortune only, but dignity, gravity, weight, sagacity, and physique were respected in the election of their captain, or *Tanisht*, *i.e.*, military commander. According to Spenser, they installed him by placing him upon a stone consecrated and reserved for the purpose, and erected generally on a hill or mound, when a sword was delivered to him as the symbol of his office. Sometimes the mark of the foot of the first great chief figured upon the stone on which the new chief stood, as he made an oath to preserve all the ancient customs of the country inviolable, and to peaceably deliver back the symbols of his office, should age or misfortune incapacitate him from the discharge of its duties. This last oath they exacted, because they considered the occurrence of these as an intimation on the part of the higher powers that he should make way for a successor.

Fig. 8.

Fig. 9.

(*e.*) *Druids or Ministers.*—These were the highest, or most sacred class. Besides being considered prophets, whose persons were inviolable, they were held in high estimation for their virtues, and were generally appealed to to determine disputes of a public as well as of a private nature, both by the Britons and Gauls. By means of augury and the inspection of sacrifices, Druids undertook to foretell the events of the future, and interpret the duties of religion; and they kept the multitude in awe by the authority they assumed—deciding controversies, bestowing rewards, and inflicting punishments. They had the direction of the education of the chiefs, and controlled all matters of State, as well as performed the rites of religion; they had the first division of the spoil taken in war, and it was considered unlawful to offer up a sacrifice without their assistance. They had absolute authority to reward and punish. In return for such important duties, they paid no taxes to the State, and had immunity from military service and public burdens.

Cæsar supposed that the Druidical system was native to Britain, and that it was transplanted from thence to Gaul; and he says that those who desired to acquire a thorough knowledge of its precepts used to cross over into Britain, and put themselves under the instruction of British priests. On account of the great celebrity of the Druids for wisdom, one of them was always in attendance on the person of the chief, to act as counsellor and judge; and as a bard he sung the praises of his ancestors; as a chronicler he registered his deeds; as a physician he attended him in sickness, and as a harper or musician soothed him when wearied, and cheered him when sad. These officers were rewarded with grants of land, which fell to their families along with the right of succession to the office itself.

The doctrines and learning of these Druids, or Western Brahmans, resembled, according to Cæsar, those found by the Greeks on the banks of the Ganges, and both appear to have sprung from a common root;[1] although we should not be warranted in inferring from the resemblance in some of their customs, their superstitions, and even from the doctrines of Druidism and the mythology of the Sagas, a common origin for the

---

(1) "à l'égard des Perses;" and the same may be said of the Hindus, "Je ne doute point du tout qu'ils ne fussent le même peuple que les Celtes. Ni la langue des Perses, ni leur coutumes, ni leur religion ne différoient pas assurement de celles de Celtes." Pelloutier Histoire des Celtes, p. 19.

natives of Europe and Asia, did we not also know that they possess as well the same common elements of speech. Corroborative evidence is supplied in the fact that the Druid and the Brahman hold similar opinions in regard to the immortality of the soul, and its transmigration from one body to another, founding thereon their common contempt for death.[1] The sages of the Druids were fond of discoursing on the magnitude of the world, the number and character of its denizens, with the movements, glories, and influences of the heavenly bodies, and the virtues and powers of the immortal gods.

The priest-bards, who wore peculiarly-colored robes, were entrusted with the education of selected individuals, instructed the people in worldly knowledge, as well as the tenets of religion, and undertook to cure their diseases. We may venture to surmise that the system of education they practised, would resemble that of the Buddhist: that it consisted in teaching the pupils to read and cast accounts, to be honest and self-sacrificing, to speak the truth, to be gentle and tender at all times, to abstain from war and vindictiveness, and to avoid everything that could lead to vice; to be obedient to their parents and superiors, to reverence old age, to provide food and shelter for the poor, the aged, and oppressed; to despise no one's religion, to persecute no man, to love their enemies; to practise humanity, endurance, patience, and submission. They taught them also to respect the value of time, which is reckoned of so much account in civilised communities, and held as of no importance among rude nations. Like the ancient sages, the Buddhist priests conveyed much of their learning in short precepts or proverbs; a method of instruction early practised by Eastern nations, and still used by the Hindus and Arabs, who teach aphorisms, such as those which compose the proverbs of Solomon, the songs of Moses, Miriam, and Deborah, and many others belonging to the same period.

The influence and authority of the Druids depended on their reputation for superior wisdom and learning. Among a primitive people, much depended on their commanding presence, and the charm of their eloquent and persuasive speech,[2] but most of all on their assumption of knowledge and supernatural power. By this knowledge they affected to resolve difficulties of state; and by this power they professed to heal bodily disease; though doubtless they knew better and were wiser than those they counselled. They were acquainted also with the healing virtues of leaves, roots, and herbs.[3] The knowledge they had, they deemed it politic to keep to themselves, and they did not commit their learning to writing.

According to Cæsar, the Druids presided over all public and private sacrifices, and directed, if they did not conduct, religious ordinances. They tried criminals, were the judges and arbitrators in all disputes, and had the power of excommunicating the refractory, if not from the favour of heaven, at all events from the advantages of society.[4] They had the power of life and death; they deposed princes from their thrones, and sometimes devoted them to destruction. We are told by Martin,[5] that in his (1703) time, every great family of the Western Islands, kept a Druid priest, whose duty it was to foretell future events, and to decide all causes civil and ecclesiastical. They were supposed to work during the night, and rest in the day time.

The Druids considered the oak tree the symbol of their deity, and their sacred places were overarched by its branches, under the shadow of which they lived, like the Buddhist saint under the Bhoda tree. The leaves, flowers, and branches of this tree were supposed to be possessed of a virtue which was concentrated in its parasite the mistletoe, which grows from its bark and was much prized for its eminent qualities.

In the book of Deer, we meet with Matadan "the Brehon," as a witness in a particular case. The laws found in the legal code of the Irish people were administered by these Brehons. They were hereditary judges of the tribes, and had certain lands which were attached to the office. The successors of this important class are the Sheriffs of Counties.

---

(1) Lucan, vol iv, 460.   (2) Martin's Description of the Western Islands, p. 104.   (3) Plin. Nat. Hist., xvi, 95.

(4) Si quis aut privatus, aut publicus, eorum decreto, non stetit sacrificiis interdicunt. Hæc pœna apud eos est gravissima. Quibus ita est interdictum, ii numero impiorum ac sceleratorum habentur; neque iis petentibus jus redditur neque bonos ullus communicatur. Cæsar Com. Lib. vi, c. 23.

(5) Desc. of Western Islands, p. 105, 1703.

CHAPTER II.

DOMESTIC MANNERS AND CUSTOMS OF THE INHABITANTS OF CALEDONIA DURING THE MEGALITHIC AGE.

HE most simple contrivances employed by the primitive natives of a country for domestic purposes varied with race, soil, climate, and character. Tacitus informs us that the Celtic Britons resembled the inhabitants of Gaul in their manners and customs; consequently, the examination of the monumental remains of the latter will assist us in understanding the general customs and primitive social condition of the former. At this early period a portion of the southern inhabitants of Caledonia were driven by the Romans into the north, and these, for their mutual protection, combined to form a state in the N.E. of Caledonia, known by the name of Pictland, which included the greater part of Forfarshire, the Mearns, Aberdeen county, and the neighbouring districts. The brave and hardy inhabitants of this region engaged in frequent warfare with the Roman invaders, as well as with their lowland neighbours, against both of whom they defended themselves with courage and determination. They were called indiscriminately barbarians; but in some respects they did not deserve the appellation. They were a fair-complexioned and intelligent race; individuals among them were even educated in a sense, and their social affairs were regulated by Druids more with reference to the cultivation of the arts of peace than the conduct of warfare.

When Claudius found that the chiefs of the British were encouraged and directed by their spiritual teachers, an edict was issued dooming them to the sword. Their chief establishments were destroyed, and their last refuge in the Island of Angelsea was devastated by Suetonius Paulinus. Nevertheless, their civilisation was not wholly lost; a portion of it was carried away by the Picts, and planted in the north-east of Caledonia.

SECTION I.—DWELLING PLACES.

(a.) Huts.—The ancient inhabitants of Caledonia lived in much the same manner as Julius Cæsar describes them. The huts they occupied during the summer months were circular, of from nine to twenty feet in diameter, erected on a raised floor of packed clay, slightly depressed in the centre, where the fire was placed. There was a doorway four feet wide and five feet in height, turned towards the south-east. This aperture, which served for entrance to the hut, was the only one for the admission of light and the outlet for smoke. The circular patches of packed clay which are so often found in groups on the mountain slopes are most probably the foundations of the houses which Tacitus describes as being circular, and Cæsar informs us were the same as those of Germany; and these remains are still to be seen in Scotland, Ireland, and England. The walls of these huts were formed of wicker-work, plastered up (Diodorus, Lib. liv) with prepared moist clay, and their sloping roofs were thatched with faggots, reeds, or straw.[1]

---

(1) *See* Hoare's Wiltshire, and the Rev. S. Rowe's Perambulation of Dartmoor.

These clusters of huts were usually surrounded by a dry stone wall, an earthen wall, or a wooden fence, to protect the inmates from their enemies and the savage beasts of the forest, such as the wild bull, the wolf, and the bear. Not only the raised earthen foundations of these huts, but the cultivated gardens and fields connected with them may still be traced on the elevated slopes of hills, with a south-eastern aspect. Elsewhere these remains are found on the elevated sloping banks of rivers. In other situations the walls of the hut were three or four feet thick, and four or five feet in height, or less. The floor was laid with clay, and sometimes with stone. These remains resemble those of Orkney in Scotland, and the bee-hive houses on the west coast of Ireland, with peculiarities due to variety of climate, and the quality of building material found at the place. Where stone abounds the circular chambers were covered with stone, mingled apparently with grass, reeds, or straw. In all these cases the hovels were low circular chambers, surrounded by thick walls, formed of rough stones or earth, faced externally with stone without cement. There is an entrance to the south-east, guarded on each side by pillars or jambs, and leading to the small apartments constructed within the breadth of the main work. The remains of several of these dwellings are near each other, and they have underground chambers; other villages of the same kind are found at Busallor Mulfra, etc.[1] Many of them are situated in the vicinity of cromlechs and druidical circles. That of Chysanter (Abor) is a little to the east of Mulfra Cromlech.[2] At an early period grain, etc., were probably stored in these subterranean caves for winter use.

(b.) Caves or Weems.—During the long winter season the primitive inhabitants of Pictland sheltered themselves from the inclemency of the weather in caves of rocks, in chambers, or weems, dug in the ground. These pits were covered and protected from the inclemency of the weather by boughs of trees and sods of turf. In most situations little stone houses were built underground, and called earth houses. In these caves, or weems, to which the inhabitants of Scotland retired during the severe weather, and in times of danger, they used to house their corn and other food on which they lived through the season during which either frost or foe beset them. There, in the midst of the smoke of their wood fires, they kept themselves secure and warm, though with but scanty covering.

These caves are found in most Celtic countries in a good state of preservation. They were made by digging a large oblong hole on an elevation, in a gravel soil, and not far from water. The sides of the excavation were built up with dry stones, which overlapped each other so as to incline inwards, and on these, as the wall rose to a sufficient height, large stone flags and earth were put to complete the roof and strengthen the structure. Thus the same device was used as in forming the Cyclopean structures of infant Greece, the palaces and temples of Mexico, and Yucatan, in South America, and the magnificent Buddhist and other temples in India, although in the Celtic houses there is often apparent more unity and compactness. The entrance to the weem is generally concealed, and a long curved passage, $2\frac{1}{2}$ feet wide, leads to the chamber. Its doorway is filled up with a large broad flagstone. The passage slants downwards to the chamber below, which is often from 12 to 20 feet long, by 6 or 12 feet broad. The wood-fuelled fires were in the middle of the room, and the smoke escaped by small apertures at or near the entrance.

Sometimes human bones are found in these weems. On Dunannon hill, in Strathmore, I found three skulls in a recess, two of adults—one a male and the other a female, and the third that of a child about 12 years of age, with the parietal bone fractured, as if smashed into the brain, probably by a bludgeon; and Mr. Rhind found four pieces of a human cranium in heaps of ashes, which were probably part of the skulls of enemies slain in battle, and kept as rude trophies of valour. Diodorus[3] and Strabo[4] state, however, that the inhabitants of Ireland in the first century of our era had a relish for the flesh of their relations. St. Jerome avers that "an obscure Scottish tribe were cannibals;" the truth of which Gibbon finds no reason to question.[5]

In Caves the archaic sculpturings in many cases are of very ancient date, in others they are more modern. The *Cave-men*, as the inhabitants of these caves were called, were without pottery and domestic

---

(1) *See* Wright, p. 134.   (2) Martin's Western Islands, p. 154.   Penant's Tour, vol. iii, 223.   Stat. Account, viii, 489; and xvii, 231.
(3) Lib. v, ch. 32.   (4) Lib. iv.   (5) Gibbon's Decline and Fall, vol. iii, p. 270.

animals, and belonged to a primitive age. These caves were probably inhabited by a race who sought shelter in them from their enemies; they were high, and covered with a thick covering of grass, and looked at a distance like a barrow or tumulus.[1] They were generally surrounded with wood, their approaches being defended by ramparts of earth or trees (Cæsar).[2] According to Strabo, a rampart of trunks of trees would sometimes enclose a round clear spot of ground, and the huts and folds for cattle. Julius Cæsar and Tacitus describe the dwellings of the ancient Britons, though smaller, as resembling in form those of Gaul.[3] They remind one also of the round and dome-shaped buildings depicted as British on the column of Antoninus at Rome, and the Pictish houses both of Scotland and Ireland.

On the western and southern brow of the hill, which formed a part of the old forest of Cluny, in Strathhardle, are the remains of a fine circle of boulders, and above it the foundations of numerous groups of huts, as well as a large cairn, which I examined, without finding any remains, and on the northern side of the hill there are the remains of another village, with a rocking stone and tumulus. The form of these huts probably resembled those still used by the hereditary charcoal burners of the present day, who are required to reside in the forests of Ireland, during most parts of the year, engaged in the preparation of charcoal for gunpowder (fig. 10). My attention was once attracted to two of these huts, on the side of a wood, which had the external appearance ascribed to the Celtic huts of Britain and Ireland. They were built on a rising ground, were ten feet in height and about twelve in diameter; and were constructed of a number of straight branches of trees. The extremities of which were thrust into the ground in a circle, and the other ends fastened in the form of a cone. Over this grass, faggots were placed in a way to overlap each other. These huts had no other opening than the door, which was two feet and a half wide; each accommodating three men, their beds being marked 1, 2, 3, and the floor boarded by dressed logs of wood, a little raised above the ground. At the end of the passage and opposite the door, was the fireplace for heating the hut, and preparing their food, and b, b, spaces for stowing away their personal effects. The inmates enjoyed good health, and lived, they said, to a good old age; but on observing that the chief of the tribe had lost his teeth, and that he wore a somewhat wasted look, I remarked to him that I supposed he must be sixty, when to my surprise I was told that he was only forty-five. His father had died, I further found, at the age of fifty-six.

Fig. 10.

They burnt charcoal in the fireplace, and were aware of the noxious nature of the "nitrogenous" vapours, which, however, had free egress through the chinks formed by the spaces between the faggots. They were careful, they said, in the selection of a dry elevated place for their huts, as they found it healthy, particularly in the dry season.

The cave in the parish of Airlie is an example of a weem (fig. 11). It is situated near the top of a gravel hill, and is of an oblong rounded form, ten feet deep, fifteen wide, and thirty long. This space is walled round with rough stones, without mortar, two or three feet above the floor, which was laid with clay. Two chimneys (*e.e.*) conveyed away the smoke of the fires, and afforded access to a scanty supply of light and fresh air. In other caves the chimney is at the further end. which would improve the air; and this was necessary, as I found the light burnt dimly at that end, which was lower than near the entrance, owing probably to the falling in of earth. Sometimes a sort of well-pit, as at Kittleburn, is found inside these caves for drainage and convenience. The entrance into this cave looked in a north-eastern direction, from between large stones slightly under the level

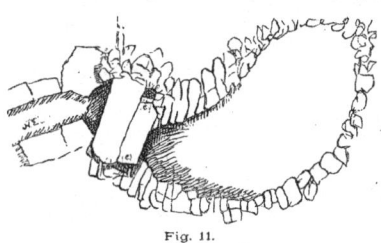

Fig. 11.

---

(1) Fosbroke's Essay of Antiquity.   (2) De Bell. Gall., lib. v, ch. 12.   (3) *Loc. Cit.* lib. i, ch. 4.

of the surrounding ground. This entrance was six feet long, sloped inwards, and was entered obliquely, and being only eighteen inches wide, was entered with some difficulty. On sliding down this inclined plane, for five or six feet, you find yourself in a large dark vault.

When preparing a new road to the Manse of Ruthven, Forfarshire, the workmen came upon a large flat stone, and in attempting to raise it the crow-bar slipped out of the workman's hands, and it dropped into a hollow below. On removing the stone a large cave was discovered of a curved oval-form, nine feet four inches broad, thirty-one feet nine inches long, and when the gravel was removed to the foundation, it was found to be ten feet deep. The walls near the foundation were formed of large undressed stones, and as they rose higher large irregular blocks of red sand-stone were placed above one another, with their ends overlapping those below, and generally extending outwards, and kept in their places by the earth on their outer extremity. The roof was formed of large flat, undressed red sand-stones, which must have been brought from the neighbouring River Isla, and transported to the spot by considerable mechanical ingenuity. Some of these were water-worn, and two tons in weight. Near the north-west end of the cave, an entrance was discovered a little more than three feet wide and four feet high, which increased in height after passing the large stone that supported and formed the covering to the doorway. This was completely filled with black earth, intermixed with pieces of charcoal. On following this it was found to take a northern direction, swelling out into a sort of ante-chamber, and terminating seventeen yards from the cave's mouth in the high and precipitous south bank of the River Isla as it flows east. The entrance was flagged, while the cave itself appeared to have had a flooring of gravel, probably smoothed with clay.

The following year the digging operations were resumed, when it was found that the caves extended in a curved direction, were built with stone, without mortar, flagged below and covered by large flat stones above. At one place were four erect stones forming a sort of stone doorway, where the flooring was more raised and the passage contracted, with a small recess. In several places near there were two layers of covering stones, and at one place the covering stones had been removed. There were found here two bronze rings, one with an imperfect screw outside, a worril, a broken stone vessel, and a large piece of iron, which might have accidentally got there. This is a Caledonian habitation, which must have been warm even in the cold winter nights, and, from being in a gravelly soil and so high above the river, was easily kept dry. One of the large key-stones, forming the roof, contained carefully-prepared circles (round cups), such as are described in Chapter IV.

Another variety of the Celtic caves appears to have had the roof supported by rafters and the walls built of a compound of clay and small stones. Caves of this kind are found excavated out of the bank of a rising ground at Gourdie, in Perthshire. The local name given to these caves is "stud stalls," from their fancied resemblance to stalls for horses. They are not far from the Roman camp at Delvin, and were supposed to be for a picket of Celtic cavalry as they watched their enemies in the plain. This is probably incorrect, for if they required such a guard the hardy horses of the natives did not require such stables. There were seven of these circular chambers, fifteen feet in diameter, dug out of the side of the northern bank of a steep hill. They were with one exception separated from each other by partitions twelve feet thick, and the passage was forty-two feet long and four feet wide. This Pictish village was elevated above the damp and unhealthy country, which was covered with wood and morass; and the houses themselves were a sufficient shelter from the winter cold even with poor clothing. I excavated one of these caves, and could not only trace the hard prepared walls by the black mould, mixed with charcoal, which had been washed into the floor of the cell, but could distinguish, from the appearance of the surface, the flat stones used as a hearth for the fire to heat the house, and to prepare food for the inmates. The roofs were probably of earth sods, supported by rafters. Here the rude tribe lived together for their mutual protection and comfort. . These cells were adequate to hide the inmates from their enemies, and defend them from the weather.[1]

These subterranean houses, when discovered, after being forgotten for ages, were found covered with a thick layer of this mould, which had slowly accumulated by percolation from above, and contained the fine particles

---

(1) *See* Statistical Account of Scotland, vol. xix, p. 359.

of the soil. Before removing this covering of earth the remains of charcoal and wood ashes were met with, mixed with fragments of large deer's horns and horses' bones, portions of them chipped off by edged tools to get at the marrow. These bones were of oxen, small sheep, goats, pigs, tusks of boars, and of dogs large and small. In Caithness, in situations near the sea, bones of the haddock, and other fish, of whale and seal, with whelk and limpet-shells, are often found.

(*c.*) *Lake Dwellings or Crannoges.*—In districts where lakes abound, the inhabitants at an early period formed lake dwellings or island forts, Celtic pile-dwellings. These pile-buildings were of considerable extent, and of different forms for the accommodation of several families. They were constructed upon platforms, resting upon piles driven into hollow places round islands, at some distance from the margin of the lake, and communicating with the mainland by narrow causeways constructed in the same way, defended by a primitive drawbridge. The Crannoge of Loch-an-Eilan in Stathspey, was constructed at the end of the 17th century, and was found "useful in time of trouble or war for the people to put their goods in, and leave their children, as it was easily defended." Such places of security were often prepared at an unknown, but very ancient time, during the stone period. The castle on the Loch of Clunie may be mentioned as an interesting example of most probably an ancient Crannoge, which was afterwards converted into a baronial castle, with its moat, and the Lan for the distribution of justice on the mainland. It was the birthplace of the "admirable" Crichton, and the place of security where the Bishop of Dunkeld deposited the treasure belonging to his church in times of danger.

These Crannoges presented different features in different countries, and their nature was only discovered in Switzerland, during the dry winter of 1854. When the lakes and rivers sank very low, the inhabitants of Merlin, on the Swiss lake of Zürich, resolved to raise the level of some ground by the accumulation of mud dredged from the shallow water. During the dredging, Dr. F. Keller discovered the remains of rows of piles driven into the bed of the lake, and among them were many flint weapons, stone hatchets, polished and sharpened by rubbing, tools and utensils of stone and bone, hammers, axes, celts, and other instruments. All these belonged to the stone period, with the exception of an armlet of thin brass wire, and a small bronze hatchet. Rude pottery, fashioned by the hand, was abundant.

The interest of Antiquaries in this country was attracted to the lake-dwellings in 1857, by Sir William Wilde,[1] through observations he made in connection with the small Lake of Lagore, near Dunshaughlin, in the County of Meath, Ireland. The lake had been drained, and a circular mound, which had been an island in it, was found to be thickly strewed with bones. As these were being carted away for manure, it was discovered to be an artificial structure. Sir William found that the mound was formed of piles of oak, seven feet in length, driven into the marl, tied together by cross-beams, forming compartments, and mortised into oak planks laid flat upon the marl and sand at the bottom of the lake. The compartments formed by the cross-beams were filled up with stones, sand, and marl; and a second tier of upright piles rose from the first. The mud was found of a dark colour, and copiously sprinkled with the bones of a variety of oxen, &c., such as the *Bos urus* and *B. bison*, liver seal, swine, red deer, lynxes, goats, sheep, dogs, foxes, wolves, horses, and asses. The dog appeared to have been the only domestic animal. From the Vegetable Kingdom were found carbonised wheat and barley, crushed by stone rubbers, querns, and pestle and mortar. There were the remains of a small variety of crab fruit, carbonised apples and pears, stones of wild plums, seeds of the raspberry and blackberry, nuts and hazel nuts, and beech, oak, and ash trees. Along with these antiquities were found weapons, ornaments, and utensils of stone, bone, wood and iron. The ancient annals of Lagore (Loch Gabhor) show that this lake dwelling was plundered and burned by a hostile Irish chief in A.D. 848. In the year 933 it was again destroyed by piratical Norsemen, which proves it to have been a place of importance, having been, probably, the residence of an Irish chief.

Since the description of this crannoge was made public, many others have been found both in Ireland and Scotland, as well as in Switzerland. In these lake-dwellings there are found no iron or bronze implements, no

---

(1) Archæologia, vol. xxxviii, 1859, On Swiss and Irish Lake Habitations.

bones of extinct mammalia, and no human bones, from which fact we may infer that the dwellers there were not cannibals. The changes that took place in these lakes after great floods sometimes swamped these habitations; remains of them are occasionally discovered after periods of dry weather, or in consequence of agricultural improvements. Several of these crannoges have been discovered in Scotland,[1] in which the early Celts must have lived, what they contain having been but little changed during the many ages which have elapsed since they were abandoned, in consequence of their having been covered with water.

Herodotus gives the earliest historical account of such a dwelling in the year B.C. 520. It was in a small mountain lake in Pœonia (part of modern Roumelia),[2] and re-discovered by M. Deville.[3] Some of the earliest of these lake-dwellings are so old, that the inhabitants did not know the art of manufacturing pottery, had no corn, and knew little of agriculture. They lived where the colossal elephant, or mammoth, the woolly-haired rhinoceros, the gigantic cave bear, and the great hyæna existed; when the British lion was a reality, and not a heraldic myth; when England was still united to the Continent, and anterior to the advent of the British and even European Celts.

(d.) Refuse Heaps.—Mounds of the kitchen refuse have been found near these ancient dwelling places, particularly on the sides of mountains, and near the banks of streams. These contained charcoal with fragments of coarse pottery, and the shells of edible cockles, muscles and periwinkles *(cardium edule, mytilus edulis,* and *littorina littorea),* as well as the bones of herrings, cods and flounders, caught by hand, by hooks, and by nets, mixed with the bones of deer, sheep, and one or two extinct animals, the long bones being split lengthwise for the sake of the marrow.

SECTION II.—HOUSEHOLD FURNITURE.

The habits and customs of the early inhabitants of the British Islands may be inferred from the remains found in their burrows, where the most prized and serviceable utensils were deposited for the use of their departed relatives in another world. The whole domestic riches of these primitive people consisted of a few articles of household furniture. At an early period, and among such a race, wooden logs or rude stools, and wooden benches were used to sit on. They slept on straw or grass spread upon the floor, on which were extended the dry skins of dogs, wolves, or wild beasts as bedding, not as coverlet, for what served as mantle by day was sufficient as coverlet at night.

Their household *utensils* consisted of platters or bowls of wood, in some cases of coarse earthenware, which they used to hold, and out of which they ate their food, while not unfrequently the leaves of plants served the purpose of plates. There were also the stone implements which must have been employed as hammers, and these round and oval in shape, sometimes sharp-edged and sometimes pointed. There were also stone celts with rectangular, rough or smooth edges, and articles made of flint—some adapted for spear or arrow heads, some for saws, and some for knives and hatchets.

Stone celts were lately found at Jubelpore, in India, resembling those of Europe, though somewhat larger in size, being six inches from the head to the sharp edge, 3 in. at the broadest part, 7½ in. in girth, and a pound and a half in weight.[4]

---

(1) Herod. Lib. v, ch. 16.   (2) Nat. Hist. Review, Octr. 1862, vol. ii, p. 486 ; Lyell's Antiquity of Man, p. 18.
(3) Proc. Soc. of Antiq. Scotland, vol ix, p. 368 and 388.
(4) Archaeol. Scot., vol. iv, p. 39. Mayweek's Customs and D. Lakes's Ath., p. 232.

Section III.—Hunting and Fishing.

Hunting and fishing formed the chief occupation and also the chief source of subsistence among the primitive inhabitants of Caledonia. They fished in the sea, the rivers, and the lakes. They often exhibited both an intimate knowledge of the habits of the fish and great dexterity in catching them. They caught the fish partly by the hand, under rocks and stones, partly by bows and arrows and harpoons, armed with flint-pointed extremities, and partly by hooks and lines. They made nets, too, of vegetable fibre, by means of which they netted birds as well as fish.

In hunting the smaller animals they used bird-lime or stones, but to kill the larger game they were generally armed with bows and arrows and lances of wood, the arrows and lances with their points either hardened in the fire or tipped with flints or hard stones; at times they used snares and pit-falls. They would arm themselves, too, with knives and clubs for the destruction of large animals, and to take their skins, of which they made their garments. Their dexterity and courage in the chase was great, and they evinced a remarkable instinct in finding out and following the trail of their game. They likewise employed [1] decoy-birds in duck-catching. The habits of birds were carefully observed, and the hunters caught them by placing water-pots over their own heads and floating with the current towards the ducks as they were engaged in feeding. When in the midst of them, the sportsman suddenly seized a duck by the leg, and pulled it under water before it had time to give the alarm. The other ducks, supposing it to have dived, continued feeding, and were in succession captured in like manner. In this art great precaution required to be observed, for had the alarm been given, and the secret revealed, the ducks would have afterwards become too chary of such floating vessels.

Among some tribes the lower classes were not allowed to eat hares or geese, and in some cases fish; and the better class lived chiefly on game, fish, and shell-fish. But the character of the food depended much on the nature of the ground, whether it afforded game, or was more favourable for the rearing of domestic animals, and the cultivation of grain crops

The domestic animals were dogs, fowls, cows, sheep, deer, and pigs. As they had no grass in winter and small store of fodder, in consequence of ignorance of the art of preserving the herbage for the winter, they killed the greater part of their small-sized sheep and cattle before the frost set in. Those that they kept alive suffered much from want of food.

The Celts gradually learned to domesticate animals and acquired the art of providing them with food against winter. Thus were introduced the rudiments of a pastoral and agricultural life. They even made feeble efforts to keep fish in pools to feed the increasing population. In the eastern countries the natives were specially favoured. Here as the rivers dried up during the hot season, the fish buried themselves in sand-beds, and retained their vitality by hibernation until the wet season. The natives, aware of this, dug them up and thus temporally replenished their larder. I have seen the natives in India take fish alive out of the moist mud, in which they had buried themselves. At a distance from the sea, where there were no lakes or rivers, the natives depended more on their flocks wandering from spot to spot in search of pasture. The Caledonians had in general few opportunities of associating with their neighbours; and the inhabitants of the mountainous parts remained in small communities, and made slow advances in the progress of civilisation. Yet the quantity of bones and other remains found in the caves and weems of the lowlands, prove that they subsisted chiefly on animal food, fish, milk, and vegetables.

---

(1) A fishing-rod was also used for catching birds, its small end tipped with bird-lime.

Section IV.—Canoes and Coracles.

In hilly countries where rivers and streams abound, and where no artificial means are employed for keeping the beds clear, they become obstructed by falling rocks and trees, and the country to the rear becomes inundated, and covered with lakes and marshes. After heavy rains, the pent-up water accumulates and forces its way along the obstructed channel, carrying away the cliffs and trees, or else opens up a new one. These accumulations of water alter the form and size of the beds of streams, and render their courses tortuous and rugged. It was in such lakes and obstructed rivers that canoes were used by the Celtic inhabitants of Scotland, and became necessary to keep open communication with the neighbouring districts in the low marshy lands near rivers. These canoes were hollowed out of the trunks of large trees, by charring the wood with fire and chopping the charred bits with stone hatchets and hammers; while their bulwarks were made of wooden planks, fastened together by twigs or thongs, to enlarge the size of the boat, and render it capable of bearing a greater number of people, who sat upon low cross benches.

Fig. 12.

Fig. 13.

These canoes must have been employed at a very early period, for they have been found at great depths, and embedded in sand; some of them are upwards of thirty feet long, four in breadth, and two in depth, and they resemble those still used in many parts of India. I have given a drawing of one of these canoes found in the Bengal Sunderbunds in that country. The stern is of two pieces, fixed into grooves in the sides and bottom, and the junction of the two sections is formed by what is called a "groove and feather." The canoes are propelled by paddles, and by punting; and the sides, where the oars are attached, are strengthened by lateral pieces of oak, fastened by strong wooden pegs, the holes for the oars being often clean and well rounded. In the bottom are projections to support the feet of the rower.

Coracles.—When large trunks of trees could not be procured, they made a framework by bending tough branches of wood, keeping these in their places by interweaving small twigs. Over this framework a fresh hide, 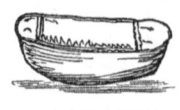 with the hair on the inside, was drawn, and laced with thongs, the keel, gunwale, and benches being of wood. As the hide dried, it shrank and tightened all. These boats were often of such a size as to afford accommodation for several people, and even to ferry cattle across rivers. Canoes of this kind are very buoyant, and although they suggest ideas of insufficiency, they are really strong, and are propelled by club oars. I have been in them in rough weather; once in a gale of wind off the coast

Fig. 14.

of Galway. I found they behaved well, and could be used with safety in visiting places at some distance. They were used by Columba and his party in crossing the Irish Sea, and even in crossing from Britain into Gaul.[1]

The coracle, according to Strabo,[2] preceded the canoe, and was prepared, he says, by stretching a hide over a framework of wicker, which formed the ribs of the boat.

---

(1) *See* Ulster Archæologia, vol. i, p. 32. (2) Lib. iii, ch. 3, § 7.

Section V.—Agriculture, Barter and Trade.

The primitive inhabitants of the more central and northern parts of Caledonia retained their pastoral nomadic and predatory mode of life, and Boadicea is represented as pleading that the Britons had no skill in husbandry, and as complaining of being compelled to till the ground for the Romans. Galgacus, in his speech before the battle of the Grampians, spoke of the Northern Britons as possessing no arable land, a state of things which continued for nearly two centuries later; and when Severus explored the northern part of the island, the Meatæ and Caledonians were still represented as having little ploughed land, and paying little attention to the cultivation of cereals. Corn appears to have been raised only in small quantities; and as the soil was not manured, it was soon worn out by the repetition of the same crop, so that from time to time new soil had to be broken up, and additional labour expended in preparing it. Their ignorance of the management of land, and the unnecessary toil they gave themselves in consequence, confirmed the inhabitants in their nomadic habits, so that they did not rise above hunters, fishermen, or wandering shepherds. As their necessities increased and their ideas enlarged, the provisions which chance threw in their way no longer satisfied them : they began to sow and plant in convenient situations, and to learn how the soil could be so cultivated as to yield a better and a larger crop. This labour would soon come to constitute that right to property in land, which had previously been confined to houses, arms, and nets, and to gifts from their chiefs to supply their immediate wants. They thus began to clear and cultivate the soil in order to retain and support the flocks they had collected. It was so in other lands, as well as in Britain.

The large and fruitful plains of Hindustan, and the banks of its great rivers, must in like manner have early drawn to them hordes of people in pursuit of the necessaries of life; but only by degrees would these penetrate into its forests and secluded valleys, either because animals of prey would debar their entrance, or because they might feel satisfied that the possessions they had were sufficient for their wants. These causes naturally separated mankind everywhere into small communities; and as the land they held would attract the envy of their neighbours, it became necessary for them to protect it against attack, and to elect some one with authority, to preserve it in well-being, and provide for its defence. Thus secured and organized, they would acquire importance as owners of the soil, and members of a commonwealth, while their advantages, and their sense of them, would from generation to generation increase. Superiority in numbers, physique, valour, enterprise, and favour of fortune, would contribute to raise some of these communities above others, till they became large and flourishing states. These happy changes would rapidly promote and encourage population, and, by the protection afforded, as well as the exemption accorded to certain classes from military service, would render their ingenuity more active in the cultivation of the industrial arts. The superfluous things which industry might thus produce, would be very soon exchanged for other articles, of which the citizens might feel the want, or vanity desire the possession; and thus would spring up a new and still further enriching industry in the form of trade.

As the southern and eastern parts of Scotland are in the main level and fertile, they were capable, even in a rude state of tillage, of producing considerable quantities of oats, wheat, barley, and pease, which constituted the chief food of the southern Caledonian Celts. It was from this that the Lowlanders got the name of Cruitnich, or wheat-eaters, an epithet of contempt or envy given them by the Highlanders who inhabited the wild and barren hills to the north, which scarcely repaid the labour of cultivation, and only afforded a scanty pasturage for their cattle, and a retreat for game, which, with the milk and flesh of the cattle, yielded them food. The cultivation of the fields in the Lowlands, whilst it increased the means of subsistence, and led to a settled and civilized state of society, rendered them at the same time a more tempting prey to the Romans; while the northern inhabitants, with a barren country, were allowed to retain their liberty, and to assert their rights by force of arms. Accordingly, to a late date, they kept up the ancient habit of painting the upper part of their bodies with gaudy colours and fantastic figures, and in the day of battle fought with a fierce and desperate valour. The number of Roman camps in the plains of Strathmore, at Delvin, Auchtertyre, Deanside, Castle Hill, and many other places; and the number of Celtic forts, bidding defiance to their enemies, upon the neighbouring Sidlaw and Grampian mountains, such as Dunoon, Finhaven, Catherthun, Forthill, &c., formed so many stores for grain, as well as places of protection and defence.

The ancient Britons, in some places, raised cereals to a considerable extent. The mortars and querns that have been found near the quarters they inhabited, were used to grind barley and oats,[1] of which they made their bread and oat-cakes. These when baked were hard and gritty, which explains why the human teeth which have been found are so much worn down, just as hard biscuit wears down the teeth of the British seaman in modern times.

Barter, or giving the commodities of one place for those of another where they were more required, was a medium of communication between neighbours from the earliest times, and is still employed in a modified form. The northern Celt obtained for skins, wool, and horns, to a late period, a few of the comforts and luxuries of more civilised life.

Trade.—Mutual wants occasioned the exchange of natural riches for the productions of handicraft, and slowly united rude tribes with more civilised countries, thus spreading moral and social cultivation over the country. In ancient times trade subdued the rugged wilderness of Caledonia, and has now cleared away the primitive forests, and drained the waters of the plains. The merchandize brought from Gaul to Britain, before the latter was subjugated by the Romans, consisted of trifling objects of luxury, such as looking-glasses, blankets, knives, axes, &c., and of personal adornment, such as bracelets of ivory, armlets, and torques of bronze for the neck or loins, amber and glass beads for necklaces, ornaments for the ankles, buttons, tweezers, pins, bodkins for the hair, adder-stones, &c.

Section VI.—British Carriages and Cars.

Ancient British Carriages.—We are indebted to Roman authors for our knowledge of these cars, as the Celts of Pictland had neither the ability to contrive nor inclination to indulge in such luxuries. The men of rank rode on horseback; and even their ladies seldom used cars. Hence these are rarely represented on their monuments. The only one found is that in the margin, copied from a sculptured slab at Meigle.[2] It represents a chariot drawn by two horses, with plaited tails. The driver is in front, and two persons are in the carriage, which is a covered one, the chief being in front.[3] At the foot, to the right, is represented a man on his back, with his head in the mouth of a mythological bear, who is pressing his chest. A dog is in front barking, and a man with a cross-bow is shooting at the monster. The dog behind the archer indicates the rank of the travellers. The chariot wheel is an example of Eastern ignorance of perspective in drawing.

Fig. 18.

---

(1) "A quern will, it is said, grind a boll of dried corn into meal in one day.—By the law of Scotland in the reign of Alexander III, in the year 1284, it was enacted, 'that no man shall grind quheit, maislaock or rye, unless in storms he is in lack of myldner to grind the samen.'"—*Currie's North Knapdale*, p. 7, (Glasgow, 1830).

(2) Jour. Arch. Assoc., vol. vi, p. 252. Sculpt. Stones, vol. ii, p. 59.

(3) This stone was destroyed some years ago, when the church, in which it had been placed, was burnt.

The Celts, with great daring, made their assaults on their enemies in war-chariots, and sometimes, particularly in the South of England, in double-manned chariots, drawn by horses, which would have proved irresistible, had they been trained. Cæsar[1] extols their valour and the impetuosity of their attacks, as they drove with great fury against the enemy, provoking them with their darts, and often throwing their ranks into disorder. The driver could stop the strong active horses as they swept down a steep descent, by turning them round in a small circle, while the fighting man would run along the pole, sit upon the yoke, and quickly return in case of need to the body of the chariot. When they attacked horsemen, the fighting men left the chariot in a convenient position, and fought on foot. If overpowered, they would re-mount and retire, or else take further part in the action.

Section VII.—Food and Drink.

(a.) Food.—The inhabitants of ancient Caledonia subsisted during the summer months chiefly on different kinds of fish, roots, acorns, and berries, and followed a rude system of agriculture, using implements made of stone, horn, and wood.

The mortar and pestle, and quern, may be considered as the earliest instruments used for pounding and crushing corn. But as this process was laborious and ineffective, it was soon superseded by the handmill (*mola mannaria*), or quern, which was first of oak, but erelong exchanged for the stone-rubber and corn-crusher. These simple round handmills were very generally used. They are found in great numbers in the caves of the Picts, and were from fourteen to eighteen inches in diameter. They resemble the mills used for the same purpose from time immemorial in India, where they were worked for ages by bondmen and bondwomen; and were generally employed in the preparation of cereals for food. In some places they were formed of a flat oblong stone, hollowed upon its upper surface to receive the parched grain, and an oblong oval-shaped rubber was passed backwards and forwards by the hand, so crushing the corn into a coarse meal. A quern of this kind was found in Anglesea,[2] and another of a similar description by the author at Rostellan, county Cork, Ireland. The meal was ground and the bread baked daily. The mills after improvements gave place to the "*molæ jumentoriæ*," or mills driven by oxen or horses, which were at an early period introduced by the Romans, and were naturally superior in structure as well as more efficient in work. Watermills were introduced, according to Strabo, Vitruvius, and Palladius, in the reign of Julius Cæsar. Nevertheless, handmills were used in Scotland till a late period, and they are still sometimes used in the Orkney Islands.[3]

The Celts made their bread by first kneading the meal into dough, and then baking it upon flat disks of red sand-stone, chipped and rounded on the edges. I found several of them that had been so used in the ruins of the small fort of the Hill of Barry; and two of them are now before me.[4] They are smooth and convex, from three and a-half to eight inches in diameter, and from half an inch to an inch in thickness.

(b.) Drinks.—The Britons used wooden and stone cups and coarse earthen vessels to drink from, water being their chief liquid. They likewise brewed a kind of beer or malt liquor called Curw,[5] in the preparation of which heather and other bitter herbs were used instead of hops; which latter were not known in England until

---

(1) De Bell. Gal., ch. iv.
(2) Archæologia, vol. vii, pp. 4, 245.
(3) Statistical Account of Scotland, vol. vi, p. 406; vol. xiii, pp. 117, 119, 207; vol xiv, p. 526.
(4) One of the workmen trenching the ruins of the Fort, said he had found a "gei curn," *i.e.*, a considerable number, of these stones. See Arch. Cambriæ, vol. xxxiv, p. 135.
(5) A name which it still bears in Wales.

the reign of Henry the Eighth.[1] The fermented beverage composed of honey boiled with water, was the mead, metheglin or madder,[2] which formed the favourite beverage of the Celts.[3] It was drunk out of a double-handed cup made of wood or horn, and sometimes of stone called a mazer bicker, occasionally neatly girt with a small silver ring or hoop. This ancient beverage of the Caledonians and other British nations in the 3rd century[4] was a generous liquor, which was little inferior to wine either in colour or flavour.[5]

The Drinking Cups of the Celts were of wood, horn, stone, and pottery,[6] some with straight sides perpendicular or converging, others with concave or convex sides. Those found in ancient barrows are of the finer sort, and were obviously placed there, with water or some favourite drink, for the use of the deceased in his passage to the other world. The bone and wooden vessels must have been destroyed by age and damp. An ox-horn is a more modern form of drinking vessel. The cogue, or coggie, was composed of wood, like the bicker, but had no handle. Drinking vessels, or dram cups, made of silver or horn, were called tassies, from the French *tasse*, viz., stoup, or jug with a handle. The *paterae*, or stone cups, like the rock basins, appear to have been in use at the earliest period, but owing to the want of metallic tools, they were fashioned into the rudest shapes: they are always found in the vicinity of Druidical, or primitive monuments. These monuments must have been erected for some religious purpose, and, on this account, they are found in the rude Megalithic age. Earthern cups are frequently found in the barrows, four, five, and six inches in depth, and they were apparently intended to hold a favourite drink, as they do not contain any of the ashes of the dead, and were probably placed inside coffins. Those found in the Scottish cists are placed near the head of the body.

Such cups or jars have been found in Derbyshire, a foot in height, with a small mouth, and of a different shape from the cinerary urns, and in them a small quantity of ashes is sometimes discovered. Cups of another variety, but much smaller, are called by Sir P. C. Hoare "Incense Cups." Besides these, large earthen vessels are sometimes found in Celtic houses, which were used probably for keeping stores; and the fragments of such pottery that remain, are generally without any attempt at ornament. Small stone cups (like "luggies"), with a handle or ear, are sometimes found in stone coffins. One of these was turned up when trenching the circular fort on the Hill of Barry, in Forfarshire; and another was found near Belmont, in Strathmore. They are known in Scotland as Druidical *paterae*. They seem to have been hollowed out of a solid stone, by repeated blows of a harder one. This operation must have required skill and great perseverance, and the vessels, being more expensive than the wooden "bicker," or drinking horn, must have been used by the chiefs on high occasions. In burying places various other household articles have been found, as well as shields and arrows.

At one time, pottery must have been of frequent use in the Celtic or British household, if we may judge by the number of specimens which have been preserved. These consist of various kinds of urns and other vessels, formed of clay, rudely manufactured, without the help of the potter's wheel or lathe. The earth they were made of was coarse, and sometimes mixed with spar. The urns are generally wide-mouthed, and ornamented with incised zigzag work; the figures on them are circles, bands of small lines, rows of dots, lozenges, and other simple devices, arranged in rows. The clay had been hardened in the sun.

---

(1) Wright's Celts, p. 70.
(2) Was so ancient that Sir Wm. Jones supposes it was the drink which made Noah senseless. The Teutons who inhabited Northern Europe used to drink metheglin for 30 days after marriage; hence the expression "honey-moon."
(3) The modern "ale" is derived from the Dutch word *Oalei*.
(4) Diod. Sic., pp. 4. 41, 242; 348.
(5) Low's History of Scotland, p. 247. Ossian, vol. i, pp. 74, 116.
(6) Principally taken from Dr. Lake's paper in "Archæologia," No. 35, p. 232.

Celtic Urns may, according to shape, be divided into four classes:—

1. Straight-sided, which seems to be the primitive and rude form.

2. Concave; thick and uneven.

3. Convex; thinner and finer.

4. Bell-shaped; are the most elegant as well as the best finished form. These are most commonly decorated with figures, some of which were made by the pressure of a cord, and the patterns in others engraved with a pointed instrument.

These urns are of a brick-red, yellowish, or black colour, and as they are better baked below, it would appear they were heated more at that quarter than at the upper margin, which is often black. The rounded form appears to have been due to a certain rotary movement in the making. None of them are glazed; but some have knobs, sometimes perforated vertically, for suspension by a string. Their capacity was from two fluid ounces to at least four gallons. They were intended to hold food and drink for ordinary purposes, and for libations in honour of the dead.

Celtic Urns may, according to size, be arranged in three classes:

1. A large-sized urn, wide-mouthed, with its mouth turned upwards or downwards, and containing fragments of bones, when found in graves.

2. A smaller-sized urn, with rude ornaments, capable of holding about a quart.

3. A still smaller urn, more fancifully ornamented, of a dark grey or black colour, and often perforated with small holes.

Section VIII.—Celtic Weapons.

Endowed with great powers of endurance, with courage and with patriotism, the Celts were always formidable enemies even to the Romans. Their religion required the display of warlike qualities; it was considered necessary for them to die in battle, or by their own hands, in order that an entrance might be insured into heaven, where they would exist in renovated strength, continue the excitement of the fight, and enjoy the luxury of drinking beer out of the skulls of their enemies.

The constant necessity of defending themselves from the attacks of enemies with skill as well as valour, required the possession and the practice of arms for defence, as well as of implements for providing the means of subsistence. These occupations left no time for the acquisition of learning, which was confined to the priests; and study being considered unmanly, was despised by the upper classes. These latter were satisfied with the glorification of their warlike deeds by poets or retainers, who exaggerated facts to gratify the humour of their chief, whose ambition was that his acts should be favourably spoken of by posterity. The personal armour of the Celts was intended to strike terror into their enemies, as well as to defend themselves. Their chiefs had distinguishing head-dresses and cloaks, and the weapons they used, besides clubs and bows and arrows, were arrow-headed spears, stone knives and axes, bronze knives and daggers, and short javelins or spears, having a knob at the extremity to terrify the enemy by the noise they made with them on their shields. The Celts were expert swimmers, and in their advance or retreat before their enemies; rivers and lakes offered but little impediment to their progress.

Other stone weapons are often found near the habitations or graves of the ancient inhabitants of Britain, and consist of chipped or smooth flint arrow or spear-heads of different sizes and shapes, with sharp cutting or irregular sawing edges. These are found along with celts, or sharp wedges, used in splitting wood and for skinning and cutting up the animals taken in the chase. The arrows or spear-points with which they slew their prey and defended themselves from their enemies, were fixed in hafts, or wooden handles. These were the earliest instruments fabricated by primitive man, and are found in conjunction with the bones of the *Elephas primigenius*, at Hoxne, in Kent's Hole, near Torquay, on the Continent at Amiens, and at St. Acheul, in the Valley of the Somme. The ancient Caledonian Celts used slings for throwing stones,[1] which they hurled with great precision from their fortified camps. They wore large, straight and broad bronze swords, and carried oval or round targets. They were also famous for the use of their battle-axes and sharp balls of flint attached to a thong, with which they used to brain their enemies.

SECTION IX.—CELTIC FORTS.

Like all rude races, being generally in small communities by themselves, and surrounded by enemies, the Celts required not only to protect their persons with arms, but to defend their houses, villages, and towns with fortified works. These were of various kinds:

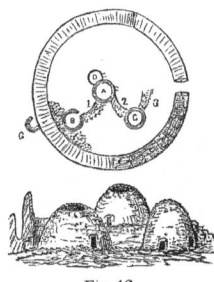

Fig. 16.

(a.) Fortified Villages were generally built in the secluded retreat of a forest or on the elevation of a hill, and were defended by a circular wall of stone and earth, as protection at once from the wild beasts of the forest, and from the more treacherous and no less savage assaults of human enemies. The risk of attack required the inhabitants to be always in arms, to guard against its possibility. Prepared with weapons of self-defence and practised in the use of them, they secured themselves further by the erection of palisades round their huts and villages, and where they could, with stone walls and ditches. Where stones abound, as in the county of Kerry in Ireland, ancient circular dry-stone forts, having stone ramparts and deep ditches, are still to be found, as in the example in the margin. This fort surrounded four bee-hive houses of the ordinary form and structure.

(b.) Primitive Celtic Forts.—The ancient Celtic forts may be grouped under three varieties: the earthen fort, the stone fort with uncemented, and the more modern one with cemented, walls. These forts are among the most ancient Celtic monuments, and differ in construction according to the nature of the country in which they were erected, and the use to which they were put. Many are elliptical in their form, while the Roman forts are usually square, near water, and built with mortar, as well as constructed in places where disciplined troops can act.

(c.) Earthen Forts in Ireland and England.—The materials with which these forts were constructed differed with the situation. In the open plains they were made of earth, and were enclosed by deep ditches and high ramparts, such as the mud-fort near Waterville in Kerry, Ireland, and Old Sarum, the British fort near Stonehenge.

The *Anglo-Saxon Chronicle* mentions that the Cymrii "fought against the Britons at the place called Searobyrus (Sarum), and put the Britons to flight." This place, though it lost its independence, was strengthened and became a stronghold of vast importance to the Romans, as proved by the great public roads which

---

(1) This is proved by the number of oval-shaped stones in their fortified posts.—Hoare, Ancient Wilts, vol. i, pp. 55-56.

proceed from it to different parts of the country. The subsequent history of this fortified place is interesting. The town was contained within the entrenchment, and after the Norman Conquest, William the Conqueror gave the lordship to Osmond, Lord of Seez. In 1076 the bishopric of Wilton was removed to it. William held a Parliament in it in 1096, and his successor, Henry I, held his court there in 1100, soon after his accession to the throne. As the country became more secure, and the clergy more powerful and independent, the custody of the fortress was entrusted to them; and in the time of Bishop Roger the splendour of the cathedral and the strength of the fortifications were such as to attract the attention of contemporary annalists. In the civil wars of Stephen, Roger was disgraced, and the fortress garrisoned by troops. The ecclesiastics were coerced and insulted by the soldiers, and they got the sanction of Richard I to remove the church to a spot in the neighbourhood.[1]

This, and other British forts, had lofty conical mounds or citadels in the centre, as we see also at Tottenhoe in Bedfordshire, and at Lancaster, where a modern baronial castle was erected. They were so favourably situated that even the Romans and Danes did not disdain to occupy some of them; and even armies of more recent date have held them and found them serviceable; a circumstance which explains why cannon balls and pieces of modern armour have since been found in or near them: even coins and pieces of sunburnt clay have been picked up. The Fort of Old Sarum, which is near Salisbury, affords a good example of ancient fortifications in the South of England. The Saxons called it Searobyrus, or Sorberdunumburgh, which was latinised into Sarum. According to Sir R. C. Hoare, the fort is 7 furlongs 26 yards in circumference, and comprises an area of 27½ acres within its walls. The *valla* of the inner and outer work are nearly of equal heights; the former is 100, and the latter 104 feet thick; they are surrounded by a wall cemented with lime. The principal entrance is in the east, and is defended by a horn-work and deep ditch. Towards the west a postern gate is similarly defended. Fragments of hewn stone are to be seen in the outer rampart.

(d.) Primitive Stone Forts.—The large fortification of Doonbey in Kerry is remarkable for its size and peculiar formation. It consists of an immense wall of large undressed stones, laid flat with great accuracy, and without cement. There is no appearance of the arch, and the erection is cyclopean. The fortification crosses an isthmus, which juts out into the Atlantic, and whose precipitous sides rise several hundred feet above the ocean.

The large fortress of *Aran* has several walls surrounding it, one within the other, so that, if the outer wall was scaled, the enemy had to face another, and sometimes another, of solid masonry within, which had to be surmounted before the place could be taken. The outermost of these was a massive circular wall, which surrounded the *bee-hive* shaped houses, and ordinarily defended the inhabitants and their cattle. The walls and the cyclopean dome-roofed dwellings of Lough Curran are referred by Dr. Petrie to the time of St. Finan. These buildings, however, are so peculiar, and resemble so much in their form and construction those of the East, that we may suppose they were first constructed by strangers from that quarter to protect themselves from the wild beasts which were in the surrounding woods. The stone *Caher* of Ireland was built by a Celtic race, of the same kindred, though not perhaps identical with the people that built the Pictish towers in the north of Scotland, and those in Caernarvonshire in Wales.

According to the historical records in the Book of Lucan, those on the island of Aran were built at the commencement of the Christian era, by the sons of Raithmore, after their expulsion from the mainland by the Scoti, or Milesian Irish.

The Hill-forts in Scotland are elliptical in form. They are built without cement. The Celtic forts of Catherthun in Forfarshire are interesting specimens. These are erected on two conical hills, one,

---

(1) Sir R. C. Hoare's Modern Wiltshire.

the White, is oval, and fortified with stone, and the other, the Brown Catherthun,[1] nearly circular, with earthen works. The view from these hills is very beautiful: to the north, a rich valley with a winding stream separates them from the magnificent range of the Grampian mountains, and Strathmore with the Sidlaw hills is on the south; to the east is the German ocean and the bay of Montrose, and on the south-west a rich and undulating plain extends as far as the eye can reach. In the midst of this plain rises the hill of Finhaven, and more to the south the hills of Dunnichen, the Laws, and the Law of Dundee, each with its Celtic fortification: but history is silent as to the time when they were erected, and even as regards the race of Celtic people by whom they were raised. An anonymous writer, more than a hundred years ago, is said to have found stones in them with hieroglyphic characters, bits of broken statues, and old coins.[2]

The conical head of the eastern hill, or Brown Catherthun, is surrounded by the remains of two circular ditches, and breastworks; but the west, or White Catherthun, has an immense collection of loose stones round its top, which is of an elliptical form. In this are the foundations of rectangular and small circular buildings. Round the base of the mass of stones is a deep ditch, and 100 yards lower down the hill are two small ditches, which may have formed defences, strengthened by wooden palisades.

Beyond the stone breastwork of the White Catherthun were shallow concentric circles, that could not of themselves have formed defences, but may have had a religious significance. Can they represent the coils of the serpent, so often seen in India as an early object of worship, and so have acted as a charm to protect those within from their enemies? In this case, these convolutions may have formed the figure of a serpent, with an oval space on the east side, representing a winding of the serpent, and intended for the performance of sacred ceremonies. The Brown Catherthun, surrounded in like manner by a serpent, may have been intended for the protection of the cattle and other purposes.

The Fort of Barry, near Alyth, in Forfarshire,[3] is an example of a primitive stone fort. It is situated on one of the hills of the lower range of the Grampian mountains, 676 feet high above the surrounding country. Three sides of the fort were built along the edge of the gorge, and portions of the walls were vitrified. The other sides were defended by a strong wall of an irregular oval form, strengthened by palisades and ditches, which descended in a circular form towards the right, where the ground was precipitous, and led to a gorge in the Grampian Hills. Another road from the fortified height led to the left, where an oblong fort, defended by a wall and ditch, was situated. This was 200 yards from the large fort, acted as a rampart, and between these two forts was a level space, where, in times of danger, their flocks and herds were left in security.

So irregular is the vitrifaction of these forts that it appears to have been due partly to the peculiarity of the stone, and partly to the violence of the fire. The stone which is vitrified is either the plum-pudding stone, or red sand-stone, and the effect is due to fire, which had been used partly for culinary and other purposes, and partly by way of signal to the other hill-forts. This vitrification is therefore to be considered in general as accidental, rather than intentional, as it was not required in the absence of gunpowder. In the construction of these forts, gneiss, quartz, granite, mica-slate, clay-slate, pudding-stone, and other rocks were employed; and the large fires that were made for social and religious purposes, were sufficient to vitrify portions of these rocks exposed to their influence, so that the extent of the vitrified portions would depend on the extent of the fires, and the more or less fusible nature of the stone. As this effect of the fire must have been observed, they did not use mortar to bind the stones together; it is probable that they used it for strengthening the walls, especially where they required them to be more than usually strong. Thus, in the construction of the Barry hill-fort, no

---

(1) From *cader*, a fortress or stronghold, and *dun*, a hill. Others allege that the northern freebooters or Catterns used the fortification, and it got the name of Catherthun, or thieves' hill; but in this case it must be a modern name.
(2) See *Ruddiman's Magazine*, August 30, 1775.
(3) Archæologia Scotica, vol. iv, p. 184.

HISTORY OF PAGANISM IN CALEDONIA.

vitrified portions have been detected in the encircling wall, but portions were found at the extremity of the bridge, and at the bottom of the large ditch which surrounds the fort. This could not, from the situation, have been meant for a beacon-fire to alarm the neighbourhood in the time of danger, and was therefore most probably intended to strengthen the wall.

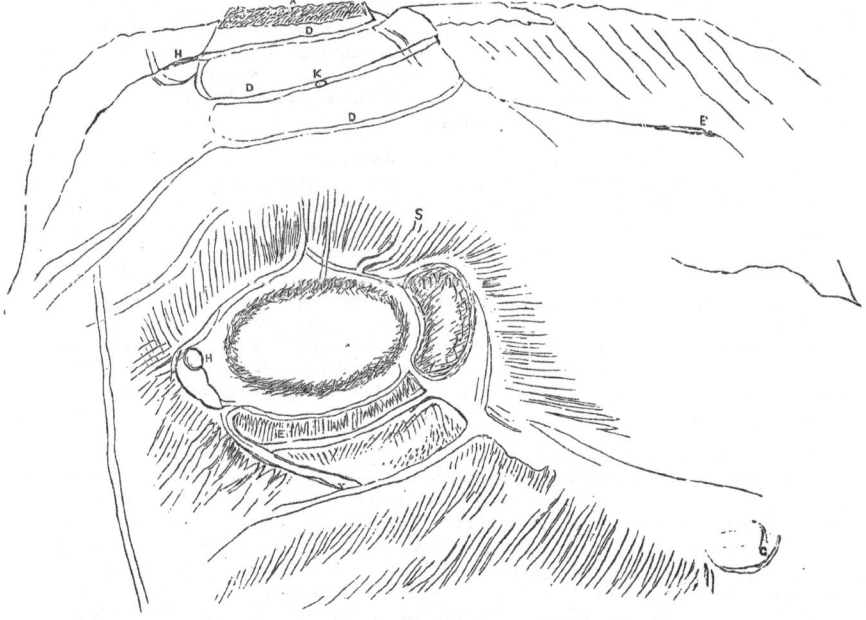

Fig. 17.

The flat top of the hill is surrounded by an immense collection of unhewn stones, which had been found near the spot, or brought from a distance. The quantity of these stones is such that the whole population must have been employed in collecting them. They appeared to have formed a wall of considerable thickness, built without mortar,[1] but the stones are now lying in a long mass, 20 feet broad, though still retaining the oval outline. The hill commands an extensive view of Strathmore, with the Sidlaws and neighbouring hills. The ascent is very abrupt on the north and west sides; and it is on the south and east that the remains of approaches and artificial defences, D D, are still visible. The upper fort is of an oval figure, 210 feet long (eighty-four paces) in an E.S.E. direction, by 53 feet wide at its broadest part, within the wall. There are the remains of a deep ditch beyond the oval wall, on its eastern and southern side; and towards the south-east, there is the appearance of an outlet from the fort, leading to a small bridge across the ditch. Chalmers informs us that this was ten feet broad; and about eighteen feet long and two feet broad, and was composed of plum-pudding stones, which had been built without much art, and vitrified on all sides, so that the whole mass was firmly united. This is the only part of the foundation which appears to have been

---

[1] The Romans introduced the art of building with lime or cement.

intentionally vitrified :"[1] and it must have been done to strengthen the bridge. This led to the south-east of the fort, which was well defended on the north-west and east sides by the steep form of the hill. The chief entrance seems to have been from the north-east, the approach being along the verge of a precipice, which was strengthened by an escarpment of stone, that must have rendered it there almost impregnable. To the south, another road appears to have wound round three parallel ditches and ramparts, which were further defended by wooden palisades. At K, there is a large round stone resembling, though much too large for, a mill-stone, with a deep round hole in the middle, six inches in diameter and a foot deep, probably for receiving a standard. On the west, upon a small level piece of ground lower than the large fort, was the well, H, which supplied the garrison with water. The oval space in the fort was covered with luxuriant grass, where houses had been, and where subterranean caves probably still exist.

The small fortification on the brow of the hill was 250 paces from the large fort in a S.E. direction. This space was extensively excavated, and may have been intended as a place of security for the cattle in times of danger. It resembled the small, or Brown, Catherthun fort. The small outfort had remained undisturbed for many generations, until the year in which I described it, when it was unfortunately destroyed in the course of agricultural improvements; and during its removal I had frequent opportunities of examining its original plan. It was oval in form, thirty-five yards long by thirty-three broad, in the oblong diameter, like that of the large upper fort, in an E.S.E. direction. This fortification consisted of an outer wall, the foundation of which was twelve feet broad, formed of large packed boulders, and upon this a wall had been built several feet high, which must have afforded an excellent protection to those within. In the formation of this wall no cement seems to have been used, and in the course of time the stones had fallen down, so that when I first saw it, they filled up the outer ditch,—this was two feet deep at the bottom of the wall, and sloped outwards and upwards for six feet, from whence the ground shelved outwards.

The northern and southern entrances of this fort were joined by a passage three feet three inches broad, which, for some distance from the northern opening, was bounded by a wall on each side, two feet high and two-and-a-half feet thick.[2] This was likewise built without cement, with its face inwards, and this passage intersected the fort in its long diameter, and joined the entrances in the S.E. direction. The space between the outer wall and the central passage was laid with undressed flags, rather under the surface of the surrounding ground. This space was filled with black earth and stones, with several large patches of charcoal and red powder, most probably brick-dust, or the remains of imperfectly baked pottery; among which I could distinguish a few bones much decayed. Numerous well-worn and broken querns were found among the stones, with a considerable number of small, flat, round-shaped stones, which may have been used as baking stones; and a stone vessel, known in Scotland as a stone cup, or Druidical *patera*. I also found a much-corroded iron knife, with a bronze nail to fix it to a deer's-horn handle, and also the iron stalk of a button. These fortifications had ramparts and ditches; and the garrison was, when threatened by an attack at the hands of enemies, increased by accessions from neighbouring hill-forts, which were so erected that all were within view of each other.

These circular or oval forts—Raths, Duns, Lises (Irish); Cathair (Gaelic)—are all Celtic, and are found over many parts of Caledonia. They varied in strength and form, according to the situation and importance, and were usually erected on elevations in flat districts; the entrances were flanked by mounds and ditches, and strengthened by palisades, or by double walls, with narrow openings at right angles to the main entrance; but the area was not always sufficiently large to contain huts for the accommodation of the chief and all his followers. Where stones abounded, the fort had high ramparts of stone. Many of them were erected on cliff-protected heights, and were strengthened on the side where they were open to attack. Examples of the first variety are found in Britain and Ireland, but of the second, in Ireland only.

---

(1) Caledonia, vol. i, p. 90.   (2) This resembled the entrances in the Strathardle circles.

HISTORY OF PAGANISM IN CALEDONIA.

Many places of refuge and defence, constructed by the Britons, were on the summits of hills, conveniently situated for the purpose. The heights so fortified were always detached, and commanded an extensive view of the neighbourhood; while the quality and figure of the fortifications depended on the country they were in, and the character of the post to be defended. Examples of British camps are not only found at Old Sarum, South Wilts, but at Marsden Castle, Dorsetshire; Mole-Arthur, Malvern Hills; and there is one on Wittenham Hills, near Doncaster, in Oxfordshire, &c. Cœr-Craddock, in Shropshire, is supposed to be the camp of the brave but unfortunate Caractacus.

The vitrified hill-fort of Knockfaril, near Strathpeffer, four miles west from the town of Dingwall, is upon the apex of a beautiful green conical hill on the south side of the valley. The fort is of an elliptical figure, the major axis being in an east and west direction. The wall was three feet high and two feet thick, and vitrified to its very centre. It resembles the portions of vitrified matter in the inner face of an old lime-kiln. The wall was vitrified to strengthen it: wood being easily obtained, while stones, and the means of transporting them, were difficult to get.

(*e.*) *The Celtic hill-forts built with Mortar.*—The large and fruitful valley of Strathmore is bounded on the north by the Grampian Mountains and on the south by the Sidlaw Hills. In the former are numerous gorges stretching from the north, and at their termination in the low country are the villages of Dunkeld, Blairgowrie, Alyth, and Kirriemuir, originally built with mortar, where the Highlander came and bartered or sold his cattle; and further south the towns of Dundee, Perth, Forfar, Brechin, and Montrose, where he obtained the necessaries he required for his family among the mountains. In earlier ages, this large and fruitful valley was surrounded by forts erected upon the hills, to which the natives retired when threatened by their enemies in the plains. The Romans established camps, as at Castle Hill and Delvin, to defend their crops and herds against these northerns, who, brave to audacity, intelligent, and enterprising, took advantage of every opportunity of attacking their rich neighbours from their hill-forts, where they kept their cattle, which constituted their wealth. The access to the forts was protected on the north-east by the mountains, and on the south by large ditches and winding pathways.

CHAPTER III.

PRIMITIVE SYMBOLIC STONE MONUMENTS IN ASIA AND EUROPE, WITH AND WITHOUT INSCRIPTIONS: DESCRIPTION AND USES.

THE uninscribed symbolic stone monuments are of three classes :—Simple and pillar monoliths; Circles of erect stones; and Sepulchral monuments. Examples of each of these are found in Asia, and other regions. In Europe they are only found in their simple form, in consequence of the people having become Christians at an early age, and advancing in civilization in other directions.

SECTION I.—PRIMITIVE SYMBOLIC MONOLITHS.

In the East these monoliths are boulders, employed as the symbols of the Deity, for "prayers," or charms, for boundary-stones, as memorial and burial erections, and for coronation purposes.

There is between the ancient monuments of Europe and those of Asia a resemblance so marked and peculiar, that it can only be explained on the supposition that the nations which erected them were originally of the same race,—that primitive Aryan race which has spread itself over Europe on the one side, and Hindustan on the other. General Yule, in his interesting remarks in the Proceedings of the Antiquarian Society, has reckoned up the various parts of India where such remains are to be found; and many more examples might be given. Our present object is, by some references, to throw light on the common origin of the monuments in question, and to account for the modifications which the primitive idea and plan of some of them, associated with the idolatry of the Hindus, have undergone in the lapse of ages; only the investigation will be complicated by the fact, that, while the Asiatics remained pagan, and these monuments among them were modified by the advancement in the social condition of the people and by changes in the form of pagan usage, the nations of the West became at an early period Christian, and gradually rejected the pagan peculiarities.

The Simple Stone in Asia.—The late Colonel Mackenzie, Surveyor-General of India, has left drawings of the stone monuments which he found in Southern India, and these exactly resemble the single erect stones, the stones in groups, and the stones in circles, so well known as occurring in the Celtic countries of Europe, while in both Asia and Europe these megalithic monuments are rendered particularly interesting as enabling us to trace the advancement of the arts in their change from the rough boulder monument to the dressed stone, having sculptured on it objects of worship. In Pictland, as elsewhere in Christendom, the simple boulder ultimately passes into stones beautifully and elaborately sculptured with Christian symbols.

(a.) As symbol of the Deity.—The great antiquity of the erect pillar stone is proved by ancient writings, especially by the Sacred Scriptures. The upright pillar stone was the first symbol of the spiritual Deity worshipped by the primitive races of Asia; and this explains the frequent mention of the pillar in the Bible, viewed as a token of the divine presence "The Lord went before them [the Israelites] by day in a *pillar* of a cloud, to lead them the way; and by night in a *pillar* of fire, to give them light; to go by day and night."[1] And again, "Him that overcometh will I make a *pillar* in the temple of my God, and he shall go no more out," &c.[2] Jacob erected several of these stone pillars on different occasions. When pursuing a lone dangerous and distant journey, he erected his first monolith at Luz. After his well-known dream, full of holy dread at the vision of God and His angels, and inspired by a most grateful sense of the Divine goodness, he raised a pillar to mark the place where he had been so highly favoured: "And Jacob rose up early in the morning, and took the stone that he had put for his pillows, and set it up for a pillar, and poured oil upon the top of it."[3]

Instances of the worship of these rude and venerated (boulder) stones are numerous in Asia and Europe.[4] The pillar required to be a boulder, and to be dedicated to God by having oil and wine poured on it, as was done by Jacob on the occasion referred to, and as we again find him doing when setting up a memorial pillar at the birth of a child, on the completion of the covenant with his uncle,[5] and on the death of his wife Rachel.[6] The respect paid to these anointed and other monumental stones as symbols of Deity, in the lapse of ages, degenerated into the rankest idolatry. Many of the ancient gods of the Arabians were no other than large rude stones, the worship of which had been thus first introduced by the posterity of Ishmael. It seems most probable that these great stones, pyramidal boulders fashioned by the hand of Providence—hierograms of God, were the first places of divine worship among the Arabs, on which they poured wine and oil as Jacob did. Thus we read of *the place of sacred stones* at Bethel, to which Saul on one occasion met three men proceeding, that they might worship God there, one carrying three kids for sacrifice, another three loaves of bread, and the third a leathern bottle of wine, to be consumed with the flesh of the kids as a feast-offering. These ancient places of worship consisted of a plot of ground, containing an upright boulder, supposed to be animated by the Deity to whose honour it was erected, in the midst of a grove of oak or other trees. Among the Israelites it was the sanctuary of the Lord, commemorating some solemn covenant with the Almighty to recall His mercies and obey His voice. Such a place was kept sacred, and dedicated to sacred purposes, the vault of heaven being considered its appropriate covering, and the horizon its boundary fence. At these sacred spots the primitive inhabitants bowed down and worshipped, as in the presence of a symbol of the Divine power and goodness. When Joshua, about to die, exacted a pledge of the people that they would serve Jehovah as their Lord, he took a great stone, and erected it under an oak tree, that was by the sanctuary of the Lord, as a witness to Israel, and poured oil upon it, and wrote down in the book of the law the terms of the covenant, and for a more public testimony, said unto all the people, "Behold this stone shall be a witness unto us; for it hath heard all the words of Jehovah which he spake unto us; it shall be therefore a witness unto you, lest ye deny your God."[7]

The Patriarchal form of worship was performed in the open air without any enclosure or temple, now in high places, and now under trees or in groves;[8] and the unwrought boulder, erected and consecrated for a memorial, was undoubtedly the prototype of the unhewn altar of the Mosaic law, in which there was a religious appropriation of the monolith as marking a covenant with God. And although in later times the Israelites were, under the Theocracy, forbidden to worship such objects, they elsewhere were directed to prepare an altar of earth and stone, but to prevent any approach to idolatry, to which they were so prone, the injunction was added, "Thou shalt not build it of hewn stone, for if thou lift up thy tool upon it, thou hast polluted it;"[9] "And Moses the servant of the Lord commanded the children of Israel [to erect] an altar of whole stones, over

---

(1) Exodus xiii, 21.
(2) Rev. iii, 12.
(3) Gen. xxviii, 18, *et seq.*
(4) Kitto's Hist. of Palestine, i, 404.
(5) Gen. xxxi, 45.
(6) Gen. xxxv, 1-20.
(7) Josh. xxiv, 24-27.
(8) *See* Gen. xxi, 33.
(9) Exod. xx, 24, 25 and 26.

which no man hath lift up any iron; and they offered thereon burnt offerings, &c. ;"[1] "And there shalt thou build an altar unto the Lord thy God, an altar of stones; thou shalt not lift up any iron tool upon them; thou shalt build the altar of the Lord thy God of whole stones," &c.[2] Such stones, being fashioned by the Almighty, were thus regarded not as altars dedicated to a local god, as among the heathen, but as "temples made without hands," where the creature might worship the Creator, as through His own handiwork, face to face.

To Bethel, the place of Jacob's sacred pillar; to Gilgal, heaps of stone;[3] to Mizpeh, a stone or pillar, Samuel went every year, and there judged Israel.[4] And these same spots were used besides as places of assembly for public transactions.[5] It was to the altar at Gilgal that Samuel directed Saul to go down, adding, "I will come down unto thee, to offer burnt offerings, and to sacrifice sacrifices of peace-offerings"[6] Saul, it is noticeable too, was chosen king at Mizpeh; and, again, after he had delivered the people, Samuel said unto them, "Come, let us go to Gilgal, and renew the kingdom there: And all the people went to Gilgal; and there they made Saul king before Jehovah in Gilgal; and there they sacrificed sacrifices of peace-offerings before Jehovah; and there Saul and all the men of Israel rejoiced greatly."[7]

So much of the science and art of Europe was originally derived from Asia, that it is desirable, before we consider the stone monuments of the West, we should glance a little at similar antiquities still extant in unfrequented places in Asia, particularly in the South of Hindustan, the remains of tribes belonging to the Indo-Asiatic, and especially to the Scythian group of the Indo-Germanic race. The Nomadic races, wandering about the northern and central parts of Asia, had already colonised the South of Hindustan and even the South of Europe, before the period of authentic history. These colonists may have composed part of the original following of Tamur, who, arriving in the south of India, along with others who journeyed from the East, had already attained a certain degree of civilisation. The tendency of these races was to emigrate at different stages of civilisation, to subdue the nations that opposed them, or to drive those who preferred their liberty to the hills and less accessible parts of the country, where they retained their ancient habits and opinions.

The original Scythian race migrated at an early period to the west and south, and their stone monuments [8] are still found along the routes they traversed through the north of Africa and the south of Europe, on as far as the islands and countries bordering on the Atlantic Ocean. They may be traced through Afghanistan and Khorassan to the Caspian Sea and to Persia. They are found in Asia Minor and in Asiatic Turkey as far as the extremities of Syria, passing thence into the north of Africa; while in Europe they may be followed from Bessarabia down through nearly every part of Greece, on even to the northern and eastern shores of the Continent. By the researches of different able writers[9] much information has been obtained respecting these peoples, their monuments, and the nature of their religious beliefs. In Hindustan the monuments have no specific name, but are either referred to the tribes among whom they are found, or are known as Dravidian. The Dravidians were early distinguished as agriculturists, who, as they settled in India, adopted Hindu manners and customs, and their descendants are met with over the Peninsula under various names; a fact which may account for the similarity between the Dravidian religion and that of the races of Southern India, allied to the Scythian or Aryan family.[10] One of their offshoots was the Kalorian branch, among whom the worship of pillar stones and circles seems to have prevailed extensively. Another branch was the Tudas, the inhabitants of the Nielgherry hills, who appear

---

(1) Joshua viii, 31.
(2) Deut. xxvii, 5, 6.
(3) Gen. xxxi, 48 and 49.
(4) 1 Sam. vii, 16.
(5) Judges xx, 1.
(6) 1 Sam. x, 8.
(7) 1 Sam. xi, 14 and 15.
(8) Bishop Caldwell, loc. cit., p. 579.

(9) Bishop Caldwell, in his Comparative Grammar of the Dravidian Races. Col. Marshall, a phrenologist among the Tudas. Col. Yule, M.Roy.Inst.Ant. Rev. F. Nietz. Rev. M. Phillips' Indian Antiquities. Col. Dixon. Capt. Newport. François Linorman Mitchell, ch. xxii, pp. 186-189. Mr. Buck's (Madras C. S.) Manuel d'Hist. Ancienne de l'Orient.—Tome i, p. 52, Tome iii, p. 458, *et seq*.

(10) Caldwell's Introduction to the Grammar of the Dravidian Language, pp. 592-596. *See* Geo. Smith's translation of the account of the Deluge.

to have originally come from the centre of Asia, and have many of the customs of the ancient Aryans. They believed in a spiritual deity, abhorred idolatry, and were worshippers of the sun and sky, fire, water, and the other elements of nature, mostly personified as heroes and heroines (Bishop Caldwell, p. 579) and had a distinct order of priests, who were the depositories of their ancient traditions. This spiritual deity they considered it impious to conceive of as confined to a house, however large. His dwelling-place was the heavens, and the pure and simple fire his emblem on earth. They reverenced the manes of their ancestors, and offered to them as peace-offerings libations of wine and clarified butter. Yet we find among this and the other branches referred to remains of simple upright stones, evidently of religious import, long before the erection of the sculptured Buddhist monuments, exactly such as we find among the Celts bearing the name of Druidical. They performed some of their rites, too, in the deep gloom of sacred groves, cremated their dead, and sacrificed to them at their funerals the flesh of animals, as though they regarded them as still in need of bodily nutriment; and these notions and practices they received from the Aryans.

While the primitive inhabitants of Hindustan are to be found, in different retired parts of that country, still retaining many of the monuments, customs, and manners of the old races, such as we find to have existed among the Celts, in modern India a small unhewn stone is even now regarded by them with veneration and held as a symbol of the Deity. It is considered sacred after being daubed with red paint, having oil poured on it, and being afterwards erected on a small cairn of stones under one of the sacred trees. This upright stone, too, is actually worshipped as a symbol of the great and good God, and the act of worship is preceded by an offering of flowers and fruit, the effect of which is that the worshipper hopes thereby to conciliate the Deity against the ravages of wild beasts and the attacks of venomous serpents; and no doubt in this act the modern Hindu sees, as the ancient Celt must have done, in the upright stone the token of the presence of an Almighty power that was spiritual, the more as we know neither of them at first had any idols, and both did homage to sun and star, not in themselves, but as material embodiments of immaterial and spiritual realities, nay personalities.

The upright pillar stone played an important part in the rites of the Druids, and seems to have been a symbol of their great spiritual deity, dedicated to his impersonation in the sun, the kindly generator and developer of all life. The Tot or Tent of the Celts—like the Egyptian Thoth, and the Greek Hermes—was worshipped in the form of a large stone or cairn placed on an artificial mound or upon a hill, called the Tot or Tent hill. All through the British Islands such upright stones abound, and they remain almost as they were when first erected, except a few on which certain symbols have been added, which will be mentioned in the next chapter. They stand sometimes alone, at other times near barrows and circles, sometimes earth-fast, at other times reared on the native rock, where they have weathered centuries of change; the tribes that witnessed their erection having long ago vanished from the scene, leaving not a single document behind them to tell their tale. These stones were selected with great care, and must, notwithstanding their great size,[1] have often been conveyed considerable distances.[2]

There are standing-stones found in Scotland, known in different districts as stones of Odin, and called, not inappropriately *amad* or speaking stones, which the barbarous tribes of early times could not have executed, nor even understood the meaning of, such the art and symbolism with which they are sculptured; but there are others of an earlier date, called in Gaelic *cran-leaca*, or *clach o' leuchda*, stones of worship, which are emblems of the Deity who sustains the universe, as a pillar does the transitory works of man, and which, as the direct workmanship of God, were regarded by the simple rude inhabitants as objects of worship and symbolic of the Deity.

---

(1) One near Dol, in Brittany, is 32 feet above ground, 15 feet beneath, and at the largest part 28 feet in circumference.—Trollope's Brittany, vol. i, p. 184.

(2) The ancient races had enormous command of brute force, and had some familiarity with the principles of mechanics. I have seen a number of Asiatics move a ton weight by means of compound levers, each man sharing his individual proportion of the weight.

The standing stone of Balcallo on the south side of the Sidlaw Hills may be taken as an example of these. It is 9ft. 8in. in height above the ground, 2ft. 4in. in breadth, and 1ft. 9in. in thickness. Being splintered and worn, it must be of great age, and is to be regarded as one of these symbols of the Deity.

In Brittany, long after the people who had raised these stone pillars had passed away, and the object for which they were erected had been forgotten, these monoliths were held in reverence by the peasantry. To the ponderous monolith *(Minar)*, 25 feet high, near Plumen, a mysterious awe was attached by the inhabitants, which degenerated into a sort of superstitious fear, that induced the peasantry in passing to bow and touch their hats as a mark of respect (*Fig.* 18). To it, men and cattle were brought to be cured, or preserved from disease, and before it women, desirous of having children, worshipped. The priests in vain prohibited such homage; and at length, to prevent the scandal, placed a cross on the top of one of these stones, so that the sacred emblem might receive the adoration (*Fig.* 19). To such an extent was this superstition carried that it was found to be an obstacle to the introduction of Christianity into the country, and in the year A.D. 658 a Council held at Nantes had amongst its canons against the idolatrous practices of the people, one which notices that there were certain oaks and stones hidden in the profound recesses of the forest, before which the people burned fires and placed offerings. The Armenian Bishops were strictly commanded by the Council to order the trees which were worshipped to be cut down, and the stones to be removed or hidden in places where the peasants could not find them.[1]

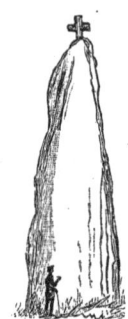

Fig. 18.   Fig. 19.

(b.) Boundary Stones.—The use of these pillars as boundary stones, or land-marks to denote the limit of right for a tribe or for a family, must date from a very remote period. The most ancient example on record is connected with the covenant made between Jacob and Laban. In this case a stone was set up as a pillar at or near a cairn, as evidence or as witness of the solemn compact of peace entered into between them. "Behold," said Laban, "this heap, and behold this pillar, which I have cast betwixt me and thee; this heap be witness, and this pillar be witness, that I will not pass over this heap to thee, and that thou shalt not pass over this heap and this pillar unto me, for harm."[2]

Cairns were cast up in Europe as actual boundaries, which were held in superstitious regard, and near them pillars of stone are often found.[3] These pillars were the land-marks, the removal of which was so strictly forbidden by the Jewish law: Whoever removed them, or caused them to be removed, was to be accursed to the last of his race.

After the Christian epoch, the sacred character of the boundary stones was enhanced by the incision on them of the Christian cross; and the veneration for them was often deepened by their association with the name of some sacred or honoured person. In Scotland, for instance, when David I settled marches, forest rights and rights of pasture, he recorded his decisions by marks on the oak tree, which were shown for generations after, and by cutting ditches in the hill-side; and tall stones were erected by the king in person.[4]

(c.) Charter and Coronation Stones.—(1) *Charter Stones.*—These stones indicated the grant of a charter by the king, showing that the districts in which they stood possessed, by royal gift, the power of making bye-laws

---

(1) Trollope's Brittany, v. 2, p. 229.   (2) Gen. xxxi, 47-49, *et seq.*
(3) *See* Rowland's Mona. Antiq., p. 51; Martin's Western Islands of Scotland, p. 259.
(4) Cosmo Innes, Legal Antiquities, p. 221.

for the regulation of their own internal affairs, the limitation being usually added—provided nothing so enacted be contrary to the laws of the commonwealth. The charter-stone of Inverness, set in a frame hooped with iron, is preserved at the entrance to the market-place of that town. And the high value attached to the possession of such a title-deed, was shown by the demand made for many years on the part of the inhabitants of the large village of New Dailly, in Ayrshire, for a stone of the kind that stood in the old village. The demand was made on the ground that the new village was the larger and more important of the two, but the inhabitants were inexorable, and refused to part with their ancient right. At length the people of New Dailly conceived the idea of taking it by force, when a desperate fight took place before the intruders were driven off, and the treasure —a blue stone—was preserved in perpetuity to the old village. In the neighbouring town of Girvan there is a charter-stone against which at one time if a debtor placed his back, he could not suffer arrestment, and where cattle, if fastened to it, could not be touched by a creditor in his right.

(2) *Coronation-Stones.*—Coronation among ancient tribes was part of the ceremonial connected with the installation of a chief. The newly-elected chief stood by, or was placed upon, a sacred stone before the people, when he gave a pledge in the most solemn manner to protect their rights, while his own person was at the same time rendered sacred by being anointed with oil. When Abimelech was made king, it was " by the plain of the pillar that was in Shechem;"[1] and when Jehoash was anointed king by Jehoiada, " the king stood by a pillar, as the manner was." [2]

Dr. O'Donovan informs us that the inauguration stone of the O'Donnells stood on a natural or artificial eminence in the centre of a large plain. The elected chief occupied a stone chair, or stood upon a flat stone, sacred to the purpose, and named the flag, or stone of the kings. At an assembly of the nobles and other orders of the state, one of the senior lords rose and presented a white wand, perfectly straight, to the chieftain elect, saying : Receive this emblem of thy dignity, and may the unsullied whiteness and the perfect straightness of this wand be a sign to thee on all occasions, so that no impurity may stain thy life, no injustice mar thy administration, and thy government be not for evil but for good to the people. Whereupon the chief took oath that he would respect the symbol, and enforce the rights as well as guard the liberties of his country.[3] Among some tribes, as we have elsewhere remarked, there were engraven the feet—one or both—of the first chieftain ; in others, part of the ceremony consisted in binding shoes or sandals on the feet of the chief, as a pledge that he would be alert and swift in the performance of his duties. The cylindrical obelisk, standing in the Rath-na-Riogh, is 6 ft. above ground, and, according to Dr. Petrie, is sunk 6 ft. in the earth.[4] There are monuments of this kind also in Denmark ; and M'Donald was crowned king of the Isles, standing on a stone, with a deep impression on the top of it made on purpose to receive his feet.

In the East, I witnessed the coronation of the Maharajah of Tipperah, which took place upon a musneed resembling Solomon's throne, upon which one hundred and thirty Maharajahs were said to have been crowned. The ceremony consisted in the Maharajah being purified, and sworn to defend the kingdom, and to rule his people in equity, according to the forms of his religion, and the directions of the Brahmins. He was then assisted to mount his throne by the representative of the English Government, and on being presented with a gold-mounted sabre, received the congratulations and offerings of his chief subjects. After ascending the throne the first order he gave was that coins of the new dynasty should be struck, which was done in our presence by a disk of gold or of silver being placed upon an anvil and struck by a sledge-hammer.

---

(1) Judges ix, 6 (2) 2 Kings xi, 14.
(3) Dr. Petrie's Essay on Tara Hill in the Transactions of the Royal Irish Academy, xviii, part 2.
(4) *Ibid.*

SECTION II.—THE OBELISKS AND PYRAMIDS OF EGYPT.

The Egyptian obelisks, which are usually sculptured all over with the titles and honours of the Emperors that erected them, and the praises of the gods to whom they are dedicated, are, properly, symbols of the rising sun, a pencil of whose rays, as seen piercing through a dark cloud, they not inaptly represent; while the pyramids, which are huge tombs, are symbols of the setting sun, as, with fire-radiance, it beckons its farewell from the entrance to the under-world into which it is rapidly making its descent. The obelisk, accordingly, was erected to the east of the Nile Valley, and the pyramids to the west: the former being suggestive of the dawning and the latter of the departing and departed light, as it in both cases triumphs over an element that would swallow it up.

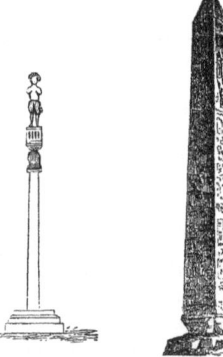

Fig. 20.

Fig. 21.   Fig. 22.

Fig. 23.

The pyramids of Egypt are the largest and most mysterious, as they are probably the oldest, monuments extant of man's art; and yet when they were first descried by me, they appeared like small conical spots in the vast plain which lay stretched out before me; and quite insignificant when compared with what I conceived to be their prototype in nature. They are examples of the nothingness of man and his works, even at their greatest, when contrasted with the power and wisdom of the great Creator of the universe, whose Spirit, as He retires, so to speak, every evening, they seem to shadow forth. At first I looked in vain for the pyramids. A large mass of *cumulo-stratus* hung over the plain below, not many degrees above the horizon, and the sun threw his diverging rays, pyramid-like, over the yellowish haze which stretched along the lower part of the sky. As I looked upon this beautiful phenomenon, I could not avoid the conclusion, that the pyramids must have been designed to represent such an appearance. Might not the kings of Egypt, who boasted their descent from the great god whose emblem is the sun,[1] have adopted this very form which the sun's rays took as the type of the repository for their own remains, and the symbol of their departure in like manner from the earth which they had been sent to illumine and bless?

The large blocks of granite of which the pyramids are composed, are from 2 ft. 2 in. to 4 ft. 10 in. in thickness. They are regularly built, and the courses of the casing-stones are so accurately put together that their joints are scarcely perceptible, while the mortar with which they were joined is still so adhesive, that the stones, in some places, break before they give way at the joinings. If they were erected for sepulchral purposes—a

---

(1) The Egyptians named their kings Pharoah, from Phrath, the sun, and worshipped them when dead.

conjecture the truth of which seems to be attested by the sarcophagi [1] found in them, and by the monuments of the dead that surround them—we may well regard them with astonishment. The original dimensions of the largest was 764 ft. square at the base and 480 ft. of perpendicular height. It consisted of 89,418,806 cubic feet of stone, weighing 6,878,369 tons, and occupying an area equal to 588,939,595 superficial feet, or about 13½ English acres. It would have cost probably about thirty millions to build it. Well might the constructor regard it as an imperishable monument, for no building could be more durable, and no effect could be more sublime than that of this stupendous structure, as I stood beside it, surveying it with the mind's eye as well as the bodily.

These structures have been the subject of much debate, and various, often wild, conjectures have been conceived at different times in regard to the purpose of their erection; but the assumption that they are tombs seems now to be established beyond a doubt by the latest excavations. They are an expression more stupendous than was, perhaps, ever given either before or since of the desire of man to rear for himself a memorial that might prove everlasting. Of this desire for immortality, and the attempts to attain it, there have been few such emphatic exhibitions, yet few that have more overshot the mark, and fallen, so to speak, on the other side. They are monuments of what one man had the power to coerce thousands of other men, remaining slaves, to rear at his bidding, but who and what, otherwise, their author was, much as it would appear he wished that to be remembered, seems to lie buried, as we may think it deserved to do, in the depths of oblivion. Nevertheless, it was out of Egypt the religion came on which henceforward any rational immortality can ever be grounded; but that religion bases it not on the power to rear masses of stone, however profoundly symbolic, but a career in the spirit and for the spirit as that appears at once constitutive and regulative of the true life of humanity. The Pyramid is at best a bare symbol of the idea of eternity, to which man is ever fain to link on himself and his works. Christianity, of the Author of which it is said, "Out of Egypt have I called my Son," is more than a symbol, for it is itself that which both *is*, and is everlasting. It was by it first that the true basis, other than merely "physical," of life and immortality was laid, and that enduringly, in this world of ours, otherwise so transitory.

Section III.—Circles of Erect Stones and Wheels.

The circles, like the upright stone, may be traced all along the routes by which the Aryan Celts travelled westward from India, through Persia,[2] Asia Minor, Northern Africa, Malta, and the South of Europe, northward to Denmark, Sweden, and Great Britain. They are also to be found in the Islands of the South Seas and in North America.[3] They are either symbols of the sun-god, in himself or in his orbit, or connected with religious ceremonies and the administration of justice, or they are memorial and sepulchral. Sometimes the single stone had others placed beside it, so that the plan of the whole was circular, and formed a symbol of the sun or a hierogram of his self-beginning, self-ending, beneficent action and influence. At other times, when the erect boulder was employed as a symbol of the Deity, a space around was considered holy and marked off by boulders arranged in an enclosing circle. This space was regarded as sacred as any most awe-inspiring pile reared for worship, and the enclosure was conceived of as no less than consecrated by the presence of the Deity, who looked down on it daily from the open firmament. There seems to have been no rule regulating either the number or the size of the stones in the circle surrounding the sacred place. Where there were only four stones they were placed severally towards one or other of the cardinal points; where they were more numerous they were placed according to the next subordinate division of the compass, one of the stones, larger and flatter than the other, being generally found towards the south-east. In general the altar of sacrifice appears to have been outside but near the circle, and to have been made of unhewn stones.[4]

---

(1) Col. Howard Vyse has discovered the coffin of King Mycerinus, who built the third pyramid of Ghizeh 4,000 years ago.
(2) Camden and Ousely's Travels, vol. ii, pp. 80-83.
(3) Professor Daniel Wilson found a circle of stones on a high hill, a mile from the town of Hudson, New York, U.S.
(4) Exodus xx, 25. Josh. viii, 31.

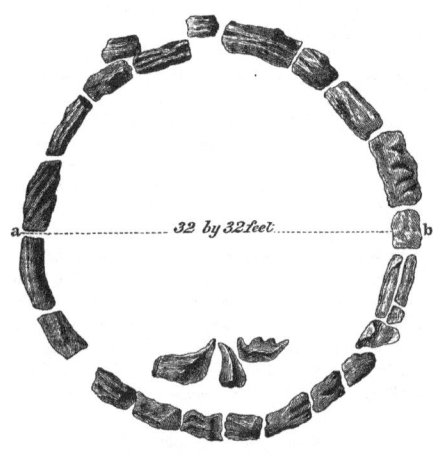

Fig. 24.

In India, in the Deccan, these monuments are found of various sizes, and are circular or oval in form, sometimes plain and sometimes ornamented with sculptures. Great numbers, considered to be the work of the Pancha Pandawars, although the natives can give no account of their history, are scattered over the hills a mile west of Darmacotta. The stones composing these circles are of a pale blackish granite, and very irregular in shape, measuring about three feet in length and breadth. It is said that such circles are very numerous among the skirts of the neighbouring hills. Some of them, having been opened by the direction of the Rajah Vassariddi, were found to contain human bones of a large size, and in some were earthen pots curiously arranged and containing ashes and charcoal.

The sacredness conceived to belong to the space enclosed by the circle may be exemplified by reference to what happens daily in Hindustan in preparations for cooking. The Hindu selects for the preparation of his food a place at once clean and elevated, unpolluted anyhow by man or animal. Here he traces a circle of convenient size, and the enclosed space is carefully cleared of grass, stones, and impurities of all kinds. This space is then smeared either with Ganges silt, mixed with water, or still better, with cow-dung, also mixed with water. In this circle a hole is dug for the fire, and upon its elevated margin is placed the earthen pot for cooking the rice and vegetables, to be eaten within the purified circle; but should a stranger enter the circle when the food is in the course of preparation, it is considered unclean, and, with the vessel that contains it, is thrown away. When a Hindu has settled in a place, a more permanent circle is prepared and kept clean for the purpose, and smeared daily with a mixture of cow-dung and water. A circle, also in a clean place, is sometimes seen drawn before or above the door of the dwelling, to prevent the entrance of devils or of evil of any kind.

The circles in the Deccan were dedicated to Vetal, or Betal, and throughout the East the people perform religious ceremonies and hold councils at them on important occasions. At such times each representative of a family has, according to his rank, a particular stone of the circle at which he stands, while the chiefs and priests stand opposite one or more of the large stones, or at a flat stone where sacrifices are offered up.[1]

Homer more than once alludes to councils being held within or at circles:[2] "The council was summoned by Alcinöus to confer upon the affairs of Ulysses; the herald appeared," &c. (viii, 5). Epiphanius, who was born and lived in Syria, describes an open circle formed by the ancient Samaritans as a place of prayer. Among the Celts, as in India, these circles were temples; and even after the introduction of Christianity they were for a time used as places of worship, a long period no doubt elapsing before walls were built round them or any attempt made to have a roof overhead, for the ancients believed that the gods were not to be confined to

---

(1) Forbes-Leslie.
(2) *See* the remarkable passage of the *Iliad* (xviii, 585), which Pope has given incorrectly. The place of sacrifice was on the outside of the circle on the south-east side, as in the Snago circle.

buildings made by hands: "Quibus omnia deberent esse patentia ac libera, quorum hic mundus omnis templum esset ac domus." Virgil thus describes Priam's chapel:

> "Ædibus in mediis nudaque sub ætheris axe
> Ingens ara fuit; juxtaque veterrima laurus
> Incumbens aræ, atque umbra complexa penates."

On this ground a round hole was left in the middle of the roof of the Pantheon, and the same was the case with the temple of Terminus, of which Ovid writes:

> "Nunc quoque supra ne quod nisi sidera cernat
> Exiguum templi testa foramen habet."

(a.) Circles as Symbols of the Sun-God.—The practice of erecting stone-circles or wheels, in honour of the sun, is of very ancient date, and most of those so dedicated must have been erected by men of the Indo-European race in connection with rites similar to those practised in India still among the fire or sun-worshippers. The twelve stones which often composed the circle, may have been suggestive of the twelve signs of the Zodiac,[1] while the large stone in the centre represented the sun, as another outside the circle, on the south-east, did the point of sun-rise at the summer solstice.[2] The circle is often double, and in the inner wheel there are very frequently nineteen stones, representative, in all probability, among the Celts of Britain of the years of their religious cycle, at the end of which the island was regularly favoured with a special visit of the Sun-God. The priests alone were admitted within the circles, while the people stood without, the outside circle being often so arranged as to preclude observation as well as access, groves of trees being frequently added and avenues from the four quarters marked off, as at Callernish, for the approach of the priests and different ranks of the people. In some cases there were more than two concentric circles, and they varied in number, as well as otherwise, according to the nature of the rites.[3] In some examples, where the stones are smaller and more numerous, they are supposed to represent the worship of the sacred host of heaven; and when the circle is surrounded by a ditch or vallum, this has been taken to symbolize the sacred serpent, never-beginning, never-ending, viewed as surrounding and protecting the consecrated spot. In other cases there are only three or four large boulder-stones, the circle being completed with smaller stones, as at Snago.

(b.) For the administration of justice.—These circles were often used for judicial purposes, of which that at Balcathro, near Invergowrie, may be instanced as an example. Indeed, they were formerly more numerous than the religious circles, or *kills*, which were so systematically destroyed by the jealousy of the Romans, and the blind zeal of the early Christians in their eagerness to outroot paganism. The judicial circles were often constructed of earth, of which those to the south-west of Stonehenge may be taken as examples. They were probably used for purposes of public deliberation and places of refuge, as well as for the dispensation of justice, and in Norway and Iceland are distinguished by the epithet *dom* or *thing*. It was from the circumstance of these conventions for civil and judicial purposes being always opened with a religious ceremonial, conducted by the priests, to impart solemnity to their proceedings, that these circles were erected in the neighbourhood of religious ones. Cæsar tells us that the Druids of Gaul sat in a consecrated place, to which all who had any contention came from all parts around, submitting to their judgment. There were decided all disputes, public and private, affecting matters of morality, the rights of inheritance, and the boundaries of land.[4]

---

(1) Cf. the Dii majorum gentium of the Romans. *See* Observations on the Ante-Brahmanic Worship of the Hindus in the Deccan, by J. Stephenson, D.D., Jour. Royal Asiatic Soc., vol. v, p. 189.

(2) *See* Tolo's MSS., p. 445, referred to in Sir J. G. Wilkinson's book, p. 14, though there is a mistake about Stonehenge.

(3) Wilson's Archæologia Scot., p. 113; Herbert's Archæologia Scot., iii, p. 141; Per. Jour., i, p. 279; Heysius' Religion of the North, pp. 185 to 205; Exod. xix, 12; xxiv, 4; Kitto, v. i, p. 407.

(4) Cæsar De Bel. Gal., Lib vi.

(c.) For Sepulchral and Memorial purposes.[1]—(1) *Sepulchral.*—Some of the larger and grander circles, such as Avebury, Stonehenge and Stennis, may have been used for burial as well as religious rites, and for the administration of justice; but the mere sepulchral circles are generally small, and surrounded by cairns, kistvaens, cromlechs and subterranean chambers.[2] The cairns often occupy the highest part of the ground, whereas the circles and cromlechs are mostly placed, not on the highest point, but on the first slope. The stones vary in number from four to thirty-seven, and they also differ greatly in height. Inside the enclosure, a foot or two from the surface, and defended by a small stone cist, an urn is usually found, containing ashes, and along with it often a flint stone and bronze implements. Dr. Stewart, in "The Sculptured Stones of Scotland," has given an account of the examination of several of these monuments in Aberdeenshire.[3] Where the bodies have been buried entire, they generally lie with the feet to the west and the head to the east, or rising sun, the renovator and reviver of a sleeping world. (2) *Monumental.*—The graceful Khotubs of Delhi, and of Pubna, near the Hooghly (*Fig.* 25) were erected to commemorate great events. This latter pillar has five resting places, with passages at each, round the exterior of the towers. The height of the pillar at Delhi is 265 feet, the other is considerably less. The desire to commemorate a victory with its circumstances by a tower, induced a conqueror sometimes to avail himself of a Buddhist pillar-tower; as appears to have been the case with *Feroz Shah*, after his conquests in India (*Fig.* 26). In this case the tower was in the ancient city of Gowar, where the kings of Bengal reigned in the 15th century. It must have been originally a Buddhist tower of safety: Dr. Ferguson, a high authority, considered it very like a transformed pillar-tower; a procedure that was often followed by the Moslem. Mr. C. Horne describes a tower near Benares as having undergone such a change. It was capped with a dome, and formed into a Mohammedan mausoleum.[4]

Fig. 25.

Fig. 26.

SECTION IV.—WROUGHT AND COMPOUND CIRCLES OF STONES IN ASIA.

As the arts advanced in Asia these circles gradually developed into novelties of form and varieties of symbolism, to the concealment often of the primitive type, whereas in Europe, the early introduction of Christianity nipped such developments in the bud by requiring the rejection or the transformation of all idolatrous emblems. The consequence is that in Europe these circles are still found in their primitive integrity, and that wrought stones are as a rule very rare in this quarter of the world, while in Asia the stones are met with in all stages of symbolic elaboration and arrangement.

---

(1) The Celtic usages after death will be explained in chapter ix.   (2) *See* Wilkinson.
(3) Sculptured Stones of Scotland, vol. i.   (4) Asiat. Journal, Calcut., v. xxxiv, pp. 9 *et seq*.

HISTORY OF PAGANISM IN CALEDONIA.

(a) Culna—An instance of this exists at the village of Culna, situated on the banks of the sacred Bargaretta or Hooghly Rivers, at which I saw religious services performed when on a visit to the late Maharajah of Burdwan. This modern temple has all the essential features of a stone circle. It consists of two concentric circles of upright stones in marble, each resting on a flat surface, representing the sacred *linga*, and canopied by a separate temple or chapel. The external circle is formed of seventy pillars (two being absent for the entrance), composed of marble, alternately black and white. The inner is formed of thirty-four pillars (two here also absent for entrance), all of white marble. The outer circle has its entrances north and south, and the inner east and west, much in the same manner as the large temple of Depaldinna, in Central India; and while in the centre of this there was a tank, the temple in Bengal, where worship is regularly celebrated, has a well of water, the *yoni*, or symbol of Parvati, the female energy of the world, as the encircling *lingas* are of the male.[1]

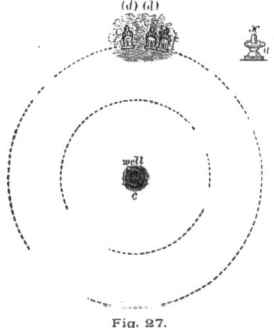

Fig. 27.

A second circle of temples in the immediate neighbourhood of Culna appears to be merely a modification of the first. There is a central circular stage which revolves, and upon this the image of Krishna is placed. The circle is formed of thirty-six small temples which surround the stage. They were empty when I saw them, but, during the Katic-pajah, gods are placed in them, probably effigies of Krishna.

(b.)—Depaldinna, *i.e.*, the hill of light, is another example of the influence of the advance of art in the work of

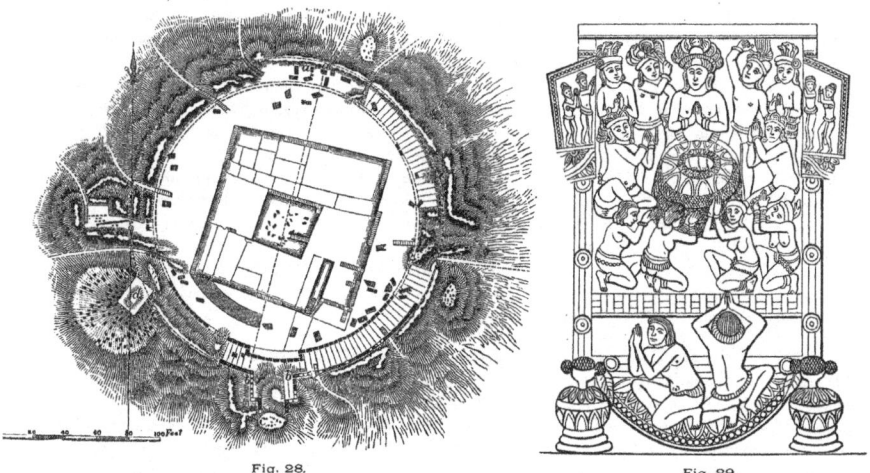

Fig. 28. Fig. 29.

(1) See Notes on some of the Buddhist Opinions and Monuments of Asia compared with the Symbols of the Ancient Sculptured "Standing Stones" of Scotland; by Thomas A. Wise, M.D.

construction. This immense structure[1] is situated on a small hill at the mouth of the river Krishna, near the site of the ancient city of Darancotta. It is surrounded by concentric circles of flat oblong stones, many of which have been displaced, broken, and taken away, such as remain being earth-fastened and covered with beautiful sculptured mythological figures. The centre of the circle had been excavated in an irregular square, twenty-four feet deep, and contains water. The inner circle is one hundred and sixty-two feet across (*Fig.* 29). I have selected part of one of the flat, upright stones as a specimen. It is covered with sculptures executed in relief, representing scenes in the life of Buddha (*Fig.* 29) who is crowned with a number of the heads of the sacred hooded snakes, which likewise surround the heads of his attendants, as symbols of royal state; while the convolutions of the great serpent encircle the body of the former at the centre or navel, and the soles of the saint's feet, the least sacred parts of his body, appear as the objects of worship, and fill up the centre of the coils.

Section V.—The Gigantic or Compound Circles of Stones in Europe.

Examples of these are to be found in Stonehenge; Long Meg's daughters, near Penrith; Callernish, in the Hebrides, Glendallock, and the circles of Stennis in the Orkneys, with other such circles. No appearances of interments are found within the Stonehenge circles, while barrows for burial purposes of different kinds surround them; but, even if remains of the dead were found within the circles, the dead may have been buried there for protection, as in a holy place, long after its original use was forgotten; as they were, and still are, in the Christian churches, buildings not for burial, but for prayer and praise. Cæsar says, as we have seen, the Druids held assemblies and pronounced legal decrees and judgments in the consecrated places.[2]

(*a.*) The Snago circle, on the estate of Snago, Perthshire, is very imperfect. It consists of only three stones, of which the western is the largest and highest, while the eastern is of a square form, and lies on the ground with its upper flat surface sloping towards the south-east. This is covered with cup-like excavations, that seem to have been hollowed out by rubbing with a harder stone. Such holes are often found on altar stones, and are generally formed with care. In the present case they have been formed for the purpose of receiving the blood of the victim, which was offered up by a priest standing within the circle with his face to the rising sun, and for retaining the blood till it was drunk up by the sun-god to whom it was offered. Here I found that the stones still standing formed a small arc of a circle of smaller stones which had been broken up on the spot and utilized for making dykes, or dry stone walls, as field-marches. A mile to the west of the circle is a cairn similar to one to be met with near Hyderabad, in Central India, which is described, and of which there is a drawing, by the late Col. Mackenzie, Surveyor-General of India, as there is of the one at Snago, as examined by myself and Principal Campbell. There were in the latter a vallum and a circle of boulder stones, 30 feet in diameter, surrounding the cairn. A trench was made through the barrow, and in the heart if it, at the depth of 4 feet, a concave packed circle of stones upon which a broken sun-baked urn—which crumbled into dust on being dried —was found, containing black earth and particles of charcoal.

(*b.*) On the south side of a natural elevation in the small sequestered valley of Glendallock near Blairgowrie in Perthshire, are four boulders, forming a square, facing the cardinal points, in which was found a beautiful Celtic cinerary urn, $25\frac{1}{4}$ inches high, protected by stones built round in a beehive form, and filled with bones, a flat arrow-head, &c.; and some years before, a flat stone, with cup markings, was found upon it to the S.E. of a pyramidal stone.[3] Two hundred and fifty yards from the circle, on the north side of the valley, and in a north-east direction, is a large pyramidal-shaped whin-stone,

---

(1) See Colonel Mackenzie's drawings in the India House, and Mr. Buckingham's newspaper, Calcutta, for March, 1822,
(2) Cæsar De Bel. Gal., Lib. vi, 13. (3) *See* Allen's Account, Proc. Soc. of Antiq., Ed. for 1880 and 1881, vol. iii, p. 87.

HISTORY OF PAGANISM IN CALEDONIA.

ten feet high, and seven or eight tons in weight, forming the pointer stone. On its south-east corner, near the surface of the ground, are cups and grooves of different sizes and depths. They are nearly opposite the four boulders on the south declivity of the valley. The cups appear in groups, and two are separated from the others by a natural fissure or groove, which extends from the base of the boulder to nearly two-thirds of its length. There is also a well-defined cup at the end, and probably there may have been one at the extremity of the lower groove, proceeding from the parallelogram. If so, the cup has been destroyed by the enlargement of the natural fissure. In this case we find the cups and grooves opposite the circle of stones marking the summer solstice.[1]

(c.) Crichie monument is a simple circle, of a common arrangement, which may thus be explained. It was formed of a circle of nine stones, inside of which have been discovered the remains of bodies that had been burnt, the ashes being contained in urns. This monument is 51 feet in diameter, the ditch surrounding it being 20 feet wide and 6 feet deep, and the entrances, to the north and south, each 9 feet wide; and there is a vallum on the outer side. The stones are from 4 to 7 feet high. Dr. Skene believes that there were originally ten stones : when I saw them, there were only three. The outside stones consist of one which marks the solsticial point (*Fig.* 30—*1*)—the period of a native chief festival—and (*Fig.* 30—*2*) an engraved stone, containing the sceptered segment of the circle with the elephant over it, marking the equator. About three miles to the north is a mound, or law, for open-air assemblies (*Fig.* 30—*3*), called the Bass of Ury, with a boulder several feet high. Here meetings were held and public ceremonies performed. Like the Sabæans of the East,[2] those of the West worshipped the rising sun, which typified God, so that the worshipper, standing in the circle, regarded the rising sun from it.

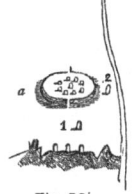

Fig. 80.

On removing the earth from the spot where the central stone of the Crichie circle had been placed, a cairn of stones was found, at the bottom of which was a rude cist, having the remains of a skeleton at full length within it; and 18 inches or 2 feet under another of the stones, rude earthen urns were found of an oblong form, with their wide mouths turned downwards, and each resting upon a flat stone. In one case, instead of an urn, a cavity, formed of water-worn stones, was built in the form of an urn, also resting on a flat stone, in which were the remains of bones, &c. The skeleton under the central stone was probably that of a chief, and his having been buried at full length without being purified by burning, would seem to indicate a comparatively recent entombment in a sacred spot, like burial in the interior of modern churches. In only one of the other boulders was any metallic article found, and that was of bronze. This examination proves that these circles were used for burial purposes, which, however, by no means excludes the idea that they were also used for worship.[3]

---

(1) *See* Allen's Account, Proc. Soc. of Antiq., Ed. for 1880 and 1881, vol. iii, p. 87.

(2) The Jews had a room in their houses directed towards the holy city Jerusalem, towards which they prayed (Daniel, ch. vi, v. 10) : "Towards the city thou hast chosen, and towards the house there built for thy name." "There God dwelt, and there revealed himself."—Tobit, ch. iii, v. 2. It was an Eastern custom for the worshipper to turn his face to that part of the temple whence he supposed the presence of the Deity was specially manifested; this part is called the Kebla : "And he brought me into the inner court of the Lord's house ; and, behold, at the door of the temple of the Lord, between the porch and the altar, were about five-and-twenty men, with their backs towards the temple of the Lord, and their faces towards the east; and they worshipped the sun towards the east."—*Ezekiel*, chap. viii, ver. 16.

(3) These stones may have been erected somewhat in the fashion of the great ceremony of Ebal and Gerizim, at which great stones were set up covered with inscriptions from the words of the law. There was connected with them an altar of unhewn stones. This was apart and distant from the great stones.

In the river Don, half-way between the Crichie circle and the Bass of Inverury, was found an oblong piece of granite with the sculptured spectacle ornament, a fish under it, and a comb and looking-glass below. It is probable that this circle existed in connection with the Bass of Ury, which, being composed of fine black mould, is in danger of being removed for agricultural and other purposes, as has been the case with the mound at Kintore in the same neighbourhood. If the Bass, like the famous Hindu Mount Meru, is the emblem of the world, the two stones outside the circle would show the solsticial point, when the great Celtic feast was held.

The similarity in so many particulars of the stupendous mound at Avebury to that in Aberdeenshire, induces me to hope that some attempt will be made to examine the ground under the great and small circles of the former, so as to discover whether there are any remains, and what, if so, these are. This would be

Fig. 31.

Fig. 32.

Fig. 33.

interesting, as it might indicate the purpose for which these monuments were erected, as well as their probable age. The absence of stone implements and the presence of articles of bronze or iron, for instance, would imply a more modern period than archæologists imagine.

(d.) Huntly Tumulus and Stone Circle.—Several miles below the circle of Crichie, and on the same side of the River Don, stood the Castle Hill of Kintore, which was removed on the formation of the railway. On the earth being cleared away from the top, the remains of a small stone circle were found, with what seemed a semi-circle of sculptured stones, which had been on the summit (*Fig.* 31); but only two of these large sculptured stones have been saved (*Fig.* 32), the others having unfortunately been broken up. On one of these was a mythological elephant, nearly all defaced by age and exposure, and the spectacle-ornament, which seemed to have been of a later date. The back of this stone bore the rough outlines of an elephant with a triad under it. The other stone had sceptered crescents touching one another, with a pronged instrument at the side. When I saw them, they were in Mr. Watt's garden; they were much worn, and when found were covered with charcoal and burnt matter. *Fig.* 33 is the remains of the circle of stones. Mr. Watt sketched their general form (*Fig.* 31) representing the Hill of Kintore when its top was removed, their supposed relative position on the semi-circle, with a circle of stones before them as a sacred place of worship, also in their relative position.

CHAP. III.]   HISTORY OF PAGANISM IN CALEDONIA.   43

A similar semi-circle (*Fig.* 34) was found at Lackin,[1] which resembled that of Kintore, and may have been in Northern India used for the same purposes: the images represent kings and saints. The sculptured stones on the hill of Kintore, as described by Mr. Watt, probably stood, when *in situ*, in the S.E. direction from the circle.

Fig. 34.

(*e.*) *Stonehenge.*—On the undulating plain of Salisbury, where it stretches out to the west and south, and sinks gently towards the north and east into a valley rich in verdure, and upon an elevation eight miles from the

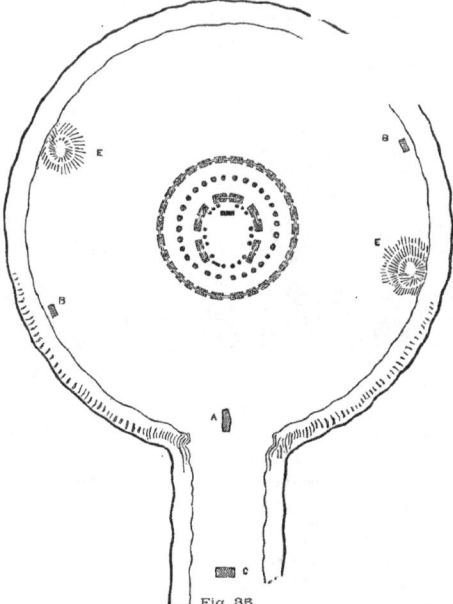

Fig. 35.

ancient fort of Old Sarum, stands Stonehenge, one of the most stupendous of ancient remains, as it is the most celebrated of British antiquities (*Fig.* 35). It was when the Romans, who had subdued the inhabitants and

---

(1) Gen. Cunningham "Lackin."

forced them to yield up their religion along with their liberties, had been compelled to evacuate the island, that the people, once more free to resume their venerated religious rites, and full of zeal for the faith of their fathers, would appear to have set about the erection of this monument, which is quite as remarkable for the mechanical resource it displays as for its stupendous magnitude.

Stonehenge consists[1] of a number of rows of stones in circular or oval arrangement. The outer circle is formed of 60 stones tapering slightly towards the top, 18 to 20 feet in height above ground, 3½ feet apart, and with 30 imposts secured by mortices and tenons, the part embedded in the ground being undressed, but that above being worked with much care. Inside this, and at a distance of 80 feet from it, is another circle, with a circumference of over 300 feet, composed of 40 smaller stones without imposts. These taper slightly, and are in general about half the height, breadth, and thickness of those of the outer circle. Within the second circle are five trilithons, arranged in a horse-shoe form, each consisting of two upright stones, with a third placed horizontally across their top. They increase in height from east to west. The uprights are grooved along their sides, the inner faces directed towards the altar being more smoothly finished than the outer. Within these trilithons, and sheltered by them, and encircling the oblong flat stone called the altar, are a number of boulders about 3 feet high, arranged in an oval form.

Near the upper extremity of this the altar lies flat on the ground. It measures 16 feet in length, 4 feet in breadth, and 26 inches in thickness; and appears to have been placed across the oval near the western bend. By one standing at the middle of the eastern border, and looking to the east, the ellipse is seen to lie nearly due east and west; but if allowance be made for the variation of the compass, the longer axis departs considerably from an easterly direction; and this seems to prove that this line was directed towards the stone (*Fig.* 35—*c* and *Fig.* 36—*b*)

Fig. 36.

and indicated the point where the sun rose on the auspicious morning of the summer solstice. About 100 feet from the outer circle is a fosse or ditch 30 feet broad, with a vallum a few feet in height on the outside, and with a slight elevation on the inner margin sloping towards the interior, and forming a large circular terrace. This is defective in the S.E. direction, where was the entrance leading to the avenue, which can still be traced by banks of earth visible on each side. On this terrace, near the ditch, are three stones. The first, 16 feet in height, is on the east side. It is named the Friar's Heel, and marks the rising of the sun at the summer solstice (*Fig.* 36—*b*).[2] The other two (*Fig.* 35—*e e*), one in the N. and the other in the E., may indicate the rising and setting sun at the winter solstice, the great conventions being regulated by the primary divisions of the ecliptic into solstices and equinoxes. The flat stone (A) is the outer altar stone where the pilgrim presented himself for admission to the temple, and tendered his offerings to the presiding priests. The mounds were probably the judgment seats.

Some of the largest of the stones are very heavy, and must weigh from 30 to 40 tons, most of them taken from boulders (grey withers), found in large numbers in the neighbourhood, although several of them have been brought from considerable distances: some, Dr. Buckland supposed, all the way from Wales. Sir R. C. Hoare

---

(1) We speak of it here as it was originally finished, or in design. It is now, as is well known, a ruin.

(2) Dr. Smith believed that the sun, at the summer solstice, rose over the summit of the "Friar's Heel;" and Dr. Thurman confirmed this belief by a visit to Stonehenge on the 25th June, and "as the long-looked for moment arrived—one friend being stationed at the outer circle and another on the altar stone—the sun gradually rose, a globe of fire, immediately behind the Friar's Heel." Long's Stonehenge, p. 57.

sent specimens of each to Mr. Sowerby, the mineralogist, who determined the stones forming the large circle and the trilithons to be a fine grained species of silicious sandstone, and those forming the inner circle, the oval and the altar, to be an aggregate of quartz, felspar, chlorite, and hornblende.

The builders of Stonehenge were, according to Dr. Thurman, those brachycephalic, or round-skulled men, who used to bury their dead under round barrows, and who occupied the centre, west and north of England at the time when Cæsar invaded it. Certainly, this stupendous structure could not have been erected during the stone age, as the stones could not have been dressed, and the mortices and tenons could not have been formed, with flint tools. Those who erected it must have advanced far beyond the rude condition of the primitive inhabitants before they could quarry, raise to the surrounding heights, and set on end blocks of stone of such weight, not to speak of the fitting of the mortices. It is doubtful whether even bronze tools would have sufficed, and there is every probability that iron ones were really used. The erection must date anyhow, it is clear, from a time later than the first Roman occupation, for a digging was made in the centre of Stonehenge by Mr. Cumrington, who found near the altar stone Roman pottery, three feet below the surface, and when a great trilithon fell in 1797, stoneware of the same people was found in the earth at the bottom of the pit in which the stone stood.[1] This conclusion is not invalidated, though, on the other hand, an examination of the numerous barrows by which it is surrounded, shows that out of 152 emtombments 39 contained bronze implements and ornaments, while in 129 cases the bodies had been burned, as was customary during the bronze period.

Hecatæus, the Greek historian,[2] and others mention an island over against Gaul as large as Sicily; of which the soil was rich and fruitful, and the climate temperate. The inhabitants worshipped Apollo Belanus, the sun, as their chief and most honoured god. The priests sang hymns of praise to him daily, and his temple was splendid, in a stately grove, and adorned by many rich gifts. They had likewise a round temple and a city consecrated to Apollo, and the citizens employed themselves in chanting sacred hymns and tuning their lyres to the god. The inhabitants of the island who had a language of their own had been visited by Greeks, who had given to the temple divers gifts inscribed with Greek characters. Moreover, in this island the moon seemed nearer the earth.[3] This island is supposed by some to be Britain, and the round temple and city, Stonehenge. Major Forbes-Leslie supposed the great temple to be the magnificent temple of Avebury.[4]

Stonehenge presents some curious points of resemblance to the great temples of Adjanta and Sánchi, as well as other Buddhist sacred structures in India. The circular enclosure of the tope at Sánchi (*Fig.* 37), was surrounded by a railing, resembling in structure the outer circle at Stonehenge, blocks of stone being inserted in the earth, and connected together by oblong stones placed across the top. The spaces between the uprights are filled up with oval blocks let into grooves in the upright pier, and forming a screen for the holy place.[5] This is a common arrangement in the topes and in the older cave-temples, and similar screens appear to have been used at Stonehenge; for we may suppose that the grooves formerly noticed as existing in the uprights there were intended for this purpose.

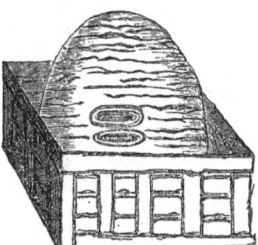

Fig. 37.

Judging, then, from our present knowledge of other countries, we may, by analogy and reasoning, conclude that Stonehenge was a sacred temple, in which offerings were made to the Deity, and religious ceremonies and the last rites of the dead performed, while the area around it would serve for the shows and games usual on the annual festivals.

---

(1) Wiltshire, vol. i, page 159.
(2) He accompanied Alexander the Great to Syria, and may have derived his information concerning Britain from a Phœnician source.
(3) Booth's Diodorus, pp. 138, 139.
(4) A temple of the same form was situated upon Mount Zelmissus, in Thrace, and dedicated to Apollo, under some local name.
(5) See Cunningham's Bhilsa Topes, pl. 2, p. 296.

According to this view the inner circle and the central oval are to be considered as the sacred part of the temple, while the large outer circle and the trilithons served in the absence of "similar rows of large oak trees, set close together," as screens to the ceremonies performed within the circle.

The inner circle and the oval, where they approach one another, were united in two granite trilithons. The latter lies prostrate where it appears to have stood, and the other has been removed with a number of the smaller stones. These two granite trilithons appear to have separated the sacred part from the sand-stone trilithons.

Stone avenues, those parallel lines of large oblong stones fixed in the earth at equal distances, inscribed often with sacred symbols to protect them from profanation, are supposed to have been erected at a very early period by mysterious races from the East in search of the happy land of the setting sun. They advanced until they were arrested at the shores of the Atlantic Ocean, one of the farthest points to the West they could approach. There the evening sun was supposed to descend, in all his gorgeous beauty, into the mansions of the blessed. Such situations became their resting-places, where they erected their monuments, which are still to be seen along the western shores of Cornwall, upon the great cliffs of the Island of Arran, and the elevations of the western island of Lewis. There they erected their altars and their tombs, leaving no record, but rude stone tools and ornaments, mounds, and monoliths, circles of stones, and the mysterious chambers of the dead. Such spots were believed to be the most appropriate to enshrine the relics of saints, which were presumed to be of inestimable benefit to those penitent pilgrims who undertook long journeys and dangerous sea-voyages, for the purpose of repeating prayers and presenting offerings at the holy shrine: by such visits they ensured the removal of loathsome diseases, and guarded against threatened misfortunes, as the darkness and coldness of the night is removed by the returning light and warmth of the morning sun and life of the world.

(f.) At Callernish, *i.e.*, "bleak or cold headland," on the west of Lewis, we have a circle of gneiss stones 42 feet in diameter, the centre *(h)* stone being 16 feet above the ground, the others about 12 feet. The avenues commenced from the cardinal points of the large circle, and consisted of four lanes of stones 8 feet high, with flat side turned *inward*, and the two end stones *with their flat side turned to the circle*. These stones were for centuries covered with peat and moss, on the removal of which they appeared white in the lower part.

The small circle *(b)* on the east of the large central stone *(h)* consists of small boulder stones placed close together round the outer margin of the cairn *(c)*, which is two feet in height, and twelve in diameter. This circle is one-and-a-half feet from the large stone. Under this cairn there was an oblong cavity terminating in a ditch, which communicated with the outer world. When this hole was opened, a "black-looking deposit" was found, like a mixture of tar and moss, containing animal matter, probably a relic of some saint. The whole was surrounded by the large circle from whence the avenues commenced.

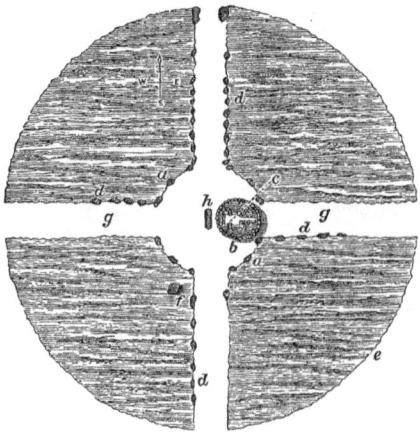

Fig. 38.

The religious ceremonies of the ancient Celtic races being little known to us, we turn with interest to similar monuments in other countries, and to the modification of similar temples in different parts of the British Islands, and among alien primitive races in distant lands worshipping the same deities and observing the same rites. The religious ceremonies of the Celtic races were performed in secret, and their temples were approached by avenues of trees, by standing stones or other screens, or by subterranean approaches through a tumulus.[1]

The resemblance of modern monuments in distant countries to those of the ancient Romans in Europe is often remarkable; and the form of introduction into the tribe is curious. In New South Wales, when a young man is to be received into the tribe, the men, women, and children are sent to a distance, to ensure secrecy, and the candidate is conducted by the elders up a long avenue to a circular temple, which is situated in a secluded valley in the deep recess of the forest, where Priam (the deity) is represented as asleep, with his face to the earth, in the form of an immense oblong mound of earth. In this condition it is believed he will remain for a certain time, and then he will awake. Within the enclosure, a narrow pathway turns off to the left, and terminates in a circular wall of earth, into which the neophyte is taken. There he is instructed in the mythology of the tribe. This consists chiefly in explaining the different figures on each of the trees, with the ceremonies to be performed, and the precepts of morality to be observed. He then takes a solemn oath, with fearful imprecations, to be faithful and obedient, and not to disclose the secrets of the religion revealed to him, while the spears of the elders are brandished before him, to impress upon him the consequences, should he prove unfaithful to his oath. The neophyte is then seated upon a piece of bark, and is seigniorated by having an upper front tooth rudely hammered out by a stone. He is then sent into the wood for a certain number of days, secluded from all the tribe, and is fed privately by one of the seniors. When the specified time expires, he joins the tribe, puts on a girdle of opossum skin, and carries the spear and other arms of the men.[2]

The dromes of Sphynxes leading to the temples of Egypt, and the avenues leading to the Hindu temples, and those of the Assyrians, Chaldeans, Persians, and ancient Greeks, have a close resemblance to each other, and much in common with those of the Celtic monuments of Scotland both in symbol and doctrine. The avenues leading to the circles in the British Islands were often lined with erect stones, a large boulder being at the centre of the circle, near which sacred ceremonies were performed. In other examples, circles of stones surround cromlechs, cairns, or excavations, as in the Maes Howe, New Grange, Callernish, and Clava monuments. These sepulchral erections are found covering kistvaens, cromlechs, and circular erections with central domed roofs. In the valley of Clava, near Inverness, they consist of single or concentric circles of boulders.

(g.) The sepulchral chamber at Maes Howe in the Orkney Islands is a chambered cairn or barrow, situated a mile and a-half from the stones of Stennis, or Ring of Brogar. It is of a conical shape, 92 feet in diameter and 36 feet in height, and is surrounded by a trench 40 feet wide and from 4 feet to 8 feet deep. The central chamber of the barrow is 13 feet high, 15 feet 4 inches long and 14 feet 10 inches wide, connected with which by openings 2 feet 5 inches square are three small cells pointing towards the three cardinal points. The west and south are 5 feet 5 inches by 5 feet 8 inches, and the north 7 feet 6 inches by 4 feet 6 inches. This sepulchral chamber has many points of resemblance to the New Grange, the Scottish mounds, and the Asiatic topes. The diameter of the chamber lessens as it rises in height, and the form passes from square to octagon (as often happens in Asiatic mosques, &c.,) and it terminates in a vaulted roof, formed of long slabs of stone, the edge of each of which reaches beyond that below, gradually closing towards the apex, upon which a flat stone is placed. This construction must have been the work of a people for the most part unacquainted with the arch. It is interesting and suggestive to find on an Orcadian plan a style of architecture exactly similar to that of the roofs of the temples of old Delhi. A long narrow passage, 54 feet in length, leads from the

---
(1) Such avenues are found in the native temples of New South Wales, of Siam, of China, and those of New Grange, Clava (Inverness-shire), and the Maes Howe in the Orkney Islands.
(2) Dr. Henderson's Observations in New South Wales, p. 148.

outside to the central chamber, and varies in size from 2 feet 4 inches at the mouth, widening to 3 feet 5 inches by 4 feet 4 inches for 26 feet, when again it is narrowed by two upright stone pillars to 2 feet 5 inches. All this structure is of sandstone.

The Celtic tribes in Europe belonged to the same race as those of Asia, and had a marked resemblance to each other, believing in the same religious precepts and observing the same practices and customs. They each respected simple boulder stones, circles, cromlechs, and tumuli. In distant countries such monuments varied in size and in form according to the fancy of the individual, the nature of the district, and the stage of advancement in civilization. In the East, the usages of the people, explained by their records and religious beliefs, as well as the manners and customs of modern times, afford us hints as to the purpose of the ancient remains. In Europe, differences exist, as we see in the Maes Howe monument, which is surrounded by a ditch, as before mentioned, and not by a circle of stones, and the monuments of Clava and New Grange, which have separate chambers and not mere compartments. But these varieties are rather peculiarities than differences.

Among the Asiatic nations differences of opinion regarding the spiritual world may be explained by their earlier civilization, their more direct descent from the primitive races, and their more exact information derived from that source. The Eastern sages, as well as the Celtic priests, had arrived at the conception of a world after death, and entertained the belief that disembodied spirits were endowed with individuality, volition, and immortality. They further conceived that the spirit lingered near the corpse until it animated another person, or until it passed by transmigration into some other body, according to the character the individual bore in his previous lifetime. As the spirit was at liberty during this period to move about, and revisit the world at will, it was often the custom to leave in the side of the tomb an opening through which it could pass in and out freely. Examples of such openings are given by Dr. Fergusson.[1]

The race from which the Celts sprang carried with them, in their emigrations to distant countries, the same ideas, and stamped them on their monuments in different forms; and this may enable us to explain some of their peculiar religious ceremonies. In such chambers as in that of New Grange and of the Maes Howe in Orkney, the Deity may have been supposed to reside; and on special occasions, when particular ceremonies are performed, the presence of the Deity was supposed to make itself specially manifest.

The Callernish circles of stones resemble in many particulars those of New Grange, Clava, and Maes Howe; the difference being chiefly in their size and arrangements. Each had a circle of stones or a vallum surrounding it; each had a cairn with long, low, and narrow passages, with avenues extending into a chamber with lateral cells, which, from their central position, and from being surrounded by cairns, tumuli, and sacred boulder stones, appear to have been considered of special sanctity. We therefore believe the tradition, as stated by Martin,[2] to be near the truth, "that it (Callernish) was a place appointed for worship in the time of heathenism, when, on sacred occasions, the chief priest stood near the central stone." Such a chamber was considered a holy place, "the house of God," and became a place of pilgrimage for religious purposes. As such, the avenues were intended for the approach of the worshippers, and in them they remained during the commemoration of feasts. On the approach of a pilgrim, according to the Eastern custom, the priest, we may suppose, standing by the side of the central stone, would demand, "Who art thou that askest assistance?" and the pilgrim would reply, "An honest supplicant." And the offerings of flowers, fruit, and articles of food, etc., being made, silence would be imposed, and suitable prayers offered up, with sacred hymns and chants.

From the evidence collected from distant countries and races, it appears that the general stone structure of the Callernish monument remains much as it originally was, with the exception of the usual palisades, to complete the four approaches to the central temple.

---

(1) Rude Stone Monuments, 1872, *Figs.* 127, 128, 192, and 193.   (2) Description of Western Islands, p. 9, 1703.

CHAPTER IV.

PRIMITIVE MONUMENTS WITH ARCHAIC MARKINGS IN ASIA AND EUROPE.

PRIMITIVE people, unacquainted with letters, and without those arts dependent upon knowledge, are usually incorrect in their ideas, and feeble in their judgment. The members of a race at such stage would, for ages, remain satisfied with obtaining the means of self-support, and defending themselves from their enemies, communicating their simple wants to each other by rude sounds, and assisting the comprehension of these by means of signs made by attitudes and with the fingers. As these tribes allied themselves with one another, for the purpose of obtaining the necessaries of life, barter was at an early period established, though without any fixed rules, so that these varied in different states. The measurements were generally taken from different parts of the body:—thus, a handful, or an armful as to quantity; and as regards length, a man's arm from the elbow to the extremity of the middle finger, which was called a cubit, the length of the ulna bone, a span, a hand, a digit, a foot, a fathom, a pace, and a yard or ell. This standard varied, of course, with the size and height of the individual.

As the intelligence of the people advanced, artificial aids were invented, which at once strengthened their faculties and improved their memories. This was sometimes accomplished by pictorial representations of objects or ideas. The Egyptian hieroglyphics and Mexican pictures are examples of such methods, as are the letters in use among the Hebrews. These symbols gradually gave rise to the art of writing, by means of which thoughts were reduced to the form of words that might be spoken or sung, and words thus written or symbolized constituted the first form of a written language. Some of the ruder forms of ancient symbols may still be seen, often somewhat modified or changed, on primitive monuments in Asia and Europe; such as markings, cups, basins, hole-stones, foot-prints, oghams and runes.

SECTION I.—PRIMITIVE MARKINGS.

These were chalk-lines, scores or tallies, and clog-almanacs.

(a.) Chalk-Lines were employed to assist the memory in keeping note of purchases of the common necessaries of life, required frequently and in small quantities, and paid for periodically. In place of such lines were often used *(b.) Scores* or *Tallies*, or notches in wood, effected by means of two oblong pieces of wood placed side by side, and a nick cut across them. This notch indicated a certain quantity, and for the prevention of tampering, one of the sticks was kept by the tradesman and the other by the purchaser. Such an arrangement saved trouble, and the articles, as loaves by the baker, &c., were counted off by dozens or scores. Similar means were employed in the Court of Exchequer for recording the taxes until a late period. *(c.)* In the somewhat

similar *clog-almanac*, time was recorded on an oblong, log-shaped piece of wood by means of notches, which marked the days of the week, the month, and the cycle of the moon. Remarkable days were denoted by symbols on the margin.

SECTION II.—PRIMITIVE MEASURES AND CUPS.

(1.) *Measures.*—Those of capacity were indicated by certain shells, or other vessels employed in carrying a fluid; and, of weight, by the number of certain seeds.[1]

(2.) *Cups.*—During the long period when the early tribes remained ignorant of letters, artificial means were employed for recording important events or the deeds of great men. This was effected at first by the erection of cairns or boulders; the boundaries of property, or rights of individuals and tribes to lands, being marked in the same way. As civilisation advanced, and property became more valuable, certain marks were added to these stone memorials. Of these, one of the first appears to have been cups,[2] or hollow circular excavations, of different sizes and groups on stones and rocks. Such cups had the advantage of requiring a degree of art to establish the individual claim, and the grouping varied with different individuals, tribes, and places. In this way, as the late Sir James Simpson believed, it was not improbable that, of old, "rights to an inheritance, in many instances, were conveyed by hieroglyphic symbols similar to the ogham characters,[3] as well as by the cups." Neither of them conformed to any fixed rules, both varied in their form and meaning according to individual or family fancies, which has rendered them difficult to understand. The peculiarities of these cups may be considered with relation to their forms and their surroundings.

(a.) Forms and situations.—These cups are smooth, round, shallow, artificial depressions on stones, from half-an-inch to three inches, or more, in diameter. Occasionally they are oval, with cruciform ornaments, and in a few instances they are square. They have been formed with care, and are often surrounded by one or more incised circles, with a radial groove proceeding from the central cup across these incisions, and terminating beyond the outer circle. Others have spiral circles round them. Care must always be taken to discriminate them from the depressions arising from disintegration of the soft parts of rocks. They are usually found in pastoral glens, or upon the summits of mountains. They occur over a wide range of country, and have been found in Argyleshire (where the Dalriadic Scots had a kingdom), Inverness, Forfarshire, Derbyshire, Northumberland, Kerry, and the east of Ireland, in France, Palestine, Hindustan, and America.[4] In India they are often near temples. They are found carved on rocks, on standing stones, on buildings, in circles and avenues, and on the flat surfaces of stones connected with cromlechs, chambered tumuli, and cists, as well as on the covers of urns. The rocks and stones upon which they are found usually occupy elevated positions that have a fine prospect, particularly towards the south and east. No determinate design seems to be necessary, or of any importance, and any peculiarity may be explained by the different purposes for which in different places they were intended. In Galloway I found a singular example of cups surrounding a "Swastika," or mystic cross, which is so commonly found in different parts of the world on dresses, for ensuring good luck, &c.

Nearly all the cups on boulders and rudimental rocks have been formed with much care, and often have radials proceeding from them. The carefully incised circles round most of them are ancient symbols of the Deity, and were probably added to impart sacredness to the object for which they were prepared. The summit of

---

(1) The ounce weight in the reign of Henry III. of England was 64 grains of wheat taken from the middle of the ear.
(2) Mr. Langland, of old Berwick, Northumberland, discovered cups and ringmarks on rocks in 1825 (Proc. Soc. Ant., Scot., vol. vi, appendix); Mr. Archibald Currie, ring cuttings at Carnban, in Scot., *ibid.*; Sir G. Wilkinson, in 1835, Long Meg, in Cumberland, Jour. Assoc., 16, p. 118; Simpson, in 1867, Pro. Soc. Ant., Scot.; Very Rev. C. Graves, in Ireland, from Roy. Ir. Acad., 1848. D. Collingwood found them in the Isle of Man and in Guernsey. They have also been found in Central India.
(3) See Archibald Currie's Antiquities of North Knapdale, p. 34; and Simpson's Archaic Sculp., of Cups, &c., p. 59.
(4) Dr. Wilson found them in the valley of Ohio.

the Chatton Law, a rugged sandstone hill in the north of Northumberland, is occupied at its western end by an ancient British or Celtic fort, about which are numerous graves.[1] On the face of two rocks, which crop out of the soil on the higher part of the hill, are sculptured a number of cups, some within the fort referred to, and others about 200 yards to the westward. Here we meet with concentric circles with a central hollow or cup, from which an incised radial line, either straight or waved, proceeds through the circles, terminating beyond them.

(b.) Their uses.—Cups were used for religious or social purposes. The chief of these are on the rocks and on the more cultivated flat and meadow land, and may have served for the division of the land. Upon the face of the Haliton Hill, which is 3 miles from Grantown, and some distance from the Grampian Mountains, numerous red sandstone rocks and light brown limestones of irregular form were found cropping out of a thin covering of earth, most of which had cups on them, some in clusters, others in lines, some nearly straight, and others bent and irregular. On one flat stone only 2 feet long, ½-foot wide, and 1 inch in thickness was a cup 1½ inch in diameter and ½-inch in depth.

Near the top of this sloping hill is a rock of mica-slate, of a somewhat triangular and truncated form, and rounded at the top. *(Fig. 39.)* It is 9 feet wide at the base, and 4 feet thick. The flat surface faces the S.E., or the solsticial rising of the sun, and slopes at an angle of 45°. On this rock the cups are numerous, and cover a large portion of the face of the stone in irregular groups. They have no circles round them, are of different sizes, and have their edges often indistinct, being worn away by time and weather.

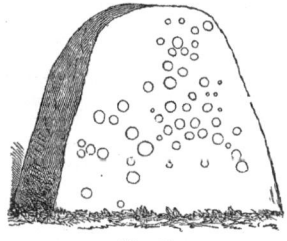

Fig. 39.

A large boulder stone, some 12 tons in weight, situated within the policies of Belmont Castle, in Strathmore, Perthshire *(Fig 40)*, is supposed to have been erected on the spot where Macbeth was slain. Two feet above the ground this boulder has a belt of cups of different sizes, and in irregular groups. None of these cups are surrounded by incised circles or gutters. This boulder was probably intended for some sacred purpose, and it faces the S.E.

Fig. 40.

At Turin, in Forfarshire, there is a large boulder which had formed one of the stones in a circle. On the flat top are several cups arranged irregularly, and without any enclosing circles. This boulder-stone is on the N.W. face of the circle. The other side was towards the S.E., facing the rising sun.

In Galloway—the country of the Gaels—is a valley, on the northern border of Wigtonshire, 20 miles from the sea, both sides of which are formed by hard silurian rocks, that crop out in different places. Wherever a part of the rock is smooth, cups are found of different sizes and depths, and at different distances apart. When seen by anyone for the first time, these cups are generally supposed to be the effects of the disintegration of the stones by the weather; but a careful examination has proved that they are artificial, their sides being smooth and their bottoms semi-circular. A portion of one of

---

(1) G. Tate's Sculptured Rocks.

these rocks larger than the others, and measuring 6 feet by 4 feet, has been selected; the rock faces the S.E., with a slope of 45°. There are no circles round their edges, and no gutters proceeding from them.

A quarter of a mile from a farm near Aberfeldie, we have seen a large smooth boulder, of many tons weight, upon the rounded top of which were groups of cups. These were a good deal worn, or disintegrated by exposure to the weather. There were various deep cracks across this gigantic boulder, which will gradually fall to pieces.

The numerous cups carefully prepared in irregular groups and figures, upon natural rocks and boulder stones, upon flat and elevated surfaces, seem to have a religious character; but might they not, in the same way, be representative symbols and records of patches of land near and facing them? Could the possessors of such landed property have the counterpart in a small stone, and thus establish their claim to possession? In the systematic explorations conducted in the Desert of Sinai, in which there have been discovered remains of primeval dwellings and of ancient tombs, almost identical with those of Great Britain, large stones have also been found which had been set up of old by the inhabitants to mark the boundaries of land. Each stone has cut upon it the symbol of the family or tribe to which the district belonged;[1] and a recent writer states that "he had seen notched mystical signs on an ancient bridge, on the borders of the Dead Sea," and adds, "I have seen similar signs on the flanks of Jellaher camels, and believe it to be a Bedouin mark for the district or tribe."

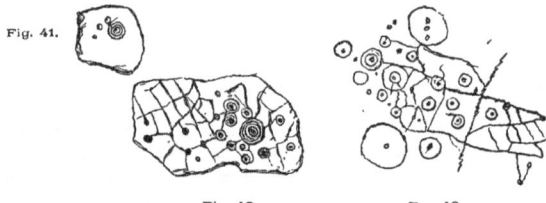

Fig. 41. Fig. 42. Fig. 43.

Some cup sculptures that might be described as *maps*, have been found in Scotland, and in the north of England. Others have been found in Kerry, in the south-west of Ireland, which have been treated of by the Bishop of Limerick in papers explaining the copies of the cups and circles which he found in Ireland.[2]

It is noticeable that there are two kinds of these cups—some have no circles round them, they face the S.E., and the cups are on the face, and not on the ends or backs, of the hard and solid rock or stone; and the others are on small unattached stones, on solid rocks, of a friable or scaly nature. *Fig.* 43 looks like the map of an estate belonging to some person, so registered and recorded. *Fig.* 42 might be the map of another, given with greater care, and with the separate farms and forts marked, and *Fig.* 41 the record of a farm.

Landmarks.—To fix individual pieces of common land in Europe, symbols were extensively used in the middle ages, especially among the ancient Ditmarshers.[3] A symbol or sign distinguished the boundaries of the lands; it was cut on the sod, or on stones erected along the lots. Sometimes it was also put over the principal entrance of a house—a custom still frequently met with in Asia,—and in Ditmarsh, and Denmark, not only is it

---

(1) Palestine Exploration Fund, Quarterly Statement, 1869, p. 148.
(2) Cup and Circle Sculptures. By Very Rev. C. Graves. Jour. R. H. and A. Assoc. of Ireland, vol. iv.; Fourth series; No. 30; April. 1877.
(3) *Dit* or *Dyt*, to clear up; *Marche*, a land mark, or riding the marches.

CHAP. IV.] HISTORY OF PAGANISM IN CALEDONIA. 53

cut in stone over entrances, but lands and cattle, seats in churches, and graves are thus distinguished. Among these signs, that which designated the priest, was formed by two concentric circles. Professor Nicholson, a late writer, informs us that in the north of Europe the mode of dividing land by lot was as follows :—Runes were cut on small pieces of wood, each owner of a hide of land choosing one. These pieces of wood, being put into an apron or bag, were drawn in succession, and after the drawing, a corresponding "*signum*," or mark, was cut on a piece of wood about 6 inches long, and driven into one of the divisions of the ground, symbolising the possession of the lot *(hasta)*. A similar mode was used in England for the common meadows, except that the mark was cut out on the turf itself. Professor Nicholson traces these marks to a pre-historic period. A modified form of such marks is to be found in the British Islands in some country parishes. Thus, in Somersetshire the Rev. J. Collinsbury mentions that the two large pieces of common in the parishes of Congresbury and Paxton, called the East and West Dolemoor,[1] were divided into single acres, each lot being marked out by different and peculiar symbols cut in the turf, or upon strong wooden and stone posts placed to mark the boundary of the ground.[2] The names given to the English landmarks have been different at different times and in different districts, and expressed ideas that were uppermost at the time in the minds of our yeomen. One of these marks, formerly called in Oxfordshire the peel, and in Sussex the *doter*, is represented by a short stick with a wooden knob. The following table exhibits the number of each tenant in an ancient common in Somersetshire, in which we see the marks take such forms as a horn, a pole-axe, a cross, a dung-fork, a duck's nest, a hand-rail, a hare's tail, &c. :—

Names.	Number of each.	Figures.	Names.	Number of each.	Figures.
Pole-Axe	5		Seven Pits	1	
Cross	4		Horn		
Dung-Fork or Pike ...	7		Hare's Tail		
Four Oxen and Mare...			Ducks		
Two Pits	1		Oven		
Three Pits	1		Shell		
Four Pits	1		Soil		
Five Pits	1		Hand-Rail		

The Saturday before old Midsummer day the several proprietors or tenants who have a right to a portion of the common assemble on it. A number of apples marked in the same manner as the acres, and equal in number to the persons entitled to shares in the common,[3] are put into a bag, and from this each draws one or more, when the plots marked with the same figures as the apples he has drawn fall to his share, and he takes possession of this allotment for the ensuing year.[4]

In other cases, the land was divided into portions called furlongs, which were marked by strong permanent posts placed at regular distances from each other, and upon which the mark of the apple that had been drawn by the proprietor was deeply cut. In 1772, an attempt was made to abolish this ancient custom, and to procure an act of Parliament for allotting these moors in perpetuity. This was abandoned, but in 1811 the common was enclosed, very much to the improvement of the land and the benefit of the tenant. A book used to be kept by the clergyman containing an account of the marks in the field and the name of each proprietor.

---

(1) The Saxon word "*Dole*" signifies share, or part.   (2) "Steward," Spalding Club, vol. ii, p. 29.
(3) The tenure is often service in the field.
(4) Hist. and Condition of the County of Somersetshire, by the Rev. J. Collinsbury, vol. ii, p. 918, and vol. iii, p. 386; 1791. See also Harris; Every Day Book, vol. ii, p. 916.

54   HISTORY OF PAGANISM IN CALEDONIA.   [BOOK I.

In Plate X of the first volume of the "Sculptured Stones of Scotland," are drawings of fragments of engraved stones, which are described as having been found upon a large, abrupt, flat, isolated rock, named Dinna-care, that juts into the German Ocean to the south of Stonehaven. The rock is 100 feet high, 200 feet long, and 30 to 40 feet wide. The top is flat, and on it a church had been erected, connected with which was a wall covered with small flat stones of red sandstone a few inches square, and with certain figures on them. In the course of time the rock has become so broken and disintegrated by the action of storms, that it is detached from the mainland. The perpendicular face of the rock in its present isolated state is so steep, that access to the top is almost impracticable; but many years ago two young men succeeded in reaching the platform,[1] and found the remains of a low wall along part of the edge, when they began to amuse themselves by throwing the stones covering the face of it into the sea below. On these stones figures were noticed; and when, in after years, the Spalding Club was publishing the "Sculptured Stones of Scotland," Mr. Andrew Gibb, F.S.A. Scot., the able artist engaged in executing the drawings for that work, searched for, and, at low ebb tide, found several of the stones that had been thrown down. It is drawings of some of these that are given in Vol. II of the "Sculptured Stones," and some of these I have copied.

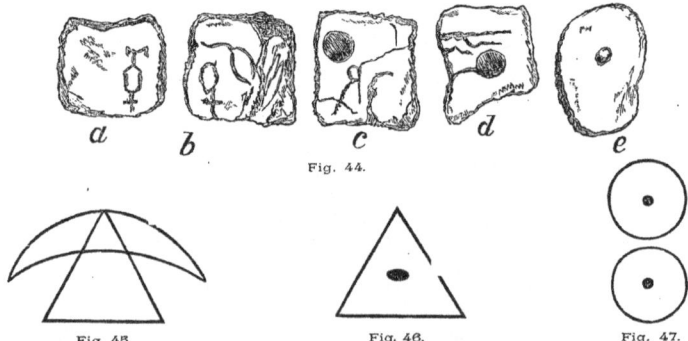

Fig. 44.

Fig. 45.   Fig. 46.   Fig. 47.

The importance of this variety of the cup becomes more evident in connection with those small stones marked by figures, which appear to refer to particular portions of neighbouring land marked by like figures. *Fig.* 44 seems to represent different portions of land, marked *a, b, c,* &c.; *Figs.* 45 and 46 represent other portions; the latter, with the right of fishery; while *Fig.* 47, consisting of two circles, with central points, and another *(e)* marked by a single cup, are other portions. The late Alexander Thomson, Esq., of Braemar, and James Christian, Esq., visited Stonehaven, and gave an account of these stones.[2]

Rocks and slabs so sculptured are met with in the neighbourhood of British forts both in England and Scotland, and sculptured stones of a similar type, and probably used in a similar connection, have been found in a Pict's house in Orkney.[3] In Southern Ditmarsh, other varieties of marking occur. A stone slab of a sepulchral chamber in one of the "*Hunengrabi*," or gigantic tumuli of the stone period, has been discovered, rudely engraven with a mark of a type which is still popular; and weapons of stone and of metal were also found marked in the

---

(1) Proc. Soc. Ant. Scot., vol. iii, p. 70.

(2) See 3rd Volume of the Proc. of Soc. Ant. Scot., p. 69.

(3) Proc. of Soc. Ant. Scot., vol. iii, p. 75. A clergyman in the Orkneys informed me that in his youth he had seen in a drawer belonging to his father, a man of condition, a number of small stones connected with the rental of properties in Orkney. I could, however, at Kirkwall, get no intelligence of such a custom, so completely had it died out.

same way. Such marks are placed on horses, sheep, eider-ducks, harpoons, stone hammers, &c., and were not assumed arbitrarily, but only after the owner had announced his intention before five neighbours at the spring convocation *(Thing)*. The similarity of most of the English marks to those of Ditmarsh, and of the old Welsh stick books, is apparent. Many of the old English landmarks, as well as the private marks of our yeomen, are also found in the Etruscan, Greek, and Eastern alphabets.[1]

The cups are the work of neither Romans, Saxons, Normans, nor Scandinavians, but are confined to the countries where the primitive Celtic races dwelt[2] before immigration set in from the East in a more modern and bronze age. By that time they had relaxed their religious strictness.

Sometimes the natural features of the country, such as rivers, lakes, ridges of high ground, &c., were the ancient boundaries of land in Scotland; at other times, objects of antiquity were taken for boundaries. Anselm of Molle, in assigning land in that territory, defines it as bounded at one point, "*per quosdam magnos lapides veteris edificii;*" in another place we find "*magnam petram in testimonium exercuerunt*." Roads, too, are mentioned as boundaries, *e.g.*, *magna strata, via alta, via regia*, &c.[3] As early as the reign of William the Lion, the boundaries of land were marked by such objects as "the old elm," "the cut in which a cross was made," "the well beside the white thorn," "the cross beside the ozier bed," the "cross and trench made on the hill-top by King David," and numerous others. But when patches of land were small and numerous, such marks were not sufficient.

One of the most important privileges of the burgesses of towns which existed so late as the end of the last century, was the right of grazing their cattle on the neighbouring arable lands—commons or hills—belonging to the town. Each burgess was entitled to an equal share of the good arable or inferior lands; but as there was no stated boundary, there were endless disputes about trespass, &c.,[4] one person holding portions of the townland in different places without any mark or fence. This was called *runrig. wodrife*, or borough acre, and it still exists in some parts of Ireland.[5] A large portion of the arable land of Scotland, England, and Ireland, was formerly cultivated on this *runrig.* system.

Commemorating Events.—Previous to the introduction of letters into the country, cups were in use for commemorating extraordinary events. Sir James Simpson, we have seen, thinks that they were probably used for marking boundaries, or the right of proprietorship to the estate where the rock is, and on which they are engraved, and that of old, rights to inheritance were, in many instances, conveyed by means of hieroglyphic symbols, similar to those already described.[6] "I am informed," says Mr. Currie, "on unquestionable authority, that the right of Macmillan to the estate of Knap in South Knapdale was cut in rude characters, in the Celtic language, upon a rock on the shore, at the point of Knap, which is now obliterated by the action of the waves on its surface."[7]

There may be another purpose served by cup-markings, and other symbols on stones which we meet with in the prehistoric age; perhaps in connection with altars, to indicate the signs of acceptance of sacrifices offered up to the sun. I found a specimen of such a stone, covering one of the long passages of a weem, or underground Pict's house, in which are cups, large and small—some with one or more circles around them, delineated in the

---

(1) The peel and duck's-nest and the mare's-tail are Greek letters, and the first two are Etruscan also, as well as the symbols of the sun and moon. The ⌓ is one of the earliest known pictorial letters, and "looks very Celtic."

(2) See Cup Marks in Central India, by G. R. Carnac, C.S.I., Asiatic Bengal, for 1870, p. 57; *ibid.*, Part I., No. 1, for 1877.

(3) Prof. Innes' Sketches of Early Scottish History, pp. 104-106.

(4) As recorded in the Mayor's office.　　(5) See Laing's Lindores, p. 306.　　(6) Archaic Sculptures, p. 59.

(7) Description of the Antiquities and Scenery of the parish of North Knapdale, Argyleshire, published at Glasgow, 1830, p. 34. The late Principal Campbell, of Aberdeen, knew Mr. Currie. He was a clever teacher, especially of mathematics, and a great authority in his neighbourhood; like many such characters he was improvident, and died young.

margin. There are three cups in a line, having two concentric circles around each of them, and from each of them a waving radial duct ascends to three smaller and simpler cups, above which are likewise three small cups of the simple kind in a line, while near the top a larger cup is surrounded by three concentric circles, and near the bottom is a single cup, larger and deeper than the others. These cups and circles were partly covered by the other roof-stones of the house; from which circumstance I conclude that they had been formed for some special and unknown purpose, before the stone was used as a common building stone.

Among the foundation stones of the Pict's house of Latham-Grange, Forfarshire, Mr. Hay found a sandstone block, rough and broken, which had numerous cups on both sides. Some of these were connected by ducts or gutters, and the largest had one or two irregular circles round them. As the cups were on both sides, the stone must at one time have stood erect. It thus appears that at that remote period, even when the Picts' house, one of the earliest class of dwelling-houses in Caledonia, was being erected, the sculptured stones had been used as common building stones;[1] so that even at that early date, notwithstanding the important and solemn purposes to which they must originally have been consecrated, the signification of the cups had been forgotten, and the stones on which they were marked were applied to common purposes. We meet with, and have elsewhere described, similar desecrations.

An interesting obelisk had been used in building the church at Dingwall, and W. C. Joass, C.E., discovered it when superintending the repairs of the church. The front (*Fig.* 48) represents the sceptred *dorge*, one of the circles being larger than the other, and a sceptred segment of an arch below, with four cups of different sizes one on the right side of the segment, one at the middle of the stone, and two near the *dorge*. The upper part of the right or front of the stone (*Fig.* 49) has concentric circles of different sizes, representing a triad, and under it a large sceptred segment, with a cup on the left side of the triad, two in the inner side of the segment—one under this symbol, and two, a large (with a circle) and a small cup, near the bottom of the obelisk. We have thus on the left circle of the sceptred *dorge* two cups under it, two above the segment and three cups underneath, one between the *dorge* and the sceptred segment at the bottom, indicating symbols arranged for important purposes.

Fig. 48. Fig. 49.

The *Fig.* 49 has the triad at the top, with a cup on the lower and left-hand side, with a large sceptred segment, and a small cup near its left-hand side; and one near the middle of the obelisk, with a large cup near the bottom of its left side with a circle, and a small cup more to the right-hand side. These cups represent some important unknown sacred arrangements, which may be at some future time discovered.

At the Grange barrow, in Ireland, in the eastern recess of the shallow stone basins, are two simple cups near the middle of the upper third. Their size and form disprove the idea of the basins being sarcophagi; while, after a careful examination, I could find no appearance of the effects of heat on the stones, which seems to prove that fire was not employed in the ceremony which had been performed there.

On a cross—the only one in an ancient grave-yard—near Inverussie in North Knapdale, in Agyleshire, were bosses on both face and back, which may represent cups (*Fig.* 50). Those within the cross may have been

---

(1) See Sir James Simpson's Work, p. 44, pl. xx., fig. 1, 2.

prepared when it was made (as A, A); the boss marked B might have been prepared afterwards; and the *relievo* boss was made out of the cross, and was surrounded by a ditch, which might represent a river, while the surrounding lines (D, D) might represent a boundary. The opposite angle (E) might represent other boundaries. The two crosses near two bosses, one within and the other without the lower angle, might represent land, the gift of the church, and be an "after-thought." As in most early markings, the exact plan may have varied with the worker—one using cups and another bosses, though for the same purpose, after once allowing the sacred boulders to be polluted by having cups formed on them.

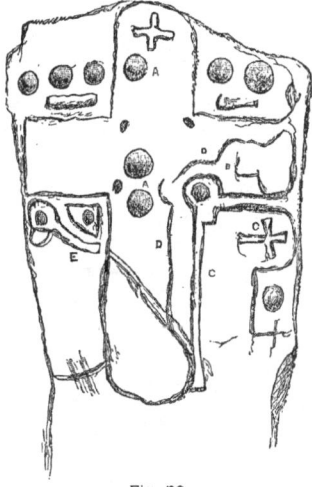

Mr. Rivett Carnac observed a striking combination of large and small cups, which he supposes may belong to Vishnu worship; and he found in the tumuli of India remains resembling those of Europe and facing the south (-east?). The cup-marks were on boulders surrounding Indian tombs, in the same manner as on those round tumuli in Europe. The rude stone monuments, in form circular, sometimes in cromlechs or kist-vaens, occasionally both together, probably the work of the same people, are found in the N.W. near Peshawur. The rocks and stones upon which the cups are marked, are generally situated on an elevated position and with a fine prospect, especially towards the east and south, perhaps from religious motives. When the cups were for other purposes, and occurred in a valley, perhaps regarding the north "star" symbol,

Fig. 50.

the symbol of the sun was placed round them, as in Yorkshire. Cups and rings are found in the United States of America (J. So. Ant. Scot. v. xi, p. 266). The former are also found on moon stones and sepulchral stones.

Cups on supposed altars.—Cups on altar-stones are less carefully prepared than those connected with social observances, and are always in or about circles. The stones on which they are found we call altar-stones, from their form and their position, which faces the S.E., generally with a slope in that direction. That of Snago, already mentioned, has, from its size and weight, been left in its ancient position in the S.E. of the circle, while most of the other stones have been removed for agricultural purposes. Are we to suppose that bloody sacrifices were offered upon these altars at the rising of the sun, and that the acceptance of the offering was decided by the manner in which the blood flowed and filled the cups?. This conjecture is rendered not improbable by the distribution of the cups. The upper and middle parts—where the sacrifice would be placed—have fewer cups than the lower and lateral parts, where sometimes two cups are connected with each other.

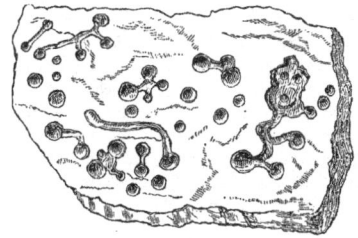

Fig. 51.

An altar-stone stands by the side of a road in front of the seat of Sir James Clark, near Balmoral. It is large and of circular form, having its upper flat surface covered with numerous cups grouped irregularly, and of greater depth than those at Snago. Some of them are joined together. This stone was near the site of a sculptured stone which Sir James had removed for safety to the neighbourhood of his dwelling-house.

I found such a stone at a place called Aghnacerribmas, near Dingle in Kerry, Ireland. It appeared to be in its

H

original position, was 5 feet 8 inches square, and had a dip towards the S.E. There were other Celtic monuments in the neighbourhood. I made a careful drawing of this stone, which I lent to the late Sir J. Y. Simpson, but he did not give it in his book, nor, unfortunately, did he return the drawing to me. The cups were of different sizes, carefully prepared and surrounded with circles, of which two or three were concentric and drawn with geometrical precision. There were no radial ducts or grooves traversing the circles. Upon the top of a cromlech at Loch Muich, four miles from Carr Bridge, Inverness-shire, was a cluster of cups. The cromlech was on the elevated brow of an inclined plain, having an eastern aspect and sheltered by a high mountain in the west. On this plain are different Celtic monuments, the remains of a fine cromlech, and numerous cairns.

Monumental and Burial Uses.—Cups are often found on stones connected with the monuments of the dead, such as on the covering stones of kist-vaens, particularly those of the short or rarest form, on the flat stones of cromlechs,[1] on stones of chambered graves, and on stones of circles,[2] such as those found on the top of the oblong stone (*Fig.* 53). On the top of the cairn at Glen Urquhart, Argyleshire (*Fig.* 52), is an oblong mass of slate-stone resting on the cairn of stones so situated as to face the south-east. By cleaning the stone, I found the cups of different sizes and depths, some in groups, and others in single or double lines. This cairn is surrounded by blocks of upright boulder stones, in two concentric circles, near each other. One of the stones (*Fig.* 54) in the inner circle has cups on it facing the north-west, so that a person facing the south-east would be opposite the cups and the rising sun of the spring solstice, at which moment certain ceremonies were performed, to render agreements more binding, &c.

Fig. 52.

At the Clava tumuli, near Inverness, were two slabs, supporting the facing of the walls and the entrance leading to the interior. My able and energetic friend, the late[3] Sir Jas. Simpson, mentions the cups on two of the slabs at Clava supporting the facing of the walls leading to the central room,[3] and Mr. Jolly has discovered other cups upon a small open circle of boulders, at which were found black earth and charcoal, fragments of burnt bones, stone hatchets, and forty or fifty large chipped flints.[4]

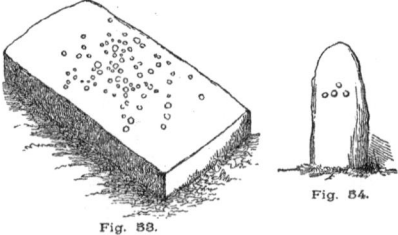

Fig. 53.

Fig. 54.

The coverings of urns often consist of fragments of stones marked with these cups; and this may have been for the purpose of indicating the property that belonged to the deceased. Mr. Wakeman, in his interesting account of the remains found in a pagan cemetery at Drumnakelly, near Omagh, in the county of Tyrone, Ireland, describes beautiful urns, inverted, and resting on small flat pieces of red sandstone or mica-slate, fourteen inches long, by eleven broad, and four thick, with one, two, or more cups.[5] Ancient graves sometimes had their walls covered with cups; and portions of deer bones, pieces of broken and very rude pottery, balls of cyenite and ironstone, and beads of a stone necklace, flint arrow-heads, flint flakes, sea shells, rounded white sea pebbles, bone implements, bone tools and combs, with carved figures, carved lines and circles, broken pieces of bone

---

(1) Archæo. Journal of Ireland, vol. iii, 4th Series, July, 1878, p. 45.   (2) *Ibid.*, p. 147.
(3) Sir Jas. Simpson, p. 29.   (4) *Ibid.*, p. 32.   (5) Archæo. Journal of Ireland, vol. iii, 4th Series, July, 1878, p. 499.

(smooth with cross lines), bronze pins, pieces of jet, amber beads, bronze rings, portions of glass or glass-beads, rings of iron and iron panel, have been discovered within them.

The cups are sometimes found on isolated rocks. On a rock, the surface of which is level with the site of it, there are cut groupings of concentric circles, three in line, and fifteen in number. Some of these concentric circles have five cups in each of them, probably to correspond with the number of the planets; and it is not improbable that these circles represent the right of the proprietor to the estate on which the rock lies— as, of old, rights to inheritance were in many instances conveyed by hieroglyphic symbols. The right of Macmillan to the estate of Knap, in South Knapdale, was, as we have seen, cut on a rock on the shore in the parish of Knap, in rude characters in the Celtic language.

(*c.*) *Ages of Cups.*—The age of the cups and the manner in which they were prepared has been discussed by Mr. Stephens, in his interesting "Incidents of Travel" in Central India. He suggests that the elaborately sculptured stones at Copan and elsewhere may have been prepared with pieces of flint or obsidian, or by the rotation of a piece of hard wood; and he found that circles and cups could be thus prepared without difficulty on whin-stone, on the Argyleshire schist, and even on hard Aberdeen granite. The megalithic catacombs, or cists, with rings and cup cuttings, have no kind of metallic tools or instruments in them. There were cups found on the covering stone of a barrow in Argyleshire, in which flint-flakes were found; so that it must have been prepared during the stone age. The pottery found showed usually on its surface dots, nail marks, and patterns of straight lines, prepared by the marking of cords upon the soft clay, and rarely displayed any of the circular or spiral lines that characterise the pottery of the bronze age. General Vallancy supposes that the ancient Irish represented the *Ti-mohr*, or Great God, by a circle, and also by concentric circles and volutes. Petrie would probably refer the monuments to an early Christian period, as Bishop Graves does.

Section III.—Sacred Shells, and Rock-Basins or Depressions.

The univalvular shell is considered sacred in Hindustan; and when the small end is cut off, it is used as a horn, and is blown on days of rejoicing and divine worship. When the volutes or whorls turn to the right they are, either from their being rare, or from some fetish idea, held in peculiar esteem, and are considered emblems of Vishnu, the preserving spirit of Brahma, the supreme being; and the more convolutions the shell has, the more highly prized it is. In one of his avatars, Vishnu is represented as having descended upon earth to save the world by restoring the sacred Vedas, destroying the giants, and punishing the wicked; and as he comes forth to carry out this purpose, he appears emerging from the mouth of a fish, rising from the primeval waters, the fountains of all being. Mythological fancies, such as these, have rendered shells objects of worship.[1]

The nature and use of the rock-basins or depressions in stones will become more evident when we consider the use to which the sacred Shelgram is put among the Asiatics, and the superstitious fancies connected with it in the Hindu religion. These small ammonites—often perforated by a slug—are used by the Unitarian Brahmin in his daily prayers. Ward says that such stones are sometimes sold for 2,000 rupees. They are valued not so much for their size, as for the shape of the curves in the perforation. Should they take the form of a cow's foot, or a wreath of flowers, they are supposed to form the residence of Vishnu and Lakshmi, his consort, the Hindu Ceres, or goddess of abundance. This valuable specimen is perforated in one place, and exhibits, according to Colebrook, four spiral curves in the perforation, which have sometimes fanciful sacred forms. A stone of this sort is more valued when found in the bed of some sacred river. It is purified by certain

(1) See Colman's Hind. Myth., pl. 4, figs. 1 and 2.

prayers and ceremonies, to ensure the deity's taking possession of this his cherished abode. It is then placed in a pure and retired place in the dwelling of the possessor. When the latter has performed his ablutions in the neighbouring river or tank, he retires to his mandala, or open hall, upon the floor of which he spreads his mat, and places his lota or brass vessel containing the sacred water, a lamp formed of a statue of some divinity, a cup of oil, sacred flowers, and offerings of grains, areca-nut, and betel leaf. He tinkles the bell, held in his left hand, as he places the sacred Shelgram upon a small stand. He then sprinkles it with the holy water, lights the lamp before it, adorns it with flowers, impregnates it with incense, and offers the repast he has provided. Each of these acts is accompanied by an invocation. In conclusion, he walks round the symbol seven times, and finally raises his hands in adoration, and utters "*O! Paramis wera*"— Forgive the sins of a poor ignorant mortal.[1] By these daily prayers to God the body is protected from accidents, and the soul is purified from sin. So holy is the Shelgram considered that it is placed near the Hindu when dying, as it ensures his soul an introduction into the heaven of Vishnu. It is worshipped at funerals, and at the ceremonies performed to the manes of particular individuals and deceased ancestors. It is also worshipped at stated intervals, during the first year after a person's death. I remember the look of contempt which an excellent and learned Brahmin exhibited when charged with being an idolater on such an occasion! He explained that it was the great God whom he worshipped with the Shelgram before him in his retirement, and that the empty hole was only to assist him in concentrating his ideas on the great and mighty Creator and Preserver, who but opens his hand and the whole world is filled with his benefits!

Fig. 55.

Fig. 56.

Basins.—In Europe the basins are large and are superstitiously fancied to be endowed with preternatural powers and virtues. They are found on both perpendicular and horizontal rocks, particularly on the shores of lakes and rivers, and sometimes in chambers, as in the examples at Dowth and New Grange. While some are undoubtedly artificial, others are mere natural hollows, produced by the wearing of some soft part of the rock under the influence of the weather. The hollow stones or rock-basins, near Carew Bré Castle, are supposed to be caused by natural disintegration. In Cornwall and the Scilly Isles the granite rocks exposed to the ocean waves show such natural basins in numbers. They abound in the rocky beds of rivers, where they are formed by the churning of stones, and some of them on the exposed summits of mountains.[2] Whether they are natural or artificial, the tradition generally connected with them is, that they are impressions produced by the fingers, feet, or knees, sometimes of giants, sometimes of holy persons; and they are always supposed to possess remarkable properties, such as the power of curing bodily pains of different kinds, inflamed eyes, head-aches, &c.; of removing barrenness; of facilitating labour, &c.

Upon a small perpendicular rock, near Galway (*Fig.* 55), which is famous for the cure of headaches, are three basins, supposed to have been made by the head and knees of St. Patrick while engaged in prayer. In order to procure relief, certain prayers must be repeated, and certain forms prescribed on two Fridays. When I visited the neighbourhood to examine the stone, I asked a woman, whom I met with near the spot, what her experience was of its efficacy. She answered, with a laugh, "Its power is very decided." She then told me how she herself had been a great sufferer from headaches, and when she was one day in the

---

(1) Moor's Hindu Pantheon, &c., edited by Rev. W. O. Simpson, p. 357.   (2) Wilson's Prehistoric Annals of Scotland, pp. 148-9.

prescribed position, viz:—with her knees and head in the basins, carefully attending to the injunctions of the priest, and repeating her prayers, in order to get rid of a "splitting" headache, a cow commenced lowing near her so loudly and suddenly, that she believed it was the Evil One. Greatly frightened, she at once fled, and did not stop until she reached her home, and since that time she had never had a headache. "What do you say to that?" she added, laughing, as she tossed her head, and ran away. There are several deep basins upon boulders in the High Street of Dingle, and others upon a flat rock near the church of Kinneller, in Kerry, Ireland. They were artificial, and so old that I could find no tradition as to their use. On the summit of the Three-Rock mountain, in Cornwall, are three huge heaps, formed of rocks piled one upon the other, and rising eighteen feet above the ground. On the top of one of these large boulders are several basins, the size of the inside of a man's hat. One is larger, and forms an oval 2 feet 6 inches long, and 2 feet broad, and 9 inches deep at the centre. They are artificial. The rock is supposed to be an altar, and the basins intended for the blood of sacrifices.

On two huge granite boulders, 20 feet in height, on the Loch Avon side of the Cairngorm mountains, there are four basins, 1 foot, or 1 foot and a-half long, and 6 inches wide at the top, rounding off to 1 inch in the bottom. They are supposed to be efficacious in barrenness, and people still living remember pilgrims coming to sit upon them for some time, that they might obtain what they wished. A visit to them was by no means an easy task, as the ascent was difficult, and to sit on them required a steady head, as they are on the brink of a rock overhanging a precipice. These basins are the "woman's stone" mentioned by Tennant. They are supposed to be the resting place or throne of a certain fairy queen; but however efficacious they may have been, they have lost much of their celebrity; and as the shepherd, who acted as guide to the pilgrims, is dead, and has left no successor, they are now rarely visited. Tennant mentions that in the Highlands the dairymaids used to pour daily or weekly libations of milk upon such hollows or cups on the Grugaich stones, to preserve cattle from disease.

SECTION IV.—HOLE-STONES—*Dolman men-an-tol.*

In the course of time sacred monuments were subject to alteration at the hands of new sects of Eastern worshippers. To the standing stone they often added a circle, to render the stone more holy, and from the back of the stone they pierced a hole which reached through to a sacred symbol. Hole-stones may be considered under two classes, according as the hole is small or large. The former were chiefly made in the Stone or Pagan period, by means of a piece of alderwood and sand impacted into the soft wood, which, on being made to revolve by a piece of string wound round it, slowly formed the required hole. The larger hole may have been formed by deepening and widening a circular groove and chipping away the centre.[1] Hole-Stones are generally associated with historical remains (Wakeman), and are connected with the earliest ecclesiastical establishments.

(a.) Small Holes.—There are two varieties of the small-holed stones, according as they are either completely or partially perforated, the one for the passage of the soul, and the other for placing a finger in the hole, which extends to a sacred symbol, when ratifying a sacred promise, which was afterwards done by repeating a portion of a sacred writing—as the Bible or the Koran. The small hole may have been formed for the passage of the soul, the hand, or a finger; and the large holes, as are often seen in cromlechs, were employed for the passage of larger objects. In the cromlechs of the Deccan, in Southern India, which consist of four dressed stones, supporting a roof slab,[2] one of the sides is perforated by a circular hole, through which the spirit might be free to pass as it lingered and moved about near the body it had animated. At Towety, in Cornwall, there is a hole in one of the props of a cromlech,[3] and there is a similar one in France. Bertrand,

(1) Jour. Arth. Inst. vol. ix. No. 11, p. 154.   (2) Capt. Meadows Taylor, Trans. Roy. Ir. Acad. vol. 25.
(3) Voyage chez les Celts.

in his "Monuments Primitifs de la Gaule," states that perhaps a dozen cromlechs have holes in their supports;[1] and M. Férand found hole-stones in the cap-stone of a cromlech at Ciudad Maham, in the province of Constantine, in Africa.[2]

Though the Celts, like the Brahmins, did not worship such stones, but looked on them as being merely the symbols of the deity they worshipped, yet the holes in them are often supposed to be produced by nature for the habitation of the gods. I have seen a flat piece of sandstone, which had been perforated by a slug, used as a charm, and as such hung up at the door of a cabin. At Kildare, in Ireland, there is an upright stone with a well-worn hole through it. People resort to it, and may be there seen making solemn vows not to break engagements. In ratifying agreements, one of the contracting parties passes his hand through the hole and touches the hand of the other on the opposite side of the stone.

Like the basins, such holes are often regarded as efficacious in connection with birth, and they are visited by women, who pray for children, or for a safe and easy delivery. Such a practice is common amongst most nations; and the like efficacy is ascribed even to the graves of those who have borne many children. Among the ruins of the mausoleum of the Emperor of Morocco at Rahat, Mr. Blackmore found one of the monuments that was regarded with peculiar veneration by the Moors, and more especially by the female portion of the population. It is a marble tablet, 2 feet 4 inches by 1 foot 6 inches, inserted in a wall, and bearing an inscription in raised letters, the top and border being ornamented with well-carved arabesque scrolls. At one side, a hole 4 inches in diameter has been cut through the tablet, destroying several of the letters and part of the ornamental border. "I was informed that it was a custom for *enceinte* women to thrust one hand into the aperture, repeating at the same time prayers for safe delivery, at the time of childbirth, and that such petitions were usually favourably answered. I was further informed that the tablet was erected in memory of a Sultan, and two very prolific wives, who were buried with him."[3]

Of the smaller holes in flat, upright stones, near circles, those in a stone between the Merry Maiden's Circle and the Piper Stone, in Cornwall, may be taken as an example. Its flat surfaces are turned to the east and west, while the hole is near the top, and is 5 inches in diameter on the west side, widening to 6 inches on the east. Executed with much care, and smooth on the surface, it must have been employed for some solemn purpose, possibly to ratify engagements, the contracting parties standing with their hands in it opposite the rising sun.[4]

The adder-stones—perforated beads of striped glass of different colours—were probably connected with the same idea. They were considered sacred by the Celtic races, and were supposed to be eggs produced by sacred serpents in summer. This egg was supposed to be seized by a Druid[5] before it fell to the ground, who was required immediately to hasten to cross the nearest stream, in order to check the pursuit of the parent adder, and thus save his own life. In Wales, stones are still supposed to be perforated by the saliva of the adder falling upon certain objects. As adders are rare in the Highlands of Scotland, these perforated stones are known by the name of snake stones, puddock stones, &c., and have attributed to them the same virtues of preventing and curing disease. In Cornwall they have their *Naen Magal* and *Glain Neidr Milpren*, or *Melpren*, and persons here pretend to have a snake charm to cure diseases.[6]

---

(1) Mon. Pr. de la Gaule.
(2) Rev. Archæo. pour mars, 1815. See also Brash's Essay on Hole-Stones; and Simpson's Work on Cups, p. 27.
(3) The Athenæum for September, 1875.
(4) There are said to be upwards of thirty hole-stones in Cornwall.
(5) For an account of the serpent's egg, see, in Toland's History, Huddlestone's learned notice of the Druids, based on Pliny's relation; especially his ingenious explanation of the Druid's egg. Note xii, p. 69.
(6) Lhwyd's Archæo. Mona Antiqua, p. 338; Pliny Nat. Hist. Lib., xxix, c. iii.

Sometimes the hole is much larger, to admit of the passage of children, of wearing-apparel, and of bed-clothes; and it is supposed to protect from, as well as cure, diseases in general. So common is such a belief, that a cleft in a rock on a promontory in the Island of Bombay is considered as a *Yoni*, and numerous pilgrims resort to it for the benefit of the supposed regenerative effect of a passage through it.[1]

As the Hindu is sworn while holding holy water in his hand, the Mohammedan on the Koran, and the Christain while holding and kissing the sacred Bible, so an equally sacred use was made in ancient times of the sacred symbols drawn on stone among rude races, who had no knowledge of writing, in offering up prayers and performing sacred offices; and as this custom has not been noticed before, I shall give an example of it, as evidence of a belief that the sacred stone, especially that with symbols, indicated the sacred influence of the Divine presence.

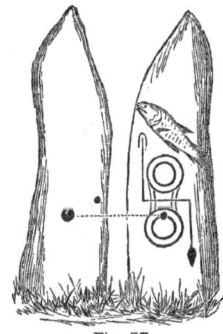

Fig. 57.

At Edderton, in Ross-shire, is a sculptured flat sandstone, of about 12 feet in height, having its flat sides facing the S.E. and N.W. (*Fig.* 57). On the south-east side, near its centre, the figure of a fish crosses the stone obliquely, and immediately under it, is a perpendicular sceptered spectacle ornament, with two concentric circles. In the upper one, the outer circle is 7¾ inches in diameter, and the inner 6 inches. At the upper part of the inner circle of the lower set, there is a hole 1½ inch in diameter, and ⅝ inch deep. The back of the stone is irregular, and is quite plain, except for a hole near the centre, three feet from the ground, and a small superficial hole near the edge; the central hole is 1⅛ inches in diameter, and 5¾ inches in depth, and the other hole is ⅘ inch in diameter, and ⅜ inch in depth. On examination, I found the hole in the inner circles of the under set, opposite the central hole on the back of the stone with a partition separating them. When any solemn vow was taken at the stone, the votary would have his index fingers inserted in the holes and touching the centre where the spiritual deity resided.

This is an example of the use of the hole during the pagan period; and we shall find examples of a similar use of it when the same race of people became Christians. They had no printed Bible, and the cross was its substitute. A hole was made in the back of the stone, so as to reach the lower limb of the cross, and with the finger in the hole touching the back of the cross, the oath, &c., was administered, or the sacred rite ratified.

The following examples of hole-stones are from Ireland :—

The *Figures* 58 and 61 are pagan, and are near the Church of Kilmakedar, Kerry. The former is a circular pillar stone, with a rounded top, which was probably intended for repeating oaths and forming

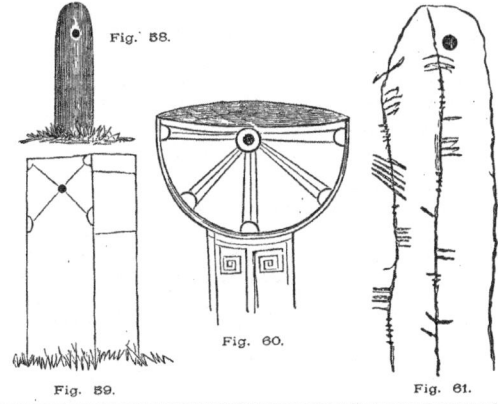

Fig. 58.

Fig. 60.

Fig. 59.

Fig. 61.

(1) Moor's Hindu Pantheon, edited by the Rev. W. O. Simpson; p. 307.

engagements with prayers. *Fig.* 61, besides its purpose for sacred engagements, &c., had probably the names of the persons and the arrangements stated on it. It is 3 feet 6 inches high.

Figs. 59 and 60. The sacred cross of St. Patrick is to the east of the pillar stones. It has an oblong square top and a hole in the centre, with two radii joining semi-circles, 12 inches apart. The prayers were repeated, and ceremonies performed, while the person faced the rising sun.

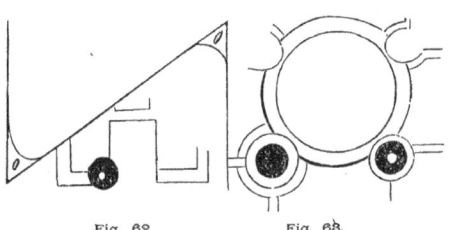

Fig. 62.   Fig. 63.

The obelisk at the church-door of Aberlemno, in Forfarshire, is another interesting example in which we have such a hole,[1] passing from the pagan symbol to the Christian cross. Upon the upper part of the stone on the reverse side, and on the inner limb, is a hole (*Fig.* 62) which will admit several fingers, or even the fist, being pressed into it. On the obverse of the stone, to the right, is an irregular hole ; (*Fig.* 63), penetrating through one of the circular depressions of the Latin cross, which has probably been accidentally broken by some violence applied from the reverse side. Here we have thus a hole penetrating through a Celtic symbol (*Fig.* 62), and terminating in a Christian cross (*Fig.* 63), and both pagan and Christian symbols were thus touched at once, as the oath was taken, or the ceremony performed. These hole-stones are usually found near Celtic monuments, such as circles of stones, and, as in this case, near Christian monuments and Churches.

On the back of a cross on a roadway in Cornwall, is a hole $1\frac{1}{2}$ inch in diameter, which had been cut, so as to reach the lower limb of the obverse side of the figure of the cross. When a witness was to be examined or a suppliant to be absolved from his sins, he was placed on the left side of the cross, and his index finger was placed in the hole, and deep enough to touch the cross. He was then examined while facing the magistrate or priest, received the prescribed oath, gave his evidence, and entered into a solemn engagement. In the example in *Fig.* 65 we have on the front of the Greek cross, with a staff (c) rounded at the top. The witness would stand behind and at the side, with the index finger inserted in the hole (A), and touching the sacred cross. In this example the edges of the stone and the edge of the hole were rounded smooth, and a good deal worn. The obverse was turned to the N.W., so that the person entering into a solemn engagement retained his finger in the hole of the cross.

Fig. 64.

Such depressions were employed for ratifying sacred obligations. In a temple on the Island of Sligo, there are several standing stones fixed in the earth, one 5 feet in height and 13 inches square, with three holes, a large one on one side and two smaller ones on the other—these latter being on either side of an incised Roman cross. We were told by the islanders, that the devotee placed the fist of his left hand in the large hole on the one side, and the thumb and ring finger of the right hand in those of the other, and thus remained while the proper prayers were offered up, and other ceremonies conducted.

(*b.*) *Large Holes.*—To keep the ancient Hindus apart from all other nations, they were prohibited from crossing particular rivers, and from travelling through countries inhabited by impure tribes, under the penalty

---

(1) Aberlemno Cross, near the Church. Sculptured Stones of Scotland, Vol. I., p. 88 and 89.

of being treated as outcasts; who could only be regenerated by passing through a *yoni*, or sacred symbol of the natural passage, made of pure gold. Such was the penalty of the rich, who were at least required to pay before they could be restored to their former rank.[1]

This emblem of regeneration *(yòni)* is quite efficacious, though it be only in the form of a hole[2] in a rock, or an aperture in a tree, that will permit the person of a child or an adult to pass through or under it; and by passage through this various painful complaints are also supposed to be cured. When sick children are passed through holes in trees—especially in the ash tree—it is the symbol and sign of a new birth, and they come again into the world with all their maladies left behind them. In the parish of Constantine, Cornwall, there is a huge oval boulder, placed on the points of two natural rocks, so that a man may creep under it and between its supporters. The diameter of the stone is 33 feet, and it is computed to weigh 750 tons. The upper surface is worked, like an imperfect or mutilated honeycomb, into basins, of which one, much larger than the rest at the south end, is about 7 feet long.[2] Such a cavity occurs below the rocks at Ardmore, in the south of Ireland, and is still resorted to for such purposes. By the passage of the body through one of these, it is believed that repentance and regeneration are at once consummated, and that diseases caused by the anger of the deity are taken away.

The *Men-an-tol*, or holed stone of Cornwall, is situated on a plain in a sloping position. It is 4 feet 2 inches in height and breadth, and is pierced by a circular hole 1 foot 6½ inches in diameter. There is no mark of chisel, and the hole resembles others that are known to have been formed by the rubbing of a hard

Fig. 65.

stone, probably before the general use of metals. Opposite this there stand two upright blocks of stone, 6 feet 8 inches high (*b, b*), which were probably placed there to to indicate the sanctity of the place. They are certainly not flat stones, such as would be used in forming the sides of an oblong cromlech, as in the examples, in the Isle of Man, and at Kerlescant in Brittany.

Dr. Joass discovered the similar hole-stone of Golspy (*c, c*) in one of the brochs he examined. It resembles the *men-an-tol* of Cornwall, and is called by the same name in Gaelic—*Tull*, with the genitive singular of the definite article. "an" (with the), but in Scotland they inflect *toll* into *tuil* in the genitive case, and write *clack-an-tuil*, "stone with the hole." The word *men* or *maen*, for stone, is now disused in the Highlands; but there are reminiscences of it in the Man of Hoy, the old man of the Ord, and in isolated rock-stacks or natural monoliths. The brave Hugh Macdonald, when near his end, ordered a large flag-stone to be placed over his grave, having a round aperture in the end, through which he might see his beloved native hills, and this, it is said, was accordingly done.[3] There are many objections to the idea that the hole-stone was part of a cromlech, and it is much more probable that the hole was employed in connection with prayers and ceremonies for removing pain and curing the sick.

Near the great circle of Stennis or Ring of Brogar, in Orkney, was the stone of Odin, 8 feet in height, and perforated with an oval hole large enough to admit a man's head. Through this hole lovers were wont to join hands, while they interchanged vows and took the "pledge of Odin," as it was called. In former times the

---

(1) Asiatic Researches, vol. vi.   (2) Colman's Mythology, pp. 156 and 175.   (3) Currie's Knapdale, p. 24.

ceremony was held so sacred, that a person who dared to break the engagement was counted infamous and excluded from society.[1] This Norse custom of betrothal was continued in the Northern Isles long after the inhabitants had become Christians, and even in modern times the heads of children have been known to be inserted in the perforation, to secure them against palsy in after life.[2] The old hole-stone of Kilhouslan is used for this purpose of betrothal. The lovers join hands through the hole and are considered indissolubly married. There are two or three similar stones in the Scilly Islands, one being at St. Mary's Island.

SECTION V.—FOOTPRINTS ON STONES AND ROCKS.

There is a belief of ancient date current, particularly among Eastern nations, that special transcendent spiritual virtue has been bestowed upon those sacred personages who have been elected by the Deity to rule and teach the rest of the race. This virtue is conceived to be such as to pervade the whole person, to affect everything they touch, and to extend even to the hem of their garments and the impression of their footsteps. It remains in their dust when they are dead, and in the soil of the very spot on which their foot but once rested. Nay, the presence of a footprint of one of these invests with a certain sacredness a whole district, and generation after generation, pilgrims resort to the spot, in the belief that they will receive strength and healing from the act. It is thus that the Vishnu-pad, which is believed to be the original footprint of Vishnu, and is annually visited and kissed by thousands of pilgrims, possesses an interest to many which far surpasses that of the famed statue of St. Peter at Rome. These footprints are partly fanciful and partly real.

(a.) *Fanciful Footprints.*—These so-called footprints, though in some cases artificially formed, are often nothing more than mere natural depressions, caused by local decay of the rocks under the action of the elements. They are met with in elevated, or sequestered, and therefore presumably sacred places, and have a resemblance, closer or more remote, to a human foot, shod or naked. Connected in the imagination of the people with the presence on earth of some holy personage, they have come to be associated with religious observances; and for such uses such spots have been appropriated and consecrated by the priesthood of nearly every creed,—those of Mohammedism and Christianity not excepted.

Such, and so regarded, is the footprint Sri-pada, as it is called, on the holy mountain of the ancient Singhalese, or Adam's peak, in Ceylon, which, with its high and pointed summit, is called the peak of God, and as it stretches into the blue vault of the firmament, is accounted the navel of the world. This is the footprint of Buddha, and the source of the Mahawelli-Ganga, the principal river of the island. This high mountain (the Pedrolallagalla) had been considered sacred from time immemorial; but it acquired a new sacredness from the day (472 B.C.) when it was reported that Buddha stood with one foot on it and the other on a mountain of Siam, and consecrated it as the last highest "footstep of fortune." This footprint is upwards of five feet in length, and two and a-half in breadth, and it has been protected all round with a ring of brass, to guard it from the effects of the weather. It is not, indeed, in the form of a human foot, but as it suited the object of the priests to have it so regarded, it was not hard for them to persuade the devout, that whether like or unlike, it was what they alleged it to be. The people, being assured by them that it was the last earthly footprint of Buddha, were not slow to believe the assurance. It was with one foot resting here, they were told, he ascended direct to heaven; and the spot from that moment became sacred in their eyes, and for ages after a monition to faith, as well as a means of grace, to the believer in Buddha.

The Siamese footprint of Buddha is a discovery of modern date, having been found by a hunter as late as the year A.D. 1602. On the discovery of it being reported by him, a commission of priests was appointed to

---
(1) Archæo. Scot. vol. i., p. 263, and vol. iii., p. 122.
(2) This, and two of the pillars of the adjacent semi-circle, were wantonly destroyed in 1814 by an ignorant farmer.

examine it critically, who, finding its dimensions exactly those of Buddha's foot, viz., 5 feet by 2 feet, thereupon decisively pronounced it to be his, although "likeness to a foot there is none," according to Mr. Alabaster's sceptical conclusion. Like the footprint on Adam's Peak, it forms a depression upon the top of a mountain, and is an object of extreme veneration to pilgrims, who, in the month of February, resort to it in crowds and leave it with, as they think, Buddha's blessing. To invest this footprint with a more than usual impressiveness, a gold plate, which professes to be a *fac-simile* of the original, is sunk into the spot, inscribed with 108 devices, the sacred Wheel of the Law being in the centre.[1]

Such are samples of sacred footprints, which, although they are mostly natural depressions of irregular oblong shape, have come in after-times to be superstitiously looked upon as impressions left by some incarnate god or heroic personality. Brahmins, Buddhists, Egyptians, Greeks, Christians, Mahommedans, and others have been weak enough to regard such phenomena with feelings of religious awe, and to connect them with certain high moments in their religious history. In holy scripture we read of high places, in which the people, deeming them specially sacred, paid homage and did sacrifice to Baal as to God. The feeling which suggested recourse to these is of very ancient date, and it prevailed for a long time far and wide among the tribes of Asia. Its existence both explains the absence in many quarters of temples made with hands for the worship of the Deity, and that superstitious awe with which, in this region, men learned to regard the high mountain-summits of the world.

Besides these, other spots are met with which are supposed to possess and convey a kindred sacredness and sanctity. I have seen what is called an inauguration-stone with the impression of a foot, in which, as alleged, the first distinguished chieftain of a race, if he did not stamp it there, stood and swore he would respect as inviolable the laws and customs of the people; and with their right foot in which his successors all stood and in a similar way swore, before they were allowed to take up and wield the badges of royalty. Such was the virtue presumed to emanate from this footprint, and such the sanction it was thought to impart to an otherwise emphatic enough protestation.

The early footsteps too of the race which originated and transmitted these ideas may be traced in Asia and Europe in those megalithic monuments which survive, in evidence at once of their physical and inventive faculty. There they are to this day, in many cases in a state as perfect as when they were first chiselled and erected, having escaped the ravages of conquering hosts, who, while they sought to destroy them and the ideas they represented, have themselves perished without sign, leaving them standing there to connect primitive races and beliefs with those of the modern world, and to afford a clue to the origin of the thoughts which have contributed to raise the character as well as extend the borders of civilized humanity.

When the Hindus conquered Ceylon in A.D. 1023, the sacred mountain with its gigantic footprint came to be referred to Civa, Lakshmana, an incarnation of Vishnu, being installed as guardian angel of the spot; while the temple of Gayā came to be regarded with special veneration, as enshrining a footprint of Vishnu. This temple is frequented by pilgrims, who, believing in the sacredness of the dust it encloses, bring hither the remains of their relations, that their ashes may be sprinkled therewith, before they are deposited for good in the sacred circulating waters of the Ganges.

The Mohammedans, on the other hand, ascribe the impression on the summit, and the consequent sacredness which invests the mountain in Ceylon, to the footstep of Adam, whom they regard as the greatest of all the Patriarchs and Prophets, and who, they allege, ascended to heaven from the spot. Just such an impression, though on a smaller scale, may be seen near Damascus, which was left, they say, by the foot of Mahomet, when, half-alighted from his camel at the southern gate of this voluptuous city, he, on the summons of the angel Gabriel, suddenly sprang back and turned away, renouncing for ever the joys of earth for the joys of heaven, which this minister of God had been commissioned to promise him, should he sacrifice every other. At least, such is the

---

(1) *See* Buddhism Illustrated, by H. Alabaster. (Trübner & Co).

common tradition; for there is another, fully as expressive of the suddenness of the transition in the Prophet's history, which represents the footprint as having been that left by the angel, whose warning took such immediate effect, that, before he could alight with his other foot on the ground, the Prophet had already taken the first step in his conversion by turning away homeward. Either way it is a significant symbol, and is taken for such by the pious Moslem, who ages ago erected a charming little mosque on the spot, in commemoration of an event so momentous.

Veneration for footprints is a religious feeling common to the race, and is met with among civilized as well as savage tribes all over the world, no less than among the disciples of Buddha and those of Mahomet. The ancient Mexicans and the islanders of the South Seas, Greeks and Romans, Jews and Christians, have all pointed to spots here and there, sacred by the presence of some impress of deity.

In the district of Bhogilpore, Bengal, there is what is given out as an impression of the feet of the supreme divinity of the Jainas, which has for several years (1812) been kept by a Pundit. It is brought to the round tower (30 feet high) at the annual Poojah, when, during the ceremonies performed there, oil is poured upon it, after which it is carried back to the house of the man who was appointed its priestly guardian.

Near the entrance of the beautiful Luckea River into the old river Ganges, stands a handsome building, which is alleged to contain the last footprint of the prophet Quodam-Resúl. A flight of steps leads up from the river to the fine gate-way of a mosque, through which one enters into a little chapel attached, where a small square piece of slate-stone is to be seen with the print of the soles of naked feet upon it. These are supposed to be the footprints left by the prophet when he stepped from this to the upper world, and the slab they are impressed on is guarded with special sacredness, and kept pure by immersion in sacred water. The mosque is in high repute among the Moslems, and is surrounded by huts erected partly for the convenience of pilgrims who visit the shrine, and partly for the accommodation of holy fakirs who live by the charity of the pious; while its sanctity with that of the domain annexed was such as once upon a time to serve as a bulwark to the Empire against the invasion of its enemies. The sacred stone is, and has for generations been, an heirloom in the family of the priest who guards it, and who lives by the offerings which devotees make, who come to kiss it in the hope of deriving some benefit from its charmed virtue.

On account of the footprint at the top, the mountain in Ceylòn also is visited once a year by pilgrims—by Brahmins, who bring offerings in honour of Civa; by Buddhists, to do honour to Gautama Buddha; and by Mussulmans, out of respect to Adam, the great arch-patriarch and world-forefather. At the base of the cone of the mountain is a small shrine or chapel where the pilgrims bathe and purify themselves before they proceed to the top with their offerings of money, rice, cocoanuts, flowers, &c., in their hands, wrapped in kerchiefs which they have brought for the purpose and had worn by the way as head-coverings. Arrived at the top, they enter into a small wooden shed, erected on a sacred spot in a hollow well-sheltered from the wind, where they are shown a depression with a gilt border round it, which, though not the least like a footprint, is said to be the one on which Buddha rested with one foot as he stepped over to India with the other. Here the pilgrims, after the observance of a series of prescribed prostrations and prayers, hand their offerings to the officiating Buddhist priests, who first deposit them within the shrine and then withdraw them to the storehouse.

(b.) Real Footprints.—Dr. Joass found footprints in a passage of one of the Sutherland brochs, which were thought to be the earthly vestige of some sacred visitant;[1] and is the earliest of the marks, as far as we know, really meant to represent footprints. Sir H. Dryden found depressions in the form of two feet upon the stone at one of the entrances of the broch of Clickemin, in one of the Shetland Islands.[2]

Fig. 68.

---

(1) *See* Archæologia Scotica, vol. V, p. 113.   (2) *Ibid*, p. 203.

CHAP. IV.]   HISTORY OF PAGANISM IN CALEDONIA.   69

Spenser, in his dialogues on Ireland, of the end of the 16th century, mentions a belief in the sacred character of footprints as prevailing in that country. He speaks of the impression as of a foot which he witnessed, engraved upon a stone, erected on an eminence or artificial mound, which is supposed to be that of the first chief of a sept in Ireland, on which his successor stands and takes the oath of fealty to the laws and customs of the clan, before he receives the sword of state and is invested with the badges of authority. In the Isle of Jura, at Finlagan, there is stone with a deep depression, which received the feet of Macdonald when he was crowned king of the Isles, and on which he pledged himself to preserve the rights of his vassals. In the church of St. Radegundis, at Poictiers, is a chapel where a stone is shown, with an impression of the footmarks of our Saviour, when he appeared to the saint. In a mosque in Egypt is the footprint of the Prophet;[1] and Herodotus makes mention of an impression of the foot of Hercules two cubits long, on a rock at the back of the river Tyres, in Scythia.[2] An outline of the soles of feet is cut out on a stone on the barrow of Petit Mont, in Brittany, near some of the sculptured mounds containing the cups mentioned above, and surrounded with waving circular and angular lines.[3] In Hall's "Ireland,"[4] mention is made of the marks of feet of different saints, but these are probably merely weather-worn cavities in rocks, resembling those in Ceylon.[5]

Dr. Petrie, in describing the stone of St. Colomb, mentions the presence of similar impressions, which he says are of the length of ten inches. This stone is many feet square, and otherwise unmarked by the chisel. It is situated a mile from Derry, and was formerly a consecration stone, on which in former times the Irish kings or chiefs of the district were inaugurated.[6] It is held in great veneration, as it is believed to have been blessed by St. Patrick. The Rev. J. Graves has given an interesting account of a boulder stone, some of the cups or hollows of which exhibit a resemblance to a foot.[7] Jervis describes such footmarks in Glenesk, in Forfarshire.[8] The last footprint I shall allude to is that of Louis XVIII at Calais. It is many years ago since I saw it, and it may still be there, though the country has since undergone so many revolutionary changes.

SECTION VI.—OGHAMS, RUNES, &c.

At an early pre-historic period, when the Celts of Caledonia were rude in their manners, their language, though confined to the expression of only a few wants, was so diversified among different tribes, that even in the present day we find those inhabiting the same district often do not understand each other's expressions; and Cæsar tells us that few of the three races dwelling in Gaul understood each other, still less the language of the Britons.[9] This divergence seems to have gone on increasing, instead of diminishing, and by-and-bye to have become especially marked in Britain; for as far back as authentic history goes, we find the present Lowlands inhabited by a Teutonic-speaking people, who not only differed in language from the Celtic Highlanders, but obstinately refused to mix with them or to borrow almost a single word from them. Bede informs us that the Pictish language was not identical with that of the Scots, although springing from the same root, for he writes of "an aged man who received the word of God from St. Columba through an interpreter."[10] When on another occasion a Pictish peasant was converted, along with his whole family, it was through an interpreter,[11] we are told the saint preached and delivered the word of life, as his own language was unintelligible to the Picts.

Bede enumerates the races in Britain in his time as consisting of Angles, Britons, Scots (Erse), Picts and Latins, and says that the Picts differed from both Scots and Britons; while Camden, in his introduction, shows from the names of places in the south-west of Scotland, that the British language differed from that of the Picts. No mention is made by Ptolemy of either Scotia or the Scots, but this may be due to the obscure position the country

---

(1) Atar-e Nibbi.—Wilkinson's Med. Egypt, vol. i, p. 288.   (2) Herodotus Melpomene, 82.
(3) Recueil des Signes Sculptés sur les Monuments Megaléthiques de Mortiham.   (4) Vol. i, p. 202, 183.
(5) Emerson Tennant, vol. i, p. 547-9.   (6) *See* Ordnance Survey of Londonderry, vol. i, p. 236.
(7) Kilk. Arch., July, 1865. *Ibid.* Sup., p. 18. *Ibid.*, vol. v, p. 451.   (8) Lands of the Lindsays.
(9) Ritson's Caledonia, vol. i., p. 478; also p. 24 *et seq.*   (10) Columba, Lib. i, 33.   (11) *Ibid.* ii, 32.

and its people held in his time. They did not come into historical prominence until strengthened by accessions from Ireland. Roused by the zeal of the Irish missionaries, they took up arms and waged constant wars during the sixth, seventh, and eighth centuries, till finally, under Kenneth MacAlpin, they conquered Pictland in A.D. 843. John Major, one of the most ancient historians of the Scots, states that "almost all Scotland spoke the Irish or Celtic tongue," and Chalmers relates that the Irish tongue was the one that was commonly spoken in the celebrated school of Aberdeen, in the reign of Mary Stuart. Even still the Celtic tongues that survive may be divided into two groups, of which the first embraces the Welsh, the Armorican,[1] and the Cornish; and the second the Gaelic, the Irish, and the Manx.

Facts of this kind have an important bearing on genealogies of races, and they often add physical certainty to the historical evidence of ancient migrations, as well as of revolutions which have left no written monuments behind them; and the inference which the facts enable us to draw here, is that the European races who speak the dialects referred to, came originally from the same Asiatic centre, and in their migrations branched out into these different tribes and nations.

The resemblance in the customs, philosophical doctrines, superstitions, and mythology of the ancient nations of Europe and Asia, affords strong evidence of a common origin; and this evidence is strengthened by an analysis of their languages, which, in spite of the differences referred to, shows them to have been derived from the same source, retaining still as they do, after many ages, the elements and even many of the forms of speech of the original. The similarity of words in the Sanscrit and Celtic languages, together with their intimate affinity in grammatical structure, cannot be accidental, but is evidence in proof that the Celts are of Eastern origin, and that the people settled on the shores of the Mediterranean and Baltic seas are kindred to those that dwell on the banks of the Indus. The idioms show very different degrees of refinement; but an accurate analysis and comparative study of these languages amply warrant the conclusion that they have had a common origin.[2] "The languages of Sclavonia, Germany, and the Pelasgian and Celtic races," observes Pritchard, "although differing much from each other, are yet so far allied in their radical elements, that we may with certainty pronounce them to be branches of the same original stock."[3] The same conclusions are come to by Baron Cuvier, who says, "The Sanscrit language is the most regular that is known, and it is especially remarkable for the circumstance that it contains the roots of the various languages of Europe, of the Greek, Latin, German, and Sclavonic."[4] In another passage of the same lectures he observes, "The Pelasgi were originally from India, a fact of which the Sanscrit roots that occur abundantly in their language do not permit us to doubt." An able critic in the *Edinburgh Review* arrives at the same conclusion: "We are," he says, "free to confess that the result of our inquiries has been to produce a conviction in our mind that the affinities known to exist between the Sanscrit, Greek, Latin and German languages, are perfectly irreconcilable with any other supposition than that of their having all been derived from a common source or primitive language, spoken by a people of whom the Indians, Greeks, Latins and Germans were equally the descendants."[5] The historical inference hence deduced, according to Pritchard, is, "that the European nations who speak dialects referable to this class of languages are of the same race with the Indians and other Asiatics, to whom the same observation may be applied."[6]

The analogy in grammatical structure between these languages is equally striking (*see* Max Müller, iv, 400); but it is enough at present to refer to the character of the connection between the primitive words and roots of the Celtic language and those of the original or parent Sanscrit, in order to prove that such affinities cannot have arisen from chance or by accidental coincidences. In applying the test, such words should be selected as denote family relations, such as father, mother, brother, sister; visible objects and elementary ideas, such as the sun, the

---

(1) The Basques are more isolated and rude than the other races, and their women, who perform all the manual offices as in the East, are looked on more as menials and slaves than with the respect paid to them in the other countries of Europe.
(2) Pritchard's Celtic Nations, p. 187. (3) Researches into the Physical History of Mankind, p. 534 to 1813.
(4) Lectures from the Natural Sciences. (5) Vol. v, p. 562. (6) Eastern Origin of the Asiatic Races, p. 18.

CHAP. IV.]   HISTORY OF PAGANISM IN CALEDONIA.   71

moon, the air, water, earth, birth, dying, knowing, seeing, hearing, &c. Resemblance in such terms as these may be considered as deciding the identity in respect of origin of any two or more languages; and if we compare words in Sanscrit with words in Celtic, descriptive of such primitive ideas and relations, a family connection is at once recognisable between them.

The proper names of rivers, mountains, lakes, and natural features are the same in different Celtic countries, being descriptive of such physical peculiarities as might strike the rudest. The south and west of Europe, from the mouths of the rivers Volga, Don, and Dnieper, to the mouth of the river Rhine, and the south and west of England, and inclusive of the whole of Ireland and Scotland, thus bear evident traces of having been in possession of the Celtic race anterior to the earliest date of recorded history.

The use of letters is one of the chief marks that distinguish a cultivated from a rude people, and the introduction of them forms a new era in the history of a nation. According to Tacitus, the ancient Germans were ignorant of the use of letters,[1] but they possessed certain characters which they used as letters, and cast lots and performed divinations with small branches of trees, upon which certain marks had been cut.[2] This must refer to the Runic or modified Ogham alphabet used by the Scandinavian races. The more perfect alphabet subsequently adopted was derived from the Greeks and Romans, but traces of the Runic are still to be detected among the Gothic and Anglo-Saxon characters.

In Caledonia, inscriptions are found recorded in three forms of letters, viz., *Ogham, Runic,* and *Roman*. The first and the second were used by the Picts, and the third by the Picts and Christians.

(a.) Ogham Characters.—(1) Ogham characters consist of lines often so grouped as to denote merely numbers, and are, as such, closely akin to the chalk lines and the notches on the tallies already referred to. (2) Oghams, in the Bethluisnin or Bethluis alphabet—so-called from the first two letters "b," *beith* (birch), and "l," *luis* (quicken), as alphabet itself is from *alpha* and *beta*—appear to have been the original written language of the pre-Christian Celts, and to have been used from an early period by the Druidical priesthood; but as the Druids were careful to conceal from the uninitiated their philosophical and religious teachings, the use of Ogham writing was confined among them to monumental inscriptions, and the like; and it was, as is probable, employed at that early period to record nothing more than occurrences of merely secular significance. The characters varied in form, as well as use, among different races and at different times, and they are found as inscriptions on stones, on bones, on metal brooches and pins, and in MSS.—in this last case, as is likely, for more detailed memoranda. They are naturally difficult to read, as the alphabet varied in different districts, while there were no stops or even divisions of words. Such as have been deciphered contain generally Latinised obsolete proper names with their patronymics, both words being in the genitive case, and denoting ownership therefore. This points strongly to the monumental and sepulchral nature of the stones. On some of the stones are also incised Greek and Latin crosses, as if to intimate the religion of the deceased.

In a burying place in Kerry, in Ireland, where these characters abound, there are eight erect stones with Ogham inscriptions, of which four have the simple inscription, and four have besides an incised Greek cross, and may mark the graves of unbaptized children, or of persons who had been converted to Christianity. In Ardmore, near Waterford, is a boulder with an incised Latin cross and an Ogham sentence.[3]

The standing stones on which these inscriptions occur, whether in England, Scotland, Ireland, or Wales, are

---

(1) Tac. Germania, c. ii, 19.   (2) *Ibid.*

(3) Though used by the Celts at a very early period, the remains of the language are very scanty. Dr. Petrie writes (Inquiry into the Origin and Uses of the Round Towers of Ireland, 2nd edition, p. 83), that "it is perfectly certain that the character was used by Christian ecclesiastics both in manuscripts and inscriptions on stone, and the character was used by the Irish previous to the time of St. Patrick. Celestinus, when a student at the monastery of St. Martin of Treves (A.D. 369), before he adopted the Pelagian doctrine, wrote to his parents in Ireland letters full of piety, which proves that they were Christians 62 years before the arrival of St. Patrick."— *See* Moor's Ireland, pp. 207 and 208.

all among the most ancient monuments these countries contain.[1] They have been the subject of much curious speculation, and points connected with the alphabet, &c., have been treated by Mr. McSwin and others.[2] The Rev Jonathan Williams mentions, as a well-known fact, that the British Druids formed the letters of their (Ogham) alphabet in resemblance to the trunk and branches of the birch tree;[3] and that these resemble the Irish characters in value and arrangement.

The Chaldæan Rabbi, Nahan, speaks of the great tree in the midst of Paradise, whose leaves were letters, and whose branches, or a collection of twigs bound together, formed words. Hammer, a traveller, in Egypt, found MSS. in Arabic, containing a number of alphabets, two of which consisted entirely of trees.[4] The Hebrews and Chinese both refer to the use of trees in writing.[5]

The Ogham character may have been a primitive attempt of this kind to record the names of certain deceased persons, or to preserve a memento of certain events dear to the individual who effected the inscription; but as there was no recognised alphabetic standard, a considerable latitude was allowed at once in their form and order, as well as in the value of the letters. They appear to have been generally considered as having some resemblance to the branches of the tree of Paradise—the emblem of knowledge. In Ireland, where they seem to have been extensively employed and to have got their name—Ozam,[6] Ogham inscriptions are more abundant than elsewhere, there being no fewer than 209 of them on stones in that country. The great majority of them are in the south; thus, in Kerry there are ninety-two, in Cork fifty-two, and in Waterford thirty-eight. In Scotland ten inscriptions seem to have been formed out of these characters, and one contains a Danish, or Norse, proper name. From references in old Welsh poems the Welsh bards seem to have used Oghams in making records, but owing to the perishable nature of the wooden tablets, or other material on which they were incised, no examples exist.

There are three varieties of Oghams—viz., the line Ogham, the wheel Ogham, and the square Ogham. The alphabet consists of sixteen primitive characters and eight diphthongs, besides the letters h and p, whose antiquity is uncertain. These letters, as may be seen in any ordinary encyclopædia of science, are classed in five groups, containing five letters each. The primitives, in all probability, formed the whole of the original scale, and are so given by O'Halloran. The fifth, or final group, with the exception of the character answering to "ea," which is the only one of any antiquity, must be an after-addition appended by later writers; for none of these letters have hitherto been found in any inscription.

Oghams of Scotland.—The Celtic monuments in Scotland with Ogham inscriptions may be arranged according to their ages, as follows:—

1. The Logie Stone, in Aberdeenshire, formed part of a Druidical circle, and has sculptured on it a Buddhist symbol, the spectacle ornament, and a circular Ogham, which may be considered the most ancient form.

2. Near the Logie Obelisk is the Newton Stone, a large oblong block of granite, which has incised upon it the spectacle ornament, and a serpent transfixed with sceptres, above which is an inscription in some Romanesque, or more probably pre-Roman character, surrounded by an Ogham inscription not yet deciphered.

3. In the museum at Dunrobin Castle, Sutherlandshire, is a remarkable stone, called the Golspie Stone, which has a beautiful cross on its face and Buddhist symbols as ornaments on the reverse, with an Ogham inscription on the upper corner right hand.

---

(1) Ulster Journal, Nos. 1 to 8, p. 45.

(2) *Ibid.*, p. 102; Arch. Cambriensis, Nos. 1 and 5, p. 231. On the affinity of the Sclavonic and Sanscrit languages, *see* Took's History of Russia. Translations of the Roy. Irish Acad., 1849, by Professor Graves; and a review of it in Arch. Cambriensis, v. ii, No. 5 of 3rd ser., p. 78, for Jan., 1856.

(3) History of Radnorshire, Arch. Cambriensis, v. i, N.S., p. 133.—*See* Brash's description of the Welsh Stones.

(4) Rev. W. Haslam's Cross and the Serpent, p. 137.   (5) *See* Davie's Celtic Researches.

(6) The name is supposed to be derived from "oghaine," offspring, and "game," wisdom. This differs from the vulgar form (ogham cruor) in being constructed in resemblance to a tree, &c., and is the parent of many other fanciful varieties.

CHAP. IV.]   HISTORY OF PAGANISM IN CALEDONIA.   73

(*b.*) *Runic Character and Language.*—The German races, or rather the Celtic, were not wholly unacquainted with letters before they acquired their learning from the Greeks and Romans, although the Runic alphabet,[1] as it has come down to us, while it is the production of a simple and rude nation, is cast in a mould the invention of later times, and was all along more an apparatus to conjure by than a symbolism of familiar speech for every-day use. The Runic character [2] is distinct from the Ogham, though there are some points of resemblance; and the oldest Runic inscription is supposed to belong to the third century, and, according to Gibbon, Venetius Fortunatus is the most ancient writer who mentions the character. The oldest forms seem to be read from right to left, but in no case must the attempt be made to render them into words belonging to the comparatively modern and provincial Icelandic dialect.

It is probable that the Runes of the Norsemen are not much older than the introduction of Christianity, although it is evident there are Runic inscriptions among the Anglo-Saxons of an earlier date, which the Christian missionaries sought in some instances to supersede, in others to sanctify. The Runic character seems to be a modification of the Ogham, with the addition of eight Greek or Roman letters to the sixteen of which the Ogham alphabet was originally composed; but as there were no fixed rules for the characters in Runes any more than in Oghams, their form varied in different districts, so that the inscriptions are very difficult to translate.

The German, Icelandic, Irish, English, Scotch and Manx Runes differ from each other just as the dialects of the tribes did who inhabited the districts where they occur. The Manx Runes differ considerably from the others, consisting of fifteen letters, some of these representing two or more cognate sounds.[3]

As the use of paper and parchment was, at the time of the older Runic inscriptions, very little known, the Rune, like the Ogham, is generally found incised on some hard material. Thus we have Runic inscriptions on a hammer preserved at Upsal, and on the remains of Bleeking. They occur extensively on memorial stones of pagan date, and on some of the earlier Christian stones. In the case of the latter, the inscription is generally written on one side of the long limb of the cross. On the reverse of the stone there are sometimes carved the figures of musical instruments and weapons of war, hunting scenes with stags, dogs, horses and horsemen, all indicative of the rank of the individual. Such sculptures date from the fourth and the fifth up till the twelfth centuries. There is only one known Runic inscription in the Shetland Islands, and none are known in the Orkney Islands. The former is given by Herbert.[4]

(*c.*) *Romanesque Character.*—The few inscriptions on the obelisks of Pictavia appear to be in forms of language derived from the East, particularly from the Sanscrit, and are written in letters having a rough resemblance to the modern Latin or Saxon character. These are probably the names of individuals to whose memory the obelisks were erected. On the Logie stone already referred to, there is, besides the Ogham, also a Romanesque inscription, the interpretation of which has puzzled the antiquary, and has not yet been satisfactorily settled. The sculptured stone of St. Vigeans [5] has sculptured on it a man with a cross-bow, indicative of an erection of the tenth century. On the lower part of the side of the stone is an inscription in the old Romanesque character, the letters being in the debased Roman minuscule character common to Europe in the sixth and succeeding centuries. According to Dr. Stuart,[6] this is the only writing in the British language that has been found; but scholars are not agreed as to the reading of the inscription.

---

(1) *See* Old Northern Runic Mon. of S., by Prof. Stephens, Huker's Thesaurus.

(2) From the old word "ruyuner" or "ruynare," to notch or to make incisions.

(3) As Kemble supposes, the Runes seem to have been inseparably connected with the old idolatrous superstitions, and inscriptions on them disappear after the propagation of Christianity.

(4) Description of the Shetland Islands, pl. 6, p. 531.

(5) Nothing is known of the district down to the year 1723, when it was formed into an independent parish. The inhabitants were generally Jacobite Episcopalians or Roman Catholics.

(6) Stuart's Sculptured Stones, vol. ii, pref. xx, p. 9; Book of Deer, pref., p. xiii.

CHAPTER V.

EARLY CELTIC ARCHITECTURE AND PILLAR TOWERS.

HE primitive structures of the Celts in Britain may be distributed into Cyclopean Block Buildings and Flag-stone Erections, with Round Towers, or Brochs, while the Implements and Ornaments were of stone, bone, horn, and metal.

SECTION I.—CYCLOPEAN BUILDINGS.

The Cyclopean erections are built of stones, without dressing and without mortar, and are remarkable for their durability, as well as their suggestiveness of rugged strength. In Christian countries they belong to the pagan period and a state of things which existed prior to the introduction of Christianity. Such structures are met with in distant countries, and, however widely scattered, are strikingly similar, arguing the prevalence at the time of their erection of a kindred stage of civilization. We have divided them into (a) Block Buildings, (b) Flag-stone Erections, and their modifications.

(a.) Block Buildings.—Structures of polygon blocks, or masses of stone, forming sometimes gateways or entrances to towers in the earliest style of Grecian and Etruscan art, are examples of this form of primitive architecture; and such have been met with underneath a mound, once fortified, on the famous Duncinnan Hill. One of these buildings we examined, and found it consisted of an oval-shaped excavation and two roundish ones of irregular horizontal form, terminating in a Celtic arch, which was formed by placing horizontal courses of stones, projecting one over the other from both sides till they met, and kept in their places by large flat stones at the top.[1] There are two narrow and low entrances near the extremities of the two galleries D and F (*Fig.* 67), and on opening the inner one (H), which was closed, we found three skulls on a line with

Fig. 67.

---

(1) Westropp's Handbook of Archæology, pp. 113 and 114. This is the earliest known attempt at the principle of the arch.

each other; one of a male, another of a female, and the third, in the middle, of a female child (*Fig.* 67—1).[1] The latter had the right parietal bone flattened and depressed, and separated on the left side a quarter of an inch. This injury must have been inflicted immediately before death, and consequently there was no appearance of any healing process.[2] The skulls may have belonged to the same family and have been preserved together. The male and female skulls may have been those of the parents who had met with some sudden death; and, as in such cases we know is still done among rude nations, the female child may have been killed by the blow of a club, in order to avert the degradation it would probably have been subjected to had it survived.

In the village of Killeany, in the Island of Arran, there is a well-known Cyclopean building, called a chapel, dedicated to St. Benignus, and situated on an elevation which commands a magnificent view of the Atlantic. Standing N.E., its dimensions are 10 feet 10 inches long, 6 feet 10 inches broad, 14 feet 6 inches high. The door is 5 feet 4¾ inches in height outside, 1 foot 8½ inches in width below, and 1 foot 3½ inches in width above outside, and 1 foot 8⅜ inches below, and 1 foot 2½ inches in width above inside; and the doorway looks a little to the S. of E. The wall at the door is 5 feet 2 inches in thickness below and 2 feet 1 inch above. The window is much splayed inside. On the declivity due east of the door, and 200 yards distant, is the stump of a pillar-tower, and a quarter of a mile to the S.E. is the church of St. Endens. A few feet in front is an excavation with, towards the east, a ledge like an altar. To the west is a large clochan, with several small oblong cavities like beds for the retainers. I am inclined to believe that in all probability these buildings were halls or dwelling-houses, probably of the chief priests, and that they were erected by the same people that built the neighbouring beehive-houses and pillar-towers.

(*b.*) *Flag-stone Erections.*—The second-class of Cyclopean buildings consists of Beehive Huts, Oratories, and Forts :—

Beehive Huts.—The dome or beehive huts in their original form were constructed of branches of trees, and have long since disappeared, but in some of the inland pasture grounds, where wood was not to be had, slate-stone had been used, and the relics of them, therefore, may still be seen. We have given a representation of a cluster of such huts, surrounded by circular parapets, in *Fig.* 16, p. 22. The form of the arch is given in *Fig.* 67—A. It is so strong, that it is met with, after centuries, as stable and sufficient as when first erected.

A modification of these Cyclopean buildings is found in the island of Harris and other Western Islands, and on the western coast of Scotland. They are built of stone either above or below ground, are among the most ancient forms of dwelling-houses extant occupied by the aboriginal inhabitants of Britain and Ireland, and their similarity in conception and arrangement proves them to have been the abodes of kindred races. There are many of them in the Orkney Islands, but they are invisible, as they are concealed by tumuli. Tradition, indeed, is silent as to whether they were intended for the living or the dead, but this may be ascertained by the examination of their form, structure, and remains. Externally, these monuments resemble barrows or graves; but as they are on the retired parts of hills, sometimes at a considerable height, as well as covered with grass, they attract but little attention, and, on account of their position, often remain undisturbed. It is only in modern times that they have been explored and carefully examined, and this requires much time and labour, as the cavities are generally three-parts filled up with stones, earth, and rubbish. They are built of well-selected large stones, and are formed into narrow apartments, about a foot square at the top, and covered by a flat stone, over which stones and clay are packed in a conical form, and the whole is covered over with a thick layer of turf.

I examined one on the Wideford Hill, a few miles from Kirkwall, and not far from the Pict's house at Quanterness. The principal apartment was 10 feet 5 inches broad, 9 feet 3 inches in height, from

---

(1) *See* Thesaurus Craniorum, by J. Bernard Davis, p. 18.   (2) Pro. Soc. Ant. Scot., vol. ii, p. 99.

which the others branched, and which were respectively 6 feet 3 inches long, 3 feet 7 inches broad, and 6 feet 6 inches high; 5 feet 9 inches long, 4 feet 8 inches broad, and 5 feet 6 inches high; 5 feet 7 inches long, 4 feet broad, and 6 feet high. The apartments communicated with each other by passages 15 or 16 inches in breadth, and on the floors of both apartments and passages were found considerable quantities of the bones of cattle and various domestic animals, but no human bones. One of the passages led to the west side of the tumulus, where the entrance may have been, although it seemed to be filled up.

These houses were not always round or oval in pagan times, some having been square. Examples of such houses during the Christian period, are those of St. MacDara on the coast of Connemara and of St. Finan, built in the sixth century, on Church Island in Corraw, Lough Fermanagh, four miles north of Dunganan Abbey. These structures are externally circular, and quadrangular within; and as cement had been used in the building of them, the fact is a standing witness of the folly of laying down rules as to form and even construction.

The huts of these ancient races are met with all along the coast of Ireland, and are called cells, Culdee hermitages, or chapels, by the common people. They are often found on islands and solitary places, near secluded lakes, amidst mountains, or perched on crags, visited only by the gannet or the eagle, and on the declivity of mountains looking eastward. They are built without mortar, $2\frac{1}{2}$ to 3 or 4 feet thick, commonly of a round or oblong form, with an overlapping stone. They are on the average of from 18 to 24 feet in diameter, and of admirable workmanship; are formed for protection against wind and rain, and it is probable that they were all originally covered with earth and turf. In many of them the roofs have fallen in; in none of them is there an aperture for the escape of smoke; and the inhabitants must have been of the most primitive habits, and have had few wants.

Oratories.—The first architects in Ireland were, according to some, Belgic settlers; according to others, African pirates, called Firnorians, who are supposed to have been the earliest to colonize the country. Anyhow, they must, we think, have been strangers from the East; and the fact that the architectural remains of Ireland present vestiges only of barbarian art, and show no traces of Egyptian, Greek, or Roman refinement, would seem to justify the assumption. The dome-roofed houses and sepulchres of stone without cement that occur so frequently, and which Dr. Petrie calls "ancient oratories," may be cited as instances. These structures are all rectangular within, and built of dry masonry, the stones being carefully fitted together, and sometimes bearing indications of having been dressed. The walls, which have no sunk foundation, are very thick below, and converge as they rise, each stone overlapping the one beneath it inside, until the top is closed by a single row of stones. The convergence of both side and end walls gives the building a peculiar, but by no means unpleasing,

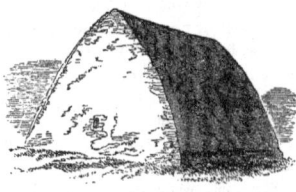

Fig. 68.

form. The doorway, which looks to the west, has converging sides, and is flat-topped, both lintel and sill being formed each of a large block of stone. The east gable is pierced by a small window or loop, and the architects show an acquaintance with the principle of the arch. The doors, except at Gallerus, are extremely low.[1]

There is at Gallerus, in Kerry, a very perfect example, which is supposed to exhibit an imperfect development of the Roman mode of construction. The window in the east gable has a semicircular head, the uncemented stones are admirably fitted, and both lateral and end walls converge in curved lines. The stone-work is quite perfect, with the exception of a stone or two, thrown down from the eastern apex. One of these contained, according to the tradition of the place, a hole, in which a

---

(1) Petrie, 2nd edit., p. 132.

smaller stone was struck, and made to play backwards and forwards, producing a sound as loud and clear as that of a bell.⁽¹⁾ The oratory measured externally 23 feet in length, 10 feet broad, and 16 feet high to the apex. The doorway in the west gable is 5 feet 7 inches high, 2 feet 4 inches wide at the base, and 1 foot 9 inches at the top. The semicircular-headed window is splayed within. The flag-stone over the door contained two holes, from which a wooden door may have been suspended, being fastened within by means of wooden loops.⁽²⁾ This door might suffice for shelter or privacy, but be a poor defence against an enemy, and may be an evidence that the building was erected for purposes purely peaceable. The gable-end doorway at the top was 1 foot 9 inches, and at the base 2 feet 4 inches, while the height was 5 feet 6 inches, and the thickness of the wall is 3 feet 6 inches. The east window was 3 feet in height and the breadth at base 1 foot 9 inches.

As regards the Use of these Oratories—1st. They were not Christian, but were erected in connection with this early, let us call it, Celtic religion. 2nd. If they had been Christian, they would have had an altar and other Christian emblems, of which, however, they show no trace. 3rd. If they had been Christian, they would stand east and west, and have had openings in those directions; whereas, after a careful examination, I found the direction varied in different oratories.⁽³⁾ They have no foundations, and no lime was used, but the stones were selected with great care and judgment, and carefully built, and the walls always converged as they rose in height.

The Maes Howe, and other galleried tumuli, show a marked similarity in the care with which the stones were selected, and in the style with which they were fashioned and placed, the upper tiers of stone projecting internally over those underneath, so that the walls approached each other. The Irish oratories, on the other hand, differ from the Maes Howe in the absence of the external covering of earth and the fosse. Perhaps the former difference may be due to climate, while the latter may be explained by the fact of there being strong fortifications near enough to afford protection in case of danger.

SECTION II.—ROUND TOWERS OR BROCHS.

These round towers are more modern than the hill-forts, and display greater variety in their plan, as well as more skill in their construction. The brochs are conical or bell-shaped towers, partially buried, it may be, as in Sutherland, in a tumulus; while in Caithness and northern situations, they are often higher and more bell-shaped. In all cases they are built of unhewn stones, laid flat on each other, without cement or ornament. The only opening is a narrow doorway, which, in time of danger, is closed by a heavy flat stone, kept in its place by a strong beam of wood, which fits at its extremities into holes let into the walls on each side, one of which is of sufficient length to receive the whole beam.

A peculiarity of these towers is, that often within the outer bell-shaped wall another conical tower is raised, so as to leave a space between the wall of the outer and the wall of the inner of about six feet at the base, and growing narrower upwards till the two walls meet at the top. In the space between the walls of some of these brochs there is a rude staircase, formed by fitting stones of varying lengths into the two walls winding round the tower, and leading into chambers, the roof of one being the floor of the next. The rest of the passage is formed into a series of chambers, which are lighted by openings looking into the inner court, which is open to the sky.

---

(1) Lady Chatterton's Rambles, vol. i, p. 143. I could not discover if there were sockets at each extremity of the ridge to keep the stones in their places.
(2) In the round Christian churches of from the eighth to the twelfth centuries the doors were generally fastened from within.
(3) Of five Oratories which I examined in Ireland, two stood S.W. and N.E., one W.N.W. and E.S.E., one N.W. and S.E., and one E. and W.

Brochs are peculiar to the north-east and west of Scotland and to the south and west of Ireland. Many of those of Scotland were used as places of refuge, especially when such enemies as the Danes made inroads. They were consequently not generally so high as to attract attention, and when on hills were at a distance from both rivers and the sea.

Dr. Anderson thinks that the age of the brochs is not earlier than the fifth and not later than the ninth centuries, that they are native to the soil of Scotland, and that they owe their peculiar character, which is unique, to the turbulent state of the country at their erection. They are eminently and peculiarly structures of defence, and not aggression. The castle holds a threat in every loop-hole of its embattled walls, but the broch is the architectural embodiment of passive resistance. Its leading idea is simply that of a perfectly secure place of refuge for men and cattle from the attacks of predatory bands, and is the suggestion of the circumstances of the whole country at the time of its embodiment, which was three centuries before the appearance of the Norse pirates on the shores of Scotland. The Irish round towers, he thinks, were for a similar purpose, and owe their existence to a kindred state of things, but argue a slight advance in the civilization of the builders, and are of their own order.

As many as forty brochs have been discovered in the Orkney Islands, besides those in Sutherlandshire and Caithness. The Mousa, or Zetland Broch, which has been lately restored, is the most perfect. It is 40 feet high, and circular in form, and articles of stone, bone, bronze and iron have been found within it. On the shores of Caithness, these towers are often of a large size, and constructed of material in a way and manner which proves the strength as well as the ingenuity of the builders, for the stone has all been brought from a distance. It is from their contents we are permitted to judge of their age, and in particular the condition of their occupants. These are bones of animals, including fish, horn and shells, with utensils of stone, bronze, and iron, belonging, some of them, to the post-Roman period, but none of them to the post-Norman. No Druidical remains have, it is remarked, been found in or near them.

These circular buildings are often in groups of different sizes and distances from each other, and where they occur in clusters, they are surrounded by walls without mortar, raised as high as the cells. Often there is a larger cell, detached from the rest, and probably occupied by the head of the community. Cairns are occasionally found near them, in some cases with a Christian cross, over spots in what must have otherwise been a pagan burial place.

The theory that these brochs were of Scandinavian or Norwegian origin was broached more than a century ago, and it was supported by such authorities as Macculloch and Sir Walter Scott, as it has been by Dr. MacPherson and others since; and there are considerations which give plausibility to this view. Nevertheless, what militates against it is that, according to the sagas, the residences of the Norsemen were not circular but rectangular in form, and that no such towers are met with in the Isle of Man and in Normandy, as well as in other parts, where it is known Viking settlements were set up and took root, any more than in other colonies of the same race. It is noticeable, moreover, that though they are nearly all on the seaboard, they must have been the settlements rather of a people who had to entrench themselves against the attacks of the sea-rover, than of men of an aggressive temper, prepared to fight for a footing where they had no right.

Danish Round Towers, as they are called, still exist in considerable numbers in the south of Ireland. A good example is the keep of Reignald's tower at Waterford. It receives its name from the builder, for we read on a stone above the doorway, that it was built by Reignald, the Dane, in 1171. It was held as a fortress by Strongbow, Earl of Pembroke, was stormed by Edward III, in 1463, and again by Cromwell, a cannon ball being built into the wall as a memorial of the Protector. These towers are built of the common undressed stones of the neighbourhood, with a considerable quantity of lime. The entrance to the lower part of the building leads into a large court in which cattle, &c., were kept. The pointed arch of the door is of dressed stone of a hard description. A narrow stone stair on the outside leads to the first story, which is lighted by oblong bevelled loopholes. The stair may have extended to near the entrance, as I found in the old tower at Kiltinnie, near Clonmel. The second story in this tower is divided into several comfortable rooms with small oblong windows. A narrow stair in the thick wall led to the third story, which, when I saw it, formed a temporary prison. There was only one large circular room, lighted by small oblong windows. Another staircase in the wall brought us to the fourth story, leading to a circular balcony or parapet, which led to small sleeping rooms. The roof has a balcony round it, with a stair on each side, leading to an oblong platform or look-out.[1]

Section III.—Pillar Towers in Asia and Britain.

When we consider how fiercely the Buddhists were persecuted by the Hindus, and how complete was the destruction of their temples and pillar towers, or "towers of safety," it is not to be wondered at, that it is only in unfrequented parts of Hindustan, in countries more or less remote, or among the ruins of Buddhist temples,[2] that the traces of the Pillar Tower are now to be found. Indeed, so utterly had Buddhism been stamped out of Hindustan, that, as we have elsewhere remarked, in the 16th century, Abul Fazl, the able minister of Akbar the Great, could not find one individual in India to give him an account of the Buddhist doctrines. To prove that these towers were common in Buddhist countries, we must refer to the descriptions left of them by travellers in Asia, and the imperfect remains of them which still exist.

Pillar Towers in Asia, as described by travellers.—Pillar towers are often referred to in Buddhist annals, and mention is made of them by the Chinese travellers Fa-Hian and Hiouen-Thsang, who visited Hindustan in the fifth and seventh centuries, to ascertain the state of the Buddhist religion in the country of its birth, since in the course of ages it had become corrupted in their own country.[3] These interesting pilgrims, especially Fa-Hian,[4] actually describe such towers of safety, as erected to keep sacred relics, such as a portion of the body of a saint, or of utensils he had used, particularly for sacred purposes. According to tradition, on the death of the founder of the Buddhist religion, eight cities contended for the possession of his body; and it was finally decided that each should have a portion. In peaceful times these relics were kept in the towers of safety, or pillar towers, and at certain hours of the day, and on particular occasions, they were removed to the neighbouring chapel (*urbaria*) or place of worship.

Fa-Hian, who was six years on the road to India, and had remained there six years, and spent three years on his way back to China, informs us that in his time (A.D. 399), as in Buddhist countries of the present day, the relics of the great Buddhist saints were considered of inestimable value. When a temple or city possessed such a treasure, its safety was secured by every possible means; and the relic was for this purpose placed in a tower, which protected the priests as well, and was also employed in calling the congregation to their devotions. Fa-Hian informs us that Na-kie, a city east of Ghuzni, possessed a portion of the skull of Buddha (Foe), for which the king of the country entertained the greatest veneration. The relic was gilt over, and covered with the most costly ornaments;[5] and so much afraid was he of its being purloined, that eight chiefs of the principal families of the kingdom had each a seal which they set on the gate of the chapel, or "tower of deliverance,"

---
(1) *See* Archæologica Scottica, vol. v, which contains an exhaustive account of these towers, their structure, purposes and history, with an interesting map, showing their situation.
(2) *See* Mr. C. Horne's (C. S.) Essay, Journal of the Roy. As. Soc. Calcutta.
(3) *See* Journal of Roy. As. Soc. of Great Britain and Ireland, No. ix. p. 108.
(4) Leland's Travels of Fa-Hian, Trübner & Co. (5) *Ibid.*, p. 83.

which contained it. Early in the morning the eight proceeded to verify the seals, and then opened the gates. On entering, the chiefs washed their hands, took up the venerated skull-bone of Buddha, and conveying it to the chapel, secured it under a bell-shaped glass upon a round stone table, adorned with all kinds of precious ornaments. Every day at sunrise, the attendants of the chapel ascended a pavilion, beat great drums, sounded the shell (conch), and struck the copper cymbals, to summon the inhabitants to worship. The king and the assembled people then offered up flowers and perfumes and performed their devotions.[1] Each one, according to his rank, placed the relic on his head and then retired to his ordinary occupation. The skull-bone was thereafter taken back to the chapel, or "tower of deliverance," and secured. The worshippers entered by the eastern gate and went out by the western.[2]

The most magnificent tower in the whole continent of India was constructed by Foe Leou Sha in honour of Buddha. In this his begging pot, an indispensable and characteristic utensil of the Buddhist recluse, was preserved. We are informed that the desire of possessing this treasure induced the king of *Yue-ti* on one occasion to invade the country with a powerful army.[3] In this case the tower and buildings in which the relics were kept were always of great strength.

All the towers were not of course equally strong, for they varied in size and form, according to the country, or the purposes for which they were intended; and often where the district was a troubled one, they were without chapels. They might have seven, nine, or twelve stories, corresponding to a certain supposed luck in the numbers, or to the twelve *Nidanas*, or conditions of relative existence. Besides being receptacles for some relic of a saint, they were occasionally erected on spots rendered sacred by some holy action. When anyone erected such a tower, "out of great faith and the impulsion of a well-directed heart," and "established the ceremonies and worship," he was promised re-birth among the gods,[4] which was the highest Buddhist reward meted out to the faithful in the next world. This doctrine is said to be taken from the sacred book, "of the names and titles of the eight great divine towers." This explains why king Nia-Kia erected a tower upon a sacred spot, more than 40 toises (about 400 English feet)[5] high, and adorned it with all manner of precious things, so that all who beheld it admired the beauty and magnificence of it, as of an object to which nothing could be compared.[6] Hence, too, it was considered by the Buddhists, that to visit and worship at the shrine of these sacred temples was an act of the greatest merit.

Remains of Pillar Towers in Asia, still existing.—If such towers existed in any considerable number, and of such a size in Hindustan, and the other countries where the Buddhist religion prevailed, we may expect to find traces of them still remaining, and this we actually do. A few of them may now be mentioned. Lord Valencia gives a drawing of two round towers he saw at Bhaugulpore in Bengal,[7] which resemble those in Ireland. The door is elevated above the surface of the ground, and the tower is provided with four large windows near the summit, and with a stone roof.[8] Captain Smith has described another such tower, which he found at Cole, near Allyghur.[9]

---

(1) Every morning dealers of flowers and perfumes collected before the gate of the temple to supply those offerings.
(2) Leland's Travels, p. 84.   (3) *Ibid.*, p. 76.   (4) *Ibid.*, p. 172.
(5) This Prof. Wilson supposes to be an exaggeration, Journal of Roy. As. Soc., 1837.
(6) *Ibid.*, p. 74.   (7) Travels in India.
(8) These towers are often referred to, but I have made various efforts in vain, when in the neighbourhood, to procure drawings of them. They are the same referred to by the Marquis of Hastings, in his private journal; and he expressly states that there are two insulated towers near Bhaugulpore, which have some resemblance to the round towers of Ireland, "but they are not above half the height. The door was on a level with the ground. Evidently those which I saw to-day were of no considerable antiquity," (vol. i, p. 95.) These cannot be considered as examples of the pillar tower; and as the late Magistrate of the Bhaugulpore district, the distinguished jurist, E. A. Samuells, C.B., could not find any trace of them, I suspect his lordship must have made a hurried sketch, or the engraver has taken great liberties with the drawing which he got.
(9) In William Bentham's Iberia Celtica, vol. ii, p. 200.

HISTORY OF PAGANISM IN CALEDONIA.

The towers were never common among the peaceful inhabitants of Bengal,[1] and were elsewhere most probably destroyed by the persecuting Brahmins and fanatical Mohammedan conquerors of Hindustan. The Buddhists of Hindustan were originally separatists from the Hindu, or rather the Brahminical religion; having rejected caste, together with the ritual, as well as the sacred books, of the Brahmins, and adopted instead a system of moral discipline, and a belief that no good work was equal to that of propagating their religion; and such was the enthusiasm of these people, that, as we have said, in a few centuries they converted a large proportion of the inhabitants of Asia to their faith. They even penetrated at an early period to Africa and Europe, where extensive traces of their presence are still found. We have already noticed, and shall notice still farther, their remains in the British islands; and a Buddhist community exists at this day in European Russia.[2] And if we find anything incongruous with original Buddhism in distant countries, and among such different races of people, that is due to the ecclecticism of the Buddhist priests, who, we are to remember, varied their forms and ceremonies to suit the fancy and circumstances of those they addressed.

Tennant states that the pagodas of Blyars, of the Circars of India, are chiefly buildings of a cylindrical or pillar-tower shape, either truncated or pointed at the summit, which is frequently surmounted with a spike bearing a round ball to represent the sun.[3] Hanway, in his "Travels in Persia," states that there are four temples of the Guetris, or worshippers of fire, of round formation, about 30 feet in diameter and 120 feet in height.

In the "Histoire des Découvertes dans la Russe et la Perse" there is an account of many round towers, "said by the inhabitants to be the work of very remote times." At Bulgari there is a round tower called Misger.[4] In the midst of the ruins of Kasimof on the Oha, which falls into the Volga, is a round and elevated tower, called in the language of the country, Misguir.[5] Among the Kisti and Ingushti, very ancient tribes of the Caucasus, most of the villages have round towers.[6]

Towers, such as those delineated in (*Figs.* 69 and 71), still exist.

Fig. 69.   Fig. 70.   Fig. 71.   Fig. 72.

These are towers where shepherds hold watch, and in them they deposit all their valuables, with their women and children.[7] When they have drawn up their rope-ladder, they occupy a vantage ground from which they can annoy their enemies with great effect. In border countries, where the people are turbulent and warlike, round towers often exist in considerable numbers, as the most useful and strongest places of refuge. There are a good many of them on the Ghauts in Hindustan; on the road between Arcot and Bangalore; and skirting the Mysore country. They are found from 50 to 60 feet in height, with a door, 12 or 15 feet from the ground, that is reached by means of a ladder, which, when necessary, is drawn up and the door secured. These towers are often of considerable size, the lower part being used for harbouring cattle. When the doors are closed, those within can easily defend themselves from their enemies, especially when armed, with merely bows and arrows, and such like.

---

(1) Since other forms of tumuli (Stupa, San.) were better adapted for the deposition of sacred relics, or for perpetuating the remembrance of some remarkable person or great event.
(2) *See* Chambers' Journal for August, 1858. (3) View of Hindustan, vol. ii, p. 123, or vol. vi, p. 133.
(4) A corruption of Muzgi, which signifies "to make a holy fire burn bright."—Richardson. (5) Guttorn.
(6) *Ibid.*, p. 145, referred to by Dr. Petrie, p. 29. (7) L'Egypte, état modern, quoted by Dr. Kitto.

In Rajputana there were numerous round insulated towers 30 or 40 feet in height, built on commanding eminences, whence the approach of an enemy could be descried from a distance, and from which the garrisons could sound an alarm over the district. The only entrance to these towers was by a small doorway, 12 or 15 feet from the ground. This was reached by means of a ladder, which was pulled up in times of danger, and the door closed and secured, so that out of danger themselves, a few could easily repel a great many, or at any rate hold them at bay. The enemies most dreaded were Pindaree horsemen; and the towers afforded a ready and secure retreat to the husbandmen, who could use their matchlocks with great effect from the loop-holes with which the tower was pierced. Even when the door was reached and driven in, the defenders had the different stages to retire to, which thus became so many successive fortresses in which to defend themselves and still annoy the assailant. Some of the towers were flanked with breastworks, and such facility did they afford for refuge, and such encouragement for continual warfare, that many of them have been destroyed by order of the English Government.[1]

The late Col. Stacy, in his advance on Cabul from Candahar, had an experience in point of the use to which these towers were often put. "Near the camp;" says he, "within one hundred yards of the road, on the slope of a hill, there was a small but high tower, with only one door, about 8 feet from the base, in which three men were concealed. They suffered the column and some of the baggage to pass, and then opened fire. Fortunately, a guard over some stores was passing at the time, and four men were sent up to the tower, which appeared to have no floor, for they placed a musket inside, pointed upwards, and brought down one of the assailants the first shot. Fearing the others might escape, a fire was kindled in the doorway below, which filled the inside of the tower with smoke, and soon obliged the other two to descend; one being killed close to the door, and the other shot in attempting to escape."[2] Colonel Smith has described a pillar tower, which from his account must be absolutely identical with those in Ireland.[3]

So well suited are these towers for defence, that the block-houses which were erected during the late rebellion in Canada (1838 and 1839) were constructed upon the same principle, modified by the nature of the materials used in the construction. In Canada this retreat was supported upon logs of wood, so as to raise the house 8 or 12 feet from the ground. The only entrance was by means of a ladder, and a trap-door, which was closed when the ladder was drawn up, and as the floor and walls were loop-holed, anyone approaching ran the risk of being shot.

The sacred character of these pillar-towers in Buddhist countries is proved by their being sometimes delineated upon coins, with other sacred objects, as in the accompanying *Fig.* 73 in which the "tower of deliverance" and the sacred tree are both represented as springing out of sacred Buddhist pots. *Fig.* 74 is that of a pillar-tower in the island of Ormuz in the Persian Gulf. Palgrave,[4] in his interesting journal of a tour through Central and Eastern Arabia, thus describes a pillar-tower: Situated just within the town walls, on the land side, and built of stone, "the edifice is, unless I confound it in my memory with what I saw at Ormuz, of elegant form, ornamented with herring-bone patterns, and pierced with loop-holes here and there; the castle alongside is irregular, more resembling a barrack than a stronghold, but is also built of stone. It appears much more recent than the town, and no one could tell me anything regarding the history of either." The solitary Pharos-tower of Ormuz

Fig. 73.

Fig. 74.

---

(1) Capt. Western, B.E., told me he had blown up some thirty or forty, to the great benefit of the inhabitants, as they were no longer required, and they had become merely nests for harbouring robbers. These watch towers are frequented by Balachu plunderers, who murder every passing stranger.—*See also* Outram's Biography, vol. i, p. 166.

(2) Narrative of Services, p. 205.   (3) *See* Sir Wm. Benton's Etruria Celtica, vol. ii, p. 200.

(4) Palgrave's Journal, vol. ii, p. 308.

is of a rounded form, like that of Sharjah, but of more graceful construction; it rises at about a hundred yards from the land's-end; it is built of brick and stone arranged in herring-bone patterns; the mortar is so excellent that it is more durable than the stone. Within, a winding staircase leads up to the top, but the lower steps are broken away, thus precluding the possibility of reaching the upper part without a ladder. From what I have seen of analagous constructions elsewhere, I should think this tower was originally the minaret of a Persian mosque, destroyed by the Portuguese, as too near the fort, and that it was subsequently applied by the Portuguese, in 1620, to the purposes of a light-house."[1] Unfortunately, Palgrave had lost his notes taken on the spot, and he does not mention where the entrance of the Sharjah tower was. He evidently was mistaken in supposing the stairs had been broken away, as the doorway was 12 or 14 feet from the ground, and this prevented him examining the interior. From the interesting commentary of Alfonso Dalboquerque, the great Portuguese Viceroy of India, edited by de W. Gray Birch, and printed by the Hakluyt Society, with a map of the island in the 16th century, the round tower appears to have been cased, probably with brick in four stages, diminishing in each stage and terminating in an oblong spheroid where the light was kept. This tower would appear to have been the same as that of Feroz Shah at Gour.

The remains of pillar towers, occasionally found amongst the ruins of Buddhist temples in Hindustan, that from their position or other causes escaped the fury of the Hindu conquerors, would appear sometimes to have been converted into a *minar*, a monument to commemorate a victory, or turned to some useful purpose. Such appears to have been the case with Feroz Shah's minaret at Gour. This able chief, who must not be confounded with Feroz Shah, who reigned in Gour A. H. 702-715, died in 1494, after a reign of nearly three years,[2] a period within which a Buddhist pillar tower might be faced and altered, but scarcely sufficient for building such a monument as the *minar*. Even in its altered form it has the chief peculiarities of the pillar tower, being a round building of stone and brick, 90 feet high, and 20 feet in diameter at the base, with a flight of stone steps all the way to the top, and no stages or flats. The door-way is 10 feet from the ground.

The people of Katar (Arabia) are exposed on the land side to continual marauding inroads from their Bedouin neighbours, who possess large droves of camels and flocks of sheep, which they bring to pasture on the narrow slip of upland that lies between the coast hills and Dahna. "Hence the necessity for the 'towers of refuge' which line the uplands. These are small circular buildings from 25 to 30 feet in height, each with a door about half way up the side, and a rope ladder hanging out; by this the Katar shepherds, when scared by a sudden attack, clamber up for safety into the interior of the tower, and once there, draw up the rope after them; thus securing their own lives and persons at any rate, whatever becomes of the cattle; for to scale a wall 15 feet high is an exploit beyond the ingenuity of the most skilful Bedouin."[3]

There was a second class of pillar towers in inaccessible situations which were changed into monasteries, where numbers resided together, in which the sacred vases, holy records, MSS., and other valuables were kept and these exist at the present day in Egypt, Syria, and other countries. There these things remain in security, and all who are allowed access to them are under the constant and keen supervision of those in charge.

Primitive Pillar Towers in Ireland.—I have selected two of these probably primitive pagan Pillar Towers erected in Ireland. They were first constructed with care, and in a style to afford the greatest security to those who erected them in defending their lives and property.

Little can be ascertained respecting the nature or uses of these towers by the etymological study of the names applied to them, and equally unsatisfactory is every attempt to solve the problem of their design and use by reference to notices of them in ancient writings or documents. The authors of these appear to have regarded them as without interest or importance; and they did so probably because, being erected by strangers no longer

---

(1) Palgrave's Journal, vol. ii, p. 319. (2) Stuart's History of Bengal, p. 106. (3) Palgrave's Central Arabia, vol. ii, p. 233.

surviving among them, they had ceased to be of any special significance to a generation with another faith, another symbolism, and other observances.

The opinions, particularly those of tradition, that prevail in regard to pillar towers, are not to be depended on. Had they been intended for any great national purpose they would be found in greater numbers in Scotland, and some also in England and Wales, where, however, there is no trace of them.

The early obelisks of the British Islands were most probably erected by pagan workmen, as the Celts at that period did not build in stone, and were not sufficiently advanced in the arts; but as the people advanced in their religious ideas, and the expression of them by symbols as well as the practice of these arts, they underwent considerable changes. It is our purpose to mark, however, the forms of the early towers; and we instance one at Drumcliff, near Sligo (*Fig.* 75). The upper part of this tower was partially destroyed by lightning, and the lower remaining portion rent in two places. The whole was built of rough stone of inferior masonry, and a very old style of construction. Another (*Fig.* 76) near Seeling, in Galway, Ireland, which is peculiar for its small size, has only one large window above the door, on a line with the first floor, for defence and for communicating with the people.

Fig. 75.[1]

Fig. 76.

They were at one time attributed to the Danes, as were also mounds, forts and raths, which certainly were not erected by them. This hypothesis must be dismissed; for these towers are not only not found in Denmark, nor in places in the north of Scotland where the Danes settled, but similar towers are found in countries to which the Scandinavian races never penetrated; and they are wholly unsuited for the purpose for which, in connection with that hypothesis, they are said to have been erected. Besides there is no proof that the Danes possessed such an intimate knowledge of architecture as these structures exhibit. They were rather like the sculptured stones of Scotland and the Ogham characters, first pagan and then Christian. And it is thus Burke somewhere sums up the argument for their native pagan derivation: "The pagan Irish," Burke writes, "were great Eastern builders. Noah built the ark, and some of his descendants the tower of Babel and the hanging gardens of Babylon. His son Japhet must also have been clever as a builder, and the pagan Irish, who were descendants of Japhet, must have built pillar towers. Hence their pagan origin."

Nor can the ingenious suggestion as to the use of pillar towers proposed by Peter Colleson,[2] and adopted by Penmant,[3] be considered more reasonable, viz. :—That they were prisons for penitents in which to expiate their sins, by remaining for a certain time of probation, first in the upper story, then in the next story, and so on, till at

---

(1) A road contractor tried the effects of gunpowder in reducing this venerable tower (*Fig.* 75) for road purposes, but failed.
(2) Archælogia, vol. i, p. 307.   (3) Tour through Scotland, vol. iii, p. 162.

length they were purified, and, being released, were allowed to return once more into the bosom of mother church. It is not likely that Christians would, even had they been able, have built such structures for the purgation of penitents, when they built such indifferent churches for the worship of God.

There are no distinctive appellations for the pillar towers in the Gaelic dialect of Scotland. If there ever were such, they are fallen entirely obsolete, owing to the districts of the country in which the towers are situated having been so long detached from the districts where Gaelic is spoken. In Gaelic they are now merely designated by the Gaelic name for "tower" *(tur, tor, turaid)*. The Irish name "*cloictheach*," "*clogas*," bell-house, or belfry, has no equivalent in the Gaelic of Scotland, and is even in Ireland a modern designation, as bells were first introduced into Ireland at a comparatively recent period;[1] and as we cannot suppose that the priests would erect such elaborate buildings to hold small bells, we conclude that they were first erected in Christian times for that purpose.

Though the idea of the pillar towers having been built for belfries is out of the question, many of them have been employed as receptacles for bells or *cloicthead*.[2] Those of Brechin, Abernethy, Ardmore, Castledermot, Cloyne, and others, were formerly, and are in some instances still perhaps, used as such. But they are ill suited for such a purpose, and some of them, as the old church of Dunnoughmore and Cossinis chapel, in the rock of Cashel, had belfries attached to the pillar towers. In the Ardmore Tower the bell rope hangs down on the outside of the building. It is known that St. Paulimus of Nola, in Campagnia, was the first who introduced bells in churches, in the ninth century. If St. Patrick had introduced them, we should have found them in Gaul, whence he came, which, however, we do not. From the inconvenience of passing the rope through the different stories of the tower, a difficulty presented itself, and it required some little management to overcome it in the Abernethy and Cloyne towers. They are not so adapted to such a purpose as we had reason to expect from the superior workmen who built them. Indeed, that the pillar towers were erected for belfries is at variance with history, for there are records of the church of Cloyne by St. Colman, and not a word about the round tower ·

> Where stands that tower, grey with age,
> And mocks the waste of time,
> The good man preached from heaven's page,
> And raised the song divine.
> His church is there, his tomb in fame,
> And we his children join
> To honour God in St. Colman's name,
> The patron Saint of Cloyne.

It has been supposed from the discovery of human remains in the Roscian, Donsuho and Cloyne Towers in Ireland, and at Abernethy and Brechin in Scotland, that the pillar towers were places of burial, and indeed a skeleton was also found on one occasion entombed in the masonry of the Ardmore Tower. Into some of these the remains may have been conveyed by accident, or the body may have been deposited there for better security, as it might well be thought to be in a building that was considered sacred; but remains are too rarely found in them to justify the conclusion that they were erected for burial; and in some cases these were in a state so perfect that we must conclude they were placed there at a modern date. Besides, the pillar towers, so large and so well-built, are very ill adapted for burial purposes. Had this been their purpose, more attention would have been given to the preparation of the actual grave at the base of the tower; for surely if a man of rank had had a pillar tower built over his tomb, a stone chamber would have been prepared and an ornamental coffin employed to receive his remains. That this was done at the same early period in cases where no tower was erected, is proved by sarcophagi of the presumed date found at St. Andrew's and at Govan, in Scotland; but

---

(1) Bentham's Etruria Celtica, vol. ii, p. 210. (2) From *cloe* or *clug* a bell, and *teach* a house.
See Dr. Lingard's, Ecc. Hist., vol. iv, p. 406.

here we are to suppose that the magnificent pillar towers were erected as monuments in honour of some illustrious deceased, and yet that the body was thrown among rubbish and without even a coffin to protect it. The most convincing argument, however, against such a hypothesis is to be found in the fact that some of these towers were built on a rock where there was no space for the deposition of the body, while the great majority of them contain no human remains whatever. Such is the case with the most perfect and beautiful Dervish Pillar Tower, Dunnoughmore,[1] and the Kennit Tower; which are open down to the rock in the interior. Indeed, the great Irish pagan kings, princes and bards are known to be buried elsewhere. A few of the towers contain a good many skeletons; and beneath the pillar tower of Turmursery there was found a cist specially constructed; but it is quite possible that in these cases they were employed for a purpose for which they were not originally erected. What applies to Ireland applies equally to Pictland, for the religious tenets and modes of sepulture were in both countries the same; and it is not at all likely that such a difference would have existed at two places in Scotland without any adequate reason. Besides, with such meagre knowledge of architecture as the Picts possessed, it was not possible for them to build such structures.

It has been urged that such towers must be the work of local builders, as none of the kind are found in any other country, not even in Asia. But how, when the Irish Church sent forth many of her sons as teachers and missionaries, not only to Scotland, but to many parts of Continental Europe, where they distinguished themselves in literature and art, are there, then, no such structures in the latter, as we might expect had the native Irish been their original builders? The assertion that there are none in Asia, we have already shown to be a groundless one. It would be difficult to speak too highly of Dr. Petrie's admirable work on the Ecclesiastical Architecture of Ireland, or of the honesty of purpose, the temperateness of enquiry, and the dispassionate candour that he shows. Still, he has failed in establishing as correct the supposition that the pillar towers were alone Christian structures, erected between the sixth and the twelfth centuries.

The general description of the pagan pillar towers will appear in the third chapter of the second book.

---

(1) Sculp. Stones of Scot.

CHAPTER VI.

LAWS AND INSTITUTIONS OF CELTIC RACES.

HE laws and institutions of Celtic races may be considered under the headings of Patriarchal Religion and Social Polity; in High Places, Mounds, and Legal Monuments.

SECTION I.—PATRIARCHAL RELIGION AND SOCIAL POLITY.

Before the inhabitants of Pictland were converted to Christianity, they were ruled by their natural chiefs and the Druids; and Cæsar, when he describes the manners and customs of their Gallic ancestry, adds that the body of the people were subject to a mild but firm despotism.

The inhabitants of Gaul, as we are told by Cæsar, were divided into Belgæ, Aquitani, and Celtæ.[1] It was the latter race that was more intimately connected with Caledonia,[2] and through the Druids, their priests, with the religion of the east. The religion of the Druids is allowed to have been of the same antiquity as that of the Magi of Persia, the Brahmins of India, and the Chaldeans of Babylon and Assyria. The Celts were so superior in intelligence, strength, and valour, that they kept aloof from intermixing with inferior tribes, and those in Britain so improved in character under the teaching of the Druids, that the Gauls sent their sons to school over the Channel, to be educated along with them.[3] These teachers devoted themselves, as no others did, to learned pursuits and the study of wisdom, and they knew how to command the regard of the multitude by withholding from all but the initiated the mysteries of their philosophy. We have already indicated our belief that their great learning was drawn from an Eastern source; and such was their acquaintance with the truths of religion that Lucian, in his poem on Britain, declares that if ever the knowledge of God had come down to the earth, it was to the Druids of Britain. Such was the class who maintained the rites of religion among the early Britons.

The office of political chief was usually hereditary, but in times of danger the supreme command was committed to him who, by unanimous consent, was deemed the strongest, bravest, and most sagacious. The several tribes, however, were jealous of, as well as faithless and over-bearing towards, each other, and from the want of union and a common interest, they were an easy prey to aliens, who invaded their shores, attracted by the rich resources and beauty of the country. They had slaves among them, but these were either prisoners of war, or the children of such.

---

(1) Cæsar: De Bell. Gal., Lib. i.   (2) *Ibid.*, Lib. vi.   (3) *Ibid.*, Lib. vi., 13.

Their form of government was at first patriarchal, but it changed into a despotic chieftainship, the Celtic community, so to speak, being broken up into clans under heads that were such by birthright. The respect for a despotic rule and a hierarchical religion, for which they were distinguished, seems to have run in their very blood, for, even when merged into free communities, it appears, they were incapable of understanding and appreciating free institutions, as witness the political character and condition of the Celtic race to this hour.

Primitively they resembled certain hill tribes of India, who live in communities under chiefs, whose right of rule is that of the patriarch, the individuals of the tribe paying for their protection against their enemies by labour or service under him in the field; retiring in times of extreme danger to caves and hill-forts in the neighbourhood, where they remain with their families and effects, and defend themselves until the danger is past. Content with procuring the necessaries of life and providing for defence against their enemies, like them too, the Celts would spend their summer months in cultivating small patches of corn, tending a few cattle, gathering certain fruits, and hunting down the wild boar of the forest.

Section II.—High Places and Mounds.

High places were either natural, such as mountains or hills, or mounds of artificial erection.

The tops of mountains have witnessed great events in the history of the race. The ark with its precious freight rested on the summit of Ararat; and wondrous scenes in the story of Jesus of Nazareth, who has been to many an ark of safety in trouble, were transacted on hills and high places. It was on a hill the Law of Life was given to the nations by Moses, and it was on a hill that the Lord of Life was transfigured into a glory more than human, before the eyes of his Hebrew forerunners. Constant allusion is made in the Bible to a belief in God as dwelling on hills, and on hill-tops. And though resorting to high places for idolatrous worship is again and again forbidden in the Hebrew scriptures. The Hebrews themselves seem to have considered mountains and high places as nearer God, and suitable for His worship and sacrifice.[1]

In the worship of the sun, as the symbol of the fire and light of the world, and in that of other symbols of the Deity, altars were erected and sacrifices offered in honour on the hill-tops. From the pure air of a mountain top the great Zoroaster procured the heavenly fire which was worshipped by his disciples for four thousand years as the purest type and emblem of the mysterious power that warms and keeps alive animal life.

In all pagan mythologies mountains or hills are set down as the favourite habitations and haunts of the gods, whence they could survey and watch over mundane affairs. Olympus, it is well known, was the fabled abode of the gods of Greece, an honour that it well deserved, for as it rises from the sea in colossal magnificence, sunbeams may be seen playing from time to time upon its white summit, which rises above the belt of clouds, and mist that so often girds its sides and hides it from mortals. The poets have sung of its heaven-kissing top; where in serene, unbroken peace, amid eternal spring, and unaffected by clouds and storms, Jupiter holds undisputed sway, distributing justice far and wide among men, rewarding the good and punishing the wicked.

The Asiatics worshipped in high places, and erected upon them altars or cromlechs. The Hindu believed that Mount Meru formed the centre or navel of the Universe, and was the residence of the gods—the heaven of Brahma, and the paradise of Indra. This hill was typified by artificial mounds erected near the temples of the gods and religious monuments, and one of these is near the great and splendid stone temple of Depaldinna.

---

(1) II Kings iii., 8, 9 and 11. Chron. xxxiii., 17.

In imitation and typification of the sacred mountains, artificial mounds were raised near holy places in all Celtic countries. There the peaceful inhabitants met to form sacred engagements, to adjust differences, and to hear judicial decisions. There kings and chiefs were chosen, and there the fact received formal proclamation: "Yet have I set my king upon my holy hill of Zion." (Psalm ii, verse 6.) The conical earthern mound, thirty feet high, called Dum Donnel, or Donald's Mound, is pointed out in Kintyre, where Lord Macdonald of that ilk, formerly gave laws to his vassals, held courts of justice, settled differences, and received rents at Whitsunday and Martinmas. Upon one of these occasions he gave to one Mackay a right to the farm of Kilmahamaig from this day till to-morrow, and so on for ever.

On account of their prominent position, the pagan high places were in some instances used by Roman Catholic priests, both in England and France, as suitable places for preaching, and exhorting the people to the performance of their religious duties. Crosses were erected on them, and in many cases—as at the great central monument of Carnac in Brittany, and at St. Michael's Mount at Penzance, in Cornwall—they were dedicated to some friendly saint. Such sites were fitting resorts for the penitent, for nowhere is all sinful desire quenched, the soul purified, or the hard heart awakened more readily than on lone mountain-tops.

Artificial mounds are numerous in the north of Scotland, and in other Celtic countries, as every earldom, lordship, and barony had its Mote or Meeting-hill, and Gallow's Knowe.[1] Such seems to have been the nature of many of the tumuli to be found in ancient Celtic countries, such as those at Dowth, and New Grange in Ireland. The hill is usually surrounded by a ditch or fosse, mostly with one side sloping, so as to enable the people to hear the verdict, if not the proceedings of the court. The business of these courts was to hear evidence, and to determine the class and degree of the crime, and the amount of compensation prescribed by law. The chief presided at this Mote,[2] as it was called, and saw effect given to the judgment pronounced by the patriarchs (*ceaum-tighes*), which they ruled by common law (*cleach-dadh*.) After sentence was executed, or effect given to the judgment, a verdict of acquittal was pronounced. All offences or crimes were expiable by a fine, payable by the criminal to the injured party, or his nearest of kin. Capital punishments were not permitted by this law, as it so often led to feuds in families, and cruel murders, perpetrated in revenge by the nearest of kin, often even long after the event. Sometimes, when the clan was implicated, they were obliged to assist in paying the penalty, and so redeem their honour. When the crime was of an infamous nature, the criminal forfeited his name and privileges, and was banished beyond the bounds of the clan, never to return.

The Tynwald Hill, in the Isle of Man, is still used as a "rostrum" for the proclamation of the laws, when enacted. It was probably originally a mound of the same sort, and is said to be composed of earth collected from every parish in the island. It is formed of four truncated cones, raised one upon another, and its circumference is two hundred and forty feet. It is rectangular in form, each side facing one of the four cardinal points, and it rises to an elevation of seventy feet.[3] There are two large triliths, one on each side of it, and probably at one time a circle of stones surrounded the hill, giving it the appearance of a Buddhist tope. On occasions of ceremony the chief sits on a chair under a canopy with his face turned to the east. His officers, the clergy, the keys, and the magistrates take their respective places under their chief, while the common people occupy the surrounding area. The first recorded meeting was held in 1417, at which Sir J. Stanley, the King and Lord of Man presided. The duty of the keys was to record the code of rules for the guidance of the ceremonies of the Tynwald, and these were afterwards promulgated. Such meetings are still held on the 5th of July, when the

---

(1) This was the name given to an eminence at a short distance from the chief barrow, where criminals were in after times executed, prior to the abolition of heritable jurisdiction. The gallows was let into a large stone on the top of the mound, and the culprit was buried near it.

(2) Or "hills of strife," and one at Scone is called "Mons Placiti," *i.e.*, mountain of the decree that seems good to us.

(3) Bullock's History of the Isle of Man, p. 229.

chief magistrate, his subordinates and the people assemble to hear the laws read, in the English and Manx languages, which have been passed during the year. Certain religious ceremonies also took place on these occasions, such as used to be observed among Celtic nations.

Silbury Hill is within the line of road from Bath to London, and about a mile south of the great circle of Avebury, and on it, as the others, is one of the mounds where laws were promulgated, cases tried, and judgment given. The ancient road, to avoid the hill, passes round to the south of it, and that fact proves the earlier age of the hill. To the north-west is a cromlech, and to the south a Druid barrow.

The sacred high places were sometimes used as courts of justice, as the Holm, in the Shetland Islands. This holm is situated on an island in the middle of a small fresh-water lake. It is still called the "law-ting," from which the parish derives its name (Tingwan). Upon this holm are four great stones, upon which sat the judge, clerk and other officers of the court, while the litigants stood on the shores of the lake; and when called on by the officers to give their evidence, they crossed over to the island on stepping stones, and on being dismissed, returned to their former station to hear the decision of the judge.[1]

The Danes held civil assemblies, called Things, Tings, or Tingwan, on artificial mounds of earth that were terraced to afford seats to the people and chief, and surrounded by a vallum, or earthen fence, for sanctity and protection. The remains of these mounds or moats are still to be found in Scotland and elsewhere—where the Norsemen, or Danes, as they are called, had established themselves.

Section III.—Legal Monuments.

(a.) Monoliths, Pillars.—We have already seen that pillars, or upright boulders, were erected from remote ages to mark the spot where solemn agreements had been concluded and the boundaries, or marches, of fields and territories, and that to add to the sacred character of these tokens the figure of the cross was in after times occasionally inscribed upon them. The Jewish law strictly forbade the removal of such monuments, and interference with them as landmarks was uniformly denounced and condemned in the strongest terms. Jacob erected a pillar of stones at the place where God made a covenant with him, and poured a drink-offering over it and then oil.[2] The covenant between Laban and Jacob was marked by a stone, "and Jacob took a stone and set it up for a pillar" or symbol of God, and surrounded it with a cairn of stones as a witness of the covenant between them.[3] In this case it was also a boundary stone.

Cairns are often met with in Europe, which were set up in like manner as witnesses, if not actual bonds, of similar transactions, and as such were held in a superstitious regard, and near these pillars are often found,[4] as if for more emphatic and effective testimony.

(b.) Circles for Legal Purposes.—These are found near other circles of stones, and at them the chiefs and rulers were inaugurated and political assemblies were held. In the historical books of the Bible we find that the circles of stones, at Gilgal, were spots where assemblies were held and judicial affairs discussed and settled.

Judicial mounds, constructed of earth, were often rendered more sacred by being surrounded by a circle of boulder stones. Those to the south-west of the great temple of Stonehenge may be taken as examples. They were probably employed for public deliberations and for the administration of justice. In Norway and Ireland such circles are called Doms, Things (Ting) or judicial circles. As the ancients always opened public meetings for civil affairs with religious ceremonies, thus adding greatly to the solemnity and gravity of the

(1) Spalding Club Sculp. Stones, vi, p. 33. (2) Gen. xxxv, 14.
3) Gen. xxxi, 45 *et seq.* (4) Rowland's Mona, p. 51—Martin's Western Islands.

CHAP. VI.] HISTORY OF PAGANISM IN CALEDONIA. 91

proceedings, we find, as already remarked, these circles within sight of the religious ones. From an early period the same persons performed religious, legislative, and judicial offices, and their religious character rendered their judicial decisions and their expositions of law more impressive and binding. Even when the religion that founded them had passed away, the circles retained much of their sacred character, and for that reason were still used for solemn assemblies and courts of justice. It is possible, however, that certain circles or parts of circles were more particularly consecrated to civil business, while other circles or parts of circles were more strictly set apart for religious service, and others as monuments of piety, or for funeral purposes.

Several curious facts mentioned in ancient writings go to show that stone circles were used for official inaugurations and councils of state, as late as the fourteenth century, in the north of Germany, in Sweden, in Denmark, and in the Western Islands. In Icelandic, such stone circles are spoken of as Dom-things or Doom-rings, or circles of judgment; and at them all courts were held, from the national council down to the meetings held by the proprietor of the land, for adjusting disputes between his villeins and slaves,[1] and known as baronial courts. There is not far from Upsal a huge stone called Marastin, which has about twelve lesser stones lying near it with wedge-fashioned stones raised a little from the earth. Hither the new king repairs on his accession, and in the presence of a large assembly, representative of all the people, he is confirmed with solemn ceremonies by the Bishop, and bound by solemn oath to defend the faith.[2]

(*c.*) *Altars.*—Pagan altars sometimes consisted of earth, but more commonly of a flat stone in a circle of boulders, at a point a little south and east, in which direction the stone also inclined. And in the Christian period, when the altar was no longer a place of sacrifice, but a table at which the feast of love (*agape*) was held, the altar was placed at the east end of the Christian erection for the celebration of the feast, and for other sacred purposes.

There are very many references to altars in the Old Testament. "And if thou wilt make me an altar of stone, thou shalt not build it of hewn stone: for if thou lift up thy tool upon it, thou hast polluted it."[3] "Therefore it shall be, when ye be gone over Jordan, that ye shall set up these stones, which I command you this day, in Mount Ebal, and thou shalt plaster them with plaster. And there shalt thou build an altar unto the Lord thy God, an altar of stones. Thou shalt build the altar of the Lord thy God of whole stones; and thou shalt offer burnt-offerings thereon unto the Lord thy God."[4]

Fig. 77.

As examples of pagan altars, we may mention uncovered cromlechs with flat stones, such as that at Rostellan, co. Cork, situate on an arm of the sea, in Cork Harbour: so important was it considered, that it gave the name to the surrounding manor castle.

(*d.*) *Rocking, or Logan Stones.*[5]—These stones are known by different names. There are the *clacha-brath*, the irrevocable or judgment-stone of the Celts; the divining-stone, or stone of the ordeal; the moving or animated stone of the Phœnicians; the tumbling stone of the Irish, &c. Two famous ones are the Pierre Martina, in the department of the Lot in France, and the Pierres-tranlantes de Huelgoat, in Brittany. They are found both in the Old [6] and in the New World,[7] and are mentioned by Pliny as existing in Asia,[8] and by Apollonius Rhodens, as stones placed on the apex of a tumulus, and so sensitive as to be movable by the mind.[9]

---

(1) Pinkerton's Descriptions of Empires, 1802.   (2) History of the Goths, p. 12 and 13.
(3) Exodus xx, 25.   (4) Deut. xxvii, 4—7.
(5) From *logg*, moving to and fro; or *logan* or *log-ing*, a vibratory motion; or more correctly *ymain-sige*, or shaking stones, in Wales.
(6) In the British Islands, France, Spain, Italy, etc.   (7) Hodson's letters from North America, vol. ii, p. 440.
(8) Hist. Nat. Lib. I, c. 96.   (9) Ackerman's Arth. Index, p. 34.

M 2

In Britain, they are found chiefly in the west of England, where Celts and Druids longest existed, and are generally in the neighbourhood of other Celtic monuments. They consist of a ponderous mass of stone, so carefully balanced upon a rock, that they oscillate sensibly at the touch of even a child's hand applied in the proper direction, though they cannot be moved by a powerful arm applied otherwise. There is one in Strathardle, in Perthshire, placed on a hill, which commands an extensive view to the north and west, *i.e.*, in the direction of the setting sun. This stone is of a rhomboidal form, its greater diagonal being 5 feet 6 inches, and its extreme breadth 4 feet 8 inches. It must weigh upwards of three tons.[1] A pivot had been made on the solid rock, and on this the stone was poised, the pivot being received in a hollow made for its reception direct under the centre of gravity. The extremities of the stone thus move freely upwards and downwards, though only when the moving force is applied in a northern and southern direction, and not in any other. The sweep of the motion increases until the arc which the extremity of the radius traverses exceeds 4 inches; formerly, before the mutilation, it exceeded a foot. On reaching its extreme movement, and after the moving force is withdrawn, the stone makes from twenty-six to twenty-eight vibrations before it stops.

A little to the north-west of the hill of Kirriemuir, in Forfarshire, there were two rocking stones within a few yards of each other. One was a block of whinstone nearly oval, 3 feet 3 inches high, 9 feet long, and 4 feet 10 inches broad. The other was of Lintrathen porphyry, 2 feet high, 8 feet long, and 5 feet broad.[2] These unique and most interesting monuments of antiquity were unwarrantably destroyed a few years ago by the petty proprietors of the estate on which they happened to stand. There is a rocking-stone at Drewsteignton, in Devonshire, which Mr. Pollwhelle moved in 1796; but it no longer rocks: water having frozen in the joints and injured the stone, just as happened with another at Dunloe, near Killarney, in Ireland. There are others at Derricunniby; near Byrring's chapel, in the county of Cork; and near Sneen, in Kerry, and elsewhere.

There is a rocking-stone upon the top of one of the mountains connecting Orme's Head, and opposite Mosyne Street of Llandagnoa. It is a lime-stone of an irregular rhomboidal form, about a ton in weight, resting upon an irregular limestone base, disintegrated by exposure to the weather. It may have been originally placed on a pivot on the surface of the lime-stone rock. There are several circles of stone near, and a cromlech is in the valley not far off. It has, however, lost the characteristic peculiarity of the rocking-stone, as it rocks equally on every side, and with force it may be made to rock 5 or 6 inches.

Among the Ibero-Phœnicians, rocking-stones were believed to be presided over by a demon or genius, and auguries were cast from their motions. There was a logan stone 10 tons in weight, in front of the principal temple of Almora in Upper India, which was employed for similar purposes, but it did not give satisfactory replies, and the suppliants, one day, in a fit of rage, overturned it. This is the common fate of pagan gods when they no longer satisfy the wishes of their votaries. From the facility of the movements of such stones, and the number of oscillations which each stone made when set in motion, before it again came to a state of perfect repose, the priests drew their conclusions. Their motion was also used for purposes of the ordeal, and by this means guilt was detected in doubtful cases, hence, no doubt, they got the name "Clacha Brath," or stones of judgment.[3] The people believed that if the stone moved to the touch of the accused person it was an evidence of or supernatural voucher to his innocence. Mason beautifully expresses the sentiment thus:—

> ———" Behold
> Yon huge and unhewn sphere of living adamant,
> It moves obsequious to the gentlest touch
> Of him whose breast is pure, but to the traitor,
> Though ev'n a giant's prowess nerved his arm,
> It stands as fast as Snowdon." [4]

---

(1) This is less than that given in the statistical account, as several large portions have since then been maliciously broken off by some drunken masons, who (as I was told) deliberately set themselves to destroy this interesting relic of antiquity.

(2) New Statistical Account of Scotland, Forfarshire, p. 177.   (3) *See* Dr. Smith's History of the Druids.

(4) Caractacus, Mason's Works, York, 1797. Vol. i, p. 209.

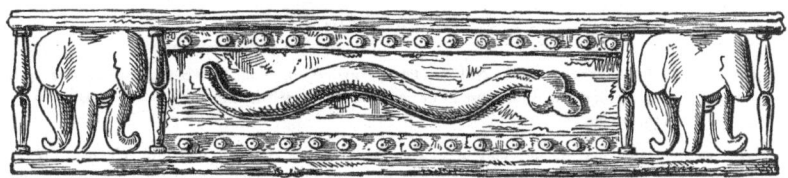

CHAPTER VII.

NATURE WORSHIP AMONG THE PRIMITIVE RACES OF ASIA AND EUROPE.

N this chapter we shall give a brief sketch of religious beliefs among the primitive Turanian races, the clever but fickle Celts, and the Scythio-Aryans; as also an account of the Hindu worship of the elements, serpents and horses.

SECTION I.—PRIMITIVE PAGANISM AMONG THE RUDE TURANIAN RACES OF ASIA.

The Asiatics generally believe in a supreme spiritual Deity, who is invisible, omnipresent, omniscient and eternal— an almighty God—the God of Gods—whose greatness and intelligence are beyond comprehension and expression. For the worship of such a being no temples were required; some of the rude races of India accordingly have neither temple nor altar. Their religious rites consist mainly of auguries of different kinds. Some of them will profess that they can foretell the future from the calls and the flights of birds, and others that they can do so by the breaking of hens' eggs upon a board, accompanied with peculiar shoutings and ejaculations. As the size and form of the fragments of the shell determine the result, should either prove unfavourable, the suppliants are encouraged to go on breaking the eggs till they get the response they seek for.

These rude Indian tribes had a superstitious dread of evil spirits. Of these spirits of evil, one of the most notorious was Vetal,[1] a demon long dreaded in the Deccan, and who is still worshipped, though in some modified form, in many parts of Hindustan.[2] He is worshipped in the form of a rough unhewn stone of a pyramidal or triangular shape, from two to four feet in height, placed on a base, often under a tree, and having one of his sides fronting the east.

Sometimes the islanders of the Indian seas try to appease the deity who brings storms, by assembling during the tempest on the beach, or on rocks overhanging the ocean, and chanting choruses.[3] Charms dedicated to such deities, and worn about the person, are supposed to be effectual in procuring their favour and in guarding against the evils they are believed to send. When a person meets with a sudden death, it is concluded that he has incurred the displeasure of some deity, and his corpse is immediately committed to the flames. When an accident happens, or a disease makes its appearance, it is thought to be impious to take steps to counteract the effect, and stay the course of the visitation, as it is considered to have been sent by one of the deities for his own

---
(1) Which has been translated spirit, or demon, viewed as animating dead bodies. (Wilson's Sanscrit Dictionary.)
(2) In the Deccan, Gujerat, &c.   (3) Sime's Embassy to Asia, vol. i, p. 159.

good purpose; and so the doomed man is left to his fate. Anything by means of which an accident has befallen, such as a tree, a piece of rock, &c., is supposed to be an instrument used by the gods, and as such becomes an object of religious veneration.

Among the more sensible members of ruder races, however, the spiritual principle in man, or the soul, is distinctly recognised; and its activity as a spiritual medium is assumed to account for the phenomena of life, as these appear more especially in diseases, dreams and visions. This spiritual principle is supposed to extend to and pervade all animal existences, and even certain inanimate objects, animals anyhow being conceived as having souls, capable of existing after death, or at the dissolution of the physical system. An extension of this idea gives rise to polytheism, which looks upon the sun, moon and stars, the heavens and the earth as animated by, and organs of, the greater spirits of the universe, and regards them and their counterparts as arraying themselves into friendly or unfriendly deities or demons, thus forming a pantheon of dualistic powers or embodiments of good, each with its antagonistic embodiment of evil.

The *Sun* was believed to be the primary source of all good throughout the year; the *Moon* was a secondary power, whose inferior agents were the genii of the woods, the waters and the mountains; and the *Stars* were the abodes of just men and of illustrious benefactors of mankind. Martin, in his Account of the Western Islands, says that in Mainland (one of the Orkneys) the sun is worshipped in a circle and the moon in a semicircle.[1] Dawe, in treating of serpents, says[2] that the temples on Dartmoor are generally in pairs—one circle being sacred to the sun, and the other to the moon, as at Avebury.

SECTION II.—THE WORSHIP OF THE ARYAN AND THE EARLY CELTIC RACES.

This we shall consider under the heads of (*a*) Sun worship; (*b*) Worship of the elements; (*c*) Serpent worship; (*d*) Horse worship.

(a.) Sun worship.—The sages of the East, Greece, Phœnicia, and ancient Britain, considered the rising and setting of the sun, as the most propitious periods for worship and meditation. Even still the modern Asiatic will prostrate himself in prayer at the moment when the first clear rays of the morning sun strike the tops of the mountains; and as soon as the rising disc appears, he begins to repeat his specified prayers, which he continues to do, until the lord of day is clear above the horizon, and shines full-orbed on the eye. The sun worshippers in Arabia observed this custom before the days of Mahomet, and they still offer up their prayers to the deity whose splendour he reveals.

These idolaters, says Palgrave, "turn their faces to the East in prayer, as being the direction of the light." "And he brought me," writes Ezekiel, "into the inner court of the Lord's house; and, behold, at the door of the temple of the Lord, between the porch and the altar, were about five-and-twenty men, with their backs towards the temple of the Lord, and their faces towards the East; and they worshipped the sun towards the East."[3]

Sabæism, or the worship of sun, moon and stars, seems to have prevailed extensively in the East from an early period.[4] As a consequence of the Assyrian conquests, the doctrines and beliefs originally current among the Chaldæan shepherds were circulated among and accepted by the conquered nations. Among the deities which these shepherds adored were the seven guardians who directed the course of the seven planets; and the seven days of the week were dedicated to these planetary gods. They had signs for the twelve constellations of the zodiac, and the twenty-four constellations of the northern and southern hemispheres.

---

(1) *See also* Toland's History of the Druids, p. 91.   (2) Dawe, p. 386.
(3) Palgrave's Customs of Eastern Arabia, vol. i., p. 8; Ezekiel, chap. viii, 16.
(4) Strabo's date of the Chaldæan observations is 2,233 B.C.

The strong hold which this worship had on the minds of the surrounding nations accounts for the repeated caution addressed to the Jews, "Take good heed lest thou lift up thine eyes unto heaven, and when thou seest the sun, and the moon, and the stars, even all the host of heaven, shouldest be driven to worship them, and serve them."[1] Joshua was commanded to drive out the Canaanites because they used enchantments and worshipped the hosts of heaven in groves and high places.

The feeling, which seems to have arisen early in the breast of primitive man, after something that never changes amid the constant change of all around him, first found rest and expression in the worship of the sun, "the most exalted," says Max Müller, "and only unchanging and infinite Being that had received a name, and that could lend it to that as yet unborn idea of the infinite which disquieted the human mind;" although, as he adds, "the man who chose the name did not mean, could not have meant, that the visible sky was all he wanted, that the blue canopy above was his god." As the idea of God grew, the sun and sky, glorious as they were, would erelong fail to express all that he was feeling, and new names would be invented, and new names employed, for the new qualities and attributes his thought might descry behind and above such merely phenomenal presentation. Well might the endless phantasmagory in cloud-colour and cloud-form at sunrise and sunset, and the splendour, grace, and beauty that then suffuse the sky, lead the meditative to dream of mystic transformations and events taking place amid the glowing scarlet and purple, leading up at length to the great final faith that the phenomenal world, so full of wonder and terror to primitive man, is but a huge shadow of the spiritual world, of which he first directly receives intimation when he looks within. For "surely vain are all men by nature who are ignorant of God, and could not, by considering the work, acknowledge the Work-master, but deemed either fire, or wind, or the air, or the circle of the stars, or the violence of the waves, or the lights of heaven, to be gods which govern the world." But not till man comes to see that the outer in nature is but a reflex of the inner in himself, does he attain to any just conception of the spiritual nature of the Universe and any really true and stable conception of God.

Nevertheless, recent scientific research has taught us to seek the explanations of nearly all terrestrial phenomena in the action of sun force. This is the ultimate source of all the motive energy which is developed on the face of the globe. It produces winds in the atmosphere and currents in the sea, and it brings about those disturbances in the electric equilibrium of the atmosphere which result in the lightning and the formation of the all-cleaving thunderbolt, and which the fancy of antiquity transmuted into the sceptre of Jove; its vivifying action enables the vegetable world to draw support from inorganic matter, to become in turn nourishment for animals and for man; it is the source of all those great deposits of dynamical efficiency which are laid up for human use in our coal strata.[2] "Nature," says Mayer, "stores up the light which streams from the sun, overspreading the earth with organisms." In the plants "the fugitive solar rays are fixed, suitably deposited, and rendered available for useful application. With this process the existence of the human race is inseparably connected."[3]

Thus, as modern science demonstrates, it is the sun's warmth which preserves the ocean in its liquid, living form, and it is by its energy and action both the air and the ocean are stirred. It is he that melts the snow on the tops and the glaciers on the slopes of the mountains, and sends abroad their enfranchised waters to refresh and revive drooping, thirsty nature. Under him it is that the vegetable world germinates, flourishes and fructifies, and, through it, the world of sentient, living beings. He urges the blood in the veins, strengthens the muscles of the body, and nerves the spiritual power of the brain; by him the eagle soars in the heavens, the tiger roars in the jungle, and the horse is fleet in the service of man. When the sun comes, come heat and light; when he goes, come darkness and cold. Yet his coming and his going,

---

(1) Deut., ch. iv, 15, 19.   (2) Herschel's "Outlines of Astronomy." Ed. 1833.
(3) *See* Proctor—The Sun and Planetary Systems. 3rd Ed., 1876.

like his power, who can understand them? Both must be regarded and studied with veiled vision; and in presence of them sage as well as savage can only bow the knee. Full of monition to us, as well as mystery in itself, this is wholly a wonder, and no one who realises the fact can fail to sympathise with the hymns which the Aryan imagination conceived in his praise.

Feelings and aspirations after an object of religious worship are, like all deep elementary desires of man's nature, in outward aspect and expression everywhere the same. If they do not find the true object to which they point, they will lay hold of a false, and even invent one for themselves. Thus, at an early stage, fetishism arises, and even under the advancement of knowledge and civilization, it lingers in the imagination, and indeed is almost the last of the brood of darkness to fly before the light. Not only do the young, the weak, and the ignorant, easily impressed and strongly possessed, cling hard to fetish opinions, as in the worship of trees, stones, rivers, mountains, &c., but we find among the educated, even in civilized nations, unmistakeable traces of a kindred belief. What could be more natural, therefore, for a simple-minded and ignorant native of Asia, as, watching the silent, pathetic withdrawal of the sun beneath the western horizon, he looked athwart at the darkness and gloom that was pressing forward from the east and invading the world—what could be more natural for him, than to suppose that what he saw was a triumph of demons and the powers of darkness over the God of light, now vanishing from the earth, and that there were powers of light and darkness continually striving for the possession of the world, and that of these, now the one, now the other, rose to the ascendant? The occurrence of an eclipse was regarded with awe, as well as the approach of darkness, and eclipses were supposed to be caused by good and evil spirits fighting together, and endeavouring to destroy each other.

It was the light of the sun as contrasted with darkness that gave rise to the dualistic conception in the Turanian creed. Though it was in later times that the all-pervading influence of sun-force first came to be fully understood, yet the attributes of that luminary are such, so varied and so manifest, that they must early have attracted the attention of the rudest races of mankind, and especially such keen observers of nature as these ancient shepherd tribes, who were so directly dependent on his gifts. The invigorating, nay, life-evolving energy of the rays of the sun, his power in colouring, developing, and bringing to maturity all forms of vegetable life, are facts that lie patent to the dullest intelligence, and must have been especially impressive to the wild rover of the desert, who therefore greeted the rising luminary every morning with prayers and adorations as to a god. It is thus easy to see how the sun came to be early worshipped as the personification of the parent and ruler of the universe—life- as well as light-giving, glorious in his rising and setting, powerful, penetrating, and all-pervading in his heat as well as effulgence; and also to see how the connection of the other heavenly bodies both with the sun and with the changes of nature, led to their being adored along with the great central orb of the high powers of the universe.

There were antagonistic principles, it was clear, of good and evil in all things, and each of these was conceived of as endowed with personality, and personally distinct. The one was the true god, *Ahura-mazda*, a much-knowing and much-giving spirit, the fountain of all that is good and beautiful; the creator of life, both earthly and spiritual; good, holy, pure and true; supremely happy; the preserver of all, and the giver of every blessing—health, wealth, wisdom, virtue, immortality.[1] The other was the dark and gloomy spirit, *Angra-mainyus*, the projector, creator and upholder of everything evil, the opposer of *Ahura-mazda*, and at perpetual war with him; the inspirer and dispenser of all moral and physical evil: who could blast the earth with barrenness; who produced thorns and poisonous plants; who caused storms and earthquakes, disease and death; who introduced the sins of witchcraft, murder, unbelief, and who stirred up wars and tumults, setting nation against nation, as well as man against man. These two great spirits had inferior spirits to wait on their persons and to carry out their wishes. Yet their worshippers were idol-haters, they had no images erected to their honour, only

---

(1) Haug's Essays, vol. iii, 96. Rawlinson's Ancient Monarchies, vol. iii, pp. 238 to 240.

symbols or emblems were invented as suggestive of their character. The supreme deity is represented by a winged circle, sometimes combined with an incomplete human figure. *Mithra,* a circle, a disc, was the sun, the light, the good spirit, and only a little inferior to *Ahura-mazda.*[1] Artaxerxes Mnemon placed the symbol of *Mithra,* united with that of *Ahura-mazda,* in the temple attached to the royal palace at Susa, and prayed for their conjoint protection.[2] As the sun is lost to view at sunset, he is believed to descend into the regions of the blessed, and the darkness, as well as the dark cloud, personifies the crafty enemy of mankind, who straightway thereafter seizes the sceptre and bears sway. As the orb of day sinks only to emerge again in renewed splendour, so in death it was believed that man too but sinks and disappears into stillness, that he may re-appear with life everlasting in the glory of the heavenly paradise, the mansion of the blessed.

It is in Persia that the dualistic conception of the Deity has received its purest and most perfect development. The religious creed of the Persians may be reduced to a belief in the co-existence of two principles, a good and a bad—a principle of light, or goodness, embodied in Ormazd, and a principle of darkness, or evil, embodied in Ahriman. These two powers, so defined and embodied, the Zeus and Hades of the Greeks, and the Jupiter and Pluto of the Romans, as they have been the active principles of the universe of being from all eternity, are also the powers which, as they confront and counterwork each other, constitute and determine the history and fortune of the time world. The Persians, however, reserve their religious adoration for Omazd, their friend and protector, and, as they fight under his banner and on his side, they are confident that they will at last share in the glory of his triumphs. In that case they expect to live with him outside and beyond the strife in a blissful eternity, where the degree of felicity will be in proportion to the degree of piety and valour they have shown in his service, while the perverse followers of Ahriman will sink into a region of outer darkness and of bottomless despair. These good and evil principles, and their contention for the sovereignty of the world, are represented in various forms in the eastern mythology, Persian and other. The dispute commences with the production of the world-egg (*mont faucon*); and, as the hatching can no more be stayed than the laying could, the evil principle in the form of a serpent works ruin on the offspring of the egg, and thereby all its issue is impregnated with its own poison.

The splendour of sunset renders it by no means surprising that there should have arisen a belief in an earthly paradise somewhere in the direction of the going down of that luminary. According to the legend of St. Brendan, the enthusiast, who set out in search of it, after wandering about for a time, at length found this paradise in the Islands of the Blessed, where the fountain of perpetual youth was fabled to flow. This is the city of Asgard, the Eldorado, the Kingdom of Prester John, the land of Cockayne of Sir Walter Raleigh, the land of Cathay, which so excited the imagination of Columbus, that he could not rest till he set out in search of it; and he discovered by the way the new world of America.

Animated by the same desire for the discovery of this happy country, enlightened and enthusiastic Buddhist missionaries from Asia pressed westward, in expectation of reaching the land of bliss, of that rest and happiness, where the sun enters the habitation of the gods, and where the secrets of past and future are yielded up. It was with that land in their eye, that these enthusiastic Asiatics kept travelling westward, until they found a halting place on the shores of the Atlantic, across which only the eye of their imagination continued to wander, but beyond which they were forbidden to pass. Upon the desolate headlands of Lewis, in Scotland, upon the stupendous ramparts of Arran and Kerry, in Ireland, and upon the majestic cliffs of Cornwall, in England, they built their last forts, erected their last altars, and found their final rest. And all this is the outcome of the primitive worship of the Sun as the fire-, or life-centre, or fountain of all being and all blessedness.

The sun was deified by the Egyptians as the symbol of the creation, and the maker and disposer of events; and the Pharaohs were reputed to be his offspring. The sun *Ra* was generated out of *toum* or *tum,* the setting sun;

---

[1] Rawlinson's Ancient Monarchies, vol. iv, p. 334; Floridan, Voyage en Perse, pp. 164, 166, 173-76. [2] Loftus, Caldæa Susiana, p. 239.

and the rising sun, therefore, becomes, at once, through this mystical metamorphosis, both his own father and his own son. Among the Egyptians, as we have said, the obelisk was the symbol of the rising sun, or life's morning period, and the pyramid of the setting sun, or life's decline and death; the former monuments being erected on the eastern, and the latter on the western banks of the Nile; and both dating from the prehistoric period of civilization, before Abraham left Ur of the Chaldees, or the Turanian races of India were assailed and oppressed by the Aryan host.[1] The power of the rising sun went on increasing till its climax at noon-day, and was accepted in the pantheistic worship, as the visible manifestation of generative and preservative power; and as such was worshipped by the name of *Ra*, or life. The setting sun, foreshadowing night, was the symbol of death, and the dark underworld, into which the human soul descends, just as the sun does daily beneath the horizon; and to this god, called *Tum*, the pyramids, the sepulchres of dead kings and illustrious heroes, were dedicated. The Egyptian temples were dedicated to *Ra* and *Noth*, the guides of life, light and truth. They had gates, adorned with pairs of obelisks, as monuments to record the names and fame of monarchs by whom they were set up. The Pharoah of the day was Horus, the incarnate stone of Ra, and the *Kheper-Ra*, the god upon earth of his age.

At Emesa, where, as at Heliopolis, there was a great temple to the worship of Baal, the sun was worshipped in pagan times under the name of Elagabalus (from *Ela*, a god, and *al Gabal*, the mountain) and in the form of a black stone, which was reputed to have fallen from heaven.[2] This form of worship attracted the attention of Aurelius, who erected at Rome a gorgeous temple in honour of the sun, and, though not a remnant of this remains, the ruins of Baalbec, which was likewise the work of Aurelius, are still objects of wonder and admiration to the traveller. To this deity the young and victorious Antoninus ascribed his elevation to the throne, and the display of this superstition was the only serious passion of his reign.[3] The moon, under the form of the Phœnician Astarte, was considered the consort of Elagabalus.

The sun religion—pure enough at first, and uncontaminated by any idolatry, for the sun-worshippers, before all, believed that the great spirit could not be represented by any figure of human workmanship—passed, in course of time, into a sensual, degraded and degrading paganism. The sun degenerated into the god Baal, who was represented by various images, one of the chief being, as we shall see, the horse (a Scythian emblem of the sun), which was carved on wooden posts, and to which sacrifices were offered. Ere long, too, the manes of the dead began to be worshipped, and a few departed heroes were so venerated, that they were raised to the rank of demi-gods, or even of gods altogether. Myths also grew up, and became interwoven with religious belief and the homage of worship; and these again wrought themselves in the fancy of the Easterns into imaginative tales. Here is one such: The sun was transformed into a beautiful female, who had accepted a king as her husband on condition that he should never show her water. When she one day asked for some, he, forgetful of his promise, brought it, and she immediately disappeared, just as the sun disappears every night on touching the water at the horizon.[4] Similar degradations of the divine to the level of the natural human led men to assign to the wrath, displeasure, and even envy of the gods, all the misfortunes that befel them, and the fanciful ideas thus arising led to offerings of flowers, fruits, vegetables, grain and cattle, and even to such cruel customs and practices as human sacrifice.

Prithri, a form of Vishnu, was the sun in the west or at nightfall; Brahma was the sun in the east or in the morning; and Siva was the sun at noon, and the same as Baal, the Greian of the Irish Druids. The three formed the triad (*trimutri*), and severally represented in allegory the earth, water and fire, while unitedly they formed the great God both as preserver and as destroyer. But from symbols they by-and-by passed into beings. Brahma, the supreme benevolent being, who was less feared as coming less into manifestation, was

---

(1) *See* W. R. Cooper's Egyptian Obelisks.   (2) *See* Mover's Dic. Phonigin, vol. i, p. 669.
(3) *See* Gibbon's Decline and Fall of the Roman Empire, vol. i, p. 280.
(4) *See* Kelley's Indo-European Traditions, p. 6. (Chapman & Hall, 1863).

soon left out, and the Hindus, like so many other primitive religionists, ranged themselves into sects, followers of Vishnu and followers of Siva, according as they took the side of the conservative interest or the revolutionary.

At an early period the sun worshippers observed the peculiarities of the sun's movements, particularly at those periods of "stopping" or "retrocession" in its course which indicated the longest and the shortest days of the year, and a knowledge of these periods was probably introduced by the eastern pilgrims who had come to Europe in search of the holy land of the setting sun—the region of the blessed gods.

The sun, the symbol of the bountiful deity—the Osiris[1] of the Egyptians, the Apollo of the Greeks and Romans; and Baal, in whose honour Baaltine or Beltane was celebrated—came, as was natural, to be specially worshipped at sunrise and sunset, and more particularly still, at times when his power began conspicuously to weaken or strengthen, grow less or grow greater; as, for example, on May-day and the first of November, at the two solstices and at the two equinoxes. In the cold winter solstice, when the sun is in the first degree of Capricorn, comes the shortest day of the year, the dark and dreary 22nd of December, after which the sun daily gains strength, till the vernal equinox on the 22nd of March, when vegetation begins to sprout into life, and the birds fill the air with their song. The radiant summer solstice on the 21st of June brings to the earth the warmth of bright sunbeams to mature the fruits of the earth; after which the sun again declines, till the autumnal equinox on the 22nd September, when the reapers begin to gather in the ripe grain with rejoicing, and the wine-press is red with new wine.

At these different periods which defined the stages of the sun during the solar year, feasts and fasts were at an early period instituted, and were strictly and ceremonially observed by the intelligent Celtic priests, the dates of the festivals being determined by the position of the sun in the heavens with reference to boulders at a short distance outside the stone circles. Less important ceremonies were observed at the four quarters of the moon's progress.

The existence of sun worship among the early Caledonians is a fact beyond debate; as also that their chief religious festivals were determined by the great moments in the movement of the celestial bodies through the heavens. This, as already averred, is evident from the structure of many of their monuments, which are so arranged, as, for the regulation of the time of a festival, to point to the quarter in the sky where at the recurrence of it the sun rises. In the Cairn Leath Broch, near the sea at Dunrobin Castle, is a stone, with markings (see Chap. viii), one of which I found to be evidently a meridian line, two oval figures on the right and left of the line, the longest the radius of the sun, and the other of the earth, indicating severally a S.E. or summer solsticial, and N.W. or winter solsticial direction, and the position, therefore, of the sun on the longest and shortest days of the year respectively. These markings are clearly of a very ancient date, and their existence argues such a knowledge of the regular courses of the sun, and of the established order of nature, as, with other phenomena, points to the derivation of that knowledge from Oriental sources, and a time prior to the age of Copernicus. They are exactly such markings as we would look for among a people who had received their astronomical science from the Chaldæan star-gazers or the disciples of Zoroaster.[2] A circle from fifteen to forty feet in diameter is formed of similarly shaped but smaller stones, in India often twelve or some multiple of twelve in number, set one or two feet apart, one or more being on the outside, and the whole without covering or temple. In some cases they are alternately large and small, while in others there is an inner circle of small stones, two feet in diameter. Dr. Stephenson found some of the triangular stones in question painted red with cinnabar to three-fourths of their height from the ground, and the remainder whitened with pipe-clay, these colours being intended to represent the hues of a flame.

---

(1) It is related in Egyptian story, that a soul on its way westward to heaven was accosted by a devil who persuaded him he was wrong, and tempted him to turn his face to the east; Osiris, however, interposed, and informed the soul that the eastern course would lead him hellward; the road to heaven lay west.

(2) *See* Ormazd et Ahriman. Leurs Origines et leur Histoire par J. Darmesteter, p. 14.

The worship at these stones consisted in certain ceremonial observances having obvious reference to the worship of fire. In sickness, and when a person was supposed to be possessed with a devil, various magical ceremonies were performed within the circle, secret prayers were said, a cock, a sheep, or a goat was offered up, and the blood of the sacrifice sprinkled over the stone.

It is interesting to observe the traces of Sabæism that still linger among peoples that have, under the influence of modern progress, long since abandoned all belief in such conceptions, and have for many ages been inoculated with the Christian faith. The festival of the sun is still observed in the Highlands of Scotland, in Ireland, in Cornwall,[1] in France, and in other Celtic countries. At Mount's Bay in Cornwall, on the eve of Midsummer day, as soon as the evening sets in, the youths of both sexes parade the streets with burning torches, which they keep swinging round their heads, till, as the darkness increases, bonfires and tar barrels are lighted, and even fireworks are discharged in every direction, so that there is quite a brilliant illumination. The torches are made of large pieces of folded canvas steeped in tar, and nailed on the ends of sticks, three or four feet long. Rows of lighted candles are placed on the outside of the windows, and along the streets. The town and the neighbouring one are lit up by the fires, so as to have quite an animated appearance. In the early part of the evening, children, wearing wreaths of flowers, dance round the fires, while others, joining hand-in-hand in long rows, play at "thread the needle," regardless of the fire, and leap over the glowing embers. Children, and sometimes cattle, are passed through the fire; as it is supposed that every living thing which submits to this ordeal will be preserved from evil during the ensuing year. This preserving influence is supposed to extend also to the surrounding fields and crops. Such meetings are always held in a conspicuous place, in full view of the people, and "in the face of the sun and the eye of light." The observances on St. Peter's eve and day, and at the fair held on the day after, are a repetition of the above on a smaller scale.

Nor are the festivities at Christmas Eve disconnected with sun-worship. A decayed stump of a tree painted, or carved, so as to resemble the figure of an old man, called Father Christmas, or old Father Saturn, is burnt on Christmas Eve, the last day of the solsticial year; and this is a surviving reminiscence of an old pagan ceremony intended to pathetically emblem the decease of the sun of the year just passing away. A piece of the log, as in the sun-worship, is carefully preserved to light the Christmas stock, and the day is spent by the rich in going about and bestowing gifts, by way of thank-offering, on their poor neighbours, an act quite as symbolic of sun, as of Christian, worship, the sun being a fit emblem and foreshadow of the grace of Christ.

The Christmas festival is in many of its forms a continuation of the old pagan festival of the *Brumalia*, "when the sun, then at the winter solstice, was, as it were born anew," a festival which a recent author derives from the Mithras-worship of the sun. On Christmas Eve the death of the old sun is commemorated, yet with accompaniments which express the joyful expectation and certain hope of his rising again, an assurance which assumes various shapes in the ritual as well as creeds of the world.

At the great midsummer Druidical festival, when the sun had arrived at its solsticial point, or rather when it had begun its retrograde motion, as indicated by the pointer boulder in the S.E. of the circle, all the fires within the boulder circle intended for prayer, were ordered to be put out. This was on the 23rd of June, and, exactly at midnight of the 24th, the holy fire was kindled and placed on the altar. Then it was carefully kept burning during the year under the charge of the priests, and from it each family was allowed, on paying a fee, to carry off a brand to kindle their domestic fire, and the brand thus obtained brought a blessing on the fruits of the earth and prosperity to the household.

---

(1) Efforts to put it down in Cornwall have proved vain, for all proclamations made against the proceedings are openly disregarded.

On the night of Midsummer eve, in the Highlands of Scotland, the tribes of witches, warlocks, wizards, and fairies are reviewed, it is believed, by Satan and his chief subordinates; new aspirants are said to be admitted into the infernal order, and, when let loose on the community, to cause misery and devastation, and to try to outstrip each other in doing diabolical deeds. Their evil purposes are superstitiously imagined to be thwarted by various agencies, such as fire; but one of the most powerful against these evils is a cross made out of the "blessed rowan tree," tied together with red thread, which, attached to the house-door, protects the whole house. There are different ways of purifying by means of fire to prevent the evil designs of the evil one, until the vivifying influence of the sun recovers its ascendancy.

The Moon.—It was by the age and aspect of the moon, that the ancients, counting by nights instead of by days,[1] measured the smaller divisions of time, and regulated the monthly religious ceremonies. Both months and years began, not from the change, but from the sixth day of the moon, when it first becomes visible.[2] Military operations were usually begun and religious ceremonies performed either on that day or at full moon.

The spring festival of the first of May is dedicated to the moon, the Saxon representative of which is the season of Easter. On this day ladies and gentlemen used to dance in the streets, and then the maypole was erected, around which they danced to music, according to the custom of the ancient Britons. Water was associated with the moon, as fire with the sun, and on May-day, accordingly, bathing in the sea and in running water, and drinking the morning dew, became as efficacious as passing through the fire at the sun festival.

Accustomed as the Romans were to the Mediterranean, where there are no tides, it was some time before they came to know of the ebb and flow of the sea, but as soon as they did so, the tides were traced by them to the influence of the moon. Julius Cæsar remarked the fact when he first landed on our shores. Speaking of the night following the fourth day after his first landing in Britain, he writes, "That night it happened to be full moon, which day was accustomed to give the greatest risings of water in the ocean, though our people did not know it." So inexperienced, however, was he as regards the effect of the rising, that, although a storm was raging at the time, he did nothing to secure the transports, left high and dry on the beach, whilst he was fighting the Britons, and the consequence was that the water rose so high in the night as to damage the ships seriously. Strabo, quoting Poseidonius, says that "Soon after moonrise the sea begins to swell up and flow over the earth, till the moon reaches mid-heaven; as she descends, the sea recedes till about moonset, when the water is lowest; it then rises again until about moonrise, when the water is again at its lowest and again begins to rise." Besides the daily current of the sea, Poseidonius writes of a regular monthly course, and of an annual one reported by the Gaditani, his description being, in fact, a fairly accurate account of what is observed at the present day at Cadiz,[3] the locality where he obtained his information. He was not aware of the double attraction of the sun and the moon.

Respect for the sun could not fail to include also respect for the moon, and hence we find the worship of the latter always accompanied that of the former, so that one equally with the other ranks among the gods. Both dispense good and dispense evil, and are provided with balm for healing and arrows to slay. Apollo, the sun, and Diana, the moon, are the two children, only-begotten, of Latona, the hidden one, and the longing affection of Selene, which is only gratified when she has kissed the sleeping Endymion, is a significant intimation of the belief that the two are at bottom one. Hence disasters to the one are as much dreaded as disasters to the other; and it was a practice, in pagan times, as it still is in the East, when the moon was under eclipse for the peasants to shout and blow horns to scare away the spirits of evil, whose fighting they supposed

---

(1) *See* Henry's History of Britain, and the Origin of the Arts and Sciences, vol. i, p. 231. Cæsar De Bel. Gall. Lib. i, ch. 50. Pliny Hist. Nat. Lib. xvi, ch. 44.

(2) Pliny, *ibid.*   (3) From Sir William Thompson's Lecture, 17th April, 1875.

was darkening the air. The crescent moon was the symbol of rising power, and the full moon was attended by troops of genii, denizens of earth, air and sea.

The Stars.—The stars were conceived to be the habitations of the spirits of the just, and of distinguished heroes, benefactors and martyrs, who, from their sky-dwelling, with hearing ear and watchful eye, regard the events that take place on their beloved earth. This idea lay at the root of the influence ascribed by astrology to the stars on individual destiny and human fortune. The festival of the stars is kept in memory of the saints by Christians on the Sunday after the Saints' Day. It used to last three days.

The heavenly bodies, and the sun in particular, figured in the imagination of the early races of mankind as embodiments of a spiritual, or rather ethereal force, whose purest essence was akin to fire, whose highest power was the light, and whose subtle action was conceived of as pervading all existence. The accompanying figure is an example of a Nepaulese chaitya, or dedicatory Tope, consecrated to the supreme invisible Being who pervades all space, whose essence is light, and was as such typified on the outside by a pair of eyes, symbols of his providence, placed on each of the four sides, either at the base or on the crown of the edifice. For the upper lights, by which the eye sees, were conceived of as eyes themselves, searching, while they illuminated, the depths of being, and watching, not without tenderness, over the fortunes of man.

(b.) Worship of the Elements.—(1) *The Fire.*—Among the primitive nations, fire is regarded as the material symbol of deity, and of that power which, pervading the universe, imparts life and energy to the organic world. The fire on the altar, a sacred hearth, symbolised this divine fire; and in token of its heavenly derivation, it was annually renewed by a spark, as it were, from the temple of the sun. The ancient Celts had their sacred fires, which were kept alive by priests, as, among some nations, by holy virgins.

Zoroaster, in his "living word" (*Zend-avesta*), dedicates four temples to the safe keeping of the sacred fire, which had been originally drawn from the rays of the sun on the mountain top. This sacred fire, so kindled, has been kept alive by the vigilance of priests for four thousand years; and being the visible, sensible image of the great spiritual incomprehensible deity, whose material embodiment and impersonation is the sun, to whom Gueber considered it was impossible to erect a temple or an altar, or to perform religious ceremonies worthy of his all-pervading influence, it was worshipped in the open air. Before this sacred fire, at sunset, at sunrise, and at particular stages of the sun's progress through the heavens, the suppliants address their daily prayers and hymns to him, and present their offerings as to the Deity. Sir James Mackintosh has given a description of a visit to one of those fire-temples. It consisted of a plain building with a hall or large room in front. The priest had been educated fourteen years in Persia, was well informed, and of agreeable manners. Through the bars of a window in the wall the visitors saw the "holy of holies," a small back room, in one of the sides of which was a small aperture, covered by a silk curtain, and with the sacred fire burning in it.[1]

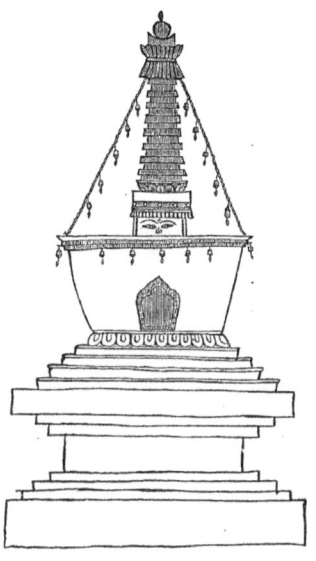

Fig. 78.

---

(1) Life of Sir James Mackintosh, vol. ii, p. 47.

CHAP. VII.]   HISTORY OF PAGANISM IN CALEDONIA.   103

Ceremonies, called the *Hurley pujah*, are held with great solemnity in the Tipperah kingdom, and I learned on good authority, not many years ago, that at these even human sacrifices were offered. The great secrecy with which the ceremonies were performed, tended strongly to confirm the suspicion that the natives of that part of India have not yet been entirely weaned from this rite, more efficacious, in their opinion, than any other, in averting evil. The Hindus suppose that the gods imbibe the spirit of the victim, which thereafter becomes assimilated to their nature, and attains immortality and other divine attributes. For these reasons it was considered an honour and a blessing to be offered up as a sacrifice. The ceremonies of this festival last two days and a half. It commences at noon, when a cannon is fired, and from the moment the signal is given, every person is obliged to remain in his house; no water is allowed to be drawn, nor any fire kindled until the end of the ceremonies. So strict are the injunctions of the Maharajah regarding this observance that it is said even cocks are not allowed to crow. The end of the festival is announced like its commencement, by the booming of a great gun, when everyone returns to his usual occupation. The sacrificial fire is kindled by the officiating Brahmin, by the friction of two pieces of bamboo, and from these all the other fires are lighted.

Among the Celtic tribes there were two varieties of this sacred fire, that in the open air conceived to be *Gall-ti-mor*, the flame of the great circle, or *Gall-Bælli*, the flame of the community; and second the sacred fire kept in the sun-tower (*Juraghan*), or the low arched building, such as that at *Gall erom*. This formed the great object of worship, and from its worship may have arisen the custom of the fire at Pentecost, while it was probably on this account that the most sacred church of the district was called the fire-house. Among these races there is a belief that good or evil prevails at any given time, according as the power of the benevolent, or the power of the malignant gods is in the ascendant, and that this strife will continue between them until the day of judgment. Then there will be a general resurrection of the dead, when the angel of darkness and his emissaries will be banished to the abode of wretchedness; and the followers of the benevolent deity will be received into the blessed realms of everlasting light. Nevertheless, the dread of the revengeful deities is apt to impart to such religions a form at once materialistic and gloomy and to confirm the low and debased character peculiar to races naturally rude.

(2) *The Elements.*—The elements, or ultimate principles of things, were in ancient times reckoned five in number: viz., Earth, Water, Fire, Air, and Ether; and most of the religions of antiquity classified their deities into groups, according as the sphere of their action was conceived to lie chiefly within one or other of these elements, so that there were gods of the earth, gods of the water, gods of the air, gods of the fire, and gods of the ether. And not only were these elements regarded as the several spheres of the activity and providence of the gods; in the regard of the philosopher they came at length to be looked upon as factors in the constitution of the universe, the earth and the water being viewed as the material basis, and air, fire, and ether as the spiritual substance or soul of things. Nothing wonderful, therefore, is it that the earlier and ruder races of mankind should have conceived of them as severally endowed with divinity, and have rendered homage to some of the more potent of them as to gods, and especially to that apparition of what is brightest in all of them embodied in the sun, the central soul, as it seemed, and eye of the universe.

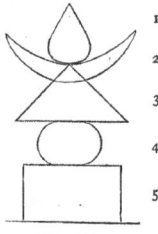

Fig. 79.

The Eastern philosophers, in particular, supposed that these elements consisted of atoms, and they so arranged the whole, as regards their cosmic unity, that underneath the fire was the earth, supporting the water, while the ether was supported by the air. The idea of this subordination is not so easily intelligible to a rude people by an explanation as by a figure, and representation of it in figure was accordingly adopted, such as we have given in the accompanying diagram. In this figure, 1 represents the ether *(akasava)*; 2, the air *(vayuza)*; 3, the fire *(vejas ya)*; 4, the water *(apas va)*; and 5, the earth *(pritrithi)*. The three first, or upper, mingle or combine more or less intimately and completely with the two last or lower elements, and each is represented by an appropriate and suggestive symbol. According to the Chinese travellers, Fa-Hian and Hiouen-Thsang, towers in representation of the several elements were erected in different forms for worship in different parts of Asia and elsewhere, and as tombs in memory of both distinguished monks and laymen.

(1) The Ether was conceived of as an extremely subtle substance of the nature of pure light, or flame, or spirit, occupying the upper sphere of being, and suffusing with more or less of its own purity, serenity, and effulgence the grosser spheres below. It is the purest essence of all being, and so subtle as often to escape remark, and be confounded with vacancy and nonentity; in the ancient philosophies, therefore, something different from that subtle, merely material element, distinct, as some think, from air, which can be scientifically demonstrated to fill the expanse of space outside the atmosphere. It was identified with the divine essence, and conceived to be the home and fountain of all the spiritual powers that pervade the universe, and especially those that embody themselves in the self-consciousness of man and the high moments of history. It was from that upper sphere the world drew the breath of its life, as well as the principles of law and order. Of this Ether the souls of men, in particular, were the purest terrestrial emanations; and, in a sense, all centres of vitality in the varied organisms of nature are of it, as well as from it, and return to it.

(2) The Air, from its extreme mobility and the intimate dependence on it of all the forms of terrestrial life, naturally stood next in rank to the subtle ether, and it was accordingly conceived of especially as the "breath" of the life of all living beings; so that the term breath, or spirit, became even in Christianity the expression for the Divine essence itself, as it had before been the expression for the Divine inspiration of the Jewish prophets in regenerate human life. It is in the form of breath, as the vehicle of the movement, action, and manifestation of this essence, that the air appears as an object of worship among ancient nations—air, as breath, seeming to convey, as it were, the soul of the ether into the vessels of plants and the lives of animals. In these last it takes the forms of respiration and of inspiration, and affects life in all its phases, especially human life, to the core. Thus of man Novalis says, "his lungs are his root; he is a child of the ether."

(3) The Fire is a less pure, but more active and energetic, embodiment of the Divine essence than the ether is, and is at bottom that ether itself in darker or brighter glow of excitation, as it struggles to overcome and subdue to itself the grosser elements of being. It is the Divine principle forcing its way, with more or less of fervour through the different grades of matter, with often the more of ardour and of white heat, the more stubborn the obstruction is that opposes its passage and resists its power. In its purest embodiment and highest power of action, as it shows itself in man, it kindles into intelligence and becomes the light of the life. Souls of men are made of it; and the more they are instinct with it, the more they, too, flame aloft into temper of white heat, often to the incredulous astonishment of those endowed with less of it. It is that passion in man which, as it takes intelligible shape in the reason, flames forth, now in scathing fire-flashes, now in mild radiance of benignant light, and in either case comes straight from above. In which last respect it is said to be at once unbegotten and unbegetting; the fire, as Christianity, too, teaches in every case coming from heaven direct.

(4) The Water is a less ethereal element than the three first, and holds more of earth than of heaven, of matter than of spirit. Nevertheless, it is entirely subject to and interpenetrated by the ethereal forces, and kept in steady flux, which is its great cosmic attribute and all-potent virtue, by their silent power. It is the universal solvent in which all things, as it were, liquify, before they come to the birth in definite, determinate forms, and in which the more solid element passes as sap into the vessels of plants or as blood into the veins of man and animals. No organism is generated or grows except by means of it, and it was early regarded as one of the great elemental powers, and even conceived by Thales, in the first

philosophic essay of the Greeks, as the beginning of all things. Nay, in the early mythologies of that people the primitive flood, in the person of Oceanos, figures, along with the Eros' egg, as the great parent womb of the gods themselves, as well as of the lesser powers that minister to health and well-being within the realm of Nature. Among the Greeks and Romans, and still more the Eastern nations, the water of the welling fountain and the flowing river was regarded with sacred reverence as a source of life and purity; while among rude races it was early worshipped as the symbol of revival, the medium of strength to the weak, quickening to the weary, and life to the dead. It distilled in gentle dews or generous showers from heaven above, and was the drink of the immortals, only withheld from man at times by the jealousy and malice of demons, with whom the gods, in man's behalf, waged constant warfare.

(5) The Earth is the solid material substance, or ground, of being, compacted of which things body themselves forth into individual, determinate, even personal forms, out of which they are made, and into which they return, as at once the womb of their mother and the grave of their everlasting rest. It is the plastic substance of all intelligible, as well as material, forms, and, as the seat or foil of their action, is even identified with sense and consciousness itself. That is to say, intelligible forms, as well as sensible, are presumed to be made of it, and so is the soul and sense by which they are shaped and seen. Without this material basis the individual soul could have no separate existence, and without the intelligible and sensible forms conceived in it and composed of it life would be an insubstantial blank. For this matter is not conceived of as a dead thing, but as the *prima materia* and reason of the forms of things, which, so long as they are formless, are nothing at all and non-existent. Without it we would have no reality either in the world of nature or the world of thought. Ether, Air, Fire, Water are alike void and formless, and first take shape in matter, which supplies at once their substance and the mould, and is as real, eternal, and divine as they.

Thus were the five great elements of being conceived of as severally divine and equally deserving of worshipful regard by mortals. Not one of them was considered as independent of the rest, and the five by their union first constitute the universe: the Ether containing the spiritual in essence, the Air conveying it as breath, the Fire fusing it into passionate form, the Water transforming it into flesh and blood, and the Earth fixing it into noble shapes, which, as they fade from sense, seem to rise again as ethereal lights to glow as suns or glitter as stars for ever thereafter in the serene of the parent heaven. Such unity as well as truth do we recognise in this worship among the ancients of the elements of nature. Most unscientific it may be, but it is not, therefore, speculatively unwise or spiritually worthless.

The Sacred Animals.—On examining the animals represented on the ancient remains of Pictland, we find that they are all Buddhist animals, and that on the stones and other monuments they represent the third member of the Buddhist triad. The most important are the serpent *(naga)*, which guarded the Brahmin Buddha; the white mythological elephant, with its six tusks, which conveyed the soul of Buddha to his mother's womb; the sacred white horse of Buddha; the sacred bull; the boar and the stag; the lion *(singar)*; the Eastern goose *(hanasa)*, the vehicle of Brahma; and they are all severally found in connection with the sacred lotus flower and bo-tree. These animals, as incised on the various sculptured stones, may be regarded as representing either sacred animals connected with the Buddhist triad, or animals offered in sacrifice during the pagan period, or animals as expressive of rank, and used in hunting and military processions during the Christian period.

(c.) Serpent Worship.—The worship of the serpent, as embodying a spirit in Deity, and therefore itself sacred and divine, is of very ancient date. The aboriginal races of India practised a rude form of serpent worship even before the date of the kistvaen and cromlech, and before the Aryan hordes had descended into Hindustan.[1] It was ultimately extensively worshipped, as is evident from the names of many places in distant localities, such as Nagpore, Widshanagra, Baylanagra, etc.; and Ferguson states that the worship of it prevailed

---

(1) *See* Balfour, Madras Reports.

throughout India, Egypt, Phœnicia, Babylon, Greece and Italy.[1] This is by no means surprising when we consider that in eastern countries the number of people annually killed by venomous serpents is very great. In India alone as many as twenty thousand natives have been known to perish in a single year by the sting of the serpent. Hence the serpent was regarded with especial terror, and worship was rendered him to purchase protection from his venomous assaults.

We have evidence both in scriptural and profane history that the worship of the serpent went side by side with the worship of fire and of the sun.[2] The sun *(surya)* and the serpent *(naga)* are antagonistic; the former representing the benign influence on vegetable and animal life of a benevolent deity, and the latter regarded as embodying the subtle malignant principle *(Typhon)*, which, because so much dreaded, was so zealously and widely worshipped (*Fig.* 80). The Egyptian serpent with a sphere in his mouth was a representation of Cneph, the great god, the creator of the world, unbegotten and immortal, whom the serpent, the bad principle, is trying to destroy. Seydes, or Seydia, is the immortal serpent, or dragon, which the Hindus supposed threatened destruction to the sun.

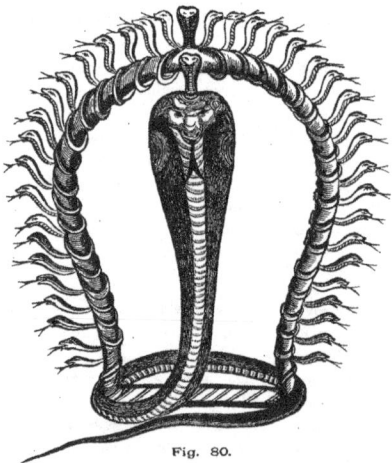

Fig. 80.

Thoth was the first who ascribed something divine to the nature of the serpent and the serpent tribe, and in this belief he was followed by the Phœnicians and Egyptians. The serpent was esteemed by them as the most spiritual of all reptiles, and of the most *fiery* nature, inasmuch as it exhibited in its movements incredible celerity, moving, as it were, by pure spirit energy, without either hands or feet; moreover it was long lived, they remarked, and had the power of renewing its youth. So Thoth taught in the sacred books; upon which account it is introduced in the rites and mysteries as a symbol of the spirit of life. It is this mystery which surrounds the serpent, and the power he possesses and exercises so widely of killing man by his slightest bite, that explains the awe with which he is regarded, and the office he holds, moreover, as the guardian of the gods. In Persia the serpent was considered the guardian of the universe. The serpent of the field [3] was for ever destined to crawl upon the earth and to be at enmity with mankind. Though the serpent, as possessing peculiar powers, such as that of moving without limbs and yet with considerable swiftness, of twisting itself into various forms, of living to a great age, and seeming to renew its vigour as it changed its skin every year, while it was endowed with preternatural keenness of vision, aptly represented the swift, subtle, potent spirit of the deity,[4] yet there was also among all nations a strong belief in its potency for evil; and the overthrow or subjugation of this evil is accordingly typified in India by the death of Kali at the hands of Vishnu; in Greece, by the triumph of Apollo over the Python; in Scandinavia, by the banishment by Woden of the malignant serpent to the depths of the ocean; and in Christendom, by the victory of St. George over the dragon.

It would appear, from its frequent occurrence on monuments along with other pagan symbols, that the serpent was had in high veneration among the ancient inhabitants of Britain. And in such sacred esteem was it

---

(1) Brosman, loc. cit., p. 494 to 499; Smith, loc. cit., p. 175, 195; Tree and Serpent Worship, p. 50.
(2) Romans, ch. i., 23.   (3) Gen. iii, 14.   (4) *See* Voss' de Idolat., p. 233.

CHAP. VII.]   *HISTORY OF PAGANISM IN CALEDONIA.*   107

held, that it is supposed to have suggested the form of some of the great temples, such as that of Avebury.[1] The great temple of Carnac, in Brittany, too, is supposed to represent the convolutions of the serpent. It is formed of huge boulders, which extend over 11 furlongs, and has a tumulus, called Kerlescant, at each extremity. These are separately situated with regard to the temple, and are nearly in the same meridian. Such may have also been the design of the wall or fence round the exterior of the Celtic hill-forts, of which Catherthum, in Forfarshire, is an example. In the same manner, we find the Hindu worshipping the imaginary sacred mound encircled by a serpent, as symbolical of the great Deity.[2]

At Ohio, in America, a fort has been discovered with an earthen enclosure, terminating in two mounds, with a paved way between them. This earthwork represents two gigantic serpents rising and contending with each other, with their heads at one extremity and their tails the other. The size of the monument may be estimated from the fact that the circumference of the area is a mile and a half.[3]

On the sculptured stones in Pictland the serpent is represented in different forms and under different circumstances, but in every case as a symbol of the divine nature in its pure or its organic form. When the serpent appears on the obelisk, transfixed by a rod, in close connection with the sceptre and under the spectacle ornament, it represents the pure divine form. When it wants the sceptre and is above the spectacle ornament, it represents mundane organic forms, as on the obelisk at Glammis, the smaller Aberlemno stone, and the Knockando stone.[4]

We have the serpent representing the divine intelligence, or as symbolic of pure life or spirit, on the Newton stone, its head raised, and the convolutions of its body transfixed by a cross-bar terminating in sceptres. Another example occurs in the Ballutherie stone, where an elephant appears above the serpent. In both these examples the unsceptred dorge appears, one above and the other below the serpent, and the serpents represent the active power, while the organic is in repose.[5] In the Picardy[6] stone, in the parish of Inch, in Aberdeenshire, the dorge and serpent are both in action.[7] It is peculiar in having both the spectacle ornament and the serpent associated with the usual bars terminating in sceptres, with a looking-glass underneath.[8] It stands upon a cairn 6 feet in diameter, into which it is sunk 3 feet below the surface. Three feet from the stone on the south side, a grave, 7 feet in length, and lying east and west, was found. It was at a depth of rather more than 5 feet under the surface. First there were 6 inches of mould and 2½ feet of loose stones, then below them about 2½ feet of loose loamy sand. The bottom was smooth, flat, and hard, being merely earth mixed with sand. No remains of any sort were discovered in the grave, nor any sign of its having been disturbed. Some of the stones were slightly marked by fire.

On the Farnell stone we have also serpents protecting or marking the sacredness of the tree under which the priests stand, the tree being under the cross, and the two serpents, one on each side of the tree, with their heads hanging downwards and their bodies in a curved form.[9] This is an unusual position; the only other

---

(1) It is said that the lower classes in the north of Scotland have pictures in which the serpent appears, which they regard with the greatest veneration.

(2) Sculpt. Stones, vol i, plates 47; also plates 33 and 34.   (3) *The Academy*, October, 1877.

(4) *See* Sculptured Stones of Scotland, vol. i, plates 71, 83, and 84, and vol. ii, plate 105.

(5) The Southern Picts were known by the peculiar name of Piccardoch. Skene's Highlanders of Scotland, vol. i, p. 66.

(6) New Stat. Account of Aberdeenshire, p. 751.   (7) Sculp. Stones, vol i, plate 2.

(8) Sculptured Stones, vol. i, Appendix to the Preface, p. 24.

(9) This interesting figure was found in the neighbouring burying-ground of Farnell. On examining it, I found that one of the apples was wanting on the Buddhist tree, and that the right figure held in its right hand what had the shape of an apple. But the worn state of the obelisk, when compared with the fresh appearance of the defaced apple and of the round design scratched on the breast of the figure, proved that the latter had been lately executed; and I have therefore left them out in the drawing.

O 2

example I know of being that in Glammis, at the Manse (*Fig.* 81). In both cases the twisting form, as in Egyptian monuments, is the mark of the evil serpent. The tree resembles the Buddhist sacred tree, loaded with fruit, and the figures under it may represent priests meditating. Had the two figures represented Adam and Eve, the serpent would have appeared in a grovelling or crouching position. Such mythological serpents are often found surrounding the reverse sides of the sculptured crosses, as, for instance, at Dunfallandy and at Glammis, etc.

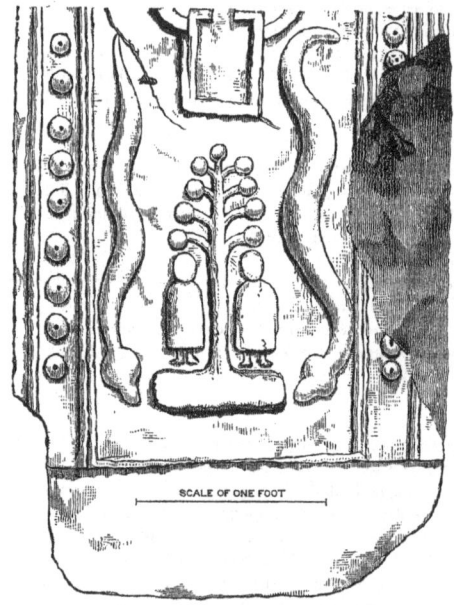

Fig. 81.

At Avebury, in Wiltshire, in a retired spot surrounded by hills, is a great temple, which has been supposed to be connected with serpent worship. This temple consists of a deep circular trench, with a high vallum or bank on the outside, and bounded by a hundred stones fixed in the earth, and from 10 to 15 feet high above the ground. Within this were two double circles, situated nearly north and south of each other, supposed to be respectively the temples of the sun and moon. The south-eastern, which had a central pillar 21 feet long, was supposed to be the temple of the moon; while the north-western was supposed to be the temple of the sun. The three central pillars were supposed to represent the division of the year into three seasons. But what we especially note here is, that from the great circle proceeded in opposite directions, in a waving serpentine form, two avenues of stone pillars, one of which terminated in a double circle of stones, and the other in a single pillar. Though it is now disputed that the monument represents a serpent at all, and Dr. Stukely's plan is supposed not to be correct, we must bear carefully in mind that he had a better opportunity of judging the original design than we have, in consequence of so many of the stones of the avenue having been since removed.

The destruction of the ophite temples put an end to serpent worship, and was considered as a victory over the great monstrous dragon, who, through their agency, had infested the earth and infected the races of mankind. The prevalence of such worship in Western Europe is witnessed to in the stories that are remembered and handed down by tradition, which magnify the piety and prowess of Christian knights in slaying fire-breathing dragons and poisonous snakes. In France a tradition exists of an enormous serpent that was vanquished by a holy saint near Vendôme, at the site of the church of St. Brière Saire.

When Jocelin, in his Life of St. Patrick, states that the saint on the Cruch Phadrine (the Mountain of St. Patrick) expelled all the serpents and venomous reptiles from Ireland, he doubtless intends to intimate that he had performed some miracle to prove more effectually to the natives the necessity of rejecting serpent worship, and depending upon God and his saints for their salvation. We cannot suppose that the serpent of evil, or the Satan of Christianity, which tempted our first parents, and upon which the curse rests, would ever be worshipped or appear upon sculptured stones in the Christian period, unless it were to reconcile to Christian teaching natives who still leant towards old superstitions. In the Christian dispensation, the treacherous serpent—represented as crawling on the earth on its belly—was the symbol of the sensual principle in man, which, being related to the powers of darkness, was called the devil, or Satan; and power was given by the Saviour "to tread on serpents and scorpions," as the symbols of this, "and over all the power of the enemy," &c.[1] Accordingly, when St. Michael introduced the Christian religion, thus supplanting the pagan worship of the serpent, he was represented as the divine or Christian subduer and destroyer of the spiritual serpent, or dragon, formerly worshipped. When the aged St. Columba visited his cornfield for the last time, to comfort his weeping children, he "raised both his holy hands, and blessed the whole of our island, saying, 'From this very moment poisonous reptiles (serpents) shall in no way be able to hurt man or cattle, as long as the inhabitants shall continue to observe the commandments of Christ.'"[2]

The serpent *(naga)* which guarded the Brahminical Buddha is the emblem of immortality. The figure of it coiled into a circle with its tail in its mouth, is an appropriate symbol of eternity with its ever-recurring cycles; while its power of renewing its age by annually shedding its skin makes it the expressive image of that eternal youth which the Greeks fabled in their conception of the ever-radiant, ever-young Apollo. Yet are serpents, in the Hindu mythology, the offspring rather of the nether darkness than of the upper light (which it is noticeable Apollo, as the son of Latona, the "hidden" one, also is), and the part they play is that of enemies to Garada, the solar bird. As nagas, they are half-human, and endowed with "knowledge, beauty, and strength." They have a city, their home, full of treasures of wealth, under the waters; and, though from their power to poison, they are often regarded with dread as demons of evil, they are charged with and impart to mortals the elixir of life. The coils of the serpent king form the couch of Vishnu, and are thus the supports on which the world rests. They were the sole tenants of the world when it was all a marsh, and their haunts are still under lakes and rivers. They are the expression of that side of life which holds of the primal watery element at feud with the sun as the source of parching heat, and they hold a high place in the regard of the Buddhist and among the symbols of his religious life. Everywhere in India they are held as sacred, and few would harm them, notwithstanding the mortality due to their bites.[3] In some of the village temples in India, dedicated to the supreme ruling power of the universe, to which all things human and divine are alike subject, the heavenly essence as it works in existence is symbolised by the form of a serpent, and is supposed to watch over the human race as dependent more or less on the genius of nature as it presides over mountain and forest, river and lake.

It is questionable, however, how far serpent worship was countenanced among the early followers of Buddha; and it is noticeable that the serpent rarely appears in the sculptures on the gateway of the Sanchi Tope, which is five hundred years older than the oldest Buddhist book we possess.[4] In the frescoes of the caves of Ajunta, three centuries later than the sculptures of Amravati, there are no traces of serpent worship. Representations of the naga, however, are found at Ajunta on the sculptured decorations of the doorways, or in detached bas-reliefs outside the caves. Dr. Ferguson, who explored these caves, and especially set himself to photograph them, so to speak, both outside and in, expressed his surprise that, intent as he was mainly on architectural features, he did not notice any of these serpent forms. "I measured everything," he says, "drew every detail, and familiarised myself with every architectural affinity; but neither then nor subsequently did I note the nagas. Now, I cannot take up a photograph of any temple belonging to the group of religions which include the Buddhist, Jaina, or Vishava faiths, without seeing serpents everywhere."[5]

The serpent, as an appendage round the neck, or otherwise, of a god, as, for instance, in the images of Siva, is, like the Gorgon's head on the shield of Athene, the symbol of terror, and, as such, an intimation to

(1) St. Luke's Gospel, x, 19.   (2) Adamnan, Book ii, ch. 29.   (3) *See* Barth's Religions of India, pp. 266, 267.
(4) Ferguson's Tree and Serpent Worship, p. 67.   (5) Tree and Serpent Worship, p. 72.

the worshipper to approach with awe, and not pry too closely into the mysteries of the god; while, in an erect posture, twined round and towering above a pillar or *linga*, it is the symbol of the sacred ire which guards any attempt to supplant the faith it protects. Only it is noticeable that while, in the Siva worship, the serpent is the symbol of the terror with which the divine is guarded, in the Vishnu worship it is the symbol of the divinity itself; the cobra being employed in the one case, and the naga in the other. Serpent worship still prevails to a great extent among the native tribes of India, and one of the aboriginal races boasts of being sons of the serpent, as others have done of being sons of the earth; and worship is paid to the serpent, not merely in deprecation of evil, but in imprecation of good. This worship prevails also in Cashmir and Nepaul;[1] and there is a serpent well in the city of Benares, which is visited once a year for the purpose of offering sacrifices to the serpent god.[2]

Serpents appear on the sculptured stones of Pictland twenty-three times; thirteen times in company with oriental symbols, and ten times by themselves. The worship of it could not have originated in Scotland, where they are so very few in number, and so small, and where there is only one that is venomous, and that slightly. On the Newton stone the inscription is undeciphered, but the serpent is the chief object of veneration, and is apparently the hieroglyphic of some god or saint. One thing is clear, that in all these cases the serpent was a divine symbol, the symbol of that which guarded Deity, as well as the symbol of Deity itself, as quickening no less than killing, in both cases in the interest of good, the ultimate interest of every form of God. It is a mistake to accept the symbol in any case as one of pure evil, or to regard the principle which it embodies as not subservient to divine use and conservative of divine purpose. Water, of which the serpent is the brood, is, like fire, a good servant, but a bad master; so the serpent symbolises that which is good or evil, according as it serves or rules. In the one case it seems a god, in the other a demon.

This early myth represents at bottom the world-wide warfare between virtue and vice, light and darkness. Such is the meaning of the contest between Indra and Vitra—the sun and the thundercloud—when the spear of Indra flashes forth and pierces the thunder-cloud, releasing the imprisoned rain, which falls, refreshes, and fructifies the earth. The same myth assumes a moral aspect, when the horse is represented as victorious over the enemy, the old dragon, as in the Christian fable of St. George, the great Python-slayer.

Fig. 82.

The Dragon.—The Dragon has been a British emblem from remote ages. It figured in Grecian mythology as a monstrous serpent, the slaying of which was an emblem of the victory of spring over winter, of light over darkness, and, in general, of good over evil, while in Christian romance the slaying of it emblems the victory of the Christian hero or saint over the powers of paganism. It symbolizes a darker and deadlier power than the serpent, and is always conceived of as a devourer and destroyer, whose end is to be slain (*Fig.* 82). He withholds the waters, his breath being of fire; and for that end he lurks about rivers, a foe to civilization and man. He is the spoiler of good things, over whom nothing less than the spell of the Cross is able to prevail. Not otherwise can he be deprived of his sting. The triumph of the upper over the nether powers is, from Vedic times onwards, a more or less effective slaying of this monster, who is, properly, an incarnation of the indolent or *laissez-faire* element in nature, which only consumes what others guard and produce. During the 12th and 14th centuries the dragon was frequently represented as devouring men, women, and children, and ultimately vanquished by the valour of some Christian knight. The figure of the dragon in early Christian art represents the temptations and

---

(1) Tree and Serpent Worship, p. 74.   (2) Sherring's Sacred Cities of Hindustan, p. 89.

evil designs of the arch-enemy of mankind. On the conversion of Constantine it was placed on the standards of cohorts, beneath the cross, as the monogram of the triumphs of Christianity.

(*d*.) *Horse worship.*—In Asia, and among the Aryan races generally, there were few animals more prized for their serviceableness and other good qualities than the horse, and few more worthy of sacred regard, as suggestive of, and identical with, what is noble among the high powers of the world. When identified with the sun, the white horse was regarded as the attendant of that deity. This gave origin to the sacrifice of *asvamedha* by the tribes of the Aryan race who inhabited the districts about the Caspian Sea, and between that and Afghanistan. It is spoken of in the early Hindu poems as observed from the earliest times. They kept white horses in their temples, and took auguries from their snorting and neighing.

It is associated with other sacred and mythological figures on Hindu coins and sculptures. As carved and depicted on the Buddhist monuments, it is represented as (1) at liberty and without trappings or rider; (2) without a rider, but caparisoned and ready for use, probably by Buddha; (3) cantering with an armed rider, who is probably Buddha; (4) sometimes it is accompanied by griffin or treading upon a serpent.

According to Colebrooke, the sacrifice of the horse, like that of *Purushamedha*, or human sacrifice, was often merely nominal, the horse being let loose after certain ceremonies suggestive of sacrifice had been performed. According to Mr. Ward, he was merely liberated for a twelvemonth, and at the end of that term he was led, magnificently caparisoned, three times round the sacrificial fire, and then killed by the blow of an axe, while the priests chanted the prescribed hymn, "Go, (horse,) to-day rejoicing to the gods, that the sacrifice may yield blessings to the donor." The flesh of the horse was then roasted on a spit, or boiled, or made into balls, and so eaten. When the Hindus, after their settlement in Hindustan, had less use for the horse, these sacrifices were abolished, or else became typical, only the head of the animal being thrown into the sacrificial fire.[1]

The Rajputan warriors sacrificed the horse to the sun.[2] A steed was the sacrifice made to the sun *(Surya)* on the Jaxartes and the Ganges on great occasions; and when a hundred horses were sacrificed, the person who offered them obtained the rank of Indra, or King of Surya. In the Indian Museum, London, is a horse in bas-relief with two attendants, one running before and the other shading the sacred horse with an umbrella (*Fig.* 83).

That branch of the Aryan race which passed from the north-west of India carried with them the belief in the sacred character of the horse, and the custom of sacrificing it on great occasions. For this purpose horses of a white colour were carefully selected and taken care of in sacred groves, and were never desecrated by the yoke. Herodotus testifies to their sacred character, and the early sacrifice of them to the sun and Tacitus makes mention of the same fact. They were kept not merely for

Fig. 83.

---

(1) Archæologia, vol. iii, p. 292.   (2) Tod's Antiquities of Rajasthan, vol. i, pp. 76 and 563.

sacrifice, but because they were believed, as we have said, to give warning and auguries of coming events. It is well known that the Romans paid deference to the ideas and religious feelings of the people they conquered, and this fact may have had something to do with the proposal of Caligula, to raise his horse to the consulship.

The white horse, which was worshipped and offered in sacrifice to Bellona, the Goddess of War, by the Celtic, Germanic, and Sclavonian races, was adopted by them also as their national symbol. The horse appears even among the insignia of Kent, the first of the Anglo-Saxon kingdoms, and it stands emblazoned to this day on the shields of the houses of Hanover and Brunswick. The first Anglo-Saxon invaders of England are said to have been headed by Hengist (stallion) and Horsa (mare), because they bore this emblem on the standard under which they conquered, and hence their final victory was called Hengistesdun or Horsedown, now Hengaston, in Cornwall. This explains the reason why, with these invaders, the eating of horseflesh was the test of adherence to heathenism, why so many places are called after the horse—as Horsham, Horsley, Horstead Keynes, Horse-ferry, &c., and why the white horse still marks the chalk downs of Wantage and Westbury. The northern heroes, Hengist and Horsa, if they ever existed, must have owed their names to the esteem in which the horse was held, and it was, as we have said, borne on their standard, as it is still to be seen on their coins.[1]

In Hanover cream-coloured horses were reserved for the use of the king alone on state occasions. The horse seems to have been held sacred in Britain, as elsewhere, and was probably worshipped as a deity,[2] for we find representations of it on high places in the south of England, and on the sculptured stones of Scotland it is placed by itself, and not as the third member of the triad. The four white horses that are represented on the chalk hills of England were formerly supposed to be the work of the Danes, and to have been formed to commemorate victories; but this does not seem to have been the case. The immense number of bones found in the cannoge at Lagon, near Danshangelas, along with a collection of articles of the pre-historic age, were probably the remains of horses that had been sacrificed. Among the Scandinavians, on the great feast day of the god Wodin, or the sun, sacred horses were offered up in sacrifice, and their flesh was eaten by the worshippers; and the old pagan Germans considered their flesh a great and wholesome luxury. The Pope in vain issued his ban against the custom of eating meat that had been offered to idols; and it was not till Winford, or St. Boniface, the apostle of Germany, prohibited the use of the meat in connection with such idolatrous practices, that the custom ceased.

The white horse of Effington in the Berkshire downs is probably a sacred mythological monument. It is of such a size and in such a position that it may be seen for many miles when the afternoon sun shines upon it.

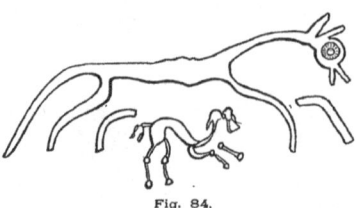

Fig. 84.

It measures from the nose to the outside of the tail 170 feet, and from the top of the neck to the forefeet, 160 feet; the length of the head is 50 feet and the eye is 6 feet by 7 feet. There is a periodical feast day devoted to "scouring" the figure, i.e., removing from it the turf and encroaching on the chalk subsoil, to form the white groundwork. When this is required, a day is fixed for a meeting of all the inhabitants of the vale. The horse is quickly cleaned or "scoured;" and during the remainder of the day, dancing, feasting, and various national athletic sports are engaged in.[3] Mr. Thom has proved[4] that it was in existence in 1072, very shortly after the Conquest, and it is probably of much earlier date. According to tradition it is the

(1) *See* Danish coins struck in Ireland. *See also* Harris's Way, vol. i, p. 206; Ulster Journal, vol. vii, p. 65; Irish Res. v, p. 656.
(2) Gough's Camden's Britt., vol. i, p. 14.   (3) The Scouring of the White Horse. Macmillan, 1859.   (4) Archæologia, vol. xxxi, p. 289.

CHAP. VII.]   HISTORY OF PAGANISM IN CALEDONIA.   113

great Saxon white horse placed here to commemorate the important victory of Ashdown (Æscendum), gained by Alfred over the Danes in A.D. 871.[1] It has, however, no resemblance to the Saxon horse, and it is extremely unlikely that such a victory would be commemorated by a figure that requires the yearly removal of the encroaching turf. It appears to be identical with the figures of the mythological horse found on British coins, belonging to the pagan Saxon times, and considered by Mr. Ackerman as identical with the horses on ancient Buddhist coins;[2] and it is, therefore, much more probable that it was connected with religious observances, and that it was formed for purposes of worship and for the protection of the Britons from their enemies. Near it is the celebrated cromlech known as Wayland Smith's Cave,[3] and all round there are numerous circles and other Celtic remains. There are also remains of a large fortification.

The sacred horse is found represented in different parts of Britain. At Inverury, in Aberdeenshire, a stone was found with the figure of a horse (*Fig.* 85), accompanied by other stones with incised figures of the spectacle ornament and the serpent, all of primitive type. The horse was marked with the usual waving Celtic lines on its body, and had, as sacred, a crest and head ornament, and may have been offered up in sacrifice, as in ancient times in India, on some great occasion. Elsewhere we have heads of horses represented on stones, as in those delineated in *Figs.* 86, 87, which are from sculptures on stones at Glammis and Meigle, in Perthshire.

Fig. 85.

Fig. 86.

Fig. 87.

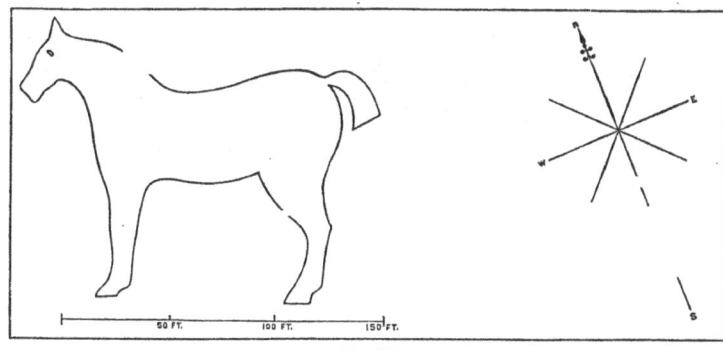

Fig. 88.

(1) *See* Annales Rerum Gestarum Ælfredi Magni, Auctore Asserio.   Recensuit Franciscus Wise.   Oxford, 1722, p. 23.
(2) Ackerman's Archæologia, Index, p. 43.
(3) The learned Francis Wise first described this interesting monument of antiquity. *See* his 1st and 2nd Letters to Dr. Meade in 1747.

There is a representation of the white horse (*Fig.* 88) in a state of excitement, on one of the brown heather hills of Morin, in Banffshire, N.B., 600 feet above the level of the ocean, and looking one-half in a S.E. direction. It is cut out of the turf, and occupies the space of half an acre. As the subsoil is black, the figure is filled with white felspar stones, to give it the sacred colour, so that it can be seen ten miles off.[1] The horse held a place in Irish mythology, and was sacred to the sun.

The Eastern origin of the symbols upon the sculptured stones of Pictland is proved by the veneration which they show to have been held for serpents, horses, and trees, and by the occurrence of representations of centaurs, lions, camels, bears, &c., which are of purely oriental derivation. These were gracefully drawn and elaborately decorated, and most certainly could not have been delineated by the rude artists of Scotland, who at that period did not know how even to work on stone. Their presence can only be accounted for by the appearance of a remarkable class of enthusiasts from Asia, who, under the direction of priestly rules, devoted their lives to the propagation of an enlightened legislation, and to the spread of the tenets of their religion to the uttermost ends of the earth, more particularly towards the fabled sacred Islands of the West, where it was believed lay the final blessed home and paradise of the immortals. Pilgrims kept constantly making for these beautiful islands; and that they might propagate, as they went, a knowledge of the faith, they multiplied everywhere the sacred symbols of their religion. This fact alone explains the number of them found on the sacred boulders of the great northern Pictish kingdom, known as Pictland.

(1) *See* Guide by the Rev. Wm. Pratt; Buchan, 1858, p. 119.

CHAPTER VIII.

RELIGIOUS SYMBOLS AND IDEAS AMONG PRIMITIVE RACES IN ASIA AND EUROPE.

N this chapter we propose to give a brief notice of the early religious symbols and ideas of the Pagan world, so far as in a general way we have to do with them here. The symbols and ideas we refer to are such as are suggestive or expressive of the thoughts and fancies of the early races respecting God.

SECTON I.—MONOLITHIC SYMBOLS OF THE DEITY.

(a.) The simple erect Boulder, one of the principal of these symbols, is expressive of the unity of the Divine Being, and as unsculptured or unmarked, perhaps suggestive of the inarticulate, unutterable awe with which that Being was in early times regarded, a memorial of one who is as yet unnamed and unnameable. It was only in later times, when certain attributes of the Deity which stood out in relief before the senses became comprehensible by human intelligence, that these stones began to be covered with marks and figures, symbolic of the ideas man had at length fashioned to himself of the hitherto inconceivable Deity, till these objects themselves began to be regarded with feelings of wonder and worship by the ruder sections of the community. Nay, we have seen that they continued to be worshipped by simple people even after the introduction of Christianity. To forestall this idolatrous practice, the priests had in some cases to cause crosses to be incised or erected on them, in order to consecrate them to a Christian purpose, and to secure for the Christian symbol the worship that had been given to them. It is probable, also, that these erect stones represented the exalted character of the Deity, to whom they were dedicated, pointing as they did to heaven above, where the simple-hearted worshipper fancies God to dwell; and that, as they stood towering heavenward, they suggested the upright attitude that was appropriate to the spirit in the worship of God.

(b.) As it was customary to employ the same kind of boulder stone which had already been consecrated as a symbol of the Deity for a *boundary pillar,* or land-mark, we are warranted to conclude that it had also a religious reference when so used. As a recognised symbol of the Deity it was a token of the solemnity of the transaction, and an intimation, as it were, of the common belief of those who reared it, that as the covenant had been made under God's eye, so God would avenge the wrong on him who should first violate it. A rude enough symbol, certainly, but an assurance of a great faith, to this day one of the very greatest, that God loves justice and will enforce it; that the claims of justice will not be baulked,—God's eye is on it.

(c.) As a *sepulchral* monument it is also probable that this unhewn native stone had a similar religious reference, and that in erecting it over the graves of their dead those early races had regard to its consecration as a symbol of the Deity. In the earliest mythologies, the god of life is also the god of death, and the soul is not left to itself when it leaves the world any more than when it enters it. It is a solar-god who rules over the dead in the Hades of India, and it is Hermes, the impersonation of the swift-darting light and lightning, who conducts the ghosts of the dead into the realms of Pluto. Fitly, therefore, might the divinely-symbolic boulder stone be selected to mark the spot where the dead, especially the heroic dead, lie buried, for by that death-porch have they first entered, under the Lord of light, the proper land of the living, to which those who live on this side of that often so dreaded other world are only on the road. Nowhere is the divine symbol more appropriately reared than over the grave of a fallen hero. It is by death he first enters the realms of the immortals, and begins from among them to hold sway over the world.

SECTION II.—SUN-SYMBOLS OF THE DEITY IN CIRCLES, DISCS AND WHEELS.

The Turanian Sandal race in India, inhabiting the Rajmal Hills, were sun-worshippers; and when in their insurrectionary movements the people of the tribe were driven from their chief village, which they left quite deserted, there was found in the yard of their chief's house under a large cover made of wicker-work a sun-circle, the symbol of their god (*Tacoor*). This was two feet in diameter, and much resembled the solid wooden cart-wheel used by the hill people. It was cracked in two places, and it was said that milk poured upon it spouted up again from the fissures. This, with other phenomena, was intended to delude the people into the belief that it was charged with and animated by supernatural influence. Around the symbol lay the heads of two buffaloes, of goats, &c., which had been sacrificed that morning as an oblation to the Deity. It was after this sacrifice that the chief had led forth his men to attack the British troops in the neighbourhood; but, though promised an easy victory, they were miserably disappointed.[1] Among the primitive races of India the circle is still drawn over the entrance, and in the pathway in front, of their huts or dwelling-houses, for the purpose of protecting the inmates from their enemies.

The simple circle by itself, while it came ultimately to denote that abstract endless continuity of being which we call Eternity, seems originally to have expressed the idea of the ever-recurring sequence of things as regulated by God in nature; how under His providence all things go and return again without beginning and without ending; no fear of the chain breaking, every link in it being held up and told out by Him; so that the circle is a rude first expression of "His eternal power and Godhood." The circle, in some such reference, occurs everywhere among the Celtic races of both Asia and Europe, as already described in chapter iii. The same idea is symbolised in the disc and wheel, though these are more a reflection of the primitive sun-worship, and express the further idea of self-centrality, as well as self-continuity and progress in the divine nature of things; the disc being the simple sun-symbol, while the wheel suggests his radiant, triumphant and progressing power.

Concentric circles have doubtless a meaning, that is, they are clearly not there merely for their own sake. They are intended to represent in rough outline such as we find elsewhere a certain relation of the Deity to organic nature, which is symbolised by a wavy line on the outside. This sphere of nature, the symbol would seem to say, depends in form, as well as in spirit, on the Deity, contains and is contained by the Deity: a rude symbol, like the rest, but an expressive, as of the free wavy movement of spirit life in organic existences. Near the church of Sancried, which is at a place called Hegenegorth in Cornwall, I found two such circles. These circles were executed with the care usually bestowed on Celtic sacred symbols. The gutter in both was perfect, and without the appearance of chisel-marks.

---

(1) Letter to the Government, dated Bhagnader, 21st July, 1855.

CHAP. VIII.]   HISTORY OF PAGANISM IN CALEDONIA.   117

Large and small circles when, as in the Lindores stone, they occur together, are to be considered symbols of the sun and moon, as embodiments of the benevolent, all-seeing, all-watchful Deity. *Fig.* 89 is taken from a Scottish example at Knockando, Morayshire, and is evidence of the worship of the sun and moon in Britain. The circle seems to correspond with the nimbus, halo, glory, or ring that surrounds the heads of Assyrian figures, which have rays to represent those that stream in dazzling splendour from the sun, the true object represented in these mythological figures. Layard derives the Egyptian emblem of the Deity, a winged globe, from these Assyrian figures; and the symbol of Sûryâ, and of the more modern Siva, appears under other types; as, *e.g.*, a circular disc of metal over the head of the Greek statue, and as a halo round the heads of the Christian saints.

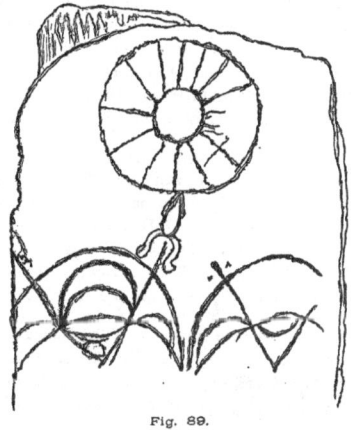

Fig. 89.

Colonel Sykes, in his Notes on Ancient India, alludes to the wheel as metaphorically expressive of universal dominion in spiritual and temporal matters; and it is thus he explains the representations of Buddha in some of the caves of Western India, in which he is seen seated on the edge of his one-wheeled chariot.[1] It is the type of spiritual progression "that which advances by revolving as a wheel (*chakraverti*)"[2] This wheel, however, is the wheel, not of the sun's disc, but of the sun's orbit.

There are many mystical and metaphysical meanings ascribed to wheels by Hindus and Buddhists, but these were probably invented more for purposes of concealment than purposes of enlightenment. "From the first," as M. Barth, in his lucid exposition of the Religions of India, affirms, "Hindu thought is profoundly tainted with the malady of which it will never be able to get rid, of affecting a greater air of mystery the less there is to conceal, of making a parade of symbols which at bottom signify nothing, and of playing with enigmas which are not worth the trouble of trying to unriddle."[3]

SECTION III.—PRIMITIVE PAGAN CROSSES.

From the dawn of paganism in the East we find the cross, equally with the monolith and the circle, one of the most common and sacred religious symbols, and it appears to have been originally employed as such by every people of any culture among the nations of antiquity commemorated in history. It is found delineated more or less artistically on walls, temples and palaces, in sepulchral galleries, on monoliths, and rocks, on statues, clothing, books, and medals, and it varied in form with the tastes and pursuits of the people and the different degrees of civilization which they had reached.

Fig. 90.

Among the most ancient of these symbols and forms is the "Crux Ansata." It is in the shape of the letter Tau with a roundlet, which seems to be an integral part of it, placed immediately above. This is frequently found on Egyptian and Coptic monuments. It is known as the mystical "Tau," the symbol of "the mysterious hidden wisdom of the Egyptians, the symbol of a future

---

(1) Trans. Royal Asiatic Soc. vi., p. 276.   (2) Vist. pur. 217 and 211.
(3) "The Religions of India," translated by the Rev. J. Wood; Trübner & Co.

life, a belief which had been adopted by them," and by the Chaldæans, Phœnicians, Mexicans and Peruvians, and other ancient peoples. In connexion with nature-worship it is the symbol of such ideas as strength and wisdom, and in connexion with human life it is that of the sacrifice of the present life for a better beyond. It was in this pre-Christian or Tau form of the cross that some of the early Gothic Christian churches were erected, such as the Santa Croce (holy cross) in Florence by the "renowned" Arnolfo. For, as Ruskin says, "the Franciscans and Dominicans saw in the cross no sign of triumph, but of trial. The wounds of their Master were to be their inheritance. So their first aim was to make what image to the cross their church might present distinctly that of the actual instrument of death."

The mystical Tau (the initial letter of the name Tamsung, the same as the ancient Chaldee) is found on coins in the form of a Latin cross. To identify Tamsung with the sun, the Tau was joined with the circle at its top, instead of the loop, and the cross included within the Maltese circle,[1] as an express symbol of the sun.[2] *The mystic cross*, as the symbol of the great divinity, was called "the tree, or sign of life," and was used as an armlet, and worn over the heart.[3] It was marked on the official garments of the priests of Egypt, Rome and Assyria. The vestal virgins of Rome wore it suspended from their necklaces, as also those of the Egyptians. The cross was used as early as the fifteenth century B.C.,[4] and worshipped by pagan Celts B.C.[5]

Fig. 91.

The Maltese cross is the oldest known, and is met with in the east and west, in China and Egypt. Some beautiful examples are seen among the Nineveh remains in the British Museum, on an oblong arched slab, having for a bas-relief king Assur-izir-pal, the earliest Assyrian monarch, who is believed to have reigned about B.C. 880. There are various sacred emblems on the side and back of the figure, and an invocation to the Assyrian god, as also a chronicle of the king's conquests. The cross figures among the symbols on the chain round the king's neck; and also in the roundlet in the left hand corner of the stile, emblematical of the sun dominating over the earth, as well as the heavens, and it seems to issue from the nave of a wheel. In more modern times the cross was found on Greek and Roman ornaments, in different forms, at right angles.

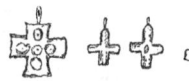

Fig. 92.

"*Swastica*," the Vedic, or mystical, cross, is so called from "*Su*," well, and "*asti*," it is well, or so be it, "contentment and peace of mind" being the only objects of pursuit worthy of the sacrifice to obtain them. It

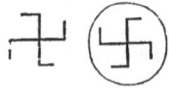

Fig. 93.

is the *Suasti* of the Sanscrit in the *Palisutras*. The Swastica, when surrounded by a circle, denotes, more explicitly than it does without one, the path from left to right of the sun round the earth, the so-called labours of which are not inaptly represented by the naked symbol. The beautiful chamber of the Roman Villa at Morton, near Brading, Isle of Wight, contains a fret pattern laid in white, terminating at the head of the chamber in a figure of a Swastica or Vedic cross as the symbol of happiness, good luck, or contentment.

SECTION V.—EARLY RELIGIOUS POLYTHEISTIC IDEAS, PARTICULARLY IN ASIA.

Originally God was conceived of as a great, incomprehensible power or spirit, to be worshipped without ritual and under the open vault of heaven; but in course of time, as now this aspect of His manifestation, now that, began to impress the worshipper with absorbing awe and wonder, the attributes manifested, and even the

---

(1) Bunsen, vol. i., p. 450.   (2) Layard's Nineveh and Babylon, p. 211; *also*, Nineveh and Remains, vol. ii., p. 446.
(3) Wilkinson, vol. i., p. 365, and Plate.   (4) Wilkinson, vol i, p. 376.   (5) Crabb's Mythology, p. 163.

earthly symbols of them, came to be considered as separate personal beings with power in their own hands to work the weal or woe of those who depended on them.

The Brahmins took advantage of this polytheistic conception to explain and recommend their religious tenets to the popular intelligence, which, under the tyranny of it, had lost the power of rising to the idea of one all-containing, all-sustaining unseen and unseeable God; and they singled out such intelligible forms of His Being as might seem real in the eye of the worshipper, worthy of his homage, and able as a person to help him in time of need. The worship of images and symbols, however much it might be countenanced by them, was countenanced merely to assist those of weaker intelligence to concentrate their ideas on some of these intelligible forms, that thereby they might rise to the conception of the Great Unseen.[1]

The ancient Hindus believed in one great spiritual God, omnipotent, omnipresent and incomprehensible, who formed and governed the world, who was known by His attributes, as seen in His works, and was worshipped in hymns inspired by Himself, and taught *viva voce* to those worthy to repeat them. Each word, each line was carefully preserved and the whole handed down by a select priesthood. These were the Brahmins who came from the north-west into the plains of Hindustan, and they taught their new doctrine to promising youths of good family. So skilful were they in forming their language, that its vocabulary is the richest in structure and the most perfect that exists. Their philosophy is so subtle and searching, too, and their ethics so comprehensive, that in many particulars they remain to this day unsurpassed. It was a reform of this system, which had degenerated into formality, that led to the rise and spread of Buddhism, and which reckons up more disciples than any other religion of the world.

Among such races as the Hindus, Egyptians, etc., the power of the priests over the religious consciousness was absolute, and any shape, form, or object to which they might attach a special virtue, was henceforth regarded as sacred, and, mayhap, even prayed to as divine. Forms, so consecrated, cover the temples and monumental remains of Buddhism, the like of which we meet with, obviously inscribed with similar intent and symbolism in meaning, as in the "Sculptured Stones of Scotland."

The figures and animals delineated on these stones are of Oriental origin, and betray an Oriental symbolism. The animals particularly are the Vaharas, or vehicles of the gods, and the sacred animals of eastern religion. The elephant, the horse, the dragon, etc., which appear on Celtic monuments, are of this description, and in a sense conventionally sacred. The camel, the bull, the boar, and the stag, which are such as became delineated in their natural forms, belong to Eastern symbolism, and suggest a similar meaning. When used as sacred symbols they are more carefully carved out, and more varied in form, than when used as ornaments.

(a.) Sacred Deities.—There are five names, representative, in a more or less partial view, of the divine nature, which occupy a prominent place in the Hindu theosophy, all from the original Vedic pantheon; and these are Brahma, Vishnu, and Siva, with Indra and Krishna, of which the three first form a sacred triad in the ranks, severally, of creator, preserver, and destroyer, and the last two are conceived of as embodying Indra the divine, in heaven, and Krishna the divine in man. In a general view, as regards the three first, Brahma is the absolute god, withdrawn, in his self-sufficiency and self-seclusion, from all observation, from whom all things issue and unto whom all things return; while Vishnu is the divine in Brahma, developing into visibility, and Siva the divine in visibility returning back into Brahma, the one more or less gaily and gladly, and the other with more or less severity of countenance and sadness of heart. Erelong the worship of Brahma retires into the background and disappears altogether, if indeed, which is questionable, it ever stood in the front, and only that of Vishnu and that of Siva survive, more or less antagonistically, in the modern Sectarian creed, with modifications which go far to darken the original belief. According to the original idea, Brahma was said to have created the dry land, out

---

(1) H. H. Wilson's Works, vol. ii, p. 54; Colebrook's Sects., Asiatic Researches, vol. vii.

of which, as directly from him, the Brahmins say they sprang; Vishnu was said to have created the water, the element in which everything takes shape; and Siva is said to have created the wilderness, thus restoring nature to the dry waste world out of which it sprang, in which, though everything lay latent, nothing did as yet exist.

Brahmá, though, as absolute and unrelated being, he has no temple specially to his honour, even as the unknown god, and has, as we have seen, now ceased to be specially worshipped, is nevertheless represented with four hands, in which some fancy there is an allusion to the four corners of the earth, which, being his special creation, not inappropriately gives colour to them, for they are always of a reddish hue, like it; if they be not rather intended to represent the four castes, considered as his ministers on earth. He is also represented as having four faces, but these are doubtless the four Vedas, boldly conceived of as containing his word. Prajâpati, who plays the same part as Brahma in the theology of the Hindus, and is likewise considered as withdrawn from all active share in the affairs of the world, is also almost without a temple, and exists more as a postulate of speculation than an object of religious belief. It is speculation too, rather than faith, which has assigned them feminine counterparts; just as the Greeks, in their reflective moods, fabled that the heavens and the earth were the progeny of a primitive pair, who held quiescent sway over the ocean on the outskirts of the universe. Their father Oceanus, by the way, was the Brahma of the Greeks, who, though the parent of both gods and men, troubles himself, like Brahma, with the affairs of neither: untroubled he, and untroubling. The Styx river too, over which all things are ferried back to the unconditioned, is a branch of the same flood which all beings cross when they first pass from the land of nothingness into the region of the upper light.

Vishnu, originally an impersonation of the fire and light of heaven as embodied in the sun, and who has stepped forth from darkness into splendour, flooding with his rays the universe, the three great regions of which he traverses in three strides, is the divine being in quest of an arena for the manifestation of his glory, and finding it on earth, where he manifoldly unfolds himself, first of all in nature, and finally in man. He is essentially the "active" one, who, as Vulcan with Venus, weds himself with Crî or Lakshmi, the goddess of gladness and beauty and victory, and is the spirit god, who, when he wakes, gives birth to, and when he sleeps, absorbs again all created things; from whose navel issues the lotus of gold, whence bud both Brahma and the demi-gods, and which these would have been as though they were not. It is distinctive of him that he descends on earth in "avatars" or incarnations, and all incarnations of the deity are, Krishna included, incarnations of him. However, as his manifestations are in time, he becomes, like Time, the devourer as well as the begetter of his offspring, so that even Brahma with the rest is made away with, being an empty abstraction apart from him. But, in the main, he is the god of birth rather than of death, and regards life rather from the birth-moment than like Siva, his rival, from that of death.

Siva, though, true to his name, "the propitious," he figures in the Rig-veda as a beneficent deity, afterwards comes to supplant the storm-god, and is, from his terrible power as a devastator, invoked as the lord both of life and death. He is allied to Agni, the fire-god, and Kali, the time-god, but to both more as powers of destruction than powers of creation, and one of his earliest appearances is that of the destroyer of the triple city of the heavens, the atmosphere and the earth. He, too, is that Time which devours as well as begets all things, and one of his symbols is the lightning, which he hurls from his height on the mountains upon the plains. Nevertheless, he is connected with generation as well as destruction, and his most characteristic symbol is the Phallus and the bull; yet, as we have said, he presides over life as culminating in death, rather than as commencing at birth. He delights in sacrifice, and is reckless of life, because he is so full of it; he gives it, that he may take it again. Ascetics and libertines, both of whom are lavish of life, alike worship him. He appears in "forms," as Vishnu in "avatars," and the most common symbols of his worship are the *linga* and *yoni*. He has three distinct characters, and the epithets bestowed on him are indicative of this triplicity of function, such as *Tri-locana*, the three-eyed, and *Nila-gantha*, three-throated, while the name Vis-ves-vara preserves his unity as lord of all. As allied to Time,

Maha-kala, or Kala, and his consort Kali, he is, first, the universal dissolving or destroying power in nature; as symbolized by the *linga* and *yoni;* he is, secondly, the restoring or reproducing power in the same sphere; and as represented in the character of an old and naked ascetic, fixed to one spot, his body covered with ashes and his hair matted, he is, thirdly, the god of mortification or that process of death-birth and death-life in which, while the flesh is systematically crucified, the spirit first begins to soar upward, until it is finally lost and absorbed in the great spirit of the universe, until it returns to Brahma.

Indra, the proper "national god of the Aryans, is pre-eminently a god of war," his battle-field being the heavens, and his great adversaries the demons, who steal away and conceal the sacred *soma*, or water of life, by which gods and men subsist. It is thus he is described by M. Barth, in the work already referred to :— "Standing erect in his war-chariot, drawn by two fawn-coloured horses, he is in some sort the ideal type of an Aryan chieftain. But that is only one of the sides of his nature. As a god of heaven, he is also the dispenser of all good gifts, the author and preserver of all life; with the same hand he fills the udder of the cow with ready-made milk, and holds back the wheels of the sun on the downward slope of the firmament; he traces for the rivers their courses, and establishes securely without rafters the vault of the sky. He is of inordinate dimensions: there is room for the earth in the hollow of his hand, he is sovereign lord and demiurgos . . . . he is the active, and, so to speak, militant life of heaven, while Varuna represents rather its serene, immutable majesty." He is also represented as riding on an elephant, and, like Jove, holding in his hand the thunderbolt (*vajra*). Indeed, he is the prototype of the Greek Zeus or Jupiter, is the lord of the day and king of the immortals, being waited upon and served by all the benignant powers of heaven; while Varuna is represented in the majestic Juno.

Krishna, though there are traces of a purely physical derivation, appears to have been a popular divinity, holding the rank of a sort of man-god, or hero raised to divinity, who, being allied with Vishnu, was at length, as a set-off belike against the personal human element in Buddhism, regarded as one of his "avatars" and "declared to be an incarnation of his divine essence." He too, in legendary story, is a fighting god, endowed at once with bravery and craft, both of which he stands greatly in need of, having, like all the gods, from the sun downwards, a sore fight of it and struggle for existence from the very first to the last; and he has a foster-brother, who, though he breaks out now and then into fits of wild, wanton, animalism, like a sort of Centaur, yet, as the animal with the spiritual should, fights loyally by his side, dealing death eternal to all manner of demons and monsters. The two fight and fall together; but it is not until Krishna sees his brother perish, and has set his adversaries by the ears to their total ruin, that he falls himself, "wounded in the heel, like Achilles, by the arrow of a hunter." Have we not here again the image of that Time, which is at once other-, and self-devouring, if not also an image of the confusion of despair and mutual dire disgust among the wicked when they find, too late, that they have been fighting against their deliverer? Anyhow Krishna is the great man-god of the Hindus, and the patron of purity, which he practised by bathing, consecrating the act into a sacrament, the observance of which came erelong to be taken as an equivalent for purity itself. He, along with others, gave sanctity to particular rivers, so that they have ever since been regarded as at once the symbol and the vehicle of divine ablution, both physical and spiritual.

Brahma, Vishnu, Siva, Indra, and Krishna, are but forms in a pantheon of gods, of whom the name is legion, but they are typical of the thoughts of deity that were deepest and truest in the faith of the early Aryans, and a witness of the original monotheistic idea thus polytheistically, as it were, broken up, evidence of the truth of the saying in the Rig Veda, that "the gods are only a single being under different names." The names, however, have here, as so often elsewhere, "hardened into things," and to this day the Hindu people, when they strive at all, mostly strive in vain, to seize and recover the original monotheistic belief in which all this theosophy originated.

(b.) Sacred persons.—Such hold a rank inferior at once to the gods and their manifestations, whether these last assume the demonic "form" of Siva, or the incarnate "avatar" of Vishnu, and are rather, at most, prophets

and priests of the Highest than incarnations of the Highest himself; the prophet as a seer and speaker ranking first, and the priest as a merely clerical or learned person being of subordinate standing. Of sacred persons, perhaps the Dalai-Lama of Thibet claims the highest place, who by divine election secludes himself from all public observation, like a sort of Brahma, absorbed in spiritual meditation for the behoof of others, and has another sacred person subject to him, who is his deputy among the people, to deliver his oracles and see his orders enforced, a sort of human Vishnu and Siva in one, alike for protection and for judgment. Standing to the people in place of God, it is as a god he is regarded, and the theory accepted among them actually is that he is the special incarnation of the divine vouchsafed to the generation. Besides these, there are subordinate grades called also Lamas, corresponding in function, some to the Grand Lama and others to his deputy. Those of the first grade profess a knowledge of religious mysteries, and lead a life of holy meditation; those of the others are some ministers of religion with a knowledge of the rites and ceremonies, some medicine men with a knowledge of diseases, and remedies, and some artists, builders and decorators of religious houses, called Lamaseries, whose art, however, with all its details of material and form, is divinely prescribed, and after a pattern that exhibits considerable architectural beauty.

The sacred caste among the Hindus, as is well known, are the Brahmins, and they are in character and function the *beau-ideal* of priesthood all the world over. Of the blood royal of Brahma, they are the chosen guardians and ministers of the *brahman*, or sacred formula, or word of power and prayer, on the strictly ritual delivery of which rests the entire order of the universe. Not till the gods themselves knew how to utter it, did they begin to exist as deities; and it is because the Brahmin alone of men knows this secret, that the rite in his hands, is of any efficacy to others. All hinges on ritual, on the use of ritual of the right kind, at the right time and in the right way; and he alone is qualified by birth and training, a severe one, to administer it, one class, by said training, one kind of it, and another another. The energy is in the formula, and the effect is magical on whosoever is legally pure to receive the benefit and believes implicitly in its virtue. Enough that the word, the *brahman*, is intelligently and rightly delivered; the spirit is in it, and is not otherwise imparted.

A theory like this—which after all is not, when rationally applied, so absurd as it seems, for the word, viewed as the articulation and evolution of a given spiritual, is everything,—is sure to become in the hands of designing men a plea for all manner of religious imposture; and such it has proved in the hands of the Brahmins. If only they can persuade people to believe in their pretensions, they can cozen them into the acceptance of the sheerest deceptions. An instance of this came under my own notice in the province of Bengal. A priest was interested in dissuading the proprietor of a useless mosque from improving his property, and his argument with him was, that the prophet was displeased with the project, as he might himself see if he looked at the mosque any day during the hour of mid-day prayers. It was the month of May, when, the heat being powerful, and a sea breeze prevailing, the mosque seemed to move as if agitated with trouble. This was explained to be due to the displeasure of the prophet, and could only have reference to the proposed profanation of his chapel. Those who informed me of this phenomenon were so numerous, and their accounts so circumstantial, that I went myself to see it, and sure enough, there was the mosque to all appearance as if it were moving. It was surrounded by tall trees, which during the hot hours of the day used to bend before the breeze; and the simple peasants, deceived by the illusion produced into the belief that the mosque was moving, had ascribed what they saw to miraculous intervention, and the mosque was left unmolested.

So much, anyhow, for the so-called sacred caste as they arose in the east, and such the theory on which they rest their pretensions. The seed which they sowed has taken wide root since, and borne all manner of fruit, good, bad and indifferent. Of such sacred persons this land of Britain has seen of all three kinds not a few, and the earliest, and perhaps not the worst, as well as the most lineally descended from the original stock, were the priests who from thence came hitherward and settled with their rites and symbols in native Caledonia.

(c.) Effigies of Sacred Persons.—One of the most noted of all the sacred personages that figure influentially in the history of the race is the Buddha who appeared some 480 years before Christ in the person of Sakyamuni, "the lion of the Sakyas." The influence he exercised was grounded more on reverence for his person than appreciation of his spirit; and if, as is the case, Buddhism is now bowled out of the India that was the land of its birth, it is because the rival sects invented for the gods a legendary set-off, and set up their effigies in imitation of his in all their sanctuaries and temples.

In the Buddhist temples are images of Buddha in all attitudes, sitting, standing and reclining. In some countries they are very numerous, and are of all sizes, from three inches high up to those of colossal dimensions. In general, Buddha is represented sitting upon a lotus throne, with his feet turned upwards and his legs crossed upon the seat. One hand is half open, turned upwards to receive gifts; and the other rests upon the right knee with the palm downwards, indicative of obedience. His hair is short, curled like that of a negro, and terminates in a spiral shape at the top of the head, or, as in Ceylon, in what is intended to represent a trifurcate flame of fire. He is usually sitting with a benign and placid countenance, and downcast eyes, in the attitude of contemplation, as indicative of the mild and humane character of the life he led and the doctrine which he preached. In other countries he is called *Aksholya*, the first of the pancha Buddhas; in Dotan he is called Gorucknuth, and is represented sitting cross-legged holding a *dorge* in his right hand, while the left supports a trident. Sometimes the trident, the symbol of Siva, transfixes three skulls, and the left hand rests on the lap and holds an asp with a jewel in it. A rosary hangs round his neck, and he has a red mitre on his head, with a sun crescent and cross marked in front.[1] These idols are considered as symbols of the spirit of Buddha, and their worshippers adore in them the spiritual image they represent. But by whatever name Buddha is known, it is his person that is especially adored, and it is to keep his person before the eyes of the devout that the sacred effigies thereof is set up in his temples. The purely spiritual has never yet carried captive the hearts anyhow of masses of men, only that which has embodied itself in some personal form, real or imaginary, demonic or human.

SECTION V.—MEANS OF MARKING THE PERIOD FOR HOLDING THE GREAT CELTIC FESTIVAL.

The ancient sun-worshippers in Caledonia, as elsewhere, at an early date, before the great discovery of Copernicus in 1540, believed there were periods or retrocessions in the sun's course, which attained their limit at the solsticial points, or the longest and shortest days of the year. At these periods it was that they held their great festivals, as they were considered to be the most propitious seasons for worship, and the offering up of sacrifices and prayers to the gods. The rays of the sun, which was regarded as the type of the great Deity, as it emerged from the horizon in the longest day, were supposed to be then most powerful. At that time, therefore, the domestic fires were all extinguished, and re-kindled afresh by the friction of pieces of wood, or the striking of flint on iron, or from a bonfire lit on the top of a mountain. The fire thus obtained was used for sacred as well as general purposes during the ensuing year. The native priests probably derived the knowledge of this from Eastern pilgrims, who had come to the West in search of the region of the gods; and so important were these periods considered, that at an early age methods were invented for marking their recurrence. Hence the construction of compasses and dials, of which the following are examples:

(a.) The discovery of a *cup-dial* was an interesting one among Celtic monuments. On a fine, erect, flat whinstone, 13 feet high, near the end of the neat modern church of Fodderty, in Cromarty, in the valley of

---

(1) Hooker's Journal, vol. i., p. 323.

Strathpeffer, I observed a basin (*see drawing*) on the south-east face of the stone, looking towards the summer solsticial point, and a smaller one on the other side; the former being 9 inches in diameter, and the latter 6. About 90 yards in the S.E. direction from the basin was a somewhat similar stone, 5 feet high, which had no marks on it, this being the gnomon or pointer; and three miles further on I noticed a flat plain. The drawing will explain the arrangement of the stone and basin—(G) the large stone—(E) the pointer—(B) the rising sun on the 22nd June (the time of the summer solstice), as it first appears on the horizon, or a flat portion of land lying between two shelving hills (A and C), and on the large basin (F), which becomes the *cup-dial*, upon the upper part of the left side of which the first rays of the rising sun fall, thus indicating the summer solstice,[1] when the offerings to the Deity were supposed to be peculiarly efficacious.

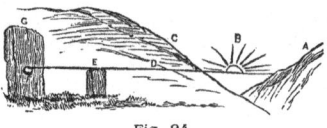

Fig. 94.

Among the ancients the great periods of the year were sometimes marked by the shadow of a vertical pillar upon a plain or flat surface; this shadow being elongated at noon in midwinter, as the sun advances towards the vernal equinox, decreasing in length towards, and reduced to its minimum in, midsummer. Such changes must have been observed at an early date, and in the course of the advancement of intelligence in science and art, the erect pillar was turned in Egypt into the obelisk or needle, and perhaps the pyramid.

(*b.*) The Cairn Leath Broch, lately uncovered by the Duke of Sutherland, under the supervision of the Rev. Dr. Joass, is situated near the sea, and consists of a central bell-shaped circular citadel, raised some 12 feet above the surrounding country, having remains of numerous outworks on its eastern and southern sides, for the accommodation of attendants, and as a protection for sheep, cattle, etc. This broch must have formed a strong fortification against enemies, or Scandinavian robbers, armed with swords, lances, slings, and bows and arrows. Upon the lintel of one of the side doors, leading to the main entrance appeared two cups, under one of which were lines, which may be the remains of an inscription in one of the varieties of the ogham character. The other group of markings consisted of two ovals, joined end to end 3½ inches long, and below and connected with them is a straight line 1¾ inch in length. This line is both sharp and deep, and with the assistance of a compass I found it to be a meridian line. The oval figure on the right of the line is smaller than the other, representing the earth, as the other does the sun. These oval figures indicate the S.E. and N.W. When complete they form a compass, and this appears to be a proof that the builders of the brochs were sun-worshippers, as the oval figures point in the direction of the horizon where the sun rises on the longest and shortest days of the year. I hope the attention of observers will be directed to the subject, in the belief that the difference of the direction of the ellipticus markings from the present points where the sun rises in winter, may give a pretty certain rule by which the age of the brochs may be astronomically determined.

Hipparchus, the Greek astronomer, having found that the interval between the vernal and autumnal equinox was greater than that between the autumnal and the vernal, conceived the idea that the earth was not, as then supposed, the centre of the sun's orbit, and that the sun moved in a circle, the centre of which was outside that of the earth. Thus, let *c, f, g, h*, be a circle representative of the sun's orbit; *b*, the position of the earth, and *a*, the centre of the circle; *a, b*, will express the amount of eccentricity; *e, d*, the line of the apsides; *f*, the position of the sun at the summer solstice; *h*, its position at the winter; *g*, its position at the autumnal equinox, and *e*, its position at the vernal.[2] On this hypothesis it appears that we not only have the discrepancy it was invented to explain in

---

(1) Such an arrangement of hill and plain are rarely to be found. In the present case both stones are in the midst of a young plantation, which surrounds three sides of the church. The late ingenious Mr. Ferguson, F.R.S., prepared one of these concave Celtic dials, which may be seen at the Manse of Keith, in Aberdeenshire.

(2) *See* the Gallery of Nature, by the Rev. Thomas Milner, p. 12.

a way accounted for, but the idea is suggested of two ovals of different sizes, the axes of which were severally *b, d,* and *b, c.* Ovals, accordingly, were adopted to symbolize the fact. It is this which is symbolized on the lintal of the Cairn Leath Broch, and the presence of the symbol is a guarantee of the great antiquity of the erection. It must have been placed by some sun-worshippers inoculated with ideas from the east, some observers of festivals connected with certain propitious seasons in the worship of the sun. Indeed, from the east came not only the practice and the symbols of sun-worship, but the faith in certain seasons connected therewith, and the devices by which reckonings of time were made at once in the course of the day and of the solar year. The presence of these on ancient monuments is proof of eastern derivation, and the spread of eastern ideas and inventions at an early date among the western nations.

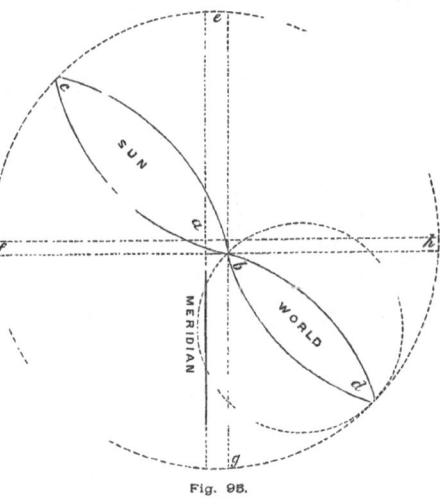

Fig. 95.

It appears that the winter solstice was a festival season as well as the summer, and this, as we see, was especially the case in Caledonia. When the winter solstice was passed it was supposed that as the earth became cold and numb, and began to settle slowly down into a death-like sleep; evil genii being abroad on the earth and having for a season usurped sovereign possession. Hence the revels which prevailed all over the north at this season, and the respect that is paid in them everywhere to the demon powers for the time in the ascendant.

These solsticial points were carefully marked by the eastern priests, and shown by the position of boulders placed outside and at short distances from the sacred circles of stones. These periods of the winter and summer solstice were the times, too, on which the principal Celtic meetings were held, while those of less importance were regulated by the four quarters of the moon.

The reverence with which the sun is regarded by the Asiatic nations in general as the image of the bountiful deity, the giver of life, and light, and heat, lead many of them to regard the time of his daily rising as the most propitious for offering up prayers and oblations; and from an early period they hailed the 22nd of December as, though the shortest, darkest, coldest, and dreariest day of the year, the day from which the sun might be expected daily to regain his strength and revive the face of nature. It is then, too, when the earth begins to wax warm and revive by the sunbeams, that the sun-worshipper specially offers up his prayers and propitiates favours, and already welcomes the far-off harvest amidst festive rejoicings. In a similar spirit, at the new moon's first appearance, the Ramadhan, the great Mohammedan fast, terminates, and food is allowed to be taken, and the voices of the boatmen on the mighty rivers of India may be heard calling—"*Ah bie chaund deca ?*"

(*c.*) *The Lindores Standing Stone* (*Fig.* 96) supplies further evidence of the existence of sun-worship, as well as of the knowledge of the sun symbol in ancient Caledonia. This stone consists of an oblong flat boulder of gneiss rock, apparently brought from the Grampian mountains. It was several years ago removed from a neighbouring eminence called the Kaimes Hill, and fixed for protection in a stone wall by the side of the roadway in the village of Lindores. It is 3 feet 4 inches in height, 1 foot 6 inches in breadth, and 2¼ inches in thickness.[1]

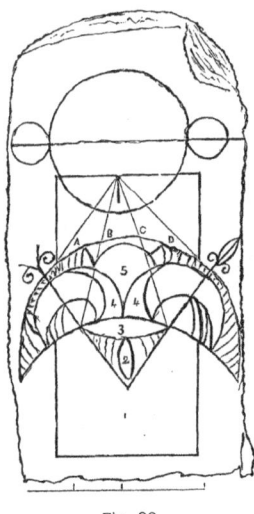

This obelisk is divided into an upper and lower part. The upper part consists of a large incised circle 12½ inches in horizontal and 13 inches in perpendicular diameter, and two small outside circles 3⅛ inches in diameter. These three circles are united by a broad horizontal line that coincides with their horizontal diameters, its one extremity ending in the outer circumference of the left circle, and the other extending beyond the right circle to the edge of the obelisk.[2]

Parallel to this line is another extending in part across and forming the top of a descending parallelogram, from the middle of the upper side of which a deep and broad perpendicular line is incised 2½ inches in length, to about an inch from the bottom of the large circle, and forming the gnomon of a segment underneath. Three inches below the large circle commences the lower half of the obelisk.[3] It consists of a large segment of a circle, extending the breadth of the stone, with two sceptres meeting below the segment and crossing it, while the space within is filled with various semi-circular devices of graceful forms, which are considered to represent severally the five elementary essences that compose the world, viz., earth, water, fire, air and ether.

Fig. 96.

The elemental earth is represented by the entire parallelogram (1), extending from the upper part of the gnomon to near the bottom of the obelisk the water by the perpendicular oval form (2), and the fire by the horizontal, oval (3), both in the apex of the triangle formed by the meeting of the two sceptres, while the large segment contains figures which represent (4) the air and (5) the ether (*Fig.* 97). The resemblance of these figures to the symbols of the several elements on eastern temples is sufficiently striking; the difference anyhow is far less marked than that which exists in the admitted western representations of the sacred animals of the east, such as the elephant;[4] or the Sanscrit elements (*Fig.* 79).

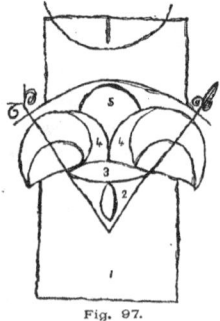

Not only are symbols of the five elements thus incised on the stone, but the divisions of the day into three parts also are as familiar to the ancient Romans. These are indicated by lines descending from the gnomon, two to where the sceptres enter, and two to where they emerge from the segment; these three divisions being represented on the convex side of the segment, the morning one commencing at daybreak from *d* to *c*, the mid-day one from *c* to *b*, and the evening one from *b* to *a*.

Fig. 97.

The power of the elements

---

(1) *See* the excellent History of Lindores Abbey, &c., by Alexander Laing, LL.D., ch. xxiv, p. 316.

(2) These two small external circles most probably represent the moon revolving round the sun, conceived of, in ignorance of gravitation, as kept in its orbit by some imaginary bond denoted by the line.

(3) These peculiar figures are found in various forms on different other stones in Pictland; and on the still more common form of Chatya, at prayer Temples, with the eyes of Providence, and on monuments to the distinguished dead, iu Napaul and other parts of India.

(4) *See* Cunningham's Bilcha Topes.

increases from morning till mid-day, when it reaches its maximum ; and it again diminishes in the evening, and is at its minimum in the dead of night, which is indicated by the crossbars. The greater activity of these elements during the height of the day is expressed by the greater collection of them towards the centre, and their less activity in the morning and evening by their overlapping only in part, and in a more diffuse form, the extremes. Thus is the worship of the elements connected here with the worship of the sun, and the principle of division indicated which regulated the times of religious observance throughout the days of the year, as well as the hours of the day. These were the days in the one, and the hours in the other, when the elemental forces in the sun began to show signs of failing and signs of revival, the failing in each case giving a pledge of resurrection.

CHAPTER IX.

CELTIC USAGES AFTER DEATH IN ASIA AND EUROPE.

IN many parts of Asia and Europe, as among primitive rude races and people everywhere, death, however naturally revolting, was often regarded, or at any rate represented, as a not unhappy transition from one state of being to another. Among the Scandinavian Norse sea-rovers and fighters, as is well known, death was rather courted than dreaded, and the heroic among them believed it to be a seal of their election that they were "chosen to be slain." It was by fighting unto death that life, in their regard, first crowned itself in victory, and with them, as among the ancient Egyptians, no man could be enrolled among the immortals till after he was dead. In India, too, from of old, the imagination, brooding on the unseen hereafter, fashioned pictures to itself of a life of happiness beyond the grave. There, as here, they would be under the rule of the sun-god, for it was a solar hero and son of that god, Yama the name of him, who first trode for all mortals that death valley from whose "bourne no traveller returns." "There," to quote M. Barth, "at the remotest extremities of the heavens, the abode of light and the eternal waters, he reigns in peace and in union with Varuna. There by the sound of his flute, under the branches of the mythic tree, he assembles around him the dead who have lived nobly. They reach him in a crowd, conveyed by Agni, guided by Pushan, and grimly scanned as they pass by the two monstrous dogs, who are the guardians of the road. Clothed in a glorious body, and made to drink of the celestial soma, which renders them immortal, they enjoy henceforward by his side an endless felicity, seated at the same tables with the gods—gods themselves, and adored here below under the name of Fathers. . India, too, was aware of the old myth, which conceives of the stars as the souls of the dead." In Christianity likewise, death is the passport to immortality. Its Author was pre-appointed to be "crucified and slain," and in the centre of its heaven is a lamb "slain from the foundation of the world." But what of the usages after death?

SECTION I.—DISPOSAL OF THE DEAD.

The treatment of the bodies of the dead varied with the intelligence and the general usages, but most of all the religious beliefs, of different races and countries. They were sometimes buried, sometimes cremated, and sometimes otherwise disposed of.

(a) *Burial.*—The ancients having had, as a rule, a sacred reverence for their dead, prepared the corpse for burial by washing it with pure and holy water, and, where possible, perfuming it with spices or otherwise, before it was disposed of. In Caledonia the practice of burial seems to have been the customary mode of disposing of the dead, even prior to the appearance in it of the Aryan race, who brought with them the belief that the body was tenanted by soul which sought, when set free at death, to house itself in and animate some other body. The primitive races buried their dead partly out of a natural wish to remove them out of their sight, and partly in the hope that they might be preserved against the dawn of some resurrection morning. In the latter case especially they would select a clean, often an elevated, and, if possible, a sacred spot, under the protection of some sacred object, such as a tree, a boulder, a circle of boulders, or a tumulus of earth or stones; and to prevent the body from being crushed by the weight of the superincumbent earth, they would lay it out straight, or in a bent or sitting posture, and surround it with erect slab stones, supporting another laid on the top. When laid out straight, the body was usually placed on its back, with the head to the west, in order that the face might look sunward when rising at the resurrection. It was wrapped in clean vestures, and provided with a vessel containing food and drink, in the idea that some nourishment might be needed; while, perhaps, to indicate the rank of the deceased, perhaps out of a feeling that what he had used and worn had now become sacred like himself, his armour and his ornaments were buried along with him. Often, and indeed in general, the grave was not dug; the body was placed on the ground, and some kind of tumulus or a cairn raised over it.

Even those who believed only in a spiritual resurrection, whether a revival, or a survival only, of the soul, used to bury their dead, probably in the belief that the spirit would thereby be entirely secluded and separated from the flesh, and freed as much as by a searching fire-process from all material impurities. The belief that the spirit had at death to undergo a more or less prolonged purgation, prevailed extensively in Asia, and especially among the Celtic nations, and the belief explains certain peculiarities in the burial customs of the latter. It is evident that in India, Persia and Egypt, and among the Celtic races of the East and West, there was a general belief in the immortality of the soul, an idea which, however it might be cherished by individuals, was unknown to the national faith of both Greeks and Romans. With these all anxiety centred in the realization of a time-ideal, and they were completely indifferent to a future existence, so be that they could achieve some worthy success in this. But the Celts not only looked with longing regard to the life beyond, they believed that the soul after death often lingered near the body by way of penance, until mayhap another suited to its deserts, good or bad, should be provided for it to animate. This idea explains the occurrence as mentioned in Chapter IV, of holes or openings in tombs in some countries, that, viz., by them the spirit might have free ingress and egress until it was fully detached from its old, and fitted for its new tenement.

The burial of armour and ornaments along with the bodies of distinguished people might in some cases have been only an expression of extreme veneration, as if no one, after they were done with them, was thought worthy to wear or use them; but they were no doubt deposited there to express the rank and deservings of him who had owned them, and perhaps as proof of a title to some regard at the hands of the Destinies who determine the future. Among the contents of the tombs it is not uncommon to meet with the iron head of a spear, with the wooden shaft of it much decayed, in such a position as to show that it had been laid, as became a warrior under command on his march, over the right shoulder, while scattered about are often heads of javelins and arrows, as if shot at him in battle. At times we come upon a skeleton with a long sword by its side, and over the breast of another lies pathetically the iron umbo or boss of his shield. The ornaments are of various kinds, and often of value, at once as precious jewels or metals and as works of art. They are more suggestive of civic dignity than of personal worth, and argue an ancient respect and reverence for lords and ladies, which runs in the blood of the Celt to this day.

The custom of laying out the body at full length was, as hinted, varied by another, apparently at the suggestion of a certain religious, or, rather, superstitious feeling. It came to be thought that the body ought to be bent on itself, either that it might have, in an expectant reference, the position the embryo had in

R

its mother's womb, the grave being regarded as a second womb; or else that it might be already seated with the face looking out towards the land of the new sun-rising. At the beginning of the bronze period, the dead were buried as in the stone age, but there was a greater tendency towards the construction of sepulchral chambers of stone covered with tumuli, such as might accommodate more than one tenant, each in this case generally bent on itself. The barbarous custom of bending the body was imitated even in Christian times. Dr. Stuart tells, in his "Sculptured Stones of Scotland," of a body in this position, found in a cist at Alloa, which had two crosses on its cover.

(b.) Cremation.—Cremation was general in the East among the ancient Hindus, and likewise the Greeks and Romans, from a belief, in the case of the former, that, by that means, the soul would be completely liberated from the body, as well as purified in the flames of the funeral pyre. The modern Hindus nearly all observe the same practice, some sects being satisfied with scorching the corpse before committing it to its resting-place, and one even burying their dead. The practice with the generality is some such as this: The body, after being cleansed and purified, is conveyed upon the shoulders of men, or upon a cart drawn by oxen, the relatives walking behind, carrying the sacrificial fire, and leading by a rope, tied to its legs, some animal, such as a cow or a kid. When the funeral pile is prepared, the animal is killed for an offering, and the fat cut out and spread as a cover over the head and the face of the corpse. The pile is then fired, and after the body is consumed, the ashes and remains of the bones are collected, one portion being put into an urn to be thrown into a holy river or tank, and the rest taken home for preservation. A piece of ground that is clean, and not overflowed with water, and under a tree perhaps,[1] is selected and prepared for the reception of the remains. Milk and water used to be sprinkled over them, and boulders heaped above them, where boulders could not be found, a mut was selected; and the mourning lasted seven days.

The Aryan and Eastern Celt believed in the power of fire to liberate the soul from its carnal prison-house, and purge it clear of the dross which adhered to it from contact with matter, and they considered it necessary it should be baptized in this element, before it could come to animate a new living organism, and hope to pass into a more exalted and ethereal stage of existence. Both Hindus and Buddhists believe in the transmigration of the soul, or metempsychosis, as it is called, however achieved, and so in the doctrine of a future state, in which the soul animates a new body in a higher or lower grade and condition of existence, according as it has deserved well or ill in the sphere which it has just left.

Cæsar states[2] that the Gauls burned the bodies of their illustrious dead, and consumed along with them their wives and slaves, their hunting dogs, their horses and their armour; and this very custom is met with among many tribes of Hindustan at this day. On the death of the late Maharajah of Tipperah the funeral ceremonies were the same as those which, according to Cæsar, were practised among the ancient Britons. A pile of fragrant wood was erected on the banks of a holy river, and after the body of the deceased had been washed, it was laid upon the pile, the officiating priests being propitiated by the present of a pony, an elephant, and articles of dress. When the fire was applied to the pile to consume the body of the Maharajah, only the interference of Government prevented his wives and slaves from being burnt along with him; but his favourite horse and dogs, along with fighting bulls and game cocks, were led or cast into the flame, that he might have the means of enjoying in the other world the sport he had found so exhilarating in this. When the pile was consumed, the fire was quenched with holy water, or with consecrated wine: and it then became the duty of the nearest relative or most intimate friend of the deceased to collect the ashes which contain the imperishable corporeal navel, a portion of which was buried under a mut or obelisk in the family burying ground; another portion of the ashes of the pile, being put into a kedger pot, and taken often a journey of many days, by the eldest son in deep mourning, to a most sacred part of the holy Ganges, into which it was thrown.

---

(1) *See* 1 Samuel xxxi, 12, 13.   (2) Cæsar, De Bel. Gal. vi, 19.

The fire that consumed the body of the late Maharajah Runjeet Singh was left burning for many days, to permit his favourite females to avail themselves of the privilege of immolating themselves with their lord. I have a sketch of several stones erected to the memory of the petty Rajahs of Kolam, in the Himalaya mountains, where some fifty or sixty unfortunate women sacrificed themselves on the altar of their master. The stones, however, have been thrown down at the instance of the Government, to signify that, however it might have been hitherto, such practices would no longer be tolerated by them.

If it was to express their belief in the continued existence of the soul of the departed that the Celts deposited bread and water in his sepulchre, it is possible that they thought they were providing for the continuity of his employments and enjoyments in the next world when they sacrificed or burnt along with him whatever—such as, his wives, horses, dogs, his weapons, implements and ornaments—ministered to either or both in this.

(*c.*) *Burial-Places and Funeral Rites.*—The desire of the Celtic warrior—not an unnatural one—was that he should be buried in some pleasant place, under the familiar shadow of some tree, or on the bank of some pensive stream. The grassy knoll or quiet dale he knew so well, enamelled with the violet, the primrose and the homely "gowan," and fanned by the gentle evening breeze, might well seem a fitting resting-place for the body of one whose spirit was henceforth to roam in a heaven of eternal bloom and peace. Near this spot, on the occasion of a funeral, feasts were wont to be held, and these were celebrated on purpose to cheer the spirit of the departed at the commencement of the more or less arduous journey ahead, before it could hope to reach the land of the blessed on the far-off western slope of the world.

There was a belief among some rude tribes that if a person fell into dotage before he died, he would enter the next world as an infant; and it sometimes happened that old people verging on decrepitude, in the fear of this doom, begged their relatives to strangle, or otherwise despatch them, that they might enter on the future life in the full possession of their faculties. It seems as if it were by the wish of the deceased that the faithful dog or horse was sacrificed to bear them company, as also that a hole or opening should be left in the sarcophagus for the exit of the spirit, and provision made in or near the grave against possible thirst or hunger.

(*d.*) *Mourning.*—The colour of the mourning dress worn by the relatives of the deceased varies, according to religious feeling chiefly, in different countries and among different people. The Egyptians, as the Jews did, wear yellow, the colour of the autumn grain, and the symbol of fading; the Ethiopians, brown, the hue of the earth, whence all things come and to which they all return, and the symbol of the vanity of life; the Chinese, white, the sign of purity, and an expression of the belief that the soul of the departed is now pure from all taint of earthly defilement; while in Christendom the colour is black, as suggestive of a more serious view of the issues of life, as winding up in something which is characterized as "eternal."[1]

In the presence of death the Hindus are in the habit of laying aside their ornaments and ensigns of dignity, cutting off their long hair, allowing it to grow in places where they are in the habit of shaving, discarding their usual clothing for sackcloth, and going without even the luxury of bathing, etc., for from thirty days to two months; and similar customs were also observed by the Romans. Thus, the practice in Asia, as also in Africa, is to disfigure the personal appearance as a token of extreme grief; and this disfigurement was often carried to the extent, in ancient times, of lacerating the face with the nails and pointed instruments, in order that the deity of the nether world might be propitiated by the sight of human blood voluntarily shed in sorrow of spirit.

(*e.*) *Embalming and Entombing.*—The Egyptians, who believed in the immortality of the soul, in early times supposed that it lay asleep for three thousand years, and that then it would resume its former body. This belief led them to preserve the body by embalming—a process which was brought to perfection at a very early

---

(1) Isaiah xxxviii, 10–12.

period, the emperors and those of sacerdotal rank having spared no expense in perfecting it—so that the body might remain unchanged during the long period it was to continue unconscious, before being awakened by the call of Osiris to immortal life. The great pyramid of Cheops, which according to the lowest computation dates centuries before Abraham came down into Egypt, was prepared to preserve the embalmed bodies of the emperors. The chemical processes used were so perfect that the countenances of some as they appear at the present day might be recognized by their friends and acquaintances, while the hieroglyphics to identify them were executed with a skill that is equally exquisite and expressive.

There are two embalmings mentioned in the Scriptures, viz., those of Jacob and Joseph. Of the former we read that "Joseph commanded his servants, the physicians, to embalm his father; and the physicians embalmed Israel;"[1] and of the latter that, when he died, "they embalmed him, and he was put in a coffin in Egypt."[2] On the death of Joseph, while the Hebrews consented that his body should be embalmed and put in a coffin, and laid in a pyramid, they bound themselves by an oath, that, when they left Egypt, they would carry his bones along with them; and so accordingly, as we read, "Moses," at the exodus, "took the bones of Joseph with him,"[3] reverencing thus the wishes and the ashes of the dead, as a sacred deposit, however little he might respect the Egyptian fancy for embalming, being, while he regarded the body as a temple, the prophet, withal, of the principle that the spirit was its own embalmer.

In the year 1850, I was shown what was alleged to be the mummy of Joseph's wife, the daughter of the high priest of *On*, in the museum of Mr. Leader, missionary and superintendent of the large Coptic school at Cairo, its identity having been proved by the hieroglyphics inscribed on it. A portion of the cerecloth had been removed, so as to expose the hands crossed upon the chest; and on the ring finger of the left hand was a simple gold ring, in which was a small blue stone,[4] the marriage ring placed there by her husband Joseph.

When a corpse was subjected to embalming,[5] certain chemicals were injected into the large vessels, and the body was washed and steeped in natron; the large viscera were removed and placed in different jars under the protection of different gods, and the cavities were filled with resin and bitumen, myrrh, and other balsamic substances and spices. The whole was enveloped in innumerable swathings of prepared linen, and a pictured shell or case protected by scarabæ and various multi-coloured cherubims with overshadowing wings, and inscribed with hieroglyphics. This was kept in a particular part of the house, and was afterwards sent to the family tomb, "the eternal abode;" where it was placed in a niche prepared for it.

The tomb of a nobleman among the Etruscans represented his house; its walls were covered with frescoes of banquets, of games, of animals, and of men, of large dimensions; it was exquisitely furnished with seats, beds, &c., with cups and other household utensils of imperishable bronze, and with vases of more fragile but more richly laboured clay. In the sepulchres of other races, gold and jewelled ornaments, with breastplates, necklaces, earrings and chains, are found, testifying to the wealth, luxury, and taste of those who deposited them, as well as the honour in which the dead was held by them.

The Burmese suppose that the soul is at death conveyed directly to Heaven, and among them the following ceremony is a common one: The corpse is immersed in a box of honey, in which it is kept until a propitious moment occurs for laying it in state. When this has been determined, which it is by an astrologer, the body is removed from the honey, and, after being cleaned, is gilded and decorated. A gigantic altar, 20 feet high, decorated with filagree work and containing gunpowder, is erected in the neighbourhood. From the altar, cords

---

(1) Gen. l, 3.   (2) Gen. l, 26.   (3) Exod. xiii, 19.
(4) I remembered it at first as a simple gold hoop, but now I think of it, it contained a stone.
(5) Embalming by one process cost £600 of our money, besides the cost of gems and gold ornaments: by other processes the cost was much less. (*See* Pettigrew's History of Egypt, under "Mummies.")

stretch to the ground, and the people in the neighbourhood stand round waiting for the ascent of the deceased to Heaven. As the lucky moment approaches the greatest excitement is evinced, and when the time has come the high priest mounts a platform and shouts, "Let the bull away;" when immediately a fiery wheel with the figure of a bull on it whizzes and flies towards the altar for the purpose of exploding the mine of gunpowder. If no result is produced, some decorated firework animal form is ordered to be launched. This is so arranged that when it reaches the altar the gunpowder explodes, and the deceased is supposed to be projected upwards thereby, and may be seen with the sharp eye of imagination ascending to Heaven. The people are persuaded to believe that the material body actually ascends, or, at least, whatever remains, that it is no longer that body.

(*f.*) *Exposure of the Dead on Terraced Towers or Towers of Silence.*—The bodies are placed on the exposed terraces upon the tops of the towers, and left to be devoured by vultures, etc., so that the corporeal part being all eaten away, the spiritual alone may remain for incorporation, pure and simple, in another body. So sacred are such places considered that the priests wear veils over their mouths in order to avoid polluting with their breath the sacred fires kept near such spots.

SECTION II.—SEPULCHRAL MONUMENTS.

The reverence in which the Celts held the dead of their own family and race led them both to the observance of sacred ceremonies in their honour, and to the erection at their graves of diverse memorials. These were—pillar stones, memorial muts and pyramids; kistvaens and cromlechs; cairns and barrows.

(*a.*) *Pillar Stones.*—Regarding the erection of simple boulder stones, in the form of slabs or upright stones, over the graves of individuals, there is no need to say much more. Jacob raised such a stone over the grave of his beloved Rachel.[1] They seem to have been erected extensively for a similar purpose among the Eastern races, and examples abound all over India. On the Khasia Hills, in Bengal, there are many such monuments, with the stones generally in groups of three, the larger in the middle.[2] Their employment for the same purpose was quite common with the ancient Celtic races, among whom the bodies seem always to have been placed in a direction S.E. from the pillar; and the custom still subsists in a modified form among us in the gravestones which are erected in all our churchyards and cemeteries.

Joshua, when crossing the River Jordan, commanded one out of each of the tribes of Israel to take up a stone as large as he could bear upon his shoulders from the midst of the river, and that they should " carry them over with them into the place where they lodged, to lay them down there " as stones with a memorial,[3] and, therefore, deathward reference. The Hebrews set up monuments, doubtless with thoughts of their slain, after their victories—such as Ebenezer, " the stone of help," raised by Samuel.[4] In many parts of Asia and Europe stones were erected to commemorate in a similar reference great victories; but at such an early period that their purpose has been forgotten. The stone set up by Malcolm, son of Kenneth, King of the Scots, to commemorate a victory over the Danes, about A.D. 1008, was of this kind;[5] as also is the stone in the Policy of Belmont Castle, in Strathmore, the spot where Banquo was slain.

In Scotland the Cat[6] stones mark the scene of an ancient battle, just as a stone was set up by the Hebrews to mark the scene of the victory of Mizpeh. Near these there are often cairns, containing cists, with urns and

---

(1) Genesis xxxv, 20.   (2) Journal Asiatic Soc., Calcutta, vol. xiii, pp. 6, 7, 8.   (3) Joshua iv, 5, 6, 7, 8; and other chapters.
(4) 1 Samuel vii, 12.   (5) Gough's Camden, iii, 431.   (6) From the Celtic *cath*, a battle.

human skeletons, fragments of arms, flint arrow-heads, and hatchets.[1] In those of later date various bronze and corroded iron weapons have been found. Recording stones were placed over the graves of chiefs, particularly when they fell in battle. In some cases they have been placed in groups supposed to be expressive of certain events; and near them skeletons are found sometimes lying N. and S., and at other times E. and W., as in India, where the gods are supposed to inhabit the western regions.

Dr. O'Donoghue gives an interesting account of the burial, in A.D. 285, of Fothadh Airgthech, an Irish chief, who had been killed in battle. Along with the body were buried his two silver ornaments, his bracelet *(burine doat)*, and his silver torque, and placed over his breast. Above his grave an earth-fast pillar-stone was erected, and an Ogham inscription was cut on the corner of the stone intimating that Eachard Airgthech[2] lies here.

(*b.*) *Muts and Pyramids.*—In countries where large blocks of stone, such as are generally in memory of the dead, are not to be found, often a pyramidal monument called a mut is erected, usually on the bank of a sacred river; and under it are deposited the fragments of bone and the ashes that remain after the dead body has been purified on the funeral pyre. The Maharajah of Tipperah erected such over the ashes of his predecessor, on the banks of the sacred river Teeta. A mut is often erected over the ashes of a favourite wife, particularly if she had become a Suttee, but in this case the mut is smaller than that of the husband. These monuments often contain a *linga*, the symbol of the generative power of Siva, or Nature, as endowed with self-destructive, self-productive life.

Of the pyramids we have already spoken (p. 34), and defined them to be colossal erections in memory of monarchs, who, regarded as sun-begotten, were considered, when they left the earth, as worthy to be represented to all time in a form suggestive of the setting of a great sun, and such as might be regarded by posterity with something of the awe with which men regard a temple of God and, indeed, ultimately as in honour of Him from whom all light comes, however dark and struggling. They have, doubtless, also an astronomical reference, placed as they are with their angles towards the four cardinal points, in the neighbourhood of temples, with star delineations, and among a people who first taught astronomical science to the Greeks.

(*c.*) *Kistvaens*[3]—The Cist- or Kist-vaens, or Stone Coffins, are formed of two oblong flat stones, vertically placed, with one or more laid across, the corpse inside being uncremated. Cists or coffins of the Anglo-Romans and Anglo-Saxons are found under monoliths, or large single upright stones; others beneath tumuli, with Runic, Ogham, or Saxon inscriptions on them. These coffins are composed of flat pieces of stone, some of them of a square form, in which the body was placed, bent double. During the tenth or eleventh centuries the body was burnt, and the ashes placed in urns, which were laid in coffins formed of rough slab-stones; neck-ornaments, weapons, and other articles being placed beside them. Some of the upright stones placed over these graves had curiously interlaced ornaments and small crosses carved on them. The covering stone of the coffin is either flat or coped. In the latter case the ridge is considerably raised and ornamented with zig-zag lines, scrolls, and interlaced patterns, combined with figures of men and animals, often in unnatural and grotesque positions. These decorations on the coffins, and the ornaments and weapons they contain, show a considerable advance in the knowledge of the arts and in the usages of the people. The Romans generally burned their dead; but sometimes they buried them in sarcophagi, or massive stone coffins. In other cases Roman tumuli contain urns with ashes.

Sepulchral caves may come under the same denomination and description of interment. They are found dispersed over the island of Guernsey,[4] in places where there are now no inhabitants; and when found in the

---

(1) Called celts, or flint stones.   (2) Four masters.
(3) From *Kist*, a chest; and *Vaen*, a stone,   (4) Journ. of the Arch. Assoc., vol. i, pp. 106-7.

HISTORY OF PAGANISM IN CALEDONIA.

vicinity of the most ancient sepulchral monuments, they are evidently unconnected with them, and appear to be the remains of a different people. Mr. Lukes examined twenty of these Cists. They are usually of the same construction, consisting of a stone chest, formed of two parallel rows of stones, fixed on their ends and covered by similar flat stones, about 7 feet in length. In these Cists were urns, shaped like barrels or kegs, of black pottery, 7 inches high, and surrounded by hoops or rims; likewise spear heads, fragments of knives, a sword in an iron scabbard, 34 inches long, part of an iron armlet, and a clay bead. No traces of human remains were discovered, but an apparatus, proving that cremation had been the mode of sepulture. The objects in metal proved to be of a later date.

(*d.*) *Cromlechs*[1] *in Asia and Europe.*—The Cromlech generally consists of a large flat stone, resting on three or more flags set up on edge. These stones are placed in a S.E. direction, with the covering stone inclined to the same quarter. This side is sometimes left open, so that the first rays of the rising sun may strike straight upon the grave underneath. Cromlechs, in their simple form, are pretty numerous in wild and retired places in India, and are the work of unknown races, called Pandus, the supposed heroes of the Mahâbharata who, according to Sir W. Elliott, wandered over India during twenty years' exile.[2] Cromlechs are either exposed or covered with earth, and are with and without circles of boulders, and with galleries. They are found in Hindustan, and in the other countries of Asia, in the north of Africa, in the Crimea, in Malta, and Minorca, in Brittany, in France, and the British Islands.

Some cromlechs contain (as *Fig.* 98) a sarcophagus, with the bones of the dead; in others are found urns of red or black glazed pottery, often of graceful shapes, with zig-zag ornaments. The urns, which have been passed through fire, often contain the remains of burnt human bones mixed with ashes and pieces of charcoal, and have beside them iron, and sometimes gold, ornaments, agricultural implements, bells, &c. Some of these monuments are reckoned to be as old as the remains of the Druids in Europe, but others are probably of much more modern date, as of much greater elegance of form, and ornamented with representations of processions of led horses accompanied with musical instruments.

Fig. 98.

As Mr. Brucks' extensive investigations have showed, there are six varieties of cromlechs in the Nielgherries. One kind called *Agârams* has small circles, which are attributed to the Hindus, who to the present day make circles round the graves of their dead. Another kind of cromlech is called Birakala (heroes'-stones). These are monuments to great men, and are some of them evidently modern.[3] Some are surrounded by one or two circles of small stones, and cases occur where small round holes are found in one of the upright stones, as in one of the sides of the cromlech on the sea margin which is near Raidrogg (*Fig.* 99). This is one of those already referred as probably intended for the passage out and in of the soul, which was believed to linger in its disembodied state near the remains of the body after death.[4] The stones of these cromlechs are more carefully rounded than those in European examples, and some are ornamented by designs on the western end. The one near Raidrogg had representations of elephants and figures with bows and arrows. In the rectangular chamber thus formed, earthen vessels were found, containing the ashes of the dead. The chamber of this one looked towards the east, and had a circle of stones round it.

Fig. 99.

---

(1) From *crom*, bent, curved, or rounded; and *lêh*, a slate. In Cornish a Cromlech is a bent slab.
(2) Page 240 of the Pre-historic Archæology for 1868.
(3) Caldwell, p. 593.
(4) "Some of these cromlechs were covered with a cairn."—Forbes, Early Races, vol. ii, p. 281.

These examples prove that cromlechs in Asia served for the reception of the remains of the dead; and those containing the remains of remarkable and holy personages were resorted to as places of supplication and prayer, as they are also in Europe. They were probably erected in the polished stone period.

There is a cromlech on one of the hills, forming a part of Orme's Head, at Llanduno, in a rich valley, on the left of the copper mines, in a field called *Mass-y-facroll*, or rather, *Maes-y-fagwyr-allt*, Stone of the female Greyhound—in allusion to the British *Ceres* or *Keridwen*, who was symbolized by the female greyhound—which consists of four upright stones, with a large capestone, a stone being wanting in the E.S.E. direction to fill up the enclosure. In this direction the hills declined, so that the rising sun could be seen at the solstice, while the mountain surrounded the three other sides. What was peculiar was a tumulus joining the cromlech on the west, although there was no appearance of a circle of stones. "Some years ago many urns were found in this cairn,"[1] containing the remains of human bodies. This is a peculiar arrangement of the cromlech and the cairn. The open side of the cromlech was where the priest offered up his morning prayers.

The cromlech has had its day; it degenerated, at length, into a stone coffin, which has varied in different ages and among different classes of society, the higher classes leading the fashion, and the lower classes following in a simpler form. In these coffins (kistvaens) are found bronze bracelets in the form sometimes of a chain, or of thick solid rings not completed.

In Europe the cromlechs occur in all forms, the simple, the roofed-in, and the chambered. The simple is the well-known square block resting upon its supports. Examples of this are the "Kits Cotty House" cromlech, in Kent, and the "Rostellan," in Ireland.[2] Neither seem to have ever been covered with earth. The former is on an elevation, and the latter is now within the sea margin. The capestones are supported by perpendicular slabs of stone, earth-fixed; and the fourth side is open, as in those of South India, and face the S.E. or E.S.E. to receive the first rays of the rising sun. Both are supposed to have contained the remains of distinguished dead, and at them prayers and sacrifices had been offered up.

Some cromlechs had a conical covering of earth; and this tumulus erelong came to be chosen as the burial place of the family in possession of the property, out of a desire to deposit the remains of their dead in what might seem already consecrated ground. The cromlech of the Phœnix Park, Dublin, is a good example of these. Here the tumuli were 120 feet in circumference, and 15 feet high. The spaces between the stones of the cromlech were filled up with small stones. In the recess, too, some perfect skeletons were found, along with the tops of the femora of another, and a single bone, supposed to be that of a dog. The skulls were towards the north, and the bodies were bent.

Chambered cromlechs are confined chiefly to Scotland, Ireland and France. Some of them are walled with upright slabs, and covered with a roof of one or more stones, and are entered by a passage of some length, formed similarly of upright stones, sometimes sculptured. The central chamber is from 20 to 30 feet long, about 5 feet wide, and 4 feet high, while the walls of the passages into it are 2 feet apart, and composed of upright stones placed nearly close together, surmounted by a roofing of flat stones. In France, some of the chambers are "free-standing," that is, formed of upright stones and a flat roof, resting on the natural surface without any artificial envelopment of earth. Others have roof stones, supported at one end on one or more uprights, while the other end rests on the ground. These are called "*demi-dolmens*," or, in English, "earth-fast cromlechs." Similar structures have been found erected on the tops of artificial mounds, and appear to have been either wholly or partially exposed to view, or else covered with earth, so as to form a tumulus, with the chamber entirely concealed from sight.

---

(1) *See* "Black's Guide to Wales," p. 49.
(2) The peninsula on which Rostellan Castle is built derives its name from *Ros*, the Celtic for temple, and *Delawin*, a plain—the temple of the plain.

In the specimens of sculptured cromlechs in Brittany, the props of the cromlechs often remain untouched, while the surface of the other stones is elaborately scored with curved semicircular concentric lines, often broken or in zigzag or chevron figures. One example shews a pattern resembling an olive branch; and in others, there are central cups and circles with the horse-shoe figure, in duplicate, surrounded in double cartouches. In Brittany, these lines form the figure of a stone celt.[1]

In a cromlech near Duffryn, in Wales, there are lines on the prop stones; and of that called Dolar Marchaud, near Loch Mariaker, the props are elegantly engraved on the inner and upper surfaces and edges; while the pattern on the under surface of the large cape-stone is in relief. In others, the blocks covering the floor are engraved.

In making a road along the top of Coolrus Hill, Parish of Ballyadams, Queen's County, Ireland, the cape-stone of a cromlech slipped down into a square pit, 5 feet deep, faced with large flags and dry masonry, the upper edge of the flags being level with the surface of the hill. When a portion of the pit was uncovered to the north and the east, a passage was found, like a gully, 3 feet square, extending 9 feet in an easterly direction from the pit, and opening on the surface of the hill. It was formed of flags and dry masonry, well built, and covered over. It was cut off from communication with the pit by the large flag, which formed the eastern side. Adjoining the western side two flags, about 3 feet high, were firmly fixed in the earth. Close to these were found the calcined bones of some large animal. At 120 feet from the cromlech formerly stood a circle of upright flagstones, and to the S.E. of the cromlech was a rude stone coffin, containing burnt bones. This cromlech seemed never to have been disturbed, and has several peculiarities. It was built with dry stones, a mode of construction which indicates a great antiquity—according to Petrie's supposition, before the 4th century. There was no urn, but the calcined bones of a long animal. There was a passage communicating with the outer world but subsequently closed with a flat stone, as in the Man of the Orkneys, and probably in the example at Callernish, in the Island of Lewis. This must have been for the purpose of admitting of spiritual communication. The circle appeared to have been sepulchral.

The Proleck stone stands in a nearly level field, a little more than three miles N.E. of Dundalk, near Ballymascoulan House. It is of granite, and is popularly known as "the big stone." The top rock is 13 feet long, 8⅓ feet wide, and about 4 feet thick. Allowing 12 cubic feet to the ton, it will weigh over thirty tons. Its direction is nearly N.W., with a slope to the westward. Supporting the top are three rocks, of which the largest is 7 feet high, 4 feet 8 inches wide below and 2 feet 8 inches thick. The other two are slightly smaller. There are several large stones about the monument, but they do not appear to be laid in any order. In the same field a few perches eastward is a parallelogram formed by large stones, which stand more than 2 feet above the level of the field, and enclose a space 20 feet long and 4 feet wide. The direction is east and west, and each end is closed by a large stone. The one at the west end is 7 feet wide, over 2 feet thick, and 3 feet high. The one at the east end is somewhat smaller. At this end there is a roof rock which measures 8 feet by 5, and is more than 2 feet thick. The rest of the space is uncovered, but many large stones are lying about outside; and there are other masses inside these. "giant graves" which are probably the remains of other roof rocks.

In some cases not only the cromlech, but also the space around it, was regarded as sacred, and marked out as such, by being surrounded with one or more circles of boulders. There is a fine example called Labacally, or the Hag's Bed, near Fermoy, in Ireland, and another at Dunmore, in County Waterford. The latter has several peculiarities. It is situated on the top of a hill and has been surrounded by a circle (22 feet in diameter) of packed boulders. The cromlech itself stands in the centre of this, and is formed of large flat boulders, which

---

(1) Davis' Arch. Trea. vol. xxv. p. 188.

enclose a space 20 feet long, 4½ feet wide at one extremity, and 3⅛ feet at the other. The widest end is closed by a large stone, the narrowest is open. The outside of the props is packed with other stones. We may well suppose this to have been the burying-place of a chief and his family.

Section III.—Cairns, Tumuli, Mounds or Barrows.

This is a class of monuments that is common to Celtic India and Europe, and consists of mounds of stone or earth. The Celtic cairn proper is a heap of stones and earth piled together, often by way of memorial of some kind, and the Celtic name for it is *crug*—heap or mound. Here the ancient Britons buried their dead, the body, when uncremated, being placed on its left side, or in a sitting position. This was the simple tumulus. Another variety contained a gallery with a circle of boulder stones, as seen in the tumulus at New Grange.

Cairns are among the earliest structures of antiquity, and are sometimes[1] found 60 feet in diameter and 16 feet high. The stones are of every size, and the whole is covered with several feet of earth and finished with a coating of sod. In constructing them a deep trench was dug round the spot, the earth thrown inwards, and stones heaped upon the earth ; and near the summit of the stones, the cist or stone coffin, formed of long unhewn flags, was placed. Sometimes this was only 3 feet 2 inches broad and deep, so that the contained body must have been forcibly bent on itself. In other cases, the coffin was of the full length, with an urn containing ashes; or the coffin was only 2 feet square, of flag-stones on their edges, with one to form the cover, and contained an urn with the mouth downwards, resting either upon the ground or upon a flag-stone.

These conical stone-heaps or earth-mounds are met with as memorial erections in most countries. Among the Hebrews a cairn of stones represented the judgment of stoning, due, in their code of justice, to particular offences, especially breaches of faith between man and man, or man and society. It appears to have been a cairn that was erected as a memorial of the covenant between Laban and Jacob, as if to intimate their mutual consent that such a heap should mark the corpse of him who should break the engagement. When Achan was found guilty of concealing the spoil of the enemy, and so wantonly disregarding the divine command, he and his were "stoned with stones and burned with fire," and "over him a great heap of stones," as a sign of abhorrence, "was raised unto this day."[2] It was so, also, that the Israelites dealt with the King of Ai, after they hanged him,[3] and with Absalom, after he had been slain in his rebellion against his father. "They took Absalom, and cast him into a great pit in the wood, and laid a very great heap of stones upon him."[4]

These cairns and barrows are a third class of monuments found in Hindustan, resembling those of the Celts. Many of them, however, are piles, not of stones loosely thrown together, as with us and among the Jews, but regularly built, and are, in fact, structures of masonry, some solid and some hollow, according to the custom of the tribe and its advancement in art. The Buddhist tope is precisely analogous to the British barrow, such as we find among ourselves in many quarters reared to the memory of some distinguished member of a clan ; and we may, therefore, conclude that the two have a common origin and express a common thought. Like the Eastern sun-worshippers, the Celts had their high places, on the top of which they raised stone-piles to commemorate some great event worthy of conspicuous regard, and, as it were, of being looked upon by the sun, as if those who erected the rude heap meant to say such is our esteem of what it commemorates ; let the sun-god hold it in equal honour.

---

(1) Wilson's Prehistoric Annals of Scotland, p. 59.   Worsaal's Hand-book of Irish and Danish Antiq.—Translated by Thoms.
(2) Joshua vii, 25 26.   (3) Joshua viii, 29.   (4) 2 Sam., xviii, 17.

In Europe the cairn on the hill-top usually commemorates some remarkable event, one worthy not only of all honour, but sometimes of all dishonour. Often it marks the grave of some chief or distinguished personage who fell near the spot, or on it, and was interred there, perhaps also to secure the body from molestation and depredation. In later times it was the custom, both in Scotland and Ireland, to bury the body in a churchyard, and then the cairn on the height was a token to all in the light of the sun of the deep and wide-spread regard with which his neighbours cherished his memory. The cairn, however small it might be at first, was often enlarged by those who passed the spot throwing another and another stone on it, out of the respect to the departed. Hence the saying in Scotland: "I'll add a stane to your cairn."[1] As civilization advanced in Celtic countries, the cairn assumed the form of a building with a spire, such as a pagoda in India, a tower in Babylon, a pyramid in Egypt, and open stones pillar in China, on which incense and sacrifices are offered as to the dead.

Tumuli may be divided into three varieties—the oval, the round, and the covered chambered cromlech. Other varieties have been enumerated, but some of these are only the results of weathering, while others are the merely whimsical device of individuals and express no public thought or conception.

(1) The oval or long tumuli are constructed of loose stones or earth heaped over human remains, the shells being of the doliocephalic, or long-headed type. The individuals of the race to which these belonged seem to have measured about 5 feet 5 inches in height, and to have had soft round pleasing features. They were probably of Southern origin. Associated with the remains are flints and bone implements and weapons of delicate manufacture, bones of animals, such as cattle and horses, and traces of fire, produced perhaps by the process of cremation or acts of sacrifice. There are indications of cannibalism, broken bones and skulls, as if the remains of some funeral feast. There are no traces of the use of metals.

(2) The round tumuli are numerous, and are placed on heights, sometimes singly and sometimes in groups. They were the sepulchres of persons of distinction, as well as of their families and immediate dependents, sometimes a skull occupying a central position. The remains are those of individuals of the brachycephalic, or round-headed race, and sometimes the bones are more or less burnt. The unburnt bodies are generally interred with their clothes on, in a bent position, in a stone cist, while the remains of those whose bodies had been burnt are found deposited in urns. Both are accompanied by the broken bones of animals—marrow-bones split for the marrow—chipped flints, frequently pottery and implements, etc. With the male remains are found stone axes, bronze swords, spear-heads, and other weapons, and with the remains of women, stone rubbers, or corn crushers, jet and amber necklaces, and other ornaments. The animal remains include the ox (*Bos longifrons*), the red and roe deer, the goat, and wild swan, &c. This round-headed race probably came from the North, as the long-headed from the South. They were probably 5 feet 8 or 9 inches in height, of warlike appearance, with large mouths, high angular cheekbones, and projecting eyebrows. They belong to a race which disappeared a century or two before the occupation of Britain by the Romans.

(3) The chambered cromlechs, as already described, are built of dry walls, covered with large flat stones, and often contain the remains of several individuals of both sexes and of all ages, with sometimes the face of the individual so placed as to meet the rising sun, some of the bodies straight, others apparently in a sitting position; and the whole structure had been covered with earth.

There are stones under the tumulus so arranged as to protect the body from injury, and also to preserve the earthen vessels containing food and drink, and other articles belonging to the deceased, deposited along with the body. The weapons and implements, as well as the earthen vessels, afford us a means of judging of the age of the barrow, and of the state of the arts at the time of the burial. Conclusions as to the age of the barrows

---

[1] See Description of British Barrows, by Sir R. Colt; Hoare's Annals of Wiltshire; also Rev. J. D. Preston's Nova Britannica; and Tacit. de Moribus.

drawn from their contents must, however, be made very cautiously, as they may contain articles belonging to a previous age, as they have been often added to since first created, and as bodies may have continued to be buried in the same barrows through a long period.

There were three forms of earthern vessels or urns used by the Celts, viz., cinerary urns, drinking cups, and incense cups, all of which are found in their graves. The cinerary or sepulchral urns are of unglazed, sunburnt earthenware, and have wide mouths. They are from 18 inches to 2 feet 3 inches in height, and have been formed by the hand, without a lathe. They generally lie about 2 feet below the surface, and rest, as already remarked, in an inverted position upon a stone. They are mostly rude in form and are ornamented with various patterns, drawn on them, when the clay is soft, with a piece of hard pointed wood. At a later period the cist and cinerary urn were decorated with a rude attempt at sculpture, and inscriptions even are sometimes met with. These urns were often used to deposit relics. " To distinguish places of sepulture in pre-historic times," says Mr. Ferguson, "the tumulus or tomb was the principal form of architectural development, and the object of special veneration, not only in northern and western Asia, but in Etruria, and as far west as the British Isles; wherever, indeed, ancestral worship was the prevailing form of religious belief. In India, the Buddhists conformed to the long-established practice of burning the dead, and the tomb became, not the receptacle of a body, but of a relic."[1]

The last tumulus found in England was the mound of earth formed in 1245, in Westminster, between the high altar and the Lady Chapel, on which was erected the tomb of the Confessor.[2]

A large ancient tumulus in Ireland, which I examined, consisted of a number of limestone boulders, upon which a coating of earth was spread. Under these, two weather-worn flagstones were found 3 ft. 7 in. by 2 ft. 6 in. and 6 in. thick. On removing the western flagstone there were found the remains of calcined human bones, with pieces of charcoal, ashes, and clay, resting on a flag of sandstone, which showed signs of having been subjected to the action of fire. The second flagstone slab being removed, a kistvaen came into view. Its sides were composed of irregular sandstone flags placed on their edges. The shape was an irregular pentagon; measured from angle to angle, its sides were from 3 ft. 9 in. to 2 ft. 6 in., and the depth was 2 ft. 3 in. It contained the remains of a human skeleton, evidently interred in a sitting position with the face to the N.E., with an urn of baked clay, which had been originally placed in the lap of the person. The skull was of the long-headed type, and had belonged to an individual of low intellect. The angles of the lower jaw were widely apart. The eastern chamber contained another skeleton with the face to the S.W. The skull was brachycephalic, and was beautifully symmetrical; the superciliary arches were rather full, the orbits were full and rather shallow, the nasal bones were vertical, and the chin beautifully formed, square and rather deep, the mouth was slightly projecting. The body was that of a person about sixty years of age. Sacrificial offerings were often made in connection with these interments, and were as follows: The kistvaen was first constructed, the body deposited in it, and a large flagstone for the sacrifice laid on the top; then the funeral pyre was erected over it, and, after the victims were slain, their blood was poured out and their bodies placed on the top, after which torches were applied, and the rites of sepulture consummated. The victims being consumed, the ashes were collected on the lid and enclosed in the urn. Classical authors confirm the tradition of this cruel custom. Homer makes Achilles sacrifice twelve Trojan youths to the manes of his friend Patroclus, who had been killed by Hector before the walls of Troy, and accompanied the oblation with the slaughter of a number of sheep and oxen, four of his favourite horses, and two of his dogs. And Virgil represents Æneas as sacrificing four of the sons of Ufens, and four youths from Sulmo to the manes of his young friend Pallas, who had been killed by Turnus, and as slaying in sacrifice sheep, oxen, and swine.

(1) History of Architecture, vol. ii, p. 477. (2) Dean Stanley's History of the Church, vol. iii, p. 127.

HISTORY OF PAGANISM IN CALEDONIA.

BOOK II.

History of Paganism in Caledonia.

BOOK II.

CHAPTER I.

BUDDHISM.

IN this book we propose to give an illustration of the nature, and a brief sketch of the history, of Buddhism, its rise and decline in Hindustan, and its extension to other countries, as well as its organization, its institutions, its symbols, and its sacred places. We have especially to note how its tenets had spread among many nations in the East and West, and at length reached the shores of Britain, being taught and in a fashion accepted in Pictland, as sculptured stones which still remain testify, inscribed as they are, among other symbols, with such as are of Asiatic origin and belong originally to monuments erected expressly in connection with the Buddhist faith.

SECTION I.—THE RISE, SPREAD AND DECLINE OF BUDDHISM IN HINDUSTAN, WITH ITS EXTENSION TO OTHER LANDS.

The chief tenets of Buddhism bear a marked resemblance in many respects to the beliefs of the Druids, who seem, as the Buddhist in substance did, to have taught the immortality of the soul and its transmigration from one body to another, to have looked at things in general in the same light, and to have run up all to the sovereign omnipotence of one God. We possess but a scanty acquaintance with the Druidical system; but it would seem to have consisted of an imperfect knowledge of geometry, astronomy, geography, astrology, medicine and physics, the latter resembling in its principles the system of Pythagoras. The Druids persuaded their followers that they were able to doom them to an inferior grade of being, that they could cause as well as cure disease, and that they had power, if not to control, at least to forestall the future. They believed in a providence of God in the world, and, in connection with the soul's immortality, they taught a future state of rewards and punishments. Courage and patriotism they especially inculcated; that men should do good and fear no evil; only fear God and shame the devil. The belief in metempsychosis made them shrink from eating any food that contained life. Like the Brahmins, they transmitted the precepts of their religion in verse without committing them to writing, and they prohibited the common people from learning the sacred language in which they were composed. Their wisdom was summarized in metrical sayings, which were committed to writing, the greatest of them all, perhaps, being the bardic motto: "Truth against the world." They grouped men into three classes: the god-like man, "who does good for evil;" the man-like man, who does good for good and evil for evil; and the devil-like man, who does evil for good. The two latter represented the wisdom of the world; it was a superior wisdom which laid down the maxim, Do good for evil. According to them there were three unseemly thoughts: thinking ourselves wise; thinking every one else unwise; and thinking all we like becoming in us.

From the fragments we possess of the writings of Porphyry,[1] we find that he divided the philosophers of India into Gymnosophists, or Braehmanes, and Samanæi, or Buddhists. The former were a sacred class by birth, and the latter by election, consisting as they did of those who gave themselves up to the cultivation of sacred learning. These last, he tells us, lived in monasteries and temples constructed by rich individuals, had abandoned their families, were summoned to prayers by the ringing of a bell (a gong), and lived upon rice and fruits.[2] Cyril of Alexandria mentions that the Samanæi were the philosophers of the Bactrians; and St. Jerome, who, like Cyril, lived at the end of the fourth and beginning of the fifth century, and was acquainted with the Buddhist religion, adds that "Buddha was believed to have been born of a virgin, and to have come forth from his mother's side." From Cyril of Jerusalem and Ephraim, writers of the middle of the fourth century, we learn that Buddhism was the taint of some of the heresies of the early Christian church, especially the Manichæan; while the former expressly alleges that the Greek Terebinthus, which in the Syrian language signifies Buddha,[3] was the preceptor of Manis, the founder of the Manichæan sect. The latter terms it the Indian heresy.

Buddhism is a native of the soil of India, and it owes its origin, as an organization anyhow, to a reactionary movement against the arrogance and tyranny of the Brahmins, or priestly caste. The claims and conduct of this caste had become so intolerable to a large body of their countrymen, that the latter, when appealed to by a teacher whom they could trust, boldly threw off the yoke they imposed upon them, and embraced a system that was at once more humane in spirit and catholic in scope. The author of this new faith and his first disciples were distinguished for their serene intelligence, their fervid zeal, and their lofty, self-denying moral character. By their firm moderation and equable human wisdom they won the confidence and moulded the character of large masses, and whole tribes of their fellow-countrymen. They shed on all hands of them an influence for good, which, however it may be repudiated in name, can never be challenged in reality, the results of it remaining to this hour, and still visibly affecting the destiny and the character of whole nations of men over a large section of the world—one-third, it is said, of the population of the globe.

Under this new influence, and after no small efforts to suppress its action, the sect, which thus originated, gradually asserted its independent existence, and declared its indifference, and consequent opposition, to the class which had ruled the situation before, the Brahminical caste, with all its high priestly pretensions. They declared off from the old gods and off from their worship, and began, under the leadership of a body of thoughtful, resolute men, not merely to accept for themselves, but to promulgate to others, a new faith, a new world-religion, founded on universal love and goodwill, the practice of virtue, and the administration of justice.

---

(1) Schwanbeck's Megasth. Indica, p. 20.; Lassen. Ind. Alt. ii, 209, 663.
(2) Prof. Wilson's Works, vol. ii, p. 314; Prinsep's Indian Antiquities, by Thomas, F.R.S., vol. i. p. 123; Asiatic Researches, ix, p. 215.
(3) Suidas calls Mania Brahman a pupil of Buddha, formerly named Terebinthus.

They ignored the supremacy of the " thrice-born," and the privilege of caste, and affirmed the freedom of the will, and the sole absolute divinity of right moral action. The question about God, and even about the soul, they held in abeyance; with them it was solely a question about conduct, and the life of the spirit, as alone determinative of itself and fortunes, as alone absolute, that holds within itself at once the power of fate and the power of freedom, so that it can, as nothing else can, decide for itself whether its course shall be an upward one or a downward one, good or evil, for ever.

Sakyamuni[1] (*i.e.*, the solitary of the Sakyas), of the family of the Gautamas, a Rajput clan of northern India, was the founder of this new religion,[2] and as such may be regarded as the regenerator of his country, and ranked with Solomon as one of the great teachers of practicable wisdom to the race. The one flourished one thousand, the other five hundred years before the Christian era.[3] Both innovators belonged to the highest ranks of their respective nations, but while the one retained his wealth and royal degree, the other, though born to royalty, cast aside all the advantages of his position, and became a monk, trusting for his success as a teacher to the truth of his doctrines, the virtue of his life, and the fervour of his piety. The one was an Israelite and the other a Hindu.[4] The one was surnamed the Wise; the other was called Buddha, the awakened, the enlightened.[5] Both were the favourite sons of their fathers, both bore the marks of their high destiny in the beauty of their person and the majesty of their mind, and both were Orientals, and imbued with the spirit and cast in the mould of the East. Each had an intense conviction of the truth and moral power of his teaching, and each thought and felt and said what was nothing private or mystic, but must find an echo in the hearts, as it should an expression in the lives, of all regenerate, and even intelligent men.

Such a revelation was the teaching of Sakyamuni to those who first embraced it, that it seemed to them that the teacher could be no ordinary mortal, but a divine incarnation, until at length he was fabled to have been miraculously conceived, and the son, therefore, of no mere man. His soul, it was said, approached her who was to be his mother, riding upon a white elephant, (Aragavarta, " the spotless one") and entered her womb, that he might one day be born, and become a great saint, to teach mankind how in self-reliance to attain intellectual and spiritual freedom, the perfection of virtue here, and of bliss hereafter, as a state which constituted the destiny, and was within the reach of every rationally endowed creature, if not of every living thing.

Such a "proper child" was he, and so beloved by his father, that every precaution was taken from the day of his birth to guard him from harm and the very sight, as well as experience, of everything evil and undesirable, while every form of pleasure which sense could enjoy and royalty procure was provided for him. His early playmates were the young, the handsome, and the high-born; all his fancies were humoured and all his desires gratified. Soon, however, the gratification of these began to lose their zest, and though new desires were called into play by the invention of new pleasures, these, too, as in Faust, yielded only satiety, and there was an end to all satisfaction from such sensual sources.

Placed at length under the care of a wise and pious preceptor, the young prince one day expressed a wish to visit the outside world, and he asked his royal parent if he might be allowed to go with his tutor, and see what was to be seen in the city. To this wish the king gave his consent, but he first issued a decree that every object which might suggest the existence of evil, in the forms especially of decay, disease and death, might be

---
(1) A muni is an ecstatic enthusiast.
(2) It has been defined to be "monastic asceticism in morals and philosophic scepticism in religion;" and it is so, if by the one we mean severe moral discipline apart from the world, and by the other ignorance of and indifference to the divine above us out of respect to the divine within us, with which alone, according to the constitution of our being, the Buddhists would say, we have any dealings. *See* Gen. Cunningham, Bhilsa Tope, p. 35, *et seq.*
(3) Sakyamuni, it is now pretty certainly ascertained, died between 482 and 472 B.C.
(4) He was the royal son and heir of Suddhodana, King of Magadha, of the line of the Sakyas, who reigned at that time on the banks of the Rohini, a branch of the Gogra, in a district 137 miles north of the sacred Brahminical city of Benares.
(5) This was the name Sakyamuni gave himself on the occasion when the light first dawned on him.

removed out of the way, so that he might not see them. This decree it was impossible to comply with, and as the two wandered about, they encountered at one point an old man bent down with the infirmities of age, at another a wretch pining under the pangs of hunger, and at another a sick man moaning under the scourge of disease. Thus the prince first saw how vain and fleeting was all the solid-seeming pageant of life, and how bitter erelong might become to him the already insipid fruit of the tree of existence. As they proceeded along, they fell in with a corpse borne on a bier, with weeping friends around it, tearing their hair, covering their heads with ashes, and smiting their breasts with anguish. At the sight he was seized with amazement, and exclaimed, "Alas! and do age and disease only end in dissolution? Is life itself as evanescent and vain as enjoyment? Can it be there is no deliverance from a fate so fearful?"

While absorbed in meditation, thus suggested, on the vanity and nothingness of life, a mendicant stepped up, wearing the dun garb of his order, and carrying an alms-bowl in his hand, yet looking calm and serene, with his eyes fixed on the ground, and with the mild air of sublime resignation. This apparition arrested the regard, and engaged the inquisitive attention of the prince. In answer to his enquiries, he was told that the man before him was a monk, who, having renounced all the pleasures of sense, now devoted himself to a life of austerity as the only pathway to at once a worthy life in this world, and an immortal one of blessedness in that which is to come. Now and henceforth the most pleasing objects of sense lost for the prince all their charms, and the question of questions which now began to engross all his attention was the high one of life eternal and death eternal. At length, his thoughts took so far articulate shape that he exclaimed: "Nothing I now see is stable on earth, nothing is real in it! Life is as a spark kindled by rubbing together two pieces of wood, of which the wise man asks in vain, ' Whence comes it? and whither goes it?' If I could attain the knowledge and art of wisdom in the way of life, it would bring light to me such as I might show to my neighbours, and would deliver the world from all this misery!"

The king tried in vain to woo his son from such weak speculations, and he had him married at sixteen to a princess, who brought him a boy, whom it was expected he might love as a father, and train to become a tutor of others. The prince, however, growing more and more dissatisfied with this life, resolved, at length, to throw up his birthright, and exchange the robes of royalty for the coarse clothing and the life of a solitary hermit. One midnight, accordingly, when only twenty-nine years of age, he left the palace of his youth for the lonely desert, carrying with him a hatchet to chop wood for his fire, a needle to mend any rent in his garments, and a filter to strain the water he drank, lest, in his drinking, he should swallow any animalculi. For seven years he meditated in the desert on the mystery of life, on the means of attaining beatitude, and on the art of teaching mankind how to escape the sufferings of existence; and the result to which he in the end arrived was this :—The suffering and entangled soul has a long and a hard battle to fight before it can break the spell and destroy the power of existence, and through stage after stage of being is it fated to pass before it can attain eternal beatitude, the blessed Nirvana, where it will be as Buddha is, beyond the region of change, and therefore that of sorrow, in the enjoyment of everlasting peace and felicity. All this misery comes with desire, and it ends only with its annihilation. Except in the death of self, first of all, there is no sight or enjoyment of life everlasting, and to achieve this first great step in life it may take æons on æons of time, and migration after migration through the successive spheres of existence.

It is here that the parallel between Buddha and Solomon comes in: it was to the study and teaching of wisdom as it bore on the immediate problem of life that Solomon, though not out of relation, but in relation with the world, likewise devoted himself. "Hear, ye children," he says, "the instruction of a father. I was my father's son, tender and only beloved in sight of my mother." "Get wisdom (*i.e.*, religion), get understanding; forget it not." "Forsake her not, and she shall preserve thee; love her, and she shall keep thee; exalt her, and she shall promote thee; she shall bring thee to honour, when thou dost embrace her. She shall give to thine head an ornament of grace; a crown of glory shall she deliver to thee." "I have taught thee in the way of wisdom; I have led thee in right paths. When thou goest, thy steps shall not be straitened; and when thou runnest, thou shalt not stumble. Take fast hold of instruction; let her not go; keep her, for she is thy life." "My son, keep thy heart with all diligence, for out of it are the issues of life. Put away from thee a froward mouth; perverse lips put away from thee. Let thine eyes look right on; ponder the path of thy feet." "Turn not to the right hand nor to the left." "Remove thy foot from evil." These, too, are the warnings of Sakyamuni; this the wisdom, hard to learn, which yet he declared to man as the light of the world. Nor did his message fall only on deaf ears: a community, which became a church of the truly militant type, took it up and preached it, as alone worth living for and worth dying for. Its adherents, though they continued to live in the land of their birth, ranked in it no longer as citizens, but as sojourners, and with the privilege of citizens, accepted the condition of the alien and the stranger. Every land was theirs, and every land was foreign to them; for, though they dwelt upon earth, their citizenship was in heaven. Subject to the law of the land, they rose above it, but it was by a spirit that was not of it. In a word, what the soul was to the body, that the Buddhist was to the world. As all the body's members are animated by the soul, so is the world by the followers of Buddha.

Accordingly, this faith, though first taught by Sakyamuni in Hindustan, did not remain and stagnate where it originated; it professed to be and propagated itself as a world-religion. Zealous missionaries went abroad everywhere and preached it, and it took fast and deep root in nearly every land in which its seed was sown. Its propagation to other lands is proved by the fact that it is still the religion professed in them, as it is by memorials of its influence where a faith in Buddha, by name anyhow, no longer subsists. What may seem singular is that it long ago died out, in profession at least, in the land of its birth, and was superseded by religions which it was thought to have subverted.

It would appear that its disappearance was in great part due to its own decadence. After converting a large proportion of the inhabitants of Hindustan to their faith, the Buddhists piously set about the erection of large and beautiful edifices for the accommodation of the different orders of its monks, who were housed and lived in them at the expense of the faithful, who looked upon them as the guardians of their religion and the ministers of its benefits. Here these priests of this once spiritual system were erelong tempted to live, and began to live, at their ease, only affecting to commemorate the life of the Master and exemplify his spirit, cherishing beside them every relic of him and his saints as nearly all their religion, and deeming it no longer necessary to fortify themselves either within or without against the attacks of their enemies. They gave themselves up to a life of indolence, which they called a life of devotion, and for this they levied an unconscionable tribute at the hands of the public. This was what no public could long stand; and they had, moreover, accumulated a large store of wealth, the gift of the lay class, which the rabble could seize with the less remorse the less the present holders were entitled to retain it. Their enemies were quick to see their opportunity; they found them a ready prey; and wherever they set upon them, they made short work of them. It was the old orthodox Hindu apparently that led on the assault, whose religion they had supplanted and whose influence they had destroyed by the rejection of caste and the sacred books and rites of Brahminism. The common Hindus were the more easily roused to take the orthodox side by the prospect of the plunder they would acquire in the case of victory. This harrying process began some time between the eighth and ninth centuries, and towards the end of the twelfth century there was hardly a Buddhist left in India. Buddhism had died of exhaustion, and could not stand before the reawakening of the spirit of what was best in its old rival. It was not fit to survive, and it was survived by a fitter. It lingered longest—till the fourteenth century, it seems—in the native district of Sakyamuni.[1]

---

[1] It is a problem of some difficulty, which Buddhism in a merely monastic form but essays to resolve—How to subsist apart from the World, and yet at the expense of it? That is to exact of the world what the World has reason rather to exact of him who separates from it, and is to invert the principle of Christian charity, which finds it more blessed to give than to receive. He is well worthy of earthly things if ministrative of heavenly.

Such of the few still genuine Buddhists, however, as escaped the sword of their enemies, undaunted by this rebuff, went forth to other lands, scattering the seeds of the faith, persuaded that the truth they were entrusted with would be received with welcome by ears that had not heard it. This propagandist work they would set about with all the more zeal that they felt it was the duty in which they had been most remiss, and for the neglect of which they had come by all their misfortunes; for Buddha, too, had required it of his disciples, as Christ of His, that they should not slumber at home, but go into all the world, and preach the gospel to every creature.

There was, it appears, at this period still some communication open between the cognate but widely separated races of the eastern and western parts of the world; anyhow, the new doctrines were carried westward especially by Buddhist missionaries in quest, as sun-worshippers withal, of the home of the gods. But these, finding the tribes they visited still unprovided with a written language, had recourse to symbols in order to express their fundamental doctrines; and they not unnaturally employed those they had used in the East. It is thus I explain to myself the occurrence of Buddhist symbols on Celtic monuments; they are a hieroglyphic expression to the Celtic world of ideas that, arising in the East, seemed as easy of credit as they were worthy of currency in the regions of the West. There the bearers of them might be received and honoured as the bearers of the bread of life, and worthy of house-room.

Though the Buddhists themselves were expelled from India, it does not follow that such was the fate of the religion they professed. The sects which supplanted Buddhism never would have made way against it, had they not given it battle with its own weapons, and arrayed, in particular, against it that broad doctrine of religious equality on the ground of which, as well as the authoritatively spiritual in man, it had originally built itself up. As a set-off against the worship of Buddha, and in imitation of the Master, in which the chief strength of Buddhism lay, they coined a host of legendary deities who embodied kindred virtues to those of Buddha, and who were quite as capable of stirring up personal devotion and kindling a passion for virtue in the breast of believers. They appealed, moreover, as it could not do, to a rich system of fable which held of the ancient religion, and by their temples and religious pageantry and symbols they overpowered the senses and subdued the heart. How far Buddhism in its original purity and integrity passed beyond Buddha himself and his immediate disciples is a question, but there can be little or no question that so far as it did pass, it still lingers in the heart of the Hindu race. Buddha, as he figures in legend, could not fail to command the homage of his countrymen, how far soever they might go from the Buddhist creed.

From all we have said it is not to be concluded that Buddhism was stamped out of India by mere force of violence or persuasion; whole masses, lay and clerical alike, must have thrown it up when they saw it waning, leaving its temples in ruins, and its monasteries untenanted or converted to other uses. A few enthusiasts of both sexes still sought refuge in the religious houses, and bound themselves by vows of poverty and chastity; but the high standard of excellence required by this religion in order to attain the state of final beatitude, persuaded many to renounce their faith and embrace one of the new sect religions, which were rapidly rising into favour, and, more accommodating to human weakness, promised access to heaven on easier terms

The rise of Buddhism in India was rapid. Its author went about preaching and teaching it for forty-four long years, and the conversions[1] achieved in his own life-time were many and deep and lasting. Its canon of faith was conceived and formed by the First Council shortly after the death of Buddha, and two centuries and a half after that event, or soon after the conquest of Alexander, it was adopted as the state religion by Asoka, the most powerful monarch in northern India, at which time it invaded the Deccan and took root in Ceylon. It was about this time it began its extensive system of propagandism, and it quickly took possession of nearly the

---

[1] "It is in Buddhism first that we come upon the notion of conversion, as well as a special term to designate it: in Pali, *sotâ patti*; in Sanscrit, *srotaâ patti*, 'entrance into the current.'"—M. Barth's Religions of India.

whole East. About the commencement of the Christian era it attracted the attention of the Emperors of China, and one of them, guided by a dream, sent an embassy to India to collect and bring to him its sacred books. In the fourth century it was adopted in China as the state religion, and it shares to this hour along with other two systems the respect of the Chinese race.

Buddhism was at its height in India during the reign of Asoka, in the middle of the third century B.C., at a time when religious teachers performed sacerdotal functions, such as were afterwards introduced into Thibet in the form of the Lama hierarchy.[1] But the duty of these early Buddhists was restricted to the performance at sunrise, noon and sunset of religious services, which consisted in the recitation or chanting of portions of the Shasters, particularly the precepts or rules of discipline, and the frequent repetition of the liturgical formula. This was accompanied with musical instruments, such as long sliding trumpets, often 5 or 6 feet in length, called holy trumpets (*chhas Dung*), a kind of hautboy, drums, cymbals, and conches. The musical sounds were slow and prolonged, and the effect solemn and even saddening.[2] During the service, incense was kept burning, and offerings of fruit, flowers, grain, and even meat were made to the figures of Buddha.

In Tartary and China, Buddhism has undergone interesting changes. These were enforced by the sheer moral power of the priests from the plains of Hindustan, as possessors of the sacred manuscripts and relics of the saints, such being considered of inestimable value, and carefully preserved in their monasteries, with the prayer-wheels and dorges, with which in their hand they constantly repeated the name and attributes of Buddha. These priests are much respected, and hold a high social position in the country.

Everywhere, except in China, learning is confined to the members of the priesthood, and the Buddhist priests are the sole instructors of youth. They are also the ministers of Esculapius, skilled in the virtues of drugs, the vendors of medicine, and the practitioners of the healing art. They profess, also, to know the secrets of destiny, and they know how to turn this profession to their own account:[3] by this, as much as anything, they hold the keys of the kingdom of heaven; shutting it against the niggard and opening it to those who bribe them with a large gift.

In most countries Buddhism, so far as it is a cultus, has degenerated into a mere priestly service, and is no better than the Brahminism against which it was originally a revolt. In some of these countries where Buddhism still prevails we find that the temples are always open and service is performed three times a-day. On such occasions the priests take their places in the chous, near the idols, before which incense is burnt, and dishes of food, with fruit and flowers, are placed. There they chant passages from their sacred books in Sanscrit or Pali, which they do not always understand, and sometimes in a more refined native dialect, with which they are, in general, no better acquainted. This is accompanied by the ringing of bells, the clashing of cymbals, and the beating of drums. Few people attend, and those take no part in the performance, which is for them, too, in a language they do not understand: they merely make offerings, and then depart.

Theoretically, the faith of Buddha has much to recommend it, but it expects too much of weak human nature as it is, and it is apt to degenerate into forms, which, while they recall some of its features, are destitute of its life. It lacks movement and growth, and is and remains all too crude. It is prone to stagnate, decay, and die out. Like all the other oriental religions, its proper spiritual virtue collapsed with the decease of the founder, and of that first, it may be more or less unintelligent, enthusiasm to which it owed its birth. Such as it is, it has

---
(1) Burnouf Hist. du Buddhisme, pp. 293 *et seq.*, Prinsep's Tibet, Tartary and Mongolia, 2nd ed., Lond. 1852. Genuine Buddhism has no priesthood. The saint despises the priest; the saint scorns the aid of mediators.—Upham, vi, Int. xxviii.
(2) Cunningham, Ladak, p. 383. Offer every morning and evening flowers, and have lighted lamps, and three times a day music, such as chanks (conch shells), and fail not in alms deeds: such was the dying admonition of King Datugomeni to his successor.—Upton.
(3) Wilson's Buddha and Buddhism, p. 377.

no power of self-revival, and when decay sets in, it issues in death. Except you graft it on some stem that has vigour, it will take no root and come to no good. To hold on, it must become eclectic, and only then has it borne any mature fruit.

This eclectic spirit, or disposition to accept and assimilate what it saw good in other systems, has always been a characteristic feature of the Buddhist as a propagandist religion; it is ever ready to adopt whatever in the practices of other religions it can turn to its own account. So much, for instance, were the Buddhists impressed with the effect of the paraphernalia and the pomp of the ritual of the Roman Catholic Church in Tartary, that in their early intercourse with the Europeans of that faith they adopted its symbols and its observances. Among these were the cross, the mitre, the chaplets, the dalmatic, the cope, the service with double choirs, the psalmody, the exorcisms, the celibacy of the clergy, the retreat, fasts, the worship of saints, processions, the litanies, and holy water. It was in some such way Buddhism absorbed what it met in the West; the transformation becoming more and more express and complete, until its entire symbolism all but merged into and disappeared in that of the Christian system.

By the seventeenth century, so completely was the once powerful sect of the Buddhists extirpated out of Hindustan, that when Abul Fazl, the able minister of Akbar the Great, made inquisition after its character as a once famous religion, he could find no one in India to explain its doctrines; and even under the more equable rule of England, there are only to be found feeble remnants who profess it, living in small communities, abstaining from carnal pleasures, and spending a monotonous existence in the routine of monastic life, without, however, even a spark of that fervid enthusiasm for which the fathers of their faith were so pre-eminently distinguished. It is worthy of note that they should be protected here in the exercise of their religious rites and the enjoyment of their worldly possessions by the descendants of a race which, in a far-off land and in a remote past, received from them some of its first lessons in civilization.

Though so few Buddhists now remain in the birth-land of their religion, yet to such an extent did the system make way in other countries that, according to Berghaus, as quoted by Lassen, there are now 470,000,000 Buddhists. The rapid and wide spread of Buddhism in these countries may be referred to various causes, and on that a long chapter might be written, which yet would fail to convey any adequate account. The service it had rendered as a political engine under the reign of Asoka, the Constantine of the system, may have recommended it to other potentates, who, it is plain, patronized its missionaries, and more or less openly countenanced them with state support. The priests of the native religions might, in these circumstances, see good to join them, and they were themselves, as we have seen, ready to coalesce with the ministers of other creeds. Or, it might be they recommended themselves wherever they went as earnest men, solely desirous of being serviceable to others, with help of knowledge, of wisdom, and of art, for which others would be ready to honour them with their substance and welcome them with a god-speed. They were accommodating, helpful men, who, as they would save their own souls, so to speak, sought not their own good, but the good of those about them. In foreign lands, too, they were not, as in India, thwarted by jealous, often unscrupulous, always potent rivals; neither were their motives, for obvious reasons, open to the same suspicion and distrust. They brought nothing with them, as they sought nothing, only the way of salvation by sacrifice of self and service to others. Their *karman*, as they called it, a sort of oversoul—for they knew no other soul, only a πνεῦμα, not a ψυχή—wrought itself upward nearer and nearer the blessed Nirvana *only so*. It was self-benefiting by being self-sacrificing.

Buddhism has two great negative principles and two great positive principles all along characteristic of it, whenever it is true to the philosophy of its founder. The two negative principles were "an absence of every theological element, and a conspicuous aversion to pure speculation," and the two positive principles are that "the *way* conducts to total extinction, and that perfection consists in ceasing to exist." It is the elimination of the theological and the metaphysical spiritually, as Comptism is the elimination of these elements scientifically. It abandons speculation, and devotes itself exclusively to the question of salvation. And yet its propagation was due less to the acceptance of these principles than to its moral discipline and the personality of its author. Indeed it was the image of Buddha more than either the spiritual power of his principles or their philosophic truth which was the factor that perhaps contributed more than anything else to its acceptance. Yet its one great rational text was: Work out your salvation.

SECTION II.—BUDDHIST PRIESTS, THEIR CHARACTER, RITUAL AND MISSIONARY MODES.

In the absence of written documents regarding the religious usages of Buddhism, we may visit with profit the country of the "wild" tribes in the south-east of India, where the Buddhists found refuge from the relentless persecution of the Brahmins about the fourth century of our era, and where, having established themselves, they are still to be found in the quiet practice of their religion. There, as elsewhere, we find that, according to their liberal propagandist principles, they had allowed the natives to retain their own simple religious practices, and even harmlessly to continue, as of old, to make their offerings of rice, fruits and flowers to the spirits of hill and river.[1] They knew nothing of caste, or inequality of rank; and they admitted anyone [2] even to the priesthood, if only of good character and naturally capable, provided only they threw up the ties of kindred, depended for their support on charity, and passed a laborious and useful life in prayer to God, in instructing the young, and in the performance of the rites of religion. These last are preceded by the ringing of bells, as if to summon the ears of the supernal powers, or perhaps only awaken expectancy, and they consist of prayers and offerings, which are placed upon a raised bamboo altar, in honour of the great Gautama Sakyamuni, the last Buddha, a service which is often performed by the people themselves, and not always by the priests.

The Burmese priests spend their time in their religious houses (*kiong*), in collecting food for their subsistence, in perambulating the village with their pupils, in teaching the young reading, writing and accounts, as well as technical skill, such as the erecting of huts, the building of boats, and other useful industrial occupations. As these priests lead an active and serviceable life, they are much respected, and they contrast favourably with the priestly class in Thibet and Mongolia, whose lazy and slovenly habits, and greedy, grasping spirit, make them shunned rather than trusted by the body of the people. The Burmese, under the teaching of the Buddhists, are in high repute for truth, honour, and self-denying, serviceable activity, while the faith they are taught softens all asperity in their relations one with another, by admitting of no distinction between man and man, and by raising the position of women, who are allowed great freedom of action, and may, in their old age, even take part in the rites of religion. For the Buddhist believes that every individual life is sacred, and in process of metempsychosis, or transmigration, from one stage of being to another. Each successive existence, if virtuous, is supposed more and more to purify the soul, until, free at length from the dross of earthly passion, it is fit for admission into that state of blessedness in which all such passion is completely purged away, and the soul is at rest, so that, as far as mundane interests are concerned, it may be said even to have ceased to exist. It is for this blessedness every Buddhist longs and labours, and the more he helps others to it, the nearer he approaches it himself. It is this belief which makes the Buddhist regard one soul quite as precious as another, and that constitutes the reason why he treats all alike, and preaches the equality of all. All are on their way to Nirvana, and it is his office, as well as interest, not to hinder but help on the process.

(1) *See* Capt. Lewis' excellent Account of the Wild Races of South-Eastern India, p. 97. (Allen & Co.)
(2) "Buddha repelled no one, and within the circle of his disciples there are no other distinctions than those of age and merit."—M. Barth's Religions of India.

Sacrifices have no place in the religion of Buddha, although offerings of prayers, flowers and sweet spices are made in memory and in honour of the Master and his saints. The order of religious teacher was instituted as early as the time of Asoka, and was pretty much such as we find exemplified in the modern Lama hierarchy of Thibet. Buddhist priests perform no offices that are strictly sacerdotal. They are rather, like the mendicants, to be regarded as embodiments of that self-surrender of which sacrifice is the symbol, on the constant practice of which, as even Brahminical philosophy teaches, rest the heavens and the earth, and the reign of the gods, still more the redemption of humanity. In their worship, besides flowers and fruits, they offer up carved work and ornaments of gold and silver, and they accompany the act with hymns of praise, and prayer, and the music of instruments. The hymns and prayers are addressed not only to Sakyamuni and his apostles, but it is even said, doubtless by accommodation, to the benignant physical powers of nature.

Buddhists scorn the idea of priestly mediation between man on earth and God in heaven,[1] and so their priests are not, strictly speaking, a distinct class with special spiritual functions, but are simply good holy men, who live as monks,[2] and seek to instruct the ignorant in the precepts of their religion. Any person, as we have already said, of a good character, and not deformed, may become a Buddhist priest, either for life or for a certain specified term. Neophytes for the order are required to study under one who is already a priest, and to attend lessons on the tenets of the religion of Buddha, which are always supposed to be delivered under the shade of the sacred tree under which the Master himself first received the light of heaven. After examination on the different points of doctrine peculiar to the system, they are, when proficient, admitted into the priesthood, on a sacred promise given that they will follow the life prescribed for the holy. They promise to give up their worldly possessions, to lead a life of poverty, self-denial and celibacy. They must not steal, must always speak the truth, and must detach themselves from all domestic and social obligations; they must employ their energies in the practice of some useful art, and in the service of religion; they must abstain rigidly from sensual indulgence, which is considered the source of all evil; they must subsist on the charity of their followers, or on the return made to them for their ghostly and other ministrations. The duties they undertake they must perform with diligence and care; the rest of their time must be devoted to the repetition of prayers and the performance of acts of religious devotion.

Fig 100.

The priests shave their beard and head, and are clad in a saffron-coloured cotton dress, consisting of a jacket buttoned up the middle, and fitting close to the body; an oblong piece of cotton cloth passed over the left shoulder, across the breast, then under the right arm and across the back, its extremity hanging over the left shoulder; the right arm, shoulder and breast being left free and uncovered, like those of Esculapius, so that they may be ready to act at any moment it may be required of them. They are kind and hospitable to strangers, and generally respectfully regarded. They are usually clean in their persons, and their only possessions are their simple yellow or orange-coloured dress, a sabert or lacquered basket to receive their food, a razor for shaving, a coarse needle to mend their clothes, a mat and a pillow to lie on, a small bucket to draw water, and a bottle to contain it, a drinking cup, and a fan, which they use as an umbrella. These priests live, or are supposed to live, in a small shed erected under their special sacred tree; they subsist on rice and vegetables prepared by their pupils, and they sleep on their mat spread upon the ground, with merely their scarf wrapped round them. On reaching the sacerdotal rank, they are supposed to live a life of retirement and

---

(1) Hodson's Sketches of Buddhism, Trans. Royal Asiatic Soc., vol. ii, p. 254.
(2) The Eastern Magi of ancient history were probably Buddhist priests, a supposition which seems to explain why the old language of Buddha, in Burmah, Aracan, Ceylon, &c., is called the language of the Mugs, or Magi.

meditation, under the shade of a sacred tree; but as their important duties do not always admit of this, they more commonly live in convents, attending to their religious duties, and teaching the young.

In order to subdue and extirpate the lusts of the flesh, they are required to observe the following twelve rules, viz.:—(1) Shun all causes of disturbance; (2) Discard all vain ornaments; (3) Check and mortify all cupidity in the bud; (4) Avoid all forms of pride; (5) Purify and elevate the thoughts by unceasing prayer; (6) Save the lives of others; (7) Be given to hospitality; (8) Search for supreme reason; (9) Search for rectitude; (10) Search for truth; (11) Dwell tranquilly in a place apart; and (12) Beg food for bodily wants and eat and enjoy it without remark.

The begging-pot is considered as an indispensable article of the religious mendicant's outfit. It is usually a small flat vessel, narrower at the top than at the bottom, and made of common material, such as clay. In it they receive food by way of alms. They do not ask any man's assistance, and are forbidden to express or feel any resentment, should anyone deny it when they need it, and they must accept no man's invitation. Such priests as these are actually to be seen in Burmah, pure in their lives, and earnest in their desire to do good to their neighbours, by propagating religion, instructing the young in the useful arts, and comforting the aged, while at the same time they subsist entirely on the free-will offerings of the charitable. The tapping of the priest upon his charity-box may be heard every morning as he perambulates the village with his pupils, to receive rice and other articles of food for the day. In other Buddhist countries where priests live together in numbers in monasteries, they are rather given to a life of idleness, under the pretence of religious meditation, and in the observance of ritual forms.[1]

In common with the Brahmin, the Buddhist, besides a faith in the necessity of the practice of good works, attaches a high value to penance, devout abstraction and prayer, as means whereby to purify the soul, so that it may arrive at Nirvana, which is to be regarded as the annihilation, not of being, but existence, of life as feverishly agitated this way and that, instead of quiescent in its own achieved self-sufficiency.[2] To attain this end, the Buddhist prohibits the destruction, under any circumstances, of the life of even the humblest creature, and all intemperance in eating and drinking. Their religion likewise enjoins the forgiveness of injuries, benevolence of heart, and the practice of charity, as well as reverential respect for superiors in wisdom, submission to discipline and to reproof, moderation in prosperity, submission under affliction, and contentment and cheerfulness at all times. Five evil habits are prohibited: inebriety, gambling, idleness, improper association, and frequenting places of amusement.[3]

These wise and benevolent doctrines were at first inculcated by intelligent as well as zealous preachers, and the religion they professed extended rapidly among the mild and peaceable Hindus, who received it with all the more favour that it was so opposed to the haughty exclusiveness of the Brahmins. The active, intelligent and persevering Buddhist missionaries emulated the royal Sakyamuni by their unwearied zeal during his life; and after his death relics of his body were distributed among eight cities, where divine honours were paid to them. The founder was succeeded by others who represented him, and who had passed through a life of kindred sanctity; their memory, too, like his, was respected, and the relics of their bodies religiously revered and cherished. These were carried about by their followers in all their journeys, and were a source of support to them in all their trials and privations. Among their precepts is one which requires them, while they hold fast to their own belief, not to think uncharitably of that of another. They were consequently tolerant in their creed, and if there happened to be a great difference between their own procedure and that of the countries they visited, the necessary compromise was made by a change in their rites and ceremonies. The points on which thoughtful minds differed were from time to time settled by meetings of councils, which generally allowed considerable latitude of interpretation in

---

(1) Capt. Malony's Remarks, Asiatic Researches, vol. vii, p. 32.
(2) *See* Psalm ii, 4, and especially Proverbs xiv, 14.   (3) Manual of Buddhism, p. 46.

regard to their tenets in intercourse with their co-religionists in distant countries among a people with different manners and customs. From this cause changes in their forms of worship necessarily resulted, but by that means the sect rapidly extended over Asia and other parts, far as well as near, of the world.

The mild, conciliatory spirit of this system, which addressed itself directly to all, without exception, the zeal and ability of its first missionaries, their strictly moral lives, and the high examplar they set before themselves and others, were such as to bespeak the respectful regard of all classes and a considerate attention to all they said and did. For long, and far and wide, they were welcomed as the ambassadors of the Highest; men sought their counsel and followed their direction everywhere; and never did a purely religious movement anywhere else achieve a like triumphant success. Not everywhere, however, did they meet with the same intelligent ears or a speech or body of symbols all ready made to represent their ideas and convey them direct to other hearts. Often in far-off countries they came upon peoples of whose speech-vehicle they had no knowledge, and could, therefore, make no use; nay, to whose ways of thinking and manners of life they were utter strangers. Among them their progress was necessarily slow and limited; and such as it was, it was possible only by accommodation to religious ideas and the employment of religious symbols with which the people were already more or less familiar. They even, as we have said, adopted many of the opinions as well as observances of those among whom they settled. In the West they are Sabbatist, and like the Greeks and Romans, although from a different motive, they would appropriate the chief gods of a country, such as, we may suppose, Jupiter Capitolinus in Rome, Jupiter Olympus in Greece, and Jupiter Ammon in Egypt; and they did as the Hindu sects afterwards, when proselytizing among the wild tribes of the peninsula: if they fell in with an idolatrous object of worship, they utilized it as an attribute or avatar of the god for whose worship they sought acceptance.

It was a reform of the Brahminical worship of the ancient Asiatic races, so as to sweep away its idolatrous practices, that gave rise to the Buddhist religion in India; and it recalled mankind, by contemplation and holiness, by the spirit of mildness, equity, and fraternity, to a religion of virtue, justice, and benevolence. In its more modern form Buddhism has distinct recognised doctrines regarding the Deity as the creator and the ruler of the universe; and having had a fancy for symbols as vehicles of instruction, it employs them still where for that purpose they are no longer necessary. The Buddhist teacher still explains the tenets of his religion to his pupils with his *dorge* in his hand, which was a symbolic device for his ideas when there was no written language to convey them, but which is now superseded by the far more expressive device of literal explanation. These symbols, however, are so identified with the system as originally delivered, that their use may be accepted as a pledge that whoso employs them does so in the name of the religion of Buddha. Wherever he travelled about he carved the sacred motto, *om, mani pampi, hom,* on every available stone which stood near the highways.

In Caledonia, however, as the symbols they used were there unknown, the Buddhists had at first recourse to such as already symbolised kindred religious ideas current in the country. But it was less by force of abstract truth than by force of their moral principles and character that they first established themselves among the rude inhabitants of the West, and acquired an influence as the ministers of religion. When they migrated into Pictavia, it was, we may be sure, the charity of their principles, the sincerity of their belief, and the unselfishness of their conduct, that early gained for them the full confidence of the natives, so that they were allowed at length to incise their own symbols upon the chief boulder stone of the sacred circle, which was always the one facing and farthest from the sun when rising. This particular stone was selected by them, not only because it was the chief, but because it was before it, and outside the circle, that the worshipper stood as he paid homage to his native deity, the sun-god, at daybreak. The influence thus acquired they increased by adding more symbols, as they do to-day in Thibet, and by multiplying their sacred texts, which the natives might look upon as so many more charms to conjure with, and would feel grateful to them for, as for a good action.

However these superstitious tribes might receive them, the symbols they employed were, as we think, no doubt, meant to aid them in the imperfect oral delivery of their principles, and they were probably first inscribed on the common unconsecrated rocks, such as that of Anworth in Galloway (*Fig.* 101). The artist who traced the markings on this rock was, we may suppose, some zealous missionary, who would naturally avail himself of a rock cropping out of a hill-top as the readiest tablet that offered, to trace the sacred symbols of his religion, with such additions as he might find likely to render them more intelligible to the ignorant people for whom they were intended. Or, whoever traced them might only have done so as those companies of priests do at the present day in Thibet, who, supported by rich and zealous Buddhist laymen, traverse the country, chisel and mallet in hand, engraving their sacred formulas on the rocks and stones in all quarters. If we assume this to have been the practice of the Buddhists who visited this country in Pictish times, it will at once explain why so many standing stones in Pictland have the sacred symbols and sacred Eastern animals engraved on them, such as a judicious teacher might presume to be within the comprehension of the natives.

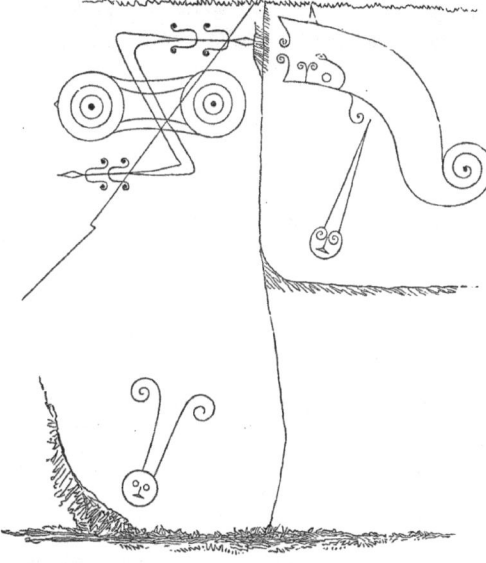

Fig. 101.

These men must have established themselves very firmly in the island, and in the confidence of the people, to be allowed, as they probably were on the decline of the native religion, to desecrate the boulder circles of the ancient worship, by inscribing upon them their own peculiar symbols, such as we find to-day on the stones at Kintore, Kineller and elsewhere in the country. The morality they taught was already more or less familiar to the people by the teaching of the Druids, from whose instruction they must have benefited before they were driven northward into Pictland by the Romans; and this fact, together with their knowledge of certain arts, as well as their moral character, must have made a powerful impression; while their zeal and perseverence, extending over the neighbouring country, would prevail over every opposition, and secure for them the liberty, if they chose, to cover with their symbols every rock and stone over the length and breadth of the country.

CHAPTER II.

TENETS, ORGANIZATION AND SYMBOLS OF BUDDHISM.

N this chapter we propose to consider the Buddhist Triad, or Triratna, as it is called, viz., Buddha, the Dharma and the Sangha, and some of its sacred forms, particularly its wheel and triad symbols.

According to a Buddhist catechism, it is the duty of a Brahman to believe in one true God, to worship Him as a living Being, and to do the things He loves. His proper temple is a pure heart; the ceremonial observances of the Brahman are good works; and his sacrifice the renunciation of selfishness. His austerities consist in abstinence from sinful disposition of mind, speech, and action, and in performing penances where needful, but not such as dry up the body. His places of pilgrimage are the haunts, and his church the company, of good men. Divine knowledge is superior to all the Vedas, which are at best only its reflection, its verbal shadow and expression. The knowledge of all the Vedas, the Rig-Veda, the Atharva-Veda, the Sama-Veda, and the Yajùr-Veda, is inferior knowledge. The superior knowledge treats of God, and is the true knowledge, the knowledge, as the Mundaka Upanishad has it, of the âtman, or self, which "reveals itself in the human heart." The most sacred formula of the Brahman is: Be good and do good; and the true Brahman is he who lives apart from the world, knowing God.[1]

Section I.—The Buddhist Triratna.

As Avalokitesvara,[2] a Hindu deity, came erelong to be conceived as the Buddhist's god; he was in course of time identified with Bodhisattva Vajruhhura, the bearer of the thunderbolt, and Vajrapani, the thunderbolt-handed, both of which epithets had been previously applied to Indra, the lord of the firmament. Thus Avalokitesvara came to form along with these two Bodhisattvas, or Buddhas elect, the earliest trinity of northern Buddhism.[3] The innovation of these three, which was a modern one, introduced a doctrine into the original teaching of Gautama, resembling that of the Hindu triad of Brahma, Vishnu and Siva, and giving rise on the one hand to the philosophical triad of spirit, matter and organized matter, and, on the other, to the theological triad of Buddha, the Law and the Church.

---

(1) As given in the fourth volume of Max Müller's "Chips from a German Workshop."
(2) See Beal's "Fa Hiam," p. 167.   (3) Rhys Davids' Buddhism, p. 200. Lotus de la bonne loi, pp. 493 and 511.

This is merely a modification of the belief of many of the nations of antiquity, as of nearly all the Asiatic races of the present day. They believed in a spiritual deity and a fruitful earth; in a male and female principle; in mind and matter; Osiris and Isis; Phallos and Venus Genetrix; Pater Ether and Mater Terra; Yong and Yin (Chinese); Linga and Yoni; Brahma and Sarasvati; and other gods, and their wives.

The Buddish trinity proper consisted of (*a*) Buddha, the sovereign intelligence, spirit, or wisdom; (*b*) the Dharma, the law or teaching, and (*c*) the Sangha, the sacred brotherhood and hierarchy. In this triad Buddha is the first; the Dharma, the second; and the Sangha, the third; and there is no genuine Buddhism which does not acknowledge all three as at bottom one. In philosophy they denote, the first, mind; the second, matter; the third, the concretion or organization of the two; whereas, in religion, as we see, the first is the author of Buddhism; the second, his Law; and the third, his Church.

(*a.*) *Buddha, the supreme intelligence, spirit or wisdom.*—The generality of Eastern Buddhists, while believers in an invisible first cause, in the form of an intelligent personal deity, are yet at the same time worshippers of the image of the saintly Buddha, whom they figure seated, looking abroad over the earth with a placid benignant countenance. Their worship of him is an exemplification of devotion as possible only to a recognisable, conceivable object, embodying and revealing in a concrete form that virtue and goodness which, however, have their proper centre and seat in the incomprehensible nature of an absolute deity, who in Brahminism is called Brahman or Brahma. These attributes shine out in the lives and sayings of a saintly class, who give themselves up as organs and ministers of the divine, which is otherwise unspeakable and unapproachable, and whom others regard as beings of higher order, and worship, kneeling before their very images, and collecting and enshrining their very dust in temples, which, as containing these mementos, are regarded as shrines of the Highest. In the worship of Buddha, who ranks as perhaps the foremost of this saintly class, and who came to be regarded at length as an express avatar of the Divinity, symbols are employed, as well as images and relics, and among these are the sun, the already accepted symbol of the Deity, the circle, the prayer-wheel, and the wheel of transmigration, each of which will fall to be considered separately by-and-bye.

The Buddhists, or rather a speculative class among them, identify the apparition of Buddha with the ninth or last avatar of Vishnu, whom we have already seen as the active preserving or upholding spirit proceeding from the supreme deity Brahma, as he manifests himself in the life of man and nature.[1] The object of his manifestation, was, it was said, to reform the Hindu religion, by exemplifying and inculcating a more spiritual and humane form of worship and code of morality. Buddhists acknowledge, indeed, and pay homage to a number of Brahminical gods, but they regard, and must regard, them with feelings of gratitude and reverence far inferior to those with which they look up to Buddha, for he, and not they, first taught them the "way" of salvation; nor do they to the extent he does represent and embody to their faith so much of the character of Deity. He, and not they, is their life-divinity and saviour.

Buddha, as represented, ranked in sheer capacity of intellect and rightly directed will far beyond aught that was known of Brahma and his companions in the Hindu pantheon, and stood on a tripod as a proper spiritual, or living god, high above them. He was by himself the lord and teacher not of one section of the universe, but of all *three* worlds,[2] and had alone, as Vishnu did only in fable—whether by three steps or three million, it matters not—really transversed the spiritual system of things through all stages from highest to lowest and from lowest to highest, and through all shades from brightest to darkest and from darkest to brightest. He is the embodied law of the universe in self-directed action, and shows how nothing is valid that is merely personal,

---

(1) Buddhists give a list of as many as twenty-four Buddhas who appeared before Gautama, all sent, as he was, at the proper time to regenerate the world, as many more will, and must needs be, in the æons upon æons of the future.

(2) Thus early do we meet with the Dantean conception of the unseen universe.

and not also cosmic. He, though worthier of favoritism at the hands of the gods than any man, is an instance of how rigorous and irrespective of persons is the law of retribution, the law, for instance, which connects evil with transgression. If it was so with Buddha then, how much more with the Buddhist?—if he sins, the penalty attached in the nature of things to the offence will inevitably take effect; the law must have its course. To this law Buddha, like the Son in the Christian Trinity, had to submit himself; and he encouraged no one to expect that it might relax itself in his favour. He had no idea that by penance, propitiation, or satisfaction, its severity could be infringed or its sanctions evaded. He was aware, as Sir Emerson Tennant observes, that neither in heaven nor on earth could a man escape the consequences of his own actions, and he regarded man, because a spiritual being, as directly working out his own salvation or his own ruin. In his religion, therefore, the ideas of forgiveness and atonement are unknown. He was the spiritual human incarnation of a will that is, so to speak, impersonal, of a law which is not a law for one, but a law for all—a law for the universe.

(b.) The Dharma, the law or teaching.—One great peculiarity of the Buddhist system is its perception and profession of the equality of all men, and its insistance, as its first law, on the suppression of merely private emotion or affection as the one great disturbing element in life, outside and above which alone one must rise to attain any authoritative standing or rank in the spiritual world. To those who have succeeded in breaking the power of these passions, and soaring aloft to the ether of pure universal goodwill, Buddhists pay supreme devotion, and they either render no homage to the unseen Almighty who sits retired in the heavens, or, like the Brahmins, in their worship of such deities as an Agni or an Indra, personifications of the fire or the sun-god, stop short with the manifestations. They are less intent to know whence they have come than whither they are bound; and are more grateful for guidance in a new life than for the gift of an old one, as men always are more grateful to their spiritual than to their natural parents. Accordingly, after conversion, the Buddhist frequently drops his paternal name altogether, assuming a new name corresponding to his new nature, just as the Italian artists used to do, when they named themselves after their master.

Buddhist teaching has respect to perfection of moral being, and it explains how this state is to be attained by purely moral methods, such as detachment from the gratifications of sense, absorption in spiritual meditation, the surrender of self to a higher law, and the cultivation of purity of thought, gentleness of heart and charity of affection. Its moral doctrine is summed up in eight precepts: (1) right views; (2) right feelings; (3) right words; (4) right behaviour; (5) a right mode of livelihood; (6) right exertion; (7) right memory; and (8) right meditation and tranquility. It aims at the extinction of suffering (which it traces to desire), by the avoidance of thoughts, feelings and actions that are impure or selfish, and the cherishing and cultivating of such as are gentle and sincere and loving. The more rigorously men follow this law, the sooner they pass into blessedness, which is otherwise absolutely unattainable. By wrong living, by every wrong act, they prolong the state of suffering, and postpone indefinitely the day of their final escape from trouble. Every separate thought, word and act has its inevitable fateful effect on the soul's course and destiny: if evil, enslaving it still more; if good, ensuring it greater and greater emancipation.

Teaching, or Dharma, like this, could not but have the most wholesome effect on those who accepted it. Such surely indicates the right way, in which, if a man walk, he cannot fail of the goal appointed him, whatever mistakes he may make in other matters, be it in reference to the God above him or the life beyond him. To reach the goal it needs only that we ascertain clearly the right road, and with dauntless heart and firm step press steadily along it. Anyhow, it is good, and for good, to be taught and to learn not to destroy life, not to be unchaste, not to deceive by word or deed or look, to return good for evil, and to avoid excess and sensual indulgence.

By such self-denial and the positive discipline and practice of charity required in this creed, the soul was believed to be gradually cleansed from all impure affection, and made meet for a felicity of being which is so ineffable that the terms employed by Buddhism to describe it are the negation of the totality of attributes that constitute finite mundane existence. Here we are in a world of change, where death succeeds life and life succeeds death, and men and all living things are involved in a series of transmigrations, passing by necessary sequence from one stage to another, and the rank we shall next hold needs not be a lower one, it may be a higher, but this depends on our power of detaching ourselves from the petty interests of our present state, and qualifying ourselves for a larger and a broader, which shall not be the less real that it is less limited, until at length, under the action of the same principle, we acquire a catholicity of spirit and being, the true Nirvana, wherein, all lesser interests being swallowed up, we lose ourselves in the great parent ocean of eternity and immensity. This, with or without material metempsychosis, with or without denial of immortality, is the soul of the Law of Buddha, the struggle upwards from the finite to the infinite, from time to eternity, from earth to heaven, by naked, unaided right moral behaviour.

Buddhism confined itself to the teaching of a pure morality, and, in terms anyhow, neither recognised nor rejected the soul's individuality through its changes, although it may be considered to have, without saying it, given that up, seeing that from the first it made perfection to consist in the soul's extinction and absorption in the infinite; and it was not without warrant that one of its philosophic systems merged the being of the soul altogether in the higher life of the spirit, the *karman*, which alone passed onward and upward to the invisible. It lifted the material pantheistic view of God which the Brahmin held, as it did the individuality of man, into a spiritual region, and the worship, which in the other systems was paid to a mechanical God, was paid in this to a spiritual, that is, to one who *had become*, and could, therefore, lead the way to life everlasting. It mattered not that he was a man and a mortal, enough that he had gone the "way;" and they did homage to his very image as to an image of the Eternal. It was only the later Buddhism which, to justify itself to the religious sense, regarded Buddha as an incarnation of God independently existent; but they made him only one of many such, thousands even, that had appeared before him and would appear after him. Their God was the Son of God, and His servant, and who, having come from, had gone back to Him.

(*c.*) *The Sangha, or sacred brotherhood and hierarchy.*—Sakyamuni, the solitary, who originated this religion, was the first preacher of it, and he began preaching in the district where it had in him first taken root. He carried it himself to Benares, the centre of Brahminism, and personally scattered the seed of it over northern and central India. Wherever he went, he fascinated multitudes by the austerity of his life, the gentleness and suavity of his manners, the ardour of his faith, and the touching eloquence of his utterances. This display of the grace and goodness that were in him made his followers early regard him with the reverence due to a god or some divine incarnation, and when he died and entered into Nirvana at the age of eighty, his disciples looked on his decease as those of Christ did when they saw Him ascend to heaven and a cloud receive Him out of their sight. Then it was, in all probability, that they first realized the weight of Buddha's words, and first began with zeal to walk in his footsteps. It was then first the Buddhist community attained an independent existence, and its members first felt their dependence on one another in the spirit of the Master, now that he was no longer himself among them in person. So long as their life in common was thus spiritually derived, the action of the Master prolonged itself in the church; and it was only when they ceased to believe in the power of his spirit, and their faith transferred itself to external helps, that the life of the church deceased, and degenerated, as it appears it has everywhere long since done, into a more or less spiritually worthless secular organization. Originally the Sangha was the third member of the Buddhist trinity, and represented its community-life inspired by the Spirit and trained in the Law of Buddha.

Buddhism, so far as its outward extension in India goes, owes a great deal to the zeal with which Asoka, the grandson of Chandragupta, embraced it and the enthusiasm his respect for it kindled. He employed the ablest men the church afforded to preach it, raised it to importance and elevation, though of questionable solidity and multiplied monuments to it all over the country. He built numerous towers, chapels, cave-temples, veharas, monasteries and topes, the stones of many of which, as well as much of their wood-work, are skilfully carved over with its symbols. These structures, many of which were magnificent, were some of them for preaching and offerings, some of them, surrounded by groves of trees, for seclusion and silent meditation, but all of them were without defence against attack, and an easy prey to the sacrilegious.

It was by means of the church, or Sangha, the order of which was organized in the name of Buddha and originated by himself, that Buddhism began to spread and finally extend itself over the East; and council after council of the order was held after Buddha's death to determine at once the articles of its creed and the rules of its discipline. And it was by its proselytizing character, displayed in the action of this Sangha, that it differed from the other oriental religions before and around it; for neither the Jews, the Egyptians, the Greeks, the Romans, nor the Hindus thought of converting others to their religious beliefs or observances, these, with the gods they worshipped, being considered national property, the inheritance of the race and its peculiar privilege. Nay, it is only the Christian and the Mohammedan religions that have since sought to extend their sway beyond themselves, and to lead captive the minds of others. With such self-devotion did some of these Buddhist missionaries give themselves up to this proselytizing work, that they came to be regarded as zealous as Buddha himself, and identified with him in his worship. Some of them were even deemed worthy, as Elisha was by Elijah, to wear his mantle, and use his alms-bowl in their mendicant wanderings, as his proper spiritual successors, such the self-surrender with which they sat at his feet, imbibed his spirit, and delivered his message. Others who followed in their footsteps fell heirs to these badges, and their names were added to the group of saintly sages which erelong figured as a constellation round the person of Buddha.

The Buddhist laws and doctrines were for centuries handed down orally, and they were necessarily subject to great modifications, as they passed from mouth to mouth in the different countries in which the religion of Buddha flourished. Œcumenical councils of the Sangha accordingly were from time to time convened to correct divergencies from orthodox belief; but the result was, ás the rule is in such cases, a series of compromises, to the damage of the original creed and the consequent emasculation of its spiritual virtue. Thus arose the changes which the Buddhist religion underwent in different countries where it was established, changes which, in the main, contributed to lower its character and weaken its influence. This result was chiefly due to the rise of a worthless and slothful priesthood, and the introduction and countenance of superstitious fancies and savage rites among the Buddhists of Thibet and Ceylon. In Mongolia and other countries, where it had maintained itself in a state of decline, Buddhism experienced a semi-revival by accepting the dogmas and copying the ritual of the Roman Catholic Church.

Some writers have affected to trace the origin of Christianity to the influence on the mind of its Author of ideas derived from Buddha, but it can be proved that every single trait of the Christian spirit which Buddhist tradition ascribes to the character of Buddha was first ascribed to it in recent years by those who had philosophically studied the Christian system. There is not a single Buddhist MS. extant which can vie in antiquity and authenticity with some of those of the Christian Gospels. Besides, in the ancient lives of Buddha no prominence is given to any characteristics specifically Christian, and hardly any of the legends regarding him which refer to events prior to the Christian era were in circulation earlier than the fifth or sixth centuries.

In Asia the Buddhists are usually classified according to peculiarities that are of local derivation, and chiefly into Southern Buddhists, such as those of Ceylon and Burmah, and Northern Buddhists, such as those of Nepaul and Thibet. It is among the Cingalese and the Burmese that, from their detached position, we meet with some of the earliest traditions regarding, and some of the personal relics of, Buddha. Ceylon boasts of containing the impression, already referred to, of Buddha's foot; and it is in the temple of Kandy here they still preserve as an object of worship the tooth of Buddha, on the possession of which, as well as the observance of festivals in its honour, depends, it is alleged, the right of any one to rule in the country. It is among the Southern Buddhists that the relics and symbols of Buddhism are held in the highest regard, and whoso possesses them possesses a charm to conjure himself into imperial fortune. The white elephant of Burmah, sacred to Buddha, bestowed on the emperor the rule of the world.

The extent to which Buddhism accommodated itself to the prejudices of others whom it sought to influence, may be seen in the readiness with which those who accepted it embraced along with it idolatrous forms of worship, to the length even of that of demons, as happened in Ceylon. When the Portuguese, Dutch, and English brought among them a religion which laid so much stress on the teaching and practice of the social virtues, many were induced to combine an outward profession of the foreign religion with a secret regard for the native. In the writings of Turnour, Harding, Forbes-Leslie, Tennant, and others, the tenets of the Cingalese are accepted as the tenets of Buddhism, but frequently no allowance is made for the influence of manners and customs peculiar to the people and native to the country. Much exploration has yet to be made in this field, and we must have more light than we yet possess before we can trace with greater clearness the history of Buddhism.

The first country to embrace Buddhism outside the peninsula was Kashmir, and it began to shed its mild influence in the empire and at the court of China at the very time when Christianity, under the seal of its first apostles, was subduing the kingdoms of the Western world.

SECTION II.—BUDDHIST CIRCLES AND WHEELS, PRAYER-WHEELS, AND WHEELS OF TRANSMIGRATION.

As we have seen, the first religious symbols in Pictland were of a simple form, such as a circle, a boulder-stone, &c., but on the boulder-stone symbols were at length inscribed, among which was the spectacle-ornament, as representing the Buddhist triad; and when carvings of animals were added, they were Asiatic and such as are held sacred among the Buddhists. The simple upright boulder, or obelisk, merely symbolized the incomprehensible supreme Deity, whereas the ornament referred to represented the Buddhist triad in the form of Buddha, or spirit, Dharma, or matter, and Sangha, or organized matter; or the breathing spirit, the plastic medium, and the organized unity of the two. The first two members of the triad were represented in the spectacle-ornament by the two circles, and the third, their union in one, by the belt or connecting bridge, as in the Deer Obelisk. This same idea was often represented by two concentric circles, the outer denoting matter, the inner, spirit, and the inclusion of the former by the latter, the living organism which connects both.

The Buddhist missionaries would necessarily be ignorant of the Western languages, and would seek to explain the precepts of their religion by means of sacred symbols. The symbol of the sun gave them one starting point, as well as the arrangement of stones in circles as representing that Deity, while on the single erect stones were placed Eastern symbols and figures of Asiatic animals, whose sacred character was indicated by the mythological aspect under which they were presented.

(*a.*) *Sacred circle representing the Sun-God.*—The circle, as without beginning or end, is the emblem of, among other attributes, absolute power, and, as such, is often represented as held in the hands of pagan gods or monarchs to indicate their supreme or imperial dominion. It was the circular form of the sun's disc or orbit,[1] in connexion with the prevailing sun-worship, which in all probability suggested the adoption of the circle as a symbol of the Deity in his benign sway over the universe of being. In this worship the presence of the light was a token of the presence and favour of the good god, whereas the darkness was regarded as the triumph over him and his empire of a demon race; and prayer to him was held to be most efficacious at the moments of his rising

---

[1] Perhaps it was that of the all-encompassing horizon.

and setting. When the shadows began to lengthen and stretch out along the plain, and a feebler and feebler light to suffuse the landscape, as the sun gradually withdrew, leaving all things in coldness and darkness, and handing them over to the evil spirits of the night, who shed down on the earth their malign influence from the cold gleam of the moon and stars, the sun-worshipper, as he stood in front of this sun-symbol, would pray the departing deity not to leave him alone, but shield him from evil against his dawning. So, too, in the morning he would wait and watch his first rays as they struck the mountain-tops and announced his return to an expectant world, ready to greet the first streak of light and glow of warmth that shot upward from the far-off horizon, until the god himself appeared as a red-glowing speck in the east and finally a huge ball of fire, the shadows of night all driven away before him, and the vapoury atmosphere all melted into transparent clearness and brightness; at such a moment our worshipper would veil his face from a glory too dazzling to mortal vision, and prostrate himself to the earth with a heart swelling with gratitude to so gracious a visitant and bountiful a giver, while all he could or perhaps durst do to symbolize his sense of his confidence in the ever-returning God's grace in the benefit, was to trace some round circle on the earth or rude wheel on a boulder. Anyhow it was when at sun-set the worshipper recalled the sun's bounties and at sunrise he forestalled them, that he felt most emboldened to supplicate the grace of the Deity and best assured that his petition would be granted.

Fig. 102.

(*b.*) *Wheels.*—The mythological circle, or *chakra*, as it is called, is often a symbol of the fire as shedding its rays in all directions around. It is worn as a ring round the middle finger of many of the Hindu deities; and it is launched against the wicked, whom it slays, though, like the bomerang, it returns to the hand that hurls it. It is usually represented by a double circle, as in the bronze symbol given in *Fig.* 102, which most probably was used in worship as the symbol of the deity of the sun, the great fire-god, and it is often represented as resting on the palm of the left hand of Buddha. From the margin of the outer circle at the four quarters of this figure proceed tufts of flame (*a, b, c, d*), and in the centre is a rude face, from which radiate eight pyramidal rays reaching to the circle. The great Deity is symbolically represented sometimes by an equilateral triangle *Fig.* 46 (p. 54), and sometimes by circles, with or without a girder, thus:

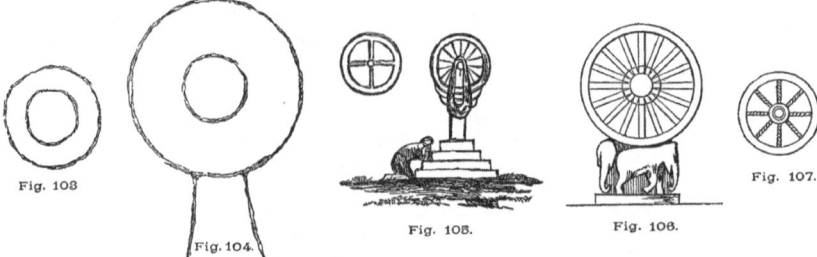

Fig. 103. Fig. 104. Fig. 105. Fig. 106. Fig. 107.

The circle, so regarded, was supposed to be possessed of such potency that the primitive tribes of India used to draw the figure of a wheel, and worship before it; they also placed it, as already remarked, before or over the entrance to their houses, to protect the inmates from their enemies,[1] human and demoniac. This circle and wheel was considered in Asia, and elsewhere among ancient nations, as the expression of a great religious truth common to them all: it symbolized the absolute power of the Deity over the affairs of the world, the "circle" representing his absolute universal dominion, and the "wheel" his conquering and triumphant authority. It was thus it was employed by the Hebrews, the Hindus, the Buddhists, the Persians, the Assyrians, the Egyptians, and the Greeks, in their temples. It is as such that among the Celts sacred boulder-stones, as we have seen, were arranged in wheels or circles of various sizes, and that, as just stated, among the aboriginal Hill-tribes of India we still find the wheel placed, with certain forms and ceremonies, in front of their houses, as the symbol which will protect them from evil. The goddess Durga holds in her right hand the wheel (*chakra*), which is represented as having mirrors between each of the spokes and from the periphery of which there issue flames. With this the Javanese believed she could transform herself into whatever shape she pleased.

(*c.*) *The Wheel of the Law.*—The *Dharmachakra*, the so-translated Wheel of the Law, is the emblem of the teaching of Buddha viewed, it is thought by some, as advancing to the conquest and possession of the world, the "wheel" representing the career of the triumphant chariot, and the "law" being the doctrine of life, or the "way" laid down by Buddha. It is just possible it may have stood originally for the discipline prescribed in the law of the Master, as it afterwards stood for a symbol of that recurring cycle, or system, in the universe of things which revolves as a wheel, and begins and ends with the advent of a Buddha. For it is part of the Buddhist creed at length that the movements of Providence proceed in cycles, and every new cycle begins with a new incarnation of the Lord of the Universe. But the radical idea which unquestionably underlies the symbolic use of the wheel in the religion of Buddha is that of spiritual power accomplishing and achieving itself in cyclical revolutions, beginning where it ends and ending where it begins, in a word, from itself to itself, and through itself, and neither more nor less at the developed end than it was at the undeveloped beginning.[1] It is so with the successive stages of the soul, it is so with the successive cycles of Providence, it is so with the preaching of Buddha, it is so with the triumphs of religion, it is so with the prayers of good men, nay, it is so with the Trinity in unity of God Himself; and all these are in Buddhism symbolized by the revolving wheel.

Fig. 108.

An example of the Buddhist wheel with a symbol of the triad is found over the eastern gateway of the Sanchi Tope. The central symbol (*a*) is typical of the absolute intelligence or power that rules the world, while the symbol (*b*) represents the philosophical triad of Buddhism, which reveals itself in the concrete phenomena of existence. Here Buddha, the spiritual power of the universe, is represented by the inner wheel portion (1), and Dharma, the material power, or matter, by the outer circle (2). The wheel is crowned by Sangha, which is a spiritual concretion of the two others (Buddha and Dharma). The one central idea represented by the wheel is movement, and that idea is radical to any just conception of the spiritual in either man or his Maker. When the spirit ceases to move, it ceases to be. Life, according to Hegel, is *der Process des Geistes*—movement of spirit, as spirit, onward.

The wheel is in the right hand of the Lamas of Thibet, and heroes are, in oriental symbolism, represented as being protected by this symbol in the day of battle. Such a symbol is intimately connected with the idea of a triad as it ever develops itself in every religious consciousness that is at all spiritual, the triad in this case being, first, the point circulating; second, the power of circling; and third, the circle itself.

(*d.*) *Prayer-wheels.*—According to the Buddhist belief, meditation and prayer are the two great means of attaining sanctity, and especial potency is ascribed to the latter. Accordingly, in a country like Thibet, where

---

(1) *See* Sketches of India, p. 19.　　　　　(2) *See*, too, St. John, chap. i. ver. 1.

they have a written language, instead of repeating prayers with the lips, which they usually do in a low, humming, bass tone, they consider it equally efficacious to inscribe their magic form of prayer—*om, mani padmi, hom*—upon a cylindrical wheel, and set it revolving. The Lamas often paste numerous copies of this prayer upon the barrel of the wheel, and they suppose that by that means they obtain credit for having repeated the prayer as many times as there are copies, multiplied by the revolutions of the wheel. This prayer literally means, "Hail to him of the lotus-jewel," and is a salutation to the sacred triad. A special merit attaches to its presentation, and hence there are Lamas who spend nearly all their lives in so offering it. From hour to hour and day to day they keep turning the wheel, in the hope that they may thereby earn for themselves exemption from future misery, and qualify themselves the sooner for entering on the state of the blessed Nirvana. The office of turning the prayer-wheel is often delegated to a servant, and, indeed, the end of its erection is answered just as well if it is planted on the house-top to be driven by the wind. Nay, in some villages, near running water, the cylinder, erected inside the houses, and kept revolving night and day by the wheel being sunk in the stream and attached to its axis, is believed to draw down blessing after blessing from heaven upon the occupants.[1] This prayer is often stamped on linen cloth, and engraved on wood and stone; and the sacred letters confront you on road-sides and houses, as well as temples, and wherever they can be written. This is done in the same hope which induces the Buddhist to multiply images of Buddha made of clay, sometimes mixed with the ashes of saints and stamped, and to place them in temples or small square rooms, near religious houses, called Joss houses, which are often filled with these offerings.[a]

The mysterious meaning of the words "*om*" and "*hom*" of the prayer *Om, mani padmi, hom*, may be interpreted in one or other of the following ways:—

I.—We may take "*om*" as the beginning of an inspiration or breath, and "*hom*" as the ending of the inspiration or the beginning of the expiration, implying (*a*) that in connexion with the name of the divine being, *mani padmi*, the lotus-jewel, there must be no other words; or (*b*) that life and death depend on the words *mani padmi*; or, (*c*) that "*om*" is as spirit at one end of the symbol of the trinity, "*hom*" as matter at the other end, and "*mani padmi*" as the resultant or concretion of the two, viz., organised matter. This interpretation is entirely new, and never, so far as I know, advanced before, till I explained and printed it some years ago.[3] This formula shows in word, as the dorge does in symbol, the trinity of the Buddhist faith. Compare the "Ya—ha—vah" of the Hebrew as corresponding respectively to (1) inspiration, (2) expiration, and (3) what issues.

II.—We may take "*om*" as expressive of musing silence, "*hom*" as still more so.[4]

My own interpretation would be that given in I (*c*) or in II: I (*c*), for reasons very obvious and too long to be detailed; II., as it is the simplest explanation. I incline to the opinion, that in ancient times, words which have now become dark were originally very simple, and have for this very reason lost their true meaning, and now present insuperable difficulties.

(*e.*) *Wheel of Transmigration.*—Most of the Buddhists adopted the Hindu opinion that there are separate places for rewards and punishments in the next world, and that there are gradations both of bliss and misery there. But, as disembodied spirits are incapable of rewards and punishments, the good man after death is raised to animate a higher, and the bad man is degraded to animate a lower, form of being.[5] By successive stages of

---

(1) These wheels appear to be peculiar to northern Buddhism.
(2) *See* Transactions Roy. Soc. Edin., vol. xxi, and particularly second essay in the Jour. Roy. Soc. Edin., and Asiatic Soc. Jour. Calcutta, 1865.
(3) *See* Roy. Soc. Trans. Edinburgh, vol. xxxi.
(4) This corresponds to a sense attached to the Hebrew word "Selah" found in some Psalms, and may be the same as the English "*um*," when one hears something strange.
(5) Lakan, Loc. Cit., p. 365.

CHAP. II.]   HISTORY OF PAGANISM IN CALEDONIA.   165

promotions individuals may be thoroughly purified from all earthly grossness, and, according to some Buddhists, be raised to the rank of demi-gods; while, according to others, the soul of the purified individual is absorbed into the great spiritual deity and extinguished, to gain which extinction is the final aim of existence. In a canon later than Buddha, a place is assigned to the devout Buddhist in another world; and we know that the doctrine of metempsychosis was borrowed from the earlier systems of Hindu philosophy, and more particularly from the Sankhya system. Brahminism presumes and affirms that there is a real world which exists beyond the world of phenomena, and Buddhism does the same; but whereas the former believes in it as a final reality, the latter for the most part does not. Both alike give utterance to the grief which, as things are, preys upon their inmost being, but the Buddhist sorrows as a man without hope, and his philosophy is therefore the philosophy of despair. The generality of Buddhists, however, like the Hindus, believe in the ultimate absorption of the pure spirit into Brahma—or absolute deity; and a nihilism of this type is actually put into the mouth of Buddha after he had entered into Nirvana, and is spoken of as living and as showing himself raised to the rank of a deity to those who believed in him![1]

There are supposed to be six grades of organised beings: angels, demons, men, quadrupeds, birds and reptiles. The soul occupies one of these, according to the grade of character the individual has attained in his previous life. This fact the Chinese represent in the wheel of transmigration, as that is understood by the Chinese Buddhist, the wheel in this case representing the continuity of transmigratory changes when normal, or their cyclical transition.

The Buddhists recognise ten mortal sins: three of the body, such as murder, robbery, and fornication; four of speech, such as lying, slander, swearing, and vain conversation; and three of the mind, such as covetousness, malice, and scepticism:[2] as well as venial sins, such as killing animal life, &c. Thus, the possessor of the most illustrious throne on earth may, in the next generation, in consequence of sin, be writhing in the agony of the place of torment, while the humblest individual may, in the course of ages, become a Buddha.

SECTION III.—THE DORGE SYMBOL.

Mundane Triad—the Dorge.—The mundane triad is symbolized in Asia by the dorge and the priest in an attitude of action (*Fig.* 108). This instrument, as engraven on an upright stone, is represented, as we shall see (in Chap. III.), by two circles united by a band and crossed at angles by a bar, from the extremities of which two trident-sceptres extend in opposite directions. On the angle of the junction a portion of it is cut off by a waving line where an eye appears, dividing the space into two halves, indicative of an active condition of the dorge.

The Buddhist had two varieties of symbols of the Deity, one in the form of a pillar, and another in that of a double circle, representing the two elements of the world, viz :—matter and spirit, which, in the hands of a priest who represented the third organisation, became the symbol of the Trinity. This sacred instrument, which was portable, is carried about by the Lamas of Mongolia and Thibet, and employed by the Buddhist priests of Tartary in the performance of religious worship. It consists, as seen in *a* and *b* (*Fig.* 109),

Fig. 108.*

(1 *See* Müller's "Chips of a German Workshop," vol. i, especially pp. 225 and 233.
(2) *See* Buddhism, by T. W. Rhys Davids, pp. 142 and 143.

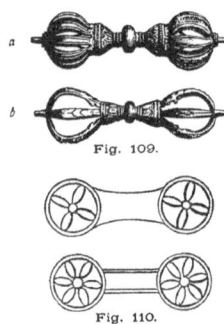

Fig. 109.

Fig. 110.

of two dorges, each of two hollow ribbed spheres or ovals of brass, united by a handle of the same metal, about 2 inches long. When represented on a flat stone with its axes or poles towards the spectator, one of the dorges (*c*) resembles the spectacle-ornament (*d*), as seen on the smaller Aberlemno stone in Forfarshire. These triad symbols are easily carried about, and from what they represent and suggest, are supposed to add authority and dignity to the priestly profession. They are constructed with great exactness, and on measuring the circles I found that they showed a difference in their diameter, in consequence of their representing the one spirit and the other matter.

Of two Buddhist dorges I examined, one in the British Museum gave for the sphere representing matter 1·43 in., and 1·4 in. for that representing spirit, while the other in the Indian Museum gave 1·21 in. for the former, and 1·19 in. for the latter.

It is held in the right hand of Durga in the bas-relief, on a pillar to the right of an Eastern gateway which dates from the beginning of the Christian era, and in an upright stone facing a part of a circle in her honour. It also appears in the right hand of Durga, sculptured on a rock, of the date of the seventh or eighth century.[1]

The dorge is in constant use by the priests, and it has been so employed by them from an early period in Buddhist countries, as one of the portable symbols of the Deity. Owing to its still sacred, and therefore unchangeable, character, the spectacle-ornament, first inscribed on the sculptured stones as representing it, does not vary from it in form; but in the Christian period, after it had become a merely ornamental symbol, its form began to vary on these stones, and with accompanying decorations according to the taste of the artist and the fashion of the period. The dorge so represented on the monuments appears to have been carried by the Buddhist missionaries to Pictland, and used there.

M. Huc informs us that there is a dorge (*Fig.* 111) in the chief temple of Siva, where it is religiously preserved, being reputed to have been wafted miraculously thither through the air from India. It is of bronze, and consists of two oval extremities covered with figures of elephants and other sacred emblems. It is an object of great veneration, and before it pilgrims prostrate themselves. At new year time it is conveyed with great state to Lassa for the adoration of the Dalai Lama and the people of that city. As symbols, carved on stone, could not be carried by the Buddhist priests when moving from place

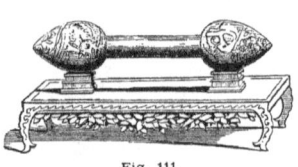

Fig. 111.

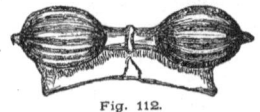

Fig. 112.

to place, and country to country, they adopted the dorge. Buddha being considered by the modern Hindus as the ninth avatar of Vishnu, I found it under the stone image of Vishnu, in Kensington Museum (*Fig.* 112), and it is sometimes found in the right hand of idols.

A figure (*Fig.* 113) of Buddha himself, surrounded with two halos, one investing his person, and the other his head, and issuing armed with his symbols of authority from the lotus-flower, represents him as wielding in

---

(1) Ladak, p. 373; and Captain Austin's Jour. As. Ex., vol. xxxii., p. 151, for 1864. See transactions of the Roy. Soc. of Edinburgh, vol. xxi., particularly the Jour. of the Roy. Soc. of Edinburgh. See also the Asiatic Jour. of Calcutta.

his right hand the sacred dorge, and thereby exhibiting himself as embodying all that the dorge symbolizes. Or, this figure may be viewed as that of a Buddhist priest, considered as representing Buddha, and the halos round the body and head may be regarded as symbols of his sovereign power and sacred, inviolable character. In the Temple of Ajanta there is delineated a battle between the orthodox and the infidel, or the good and the bad races, in which the former are represented as protected by the sacred wheel, as an ægis, whereon all the shafts of the enemy directed against them are broken.

Fig. 118.

CHAPTER III.

SYMBOLS OF BUDDHISM IN PICTLAND.

 HE doctrines of Buddhism were embraced by the intelligent before they were accepted by the poor and ignorant, and it was the beauty of its sentiments as well as the truth of its teachings that attracted them and enlisted them in its behalf. The presence of the latter class rendered the introduction of symbols necessary, and these were admitted in deference to a principle which afterwards became a ruling one in the Buddhist community. As they made advances upon Christendom, they acted upon this principle, while they brought with them their native symbols, which they retained in combination with the cross, the emblem now also of their new faith. This rule was followed in order that the Pagans, as well as Christians by whom they were surrounded, might not be shocked by the suddenness and completeness of the change introduced; while to humour the tastes of the upper classes, processions and hunting scenes were afterwards added.

SECTION I.—SYMBOLS OF THE SACRED TRIAD.

In the different countries to which the Buddhists extended their religion, and in which they found it necessary to employ symbols to explain their religious tenets, *Spirit* (*Buddha*, the creative power) was represented by a circle or wheel, as typical of the divine intelligence and the energy which developes all things, and as expressing the passage of the soul through the cycles of existence; *Inorganic Matter* (*Dharma*, the law, or that which regulates) was represented by a circle, or by a monogram formed of the initial letters of the names of the elements of matter, viz., the four material and visible elements (*Fig.* 79), together with the radical or initial letters of mense or mind, the ether of the Greeks, the akás of the Hindus,[1] or the soul, which was supposed to be an emanation from the self-existing God; and *Organised Matter* (*Sangha*, that which has been created and regulated), was represented by a third circle, which, according to the *exoteric doctrine*, was often formed of the terrestrial union of the two former symbols, as on coins, or as on the erect sculptured stones of Scotland, by segments of a circle (*a*), or organised animals, as the elephant (*b*), or a flower, the sacred lotus perhaps, gracefully bending over the

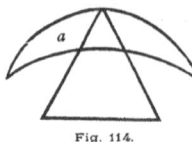

Fig. 114.

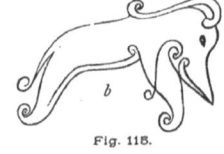

Fig. 115.

---

(1) Gen. Cunningham's Bilsa Topes, p. 355, *et seq.* plate 31; and Book I, ch. VII, p. 103, the Towers of the Elements.

HISTORY OF PAGANISM IN CALEDONIA.

symbol of Deity, from whence it received its spiritual energies, thus indicating, according to the Buddhist idea, that all organic matter was spiritually derived from God, and all animated beings in different degrees of purity, up to man in a condition of perfect purity. The Hindu trimutra, the three-headed Deity—the creating, preserving and destroying god (Brahma, Vishnu and Siva) in its original symbolic form—was adopted by the Buddhists in the form of three circles in the Temple of Ellora, and upon coins forming the *chaitya*, and taken by them to represent their own peculiar trinity.

In the progress of the arts, the symbols of the Buddhist triad assumed a more complicated and elegant form, as it appears in the examples of India. The spiritual deity, Buddha, was represented by a central golden wheel surrounded by the material element as Dharma, and crowned by the third, organic matter, or Sangha, the combination of the two former in an active state.[1] These three "precious jewels" are distinct and dissimilar, and yet of one nature and constitution.[2]

(*a.*) *Circles.*—Examples of simple triad symbols were found by Col. Sykes in the Buddhist temple of Ellora, in India. Among these the members of the triad were each represented by a circle, one above and two below, while on coins the same triangular arrangement of circles was met with, a semi-circle above forming a Buddhist chaitya.[3] Circles in similar arrangement to those on the temple of Ellora are frequently found in Pictland. On a stone in Ross-shire there may be found an example of the same. (*See Fig.* 108—Dingwall stone). Three circles like those in this temple, when occurring on the sculptured stones in Pictland, may therefore form a symbol of the Deity, considered as manifested in the Trinity. Should this hypothesis be correct, they will always be found to differ in size as representing different objects—spirit, inorganic matter, and organic matter.

In the parish churchyard of Kinnellar there is a circle of boulders, of which a considerable number still remain, though they are no longer erect but prostrate. A fragment that either formed a part of one of the stones of the circle, or of a stone in connection with it, is built into the wall of the churchyard. It is 2 feet 3 inches in length, and 1 foot 7 inches in breadth, and at the bottom 1 foot 6 inches opposite the circles. It has incised on it a circle enclosing three smaller ones, the diameter of the large circle being 1 foot 1¾ inches; the greater circle representing Brahma, the self-existent and absolute creator, and the smaller representing severally Vishnu, Siva, and personal life.[4]

Fig. 116.

Fig. 117.

One of the simplest (*Fig.* 117), and probably most ancient, of the British symbols, is formed by three small circles enclosed in a larger one; and of this the stone

---

(1) Journal As. Soc. Bengal, vol. v, p. 37.   (2) *See* Transactions and Journal of the Royal Soc. of Edin., vol xxi, p   .
(3) "I may mention," says Colonel Sykes, "that the three circles form, when close together and surmounted by a crescent, the Chaitya or Buddhist monument, engraved on several of the Buddhist caves, although the circles are not quite contiguous."—On Elephanta, Royal Asiatic Soc., p. 8.
(4) Professor William's Hindostan, p. 87; Colbrooke Essays, vol. ii., p. 254.

of Rothienorman,[1] in Aberdeenshire, is an example. The canopy in this case may represent Providence hovering over, while the three small circles most probably represent the triad. The sceptre ornament, so often associated with this triad, represents animated nature, under theocratic rule, subject to and fulfilling the purposes of God.

A stone (*Fig.* 118) found in the Western Highlands, and now in the Antiquarian Museum, Edinburgh, has a double circle including three other circles, with a book above. The diameter of the large circle is 12 inches, of the right hand small circle $5\frac{1}{4}$ inches, of the left hand one $5\frac{1}{4}$ inches, and of the lower one $5\frac{3}{4}$ inches.[2] The three incised circles within the large circle exhibit the same differences as those on other ancient stones, viz :—two are of the same size, and smaller than the third.

Fig. 118.

The late Mr. Jervis found that the smaller Aberlemno obelisk occupied at one time the north-west part of a primitive circle, now covered with earth, the circle being 6 feet in diameter, and of packed boulders. Both stones appear *in situ*; and the side with the pagan symbols faces the N.W., and is in a line with the obverse side of the cross, so that the worshipper of both the crosses and the symbols on the small obelisk looked straight in the direction of the rising sun.

The Strathpeffer sculptured stone (*Fig.* 119) shows another variety of the triad symbol, having cups with incised circles round them. It is nearly opposite Knock Farrel vitrified fort, and stands upon a small mound. Occupying the upper half of the stone is a horse-shoe, in each of the limbs of which is a cup, under a bell-shaped cover, and in the centre another, under a semicircle.[2] On carefully measuring these cups, I found their diameter was as follows : the right and the left cups were both of the same size, each 1 foot 2 inches, and the upper was 1 foot 5 inches. On the lower parts was inscribed a sacred hawk, or eagle. The cups are guarded by coverings, to indicate their sacred meaning, and the whole represents the heavens with their winged host, and the earth with its animated beings under them, as subject to the rule of the three-one God.[3]

Fig. 119.

(*b.*) *The Dorge or Spectacle-Ornament.*—The Spectacle or Dorge-symbol on the erect stones of Pictland differs, as it does in Asia, in size and form, and in the number of its ribs or radii. There is also a difference in the size of the two circles. In the sculptural stones of Pictland it appears in the form of two circles, representing the two principles of spirit and matter, united by a belt, and crossed by sceptres, indicating sovereignty, and connected with a third below or above, in the form of a segment of a circle or crescent, an elephant, a serpent, a

---

(1) Sculptured Stones of Scotland, vol. ii., Plate xiv, p. 9.
(2) See Transactions of the Society of Antiquaries of Scotland, Index 481.
(3) Through the kindness of the Rev. Dr. Joass, I procured a careful rubbing of this stone.

CHAP. III.] HISTORY OF PAGANISM IN CALEDONIA. 171

flower, &c. The spectacle-ornament is illustrated by the accompanying figure, taken from the smaller Aberlemno stone, in which the smaller circle (*a*) represents spirit, and the larger (*b*) matter, (*c*) the belt, (*d*) the cross-bar,

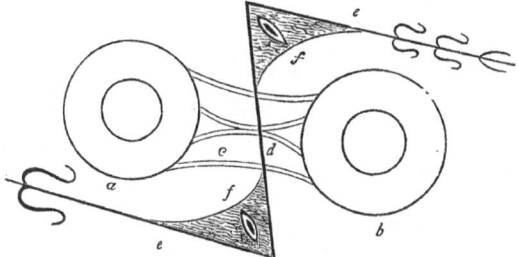

Fig. 120.

(*e e*) sceptres, and (*f f*) the eyes of Providence.[1] The relative size of the two circles will be seen from the following table:—

MEASUREMENT OF CIRCLES IN SPECTACLE-ORNAMENTS.[2]

	Diameter in Inches.			Diameter in Inches.	
	Matter.	Spirit.		Matter.	Spirit.
Aberlemno Small Stone	12 4/8	11 5/8 [1]	Elgin (Cathedral)...	10	9 6/8 [1]
Dyce Obelisk ...	10 4/8	10 1/8	Edin. Museum	5 3/4	5 1/4
Kintore	8 4/8	8 2/8	Strowen	8 4/8	8 4/7
Newton (left arch with a notch)...	7	6 5/8	,, ...	7 2/8	
,, small circle	5 4/8	4 7/8	Anworth (on a rock)	0	7 6/8
Elgin (Cathedral)	12 4/8	11	Dunnichen	10	9 6/10

The two balls, or the circles, of the dorge, the one representing the material element of the world, and the other the spiritual element, form, when united, at once the organised universe and the Deity by whom it subsists. The smaller Aberlemno and the Dunnichen sculptured stones afford examples of such dorges, and the eyes formed on both stones at the angle at the junction of the sceptre and the cross bar, are a proof of the divine nature of the symbol.[3] Stones with these symbols are invariably without reverse, or any symbol of Christianity. There are two Aberlemno stones, the larger with a cross, the small one here referred to being blank.

On the Aberlemno stone (at the church), already mentioned as having a cross, and on the reverse, there is a square or altar with an incised compartment on the upper part, and in the limb of the square is a peculiarly formed triad with a hole worn quite smooth, from the constant insertion of the finger, perhaps, while repeating prayers, or performing certain ceremonies. (*Fig.* 62, 63, p. 64.) Both the small Aberlemno stone and the Dunnichen are undressed sandstone slabs, of an oblong form, with the symbols deeply and carefully incised. Both are sculptured only on one side; and the spectacle-ornament in the former has a sacred serpent bending over it, while the latter has a sacred lotus-flower [g] bending over the sacred symbol, with the comb and looking-

---

(1) The Tope in which the Deity rests is known by an eye being figured on each side. (*See* Cunningham's Bilsa Topes, plate 3, fig. 6 and 7. *See* also a Nepaulese Chaitya or dedicatory Tope, p. 102.
(2) Measured by Mr. Jervis and myself.
(3) Stewart's Illustrations, Sp., plates, p. 15. Nos. 31 and 24.

glass under each. In delineating a dorge upon an obelisk, the two balls or circles would appear when viewed from their ends or axes, either as two sacred wheels, or as a plain circle. The former is the exact representation of the spectacle-ornament upon the small Aberlemno stone.

These Buddhist symbols, when first incised, had no ornaments, as they were the ideal representation of a religious feeling; but on the introduction of Christianity into Pictland, they were no longer held sacred, and became ornaments. The simple spectacle-ornament was used as an ægis, or a shield over the head of a chief.

A love for metaphysics being distinctive of the ancient Hindus, they early evinced this love by identifying the spiritual with the material, or rather by regarding the material as an embodiment of the spiritual.[1] This is seen in their system of sacred signs; particularly in their symbols of the mundane triad. Spirit and matter, the active and passive principles of things, are severally represented by a circle, as if each were complete in itself, but when they unite to form the universe, as represented by the connecting band, the rule they are under is symbolised by the trident sceptres, and the rigour of the rule by the transverse straight rod. To this figure was added the third member of the triad, which might be that of a priest in the ordinary use of the eastern dorge; or, as on the sculptured stones, a sacred elephant, or a flower, which, being living objects, did not require the tridents.

The Keilor Stone is an example of an oriento-symbolically sculptured obelisk. It is one of the oldest extant, is situated two miles from Meigle, to the north of the Sidlaw Hills, on the side of the highway, which stands on a tumulus 4 feet high. It is a rough, oblong mass of gneiss rock, brought from a distance, and is feet 6 inches above, and three feet under the surface. It is 2 feet 8 inches broad, and at its thickest part, near the middle, 10 inches thick. The drawing given (*Fig.* 121), which I made with care, was, on a careful inspection by the late Dr. Stuart, pronounced to be correct.[2] It shows the incised figure of the sceptred spectacle symbol of the Deity, with a sacred animal above,[3] and what may have represented a looking-glass and four cups below, the back of the stone being rough and without any figures. The upper figures were at one time supposed to be Greek letters, while an eminent antiquary, the late Dr. Gregory, described them as Gaelic hieroglyphics, so difficult is it to distinguish animal figures, particularly mythological, on a disintegrating stone. The middle figure is the spectacle-ornament, and the upper an embryo boar. This obelisk appears to have been a prayer-stone, and the spot where it stood considered holy; and it must have retained its sacred character for a long time, as I found near it not only ashes of burnt bodies, but also stone coffins both long and short, of no very antique form, and comparatively recent deposition.

Fig. 121.

Now, however, reverence for this venerable object has so completely died out, that a fire had been kindled at the lower part of the stone a short time before I saw it, and, when heated, the stone itself broken by a large stone being thrown at it. And even after this, it was with difficulty that I was able to preserve it from being broken to pieces for the purpose of mending the road. At length, Lord Wharncliffe, the proprietor, took interest in it, and had the broken stone firmly joined and imbedded in masonry, and the whole included in a small plantation, surrounded by a wall and an iron

---

(1) Witness the Sankhya philosophy. *See* Prof. Monier Williams' Hindustan, p. 490 and pp. 195, 200.
(2) *See* Plate 3 Sculptured Stones, and xxxiv of the Notices.
(3) Which resembles the embryo on the Largo silver ornament, and on other stones.

railing. During these changes I had an opportunity of examining the cairn upon which the stone rested, and found several rough stone coffins, about 6 feet long, 5 feet 6 inches wide, and 1 foot 3 inches deep, disposed in different directions, and filled with earth. The bones had crumbled into dust, and only a few small fragments were left. Other graves, which appeared older, contained ashes of bodies— those, probably, of persons of higher rank—which had been burnt, and charcoal, but no remains of urns. The graves that I explored were evidently of different dates. Some years before there had been found in the same field five oblong stone coffins, composed of flags, and containing crumbling bones. They probably marked an ancient battlefield, and the place is still called "Williewas," a Scotch exclamation of woe, supposed in this case to have been heard proceeding from the women, as in their search after the battle, they came upon body after body of their dead relatives.

The Dyce stone in Aberdeenshire (referred to Book II, ch. III, *Fig.* 120), as figured in the margin (*Fig.* 122), may be instanced as affording an example of the Buddhist triad in the form of the spectacle-ornament, with the

Fig. 122.

elephant as the third member, and the zig-zag lines, probably at first a representation of the thunderbolt, the great token of divine sovereignty, now modified into the form of the sceptre, as the symbol of spiritual power. Of the zig-zag lines which appear on thirty four of these obelisks, there are twenty instances in which they are in combination.

We have often already referred to the eclectic spirit, tending to the combination of foreign symbols with those generally belonging to itself, as a well-known characteristic of Buddhism, and instanced how in the early intercourse of its missionaries they borrowed religious ceremonies from the ritual of the Latin Church, so that the Buddhists of Tartary still use the cross, the mitre, the cope, the responsive choral chants, the rosary, ecclesiastical celibacy, monastic seclusion, fasts, processions, &c.[1] A similar combination appears to have taken place in Scotland on the introduction of Christianity, with this difference, however, that there the faith and the symbol of the cross eventually prevailed over those of Buddhism. For a time the old symbol of the Deity, the "spectacle-ornament," or, as it ought in my opinion to be styled, the "dorge-symbol," was retained along with the emblems of Christianity. From their similarity to each other, the figures on the sculptured stones of the north-east of Scotland appear to have been executed by the same Christian community, and that the very earliest inhabiting this part of the island; the community, in fact, to which Tertullian refers as in the third century inhabiting those parts of Britain, and never conquered by the Romans, and which, after gradually superseding communities that upheld the more ancient beliefs, flourished in the great kingdom of the Picts.

The multiplication of the Buddhist symbols of the triad upon the sacred boulders and obelisks of Scotland was looked upon as an act of grace, to the illumination of ignorance, the conferring of benefit, and the prevention of evil. We know that the same advantages are represented elsewhere as accruing from the multiplication of the sacred formulas and the images of Buddha; and it is thus we explain the desire of the Eastern Buddhists to multiply their symbols and sacred animals upon the monoliths of the Celtic people whom they lived among and taught, and whom they eventually, in some rude way, converted to their faith. These people gave an early proof of their faith in their teachers, by allowing them, though strangers, to delineate their symbols upon the boulders composing circles which they accounted sacred, and upon which no tool had before been allowed to be raised. And so strong was the reverence entertained for these symbols long after that it was before the monoliths inscribed with them, the poor illiterate but sincere converts used to convene at appointed times to receive

---

(1) *See* Travels in Tartary, vol. ii, p. 231.

instruction from missionaries of the Cross and the sacraments of the Christian religion. The sacred character of the stones was preserved and still further enhanced by the presence of Christian symbols engraved on them alongside of the Pagan ones.

These groups or circles of stones were called by the new converts the "clachan," or church, stones, a name afterwards applied to the Christian places of worship, until, at length, when houses were erected near them, the village with the church or monument came to be called the "clachan."[1] The Romans called such a circle of stones "circus," which was converted by the Germans into "Kirche," by the Saxons into "church," and by the Scotch into "kirk."

The practice on the part of the Christian missionary of utilising for Christian purposes erections which the converts were already accustomed to regard as holy, was afterwards authorized by Pope Gregory, in his instructions to St. Augustine. The papal edict directed that the pagan temples in Britain should not be destroyed, but only the idols contained in them, and that the temples themselves might be consecrated to Christian use, after being thoroughly cleaned and sprinkled with holy water.

From the number and size of the boulder monuments in Pictland that still exist, we may infer the earnest religious character of the original Celtic inhabitants, and the fervour of their religious impressions. On their conversion to Buddhism the same earnestness was exhibited, when they allowed the strangers to desecrate their ancient sacred monuments by engraving the peculiar symbols of their religion upon them. The stones that are so marked belong to what we may call the second age of such monuments, and from their peculiar character we conclude that the missionaries who carved the Buddhist symbols on them had come directly from Asia Minor, or thereabouts, probably at the beginning of the Christian era, about 61 A.D., when the Island of Anglesea (Mona) was devastated by Suetonius Paulinus, and the Druid priests killed or ejected.[2] Some of these, escaping as fugitives, may have received protection in Pictland, and among them, or coming shortly after them, may have been Buddhist priests, who, as they advanced northward, drew the sacred symbols of their religious belief upon the rock cropping up on the hill of Anworth, in Galloway, just as we have already seen they were in the habit of doing upon the rocks and stones of Asia. Their simple symbols they inscribed here in a form more easily understood by a rude people than the more complex symbols with the sacred animals with which they afterwards covered the sacred boulders of Pictland, after they had won the confidence of the inhabitants of that country. These symbols were inscribed on the side facing the N.W., so that the worshippers, while regarding them, stood with their faces to the rising sun, the type and manifestation of the power and goodness of the Deity, as he sheds his benefits over the world, and to whom, as to a god, cultivated Asiatics still render prostrate homage every morning and evening.

I have been able to trace on several of these obelisks parts of primitive circles and other Buddhist symbols and objects of worship, such as the sacred lotus-flower and bo-tree, peculiar mythological elephants, sacrificial horses, bulls, serpents, &c. And these symbols and animal figures are found only in Pictland or its neighbourhood, and must have been executed about the time we have referred to, by missionaries from the East desirous of propagating their faith in the extreme West. This conclusion is confirmed by reference to the Buddhist rock inscriptions in different parts in Hindustan, containing the religious edicts of the Emperor Asoka, which insist on the importance of Buddhists spreading themselves over the whole world to convert the ignorant to their faith, as well as by appeal to the zeal and ability of the missionaries themselves, which was such, that after converting the greater part of Asia, they extended their operations to Europe, previous to, or soon after, the Christian era.

---

(1) Armstrong's Gaelic Dictionary.   (2) Tacitus An. xxv, 29 and 30.

The explanation we give of many of the symbols used may not be exactly correct; it is intended merely as a first attempt:—

The Looking-glass and Comb.—These are often found on the Pictland obelisks, but they never appear by themselves. The looking-glass figure, showing a small circular mirror with a handle, is generally found under the spectacle-ornament. It is frequently met with on the old class of obelisks, and its position would seem to indicate something important, and yet from being so often absent, nothing essential. On the Sanchi Tope a royal couple are represented seated on a couch; the male raising a cup to his lips, and the female holding in her hand a round looking-glass, similar in shape to those on the sculptured stones. It also appears in the hands of Hindu goddesses and in the Etrurian tombs,[1] and frequently on the engraved stones of Scotland.[2] In some of the more ornamental stones of Book III this figure appears no longer as a symbol, but as an ornament filled up with an ornamented design.

The Horse-Shoe.—The bell-shaped symbol on the sculptured stones of Scotland has a superstitious feeling attached to it, as it is supposed to represent the figure of the firmament, or Providence hovering over the world; and this has given rise to the idea of its talismanic influence against evil spirits. This symbol, like a canopy, hovers over and protects the third member of the triad, as in the Dunrobin stone. It sometimes hovers over the sceptered segment; sometimes over the mythological elephant, the third member of the triad; and sometimes it is over a bird. The elephant and the bird have never the sceptres over them, as they are in a living state. The horse-shoe is said to indicate the Yoni,[3] and is supposed to keep off the evil eye. The Thibetan saints, or Lamas, have the horse-shoe to protect the person, as the hierogram of the ophite sanctuary, and, as we have seen, as representing the figure of the firmament or Providence hovering over the earth. It appears in many ancient monuments and temples of Egypt and rock temples of India, and upon the sacred symbols in Pictland. It is sometimes identified with the Cross, and it is most probable that the similarity of the horse-shoe to this sacred symbol has given rise to the general belief of good luck attending any one who fixes an old horse-shoe upon the door of his house, where it wards off disease, repels misfortunes, ensures success, and paralyses evil spirits in their career of mischief.[4] The horse-shoe is likewise an artistic emblem.[5] It is even stated that a witch could not pass the threshold of a house protected by a horse-shoe.[6] In Catholic countries the priests bless the cattle and pigs, and brand them on the forehead with the figure of the horse-shoe, and with the iron of Dominico, to guard them from disease.

The third member of the Mundane Triad.—This consists of a segment of a circle, of altars, of mythological elephants, as in the Deer stone; serpents, as in the Aberlemno stone; of birds and sacred trees. The segments of circles are either with or without serpents; those with serpents representing the third member in activity, and those without serpents, as in the Daviot stone, with a sceptre or segment indicating it as in an inert condition. It was usually objects from organic nature that represented the third member of the Buddhist triad. The symbols used, too, such as the segment of a circle, or a cornucopia, like that upon the hill of Anworth (*Fig.* 101, p. 155), in Galloway, were representative of living nature either in some section of it or of the whole.

The segment of a circle (or the cocked-hat symbol) is sometimes decorated with sceptres, and various exoteric symbols, as seen in the Logie[7] and Daviot[8] obelisks, which most probably represent material elements

---

(1) Cunningham's Bhilsa Topes, p. 223.   (2) It appears thirty-six times on these stones.
(3) Inman's Ancient Pagan and Christian Symbolism, p. 78.
(4) Many houses in the West-end of London have a horse-shoe on the threshold. Aubrey's Miscellanies, pp. 141, 142 (about 1696.) We have seen horse-shoes nailed on college doors, vessels, omnibuses, and in one instance, over the gate of a borough jail. (Quarterly Review, vol. ii, p. 326.)
(5) Harcourt Doct. Del., vol. ii, pp. 47, 335, 6, 47.
(6) Journal Hist. Ulster Asst., Dec. 1860, p. 331.   *Also* Arch. Journal, vol. v, p. 137.
(7) Sculp. Stones of Scotland, vol. i, plate 3, p. 4.   (8) *Ibid.*, vol. i, plate 4, p. 4.

of the world, as so remarkably seen in the Lindores stone, described at pp. 125—127, or in the Crichie stone.[1] The obelisks of Dunrobin, Thurso, &c., afford examples of the fork symbol, accompanied with fish segments, &c., as the third member of the mundane triad.

The Altar.—The figure called the *altar* is square or oblong, having a cleft in the lower part with semi-circular notches, and traversed diagonally by a bar terminating in sceptres. This symbol (*Fig.* 123) appears on stones which formed portions of circles or were connected with them; and it consequently belongs to the first or most ancient class of symbols. It is never met with in connection with the spectacle-ornament, the serpent, or horse-shoe, probably because it represents the same triad with the cross-bar. There are six examples of such altars, and stones inscribed with them are invariably without any symbol of Christianity. The only animal inscribed on the stone with them is the goose, which was considered by the Celts as an unclean animal.

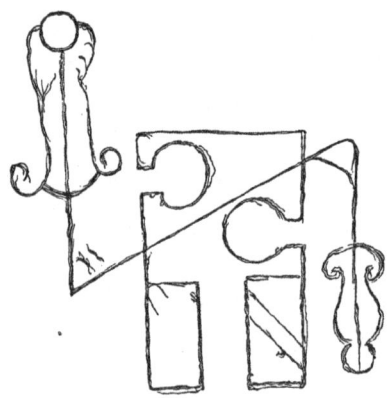

Fig. 123.

The two classes of monuments, the simple boulder monument and the Buddhist sculptured boulder, were connected with Pagan worship, and may have been prepared during the first century, and first half of the second. The sculptured stones, in connection with Druidical circles, are numerous, and the following are examples as published by the Spalding Club, Vol. I:—

Vol.		Page.	No.	Vol.		Page.	No.
I	Huntly Market Place	41	131	I	Rock of Anworth	31	97
	Drimmies	5	9	,,	Thurso Castle	11	30
	Dyce	13	39	,,	Kintore	33	110
	Inveravan	8	15	,,	Criche	6	10
	Eddeston	11	31	,,	Kineller	6	10
	Abernethy	15	40	,,	Aberlemno	21	71
	Dunnichen	28	92	,,	Logie	4	3
	Lindores	32	102	,,			4
	Bulluthorn	20	67	,,	Daviot	4	4
	Dingwall	33	107	,,	Newton	7	12
	Inverary 2nd	35	113	,,	Clatt	4	5
	Drainie, &c.	40	129	,,	Rhynie	4	6
					Brucetown	34	111

A stone with a sculptured serpent and spectacle-ornament was found on Major Grant's farm of Dumbace, Glen Urquhart, Inverness-shire. It was turned up by a plough in 1868, and is supposed to have been used as the covering of a grave composed of flat stones set up on edge. The sculpture is deeply incised and of the earliest type. The serpent has the bar passing between its folds, and its head is inclined upwards and towards the left. The two circles differ in size, and the lower curve of the serpent nearly touches the left circle, or matter, on which it bestows its influence, and which is one quarter of an inch larger than the other.

---

(1) Sculp. Stones of Scotland, vol. i, plate 10, p. 6.

A stone has been recently found on the Castle Hill towards Princes Street Gardens, Edinburgh. It formed part of a bridge in one of the walks below the castle. Its original situation is unknown. The sculptures on it consist of a sceptred segment of a circle, with the remains probably of a sacred symbol.

The peculiarities of the sculptured rock already referred to (*Fig.* 101, p. 155), on a hill near the Parish Church of Anworth, interested me so much that I paid a special visit to it and made a careful drawing of it on the spot. The circles are drawn upon a flat surface of rock cropping out of the ground, and inclined at an angle of about 45°. It is on the Trusty Hill, one of the Ballard Range, and faces in a E.S.E. direction, 200 feet above the beautiful town of Gatehouse. The top of the hill is encircled by the ruins of a vitrified fort, the wall of which is outside the sculptured rock.[1] The spectacle-ornament is horizontal, and has three concentric circles with a central point. The extreme length of the ornament is $22\frac{1}{4}$ inches; the left external circle is $7\frac{3}{4}$ inches and the right 8 inches. The bar crossing the belt is broad and terminates in two sceptres. The extremity of the upper sceptre is opposite the horn-shaped cornucopia, from the mouth of which the sceptre was conceived to receive the vital influence, conveying it to the third member which enters its body. There the embryos are seen formed, and thrown off from the navel, the great centre of organisation according to Eastern mythology. From this navel an embryonic body, with two converging lines or feelers, proceeds. Lower down in the rock is another embryo detached, but more developed, having two long arms or feelers with rounded terminations.[2] We can thus suppose that these antennæ, like those of insects, assisted the embryo in maintaining a separate existence, enabling it both to guard itself against enemies and to obtain the nourishment necessary for its development. This figure may be considered to be one of those delineated upon the rocks by Buddhist priests as they retired north before the oppressive tyranny of the Romans, and the particular delineations would be looked upon by the natives as representing fructifying nature, receiving its vital power from the Deity and throwing off organic bodies. In this case it may be considered as one of the earliest of those remarkable symbols.

These peculiar symbols are not found in any other stone monuments out of Caledonia. They may be said therefore to be peculiar to Pictland; but as they are accompanied with Eastern animals, it is to that quarter we must look for an explanation of their occurrence there. It cannot be supposed that these obelisks were brought and accumulated there by accident, or that they were executed by native artists, since they did not and could not work in stone, and had moreover never seen, or probably heard of the existence of, such Asiatic animals, certainly not in their mythological forms; and what is further remarkable, we find that the Christian crosses there are of a different form from those of other parts of Scotland and England.

The rational explanation, we again insist, appears to be, that these symbols were added to the Celtic sacred obelisks by Eastern artists, called to preach withal to a people who were ignorant of their language, and to whom they were desirous of imparting the precepts of their religion. We see that the artists retained the fundamental conception of their own religious opinions, by the care with which they executed the symbols; while they changed the form and arrangement of the ornaments, so that as a result, there are not two alike. These sacred Buddhist symbols were executed with exactness. Thus, on measuring the circles of the dorge, I found, as I have shown, that they exhibited a difference in their diameter, in consequence of their representing spirit within and matter without the symbol. The two circles of the spectacle-ornament are not always horizontal; in the small Aberlemno stone they are nearly perpendicular, and the upper one represents spirit, which is animating a serpent above it.

---

(1) I was much disappointed to find an iron cage over the monument, so that I was prevented from taking a rubbing, but I saw the necessity for it, in order to protect the relic, as a number of names had been cut in the rock by unthinking people, and the practice was fast threatening to disfigure and destroy the monument.

(2) It has been supposed that this rounding was added in modern times; but on a careful examination, I found the fresh sharp appearance of the incised figure was owing to its having been covered with turf for ages; while the edges of the remainder of the sculpture were rounded from its long exposure to the weather.

There are also very interesting peculiarities about the sculptured stones at Corgah near Grantown. The
two stones are opposite each other, apparently at the entrance to a
confused heap of field-stones or a cairn, enclosed in a circular
fosse or ditch, and said to have been an ancient burial-place for
"unbaptized children," or pagans. These two stones are 3 feet
in height and 4 feet in width, one on each side of an apparent
entrance. The one on the N.E. side has a sculptured dorge (*a*),
of which the right circle is a ¼-inch larger than the left; and *b*
is the third member. The sceptres are not united by a rigid
straight rod, but a line, passing in a curved form, so as to sweep
over the one circle and under the other, as if to suggest a freer,
fuller, and more intimate relation between them and the sovereign
power to which they are subject. This form is different from
all the other examples in Pictland, and seems to explain the
functions of the parts. The third member is in the form of a
peculiar helmet-shaped figure, like the segment of a circle, or
the third member of the triad, with an arrow-shaped rod passing
through a small circle, and a point directed to the inner side of
the left circle. Another peculiarity is in the connection of the
extremities of the segments with each other. This is not direct,
as usual, but by means of a straight line across the belt uniting
the two circles. In this example, the extremity of the sceptre
passes along the circle (spirit) and joins the opposite circle
(matter) on the outside of the connecting belt.

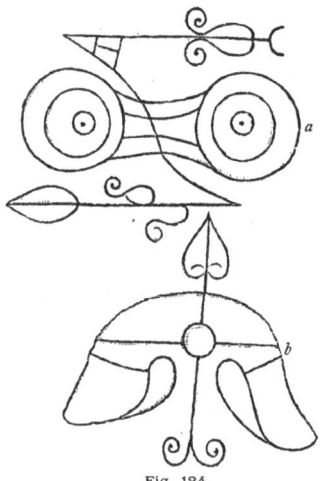

Fig. 124.

CHAPTER IV.

SACRED PLACES AND MONUMENTS.

N this chapter we propose to consider Sacred Places and Monuments, comprehending Caves, Elevations, Monasteries (vaharas), Obelisks, Topes, and Towers (Lâts), and Rock Inscriptions.

SECTION I.—CAVES.

Caves.—Caves were the natural dwellings or homes of men in early ages, and even in this country some on the sea-coast were occupied as such so recently as the time of the Romans, by a class who lived partly by fishing and partly by the plunder of ships wrecked on the shore. In the East natural retreats such as these were resorted to for purposes of worship, till at length they acquired the sacred character of temples. The cave-temples of India are well known, and though mostly artificial, there can be no doubt they were primarily natural caves sanctified to a sacred purpose. Buddhist, as well as Hindu sects, had recourse to them, and the former might naturally take to such retreats for worship in the lands which they visited in the propagation of the Faith. This, accordingly, we find they did in Pictland.[1] At an early period the Buddhist missionaries lived in the caves of Fife, and drew symbols of their religious worship on their walls. The religious instinct naturally courts seclusion in the performance of its ritual, and it was in all probability to gratify this that men at first converted caves into temples, as they, for the same purpose, sought the recesses of forests, hedged themselves round with fences, and as they still subdue the light admitted to churches consecrated even to Christian worship.

SECTION II.—ELEVATIONS, MOUNDS, HILLS, AND GROVES.

If there are elements in the religious consciousness of man which court seclusion, there are others which have no less an instinct for the open air and the upper light. Accordingly, we find that while the one set of impulses drove him to caves for secrecy, the other urged him to seek the mountains, and even the mountain-tops. There he might not only feel as retired and as awe-struck as in caverns, but there his worship was rendered in the presence of a symbolism that was suggestive to him, as no mystic shrine could be, of all that he owed to the light of heaven and the breath of life. In the cave he might well experience some sense of the mystery of being, only in the upper air and on some elevated vantage-ground could he realize its glory and sympathize in

---

[1] Smith, Collectina Antiqua, vol. i., p. 66. The Celts, Romans, and Saxons, 2nd edition, by Thomas Wright.

its joy. Here, too, his soul would feel purified as well as elevated, and see, as well as feel in some measure, what Christianity first confidently assures us of, the mercy and the grace of God. Such spots are sacred in the Buddhist as in every other religion, and we have noted several of these already in the course of our work. For the Buddhist, though he is an ascetic, is an ascetic only as regards self-seeking, and nowise as a worshipper of the sun, in whose effulgence he hopes one day to be lost.

Section III.—Monasteries (Vahara).

Monasteries were common among the Buddhists from ancient times, and they still exist in great numbers in Thibet. Here no noise or care disturbs the meditations of the inmates, and no danger threatens their peace. Here the heart is weaned from carnal affections, and the gross appetites are subdued and chastened, while the soul is wafted into the regions of philosophy, and borne on the wings of truth into higher and higher spheres. For Buddhism, like Christianity, is an anti-worldly religion, and from the first feels the need of a separation from the world's ways. Inward separation is not enough; outward is also necessary. This was necessary for Buddha himself; and, as Buddha had ordained, far more so for his mere followers. In this we recognise nothing morbid, but rather a high ideal of life, a low estimate of worldly people, and a deep sense of either the weakness of man or the seductiveness of evil. And these monasteries, if they have not served the purpose of conserving the spirit, have contributed to preserve the records, of Buddhism; for in them these records are still kept and cared for.

Section IV.—Pillar Towers, or Towers of Deliverance.

Pagan Pillar Towers in Ireland.—Ireland, being at the extreme western part of the then known world, was, as we have already described, early visited by Asiatic missionaries under the idea that it was situated near the home and the seat of the immortal gods. Being surrounded by warlike tribes, the Buddhists in Ireland first erected the primitive pillar towers for the preservation of their lives and their sacred effects, and they enlarged and strengthened them when they were more powerful and more practised in the arts. Two of these are described at page 84; they were small and rude in their construction, and the stones badly dressed and indifferently selected. One of these had merely a door for its defence, and the other had a large window besides, like the door with a large window of the ancient form, intended to admit light in giving instruction to their followers.[1]

As the Buddhists extended their influence and their experience of the character of the natives, they felt the importance of these pillar towers, and began to construct others with that skill which is so characteristic of their elevated buildings in Asia, which have never been surpassed in any country.

We have already described, page 79, how the Buddhist missionaries changed their symbolical pillars (lâts) to hollow cylindrical or pillar-towers, to protect their persons, and the precious relics which they carried with them to distant countries and valued so highly. The remains of some of these are still to be found in different parts of Hindustan. Tennent states that the pagodas of Blyars, of the Circars, are chiefly buildings of a cylindrical or "round tower" shape; with their tops either pointed, or truncated at the summit, which frequently bears a round ball on a spike, to represent the sun.[2] Hanway, in his travels in Persia, states that there are four round temples of the *Guebres*, or worshippers of fire, "about thirty feet in diameter, and about 120 feet in height."[3]

---

(1) I have called these specimens of the primitive Pillar-Towers.
(2) View of Hindustan, vol. ii., p. 123, or vol. vi., p. 133.   (3) *Ibid.*, p. 137.

CHAP. IV.]   HISTORY OF PAGANISM IN CALEDONIA.   181

The sacred nature of these pillar-towers in Buddhist countries explains why they are sometimes delineated upon coins, with other sacred objects; as in the drawing at p. 82 (*Fig.* 78), in which the "Tower of Deliverance," and the sacred tree are both represented as springing out of a Buddhist pot.

Pillar Towers were first erected in Ireland by artists from the East, with a degree of skill that has never been surpassed, and at a time when the inhabitants of Ireland and Scotland were in a state of great rudeness. The towers were well adapted for defending the occupants and their effects from the rapacity of the warlike chiefs among whom they dwelt.

The beautiful Pillar Tower of Duncliffe (*Fig.* 125) was erected at an early period in the County of Dublin, and it is remarkable for the admirable selection of the stones used, before quarries had been opened, and when they were, moreover, at a great distance and difficult to reach, as well as for the segment of a circle in which they were wrought.

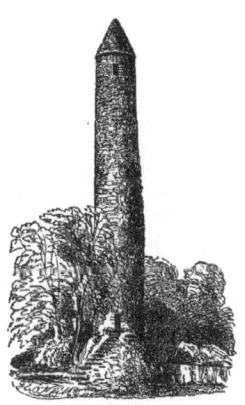

Fig. 125.

The able and enthusiastic pagan architects may have refused to construct any sacred buildings except these pillar-towers. They appear to have erected, in the north-east of Scotland, standing stones only, which at first bore only the pagan symbols. In Ireland, first a sacred pillar was erected, which afterwards became a national ornament, and Christian emblems were placed on it in a more advanced state of the arts. In no other erections of the earlier period was the same architectural superiority exhibited, as sacred structures alone were considered worthy of the exertions of the architects.

In peaceable times the Buddhists collected their followers and prepared for their sacred services, by the sound of the trumpets, and these are still occasionally found near the pillar towers. Those used were such as are drawn (*Fig.* 126), and marked *a, b, c, d, e, g* and *h*. The long trumpet is still used in modern Buddhist temples at stated times during their religious ceremonies, along with the beating of drums, gongs, &c. It is probable that the Buddhist missionaries performed some of their religious ceremonies while standing at the elevated door.

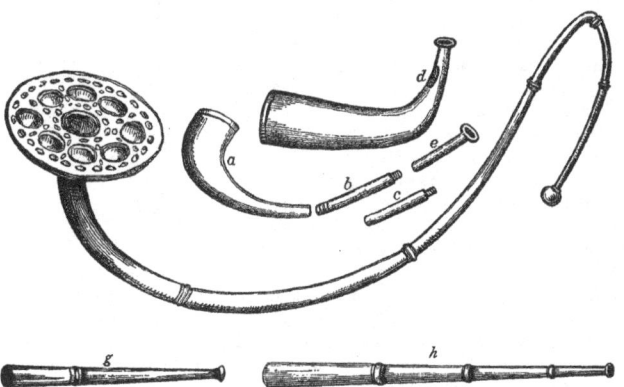

Fig. 126.

The pillar towers were first erected in Asia as religious edifices, and to afford protection to the persons, the relics, and other

AA

valuable effects of the builders; and in Ireland, as places of refuge and observation, from whence they could alarm their friends by the blast of the horn, the clang of the cymbal, or the roll of the drum during the day, and by waving a torch from the apertures at the top of the tower at night.

Fig. 127.

The Cloyne Pillar Tower (*Fig.* 127) may be instanced as an example of one class of tower. The top of this graceful tower was injured by lightning, and a battlemented top was built upon it. The reddish coloured sandstone of which the tower is built was obtained in the neighbourhood, and is still in excellent preservation. The curvature of the tower was worked with a chisel-pointed hammer. The stones are large and flat-bedded, and carefully worked into the form required. The thickness of the wall at the door is 3½ feet, and the diameter is 9 feet 2 inches throughout. The doorway looks S.E. by E., and is 11¼ feet from the ground. It is flat-topped, being covered with a lintel, and is wider below than above. This tower has six stories; the first being on a level with the door, and the others resting upon ledges projecting from the wall; while the height of the chambers is 11½ feet. The four top windows face the cardinal points, and like the door, are broader below than above, after the Pelasgic and Egyptian style. Below, there are several small openings, one of which, over the door, is larger than the others, and shows a marked modification of the arch. The modern tradition is that when St. Colman was finishing the tower, he was scared by the appearance of the Evil One in the form of an old woman. In his fright he leaped from his elevated position, and alighted upon a flat rock on the side of a hill, two miles distant, upon which the impression of his hands and feet are still seen in the form of four or more cups of an interesting description on a horizontal piece of rock.

Devenish (Fermanagh county), the most perfect of this class of Pagan pillars, is constructed of sandstone, carefully wrought, and with ornamental mouldings at the base of the cone.

Varieties of Towers.—The Tower (*Fig.* 128) of Ardmore (county of Waterford), is nearly perfect; it is of conical shape, with three weathered string courses, while the door is circular at the top, and 13ft. from the ground. The Keneith Tower (*Fig.* 129) is built of the slate-stone of the locality, and is very peculiar in its external form, having a hexagonal base, each side of which is 10 feet 4 inches in width, and 20 feet in height. Including the round part, the tower is 50 feet 4 inches, in height, and it appears to have been left unfinished; or else a portion of the original top has been destroyed. This tower is built upon a levelled rock, cropping abruptly from the ground. The door faces the west, and is 14 feet from the ground. The whole has recently undergone repair, and has been provided with iron stairs to the door, and to each of the four stories, which rest upon ledges left in the thickness of the wall, each compartment being 11 feet and 9 inches in height. The diameter of the tower contracts as the wall rises; and the breadth of each ledge, four inches, increases the splaying of the wall. There is a small bell in the upper stage, supported by cross beams, but it appears to be unused. The walling of the foundation consists of large rough stones, and the selections of the slate stones has been so skilful that it is still in good preservation. The narrow, flat and slightly concave chisel hammer still leaves a clean cut in the stone.

Fig. 128. Fig. 129.

The floor of this tower is on a level with the door, and is supported by a flat arch with a small hole in the centre, proving the advanced state of the arts at the time of its construction. A chamber is thus formed below the level of the door. The whole erection is admirably executed and cemented with shell lime, and the general effect is most graceful. This would be much more apparent but for the ivy which covers the lower part, and has already displaced some of the stones. If this ivy is not removed it will endanger the tower. This subject will be resumed in Book III, when treating of the Christian Towers.

Section V.—Pillars of Victory.

Instances of boulders appropriated or erected as monuments of victory are so familiar and numerous that there is no need to refer to them in detail. Samuel set up such a stone, and called it Ebenezer,[1] and most of them, like this one, had originally a religious reference, so that they symbolize ideas of the Deity as well as express gratitude for triumphs vouchsafed. By and by monuments of the kind degenerated into merely personal memorials, and some of the earliest known mark only graves of the dead. This may have arisen from the practice of raising memorials on battle-fields, so that they became at once monuments of victory, monuments to those who fell in the fight, and thank-offerings to the gods. Many of them found in Caledonia are proved to have been sepulchral by the inscriptions on them, as well as by the fact that cists have been found associated with them.[2] Among the inscriptions in Christian countries the symbol of the cross is usually included, as if to signify that the deceased was a Christian, and owed his victory to Christ. On a stone in Drogheda, in Ireland, there is a symbol of the Creator, just as on sacred stones of the kind among the Hindus we find often an image of Mahadeva carved.

In Egypt the simple boulder-stone, so used, passed, as we have seen, into the obelisk, where the figure, as it looked out with its four sides to the four quarters of the horizon, tapered off to a point, as if to represent a tongue of fire. These monuments usually placed before temples (*propylæa*), were, according to Herodotus, first dedicated to the sun and represented his eyes, and doubtless are memorials of victory and suggestive of triumph.

Of the stones inscribed with the edicts of Asoka, which are among the earliest sculptured remains extant, there are some which have been appropriated as memorials of triumph. There is one at Delhi which was erected by Feroz Shah as a pillar of victory in memory of his victories over the Hindus. Of these early monuments three are still standing near the river Durnerdash in Tirhoot, and one is erected on a pedestal in the fort of Allahabad. A fragment of another remains near Delhi, and part of a seventh was utilized as a roller on a road near Benares by an engineer officer of the East India Company.

The Mohammedan Tower of Victory.—The Buddhist pillar towers were sometimes altered by the Mohammedans by casing the tower in a layer of stones from the bottom to the top, and so changing the style of the doors and windows as to give a new character to the tower, while inscriptions were added giving the name of him in whose honour it professed to be erected, with an enumeration of the deeds for which he had been distinguished. (*See Fig.* 26.)

Section VI.—Inscriptions on Pillars or Lâts.

The inscription on lâts and rocks in Asia is memorial, or contains royal edicts, as in Hindustan. In Western India there are rocks inscribed with imperial edicts. One shewn in a drawing, *London News*, Jan., 1872, gives, like the others, the edicts of the Buddhist Emperor Asoka, who reigned in India about the 3rd century B.C. It is near Junagarth, in Kathrawad, and is 20 feet high and 69 in diameter. These edicts regard the building of a neighbouring bridge.

---

(1) 1 Sam., vii., 12.   (2) *See* an instance mentioned by Macculloch in his "Western Islands."

The second edict on the Gomor Rock is as follows:—In the whole dominion of King Devanampriya Preyadasin, as also in the adjacent countries, as Chola (Tanjore), Randigo (Arest), Satyaputra, Herolaputra (Malabar), as far as Tamraparne (Ceylon), the kingdom of Antiochus, the Grecian king, and of his neighbour-kings, the system of caring for the sick, both of men and cattle, followed by King Devonampreya, has been everywhere brought into practice, and at all places where useful healing herbs for man and cattle were wanting, he has caused them to be brought and planted, and at all places where roots and forest trees were wanted, he has caused them to be brought and planted; and he has caused all wells to be dug and trees to be planted on the roads for the benefit of men and cattle." Thus the second and the fourteenth edicts form the historical link which connect India and Greece. In the second the names of Gona, Gavan, Ioman, and the Greek King Antiochus occur, the latter of whom died B.C. 247, in the 12th year of Budarmed or Asoka's reign. In the thirteenth table the names of the Greek kings Ptolemais, Antigonus, and Magos occur, and the fourth, the number of Asoka's embassies, which were for victory, not by the sword, but by religion.[1]

(1) Account of Asoka by Rhys Davids.

CHAPTER V.

SACRED BUDDHIST ORGANIC SYMBOLS ON THE SCULPTURED STONES OF PICTLAND.

HE organic symbols on the obelisks of Pictland consist of Beasts, Fishes, Reptiles, &c., with forms from the vegetable kingdom, and they are all found to be among the sacred symbols of Buddhist worship.

Section I.—Sacred Animals.

Among these sacred animals are the monkey, the serpent, the elephant, the horse, the centaur, the bull, the boar, the stag, the lion and the leopard, the camel and the dromedary, together with sundry birds and fishes.

(*a.*) *Monkeys* were among the sacred animals which assisted Rama in his conquest of Ceylon. They are in consequence inviolable, and under no circumstances are they allowed to be molested. Numbers of them are found in the neighbourhood of temples; in the groves of the bo-tree near villages, where they live on nuts; and in the neighbourhood of grain merchants, where they freely devour the contents of the exposed baskets of grain, from which they are regularly enticed away to other grain-stores, so that it is with a grudge they receive their food from Buddha's followers.

(*b.*) The *Serpents* have been already noticed under the head of serpent-worship, in Book I, p. 105.

(*c.*) *The Celestial Elephant.*—It was the Celestial Elephant (asobat azaza vartvaro) that conveyed the soul of Buddha to be incarnated in his mother's womb; and this elephant is represented as white, with seven tusks for defence. The honour thus ascribed to the elephant was not so much due to its natural as to its mythological attributes, the elephant having from of old—for the myth is an exclusively Indian one—figured in the Hindu imagination as the cloud-steed of Indra, the dispenser of the gifts of heaven, and the god especially of the beneficent rain. This is evident from the perfect form of the head, and the white colour ascribed to the one which bore Buddha on his back in one of his avatars. It is represented as such in the caves of Ajunta; and it is in this aspect it has been appropriated as the symbol of universal dominion. It is owing to this circumstance that the Buddhist king of Burmah proudly claims to be the lord of the white elephant, for, as representing Buddha, he considers himself the sovereign of the world. The sacred character of these animals is unquestionable. They differ from the real animal in the qualifications required of them, and this explains their peculiar form and colours. Sometimes their members are increased in size, to indicate an increase of power in such parts: the size or number of the heads indicate intellect, the large legs power, while their imperfect movement is indicated by legs and feet terminated in scrolls. This exaggeration is seen sometimes in Asia, and frequently in Pictland; and in the Hindu mythology the elephant supports the world, just as Atlas, in the Greek mythology, figures as the world-bearer. The sacred character of the elephant, with its imperfect movement, as indicated by the legs and feet finished off with scrolls, is represented on a frieze in an old Buddhist temple at Benares, among the ruins of Manipore. I have figured this curious piece of carving in the margin [1] (*Fig.* 130). It formed a basement moulding, executed on a long slab. It may be observed that the mythological elephant is distinguished by its head. The head in this case is large; and when the lower members terminate in scrolls, this is to indicate its wisdom and aëreal nature.

Fig. 130.

The sacred elephant is represented on about a hundred of the monoliths of Pictavia in Scotland, with peculiar lineal marks on the body, and the legs terminating in scrolls *(see Fig.* ,115, p. 168). The whole outline testifies to its foreign origin, and the form is one that is carefully and rigidly maintained in the early, or purely heathen sculptures. The head of the elephant as sculptured on the stones of Scotland is that of the Asiatic and not that of the African species,[a] yet it is so delineated as not to represent exactly the real animal as the delineators knew it. In Scotland the aim of the Buddhists was to represent not the real elephant as artists, but the celestial elephant as missionaries, and this accordingly was the form in which it was incised on the stones in the Buddhist interest.

The original form of these animals as adopted for symbolic purposes, and carefully copied in a rude age by the sacerdotal caste as so delineated, was retained in India, Egypt, and other pagan countries; and, though in other cases the art of delineation went on improving among these nations, the original prescribed mode of drawing these sacred symbols was always followed, and to insure this, the preparation of them was entrusted to particular families and schools. The figures of the deities and other sacred objects were executed according to an exact geometrical scale, regulative of the size, form, and attitude of the body, the position and form of the eyes, the shape of the nose and mouth, the cast and covering of the head, body, and extremities, as well as the age and expression. There are still schools for the preparation, according to an orthodox type, of these sacred figures at Landack and Zaskar. No innovations or improvements are allowed; no attempt to copy nature is encouraged or tolerated; and the fancies, weaknesses, and blunders of early times are religiously respected and imitated by all succeeding artists. [3] It is thus we explain the form of the flowers and trees, animals and gods, represented in fresco in the temples of India,[4] and on the sculptured stones of Scotland.[5] They are not after the natural type, and their peculiar exaggerations are intended to emphasise particular attributes. This, too, accounts for the number of the heads and arms of the pagan gods, and the grotesque representations that are in different countries given of the person of Buddha. In Bengal, Buddha is sometimes represented riding a winged horse and brandishing a scimitar, but the figures in Ceylon, Ava, Burmah, and China all differ from one another. In each of these countries, when a particular symbolic representation was adopted, it was considered impiety to vary it in any way from the original form.

---

(1) *See* Journal As. Soc., Calcutta, for 1867, p. 159, v. 93; but particularly an original sketch in my possession, by G. C. Horn, B.C.S.
(2) *See* Col. Forbes Leslie's Early Races of Scotland, vol. ii, p. 416.
(3) *See* Captain Godwin Austin's Papers, Journal Asiatic Soc., Calcutta, vol. xxxiii, p. 151—1864. Wilkinson and Lane's Egypt.
(4) Ferguson's Tree and Serpent Worship. (5) Stuart's Sculptured Stones of Scotland, Spalding Club.

CHAP. V.]   HISTORY OF PAGANISM IN CALEDONIA.   187

(d.)—*The Worship of the Mythological Horse.*—There is one representation of this horse in England, two in Scotland, and one, sacred to the sun, in Ireland. The accompanying impressions (*Figs.* 131-133) of coins are British, and prove the existence of horse-worship among the early Britons. (*See Horse Worship*, Book I, chap. vii, p. 111.)

Such inscribed coins are found in the West of England, and are struck either in silver or gold. On the obverse (*Fig.* 131) *Bodvo* is impressed in large letters across the field, and surrounded with a circle of pellets; while on the reverse a two-tailed horse faces the right, with two ring ornaments above it, and below it a wheel. On the obverse (*Fig.* 132), there is, besides the name of *Bodvo*, a beardless head with a profile looking to the left; while on the reverse we have a horse galloping to the right with a ring above it, and a number of crosses and pellets scattered about. The name here may be supposed to represent that of some chief, but, after a careful examination of these coins, Dr. Evans confesses ignorance regarding them, and says, "their history is unknown."[1]

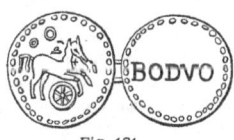

Fig. 131.   Fig. 132.

As, however, it is now generally allowed that there were Buddhists in Scotland and Ireland, and most probably in England, about the time of the Roman occupation, what more natural to conclude that these are Buddhist medals stamped with the name of Buddha. The more that we know the Buddhists were in the habit of so stamping such in the countries where they were residing, varying the impression according to the fashion of the country. In Java, among a rude people, they crowded their medals with such symbols (*Fig.* 137); but in England, among a more enlightened community, they added the name of Buddha. All that Dr. Evans can say about these coins with certainty, is, that they were struck in the West of England, at the late period of the Roman coinage in Britain. We regard them as an additional testimony to the reception, in some measure among us, at that early date of the religion of Buddha.

The horse is sometimes represented on coins with web-shaped feet, and with the sacred ægis over him, as in *Fig.* 133, while in the central countries of England he is delineated, as at Effington and elsewhere, in gigantic proportions. (Book I, p. 112.) All such peculiarities point to mythological ideas, and these, if not the modes of representing them, have clearly an Oriental source, and might well have been imported by the missionaries of a religion whose policy it was to utilize whatever they met with, whether it was indigenous or not, which might serve as a vehicle for the delivery among an alien people of the truth they had gone forth to teach.

Fig. 133.

Riding Horses, in the sculptured stones, are of different sizes. The chieftain is always known by his size and dress, and is mounted on the largest horse, with a staghound by his side, which was only allowed to be kept by the chiefs; while his follower is mounted on a smaller horse, with a small terrier dog at his side.

---

(1) Coins of Ancient Britons, chap. ix, p. 130, *seq.*

(e.) *Dog.*—The dog plays a conspicuous part in all mythologies, chiefly as a house-guard and a hunter, and sits on the threshold where treasures lie. In the capacity of guard, his place is outside the dwelling, and he watches it against the demon powers at night. In Eastern fantasy he figures as seated on the rim of the horizon where the sun enters the underworld in the evening, and is still on watch there in the morning when the sun comes back. Thus he belongs to the death kingdom as well as the darkness, and in the form of Cerberus he guards the souls of the dead. As a hunter even he belongs to the night divinities, yet as attendant on Diana is a servant of the light, his post ever on the border land between light and darkness, death and life, as a minister of the upper powers, or of the under, as in league with those above.

In the accompanying cut,[1] dogs are represented under the altar, while the two priests are guarding the Eucharist. These two dogs represent the evil genius crouching and scowling at the ceremony that is passing above. Another representative of the same species is supporting the head of the two labourers.[2]

Fig. 134.

(2f) *Centaur.*—The mythological centaur, so familiar in Grecian art, as well as the useful camel, the ship of the desert, lions, and hunting scenes, are found on the sculptured stones of Scotland, associated with representations of church dignitaries and persons of rank, in combination with the Christian cross. The former could only have been sculptured by artists from the East, acquainted with their appearance; and the latter by those acquainted with the customs and habits of the higher classes of Scotland.

The centaur is a mythological fancy which combines in one the form of a horse and that of a man, and it is found sculptured on monuments in widely different regions at once of Asia, Africa, and Europe. It is one of the signs of the ancient Hindu zodiac, the one from which we derive our Sagittarius, the archer. He is described as the armour-bearer of Osiris in the Egyptian zodiac.[3] In the ancient Greek mythology the race came into fierce collision with the Lapithæ, in consequence of one of them having offered violence to the bride of the king; the result of which was a war in which many of them were slain and the rest forced to retreat.

The earliest and the original form of the centaur was that of a human figure joined to the body and hind legs of a horse, and the idea represented was the two-fold relation found to subsist between the spiritual and the animal in man, in most cases the animal, as in the common herd of them, running away with the spiritual altogether, and in a few, as in Chiron, the spiritual holding the animal in check and bestriding it to spiritual account. The earliest modes of representation is shown in the figure (*Fig.* 135) taken from a painted vase, the name Chiron, who is the embodiment of the spiritual in the form of instinct, being inscribed near the head in Greek letters. This is supposed to have been executed thirty years before the Parthenon.

Chiron also appears on the most ancient vases, with the same folds of drapery, encircling motionless limbs, and hanging straight. When the figure was represented in motion, the bold action of well-developed muscles was exhibited, and the flow of the drapery was arranged to suit the action of the body, as seen i

---

(1) Spalding Club, vol. i, p. 28.   (2) *See* Frontispiece.
(3) Maurrus Hist., vol. i, p. 304.

HISTORY OF PAGANISM IN CALEDONIA.

Fig. 135.

Fig. 136.

the Borghese centaur of the Louvre. In this figure (*Fig.* 135) a branch of pine tree issues from the head of the centaur, the cones forming the chaplet upon his head. Two goats mounted upon his back reach up to the fruit.[1]

The centaur is sometimes represented bearing a branch of a tree with nuts;[2] and as the figure appears upon ancient British and Gallic coins, it is of a date anterior to the Roman invasion. He is sometimes represented as blowing a horn, or playing upon pipes. On the back of the large Meigle cross (*Fig.* 136) a centaur is represented armed with battle-axes for the destruction of the sacred groves, branches of which they are seen carrying away. Such a conception could not have originated in the brain of a Caledonian, but clearly points to Greece, or perhaps the mysterious Pelagians, who appear in Druidism as the worshippers of the oak. The Buddhist sages, we fancy, must have picked up these fabulous fantasies in their progress towards the West. Certain trees were respected as sacred by the Caledonians, after the introduction of Christianity, which explains their appearing in honourable positions on the same stones with the cross, as on the Eassie stone, while the centaur is represented on the lower part of the stone; and in the Aberlemno stone a bar separates the figure from the chiefs above.

The idea of the centaur appears to have first suggested itself to the Greek fancy in connexion with the tradition of a race of horsemen who wrought great havoc among the early settlers by their skill in horsemanship, and so much did the man and the horse move and act in concert, that it seemed, as they were at length believed, to form only one animal (*Fig.* 135), which we know was the fancy of the Mexicans long after, when they first witnessed the equestrian feats of the Spanish horsemen from Europe.

(*g.*) *The Sacred Bull* is pre-eminently a Hindu symbol, and the worship of it, along with that of the cow dates from the time when the Hindus were especially a pastoral people, and depended on these two for their chief subsistence. Soon the one became the representative of the male, and the other that of the female, principle in Nature; and so together the symbols of all things in that sphere on which depend physical life and strength. The bull drank of the soma, or primal liquid element, which distilled from the udder of the cow, and thus acquired the power of procreating all that lives, and so is in turn life-generative and life-supporting.

In India the bull, like the cow, is protected as a sacred animal, and more especially such as are perfect in form and uniform in colour. White bulls were held in especial honour among the Celts, who used to sacrifice them to the moon; and so sacred was this animal regarded among them, that to swear by the image of it was accepted as an oath taken before the gods. An oath of this kind was once (101 B.C.) given by the Cimbri to the Romans and accepted as a pledge that the terms of the treaty made when they capitulated would be religiously respected. Bulls of a decidedly Hindu character are met with on the stones of Scotland. There is one on the large Meigle Cross, which has the characteristic Asiatic hump upon its shoulder.

---

(1) *See* M. Baiardi (Bayard), Antichite del Ereoland Pittur and Pliny zuxes.
(2) Dennie's Cities and Cemeteries of Etruria, vol. ii, p. 18.

A bull, of the same type, was found at Burghead on the Moray Firth incised on a sandstone slab among the ruins of a stone and lime fortification remains of mouldings lying in its neighbourhood.[1] A small bronze bull was found in Cornwall with a human face and some of the features of the lion, and was therefore probably sacred to the sun As this is a Phœnician symbol, and the Phœnicians were in the height of their prosperity about 1100 to 550 B.C., this bronze, if theirs, must be very old. The Greeks are supposed to have first added the human face to the body of an animal, but this is a mistake, as the custom was of Eastern origin. The decoration of the body is more Egyptian than Assyrian; and the head looks as if we had the Egyptian Apis employed in a Phœnician superstition. The sacred bull was consulted as an oracle, and to it, as representing the sun, divine honours were paid, and festivals celebrated.[2]

(*h.*) *The Sow and the Boar.*—The sow is well known for its exceeding fecundity, and was associated as a symbol with the worship of the procreative or conceptive power of Nature, such as that of Ceres, the fertile goddess of the earth. It naturally came, at length, to be identified with mere libidinous excesses, and to represent a nature given over to sensual indulgence, as in the companions of Ulysses under the spell of Circe. The form of the sow, as well as that of the boar, is often assumed merely for purposes of disguise, and there often lurks under these forms a certain demoniacal power. This is especially the case with the boar, which is frequently represented as the divine in the demon form entering the demon world, and fighting and overpowering it with its own weapons. Thus is it at one time a pure demon, at another a god armed with demon power in the interest of the gods, doing spiritual battle with carnal weapons, the mood somewhat fierce, as we may see in the conquests of Islam. Hercules when he slays the boar of Erymanthus is the divine dealing death with its own weapon. Vishnu, incarnated as a boar, is the divine dealing death with the help of the demoniacal, or the terrible, as a weapon of Divine power, like the Gorgon's head on the shield of Athene. The mythological boar is consecrated to Vishnu; and upon a slab of argillaceous sandstone, at Knocknogail near Inverness, is the figure of a mythological boar marked as sacred. It is incised rather faintly, with the peculiar waving marks. The extremities have human hands and feet, and not the cloven feet of the animal. A concentric incised circle, with a central point, is over the boar.

(*i.*) *The Stag* is often represented as spotted, and belongs therefore obviously to the symbolism of night, the spots being the stars. Mythologically conceived, it is the light in the darkness, sometimes direct, sometimes reflected, but always pure, though cold. It is never sunlight, but at best moonlight. In the fourth century the stag appears on sculptured sarcophagi as the symbol of the companionship, through the night of death, of a spirit, which reflects the departed upper light; as the guide of the soul into the invisible world, the idea being the assurance that such light as we have enjoyed here, may be trusted as a light sufficient to guide us through the gloom that seems to lie between us and our arrival there. It is the pagan emblem of the resurrection of the dead.

(*k.*) *The Lion*, though seldom, if ever, delineated on the stones of Pictland, deserves, as a mythological animal, a passing reference. He is the symbol of all kinds of royal or self-derived strength in the hour of its triumph, representing the sun, for instance, at that season of the year when his power is at its height. He is the symbol of royalty, as making all things loyally bow to itself, and is identified with Buddha, who is called the Lion of the Sakyas, viewed as manifested and prevailing in the zenith of his might; his people, if we may say so, willing in the day of his power. His strength, like Samson's lies in his hair; stripped of that, he is weak, as the sun shorn of his rays. The demon of night knows this; and hence, when the lion of the day descends amid flame in

---

(1) Pinkerton's Inquiry, 2nd edit., vol. i, pp. 6–8.   (2) Wilkinson's Ancient Egyptians, chap. xiii, p. 319.

the evening, the blaze was fabled to be due to the demon plucking off his hair and setting it on fire. He is also, like Achilles, especially vulnerable in the feet, though that is a wound which can be healed by plucking out the thorn. The figure of a lion is at times seen surmounting the Buddhist Tope, and is doubtless intended to symbolise at once the royal degree and royal power of the founder of Buddhism.

(*l.*) *Camel and Dromedary.*—The camel and dromedary appear upon the ancient crosses of Scotland. They were probably inscribed there by the Buddhist priests in grateful remembrance of the assistance which the "ship of the desert" had rendered to the pilgrims when traversing the vast wastes of Asia. There is a camel on the Meigle cross, and a dromedary upon the cross in Canna, one of the Western Islands of Scotland, in Inverness-shire. This cross is peculiar in form, representing the transition from the Pictavian cross to the Western or Irish, and the picture of the dromedary appears on the right arm. These animals are of purely Oriental derivation, and point to the arrival in these parts at a remote time of Eastern pilgrims.

(*m.*) *Birds.*—Of Birds, such as the Indian *goose*, the *swan* of the Buddhists; the *ruddy shelldrake*, the well-known *chaqua-chaque* of the Hindus, and the Ibis, the ancient symbol of vitality among the Egyptians, there is little or no trace on the stones of Scotland, as the Caledonians were prejudiced against them, and other birds were substituted instead. Such as were delineated, however, would, we are persuaded, reveal if they were studied, some reminiscence of Eastern symbolism, and contribute to confirm our main position of the connection of these figures with the appearance of an Oriental religion.

(*n.*) *Fish.*—The appearance of the fish in several of the ancient sculptured stones of Scotland along with the symbols we have referred to, is proof that the latter were not of Celtic origin, as the Celts never used them, and would not represent them upon these stones. As Vishnu assumed the form of a fish to recover the lost sacred Veda in the ocean, so the temples of the Hindus are decorated with fish of all descriptions; and individuals weary of life sacrifice themselves to this Deity by drowning.

The fish is seldom mentioned in the sacred Scriptures. From *ichthys*, the name for the fish in Greek, containing the initial letters of the words Jesus Christ, Son of God, Saviour, it was considered emblematical of Christ,[1] and the fish became a very favourite symbol of the early Christians; while the *vesica piscis*, a rough outline of a fish, formed of two curves, making points at their extremities, was made to enclose the holy symbol. This image was sculptured upon crosses, tombs, and urns, as well as upon seals and rings.[2]

Section II.—Sacred Trees.

The Celtic places of worship were in the open air, as the Celts considered that no covering could contain the Infinite. But in a flat country recourse was had to groves of sacred trees, by which both shade and seclusion were secured for the performance of their rites and mysteries. These trees were sacred to the Deity, and particular veneration was extended to the oak, its leaves and fruit, and even to its parasite, the mistletoe. The properties peculiar to others were supposed to be increased from their being gathered by the priest, who was, during religious observances, adorned with garlands of oak leaves and chaplets of flowers. These groves of oak trees

---

(1) Ιχθυς the symbol of Christ, being composed of the first letters of the words Ἰησους Χριστος θεου υιος σωτηρ.
(2) *See* Maul's Heraldry of Fish, p. 12.

were the only temple and habitation of the gods (King), and their silent darkness inspired a sacred awe in the worshippers, and thus promoted religious feeling, as well as afforded shelter and protection to the priests. No one approached except on stated days and with the sanction of the priests and the escort of the chiefs. The place was thus regarded as holy, and was always approached with pompous solemnity.

Among the Celtic races the growth of the *Mistletoe* on a tree was supposed to mark it out as peculiarly sacred, and to be evidence that it had been selected by some deity, as his shrine. Considered as planted by the gods, this parasite had divine virtues ascribed to it, and these were considered an infallible panacea for the ills of both man and beast. Its juice taken internally imparted fertility, and formed an antidote against poison;[1] while applied externally to wounds and bruises it ensured a certain cure.

The Druid was so named from druys (δρυς), an oak; the British drew, the Irish derry, and the English dree, or tree, being the same word. Tree-worship was common in ancient countries. Tacitus alludes to it frequently in his "Germania." The Germans, he said, had no images, and considered groves of trees to be their gods. The veneration for the oak tree is as early as the time of the Patriarchs, by whom trees were held in great esteem from the usefulness of their wood, and the advantage of their shade. "And Abraham planted a grove in Beer-sheba, and called there on the name of the Lord, the everlasting God."[2] There he pitched his tent, and built an altar unto the Lord; and these trees were in time much esteemed by his descendants, partly, it might be, on account of their age, but mainly out of regard for the Patriarch, who had dwelt and sacrificed under them. Jacob buried his mother Rebekah's nurse, under an oak,[3] and Joshua[4] raised a stone or pillar under it in memory of the covenant which was entered into just before his death, between God and the Israelites. We find that worship in connection with trees were mixed up with superstition, and hence among the Jews it became infamous, because of the sacrifices and incense that were burnt in high places and groves and under every oak and green tree, notwithstanding Divine prohibitions and threatenings;[5] and even in the time of Constantine the oaks under which Abraham dwelt were resorted to with great devotion by Christians, Mohammedans, and heathens. These oak groves served as screens during the performance of mysterious rites within the circles of boulder stones, which were the symbol of the Deity and of different sizes and segments to suit the convenience and extent of the population. Other circles did not require to be surrounded with a grove of oaks, where only a court of judicature was held or only instruction given to the people.

Olius Wormius[6] mentions a sacred hill with a circle of stones round it, which again is itself situated within a square of Druidical stones. In another place he makes mention of a similar hill enclosed within two circles of stones, one around the base, and the other about one-third below the summit. The Aggle stone[7] in the Isle of Purbeck, in Dorsetshire, is a remarkable monument of the same kind. But in many cases the reference to high places was more to the idolatrous objects of worship and sacrifices to idols within them than to their being hills or elevations. These high places were in the city,[8] in the streets,[9] and even the houses.[10]

The veneration for trees was universal over the ancient world, particularly in hot countries where the trees were selected for their shade, as well as for the silence and the gloom which groves of them offered, for the cultivation of that reverential feeling which became the worship of the Deity. Both in Asia and in Central Africa[11] the banyan or Indian fig-tree was, like the oak tree, considered sacred. The bas-reliefs of Lamhi display the

---

(1) Pliny Nat. His. Lib. xvi, ch. 44.   (2) Genesis xxi, 33.   (3) Genesis xxxv, 8.   (4) Joshua xxiv., 26.
 (5) 2 Kings xvi, 4; Isaiah lvi, vii; Jeremiah ii, 20; Hosea iv, 13; Judges iii, 8.
 (6) Monumentarium Dannorum, p. 8.   (7) *Ibid*, p. 35.
(8) 2 Chron. xxviii, 24.   (9) Ezekiel, xvi, 31-39.   (10) 1 Kings xii, 31, 32.
 (11) Livingstone's Travels, pp. 290, 495.

people worshipping the sacred trees[1] in the temples of India. In these cases the trees, like the sacred animals, are of a fanciful and mythological form.

The sages of ancient times used to represent to their followers, as teachers still do in Asia, that, while God is everywhere, He is more especially there, where we can best realize Him, and that we could best do, either in the silent and pure air of the mountain top, or, as at Dodona, amid groves of trees planted by His own hand, and ever and anon stirred by His breath blown on them. It was in these groves that the ancient festivals were held, and within and around their precincts that they afterwards erected churches. There the altar was erected, and there sacrifices were offered up, and sacred and mysterious rites performed.[2]

The imagination of Eastern sages has bestowed wonderful qualities on sacred trees. It was upon Mount Meru, the residence of the Hindu gods, that the sacred Buddhist tree of Paradise (the Kalpa Marksha), flourished. In this sacred spot the blessed inhabitants are represented as free from labour and sickness; they are decked in ornaments, clothed, and fed with food from the sacred tree. It resembles a wilderness of peaks without valleys or low places, and is free from all impurities, like the court of a temple, or a wall of crystal. The inhabitants of this heavenly region are all friends, live to be a thousand years of age, and all the time, with the assistance of the Kalpa tree, they enjoy themselves like the Divi, in virtue of their individual merit and goodness. Such was Mount Meru of the Hindus and Buddhist, round which the world was supposed to revolve. Such too was the Olympus of the Greeks, the favourite habitation of the gods, from which they could look down, if not without interest, yet without harm, upon the strife of mortals. The fabled Mount Meru, the North Pole, the centre or navel of the world, is represented as a high and lofty mountain of gold and gems among the Himalaya mountains. From the numerous glittering surfaces of its peaks the sun diffuses light into distant regions, and its sides are clothed with plants of heavenly origin, and with graceful and majestic trees, while streams of limpid water flow down it, and on every side it resounds with the music of birds, and the sweet odours of flowers. This central region is surrounded by the Ganges, which issues from the foot of Vishnu, washes the lunar orb, falls from the skies, and after encircling the mountain, divides into four mighty rivers, flowing in four opposite directions.[3]

By some more modern writers, Meru is supposed to be like the lotus flower, the petals of which are the abodes of the gods, the Ruhus, the Gandharvas, the Apsaras, and the Naga Raja, or great snake king. On its summit is a crescent, the abode of the Supreme Being, round which the sun and moon revolve. This upper region is the dwelling-place of Siva, and the heaven of Brahma. In the east of this is the paradise of India, resplendent as a thousand suns. The S.E. is the heaven of Agni, and the S. is Yamas; in the S.W. is the heaven of Surya, the sun (*viru pacsha*); in the W. that of Verana; in the N.W. that of Vayén; in the N. that of Kaviras; in the N.E. that of Siva. Vishnu has his heaven in the frozen ocean, or in the sea of milk; here, too, are the houses of the blessed spirits, and Nandanas, the grove of India.

The Brahmins, Celts, and Buddhists, and other Eastern nations have retained a faint recollection of the nature of the quarter where, according to ancient legends, mankind was first reared, and where they first offered up their prayers and sacrifices to the great God, in their primitive state of innocence. It is evident that the Aryan race had first, at the sight of the fruitful plains, crossed the Alpine frontier, and the descendants of these had in turn still further severed themselves from the primitive haunts of man; then the glorious highlands of the north were peopled, by the ever active imagination, with the groups of mythic beings. That was the locality from which the founder of the Indo-Aryan race had issued; there had been enacted all the mysteries of the ancient world.

---

(1) *See* Ferguson's Tree and Serpent Worship; Sir Stratford Raffles Java, and Stuart's Sculptured Stones of Scotland.
(2) Sir W. Ouseley's Travels in the East—on Sacred Trees.
(3) *Vide* Wilson's Vishnu Purand, p. 109, 70.

It was under the shade of the terrestrial bo-tree[1] (bodha-tree) that Sakyamuni (Foë) sat meditating, and it was under its refreshing shade that he first heard the voice, and saw the face of heavenly wisdom. It was under the shade of a large bo-tree (*Ficus Religiosa*) that Gatama wrestled in an agony from early morning till sunset with the fleshly allurements of home, and friendship, and love, and wealth, and power, before the spiritual prevailed, and the claims of religion gained the victory. His doubts and distress of mind cleared away, and his nature entered the haven of peace, when he saw that there was something higher than the love of self, and that love of self must lose itself in love for others. By this victory, he became Buddha, the enlightened. We might suppose that this tree was selected as the tree of wisdom on account of its size, for it spreads itself to a great distance, drops roots from its branches to the ground, thus forming new trees, while among its branches bees swarm to drink the honey, from which mead is made. Such, any how, was the tree under whose shade Sakyamuni rested with his back to the trunk, and his face turned to the east, where the splendour of the rising sun, the restorer of nature to life and action,[2] sent a ray of its own light into his heart when engaged in profound meditation on the present, past, and future, and revealed to him that secret for the proclamation of which he became one of the honoured sages of the world.

This bo-tree, or tree of wisdom, became henceforth an object of worship, and an offshoot from it, so sacred was it deemed, is still growing on the spot where the Buddhist pilgrims found it, and where the original tree had grown in the ancient temple in Bodh Gaya.[3] This tree is still worshipped at Beerboom, in Bengal,[4] as well as in other parts of India and Ceylon. Thither, once a year, many still repair to a shrine in the jungle to make offerings to the spirit who dwells under a Bela tree.[5] The shrine consists of thorn trees, and the one in which the spirit resides is marked at the foot with blood. These trees are said never to grow or change in any way.[6]

On a fresco on a rail-post of the Buddhist Gara[7] Sakyamuni is represented under his bo-tree, surrounded by pigs, as if to indicate his jungle residence.[8] In another fresco, Buddha is surrounded by the seven-headed snakes.

In the East, different trees were considered sacred by different Buddhists, according as their peculiar saint was supposed to have been born, to have done penance, to have preached, or to have died under the shade of it.[9] Each Buddhist had his particular bo-tree. The *Ficus Indica* (of Brahma), *F. Glomerata*, *F. Religiosa* (of Buddha), *Mimosa Serisha* are thus considered sacred, and this fact explains the variety of trees on the Buddhist coins, according as the dynasty or family who struck the coin were disciples of the Buddha or of the saint whose emblem they adopted. The seclusion of the spot where it grew, and the size of the tree, seem to have decided the selection; and in Europe the oak was chosen for the same obvious reason, the secrecy afforded by forests of these fine trees being well-adapted for the performance of mysterious rites.[10]

A tree, or umbrella, crowns the top of the Burmese pagoda, and without this the temple is not considered sanctified. This is also seen represented in the Cattack Caves, and in the splendid gateways of the Sanchi Topes. The *Ficus Religiosa* was the sacred tree represented in the Temple of Ameraphoora, in those of Java, and on many other bas-reliefs and coins.

---

(1) The Banyan tree; the *Ficus Indica*.   (2) A prevailing custom among the nations of Asia.
(3) Tree and Serpent Worship, p. 74.   (4) *Ibid*, p. 282.   (5) *Ibid*, p. 56, *et seq*.
(6) Hunter's Annals of Rural Bengal, p. 131.—*See* General Cunningham's Archæological Reports, vol. i., p. 6.
(7) Journal As. Soc. Calcutta for 1866, vol. xxxvi, p. 51.   (8) *Ibid*, xxxv, p. 51.
(9) The *Bilwa Tolusa* and other trees and plants are considered sacred by the Hindus; and as Vishnu transferred the ashes of the virtuous Binda into the toulusc plant, a leaf of it is placed under the Shalgram Stone, sacred to that deity.
(10) The peepul, or panker tree, and perhaps the buth tree, are said never to be struck with lightning, being conductors; while kuddurajain tarr and mango trees are often struck during the frequent severe storms. This might, to some extent, decide the trees that were to be considered sacred.

Veneration for the oak tree gave, as we have seen, to the Western Celtic priests the name of Druids, and it was among the oaks, the symbol of the Deity, that they resided, exactly as each Buddhist under his sacred tree, under whose shade he has supposed to have been born.

In France, tree worship (*arbores et ligna pro diis colebant*) was long continued in the north, near Beauvais, and the destruction of the tree, dedicated to the devil, (*arborem quæ erat dæoni dedicata*), is recorded as a most meritorious act.

Trees seem to have been formerly worshipped in Assyria, Greece, Italy, Gaul and Britain.[1] Seneca, in describing a sacred wood enclosing a temple of Jupiter, says, "The interwoven boughs which exclude the light of heaven, the vast height of the wood, the retired secrecy of the place, the deep unbroken gloom of the shade, impress your mind with the conviction of a present Deity." This worship is frequently mentioned in Greek history.[2]

At Dodona, a town in Epirus, was the most ancient oracle of Greece, and there the ancient Pelasgi lifted up their hands and voices to Zeus, whose dwelling place was in an oak of the forest.[3] The whole grove, indeed, which surrounded the temple was endowed with the gift of prophecy, and the oracles delivered were frequently managed by the priests, who had artfully concealed themselves behind the trees.

In Africa, tree-worship is still quite common, and in Britain it lingers lovingly in the Highlands of Scotland,[4] while many of the trees worshipped have certain peculiar irregularities in their form. In the sacred tree, at Beresov, the trunk at six feet from the ground separates into two parts, which again unite farther up, and costly offerings of every kind are placed in the opening.[5] When such trees decay with age they are still held sacred, but when they are broken, or in any way injured, the deity, or saint, is fabled to fly away, as the gods are said to do among the Hindus, also when the like befalls any of the sacred animals or images.[6]

In the engraving on a stone in the India Museum is a sacred tree springing out of a broad circle, with a rail underneath and a second rail round the pot, and the soles of the feet of the god Vishnu, with two eccentric circles in the midst. On each side are worshipping Buddhists.

Fig. 187.

---

(1) *See* Lubbock's Origin of Circles, pp. 278, *et seq*.
(2) Harris's Ancient Greece : Müller's Hist. of Ancient Greece.
(3) Classical Dictionary, Art. Dodona.
(4) Early Races of Scotland.
(5) Erman's Tour in Sylvania, vol. i, p. 464. *See* also Decr, de toutes les Nat. de l' Emp. Russe, Pt. xi, p. 43.
(6) Mariner's Tonga Islands, vol ii, p. 137 : Seeman's Visit to Viti, pp. 192-198.

196   HISTORY OF PAGANISM IN CALEDONIA.   [BOOK II.

In the procession sculptured on the Eassie obelisk[1]—the reverse of which is occupied by a beautiful Christian cross—there is a tree represented as guarded by three priests with Celtic tonsures behind, and being drawn to a temple, on a feast day, by three oxen, marked sacred, where prayers and presents are offered up. The first priest holds a long staff in his hand, before which is the sacred tree, which, during festival time, is taken to its temple, where rites are performed (*see Fig.* 138.) This tree is the same as that on an Indian Buddhist tower, and both of them rise from pots.

Fig. 138.

(*a.*) *Lotus Flower.*—In the Hindu and Egyptian mythological representations of nature, the lotus was the emblem of the great generative and conceptive powers of the world. When Vishnu, according to the Hindu fable, was swimming in the ocean of milk, the lotus was produced from his navel, and on unfolding its flower first displayed Brahma in his true creative energy. It was considered the attribute of Ganga, the goddess of the Ganges. In Egypt it was consecrated to Isis and Osiris, and was the emblem of the creation of the world from water. It is found in the bas-reliefs and paintings on the Egyptian temples (in the representations of sacrifices, religious ceremonies, &c.), and in tombs, and whatever is concerned with death or another life. Among both nations it is regarded with religious veneration; upon it the saints rest, as it rises from the ocean of milk. It is represented as the third member of the triad hanging over the spectacle ornament in the Aberlemno stone (*Plate* 71, *Vol. I.*)

---

(1) Eassie Latin Cross (Sculptured Stones, Plate 90-91, vol. 1,) in front, and following procession extended behind.

HISTORY OF PAGANISM IN CALEDONIA.

BOOK III.

History of Paganism in Caledonia.

BOOK III.

CHRISTIANITY IN PICTLAND AS ILLUSTRATED BY RECORDS, TRADITIONS, AND MONUMENTS.

INTRODUCTION.

THE similarity of the ancient monuments of Europe to those of Hindustan has been already amply insisted on, in the cases at once of the standing stones and circles, kistvaens and cromlechs, cairns and barrows. We have also referred to the gradual extension of the Eastern race, by Scythia and Scandinavia, on the one hand, and by the shores of the Mediterranean on the other, and it is known that along these routes very similar monuments belonging to this period are found. The relationship of the races occupying these districts is likewise proved by their agreement in physical conformation, by the resemblance of their manners and customs, and by the similarity in the structure and idioms of their dialects, which are Celtic, and are almost universally allowed to be of cognate origin, with the Sanscrit and the languages of Greece and Rome. The ancient names of places in the South and West of Europe, further prove that certain districts had been inhabited by the Celtic race anterior to the earliest period of authentic history. Such facts serve to clear up some of the obscurity which hangs over the history of the Western monuments.

CC 2

The Romans, in their invasion of Britain, found a formidable opposition in the Druids or Celtic priests. More enlightened from their training and intercourse with the inhabitants of Gaul than the other members of the community, they employed all their influence to induce their countrymen to resist the encroachment of those invaders. This was known to the Romans, so that when their discipline and arms prevailed, and the Britons were obliged to submit to their new masters, the Druids could expect no quarter, and many of them retired to a distance, and gradually formed separate Celtic communities. One portion withdrew to a region in the remote and barren West; which, from a chief, named Cornvealas, was called Cornwall; another portion took refuge among the mountains of Cambria, afterwards known as the principality of Wales; a third withdrew to Caledonia, and made their home among the bleak and impregnable mountains; while yet another portion of refugees went over the seas, and settled in Ireland. These separate communities proved a thorn in the side of the Romans; since they banded together to defy attacks, to which they were exposed, and which, except in union, would have issued in their extermination.

In Scotland, the Celts formed a powerful confederation, known as the Kingdom of the Picts, which the Romans were never able entirely to suppress. The country, indeed, was poor, and the inhabitants few and rude; but by their energy, union, and intelligence, they were able to defy their enemies, and leave the proud recollection to their descendants of never having forfeited their independence.

The Druids, as also the Buddhist priests who came after or along with them, from their intelligence as well as standing, naturally possessed much influence in the affairs of the nation. Evidences of their power are still to be found in the traditions and monuments which survive them, although it is a matter of regret that history proper, is so silent and, indeed, has nothing to say on the subject. We know, however, that it became the policy of the Romans, rather to conciliate than coerce, in order that by so doing, they might quietly conquer. In accordance with this policy, Agricola, one of the ablest the Roman generals, encouraged the British to build market-places and houses, to send their childr to Rome for instruction, and to wear the dress and imitate the habits of their conquerors.

From the time that the Romans obtained a permanent footing in Britain, a constant co munication was kept up between the Provincial Government and the Imperial Court. What little 1 known of the inhabitants has to be gathered from the statements of their enemies, and of cours these are necessarily prejudiced, and more or less misleading. In many respects the Britons wer influenced by the civilization and religious belief of their conquerors, while, in remote parts, the Paga element predominated, a circumstance which could not but materially affect the popular acceptance the Christian system. Of the distinct and separated Celtic communities, those of the North of Scotlan especially, defied the prowess and discipline of the Roman arms. In these unconquered tracts the i habitants retained their ancient manners, with the customs and religious observances of Druidism; b these were not committed to writing, because, as we have seen, such a mode of instruction w forbidden by the esoteric nature and express edicts of the Druid religion. It is among these tribe however, that we find early indications of Christianity. Those missionaries from the East, we ha so often referred to, took possession of the groves, cells, and high places of the Druids, to whi the Pagan worshippers had been accustomed to resort,[1] but traces of the old religion seem to ha long survived the introduction of the new, throughout Britain, for in the time of Canute a law was direct

(1) *See* O'Hally's Introduction to the History of Ireland.

against those who worshipped fire, rivers, rocks, or trees,[1] and a canon promulgated by King Edgar, while forbidding all necromancy and divination, also forbids stone worshipping;[2] just as the Council of Tours, in the year 567, openly repudiated all "venerators lapidum," worshippers of stones.[3]

We have seen that the Druids in their religious rites erected stones in particular forms and positions, surrounded them with sacred trees, and that within these enclosures, mysterious ceremonies were performed. Of these especially, the Buddhist missionaries took advantage in teaching and disseminating their own religious tenets, by means of symbols peculiar to themselves. Like the Druids, the Buddhists of Asia were at first averse to the written expression of religious opinions, and in the East it was long after the Convocation of Kashmen that those tenets were committed to writing. We are informed that in Ceylon the doctrines of Buddhism were preserved by tradition alone for 450 years, and it was not till after this date that their canon began to assume the form of a sacred Scripture.

The conversions from Buddhism to Christianity which afterwards took place—for the Buddhist missionaries were, by their adoption of the cross, virtually Christian ones—were facilitated by the eclectic tastes of the former and their readiness to accept and acknowledge the truth under any and every form of manifestation. The same honesty and liberality are still seen in their attitude towards other religious sects, and these qualities form, to this day, a marked feature in the character of the Buddhist priest of Thibet. "We found," writes M. Huc, "many of the Buddhist priests (Lamas) attaching the utmost importance to the study and knowledge of truth, and the same men came again and again to seek instruction from us in our holy religion." Such love of truth and liberality of sentiment must have facilitated the conversion of professed Buddhists to the purer Christian faith. The early Christian converts were equally exemplary, and their wide dispersion is thus strikingly described by one of their number in the first generation which followed that of the Apostles. " The Christians are distinguished neither by country, speech, nor government from other men. They neither dwell in towns of their own, use their own dialect, nor follow any peculiar mode of life. They occupy Greek or barbarian cities as the case may be, but follow the country's rule in dress and manner. Their great aim is the establishment of their faith, the purest and most easily propagated known. Among so many different races and people a considerable variety in the forms of worship and government is to be expected, but in no place is there any private creed or peculiar opinion. Just as the sun, God's creature, stands forth singly and is visible throughout the earth, so, in like manner, is the preaching of the Word diffused."[4]

The early dissemination of Christianity will not be difficult to understand if we consider the condition of the primitive Church as planted by Christ and His Apostles. The peculiarity of the early Church was, that it prescribed no dogmatic creed, but only required assent to certain events as expressions of Divine grace, and pledges of a Divine promise and purpose. Very little is known of the first introduction of Christianity into Pictland; but a tradition resting, however, on no very solid basis, existed to the following effect, that during the reign of Domitian (A.D. 81) some of the disciples of the Apostle John visited Caledonia, and there preached the Word of Life. If we accept the truth of this tradition the enthusiasm of these early missionaries might easily have removed any misapprehensions which existed, and the liberal Buddhists, open to reason and eager for the acquisition of truth, would be readily converted, and might very naturally become zealous propagators

---

(1) Wrekin's Anglo-Saxon, page 134. Quoted in Arch. Camb., vol. i, p. 8.
(2) See Lingaid's History and Account of Anglo-Saxon Church, vol. i, p. 167.
(3) Arch. Camb., vol. xxxv., p. 51.
(4) Epis ad Drog Apostolorum Discipulus. Quoted by Wilberforce in his Five Empires, p. 196.

of the new faith in its purity and simplicity. This is further shown by the statement of St. Chrysostom in his "Demonstratio quod Christus sit Deus," written A.D. 387, that "the British Islands (situated outside the Mediterranean Sea and in the very ocean itself) had felt the power of the Divine Word, churches having been founded there and altars erected."[1] Again, in the 28th sermon on the 2nd Epistle to the Corinthians, chap. xii., he says, "Into whatsoever church you enter, whether among the Moors or in these British Isles,[2] and although thou shouldest go to the ocean and those British Isles, &c., thou wouldest hear all men everywhere discoursing matters out of the Scriptures" (vol. iii, p. 3.).

The Druids of the South of Britain, who had opposed the Roman invaders with so much energy, and had so long ruled the simple, ignorant, and superstitious people, must soon have felt that their craft was in danger through the sincerity and truthfulness of the Christian teaching, and through the purity of their faith. They would, therefore, oppose its introduction with all their might, stir up their chiefs to put the Christians to death, and encourage them to do so by appeals to prodigies which they would interpret as expressing the displeasure of Heaven at the new religion.

The skilful and enterprising Phœnicians, and afterwards the Greek and Roman navigators, were at an early period the great propagators of all that contributed to civilization, and especially of that mutual acquaintanceship among nations, which began thus early to open up the commercial intercourse which was some day to weave into one web the common interests of the world. Unfortunately, however, from mercenary motives, they kept their knowledge of the British Islands, and the valuable traffic which they carried on there, a profound secret from others, and they, too, were likely to be quite as jealous of the propagation of Christianity as of any merely commercial rivalry that might accrue to their disadvantage. The same causes, moreover, that at first operated in spreading religion, afterwards acted in retarding its progress among the inhabitants of the South of Britain. For we learn that the missionaries were supposed to encourage the treachery of the Britons and to instigate their frequent rebellions. This induced the Roman emperor to try to crush the new faith. An inhuman decree was issued for the purpose from Nicomedia in Bithymia (A.D. 303), which was carried into effect by the cruel Masiminus. At this time Britain contained Christian communities, although there was not any very widespread reception of the faith or encouragement of Christianity. (*See* Mosheim, p. 449.) Though the gentle Constantius mitigated the severity of the decree which had been passed, the decree itself was to the following effect:—"That the Christian churches in all the provinces of the Empero should be demolished to their foundations, and the punishment of death be inflicted on all who shoulc presume to hold any secret assemblies for the purpose of religious worship. That the clergy shoul deliver all their sacred books into the hands of the magistrates, who were commanded, under the severes penalties, to burn them in a public and solemn manner, and to confiscate the property of the church Educated Christians were declared incapable of holding any honours or employment. Slaves were to b for ever deprived of the hope of freedom, and all who professed such opinions were to be put out of th protection of the law. The judges were authorized to hear and determine every action that was brough against a Christian, but Christians were not permitted to complain of any injury inflicted on them."[3]

Thus the Pagan population, dreading the decay of their ancient beliefs, was stirred up to lay violen hands on the churches and symbols of the new faith, and during the persecution, many Christians sough

---

(1) Quoted in Tables of Deaths in Census of Ireland for 1851, vol. v. p. 3, rendered into Latin as follows : " Britannicæ insul virtutem verbi senserunt, sunt enim etiam illic fundatæ Ecclesiæ et erecta altaria."

(2) In quamcunque Ecclesiam ingressus fueris sive apud Mauros sive apud ipsas Britannicas insulas."

(3) Gibbons Decline and Fall of the Roman Empire, ch. xvi.

protection in the Celtic communities of Cornwall, Wales, and Pictavia.[1] On the accession of Constantine, the son of the mild Constantius, to the imperial purple in A.D. 324, the Christians throughout the empire were left to the free exercise of their religion. From this period, the Romans, for nearly 100 years, remained in Britain, but notwithstanding the length of their stay and the advantages which they possessed, little progress seems to have been made so far as the propagation of Christianity was concerned.

A list of the clergy who attended the first Ecclesiastical Council, called by Constantine, and held at Arles, in Gaul, to settle a dispute among the African Christians, has been preserved, and in it Eborius, Bishop of Eboracum (York), Restitutis, Bishop of London, Adelfius, Bishop of Carleon, and Arminius, the Deacon, are mentioned as having represented the British Church.[2] In like manner, under the same Emperor, a Council was held at Ariminium (Rimini), in Italy, A.D. 360, on account of the Arian Controversy, which was said to have been attended by 400 Bishops. Sulpicius Severus, who wrote forty years after, states that provision was made for the Bishops, in order that they might not be at any personal expense during the time of the Council. A few only of the British Bishops, on account of their poverty, availed themselves of that provision.[3] It is exceedingly probable that some of them were indigent at that time; the poverty of the land being great, and their revenue being derived solely from the free-will offerings of the people.[4] Heathenism was far from being thoroughly rooted out of Britain, but the chief cities had Christian Bishops, and Christianity was, until the decline of the Roman Empire, the religion of the land. Early in the fifth century the Romans relinquished Britain, in order that they might concentrate their strength in the defence of Italy, which was seriously threatened by a new and formidable enemy; while, at the same time, many of the wealthy Roman residents left the country, and the intercourse with Rome, in a great measure, ceased. This withdrawal was followed by constant quarrels amongst the native chiefs, and these, accompanied as they frequently were, by devastating invasions of bands of the Picts and Scots, and Scandinavian pirates, soon led to a decay in the incipient religion and civilization of the people. The Roman roads and public buildings were neglected, lands were allowed to lie waste, and Paganism began again to raise its head amid the neglect of learning and general corruption. The Britons, in the hour of danger, as is well known, called to their aid the Anglo-Saxons, who, while they drove the barbarian hordes back to their fastnesses, at the same time took permanent possession of the districts which they had conquered. The Earls, Thanes, and Freemen, settling down, divided the land amongst themselves, and became, in a great degree, independent; while the native Britons were either driven away, or else remained only as serfs and bondsmen—" hewers of wood and drawers of water." The military chiefs who had taken possession of the land, effaced almost all the traces that remained of Roman civilization. They lived in houses made of a framework of oak timber, blocks rudely squared, having the interstices filled up with plaster. The windows were small and unglazed, the only means of closing them being by strong shutters. The walls were hung and ornamented with cross-bows, boar-spears, swords, bucklers, sheaves of arrows, and trophies of the chase. The floors were strewn with rushes; large planks and logs of wood, rudely joined together, formed their only tables and seats. The huts of the common people were made of timber and mud, and differed from the halls of the nobles more in size than in construction; while the forests by which they were surrounded, shut them out from the rest of the world. These military chiefs were nearly independent, and ruled their vassals despotically. They worshipped the gods of their fathers.

---

(1) Gaul, or Gael, was the ancient name for all the inhabitants of Britain. The Northern Highlanders were called the Gael-Duni (from Dun), a hill, and this was softened with Caledonia.
(2) Renovant Ecclesias ad Solium hague destructus. Bede Hist. Eccl. Lib. i, cap. viii. Gilda's de Eccl. Brit. 12.
(3) Wright, The Celt, &c., p. 297.
(4) See Sulp. Severus Sacred Hist., Lib. ii., cap. 14.

The transition from the Pagan to the Christian period dates from the time when the permission was given to inscribe the Eastern symbols on the Celtic boulders, "formed by the hand of God." The recognition of these symbols paved the way for the Christian meaning of the highest of all symbols, that of the Christian Cross. Accordingly, after an uncertain period, the cross appeared, sometimes with an Ogham inscription, as in Ireland, but in Pictland with the Buddhist symbols and sacred animals; while in each country there were associated with it marked peculiarities. In some cases in one district of country, the cross was prepared *in relievo*, on a flat surface; the very shape of it, as well as the ornamentation, being varied. These crosses have on them the Pagan symbols; but these appear more as ornaments than as sacred emblems, and are a sign that the Pagan faith is dying out of the popular conscience. The crosses in the South and West of Caledonia were of graceful proportions, evidently adapted to a people more advanced in civilization, and adorned with incidents from Bible story. The earlier Christians were very simple in their dress, and unostentatious in their mode of living; but the necessity was felt, at the same time, of showing respect to Pagan sentiment, accustomed as it was to the ceremonial of the old rites. This feeling was strengthened by more liberal ideas, better knowledge of the world, and wider diffusion of learning.

Tertullian, writing about A.D. 200, mentions it as a fact that the several races of the Gaêti—the extensive territories of the Moors—all outside the bounds of Spain—the different nations of the Gauls—and those localities in Britain hitherto inaccessible to the Romans, had become subject to Christ; together with the territories of the Sarmatians, Dacians, Germans, and Scythians, and many distant nations, provinces, and islands, the names of which we do not know, and cannot, therefore, enumerate; and, further, that the name of Christ had extended to places which defied the arms of Rome.[1] Origen, who wrote about A.D. 230, asks,—"When did Britain, previous to the coming of Christ, agree to worship the one God? When did the Moors? When did the whole world?" And answers,—"*Now*, however, through the efforts of the Church, all men call upon the God of Israel." (Fourth Hom. on Ezek.) From this it may be looked on as an established fact that Britain was a Christian country. In his Commentary on Ezekiel, when inquiring into the cause of the rapid progress of Christianity in Britain, he says, "The island has long been predisposed to it (*i.e.* to Christianity), through the doctrines of the Druids and Buddhists, who had already inculcated the doctrine of the unity of the Godhead.[2] By the third century many of the inhabitants of the Roman Empire and of several neighbouring countries having professed a somewhat loose Christianity, the endeavour was made to preserve unity of faith, and this Church discipline gave rise to an ecclesiastical tyranny, so that when Constantine the Great, in the beginning of the fourth century, extended toleration to the Christians, we see the bishops exercising the power of judges of the faith in the first General Council of Nice, A.D. 325.

The primitive Christian missionaries were humble in their walk and conversation, and earnest and persevering in their efforts to teach the truth and to do good to their fellows. The precepts they taught they exemplified and enforced by a holy and upright life, by denying themselves all worldly pleasures and the indulgence of all sensual and carnal gratifications. Poverty, self-denial and self-devotion, became, by their example, the distinguishing marks of a Christian. As soldiers of the cross they endured hardships, and rejoiced in the power that enabled them to do so as an earnest of fellowship with their great Captain who had led the way through suffering to a throne. As the Christians found themselves unable to suppress the Pagan superstitions, they allowed the use of certain cherished emblems. And so these symbols were continued under the Christian

---

(1) Britanniæ inaccessa Romanis, loca Christo vera Subdita Christi nomen regment. Christi nomen et regnum Coletum. Tert: Adver Indæ, cvii., p. 189, Ed. Regulis. *See* Keith's Catalogue of the Bishops of Scotland.

(2) Quoted by Davis, in his History of Cornwall, vol. i., p. 93.

dispensation. It is exceedingly probable that skilled artists in the course of their travels may have visited Pictland, and there expended their skill in erecting in public places the symbols of the new religion, working these Eastern symbols in stone, and adorning them with artistic taste. Possibly they may, with the assistance of the Buddhist priests, have adopted the rude unsculptured stones with Eastern animals and symbols, and made such other additions as seemed to them to be necessary, in order to reconcile the leading men to these changes. They probably also assisted to erect the pillars or round towers, some of which are found in Scotland, and still more numerously in Ireland, the object of which was to protect themselves against their enemies.

The custom of erecting crosses may be traced to the third century, but most probably it came into use at an earlier period. Constantine the Great first used the cross with the motto, "Per hoc signo vinces," as the motto or token under which he fought and conquered. He is also supposed to have been the first to erect crosses in public places. Others believe that it was not until the time of the Empress Helena that the cross became an object of worship. This was about A.D. 326. Previous to a battle, or any great enterprize, an offering to Heaven was made by the erection of a cross. This was done by Oswald in the seventh century, previous to the battle he fought with Cadwell, himself holding the cross aloft, while his soldiers knelt around and gathered courage from its presence.[1] C. R. de Fleury, in his work on the Cross, represents this drawing on an ancient tomb as the most ancient specimen of a bas-relief of the third or fourth century. In the absence of written documents we must appeal to the evidence which these remains supply us, particularly to that kind of evidence derived from the traditions of Christian communities. It would appear that the Christians in Pictland instructed the inhabitants in the Christian doctrines, and prepared the crosses, the symbols of their faith, selecting those stones that were most durable, and those that from careful observation they found could best resist the effects of the weather. Even in modern times, if you wish to select stones for the purpose of building, a standing rule is this: — " Examine the effects of the weather on a wall, and select your stones accordingly." Thus, one kind of stone will be found suitable for one situation, another kind for another. The stones once selected, they designed from an Eastern theory. They converted natural objects into mythological forms; and, from a veneration for Eastern tradition took symbolical objects as an emanation of Deity, however imperfect. Thus did there spring up a study of nature and the power of execution. This careful study of art formed the one business of their lives. In process of time, however, as some died at their posts, and others returned to their native country, the workers who were left proved incompetent, from a want either of the requisite skill or the requisite training. Palladins, and other excellent men, seem afterwards to have gathered round them many willing pupils, who left, as their only remains, those noble crosses so graceful in design and so beautiful in execution ; while in other places, where teachers were absent, the converts lapsed back into their ancient superstitions.

Primitive Christianity in Pictland was simple in its form, and the Word of God alone was received by them as the rule of faith and practice. Missionaries went forth with no other weapon than " the Sword of the Spirit, which is the Word of God." Though neither learned nor wealthy, they were clear in their belief of the truth, strong in their conviction of it, and zealous and unwearied in its propagation. It is probable that there were believers in Christ in these islands before the end of the second century.

St. Patrick, the apostle of Ireland, was as discreet as he was zealous in his missionary work. Like St. Paul, he made himself " all things to all men." He dealt tenderly with the usages and

---

(1) Bede Eccles. History, c. iii.

prejudices of the Pagans. Sometimes he overturned their idols; sometimes risked his life, and while he acknowledged himself as unlearned, he was guilty of no offensive or needless iconoclasm. The nature of the truths of the new religion, he explained in the language of the natives. By his judicious management, the Churches which were founded became self-supporting, that is, were endowed by the native chiefs, and were able to exist without foreign aid, supported alike by the priests, prelates, and people. The Irish missionaries did not confine their activity to the narrow sphere of their own island; in their boats of skin they travelled across the stormy seas of Orkney, Shetland, and Faroe. When in the year A.D. 870 the Norwegians first visited Iceland, they found there no trace of human civilization except the crosses and bells, and a book, the Irish ritual of the Papæ, as they called the monks of *Iona*. These tokens, however, proved their fervent piety, their love of meditation, and the spirit of self-sacrifice which prompted the Irish to visit the distant islands of the North, and hazard the stormy seas with which they are environed.

Thus, of our theory this is the sum: A careful consideration of the foregoing remarks and observations, drawn from various authorities, and a faithful examination of the sculptured remains of Pictavia, leads us to the conclusion that the Christian religion, though a purely spiritual religion, and as such early introduced into these islands, was preceded by, and in some cases, associated with another which employed symbols, and that these symbols were represented on the sculptured stones of Caledonia along with others, connected, on the one hand, with the ancient Pagan faith, and on the other, with ideas that belong to the faith of Christianity. The Buddhist missionaries were virtually Christian, not only as Buddhists, but as bringing with them symbols already familiar in the East as associated with the Christian religion.

CHAPTER I.

PAGAN SYMBOLS OF THE DEITY ADOPTED BY PRIMITIVE CHRISTIANS.

SECTION I.—PRIMITIVE CIRCLES INCISED AND IN BAS-RELIEF.

HE simple erect boulders and incised circles are, as we have seen, symbols of the Deity; and it was in this sense that they were adopted by the primitive Christians. A circle of this simple form was found in the middle of an erect oblong head-stone in Sutherlandshire, and on the upper part of a cross in Cornwall, in the centre of a short Latin cross in Argyleshire, and it often appears in the centre of the Christian cross. Upon the lintel of the entrance of St. Fichin's Church, at Fors, a wheel is incised. There is also one upon the church door of Ardoilen, or High Island, now uninhabited, as well as on that of the small island off the country of "Armora." The east window, the only one in the building, being semi-circular-headed, and 1 foot high, and 6 inches wide, above the altar.

SECTION II.—SYMBOLICAL CHRISTIAN MONOLITHS.

These are boulders, which, as Christianity and the arts advanced, were afterwards transformed into ornamental pillars. The size as well as the style of these varied at different times. It is stated in Scripture that[a] King Josiah stood by a pillar, and made a covenant before the Lord, to walk after Him, to keep His commandments, and His statutes, with all his heart and all his soul; and we have seen that the same symbol of the Deity was common in Celtic countries, both in Asia and in Europe.

Pillar-Stones (Maen-her), which resembled those of Asia, are still to be seen in La Vendée, in France. These, as in the British Islands, were regarded by the ancient Celtic inhabitants as emblems of the Deity, and it became the policy of the primitive Christians not to tamper with them for a time, until it was deemed necessary to cut out a cross on the top of one of them. (*See Figs.* 18 *and* 19). Sculptured crosses are found in the temples of Upper Egypt, also in Nubia; and the Druidical remains in the parish of Narvia, Isle of Man, have deeply incised crosses. By this means the meaning of the symbol was changed without directly attacking and shocking the prejudices of the simple and rude people, whom they sought not to repel but to win over to the faith of Christianity.

(1) 2 Kings xxiii. 3.

This is the explanation of the number of crosses that have pagan emblems incised on them, as it was found that some of the converts still retained a deep veneration for the ancient symbols, and the rites and superstitions of the local religion. In Brittany, much of the ancient ophiolatry, or serpent worship, still mingles with the Christianity of the peasantry; for, indeed, not only customs, but even religious ideas were sometimes adopted from the heathens by the Papal Christian Church. As there is no authentic account of the people who erected the monuments in Scotland, we have no other resource than to compare the race that inhabited the country, and their manners and customs, with the same race in other quarters of the globe.[1]

In the absence of the desired records, and as traditions are not to be relied on, it becomes instructive to examine the boulder monuments that remain, which are at once so ancient and so little changed in form since they were first erected, and are to be met with in most known countries in different parts of the world. These record the creed, manners, and customs of distant races; and when compared we find some which imply a similar advance in the arts, and a like stage of refinement, such, for instance, as the style of the masonry and the peculiar principle of the arch. "Under these circumstances," as Gordon remarks in his interesting "Itinerarium," "instead of compiling inventions and uncertain reports," he "rather searched into the remains and undoubted evidence of former times, hoping that the general result arrived at may compensate and atone for any shortcoming in the manner of handling the subject."

The ancient nations as a rule considered this life as a state of probation for another and a better, and events that seem great to us were considered unworthy of being recorded by them, and even their dates are unknown, so that we have been left to assign very different ages to particular epochs, and find it hard to arrive at the truth respecting them. The late discovery of "sand drifts" may be selected as an example, and the depths at which pottery is found in such an alluvial country as Bengal or Egypt, have been pointed to as a proof of age; but the quantities of these deposits differed much when the bed of the river was lower and the deposits deeper. Even now in such countries the deposits of silt differ much in depth, in different years, according to the nature of the inundations and the position of the part. Sometimes there is only a slight deposit, and in some years in India I have known it to be six or many more feet in depth. How then can we calculate the age of a piece of pottery when there is such a difference with deposits?

SECTION III.—THE CHRISTIAN PILLAR-TOWERS OF IRELAND AND SCOTLAND.

These pillar-towers were erected in Ireland and Scotland during the Christian period. We have already described those of the primitive and transition periods, and have now to consider the Christian pillar-towers, which form such a contrast in architectural skill and beauty to the other buildings of that epoch. When the Christian section of the community rose in social position, and had become rich and powerful, these towers, as th monasteries are found to be in Egypt and Syria at the present day, were found to be useful in protecting thei inhabitants, sacred relics, vases, books, records, and other valuables from the rapacity and cruelty of th unscrupulous chiefs among whom they lived, and by whom they were professedly protected. This ris induced the ecclesiastics to build pillar-towers in Ireland, and in some cases, as at Abernethy and Brechir in Scotland. In the third, or Anglo-Saxon period, the progress in Christian art was chiefly due t the Church, and the ecclesiastical connection with Rome, which had great influence on the early work: as well as the religious rites, of the form of Christianity that was introduced into Ireland, from the fifth an sixth to the end of the ninth century. At this time their churches were made of mud, and wattled as in Britain but as the influence of the priests increased, they absorbed much of the wealth of the country, and brought ove architects from the Continent, whose constructive, as well as artistic skill, they employed in preparing the firs

(1) Moore's Ireland, pp. 207 and 208.

stone edifices; while, to increase the splendour of their ceremonial, they enriched their altars with their most precious ornaments. This is the reason why these establishments were so frequently attacked by their unscrupulous neighbours, and the merciless Danish pirates. The pillar-towers of Ireland were found by the priests to be most serviceable erections: near them they resided, and in them they took refuge, with their most valuable effects, from the rapacity of marauders; thus following the injunction of Pope Gregory to Augustine of Canterbury, in the sixth century, to appropriate any sacred shrine of paganism, for Christian use only, making such additions as were necessary or convenient. They accordingly not only occupied such places as already existed, but built other erections after a similar pattern.

One of the first of the pillar-towers erected by the Christian community was that at Clonmason, the approach to the upper loft being through a square hole in the ceiling of the arch; which forms the communication with the chamber, under the ridge, from which the round tower is ascended. By this construction the tower was available for defence. The St. Kelone's round tower, which communicated with the church, and has the door on the level of the church floor, is supposed by Mr. Brash, in his able work on the "Architecture of Ireland," to be pagan; but Mr. Hogan, and the Rev. P. Neary, agree[1] in supposing the church (Tempul Fingin) to belong to the twelfth century (*circa* 1130 or 1150), and that it "had nothing to do with the round (or pillar) towers, which were of pre-Christian origin."

The Rev. Mr. Graves,[2] however, when exposing the bases of the tower and the church, found a Romanesque doorway, on a level with the ground, opening into the interior of the church, and both foundations appeared to be one work, and to have been prepared at the same time; so that the tower was of Christian origin. The round tower had never been isolated; and in the round tower of Aghaville, county Killarney, there is a doorway on the floor, and another at the usual elevation, both of which had been closed up. This latter class of towers may be known by their more modern construction, and by their rounded doorways being cut into a series of recesses, the angles of which are slightly rounded off; also by the addition of a moulding—a mere incision upon the face and soffit of the arch. Others of these modern doorways are decorated with the chevron and the bead ornament, as in the gold ornaments found in Irish bogs, and in some very antique cinerary urns, dug up from old Pagan and Etruscan cairns and tumuli. In some of the towers the repeated columns, and successive arches, and various mouldings of the doorway are rich and striking. The capitals of some of the columns are heads, the hair of which is entwined with snake-like animals, as in the towers at Timahoe and Kildare, the ornaments of which resemble the rich and elaborate decorations on Cormac's chapel, Cashel, executed towards the commencement of the twelfth century. It may be admitted that Norman builders executed these doorways, and decorated them with the ornaments and symbols of their religion, like their churches and other buildings. As they were in the habit of working in sandstone, the ornamented entrances in the pillar-towers were usually of this stone. So much was this prized, and so marked is the contrast between the entrance and the tower, that the former is supposed by R. B. Brash to have been subsequently inserted.

The Donaghmore pillar-tower has the ruins of a church and belfry close to it. It is one of the more modern examples, and has been used as a place of retreat. It has the door elevated, and is without the four upper windows, which were no longer considered necessary by the Christian people who had erected it. The reference of the date to Christian times is confirmed by the carving of the Crucifixion over the door of this tower. McCarthey's church, on the north-west side of the cemetery of Clonmacnois, is interesting from its having a pillar-tower built at the same time, of the same stone, and similar in the character of its masonry. Part of the solidity of the tower was sacrificed to give full space to the chaste specimen of the Romanesque chancel arch attached to it. This tower is 55 feet in height and 7 feet in diameter, and is cemented with lime.

---

(1) . The Journal of the Roy. Hist. and Arch. Asso. Ireland, vol. iv, Fourth Series, p. 279.   (2) *Ibid.* p. 281.

The conical cap is built in the herring-bone style. The door is on a level with the ground, and there are only two small windows near the top, facing respectively the north and the south. To the third variety of pillar towers belong Timahoe, Queen's County; Seven Churches, Smaller Tower, Morsida; Kildare; Antrim; Donnaghmore, Meath; and Brechin, Scotland.

Such are the three classes into which the Irish pillar-towers may be grouped. The first, or original form, was most probably erected by Eastern missionaries, chiefly for religious purposes; and the other two classes were modifications of them, introduced in the course of time, as the buildings were more required as places of defence. As such they were probably used both before the appearance of the Buddhist religion as well as after it had ceased to prevail, as they afforded the simplest and most effectual means of protection against violence; and this accounts for the number of them among turbulent races as compared with the few to be found in more peaceful countries—as, for instance, the few in Scotland compared with the many among the turbulent tribes of Ireland. They still retained their sacred character, and while used for religious ceremonies, were found most useful as places of security, when the Danes, as they swept the sea from the sixth and seventh down to the twelfth centuries, plundering in all directions, and natives who professed discipleship, did not hesitate to commit sacrilege. They were built by the side of the church or monastery, and in them sacred MSS. and vessels were preserved. They could accommodate about a hundred persons. Mention is made of one burnt in 948, " full of religious and good people;" and in 1097 one at Monasterboice, " with many books and much treasure."[1]

In the Christian pillar-towers of Kildare and Tomahoe the character of the doorways becomes of importance from their resemblance to the chancel arch of the neighbouring church Rahen, in King's County, which is still used as a parish church, and appears to have been erected by the same architects that prepared the door of the pillar-tower. Kildare, like that of Tomahoe, consists of two divisions, separated by a deep revial, and presenting each a double compound recessed arch, resting on plain shafts with flat capitals. The shafts of the external arch are decorated with human heads; the bases are likewise decorated with human heads on the alternate eastern, and with a figure resembling an hour-glass on the alternate western angles. The jambs of the recessed arch of the first division are rounded with semi-columns at the angles. There is no ornament at the base, but on the capitals at each angle on the west side are human heads, represented with moustaches, thin whiskers, and flowing beards. The hair, divided at the forehead, and passing over the ears, forms, by interlacing, a cross of highly complicated and graceful tracery. The outer arches of the second door have a semi-column at each angle, with human heads as capitals; the head on the western angle has massive curls on the forehead, while the space at the back of the head, and under the cheek, is filled with interlaced sill ornaments. The head in the east has plain moustaches, and has them arranged in straight plaits from ear to ear under the chin. Dr. Petrie says the churches were founded before the eighth century. These architectural features are not found in the Norman style in England or Ireland. The massive limbs of the quadrangular doors of Drumobo and Swords, and the semi-circular arch of the doorway in the pillar towers of Glendalock, Brechin, and Kelmacduagh, are cut out of a single stone. The masonry in the last resembles exactly that of the church, and both are attributed to a celebrated builder who lived at the time of the foundation of the church, in the year A.D. 610. The arch is found on the round towers of Oughterard and Tory Island, the latter being composed of several small stones. The ornamental door of the Antrim pillar-tower resembles the door of the church of Form. The door at Kildar is highly ornamented.

When the pillar-towers were adopted by the Christians for religious purposes, the symbol of the Christia faith was exhibited over the door, e.g., the cross over the Antrim Pillar, Ireland, and the crucifix over thos of Donoughmore, Meath, and Kells, in Ireland, as over that of Brechin in Scotland. The pillar-tower o

---

(1) See Ulster Journal, vol. i, p. 146. Edited by the present author.

Rosina has the top of its door arched with three mouldings similar to the towers of Monasterboice and Donoughmore. The latter has an image of our Saviour on the cross executed in relievo on the keystone, and on the stone above it. The crucifixion is also represented on the door of the pillar-tower of Brechin. Dr. Petrie told me that he could prove that this pillar-tower was erected by Irish ecclesiastics in the year 1020. Mr. Brusman had previously come to the same conclusion.

There are, as is known, only two pillar-towers in Scotland with the same peculiarities as the Irish towers; one of them at Abernethy, in Perthshire, and the other at Brechin, in Forfarshire; the former in one of the Pictish centres of government, and the other amidst the Pictish crosses, exhibiting Christian emblems, the one of the eighth, and the other of the end of the tenth century (A.D. 990). The tower at Abernethy,[1] Perthshire, though in the capital of one of the Pictish governments,[2] is not mentioned in any of our ancient histories. We only know that the people of the district were converted to Christianity, and the town and adjacent country dedicated to God and Saint Bridget in the fifth century (A.D. 456).[3] It is probable that at this early period they followed the heathen custom of worshipping in the open air (*sub dio*), at sacred stones; for we find in the eighth century (A.D. 711), that Nectan III., King of the Picts, being dissatisfied with the primitive custom of worship, and desirous to follow the Romish ritual, wrote to Coelfred, Abbot of Jarrow, in Northumberland, requesting information regarding certain disputed observances, and soliciting the assistance of architects to build a church, which was to be dedicated to St. Peter, the prince of the apostles.[4] The architects were accordingly sent, and the church was built of stone, like the Romish churches. This has passed away; the new church and collegiate establishment formed by the Culdees, as well as a priory of regular canons of the Augustine order, established in 1273, have disappeared; and since then another very old church has been taken down, and superseded in the beginning of this century by another of a rather superior style of architecture. During these changes, extending over a long period, the pillar-tower has stood, and still stands, distinguished alike by its striking form and by the admirable manner in which the material was selected and the building executed.

The Abernethy tower (*Fig.* 139) stands on a sloping bank at a short distance from the Ochill hills, and a mile south of the river Tay, near where it joins the Earn. The view from the tower is contracted towards the south by the proximity of the hills, where a beautiful valley stretches southwards, while to the north there is an extensive prospect of a rich and undulating country, one of the granaries of Scotland, in which direction is the entrance to the tower. The building is 75 feet in height and 48 feet in circumference; its extreme diameter at the top is 13 feet 9 inches, increasing towards the bottom, where it is 15 feet 6 inches; while the thickness of the wall at the top is 2 feet 9 inches, and at the bottom 3 feet 7½ inches. The tower is now without a roof, and the coping over the wall is probably modern. It is divided into five stages or storeys, each supported by stone abutments; and is built of sandstone, which is now much disintegrated, except on the lower and western side, where there are twelve courses of grey freestone, little changed by exposure to the weather. The stones are all carefully dressed, convex on the exterior, tapering inwards, and concave on their inner surface, in order to give a circular form to the tower, and they are accurately adjusted in regular courses with but little lime or cement. The doorway is 6 feet above the base, but in consequence of the graveyard adjoining having become greatly elevated above the general surface of the soil, the door is now only 2 feet above the ground. It is 7 feet 9 inches high, 29 inches in width at

Fig. 139.

---

(1) The name is derived from *aber*, confluence, and *nethy*, a small stream that passes down to the town, and joins the river Earn; and the town is sometimes still called by the Scotch-Irish name of similar import, Invernethy.
(2) See Four Masters.   (3) Innes' Critical Essays, vol. i, pp. 3, 122, 127.   (4) Bede, Lib. v, c. xxi.

the spring of the semi-circular arch, and 27½ inches across at the bottom. Four windows near the top of the tower face the cardinal points; they are 3 feet 10½ inches in height, 1 foot 4½ inches in width above, and 1 foot 6½ inches below, and seem to differ from each other in their architectural form. Gordon, in his Itinerary, says that at the beginning of last century "each window" was "supported by two small pillars," traces of which are still very evident in one or two of them. Those in the west windows are entirely gone. Dr. Wilson supposes [1] that the windows may be modern, but after a careful examination on the spot, I have come to the conclusion that they were prepared at the same time as the rest of the tower. Besides the four upper windows, there are three small openings below to admit light to the interior.

Thirty years ago an excavation was made within the tower, when seven human sculls were found lying together. Some of them were of a dark colour, as if they had undergone some process of embalming. Along with these several long bones were found, some of which must have been recently deposited, as they had still their ligaments attached to them.[2] The tower stands about twenty yards to the south-west of the parish church, which is a modern structure. It is now used as a belfry, and the beadle informed me that it is "pretty well" adapted for this purpose. It also contains the village clock; and the ancient jongs or pillory is attached to it.

Fig. 140.

The other pillar-tower in Scotland of this class, at Brechin [3] (*Fig.* 140) is distinguished for the beauty of its workmanship and the elegance of its form. It is supposed to have been built in the ninth century, or a century or so later than the old church of Aberlemno, which is believed to have been founded by Kenneth IV, A.D. 990.[4] The present church, to which the tower is attached, was added long afterwards. The tower of Brechin is built on a gentle elevation, to the north of the old castle and the River Esk. It commands a contracted view of a fruitful valley on the west; while on the east there stretches away from it a rich and wide plain, bounded by the bay of Montrose and the German Ocean. The stones of which this tower is built have been carefully selected, and very little cement has been employed in the building; but the nature of this cement cannot readily be ascertained, as the structure has been thoroughly repaired, and a modern octagon roof erected over it, with angular-headed windows at each of the abutments and spaces, to give it the same architectural character as the modern church, which it joins, and of which it forms the south-west corner. The old tower, previous to the repairs, was 85 feet in height; it is now 18 feet more than the height of the new roof. Its extreme circumference at the top is 38 feet 6 inches, sloping outwards to the bottom, where it is 50 feet; the interior diameter at the top is 7 feet 8 inches, at the bottom 8 feet; the thickness of the wall at the four upper windows is 2 feet 10 inches, and at the doorway 4 feet, including the projection of the door lintels, which is 2 inches.

There are seven openings altogether. These are:—(1) The doorway which faces the west; (2) two oblong openings facing the south and east, to afford light to the interior; and (3) four oblong rectangular windows near the top, facing the cardinal points. Over all these openings large stones are built into the wall, and that over the door is hollowed out into an arch. Round the doorway are large blocks of sandstone, more prominent than the other stones of the building, and sculptured with bas-reliefs. That over the door is the crucifix, and those on the lintels are the supposed figures of St. John and the Virgin Mary. At the bottom of the doorway are sculptured on one side a crouching animal, and on the other a monstrous griffin.[5]

(1) Pre-historic Annals, 595.   (2) Small's Roman Antiquities of Fife, p. 154, and appendix F.
(3) From the Gaelic name, Breaschnain, a "brae" or sloping bank.
(4) Hic est qui tribuit magnam civitatem Brechne domino.—*Chr. Pict.* Kenneth died by treachery (per dolum) A.D. 994.—*Ulster Annals.*
(5) Perhaps symbolical of evil. *See* Eusebuis' "Life of Constantine," Bk. III, ch. iii.

The lozenge ornament in the middle of the door-sill appears to have been filled with tracery. The double row of button-like ornaments surrounding the doorway bear a resemblance to those upon the Inchbrayoc and Brechin sculptured pillar-stones.[1] All these figures and ornaments are now much defaced by time. The other stones used in the building of the tower are grey-coloured freestone. There are six unequally-sized stories, with strong timber floors resting upon abutments or supports of hewn freestone, each of which projects from 6 to 10 inches. The top of the tower is reached by a series of six ladders. "Mason marks"—the only ones yet discovered in the pillar-towers—have been found in the interior of the building, and have been delineated by Mr. Chalmers.

Pillar towers of different varieties appear to have been afterwards erected for similar or other purposes in other districts of these islands, but the original type of them all is of oriental derivation, and must have been the erection of the people to whom we refer the other oriental devices on the stones of Scotland. Such erections were partly found convenient for, and partly further adapted to, Christian uses, and they continued to rise in the original plan, as of native growth, alongside of other properly Christian structures. Nay, it is possible some were erected in times and places where they were no longer necessary, on the principle on which a flock of sheep will continue jumping as their bell-wether had done, though the barrier had been removed which compelled him to do so.

Fig. 141.

(1) *See* Sculptured Stones of Scotland (Spalding Club), vol. ii, plate 1.

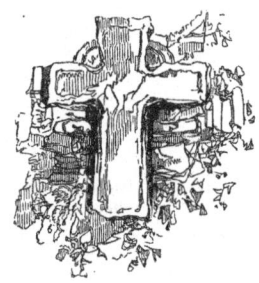

CHAPTER II.

FORM OF THE ANCIENT INCISED AND BAS-RELIEF GREEK AND LATIN CROSSES IN THE BRITISH ISLANDS.

HE Christian crosses of Pictland, as we have seen, may be arranged into four groups, and that probably in chronological order :—[1]

1. Incised crosses, without ornaments, common in Caledonia, and as such distinguished from Pagan, perhaps A.D. 110 to A.D. 260 (Tertullian).

2. Greek and Latin crosses with ornaments in bas-relief; among them Eastern symbols and animals on the obverse and reverse, *circa* 431.

3. Latin and Greek crosses, with ecclesiastical figures and equestrian processions in relief on the reverse, *circa* 642.

4. Latin crosses, with representations of the Crucifixion, &c.

SECTION I.—PRIMITIVE INCISED CROSSES.

We have remarked in Book I, p. 118, that crosses were used as personal ornaments among the ancient nations of Asia, as a symbol of virtue, as well as an ægis against the assaults of evil. The simplest form of the cross has four limbs of equal length, originally symbolical of the four seasons, and the union of the five elements of ether, fire, air, earth, and water, these being supposed by the

---

[1] It is highly uncertain whether the symbol was in use in its properly Christian reference before the days of Constantine, though Martigny refers to Perret (Catacombs of Rome iv, xvi, 74), as mentioning certain stones apparently belonging to rings on which the cross is engraved of date prior to his time. (Dr. Smith's Dict. of the Bible, vi, p. 496.)

Hindu and other ancient philosophers, as explained in Book I, pp. 103—105, to be the constituent elements of all things, both spiritual and material, throughout the universe,—nothing being regarded as annihilated, but everything as existing only under changed forms. This form of the cross was the first that was incised by the Christians, and it resembled the Eastern type, consisting as it did of scores, scratches, and furrows, without ornamental decorations. Those which occur in Pictland are from four to twenty feet in height.

Upon the flat face of a high rock rising perpendicularly by the side of a Highland road in Sutherland, are two small simple Greek crosses some feet apart, the one being higher up than the other, the lower for the penitent, as if to allow him to kiss the cross before which he had prayed. On another flat surface on a cropping of a rock, on the face of a hill in Kerry, there are two such small crosses at some distance from each other, but the one is the Greek cross, and the other a Latin cross.

This interesting class of simple crosses is found in considerable numbers in the British Islands. There are fewer in England proper, than in Wales, Cornwall, and Ireland, where they are numerous. These, though rude in point of art and otherwise similar, are all equally destitute of any ornaments. Crosses of this rude order and type are not found so frequently in Pictland;—as the Christian religion appears to have been introduced into Pictavia by teachers who were not only gifted with a more spiritual apprehension of the Christian system, but also with more artistic power of expression, and who found there already a people in some measure prepared for their teaching by the prior appearance among them of Druid priests, Buddhist missionaries and Buddhist artists. These crosses are very beautiful and form a marked contrast to the early crosses of Ireland. Indeed in general effect, form, and proportions of the different kinds, these ancient crosses are of a superior order and argue the presence of a comparatively advanced stage of at once culture and art.

The primitive incised crosses were probably the first symbols of the Christian faith in a new country, where the Pagan inhabitants already worshipped the erect boulder, as the symbol of their spiritual deity, with the blue heavens above as the only appropriate canopy. In some cases, as we have seen,- the cross was engraved upon a primitive rock, or an oblong boulder stone fixed in the earth, and beside it prayers were offered up and instructions given to the young, for here naturally those were to be found who, as religiously disposed, would be most desirous to learn the new doctrine.

The original shape of the cross, the instrument of punishment on which Christ was crucified, was an upright stake without arms to which the victim was sometimes merely bound, and on which at other times his body was empaled; and this was in reality the shape of the "σταυρος," as used for punishment in Roman times. At length, however, it assumed the form of an upright beam with a transverse beam at the top, and without any extension upward. Lucian alludes to the Cross [σταυρος] as being in the shape of a Tau; and this T was frequently prefixed to inscriptions by the early Christians in Egypt, and it is also represented on the Graffite found on the Palatine Hill. According to Didron, however, the cross of Christ was a Latin cross, formed of one vertical shaft, and of a transverse beam intersecting it at right angles. It is believed to have been in the reign of Theodorius that the Latin cross was adopted as the Christian symbol, and it was the belief of the Fathers that this was the form of the cross of Christ. The Achæan Greek cross, so frequently used as an ornamental device in Greek art, was, it appears, adopted by the early Christians as a religious symbol, not as suggestive of the instrument of Christ's death, but from its resemblance to the monogram of Christ.

Between the Tay and the Spey, there exist thirty-one boulder monuments incised with symbols; seven of which either form a part of, or appear to be connected with, circles of primitive boulders, arguing the presence of a wide-spread Celtic community. Of these, six have a cross in combination with scenes relating to religious warfare or sport. One has the cross alone, another has incised letters of an unknown language; and one alone of this number has the figure of a man seemingly undergoing crucifixion. That is to say, there is only one with a cross that bears unmistakeable reference to its use as a symbol of an instrument of death.

The obelisks which prevail in this district have no connection in style with the Celtic monuments of Western Caledonia, but are of an order peculiar to Pictland. They were prepared through a period of several centuries, during a time when the inhabitants were apparently undergoing great and important political changes.

Fig. 142.

The accompanying figure gives a rare instance of a Buddhist symbol added on to the back of a very early form of obelisk, with an incised Latin cross. It contains a sceptred segment of a circle, carefully drawn and looking downwards, immediately over a satchel. (*Fig.* 143).

Fig. 143.

The absence of intercommunication, due to the suspicious and treacherous character of rude races, which prevents them from associating with their neighbours or viewing them as friends, explains many peculiarities in the antiquities of countries accessible with difficulty before the inhabitants were converted to Christianity. Accordingly, even after the conversion of the natives to Christianity, we find stones with crosses in bas-relief were rare in Pictland. And these crosses are larger in size, and the figure of the cross in bas-relief rises upon an oblong flat surface on the obverse.

In Pagan times, as we have seen, the erect boulder-stone was the symbol of the Deity. This was succeeded by the symbol of the triad of the Buddhist belief, and this again was followed by the Christian cross as the symbol of the Christian faith. The raised crosses of Pictland have their margins filled with grotesque ornaments, animals, &c., differing entirely from those of the South and West of Caledonia. It is, therefore, incorrect to suppose "that Christianity was introduced into Scotland from Ireland, and that the sacred influence of Christianity was diffused into Caledonia, in an indirect manner, from the fane of Iona."

Near the southern end of the famous pass of Killiecrankie, which even the Hanoverian soldiers on seeing refused to enter "as the dreaded mouth of the lower regions," is a prayer-cross, in strong relief, on a block of sandstone four feet high. At this spot travellers offered up prayers for their safe preservation before entering, or rendered thanks for their safety after leaving the dreadful pass. This double use appears evident from the sides of the stone being placed opposite to the S.E. and N.W., upon each of which is the figure of the cross. Crosses of this kind were prepared by a race of Christians, who have passed away without other sign and before history began to speak. In this case it is probable that a small chapel was in the neighbourhood, as the place is still called Chapel-land, and, indeed, vestiges of the building may still be traced.

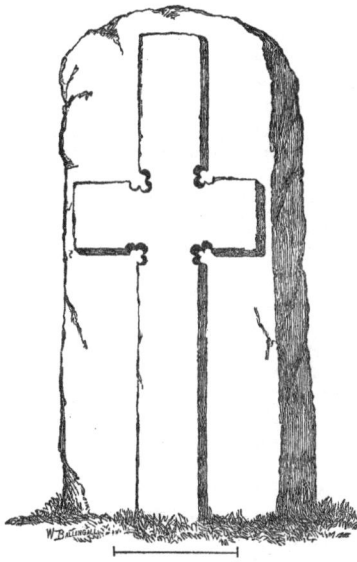

Stones with the incised crosses of the earliest type bear no extraneous ornaments, Pagan symbols, or Asiatic animals, and they appear as the symbol of a pure and simple form of religion to which the cross was added as being the sign of a faith in, and a joy over, a living Christ, which the Church crowns with flowers.

An incised Latin cross of this simple kind is at Deer, in Aberdeenshire. It was fixed in the earth, and was probably a prayer cross. On the reverse is an incised sceptred segment of a circle (one of the Buddhist symbols), with a satchel, probably containing one of the gospels, and this segment may represent the Divine power shedding His influence over the sacred book. The crosses of Pictland are often made of one stone, while the slender English and Irish examples generally consist of two parts—the top, or cross proper, being formed of one block, and the shaft of another, united by a mortice and tenon. The section of the stalk is rectangular, with sometimes the cable mounting along the angle. The faces are divided into panels filled with graceful patterns. They are moderate in size, but those of Meigle, Aberlemno, &c., are from 12 to 15 feet in height, and that of Gosford, in Cumberland, is 15 feet high.

Fig. 144.

SECTION II.—PRIMITIVE BAS-RELIEF CROSSES.—THE MAIDEN STONE.

(*See* Frontispiece.)

The Maiden stone stands in the parish of Garlock, in Aberdeenshire. It is a hard-grained granite earth-bound stone. Its height is 10 feet 6 inches, its breadth 2 feet 9 inches at the middle, and its thickness at the top is 4 inches, at the middle 8 inches, and at the bottom 9¼ inches. A triangular portion near the bottom, covered with ornament, is defective, also a similar portion near the top. The Christian cross faces the N.W., and the symbols the S.E. The back is divided into four compartments by a rod-like moulding, which runs round the compartments and along the edge. The upper compartment has three mythological animals, and a centaur, all of which are much defaced. The second has the sceptred altar already referred to. In the third there is the elephant; and in the lowest compartment are the looking-glass and comb.

The front of the stone has a Latin cross standing upon a square basis containing a circle, the diameter of which coincides with the breadth of the stone, and within this is a circle concentric with it, having a diameter of about half that of the outer. Four graceful prominent spiral ornaments, like that in the Farr cross (with knot pattern), occupy the centre, and the outer ring has the zig-zag or wicker-work pattern. Each of the upper corners is filled with a simple knot ornament, and the two lower with a more complicated form of the same, while the whole presents a combination peculiarly elegant. The limbs and margin of the cross were likewise ornamented with different patterns, now entirely defaced. Upon the upper limb are two mythological monsters like dolphins, whose heads nearly meet at the top. They are on either side, and their bodies form a semi-circle, with their tails, of a spiral form, resting upon the circle of the cross. In the circle thus formed, and standing upon the upper limb of the cross, is a figure, probably of Christianity, with arms and hands open, and surrounded by persecution, represented by the monstrous dolphins. This may be our Saviour standing on the cross, with outstretched hands, exclaiming, "Come unto Me, all ye that labour and are heavy laden, and I will give you rest;" or the whole may represent the shield of the Christian religion.

The Latin Cross with a Nimbus.—The cross of St. Orland, or St. Erland, is situated upon a slight mound, with a hollow below, where the people met to worship and to receive instruction. It is in the middle of a field, on the farm of Cossins, a couple of miles north-east of Glammis Castle. Being long quite unprotected, it was one day used as a rubbing stone[1] by a bull and broken across, five feet from the ground. Such was the mysterious veneration, however, with which it was viewed by the people, that the farmer could not sleep at night, until he had got the obelisk mended; which was done in a rude manner by large clamps of iron; and the Earl of Strathmore has since surrounded it by an iron rail, to prevent such an accident again occurring. This beautiful Latin cross [a] faces to the S.E., and is probably in its original position. It is decorated with very graceful interlaced ornaments, and entwined monsters. A tenon on the top indicates that another stone, now lost, formed a coping to protect it from the weather, and there is a ledge near the middle which was probably intended to receive a box of relics, that would be there exposed to the public on the occasion of certain festivals. On the reverse of the stone, two griffins surround the upper margin, with their heads near each other and over the centre, with something in their mouths. The sceptred spectacle ornament has the sceptred crescent over it. These symbols are on the upper half of the stone, and underneath an interlaid margin are men on horseback, and hunting dogs above with a peculiarly shaped boat. Underneath these are two monsters. Such a hunting scene probably represented a chief followed by his attendants, enjoying their favourite pastime. The chief and followers have defensive armour, and housings on their horses; this representation was probably meant as a compliment to some local chief, in return for the assistance obtained in erecting the cross.

A Latin cross, without a nimbus, in the old churchyard in the Island of Canna, one of the Western Islands of Scotland, and dedicated to St. Columba, is supposed to have been erected soon after his death. It is of red sandstone, and is both in form and decorations unlike those in the west of Scotland. It may be considered as a transition cross, from the Eastern to the Western type. It is cruciform in shape, with an ornamental margin round it, which reduces it nearly to the form of the Eastern crosses of Pictland. It has entwined mythological serpents, with griffins and other animals on the reverse, and an equestrian figure on the field. On the remaining limb of the cross, on the right side, is the figure of a well-sculptured Bactrian humped camel. This animal may

---

(1) It is of sandstone from the neighbourhood, 7ft. above the ground, 2ft. 6½in. broad, near the ground, and 2ft. 4in. above, and 10in. in thickness near the ground, and 4½in. near the top.

(2) Sculp. Stones, plate 85.

have been selected by the artist from among other Asiatic animals, out of gratitude for its service in crossing the arid deserts, and we may suppose he cherished the hope that he might require its assistance in returning to his Eastern home. The same useful animal appears on the engraved crosses in the Meigle graveyard, swinging his long neck and stretching round his inquisitive eyes, kneeling and groaning aloud, while his attendant is probably binding a heavy burden on his shoulders. A scene familiar to one who has travelled in Asia, and a picture that could not be drawn by one unfamiliar with the habits of the animal in its native country.

The numerous ancient small crosses in Argyleshire are more modern than those in Pictland, while the form of the cross is more ornamental. They are of different sizes, according as they were intended for prayer, or for monuments of the dead. Many of them are large and gracefully executed in relief, specimens similar to them are found in England, and in considerable numbers in Ireland. Cases of the Latin cross without a nimbus are not so common as those with one; that in the old churchyard in the Island of Canna being an example.

In the Edderton stone, there is on the obverse a Latin cross with a nimbus, having a division, giving it the form of a Greek cross, and on the reverse a Latin cross without a nimbus, and supported by a semi-circular bridge.[1]

The Brodie stone [2] is a Latin cross, without either nimbus, symbols, or ornaments. The cross is filled with tracery, and shows entwined monsters in the margin. On the upper part of the reverse are two horse-shaped monsters, between and below which are circles in relief. Underneath is the elephant fancifully ornamented and interlaced; still further down, is the spectacle ornament, with decorated bar sceptres.

Ancient Cornwall (Cornu-Galliæ), according to Strabo, Diodorus Siculus, and others, was early celebrated for its mineral wealth, and had, in consequence, at a very early period communication with the great nations of the East. The Phœnicians, we have seen, resorted to it in very early times, and probably formed settlements there, while the inhabitants made some advance in the arts and in civilization several centuries before the Christian era. It was there that the first regular government was established in Britain, and the first attempts were made at coinage,[3] and with this exception "all the affinities indicated by later and well defined relics of natural art point to a more intimate intercourse of community of customs and arts between the natives of Scotland and Ireland than between the northern and southern parts of Great Britain."[4] The Cornish crosses have few inscriptions. They are often sculptured at the top into the form of a rude Greek cross. In other examples the sacred emblems are incised. In general character they are ruder than those of Ireland and Scotland. They are short oblong slabs, like those of Scotland, with few ornaments. Where they are memorial crosses they have an inscription in Roman character, recording the names of the individual over whose remains they were placed.[5]

The beautiful cross of Rossie Priory,[6] has a Græco-Latin cross with a nimbus on one side, and a Greek cross without a nimbus on the other; one arm of the cross and nimbus being broken. Both are covered with a variety of graceful interlaced and Celtic ornaments. On the face, or obverse, are various mythological animals. The limbs and margin of the cross are filled with beautiful and varied ornaments, and in the lower limb is an unarmed equestrian chief, having before him the sceptred segment of a circle in the margin, as

---

(1) See Sculptured Stones of Scotland, vol. i, plate 31.   (2) See Sculptured Stones of Scotland, vol. i, pp. 22, 23.
(3) Tour in Wales, vol. ii, p. 196, published in 1781.
(4) Post's Britannic Researches and Coins of Cunobeline, &c., &c., p. 224; also pp. 139 to 146.
(5) Wilson's Prehistoric Annals, p. 467.   (6) See Sculptured Stones of Scotland, vol. ii, plate 98.

an ægis. Under the chief is another with the mythological elephant resting on a two-headed griffin. This also may be the ægis to the second horseman. A third equestrian is followed by two greyhounds, indicating the rank of chief, followed by two other horsemen. The last appearing at rest while the others are in motion.

The large crosses appear to have been respected, while the smaller ones were generally broken at the time of the Reformation, the fragments being employed as building stones. Some of these were found on removing the old church of Kincoldrum, others at an old chapel at St. Andrew's, and others on removing a malt-kiln, close to the church stones of Meigle, in 1851.[1] In like manner, according to Dean Stanley the monuments of Westminster Abbey nearly all perished at the Reformation.[2]

It is probable, that the beautiful cross of Rossie was placed at a forked road, so that the traveller faced one cross as he went, and another as he returned. The one side contains a Græco-Latin cross, with an outer border filled with symbols and equestrian figures, their ægis, and hunting-dogs. The reverse cross has a beautiful Græco-Latin cross, with the usual mythological animals on the margin. Such a cross must have been prepared in a more populous and more important part of the country, when chiefs were required to be propitiated —one of them being represented in the descending limb of the cross (*Figs.* 145 *and* 146.)

Fig. 145.

Fig. 146.

The Rose-Markie obelisk is an interesting and elaborate specimen of a graceful cross.[3] The cross is enclosed in a square compartment, in the upper part of the obverse side, and the remainder of the side is filled with graceful and varied interlaced ornaments. The reverse side contains the same exquisite workmanship. At the upper part is a sceptred segment, above and below the spectacle ornament, filled with a variety of ornaments, bosses and sceptres; and below this, is a second variety of the Greek cross, with bosses in the corners, and surrounded with graceful ornaments. The other specimens of the Greek cross are the Glenfurness cross,[4] with interlaced ornaments, and ornamented symbols; the St. Andrew's cross,[5] with corners of limbs, monkeys and serpents entwining, bosses (lid of sarcophagus); the Farnell cross,[6] with tree and priests, serpents, a Latin cross on the reverse; the Abbotsford cross,[7] with animals and horsemen on the reverse, brought from Pictland.

---

(1) *See* Sculp. St. Scotland, vol. ii, plates 49, 131. (2) Memoirs of Westminster Abbey, ch. iii, p. 177.
(3) This obelisk formed for many years a part of the flooring of the old church; in 1870 it was set up in an iron framework at the end of the church, pl. 105, 106, Sculp. S., vol. i.
(4) *See* Sculptured Stones of Scotland, vol. i, pl. 24.
(5) *Ibid.*, pl. 63.   (6) *Ibid.*, pl. 86.   (7) *Ibid.*, pl. 99.

SECTION III.—PRIMITIVE VARIETIES OF CROSSES IN THE BRITISH ISLANDS.

There are other varieties of crosses from Cornwall, Ireland, Western Scotland, Wales, South of Caledonia, and the Island of Man, besides the Pictavian already described.

Cornwall.—The early intercourse between the Levant and this part of the island, in connection with the trade in tin and copper, formed a ready channel for the importation of Christian beliefs and symbols among the inhabitants, and it is chiefly the small Greek crosses that are found there, without any remains of churches. These are peculiarly significant and suggestive of original peculiarities, as they were constructed before the separation of the Greek and Latin churches, and they are found in great numbers all over Cornwall, where the origin of the Church may be viewed under two aspects—first, in connection with the names of the saints; and, second, with the form and ornaments of the cross.

An important distinction appears in the crosses. We find them nearly divided into those of the Greek and Latin form; crosses in relief and those formed through the thickness of the stone, as in Ireland. Two-thirds are plain crosses, and the remaining third have the form of the crucifixion. The ornaments are still more characteristic; and here we find a marked difference between the Cornish and Irish crosses. The former are generally smaller, many having no stalk, and when longer are filled up with different simple dots, and in one instance with the interlaced pattern in the margin of the crucifixion, with a Saxon inscription.

SECTION IV.—VARIETIES OF CROSSES IN THE BRITISH ISLANDS.

Irish and Iona Crosses.—The peculiarity of the Irish cross consists in its being erected on a carved pedestal, from which the cross proper tapers to the top, and upon which a conical unhewn copestone[1] is placed, while the crosses of the West of Scotland are either fixed in the ground or let into a block of stone. The halo or circle in both these varieties binds the limbs and shaft together, and generally in the centre of the stone there is a crucifixion. The compartments of the Irish cross contain scenes from Scriptural sources, such as the Fall of Man, the Last Judgment, the Tree of Knowledge, the Sacrifice of Isaac, the Judgment of Solomon, &c., indicating that they were intended for a more cultured people than those of the East of Scotland. The Irish crosses, like those in the West of Scotland, are generally found in or near churchyards, and the similarity between them evinces the early connexion between the countries, from the time of St. Columba and his followers.

The crosses in the Isle of Man are numerous. They are engraved on slabs with rude figures of animals, as stags, dogs, horses and horsemen, musical instruments, weapons, and ornamental devices. Runic inscriptions record the name of those who erected them.

According to the inscription on the Kirkmichael cross, one named *Dant* made all the crosses in the Isle of Man.

---

(1) *See* Book III, chapter vi.

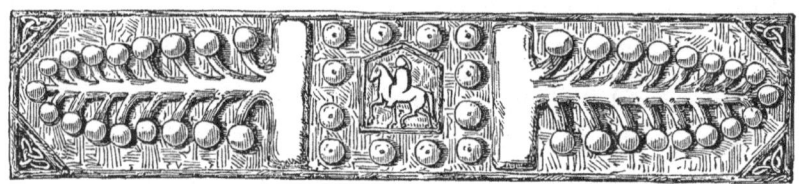

CHAPTER III.

USES OF THE CHRISTIAN CROSSES IN PICTLAND: PREACHING CROSSES, AS WELL AS PRAYER AND MEMORIAL CROSSES.

Section I.—Prayer and Preaching Crosses.

HE prayer-crosses are usually small, and without extraneous ornaments in the margin or back. We have (see p. 215) already described a small Greek cross, of simple form, which is found in retired places, and is believed to have indicated a place of resort for prayer at a very early period. A more artistic form of such a cross is found at Meigle; it is built in the wall which surrounds the Meigle churchyard, and was most probably damaged when the old church was burnt. As the Christian religion spread in Pictland, more attention was paid to the prayer-cross, and larger ones were erected and employed in connection with public exhortations, as well as placed over the graves of the dead, to impart to such spots an additional sacredness. Notwithstanding the evident skill of the Pictavian artists, as shown in their sculptured stones, it is remarkable that, with the exception of the prayer-crosses and the tombs, no remains of sacred edifices exist; from which we infer that there were no churches of stone in the early period, but expensive tombs, such as that of Govan, were erected in after times to enshrine the remains of the illustrious dead, those of the primitive type containing the serpent, comb, and mirror.[1] Three pieces of a skeleton and a bronze dagger were found near it. It probably marked the grave of a Norseman, which would account for the weapon;[2] and these peculiar stones retained their sacred character even in the Christian period, partly because of their religious nature, and partly as associated with the dead.

Another variety of cross is found at Dunkeld and Abernethy. They are of more modern date, and resemble the crosses in the south and west of Caledonia. They show graceful mouldings, similar to that on

---

(1) Sculp. Stones of Scotland, vol. i, p. 112. (2) Pref. Spal. Club. Sculp. Stones of Scotland, vol. ii, p. 5.

ancient MSS., with subjects from Bible history, proving, as we have already remarked, that the people they appealed to were better instructed than those of the east of Scotland, as well as possessed of more artistic taste. A cross, used as a mourning or weeping cross, is situated at Flintstown, near Holly-Well. These large and venerable monuments were wayside prayer-crosses, and as Dr. Lingard supposed, supplied the place of oratories, consecrating, by their sacred emblems, the ground around them. The first Christian cross was simply incised, to which was added the circle, the emblem of the Deity, or eternity; and this became the germ of the elaborately sculptured crosses so common at a later period.[1] The object of the erection of the large and beautiful crosses was chiefly that of worship, and as they rendered the place sacred, the spot came often to be used afterwards as a sepulchre for the dead, while from their sacred character they were also used to commemorate some great event, or to mark an inviolable boundary. The wayside cross, like all the others, afforded the privilege of sanctuary; and eight of these, called mile crosses, mark the boundary at Ripon,[2] while at Hixhon this is indicated by four of these, placed at certain distances from the road leading to the church There are also stump crosses, market crosses, as well as crosses representative of the crucifixion. The material is sometimes wood, sometimes stone, and sometimes metal. The first crosses were of wood, and being of perishable material, soon disappeared; bone, ivory, and metal are more modern; stone as the most accessible, workable, and durable material, is most common, the favourite being fine grained light sandstone; but red sandstone and granite, &c., are also found, while the crosses of the Isle of Man are almost always of grey slate.

Tertullian, who wrote A.D. 199, or about 120 years before the conversion of Constantine, tells us that the cross was in Pagan times regarded as a symbol of omnipresent deity, and as such invoked, and this belief paved the way for its adoption by the primitive Christians as a Christian symbol. "Before commencing business, on going out or coming in, when preparing for a journey, or going into a bath, when sitting down to a meal, when we lie down or sit up, on a light being brought into the room, whenever we have business, and whatever business we may have on hand, we should make the sign of the cross on our foreheads" (*de Corona Militis*); and Chrysostom (A.D. 350), says that "in the market and in the desert, in the highway and on the mountain, in forests, on hills, on the sea in ships, and on islands, crosses were erected for the purpose of taking possession, and to avert evil." We can understand how these crosses, being considered holy, came at a more modern period to be used for other purposes by a rude and superstitious people. It was the custom to bind men and women affected with disease or insanity, on Saturday night, or on the eve of a saint's day, to one of them, but while some were said to have recovered, the majority, from the exposure to cold and hunger, were found dead or dying in the morning.[3] During the middle ages, the cross continued to be the great symbol of the Christian religion; and as there were no parochial divisions during the first centuries of the Saxon church, the clergy resided in monasteries, whence at fixed periods they proceeded by turns to instruct the country people, and to administer the offices of religion at the cross in the open air, or in such churches as happened to be erected.

The Dupplin cross on the Island of Canna,[4] we may regard as having been prepared during the transition period, when the Christians of the different parts of the Island became less exclusive. The stones were prepared by missionaries, of the south of Scotland, in a cruciform manner, resembling those of Ireland, while they retained an outer margin, the peculiar interlaced pattern, and other points of similarity with the older crosses of Pictland. According to the account of Dr. Wilson, "the interlaced patterns and figures of dragons, serpents, and nondescript monsters, bear a close, and unmistakable resemblance to the decorations of some of the more ancient MSS. Several of the beautiful initials from the book of Kells, an Irish MS. of the sixth century, as engraved in Westwood's Palæographia, are markedly similar to the style of ornament of these

---

(1) Tour. Brit. Arch. Assoc., No. 34, part iii, p. 354.

(2) *See* Walbrace's " Guide to Ripon," p. 30.

(3) *See* Joceline.

(4) Sculp. Stones of Scotland vol. ii, pl. 50 and 51.

sculptures, while the interlaced network, in the case of the shield of St. Maido, which Dr. Petrie conceives cannot be of a date later than the eighth century, though less distinctly characteristic, and by no means peculiar to Ireland, very nearly correspond in its details with the ornamentation frequently introduced in the Scottish monuments.

The smaller of the two large crosses of Meigle (Forfarshire) is in the ancient Latin form, with monstrous figures on the margin, and has on the lower part of the back of the obelisk two processions of horsemen. (*Fig.* 147).

Fig. 147.

In the upper of the two processions, which consists of three horsemen retiring from a griffin, or evil genius, the leading equestrian is a person of consideration, as is indicated by his large size, and also by that of his horse. In the lower of the processions two horsemen issue from space, the leading figure being of a larger size, to indicate his superior rank. They are preceded by a protecting angel, in which we recognize the Christian origin of the sculpture. The upper part of the cross is surmounted by a large fish, which we may take as representing the Christian religion, and this overspreads the stone. Under it is an embryo elephant, and a large winding serpent transfixed with a rod, terminating in two sceptres. A knotted ornament is near the head of the serpent, and beyond that, the head and neck of a horse, terminating in scrolls, with a kneeling lamb underneath. Beneath the serpent is a looking glass and comb, and near these a kneeling camel. The cross is five feet six inches above the ground; three feet six inches in breadth below, tapering to three feet two inches at the top, which has a rounded form; seven-and-a-half inches thick at the surface of the ground, and six inches at the top.[1]

The second majestic and larger cross, in the churchyard at Meigle, is Græco-Latin in form (*Fig.* 148). The lower limb and its margin are filled in with figures, and mythological animals; all much worn by exposure to the weather. The beautiful cross above fills the whole breadth of the stone; its four limbs are surrounded by a circle, ornamented with knobs or bosses. There are griffins on the margin of the limb, above and below; while on the left side, a man appears trying to evade a monstrous animal. On the reverse, are warriors on horseback with staghounds by their side; the centre being occupied by a human figure surrounded by lions.

When these sculptures are extended in line (*Fig.* 149) they may be thus explained:—

The central figure represents the genius of Christianity, protected and fawned on by lions as the symbols of self-derived and triumphant strength, lambs on their backs representing the consequent state of

---

(1) From their exposure to the weather, the interstices and cracks in these sculptures fill with water every winter, and enlarge and expand under the action of the frost, so that much of their ornamental forms will soon become illegible. The late Sir George Kinloch, lord of the manor, raised a subscription among his friends, and purchased a house adjoining the grave-yard, which if used, will place them out of danger of further destruction. The beautiful stone of Eassie, found in a neighbouring brook, may be instanced as requiring sadly such protection.

Fig. 148.

peace. The open front face and attitude of the figure also indicate tranquillity and peace; while the outstretched arms and open hand, also seem to say, "Come unto Me, all ye that labour, and are heavy laden, and I will give you rest." On the left of the central figure is a centaur armed with battle-axes, carrying a sacred tree; and beyond this is a sacred bull (recognisable by its hump), which is being destroyed by a monster with an armed man over it. On the right of the central figure is a procession of equestrians. The leader, distinguished by his size as a chief of rank, is preceded by two stag-hounds, and guarded by his ægis, or an angel going before. Thus the whole would seem to be a symbol of, on the one hand, the collapse of Paganism, and on the other, the conquering career of Christianity consequent on the peaceful possession of the earth by the meek spirit of the cross.

Fig. 149.

Fig. 150.

It is of importance to know the relative position of these crosses. They are given in the margin from sketches taken by me many years ago (*Fig.* 150). They are parallel to, and only a few yards from each other. Both had the crosses directed to the north-west, so that being prayer crosses, the worshippers as they stood facing them would regard the sun as it rose in the east. We may therefore conclude, that these two crosses in the Meigle churchyard still stand *in situ.* They are called by the residents, "the twa chappies." Thus do these two stones testify, however dimly, at once to the sun worship of the Pagan and the assurance of Christian hope, which sees the sun-rise in the sunset of death.

All the figures on these stones are well executed in bas-relief; and the presence of Pagan emblems on them proves that the change to Christianity was as yet but half intelligent and far from general throughout the country. The bulk of the people believing in idolatry, and its accompanying superstitions, required the continuance of the heathen symbols. As the belief in Christianity extended however, the symbols of Paganism were relegated to a lower position, and even frequently left out, while the chiefs were delineated with the proud ensigns of the rank, which now belonged to them as freemen and knights, and processions guarded by an angelic ægis, were placed above those which could boast of none such.

The large Græco-Latin crosses, at Meigle and Aberlemno, appear to have been used as preaching-crosses. Both face the north-west, while the Celto-Buddhist symbols on them are the same. The basement stone of these crosses extends beyond the cross, so as to leave a ledge for the minister of religion to stand on in the discharge of his office as a preacher as well as a priest. Such crosses were erected among a scattered population of primitive habits and superstitions. They have the ancient ring form, but are of the more recent class of these monuments, being short and flat, and studded with knobs. As it was necessary to protect them from the influence of the weather, they had projecting stones over the top and along the sides; and though these have been lost, the mortises remain into which the tenons in the narrow oblong stones were inserted.

The Cross of Nigg,[1] in Rosshire, is one of the most graceful obelisks among the remarkable sculptured stones of Pictland. It is five feet in length, with an imperfect pyramidal head, and three feet broad, and is elaborately carved on both sides. The cross is of an irregular Græco-Latin form, divided into compartments filled with different sections of interlaced ornaments, those forming the limbs of the cross being sculptured with mythological animals of serpentine form, whilst the centre is filled with interlaced ornaments in bundles, joined to each other by entwined belts. The long shaft of the stone, too, is filled with various similar ornaments; and the margin is in compartments, with interlaced ornaments and centre knobs of interlacement in circular and oblong forms, in high relief ($\frac{1}{2}$-in.), the whole forming a cross of rich and most graceful ornaments. The back of the Nigg stone is much worn, particularly the oblong central part, at the top of which are the remains of the representation of a large bird, which occupies nearly the breadth of the space. Underneath is an elephant, a sheep, and a harp, and at the bottom a man on horseback, with a greyhound in pursuit of a deer. The broad margin is filled with compartments, in gracefully entwined varieties of patterns.

The superstitious beliefs to which the new converts to Christianity in Pictland still clung, induced the Christian ministers to allow the Pagan symbols and the sacred Asiatic animals to appear on their preaching crosses, but they were executed with less care and attention to their symbolic forms, and were placed in subordinate positions with reference to the Christian cross, which was always carefully prepared, and elegantly finished. A curious example of this is seen in the Golspie Cross,[2] now preserved in the interesting Museum at Dunrobin Castle Sutherland. This beautiful obelisk may have been prepared during the transition period, between the decline of Paganism and the ascendancy of Christianity; and it proves the great zeal of the new converts. There is a Latin cross, without a nimbus, on the obverse or face of the obelisk (*Fig.* 151). The limbs and margin of this cross are filled with varied and gracefully interlaced ornaments in compartments, the whole exhibiting great artistic skill. On the reverse of this obelisk is an incised representation of a man in an ancient dress. His body is supported on his right foot, which rests upon the bifurcated extremity of the tail of an entwined mythological serpent; while the uplifted left foot is kicking the third member of the Pagan triad, from its position over the spectacle ornament, which is in the lower part of the obelisk, and significantly without sceptres. The triad in this case consists of a segment denoting organised matter, with fictitious sceptres, and the representation of a Buddhist's chaytra, or relic-temple. The man has in his right

---

(1) Cross of Nigg, Rosshire. Sculp. Stones of Scotland, vol. i, plates 28 and 29.
(2) Sculp. Stones of Scotland, vol. i, plate 34.

HISTORY OF PAGANISM IN CALEDONIA.

Fig. 151.

hand an uplifted axe, with which he threatens an advancing sacrificial bull, marked as sacred; while in his left, he holds an open knife, menacing a fish. The figure at the top of the stone probably represents Providence, with a triad hovering over an elephant, the ægis, probably, of the Christian hero. An untranslated Ogham inscription surrounds two edges of the stone.

This remarkable monolith, as we conjecture, represents the rejection of Paganism, and the acceptance of the Christian religion. There is here no longer any halting between two opinions, but a decisive and peremptory repudiation of Paganism, the Buddhists included, root and branch. Buddha, his law, his symbols, his relics, for these are all represented here are no longer of any account, or rather as worse than worthless, and so remorselessly cast out. For Christianity has a militant aspect as well as a peaceful, and cherishes a sacred intolerance towards everything that hinders, still more opposes, the truth. No more of that idle trumpery of nature-worship; man is man, and his proper business is with himself; not to worship the sun or moon, but the spirit, and in the spirit do God's work. Such at bottom is the meaning of the rejection of Paganism, such the high warrant under which it was cast out, although the work of demolishing it was achieved by men who, as the unconscious organs of a higher Power, did not know what their action meant.

We notice here that the try-glyphs in the symbol of organised matter are joined at each end, and form tridents on Buddhist coins, which, in Asia, have no legend or character. The symbol (*b*), *Fig.* 152, represents

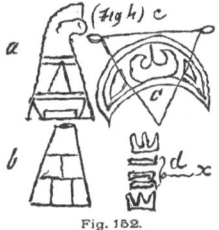

Fig. 152.

the temple or chaytra on Buddhist coins in Asia, containing the Taru or sacred law-manuscripts, symbols and coins.

It is evidently the model of the similar temple seen on Pictavian stones; (*d*) is also from Buddhist coins; the centre represents organised matter as a triad, the Eastern trident at each extremity.[1] The difference is greater in the sacred animals, as the Eastern missionaries retained these upon their monuments in Pictland. It has been asserted that no such figure of an elephant is to be found in Asia, with such waving terminal legs, but we have seen that such figures are found in Buddhist temples (*see* page 186); and, when once adopted, are always represented as the proper figure for the celestial animal. The other

---

(1) Remarks on Buddhist coins, &c., Journal Asiatic Soc., Calcutta, vol. xiii, p. 571 *et seq*: and notes on the state of Ancient India, by Col. Sykes.

animals on the crosses are lions, bulls, serpents, monkies; and the camels and centaurs are represented in their natural forms. The able artists who prepared the crosses, prove by this means that they were well acquainted with the habits of these Eastern animals. The Bactrian, and the Indian varieties of the camel are given; and the latter is represented kneeling and looking back, recalling to us the mournful cry it utters while its masters are loading its back. Along with the processions of foreign animals, there are others of Western equestrians. These manifest the social rank of those in whose honour they were erected, while the mythological monsters, on the outside of the cross, prove that the religious ideas are still mixed with superstitious fancies.

The liberty which was allowed the artist in preparing the reverse of these crosses, invests these monuments with another interest of a local bearing, and this will require more care in the explanation, particularly as such an explanation has not been before attempted. The ornaments on the reverse are to be explained by reference to that form of culture, which seeks to awaken a sense of what is beautiful in nature, and to destroy superstitious fancies regarding it. When ideas of progress also begin to be developed, and the eye, looking on the book of nature, sees its leaves written over with psalms of rejoicing to the great God, at whose word alone such a beautiful world was formed, awe-inspiring in its vast sublimity, and revealing in the minutest particle a form and beauty altogether incomprehensible, it is a noble work to develop the mind of a people, by studies of nature on its monuments, and to give as subjects for contemplation the landmarks achieved in the history of their country. The sculptured stones of Scotland, however, are but exquisitely chaste masses of incoherent symbols, and peculiar Asiatic animals that tell no story, and leave no records of heroes. They are mixed up with graceful artistic ornaments and symbols of the Christian religion, prepared by those Eastern races, who, for many centuries, migrated to the West, until they were arrested on the shores of the Atlantic ocean There they have left monuments of rude pillar stones with remarkable cromlechs for the depository of the dead, which have remained unchanged for many ages.

SECTION II.—BOUNDARY CROSSES.

The sacred nature of the cross, from an early period, induced the Christians to employ it to mark the boundary of property, and the honesty of market transactions. In the Christian period it was added to the erect stones formerly used, and the lands so bounded were called *Yermon*, or lands of the cross, and being ecclesiastical, were exempt from taxes. The Mugdrum Cross of Lindores, in Fifeshire, is an example.[1] They were considered sacred, and it was an impiety, as well as a crime, to remove any such landmark. "Wherever you find the cross, do no injury," was the implied caution,[2] it being supposed to hallow a place, and constitute a sanctuary.

In more recent times we find that crosses were erected in newly discovered countries, to signify their appropriation by Christian monarchs, in the name of Christianity. Thus the Spanish and Portuguese navigators of the 15th and 16th centuries erected crosses in the lands they discovered with all the ceremony they could command; the chiefs, as they formally took possession of the heathen country, prostrating themselves in adoration, waving aloft their swords as defenders of the cross, and displaying their respective Royal Standards.[3]

---

(1) The hunting forests of the chiefs were thus marked in Scotland, and other countries, at an early stage of society.—*See Logan's Account, Archæologia*, vol. xxii, p. 58.

(2) Ulster Journal of Arch., vol. vi, p. 55.

(3) Columbus, Balboa, Cortéz and Pizarro, are said to have used the following prayer during their voyages of discovery :— "Domine Deus, Æterne et Omnipotens, qui sacro tuo verbo coelum et terram, et mare creasti, benedicatur et glorificatur nomen tuum, ut ejus hoc? sacrum nomen agnoscatur et predicatur in hac altera mundi parte.—*Life of Columbus*, p. 93.

Section III.—Memorial Crosses.

These are generally Latin crosses of simple form, though often decorated with figures or symbolic emblems. It is not likely that the Pagan custom of cremation subsisted for any length of time after the first acceptance of Christianity. There is evidence in the catacombs of Rome that the utmost care was bestowed on the burial of the Christian dead. This carefulness was due to the belief in the resurrection of the body, and the practice of entombing the dead would spread wherever Christianity was preached, and memorial stone crosses accordingly increase and multiply. Some of these, however, have been examined, such as the "Maiden Stone," and the stone on Hunter's hill, near Glamis, without any remains being found.[1] In the sculptured slab at Govan,[2] and the one found under the foundation of the cathedral of St. Andrews,[3] the decorations appear to have been of the same character as those in the beautiful cross over them. The sacred character of the ancient crosses was, in some measure, regarded in modern times, and it is on record, for instance, that the mason who repaired the church of St. Vigean's mutilated an ancient cross, in order to make room for the coffins of himself and his wife on either side.[4]

The veneration in which the Christians held the cross, induced them to erect it over the graves of the departed, so that the spot might be rendered more sacred and inviolable. Such were small, and often of the Greek form. At an early period a small cross was placed at the top, and another at the bottom of the grave, to protect it from evil, and in some cases it was placed under the head of the deceased. The following from Meigle churchyard (*Fig.* 153) may be instanced as an example; although merely a fragment, enough is

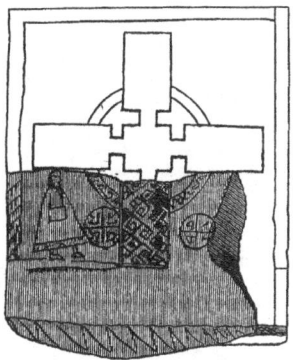 

Fig. 153.

given to justify the completed sketch I have given of it. It is interesting, as containing what is probably the figure of the deceased, in his ordinary dress; and on the back of the stone is the segment of a circle, as representing organised matter, which may be accepted as an indication that the deceased was a Pagan converted to Christianity.

---

(1) Professor Simpson was present at the examination of the grave of a criminal, the authenticated date being 200 years ago. The bones were reduced to powder. Only the teeth remained as evidence that a body had been buried there.
(2) Sculptured Stones of Scotland, vol. i, p. 134-137.   (3) *Ibid.*, vol. i, p. 61.   (4) *Ibid.*, vol. i, p. 70.

When the art of writing became known, the names of the deceased were given first in Ogham, and afterwards in Anglo-Roman characters. Considerable latitude, indeed, was allowed to the artist as to the arrangement and adjuncts, but none whatever as to the fundamental form of the emblem. Most of these crosses are exquisitely executed, but they had no human remains under them, while others were connected with rude graves, formed of slabs of unwrought stones, and contained remains, in different states of decay, proving that they were of more recent date, and of people whose remains were not particularly respected. Had these crosses been shrines an equal share of decorative art would have been expended in decorating the memorial stone which was to indicate the resting place of the remains of the holy personage. In none was this the case:[1] and the fact of there being graves near the cross, is explained, by its being considered a holy place, just as for the same reason they often became sites for churches. It is, indeed, argued, " it may be taken for granted, that these (crosses) stones are sepulchral monuments;" and this being granted, that nothing could be "more natural than that some representation should be placed upon the stone by which the family, sex, or occupation of the buried person should be indicated." Such these symbols are supposed to mean. I examined some of these crosses, and in front of the large red sandstone cross (*Fig.* 150) of the Meigle burying ground, found the remains of a body of a child, which had been recently buried, a few feet under the surface. But this is a proof of the modern respect in which the spot was held, and no proof that the stone was originally sepulchral. The Keiller stone was on a raised mound containing pieces of charcoal and the remains of pottery, most probably of urns which had held the ashes of the dead. There were stone coffins, four or five feet long, in which bones were found. In all these cases, the burial had taken place in comparatively modern times, near the sacred cross, which had originally hallowed the place.[2]

Anglo-Norman Sepulchral Monuments consist of stone coffins for men of eminence. These date from the close of the eleventh and through the two following centuries, a period when few upright stones were used. The stone coffins had often ornamented lids, sometimes appearing in the churchyard above the surface of the ground. In other cases the lids of the stone coffins formed part of the pavement of churches. The coffins of founders of churches are often placed in arched recesses in the church walls. In some cases the stone coffin is formed out of a solid block of stone of an oblong figure, with a circular part for the head. The most common coffins during the eleventh and twelfth centuries were formed of slabs of ordinary stone, with a cross incised, or sculptured in low relief with interlaced figures. Sometimes the coffin is of wood, and few have inscriptions. When the Gothic style of architecture was followed, rich monumental slabs and crosses were used, with tracery, decorations, and divine emblems or symbols, indicating the calling of the deceased. The ecclesiastic had his staff, the episcopal ring and cross, the chalice and book, with the hand in the attitude of benediction. Knights and men-at-arms had armour, such as a helmet, shield, and sword. Females had a key, and so on.

Primitive Christian Burials.—In the construction of the catacombs of Rome—the cradle of Christian sculpture in Europe—the Christians took their model from the Pagan cemeteries then in use; and this rule was followed also in other cases. In the churchyard of Peumachin, in Wales, for example, there is a small cross with a pillar-stone bearing the Christian monogram for ΧΡΙΣΤΟΣ; and the inscription, "Caraosius hic jacet in hac congerie lapidum."[3] This cairn or barrow, the oldest and most universally known, was of the Pagan and Christian form met with until the tenth century. The full length graves formed of stone slabs set on edge, had their long axis East and West. The head lay towards the West, so that the buried persons might rise on their feet with their faces to the East at the resurrection. Clay vessels and glass drinking cups, containing food and drink, were, among the early Christians, buried along with the dead, in graves just like those placed in Pagan times for the use of the deceased during the time the soul remained near the body. In France the burying of these vessels began in the stone age, and was continued through the transition period of Gallo-Roman and Pagan, to the 16th and 17th Christian centuries.

---

(1) With perhaps the exception of Govan; but here the individual was of high character and rank.
(2) *See* Book II, *Fig.* 121.   (3) Westwood Archæ. Cambriensis, vol. ix, p. 257.

CHAPTER IV

CHRISTIAN SYMBOLS WITH ORNAMENTS AND ANIMALS ON THE CROSSES.

SECTION I.—VARIETIES OF SYMBOLS UPON THE OBVERSE AND REVERSE OF CROSSES.

HE obelisks of the east of Scotland exhibit in their sculptures quite unique specimens of the peculiar Eastern symbols, and representations of various Asiatic animals, such as serpents, lions, camels, elephants, brahmin and common bulls, and centaurs. These show a familiar knowledge of the East, which could only have been acquired by Eastern artists imbued with its civilization. The presumption is, that these artists came as enthusiastic missionaries of oriental beliefs, and devoted their skill to the delineation of the symbols, and their energy to the teaching of the truths of their religion; while the Eastern sacred animals with which they were familiar, were introduced in order to impress, with additional awe, the rude people among whom they had come to minister, and lend a certain weight to their teaching. Too poor and too few in number to erect temples, as in Hindustan, but having amongst themselves those who could minister to their wants, these missionaries confined themselves to the erection and decoration of these obelisks, the Pagan symbols being often afterwards retained as ornaments in subservience to the cross, before which the worshippers offered up their prayers, and by the side of which teachers, who afterwards followed, inculcated the principles of the Christian religion. The number of these obelisks, with Pagan and Christian symbols, which still remain, is remarkable considering their great age, and the few remains otherwise of the system of religion which they symbolize. Of comparatively modern crosses, images and ornaments, there is often scarcely a remnant left to tell of their existence; while these ancient monuments, with their sculptured emblems, both Pagan and Christian, remain, often at a distance from churches and habitations, though too often in a broken down condition, and in all cases neglected. This desecration of these beautiful crosses is the more to be regretted as they display a remarkable intelligence on the part of the artists in the selection of the stones, as well as skill in their execution. There is a great similarity in the crosses, symbols, and ornaments; representations of the Eastern animals constantly occur, while the delineation of horsemen, with their attendants, accompanied by forest dogs, which could be kept only by noblemen, is a common feature. Yet in the midst of such similarity, there are such differences, that, out of the hundred crosses, in the north-east of Scotland, not two are exactly the same. Many of these are, as we have said, in fragments, or are defaced, from the negligence and the mistaken zeal of religious bigotry; but, in general, so well selected were the stones, that the figures, and graceful ornaments, still stand out almost as clear and bold, as when they came from the hands of the sculptor ages ago.

The first missionaries of the second epoch belonged to a class of monks, who were each obliged by their rule to learn some handicraft, one of which was the formation of Christian crosses, decorated according to a specified form. It is probable that these were the artists who sculptured so many of the crosses in the Pictish kingdom in after years, as they went about from place to place to disseminate their doctrines. It thus appears that these Christian missionaries laboured in multiplying crosses, in favourable positions; employing all their art and energy in the decoration of the great symbol of their faith; and with such success, that they are still objects of admiration as artistic productions. These early efforts of art on the sculptured stones of Pictland have been variously accounted for. Thus Hector Boethius thought they were relics of a symbolism derived from Egypt, and that the figures of birds, &c., were merely instances of the old hieroglyphical way of writing, practiced in the country from which the artists came. He supposes they are the remains of an alphabet formerly in use, and which, he says, was taught, even in his own day, by men skilled in it. Others have supposed that these symbols are of Danish origin, a hypothesis which Maitland is at pains to controvert; as the Danes and Norwegians were pirates, who came in quest of plunder; and it was not reasonable to suppose they could have erected such monuments, or that they would have stood, had they reared any, since they were repeatedly defeated, and at last expelled from the country. Had they been erected, as alleged, to commemorate victories, it is not likely that the inhabitants would have let them remain as memorials of their defeats. Maitland, therefore, concluded they were sepulchral, and not memorials of invasion. All this is beside the mark, as such symbols are met nowhere else except on Eastern monuments, and are, therefore, only accounted for by assuming a special and direct connection with oriental religions.

In these obelisks perspective is not observed, and dogs of small size appear in Pictavia, in full cry, right over the heads of horsemen, as is frequently the case in Assyrian and other Eastern sculpture.[1] The figures in such cases, however, are not distorted, as in many of the examples in Eastern monuments. They are well done, the higher the rank, the larger. Figures, such as the chief with the staghound, are drawn with peculiar insignia. The villains, serfs, or slaves, appear without arms, even when guiding oxen with a stick, as in the Eassie obelisk, and in the Church of Aberlemno obelisk, when engaged in battle, and when leading a bull.

"The Eastern artists doubtless followed the conventional form in preparing the sacred objects, and if their art seems defective, the result is due to excess of religious zeal, and to no lack of artistic capacity. Thus, I knew a common image maker in India who, while adhering to traditional modes in the manufacture of his images, used to execute admirable busts of individuals, in which the likeness and individuality were caught in a remarkable manner. On one occasion, a sect believing that misfortunes had befallen their craft, owing to the anger of the gods, resolved to expiate their sins, by exhibiting and worshipping the chief deities in due form. The idols prepared for the occasion were executed, indeed, after the conventional manner as handed down by tradition, but the entrance to the large building, which contained a group of the gods in their characteristic occupations, was guarded by colossal Herculi, of admirable pose and accurate development, and in the representation of the

---

(1) Sculp. Stones of Scotland, vol. i, p. 60.

contest between the good and evil genii the field of battle was covered by the wounded and slain, in all stages of the agonies of death. This seems to me an evidence that here genius only required development; and even in many of the old temples of great height, what could be more graceful than the general effect and the minute ornamentation of their detail. The conventional pattern, invented by men initiated into the ideas represented, who knew little of nature, and still less of the rules of art, when once authorized suffered no material change. The humanized figures of the deities were represented with two or more heads, so as to indicate the intellectual and other powers of the god, and if they were represented, as often happened, with more arms than natural, this was to more emphatically express the greatness and extent of their power and majesty. These distorted forms were drawn from models prescribed by the priests, who, though they knew little, either of nature or art, were yet presumed to know all about the mysteries of religion. Natural elegance and beauty were considered too mean an ornament for a god, and divine intelligence, as well as physical power, was expressed by hideous and unnatural forms. The original artists, being unable to represent superior strength or power by development of herculean muscle, had recourse to the rude expedient of gigantic size. In Egypt, and generally in Asia, large size and grotesque shapes were assumed at an early period, as the proper form in which to represent great and distinguished individuals, and these original forms are religiously retained.

The teaching of the arts and sciences was closely connected with that of the Christian religion; and an interesting question arises:—Which division of Christendom can claim the honour of having introduced these into the British Islands? The peculiar character of the early monuments is clearly a development of the Byzantine style of art, and the artists who prepared the Buddhist symbols belong to a period, probably, as early as the second or third century. We can trace the progress of change during the Christian period, the Pagan emblems being at length transferred to the reverse of the stone, and a lower part of the obelisk, or on the margin, as in the Aberlemno Church cross, where the interlaced grotesque animal, forms by means of its body, the spectacle ornament, and its legs and feet the two sceptres. Both margins of the long limb of this cross are filled with this peculiar figure (the dorge symbol) the most perfect being to the right. If this was sculptured before the seventh century, it might be a specimen of the many beautiful interwoven ornaments, in the first MSS., which are so gracefully and exquisitely executed. This beautiful interlacement having been so frequently represented in antiquarian works, it is not necessary to give the figure here, although its very peculiar mannerism in the animal windings, forming the spectacle or modified dorge symbol, has not been specially noticed before. Of the symbols of the Buddhist missionaries, who, in a few centuries had converted a large proportion of the Asiatics to their faith, we have seen numerous examples on Celtic sacred boulders. They appear also in England to have left their mark upon the coins, and to have penetrated into Ireland, where they were in danger of being robbed of their property, as well as deprived of their lives, and were obliged, as we have seen, to build pillar-towers, for the safety of their persons, relics and symbols. They seem to have remained a short time in Ireland, and to have made but little impression on that volatile people. The towers which they left behind, however, were found useful for defence, and were imitated and enlarged by their successors, with certain modifications, adapted to their new necessities.

It was natural that the Asiatic should exhibit his ideas of religion, and for a like reason that the commemorative sign of the Christian cross should be placed by the Christian missionary on the stones. Thus the despised and persecuted Christian converts in Rome used to inscribe symbols on the walls of rocks and caverns, and on the rude masonry of the catacombs of Rome, in the primitive ages of Christianity. Among these we find the emblems of holy hope, such as the undying lamp; the wreath of amaranth; the palm branch of martyrdom, suspended on the nameless martyr's tomb; the history of Jonah, the type of the death and resurrection of Christ; the raising of Lazarus, the type of that of Christ's people; of Noah, a type of Christ, the true refuge, and the ark the Church. We also find Pharaoh, and the submerging of his hosts, as a symbol of the doom of the wicked; and the good Shepherd searching out his sheep, carrying them, feeding them, separating the sheep from the goats. All these are the appropriate symbols of the fervent hope of a future state of reward which supported people in the hour of trial and threatened extirpation. But none such are found among the monuments of the primitive Christians in Celtic Britain.

The sculptures on the early Irish crosses were derived from the Byzantine style of art, which first appeared as pillars with incised crosses, and afterwards in connection with these executed in relief. This style differs from that of Greece and Rome, and was developed on the decline of these and the rise of the form of Christian art, known by the name of Mediæval, which reached a very high development in Ireland.

The Shandwick Stone is a magnificent specimen of an embossed Latin cross without a nimbus.[1] Among the numerous and varied patterns of animals on the reverse, are vultures, elephants, a tiger, a fox, a man with a crossbow in the act of firing at a deer, and two men fighting with swords and shields. Edderton is also a good example of a graceful Latin cross without a nimbus.[2] There is a man on a spirited horse in motion, in a semi-circular excavation underneath.

Section II.—Asiatic and British Animals upon the Reverse of Crosses.

The sphinx, the centaur, and the griffin, are frequent in Byzantine churches. These were adopted by the Christians on account of, as some think, power ascribed to them from Pagan times of driving away malignant spirits; although, according to others, the greater number of these odd and wild figures were only ornaments created by the caprice of the sculptors.[3] Certain it is, however, that St Bernard inveighed against the introduction of them into the sculptures of churches, as not being Christian, as well as decidedly improper. On the Scottish stones we find apes, lions, centaurs, monsters with several bodies and one head, or many heads and one body, quadrupeds with tails of serpents, and fishes with heads of quadrupeds, &c.; while on the Etruscan painted tombs are found, hippopotomi, centaurs, dolphins, sphinxes, and other fanciful figures.

We have described both the Pagan or Celtic, and the Buddhist class of sculptured stones. The former are among the oldest monuments of the country, and on some of these we have the Buddhist symbols incised with great care—the sacred triad, and sacred Eastern animals, as suggestive of religious ideas. No native artist of Pictavia, at that early period, could have drawn these with so much exactitude, or copied them from any earlier delineation, particularly as each differs from the others; and in all cases the symbols are carefully drawn according to established rules. The retention of Pagan symbols, in combination with the Christian cross, is in accordance with the order of Pope Gregory, who in writing to Abbot Melitus, gives permission to adopt, for a time, a heathen rite, with the view of giving it a new character.[4] And so we find the dorge, the symbol of God, as the ægis over priests, in the Dunfallandy stone,[5] and the eastern Pagan custom retained of praying with the face to the East. "We pray towards the East," writes Tertullian,[6] "As Christ the Sun of Righteousness rises with light and heat, and penetrates to man's heart, and mind."[7]

---

(1) Vol. i, plates 26 and 27.   (2) Vol. i, plate 31. No. 2.
(3) (De Caumont, p. 1883 and 1991.) *See* ancient Church of Louvigany, in the Bourbonais.
(4) Bede Hist: Ed. I. 30   (5) *See* Sculptured Stones of Scotland, Vol. i.
(6) Nos ad orientes regionem pecavi Apolog : c. 16 p. 688. *See* also Chan : King's Primitive Church, p. 2, *et seq.*
(7) Justin Martyr: Diag : p. 334.

Section III.—Ornaments on Christian Crosses.

The decorations on the sculptured stones may be arranged into four classes, symbolical, animal, mythological, and ecclesiastical. The symbolical and mythological representations were supposed to have been of Divine intention, and are graceful in form, and conceived of, as stupendous in size. The various ornaments are of Pagan derivation and significance, and the fact of their adoption proves that when the Celtic race of Pictland embraced the Christian faith, they did so without altogether rejecting their Buddhist opinions, the more so that their previous faith inculcated charity, benevolence, integrity, and most of the Christian virtues. For this reason they were not unwilling to retain symbols which the people had been accustomed to, so long as the cross was the chief object. Before these stones it was that they worshipped, when churches were not yet in existence, and the ancient Gaelic word *clachan* denoted, not the church, but the stone for worship. It were interesting, if we could trace the Pagan symbols of the Deity in the order in which the stones were executed, as an example of the connection of the Pagan with the Christian cross. Thus, in·that of Aberlemno, the spectacle ornament retains the upper, or dignified position; while in others, it occupies the lowest position upon the back of the cross, as on that of Fornith, while it is not found at all in the beautiful one in the Meigle churchyard. But these monuments have not yet been studied with a view to determine the comparative age of the sculptures on them.

The occurrence of interlaced ornaments separates the Celtic art from all other kinds. These patterns, which are known as knotwork or braidwork, are probably copied from the wattlework of the aboriginal inhabitants. They are of the Greek fret-type—the geometrical fret-pattern-type or key pattern, which is formed into interlacements, elaborated into foliage, and one development of these patterns shows even animals interlaced. Mr. Cumming thinks that the pelleted band suggests the sealed animal in the Isle of Man, "starting from the form of a single cord or ribbon, then of two or more different ribbons intertwined; this form of decoration has passed into floriation, assuming the forms of interlacing boughs and foliage, and at all times has a tendency to metamorphise itself into grotesque figures of intertwining monstrous animals, more especially of dogs, birds, fishes, and serpents."[1] The higher development of the sculptor's art shows often a curious mixture of Pagan and Christian legends. The St. Andrew's stone has horses, stags, and dogs well done, but with Eastern want of perspective.[2] There are figures on the reverse of crosses at Garforth, at Warwick, at Wenwich, at Arcliffe, and at St. Vigeans. The inscriptions which are sometimes found are written either in debased Latin, Scandinavian, or Saxon characters, but some are in Oghams, Runes, Latin capitals, and the Irish alphabet of the Book of Kells.

It has been alleged that the sculptured stones in Pictland were prepared by native artists, and that it is owing to the peculiarities of the country and people that the same monuments are not found in other countries. Such a conclusion might appear to be confirmed by the fact that symbols identically the same are not always to be found in Asia, but on examining the Eastern monuments, we find they have undergone considerable changes in the course of ages, according to the advancement of the arts in different countries, and among different races. To such changes the eclectic Buddhists had frequent recourse, in order to gain for their sacred precepts a readier intelligence and acceptance among a strange people, professing a form of belief not dissimilar to their own. Viewed in this light, the similarity of the monuments of Pictland and those of Buddhism in Asia, is most striking, as they include in their designs the same symbols and sacred animals.

The Pagan symbols and mythological Asiatic animals underwent considerable modifications, under altered forms of religion, some of them being converted into ornaments by the Christians, others employed as symbols

---

(1) Arch. Camb., 1866, pp. 156-167.   (2) Sculptured Stones of Scotland, pl. 61.

of evil. By the influence of the Buddhist converts to the Christian religion, the missionaries obtained permission to erect the emblems of their religion in convenient places, and probably used the sacred circles of boulders for their religious meetings, giving them the name of Church (Clachan), as of old. As the places of worship extended, they prepared pillar crosses at convenient situations, and the reverse of these had often the spectacle ornament, the segment, the elephant, and other symbols, but they were drawn without care or attention to a standard rule, and were filled with the interlaced pattern; thus the scruples of the Buddhist worshippers were satisfied, and belief was inspired that the new religion was similar to their own. The elephants and crescent ornament underwent a like change, and now appear as ornaments; sometimes there are two of them on the same stone, as on the Glenfernis obelisk, differing from each other in size and form, and intended merely to fill up an unoccupied part of the stone.[1]

At an early period a cross, similar in form to that now called Greek, was long worn by the Assyrian monarch as a sacred emblem, and a charm to protect his person from danger and the effect of evil influences. This emblem, in a simple form, incised on rocks was introduced into the British Islands at an early period, and used by the pious in worship. The veneration in which crosses were held, and the sacred character with which their presence invested the neighbourhood, accounts for their being frequently surrounded with graves, such holy ground being considered advantageous to the souls of the departed. The limbs of the cross were often filled with ornaments, resembling those of the decorated MSS. They form a series of zigzag interlaced ribbon patterns, like those of the Christian crosses of Ireland, which are known to have existed there between the seventh and the eleventh centuries. Those on the sculptured obelisks of Pictland had been executed at a much earlier period, but both have been derived from the same source.[2] In the one case, the designs have been cut on stone by artists accustomed to work on that material, in the country from whence they came; and in the other, at a later period, they have been executed on stone and parchment. Differences have no doubt also arisen from the fact, that ancient Caledonia was inhabited by Celts belonging to different tribes, who were often separated from each other for considerable periods. Columba, when he visited the north of Scotland, was obliged to employ an interpreter.[3] This we still find to be the case with primitive inhabitants of India, where two or three tribes on the same mountain do not understand each other's language. Intercourse might have become still more difficult, owing to the races having become converted to Christianity by missionaries from different countries. These interesting stones afford remarkable specimens of the taste and skill of the Christian, conniving at and humouring the superstitions of the weak and ignorant converts, by inserting their symbols and portraying their habits and opinions. The elegant and elaborately decorated crosses are always in the most dignified and honourable position; on the reverse of which, are often the representations of monsters extraneous to the holy religion. The same idea was carried out by the architects of the gorgeous Gothic structures—there, they represented devils and monsters of all kinds.

Christian Crosses.—Celtic ornaments will be seen in the drawings given in the next page (*Plate II.*); and I shall here confine myself to the chief specimens of these which were taken from the following crosses; (*No.* 1) at Nigg, Ros-shire; (*No.* 2) Mountblow House, Lanark; (*No.* 3) Maiden Stone, Bennahu; (*No.* 4) St. Andrew's; (*No.* 5) Dunfallandy; (*No.* 7) *ibid.*; (*No.* 8) Killon of Cadboll; (*No.* 9) Meigle; (*No.* 10) Eassie; (*No.* 11) Rossie Priory; (*No.* 12) Rosemarkie; (*No.* 13) *ibid.*; (*No.* 14) Falkirk; (*No.* 15) St. Andrew's; (*No.* 16) Meigle; (*No.* 17) St. Andrew's; (*No.* 18) Chandwick, Nigg; (*No.* 19) *ibid.* The two patterns at the foot of the page are the most remarkable, being intricate designs of respectively interlaced serpentine forms and dragons. Another beautiful variety is found on the Aberlemno cross, being the serpentine interlacement forming the

---

(1) Sculp. Stones of Scotland, vol. i., p. 24.

(2) *See* Journal of Archæological Association, vol. xv, p. 63. (3) Victa Sancti Columba. Lib. i, ch. xxviii.

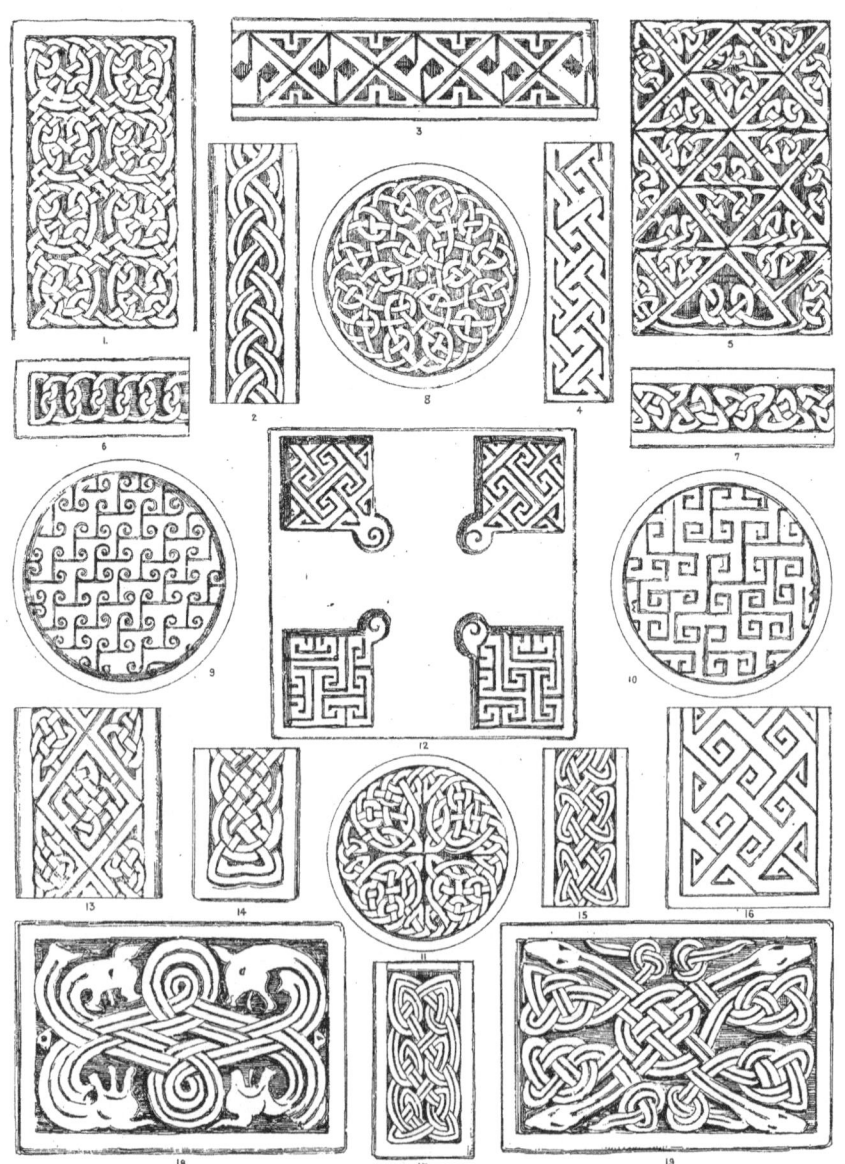

FORMS OF CELTIC ORNAMENTATION.

modified dorge. The same exquisite taste and skill were shown by the ancient Celts in their stone ornaments in the course of time, but these were somewhat varied in form, and later on the ornamentation passed into the beautiful metallic style of art, found in the ancient British arms, shields, horse-trappings, and the graceful Irish metallic work and illuminated MSS. These are still the admiration of modern adepts, and continue the glory of the race, but do not come within the purpose of this book. One class of figured ornaments is composed of interlaced figures in the oblong divisions of the cross, and knots, each being separated by a moulding. Sometimes portions of the limbs and the centre are filled up with interlaced patterns, as in the Dyce Stone of the ninth century, sometimes in separate bodies. The national style delineated the beautiful forms and divisions, from the minutest ornament to those of large size. Such structures admit of a series of arrangements, without admitting of divergencies or digressions from the original form. This natural and beautiful style of art belongs to the Celtic race, and is seen at an early age in the ancient Asiatic, Assyrian, and Egyptian ornaments, and in more modern times in the beautiful Irish and British ornaments, particularly in illuminated manuscripts. The early age of the hieroglyphics of Egypt is known by the beauty of their mechanical execution, but unfortunately, the hierarchy under which they worked rejected the human form, and required them to follow a fancied, ungraceful conventional model.

See description, page 242.

CHAPTER V.

PROCESSIONS AND ÆGIS OR SACRED SHIELDS.

SECTION I.—DEVELOPED PROCESSIONS.

PROCESSIONS on the crosses of Pictland are either ecclesiastical, civil, or military. They usually appear on the reverse side, and are preceded, or overshadowed by the ægis. The processions are representations of various Pagan and Christian customs of the period to which they belong, and the ægis expresses the prevalent ancient belief, in the interposition and protection from danger, accorded by the Deity, or His angels. This idea is clearly indicated on the various Asiatic monuments, as expressed by their symbols; it passed into Europe with the Eastern creeds, and finds a conspicuous place on the crosses of Pictavia.

Fig. 154.

At Meigle, several oblong fragments of sculptured stones have been built, for preservation, into a wall six feet high, standing in the middle of the churchyard.[1] On one of these fragments is a procession of equestrians, all bareheaded (*Fig.* 154). The first horseman is somewhat larger than the others, though he is not accompanied by the staghound, the usual indication of rank, but by a small terrier. The two first horses have their ears turned forward, while the last has its head and ears thrown back, as an indication of a state of terror. This is explained by a representation of the evil one, from whose extended mouth issues forth

---

(1) Sculp. Stones of Scotland, vol. i., p. 76.

pestilential vapours, and whose foot is raised as kicking the terrified horse. The composition of this group would seem to indicate that it represents people of ordinary rank, but the situation symbolised, is evidently that of the Christian flight from the genius of evil, in the form of a persecuting power, alien to the Christian spirit.

There is a procession on the stone of Hilton Cadbolt, Ross-shire (*Fig.* 155), which formed one of three obelisks, remarkable for the beauty of its ornamentation, and resembling those of Nigg and Shandrie, on the coast of Ross-shire, and on the north side of Cromarty Firth. The Hilton cross has been greatly defaced, and barbarously tampered with. The reverse shews a broad margin of entwining mythological animals in compartments, with waving circles below, and a spectacle ornament above; while the upper and central part is occupied by the segment of a circle and Eastern symbols, filled in with the ornamental entwined pattern. Below these are two women on horseback, with curled hair and padded jacket. They have a looking-glass and a knife, to represent their ægis, and two trumpeters step behind, followed by an armed chief and servant, accompanied by two greyhounds; the whole indicative of their rank. The total absence of perspective in the chief figures is a further proof of the Eastern origin of these sculptures. For a similar representation of trumpeters behind a Celtic chief we may notice the large Aberlemno stone.[1] See also for Celtic trumpets the illustration in Book II.[2]

Fig. 155.

The fine Latin cross of Fowles[3] shews on the reverse a group consisting of an equestrian chief with attendants (*Fig.* 156). The chief, with a staghound by his side, is followed by his attendants, also on horseback and attended by dogs, while behind them is a slave, his degraded position indicated by the want of arms, leading a sacrificial bull, and guarded by foot soldiers, who march behind. The sketch in the margin is an extended view of the figures, being evidently a sacrificial procession, conducted by a chief of rank; distinguished as such by his horse of greater size, by the elegance of his dress, his wig, and the accompanying staghound, only allowed to be kept by kings and chiefs. The mounted head-men who follow have their terrier dogs, two of which are in this sculpture seen, regardless of perspective, and after the Eastern manner, running over the shoulders of the horses. We notice, also, that the horses are different sizes, according to the rank of the riders, and the double lines, as is usual in these early sculptures, both of men and animals, are used to denote a troop of several horsemen.

Fig. 156.

---

(1) Sculp. Stones of Scotland, p. 80. (2) *See* Celtic Trumpets in this work, Book II., chap. iv., *Fig.* 126.
(3) *See* Sculp. Stones of Scotland, vol. i.

Reverse of Crosses.—On the reverse of the elegant crosses of Pictland, hunting scenes were often depicted as expressive of the rank of local chiefs. These are evidences of a transition period in the religious history of the country, and appear to have been prepared before the middle of the 9th century, when the Scots became a prominent nation, and the northern part of the country formed one kingdom. The following considerations tend to show that these crosses must have been prepared by artists belonging to the Eastern Church: (1) The form and decorations belong to the Eastern style of art, and the symbols and animals in the earlier specimens are Asiatic. (2) The early Scottish Church proves her Eastern derivation by the fact that she, for long afterwards, adhered pertinaciously to the date of the Jewish Passover—the 14th day of the month of Nisa as the date of Easter, in place of the succeeding Sunday, as observed by the Western Churches, headed by Rome.[1]

Some of the most beautiful and elaborate of the Pictland crosses are of this Eastern type, of which the cross at Nigg,[2] Ross-shire, is an elegant example. It has no Pagan symbols, these being superseded by ornaments and devices of a different description. Above the cross is a representation of the Eucharist—a descending dove, hovering over a moveable altar, with the wafer in its beak. On each side are two stooping figures in the act of devotion, while under the altar are the figures of crouching dogs, representing spirits of evil on the watch to take away from the supplicants the expected blessing. This obelisk is probably more modern than others of its class. On the reverse are a dog in pursuit of game, a man on horseback, another playing a harp, a sheep, a man armed with a spear and shield, an eagle, and other figures of men and animals in apparent confusion. The broad margin is filled with beautiful and varied interlaced ornaments in compartments. It is lamentable to think how many of these beautiful crosses have been destroyed by wantonness and superstition, as well as by neglect and ignorance, and the tempting convenience of the stones for secular purposes. A few instances in evidence of the barbarism which has been perpetrated will suffice to justify the better feeling that now exists, and may lead to the protection of these monuments from further desecration.[3]

The beautiful obelisk of Cadbole[4] is "one of the most remarkable in Scotland, from its elaborate finish and varied representation." It has the sculpture on one side erased, and the face smoothed to afford a tablet for the following inscription substituted instead : "He that lives well, dies well, says Solomon the wise. Here lies Alexander D——- and his three wives;"—a remarkable proof of the advanced state of the arts, and subsequent decline of intelligence, ages afterwards. The fine cross, too, of St. Vigean's was broken, so as to leave an opening on each side, in which the coffin of a man and his wife were placed.

The reverse of the beautiful cross in the churchyard of Aberlemno,[5] when extended, affords an interesting example of a procession in which guardian symbols appear (*Fig.* 157). Of the three central figures representing foot soldiers the foremost is armed with shield and sword. the next with a lance and wearing a modern head-piece, and the third is a slave without arms. They are attacked by a man on horse-back armed with a lance. These three are defended from behind by a bird and disc, repelling the enemy. The higher class represented, are equestrians with head-pieces, one of whom is attacking another with his lance. On the extreme right a horseman is galloping away, protected over-head by his ægis, in the form of the triad symbol

---

(1) The question of the date for the observance of Easter was matter of early controversy in the Church. At the Council of Nicæa (A.D. 325) the Eastern Greek, or orthodox Church party, held the historical traditions, while the Western Church, headed by Rome, pronounced for the following Sunday. (*Dean Stanley on the Eastern Churches*, p. 155.)

(2) *See* Sculp. Stones of Scotland, vol. i, pp. 28, 29.   (3) *See* Book II, chap. v, sec. i, p. 188, *Fig.* 134.
(4) *See* Sculp. Stones of Scotland, vol. i, p. 25.   (5) *See* Sculp. Stones of Scotland, vol. i., pl. 78 and 79.

CHAP. V.]   HISTORY OF PAGANISM IN CALEDONIA.   241

of the deity, and pursued by a spearman, who is thrusting at him with his spear, and about to kill him, when the weapon is diverted from its object by an ægis or wheel, which throws back the spearman, and retards the horse. This procession seems to be an allegory of the struggle between Christianity and Paganism—the Christian figures proceeding to the right, and the Pagan to the left,—but helpless against the Christian ones protected by the ægis of their faith.

Fig. 157.

The Græco-Latin ring cross of Eassie,[1] in Strathmore, lay for many years in the bed of the small Eassie stream, from which it was removed by order of Lady Arbuthnot, and erected on the left bank of the Eassie river, behind the old church of the parish. The upper limb is guarded on each side by angels, with a messenger on the left margin carrying a spear and book, and a deer and other animals on the right margin in repose, with a hound in pursuit. The central portion of this interesting cross is filled with a square pattern, and the limbs with varied graceful interlaced ornaments. On the top of the reverse of this obelisk is represented the head of a sacred elephant, nearly defaced, under which appears the sceptred spectacle ornament. When the sculpture is extended it shows a procession in honour of the sacred tree festival, such as may still often be seen on anniversaries in celebration of such sacred objects in India, and other heathen countries. It consists of a platform dragged forward by three oxen marked as sacred; on the platform rests the tree, before which the enslaved driver stands, and behind appear three priests. These have frontal or Celtic tonsures, the chief priest holds a pastoral staff, and they have the sceptred dorge as their ægis.[2] They wear similar dresses in the Christian period; as seen in the cross of St. Vigean's, the tonsure is conspicuous, and one carries a lighted candle, followed by a superior holding a pastoral staff, and robed more elaborately, these have no ægis.

Fig. 158.

There are on this cross of St. Vigean's several figures besides the two priests represented (Fig. 158), and who have Latin tonsures; above these, although much defaced, we can trace two similar figures, with fringed robes and boots; these have between them an unrobed figure, with the Celtic tonsure, who is placed head downwards on a block. If these sculptures were extended in line it would represent a procession of Latin priests, the two going in front, having between them the degraded Celt, and the two superior priests following.[3]

The stone has suffered much from being so long in the water, and the exposure to the weather has already defaced many of the figures. It might with advantage be removed to the house prepared for the Meigle crosses, as it is not *in situ*.

---

(1) Sculp. Stones of Scotland, vol. i, p. 90.   (2) See p. 196, Fig. 138.   (3) See Book II, p. 196.

The processions on the large Meigle crosses, [1] with various others, have been described in a previous chapter; those enumerated here have especial reference to the singular grouping of the various figures, forming what we have termed processions, which we believe has not been before commented on, or any explanation attempted. By extending the figures in line, according to the exact order found in the sculptures, we seem to arrive at a clearer idea of the scenes represented. There is also a very interesting group on the beautiful Rossie cross, not included here, which will be the subject of remark in the following chapter.

SECTION II.—THE ÆGIS OR SACRED SHIELD.

The ægis, or sacred shield, as seen in the form of the guardian angel going before, to protect from danger, is also figured in the Buddhist symbols hovering over the heads of the protected from evil influences. [2]

The ægis was the fabled shield of the Greek Jupiter, said to be too dazzling for mortal vision, and as appropriately representing the protecting care of the Heavenly Father, was in that sense adopted by the Christian Church. It came to be regarded as a synonym for the cross in its divine and strength-giving power. Amongst the primitive Christians the Holy Spirit was believed to improve the development of the bodily power, and this is exemplified in the sketch at the head of this chapter, [3] in which is represented a strong man resting his head upon the Christian cross as his ægis, while his feet are upon the sacred bull, the Buddhist symbol of power and procreative energy. This mingling of the Christian and Pagan symbols of power has evident reference to the transition period already alluded to in the Pictavian sculptures. In the character of an oarsman the strong man is represented as overpowering the resistance of two other oarsmen, one of whom rests his head against a foul cur, and the other his feet upon some degraded animal, as indicative of man's debasement. In other words, the contest represents the feeble efforts of Paganism, in contra-distinction to the success which must ever accompany faith in the Cross of Christ.

The early belief of the Orientals in the personal influence of the Holy Spirit is evident. Thus the Jewish Prophet says, "The Lord God and His Spirit hath sent me." [4] And later on the Apostle St. John writes: "I saw the Spirit descending from heaven like a dove, and it abode upon Him." [5] The "rushing mighty wind," and the cloven tongues like as of fire, "which sat upon" the assembled apostles in the upper chamber, testify to the personal presence of the Mighty Spirit. [6] And as Ambrose Serle has it, "The Holy Ghost is a person;" for, as Job states, "He creates and gives life; [7] is seen descending in a bodily shape; commands apostles; sends messengers; bestows gifts; hath worship." [8] We cannot wonder, therefore, that with the fervent faith of those early times, the protecting power of the Divine ægis was inscribed on these primitive Pictavian monuments. We have already adverted to the retention, in the earlier years of Christianity in Pictland, of the Pagan and Asiatic symbols as protecting influences seen over the heads of the sculptured figures, and in still later times to the introduction of Christian emblems, combined with the former, intimating an advance in religious teaching; in all these various emblems we may trace the profound impression made on these primitive people by the oriental idea of a pervading spiritual influence, shewn in a very striking manner by the constant recurrence on the Pictavian monuments of the protecting ægis or Divine Spirit hovering over the persons of the faithful.

---

(1) *See* chap. iii, sec. i, p. 222.

(2) Ægis: a goat-skin shield, from the Greek goat, originally applied to the shield given by Jupiter to Minerva. Hence anything that protects.

(3) *See* Frontispiece to ch. v. (4) Isaiah xlviii, 16. (5) John i, 32.
(6) Acts ii, 2. (7) Job xxxiii, 4. (8) Horæ Solitariæ, vol. ii, 91.

HISTORY OF PAGANISM IN CALEDONIA.

Fig. 159.

A very early Pagan form of the guardian power among the nations of the East is a pillar stone, which they capped with a small pyramidal smooth stone, as perhaps symbolic of the Divine protection. As the arts advanced, we find the capped stone in many of the beautifully sculptured Irish crosses, with an oval or semi-circular stone like a boulder, without any attempt at ornament, as being Nature's own workmanship, and therefore peculiarly sacred as from the hand of God (*Fig.* 159).

The heathen idea of the sacred character of the boulder stones is instanced in other examples, and we see a progressive idea, from the Asiatic to the European, in the capped summits of places of worship; thus indicating the gradually enfolding idea of the supremacy of the Church as representing the authority of Deity (*Fig.* 160). Another form of the Divinity surmounting the cross is

Fig. 160.

a triangle, a symbol which is evidently adopted in recognition of the Trinity[1] (*Fig.* 161). This may also be the explanation of the rude triangular stone on the top of the beautiful Irish crosses. Some of these are simply incised stones found in churchyards, and have by degrees been worked into elaborately sculptured slabs. Similar stones are found in Scotland, Ireland, Cornwall, and Brittany, from the 6th and 7th centuries to the period of the Reformation. There is an example of a Latin cross with a triangular head at Somersby, in Lincolnshire. It is fifteen feet in height and has on one side the figure of the Virgin and child, on the other a crucifix. In the Florence Baptistry is a crucifix said to be made out of the wood of the true cross. It is very old, and greatly venerated. The figure is extended upon an ornamental Latin cross, and upon the Saviour's head is a mitred or conical cap.[2] Similarly can this be an allusion to the stone church? and can we account for the peculiar boulder covering of the splendid Irish crosses, which in the more modern ones is abandoned?

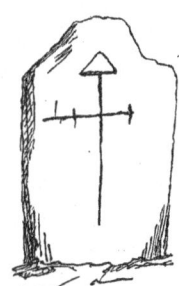

Fig. 161.

As we have already seen, the aboriginal tribes of India drew the figure of a circle, or of a wheel (*Fig.* 162) upon the ground before their houses, or over the chief entrance, to protect themselves from their enemies. The fresco paintings in the rock

---

(1) *See* O'Neil's great work on the Irish crosses.   (2) Fleury's History of the Cross, plate iii, 271.

244 HISTORY OF PAGANISM IN CALEDONIA. [BOOK III.

Fig. 162.

temples of Ajunta, in India, represent a battle between the infidels and the believers.[1] The figures on the white elephant, with warriors in white clothing, with umbrellas held over the chiefs, who are of a pale coloured race, represent the orthodox warriors; while the infidels are on dark brown coloured elephants, and are of a dark reddish race, whose arrows are broken by the ægis, and are falling harmless to the ground. This fresco is supposed to have been executed between the first and tenth centuries. The figures are sometimes types of the Supreme Being; the symbol of the sun and moon; while a vulture with wings like those of a scarabæus, as the great Deity, protects the Emperor from harm. Mr. Rawlinson supposes the circles probably to be typical of eternity, while the wheel expresses omnipresence, and the human figure symbolizes wisdom and intelligence.[2]

Fig. 163.

The Assyrians and Persians also, like the Buddhists, employed the simple wheel, and the circle with wings (*Figs.* 162 *and* 163), and at one time it was the fashion for the protecting god to be represented as assuming a bodily form. In time of war the face of the Deity is represented as turned towards the enemy, and in the act of discharging his thunderbolt, in the form of an arrow, against him. In time of quiet, the god in the ægis stands with his right hand raised and open, in the attitude of offering peace, while the left hand holds an unstrung bow. A third variety of the ægis is an eagle, the type of revenge, in front of the advancing king, with the bleeding head of an enemy in his talons. The Egyptian kings were guarded by a couple of serpents below his double crown or cap, as the kings of upper and lower Egypt (*Fig.* 164).

Fig. 164.

In countries where metals abound, coins were used as sacred emblems or talismans. These are frequently found in Britain and France, and are generally called wheel-money. The same wheel is often found over horses, on the ancient British coins. The Hindu and Assyrian wheel was not used during the Christian period in Pictland, but the Buddhist discs and triple wheels. The principal protecting sacred symbols of Pagan times, found on the Pictavian stones, are the following:—The circle or wheel, the mirror, the bird, the dorge, with or without sceptres, the segment of a circle with sceptres, the mythological elephant.

Fig. 165.

In modern times the idea we have here, is expressed in the angel guarding a child from danger as the symbol of man during his pilgrimage through the world (*Fig.* 165).[3] The same idea was expanded in the banner of the Libarum, or the Standard of the Cross, which was supposed to render the fifty guards which protected it, secure and invulnerable amidst the darts of the enemy. It animated the soldiers of Constantine with an invincible enthusiasm, and scattered terror and dismay through the ranks of the adverse legions.

The beautiful cross of Dunfallandy[4] is situated by the ruins of an old chapel near Killiecrankie, in Perthshire (*Fig.* 166). It is interesting from being at a distance from the crosses of Pictland. On the reverse of this obelisk is a short cross, resembling the large crosses of Meigle and Aberlemno. The central limbs of the cross are square. They rest on a pedestal, and are divided into compartments, filled with interlaced ornaments, with the addition of bosses or knobs. On the margin outside the limbs there is a deer, and various grotesque

(1) Mrs. Spier's Ancient India, p. 302.
(2) *See* Five Great Monarchies of the ancient world.
(3) Exod. cxxiii, 20, 21.   Psalm xci, 10 and 11.
(4) *See* Sculptured Stones of Scotland, vol. i, plate 47.

mythological animals. The stone stands on a high knoll, covered with trees, and was placed immediately before a chapel, so that the priest, standing at the door or altar, faced the cross, and the rising sun in an E.S.E. direction. The slab is of friable sandstone, and is 4ft. 10in. in height, 2ft. 1in. across, and from 4in. to 4½in. thick. It is known locally as the Priest's stone, or old-cross.

The reverse side is surrounded with mythological serpents, snarling at each other above, and terminating below the cross in brush-tails. The upper division represents two ecclesiastical dignitaries, sitting on chairs, in relief. They are of different sizes and ranks. (*See Fig.* 166.) The larger is on the right, and the smaller on the left. There is a graceful little cross between them. The ægis above and before the sitting figures consists of the third member of the Buddhist triad, protecting the Christian priests. The right-hand figure has the sceptred segment before, and the spectacle ornament above him, and the figure on the left has the sacred elephant over him. The ægis in both cases is thus shedding its benign influence in unequal proportions over the persons beneath. In an under compartment is a priest upon a mule, with his head directly under the cross, and before the mule is the sceptred segment of the circle and the mythological elephant, as an ægis to guard and guide the rider, and protecting him from evil, as the Eastern chiefs are guarded by the divine ægis in the form of a circle or sacred bird. Dr. Stewart supposes the two seated men (one with a rod in his hand) represent figures at a Celtic Coronation. Dr. O'Donovan informs us that the chief held a white wand in his hand, given by the Brehon. If this be the meaning of it, we would have here a Pictish chief sitting in one chair, with his heir-apparent (tanish) on the other, with the Christian Cross between them.[1]

Fig. 166.

As the knowledge of Christianity became better known, the form of the ægis was changed from the sacred Pagan symbol for that of the figure of an angel, as the protecting shield of Providence.

The chiefs used to be, among Asiatic tribes, selected for size, beauty, and perfection of form, their imposing presence, and their superiority of mental endowments. Such persons were supposed to be destined, from the fact of their superior constitution and abilities, to rule over their fellow-men, and to be so guarded by the deity as to be assured of success. It is said in Asia of such a one that he "has the longest sword." These favoured individuals were attended by guardian angels, good and bad; as long as they behaved honourably the former averted evil from them, but should they, on the other hand, become reprobate, the evil power is permitted to prevail. An unsuccessful chief was consequently deposed, his want of success being accepted as a proof that the good angel had departed from him, and that he was no longer the elect of deity. These guardian spirits are a conception of Asiatic origin, and they vary in their character, according to the religion of the nation among whom

---

(1) Proc. of the Antiq. Society of Scotland, vol. viii, p. 102.

they were believed in. In Egypt, animals, birds, serpents, &c., such as were held sacred by the nation, are represented hovering over the inferior being or the king as their ægis. [1] In Scotland, in Ireland, and in other Celtic countries, great families have a Banshee to guard them, sometimes in the form of a swan, a woman, or a drummer, etc., and these were supposed to manifest themselves when any of the family was about to die. This superstition, formerly very common, still lingers in some districts, and has been made the subject of many poetical fancies.

(1) Layard's Nineveh, vol. ii, p 449.

CHAPTER VI.

CHRISTIAN COMMUNITIES, RITUAL, AND CHURCHES.

SECTION I.—ANCIENT CHURCHES.

N the introduction of Christianity into Pictavia, there were at first no permanent buildings in use as churches, only in after periods did some primitive structures begin to be erected here and there. These were of small dimensions, constructed generally of earth, and afterwards wattled, covered with clay, and thatched with sods and reeds. The inscribed rocks would naturally be resorted to at first as places of worship, as well as caves, which might also serve as dwellings. The wattled churches were small, generally about 12 feet by 9 feet in dimensions; the primitive altar being, as a rule, in the eastern end of the edifice, formed at first of earth, and afterwards of stone. The large stone being difficult to remove when it was desirable to change the site, the expedient of a small stone as a moveable altar was devised.[1]

The earliest churches of an improved form appear to have been erected on the north side of the prayer cross, facing towards the east, as that was "the place of light or resurrection." Trunks of trees were placed at each of the four corners, other trees split into halves, fastened side by side, formed the wall; while others, laid horizontally, served for sill and cornice, the whole was roofed with rafters, and the outer ground fenced. As time went on, hangings and decorated screens would be introduced; but it was not until the 8th and 9th centuries that churches in these islands were built of stone. In the 12th century the Celts introduced stone churches, stone coffins, etc. Though the form and character of the earliest stone churches in Ireland give evidence of a Grecian origin, in both countries the building was oblong, and rarely more than from 20 to 40 feet in length; so that they were rather oratories, in which the priests celebrated the mysteries of their religion for the benefit of the people—who stood at the decorated western door, opposite the altar, with their faces towards it in the east—than churches in which the people assembled for worship.

(1) *See* Priests worshipping on Nigg Cross. Sculp. Stones vol. i, p. 28.

A very ancient prophecy in the old Irish dialect is preserved by the Scholiast on Fiace's Hymn, and may be referred to in passing, as an evidence of the early orientation of British churches. It is in a rude rhyme, and has been thus rendered—

> —— He comes, he comes, with shaven crown, from off the storm-tossed sea,
> His garment pierced at the neck, with crook-like staff comes he.
> Far in his house, at its east end, his cups and patens lie,
> His people answer to his voice, Amen, Amen, they cry.
>   Amen, Amen.

It is clear that these verses are not the composition of a mere Pagan Druid, and that they were written when the orientation of churches was the rule, and the altar always at the east end of the building.[1]

Many remains of stone fortresses and circular stone houses are found in some of the valleys of Kilmalkedar, in Kerry, and in the neighbouring elevations are ancient oratories built of uncemented stones, that admirably fit into each other, their lateral walls rising from the base to the apex in curved lines, but betraying ignorance of the principle of the arch. These structures appear to have been erected in the sixth or seventh centuries.

In still later times, churches built of stone were erected at the instance of Wilfrid and two other Anglo-Saxon bishops, who procured artists from Italy that wrought in stone, and introduced glass. These churches were small but strongly built, so that they might afford protection to both the priest and his treasures. In the twelfth century, the sacred edifices were improved in form and style, and the erection of them in stone became general, not only in England, but also in parts of Scotland and Ireland, though for nearly a century after that, the ordinary houses in London, and the other capitals of Europe, were made of wood and roofed with thatch. For many centuries the people were not only instructed in the church, and at the church door, but also beside crosses erected in suitable places, where the priest prayed and admonished the people, a practice which continued to a comparatively modern date. A few of these early churches are still to be met with, especially in some of the more remote islands on the shores of Great Britain and Ireland. We have already mentioned the ruins of one on Dinnacair, on the coast of Kincardine. There is another on the Forfarshire coast at St. Skeoch (pronounced *Skae*), and also a very well marked set of such buildings on the Skelligs. These form a group of conical rocks on the south-west coast of Ireland, eight or ten miles from the mainland, rising to a height of 1,000 feet above the sea level, as sharp and abrupt as Alpine *aiguilles*. They are in the full sweep of the Gulf stream, and are consequently so mild in climate that, though snow falls, it never remains on the rocks for any length of time. They now belong to the Government, and the Great Skellig is occupied by a lighthouse, the lights of which are usually the first seen by ships coming from America. The never ceasing roll of the Atlantic ocean booms continually against the caves and holes, the sound being heard for miles, amidst the screaming of wild fowl as they wheel round and round. Such the lone wild retreat to which, in their tender shrinking from the companionship of a godless world, those early Christians were fain to isolate themselves.

It is probable that the Danes in their invasions of Ireland, in the eighth and ninth centuries, erected the first stone buildings there; and about that time among the Picts, in the north of Britain, buildings of stone began to be in use for churches. Naitan, King of the Picts, requested Ceolfrid, Abbot of Weremouth, to send him architects to build a church in the Roman manner, which was to be dedicated to St. Peter, and this request was complied with in the year 715.[2] We may suppose this to be the first stone church that was erected, as we find that Finan, who succeeded Ardan, Bishop of the Northern Saxons, built a church in the Isle of

---

(1) *See* Todd, chap. iii, p. 411.   (2) Bede Hist. Eccles, Lib. v, ch. 21.

Lindisfarne, A.D. 652, which, though the church of the Episcopal See, was not made of stone, but of split or hewn oak, covered with reeds, &c.,[1] after the manner of the Scots, *more Scotorum*. We may therefore infer that in Scotland, and in the north of Ireland, the ordinary houses also were built of wood and covered with thatch.

Another interesting example of a primitive church is that of Egilsay, in Orkney, already referred to, where for better security a round tower was added to the nave. It was most probably built before the conquest of the island by the Norsemen in 876, and was re-constructed in 998. It resembles the ancient Irish churches of the eighth, ninth, and tenth centuries, the size of these being 60 feet by 27 feet, and that of Egilsay being 62 feet 9 inches by 21 feet 7 inches. It is constructed of the unworked clay-slate of the district, and has an external door, probably for cattle, separated from the body of the tower by a strong, probably arched, roof. The chief entrance of the tower was from the inside or nave of the church, at a considerable height from the ground. The tower itself, with its inner door closed, formed an impregnable tower of defence, and was probably built about the middle of the seventh century. It resembles in its construction and use the round tower of Clonmacnois, which forms an integral and undoubtedly contemporaneous part of the structure (p. 271). This is still more marked in the pillar-tower of Duncliff, near Dublin (*Fig.* 25, p. 181); there it springs from the roof of the chapel, and was evidently intended as a last resource in securing the lives of the priests, and of their most valued relics and MSS. In many respects, says Sir H. Dryden, this tower resembles that of Norfolk, of the 11th or 12th centuries.

SECTION II.—THE PRIMITIVE CHRISTIAN COMMUNITIES IN CALEDONIA.

The ancient Christians of Caledonia may be considered as divided into those of Pictland and of the south and west. The Picts in the north-east of the country became Christians at an earlier period than might have been expected, considering their remote and isolated situation, and sooner than is generally allowed by our historians.

From that upper chamber in Jerusalem, where the Apostles received the gift of the "Comforter," and celebrated the first Eucharist, the new faith soon spread to the remotest lands; and already traces of Christian communities, forming the earliest church in Caledonia, appear in Pictavia as early as the first or second century, their rites and ceremonies modified by the previous existence among them of ideas and symbols introduced by Buddhist missionaries. These were preceded by the Druids, who had occupied a position of great influence in the district, a fact which accounts for the number and size of the primitive monoliths existing in it. The tenets of the eastern missionaries supplanted the teaching of the Druids, but as there are no dates on any of the sculptured obelisks of these primitive times, and no records of the artists who constructed them, excepting what art-history affords, it is only a rough estimate we can form of the chronology. The stone records taken in order are:—

(*a.*) The Celtic monuments, consisting of erect stones with symbolic lines and circles.

(*b.*) Buddhist symbols, found inscribed both on rocks and boulders.

(*c.*) The Christian crosses of the second century, probably introduced about A.D. 160.

It is probable that the rites of the Christian Church in Pictland were closely allied to those of the oriental churches from which they had originally been derived, and were such as we still find in the church of Abyssinia. In any case it was not until the Council of Nice, that Rome preferred her claim to

---

(1) *Ibid*, Lib. iii, ch. 25.

lord it everywhere in matters of faith, and it is not probable that Romish forms of worship were adopted in Pictavia before that time. The Eastern and Western churches had not begun so early as the middle of the second, or even that of the fourth centuries, to assume the peculiarities by which they were distinguished; these announced themselves first in A.D. 729. Before that time, the Latin and Greek crosses were indiscriminately in use in different countries and churches; and certainly it was not before the fourth century that the Latin cross was generally accepted as the true form of the cross. The earliest missionaries in Pictavia contented themselves with the erection of a prayer or preaching cross, by which they stood when exhorting the people, but as the Christian class grew more numerous and powerful, they erected houses, where the solemn rites of their religion were celebrated, such as we have no traces of in the earliest period.

It is not until the ninth century that we find any written records. The book of Deir, recently discovered at Cambridge, appears to have been in the possession of a Celtic monastery of the sixth century, and it is not till the time of St. Columba we find the monks employed in multiplying copies of the Gospels and Epistles, as being reckoned by them the most valuable of their possessions. In the library at Cambridge is a MS. of the Gospels, supposed to be of the tenth century.[1] It belonged to the abbey of Deir or Deer, and contains some forms of church service, while on the margins are a few charters and memoranda of grants to the Church of Deir. These entries are of high antiquity, more ancient than in any extant Scottish chartularies, and record facts still more archaic, reaching, indeed, a period of history which neither charter nor chronicle among us touches, and of which we have had hitherto only a few glimpses from the lives of the saints, or from the meagre notes of foreign annalists. The memoranda are in a Celtic dialect. Mr. Innes thinks that it proves the existence of a religious house at Deir, founded by the disciples of Columba from Hy ages before the Cistercian convent mentioned by Mr. Pratt,[2] though what he mentions has reference probably only to a new and more liberal endowment, together with a change in the occupants of the previous establishment. An old stone was found at Deir, with a rude incised cross, which was removed and placed at the end of the Cistercian Abbey, founded A.D. 1218 by William Comyn, Earl of Buchan. There were formerly upwards of a dozen circles of stones in the parish, with a small village of Pights' or Picts' houses.[3]

We know that in Ireland none opposed the introduction of Christianity more strongly than the Druids; but when they were convinced of its truth "none came into it speedier, or made a more advantageous figure than they did."[4] It is not known at what time and by whom Christianity was introduced into England and Ireland, but it was at an early period, most probably during the second century; and it is thus we explain the remarks of Tertullian, who flourished in the latter part of that century. In his work against the Jews, while enumerating the nations that had embraced Christianity, such as 'all parts of Spain, Gaul, and parts of Britain, into which the Roman arms could never penetrate, he adds, "There His name reigned; there His kingdom was established."

When Christianity was introduced into the British Islands, the priests, as the ministers of the Word, naturally began to teach the rude people letters, and to accomplish this the alphabet was sometimes incised upon the margin of a cross erected at the door of the church. A very interesting specimen of this is on a cross in the churchyard of Kilmalkedar, Kerry (Ireland). When I saw it, the upper part was broken off, and the A B wanting. At such a cross the neophyte would receive his first lessons in letters, and resort thither for study at his leisure. The lettered margin of the cross would be the *abcedarum* for instructing the scholar.[5]

---

(1) Edited by Mr. John Stuart. (2) Buchan, by the Rev. John B. Pratt, M.A., 2nd edit., ap. 1859.
(3) Statis. Acct. of Scotland, vol. xvi, p. 481, 2nd edit., 1795. (4) Toland's History of Druidism, New Ed., p. 62.
(5) *See* Harris' War Irish Writing, Book II, ch. i, Ecclesiast. Arch. of Ireland, p. 132, ed. 1845.

Section III.—Ritual and Vestments.

In the days of St. Augustine there existed a liturgy in the hands of the church in Lyons, which she had received from the church of Ephesus, under St. John, having been brought to Lyons by some missionaries, who arrived in Gaul shortly after the Apostolic age. This is corroborated by the fact that Augustine consulted Pope Gregory the Great as to which liturgy he should follow in re-modelling the church in Britain. When he asked why, since the faith was one, the customs of the church were so various? and why one manner of celebrating the Holy Communion existed in the Holy Roman Church, and another in that of the Gauls? Gregory answered: "You know, my brother, the custom of the Roman Church in which you were bred up. But it pleases me that, if you have found anything, either in the Roman, or Gallican, or any other church, which may be more acceptable to Almighty God, you carefully make choice of the same, and sedulously teach the church of the Angles, which yet is new in the faith, whatsoever you can gather from the separate churches. For they are not to be loved for the sake of places, but places for the sake of good things. Select, therefore, from each church those things that are pious, religious, and correct; and when you have made them up as it were into one body, let the minds of the English be accustomed thereto."[1]

Some of the sculptured stones of Pictavia supply us with interesting archæological details, such as priests in their robes, with books,[2] or in processions, with sacred oxen, or oxen about to be sacrificed. At other times the priests have peculiar costumes and bear candles,[3] some have peaked beards [4] and moustaches, resembling those on the south-east side of the cross of Monasterboice, in Ireland. There are figures with wigs and long flowing robes, having large sleeves and caps, and with long pointed shoes. The dress of the clergy or ministers, when on duty, consisted of a linen covering from the waist to the middle of the leg, over which was worn the coat reaching from the neck to the waist in front, and to the feet behind. These robes are probably the tunic or alb, and the cope, not differing greatly from the Latin in use. The sculptured stone of Eassie represents a procession in honour of a sacred tree (see *Fig.* 160, *ante* p. 233). Here the long hair of the head appears cut in front of the ears to form the Celtic tonsure, and twisted to form a ball behind, while a long pointed beard hangs from the chin.

In *Fig.* 168 (*ante* p. 245) we see represented two church dignitaries seated, whose dress is the usual robe of the superior clergy. Their Celtic nationality is apparent from the form of the tonsure, and the absence of sandals or shoes. The churchman riding a mule, sculptured beneath the seated priests, wears the same description of dress. As the celebrated Palladius, whom we are to speak of presently, had his chief seat at Fordun, in the vicinity of St. Vigean's, it is probable that his influence was exerted to promote the change from the Celtic to the Roman use in the matter of vestments, the tonsure, and other distinctions between the churches.

The Celtic tonsure, or that of the Apostle John, was adopted among the Greeks, Britons, and Irish; while the shaven crown or tonsure of the Apostle Peter, in emblem of the crown of thorns, was the form agreed to by the Council of Toledo, A.D. 633, and was called the *corona clericalis*. It was effected before consecration, and was common to the clergy and monks of the west of Europe. The extent of the tonsure was increased with the rank of the individual. The Franciscans left only a narrow strip of hair round the head, called the clerical crown, as if to represent more decidedly the thorn crown of Christ. The tonsure was first used A.D. 80, and it was encouraged at the council held

---

(1) Bede Eccles. Hist., Book II, ch. xxvii.
(3) *Ibid*, pl. 70.

(2) *See* Sculp. St. of Scotland, p. 25 (1 brs.) p. 5, No. 2.
(4) *Ibid*, pl. 45, 46.

at Carthage, A.D. 398. St. Benedict, the founder of Monte Cassino, sanctioned it A.D. 515 for his monks, and in his regulations, A.D. 529, it was enjoined that it should be enlarged with the age of the monks. The order of Columba used white garments, and the Celtic tonsure.[1] This tonsure appears at St. Vigean's.

SECTION IV.—SEPARATION OF THE GREEK AND ROMAN CHURCHES.

The ecclesiastical pre-eminence of Constantinople followed upon the political eminence it acquired by the removal of the seat of empire from Rome to Byzantium. Before the close of the fourth century a canon of the first council of Constantinople, held A.D. 381, assigned to it the first rank after ancient Rome. The eminent qualities of some of the Greek bishops, especially the talents and virtues of John Chrysostom (called the "golden-mouthed," from his eloquence as a preacher), led to a decree of the council of Chalcedon (451), which established the precedence of the Church of Constantinople over other churches. Many circumstances in succeeding years separated East and West from one another and led to a final rupture. The contests about image worship, the Latin doctrine of the "Filioque," with others of greater or less importance, issued in a formal sentence of excommunication of the East, A.D. 1054, by Pope Leo IX. After that, reconciliations were attempted, but since the fall of Constantinople, 1453, all further attempts have been fruitless, and the schism is complete. The earliest crosses in Britain are generally of the Greek form, which shows that the early Christian teachers were from the East. The Græco-Latin cross was introduced later, while the Maltese cross, as stated in p. 118, is the oldest known form with an unquestionably Eastern origin. When the Latin Church finally prevailed in the West, the Græco-Latin as a transition cross appears to have become general.

SECTION V.—THE INFLUENCE OF ST. PALLADIUS ON THE HISTORY OF CHRISTIANITY IN PICTLAND.

We have a very imperfect knowledge of the primitive churches in the British Islands during the third, fourth, fifth, and sixth centuries. We may suppose that the Roman legions contained believers in the new faith, and the number of the latter would be increased by the missionaries, who by way of Gaul visited the beautiful islands and intelligent inhabitants of the far West. The tyranny and cruelty of the Roman chiefs in Gaul, moreover, led many of the believers in the new religion to search for rest and peace in the neighbouring countries. Some retired to Ireland, and the new faith made rapid progress among the clever and excitable natives, already enlightened by knowledge from the East. These were increased and consolidated by the earnest and indefatigable zeal of St. Patrick in the beginning of the fourth century, who, in defiance of many obstacles, preached Christ's doctrine, made many converts, established churches and schools, ordained priests, and acquired a great name by his constant acts of piety and religious meditation and prayers. He dealt tenderly with the usages and prejudices of the pagans, being a humble man, calling himself "indoctus;" and by his judicious management with the chiefs, he obtained their support in overturning the idols, while he risked his life in the defence of his faith. St. Patrick makes no mention of a mission from Rome, but considered his call to teach barbarous nations as expressly derived from God himself. There was no reference to Rome, or confirmation of

---

(1) The community of Iona conformed to the unity of the Church of Rome, on both questions of the time of keeping Easter and the tonsure, in the year 716. Bede, Book IV, chap. ix; Book V, chap. xxii.

the bishops appointed by him, and in the hymn of St. Suchnel, written by his disciple, the son of his sister, and his successor, nothing is said of his having a mission from the Pope, nor is there any allusion to it in the Book of Armagh.[1]

St. Patrick converted a considerable proportion of the inhabitants of Ireland to the Christian faith, having been born in Scotland, according to Usher, A.D. 372, and having, after an active and holy life, died about the year 464. When Pope Celestine learned that the Christians in Ireland had become so numerous, and needed an experienced person to encourage them to be faithful to himself as head of the Church, he selected Palladius[2] who was a Greek by birth, and a learned, calm, and sagacious dean of the Gaulish church,[3] to preach the gospel, and to convert them to the faith of Rome. When he arrived in Ireland,[4] thirty years before the death of St. Patrick, he was at first well received, but on finding that his doctrine differed from that of St. Patrick, then in great favour, the Christian converts opposed him and the changes he required. This led to frequent disputes, which induced him to leave Ireland, after he had made converts and founded churches in Leinster,[5] thus leaving St. Patrick to Christianise it.[6]

Nennius, a Roman Catholic writer, reflecting on the state of the Irish mind in this matter, remarks "That no man can reverence anything upon earth, unless it be given from above;" and Probus, another Roman Catholic, observes "that the Irish being wild and barbarous, would not receive the doctrines of the Roman Catholic faith;" while Joscelin, the biographer of St. Patrick, tells us that Palladius left Ireland after a residence of one year; "the Irish obstinately opposed him" as an intruder into a Church which was complete and independent, and would not listen to his commission, or respect his foreign jurisdiction. They alike rejected the pretensions of the Pope, and those of his delegate. This was the tenor of the ecclesiastical history of the country from the second to the twelfth century. Hume says "The Irish followed the doctrine of their first teachers, and never at the period alluded to acknowledged their subjection to the see of Rome."[7] St. Iber told Palladius, on his arrival in Ireland, "That the converts would never acknowledge the supremacy of the foreigners, and consequently protested against their claims," and the able O'Halloran writes, "I strongly suspect that it was by Asiatic or African missionaries, or, through them by Spanish ones, that our ancestors were instructed in Christianity, because they rigidly adhered to their custom as to tonsure and the time of Easter." Certain it is that St. Patrick was never at Rome,[8] and found no hierarchy established in Ireland when he arrived in it. At that time the faithful Christians had simple Apostolic views, and were not disposed to submit to the authority of the Pope of Rome. St. Patrick did not come commissioned by such authority, or as the bearer of any peculiar doctrine from another country which he was bound to teach. Authors afterwards confused the name of Palladius or Patricius with Patrick, he having been known in Ireland by this name until the period of the English invasion. The fact of the distinction explains why St. Patrick, in his confessions, makes no mention of his mission to Rome, and of his having been regularly taught, but describes himself as "indoctus." It elevates the character of this excellent man, and also explains why many of the incidents in the life of Palladius were transferred to the

---

(1) *Ibid* p. 314. *See* also p. 316.

(2) Ad Scotos in Christum credentes ordinatur a Papa Celestino Palladius et primus episcopus mittitur (Dr. Todd, p. 270.)

(3) Ante cujus adventum habebant Scoti doctores ac sacramentorum ministratores, presbyteros solummodo vel monachos ritum sequentes ecclesiæ primituræ.—Fordun Scotichron, cap. viii.; Spottiswoode, Book I., p. 7.

(4) According to Prosper. Christ. Chron. A.D. 431.

(5) Usher's Antiquities of the British Church, c. cxvi, p. 413, fol. 1686; Lloyd's Hist. of Church Gov. p. 51; Bede, b. 13; Prosper Alpinus Eccl. Hist. of Ireland, vol. i, p. 44.

(6) Innes' Civil and Eccles. Hist. of Scot., vol. i., p. 53; Todd's St. Patrick, p. 278 *et seq*.

(7) Hist. of England, Henry II.

(8) *See* Todd's Life especially.

story of the Irish saint, who was incorrectly supposed to have got a commission from Pope Celestine to succeed him, although he died thirty years after the date of Palladius' visit to Ireland. Thus the acts and legends of both are mingled together in utter confusion. Palladius performed his duty with such energy as led the future chroniclers to confound him with St. Patrick; and the biographers of Palladius call him Patricius, which only made confusion worse.[1]

Ancient Church of Fordun in connexion with St. Palladius.[2]—The ancient church of Fordun is mentioned in the early history of Scotland as an ecclesiastical establishment dedicated to St. Palladius, who, it is alleged, resided there for twenty years. The liberal and Christian character of the Pope Celestine accounts for his selection of Palladius as the first missionary bishop of Ireland (A.D. 431), in consideration of the high repute in which he was held for purity of life and Christian devotedness. His willingness to encounter the trials of a missionary life in the cause of his Master, is evidenced by the continuous labour of upwards of twenty years at Fordun, amongst a semi-civilized people. Dr. Todd informs us that there is a wide-spread opinion amongst authors that the mission of St. Palladius, though authorised by the See of Rome, was in reality projected by the Gallican church. Be this as it may, we are warranted to conclude that Pope Sixtus, who succeeded Pope Celestine, A.D. 432, sanctioned the continued labours of Palladius in North Britain, and that to the influence of the latter may be attributed the fusion of the Celtic Church in his neighbourhood with the dominant Latin Church. The sculptured stones in that district exhibit the change in the tonsure and dress of the priests; these being, thenceforward, distinctively Roman. And while on previous sculptured stones we find representations of bloody sacrifices as remnants of Pagan times, the abolition of these ere long, we have no doubt, was owing to the strenuous efforts of men like Palladins, in the conversion of a semi-barbarous people to more humane and gentler feelings. The ancient church of St. Palladius has disappeared, but its site, now occupied by a modern edifice, is known. It was in front of the old and primitive building that the missionary, venerated as a saint, stood to preach to the people the good news of God; there he also instructed them in the ways of more advanced civil life, collecting them for the purpose of a market, afterwards removed from the site to a neighbouring hill, and the memorial of which is perpetuated in the annual popular fair still held there. Some idea of the work of Palladins, in the district, may be gathered from the traditional veneration in which his shrine was held up to the period of the Reformation, when the new ideas displaced in the popular regard the revered memory of the former worthies of the ancient church. Until that epoch, numbers of pilgrims from all parts of the kingdom resorted annually to the shrine. At the entrance of the ancient chapel, erected A.D. 452, to receive the shrine, the tombstone of St. Palladius, which was discovered under the pulpit of the modern church, has been placed, in order to be accessible to visitors. It was on taking down the old church that a large sculptured slab of freestone was found, 5 feet 1 inch in height, 2 feet 11 inches broad, and 4 inches thick. The sculpture on the stone is a Græco-Latin cross filled with Celtic ornaments, an equestrian figure in the lower limb, as also in the margin, and an exceptional instance of the Pagan symbols of the dorge and sceptre, of inferior workmanship, incised beneath. The back part has no sculpture, and the stone from age and exposure is in a bad condition.[3] In opposition to the Pelagian doctrine, Pope Celestine about this date had published nine articles supporting the teaching of St. Augustine on the doctrine of grace.[4] This is "a valuable testimony to the continuation of Christian faith in the West,"[5] and may serve as some index to the mission of Palladius to the Celts, who appears to have discharged his duty with great fidelity.

All writers agree that the stay of Palladius in Ireland was brief, and that he finally took up his residence in the land of the Picts (terra Pictorum) where he died, as before stated, at Fordun, in Kincardine. The

---

(1) *See* Todd's Life, ch. i, 308. (2) Little is authentic concerning Palladins, as he has been mixed up with St. Patrick.
(3) Sculp. Stones of Scot., p. 67.
(4) Fleury, chap. xii, 26. (5) Milner's Church History, chap. xi, p. 362.

annual fair, 6th July, also before alluded to, called *Padie's Fair*, or Palladius' fair,[1] is commemorative of his name, while the church and a neighbouring well were both dedicated to him, and Innes further mentions that his relics were preserved there till the Reformation. It would thus appear that from the date of his arrival in Ireland, A.D. 431, from his stay in Ireland of one year, and his twenty years' residence at Fordun, the date of his death would be about A.D. 452. In 1494 his relics were disinterred at Fordun and placed in a silver shrine by William Scheves, Archbishop of St. Andrews, where, as we have said, they continued to be venerated till the Reformation.[2] It is said that the silver shrine was removed at this time by a person of good repute in the neighbourhood, and that in after years a reverse of fortune having overtaken his family, the country people attributed the occurrence to the violation of the grave of St. Palladius, the memory of whose sanctified life and efforts still lingered amongst them. It is stated that all the incumbents of the parish, Popish, Episcopal, and Presbyterian continued to be buried in the chapel of St. Palladius, until the beginning of the present century. John of Fordun—the celebrated author of the "Scota Chronicon"—was presbyter of the parish in the fourteenth century, and was interred also in the chapel. The poet Beattie was once its schoolmaster, and George Wishart, a martyr of the Reformation times, was born and passed part of his youth here.[3] Thus Fordun has many features of interest. The scenery is picturesque and beautiful, with hill and dale, wood and water. The Luther flows at the base of the rocky and precipitous eminence, where stands the modern church on the ancient site, surrounded by fine old trees; and we are further told that the poet Beattie describes this scene in his "Ode to Retirement," in his poem of "The Minstrel." The traditional well of St. Palladius, once deemed holy, and the resort of pilgrims for its supposed curative properties, still exists; and in "Friar's Glen" are found the rude remains of a monastery.

Bodies of Christians in Britain and Ireland, are noticed in different quarters as existing before Palladius and Ninian were sent by the Popes of Rome, and long before Regulus was brought from Ireland by Columba, and their organization indicates a connection with the East. During the first three centuries of the Christian era, there are no traces of any connection with a foreign centre like Rome. All the officers of the small local sections acted each with perfect independence, and they show no sign of having received command from any superior power.

Ninian was born A.D. 360 (or 200 years before Columba), and was sent to convert the southern Picts in A.D. 400, or about thirty years after Palladius. Iona is improperly supposed to have been the first seat in Scotland of the Christian missionaries, who, along with their religion, brought some of the arts of civilized life to the savages of Caledonia.[4] But this is far from being the case, for the Christians in Pictland are a much earlier community than those of the West. We may, therefore, assume that they obtained their knowledge of religion from the Apostolic age, and that their early beliefs were modified at a later date by the teaching of the missionaries sent out by St. Columba, from the Irish, or western, and Roman church. Columba visited his Christian brethren of Pictland several centuries after their conversion, and is supposed to have founded several religious establishments, and confirmed the faith of the old and venerable church of the country. For some time prior to Columba's advent, the priests seem to have disappeared, and the ignorant natives, left to themselves, and mixing with the Celts from Scandinavia and from Gaul, appear at that period to have returned to their ancient worship. This need not surprise us, when we find that the circles of boulders are still held sacred as places for worship, and for completing contracts, etc.[5] It is a mistake to suppose that St. Drostan, the disciple and

---

(1) Innes' Civil and Eccles. His. p. 65. Lesser. Palladii episcopi et confessoria Apostolo Scotorum, minus. Brev. Aberd. (Prop. SS. Prid. non. Julii.)
(2) Todd, chap. i, 299.   (3) The Kirk and the Manse—Rev. R. Fraser.
(4) Life of Sir James Mackintosh, vol. ii, p. 257.   (5) *See* Journal, vol. i, p. 232.

companion of Columba, introduced the Christian religion into Pictland; but he with St. Columba are believed to have founded the Monastery of Deir, in Buchan, Aberdeenshire. The name, if not the memory, of St. Drostan survives in a fountain, known as Drostan's Well, and in a piece of land, on the banks of the river Tarf, called Drostan's Meadow.[1] It appears to have been the custom to found monasteries on the model of that of Iona in the various centres of population, under the auspices of the local chiefs. The church of Glenesk (Glean-uisk, glen of water) or Lochlen (the smooth lake) was supposed to have been founded by St. Drostan, Abbot of Donegal, in Ireland, who, desirous of a retreat where he might lead a hermit's life, retired from the sister island, as probably Palladius did to Fordun in the eighth century, and in the wilds of Glenesk found a suitable spot, where he erected a church.[2]

On the decay of the Celtic Catholic church, shortly after the middle of the 12th century,[3] the lands belonging to the chief monasteries of Scotland became secularized, and passed into the hands of laymen, who retained the name of abbot, and whose spiritual offices were performed by ecclesiastical deputies. In the chartularies of the Scottish bishoprics and monasteries we find traces of lay abbots in possession of the lands of early Celtic institutions throughout Pictland, as at Abernethy, Dunkeld, St. Andrews, Old Montrose Ecclesgreig, at Madderby in Strathearn, at Kirkmichael in Strathardle, and many others.[4] The Southern Christians derived their tenets from the south; and it was owing to this that the disputes which arose, were chiefly about such forms as the style of tonsure, and the period at which Easter ought to be kept. The Western Church of Caledonia consisted of the Dalriads and the still more celebrated Church of Iona, fifty years afterwards. There is an ancient belief in the west of Caledonia that Christ's name was known in that quarter as early as the third century.[5] The Dalriads came with a colony of Christians, headed by St. Ternan, which settled in south Argyleshire. The church and cave of the more celebrated Columba still exist near Campbeltown, in Kintyre, one of the ancient and great centres of the Christian communities.

A.D. 81, Tacitus mentions the existence of two Scottish tribes. A.D. 230, Dio still mentions two. A.D. 296 is the first mention of Picts by Roman authors. The Picts[6] disappear suddenly in A.D. 843. Fordun's words are—"Not only were the kings and chiefs of that nation destroyed, but the very race with its language utterly perished."[7]

SECTION VI.—THE DISPERSION OF THE PICTAVIAN CHRISTIANS UNDER THE NAME OF CULDEES.

Having now completed our purpose, that, namely, of tracing the early history of Pictland by its antiquities, it only remains that we briefly refer to the final dispersion or amalgamation among other races of the Pictavians, afterwards generally known by the name of Culdees.[8]

---

(1) Registrum de Panmure, vol. i, app. to preface, p. 92.
(2) Breviar, Aberdon, fol. xix.
(3) Chron. of Picts, p. 138.
(4) Registrum de Panmure, app. to preface, p. 93.
(5) Mull of Cantyre and Island of Arran.
(6) Bede refers to a tradition that the Picts were a foreign race who came in as aggressors and settled in Scotland.—McLauchlan, chap. iii.
(7) McLauchlan Early S. Church, chap. ii, p. 16-18.
(8) The Latin *servus Dei* would appear to be the origin of the Celtic compound *Cile-Dé*, which in the course of time underwent modifications according to circumstances. In Scotland, Hector Boece, followed by George Buchanan, gave currency to the term *Culdens*, out of which grew the vulgar form *Culdee*, which has come into general acceptance.—*Dr. Reeves on the Culdees*, vol. xxiv., p. 123.

CHAP. VI.]   HISTORY OF PAGANISM IN CALEDONIA.   257

The three periods into which the history of Pictavia resolves itself, as traced by us, may be thus classed:—

(*a.*) *The Celtic period.*—At this time the inhabitants of Pictavia were marked for their bravery and intelligence, their singular power of combination, the influence among them of the Druid priests, and their strenuous resistance amidst their mountain fastnesses to the efforts of the Roman power to bring them into subjection.

(*b.*) *The Buddhist or Eastern period.*—This is distinguished for the introduction of Buddhist doctrines from the East, impressed unmistakeably on the numerous boulders or sacred stones, with their subsequent incised symbols; the gradual corruption of the purer and primitive doctrines of Buddhism, as shewn by the introduction on the monoliths of representations of bloody sacrifices, as witness the cross of Fowlis, where the bull is being led to sacrifice by a slave, also the cross of St. Vigean's, where the animal is represented as being slain by a slave kneeling before him with uplifted knife.[1] The declining influence of Buddhism is shewn in contemptuous treatment of their sacred symbols.

(*c.*) *The Christian period.*—During which peaceable arts and religious sentiments were introduced by later missionaries from Gaul, and the influence of Byzantine art is visible in the Pictland crosses, while traces of successive impressions and distinctive Christian teaching, left by the Roman legionaries during their long occupation of Britain, necessarily follow.

As regards the obscurity and uncertainty that invest the history of the Culdees, the following observation from the pen of an accomplished scholar is appropriate. Speaking of these interesting people, he says:—"Their transactions are abundant as we become familiar with them, and but for their antiquity, their unintelligible name, and unknown founder, we should seek in vain for the grounds of the hot controversy it has been their singular fate to excite."[2] Dr. Reeves also states, that "In Scotland, where Celtic usage when brought into competition with Saxon institutions gave way, the name and office of the *Céle-dé*, or *Kéledei*, disappear from the page of history, A.D. 1332.[3]

We have already stated that there were Christians in Britain before there is any vestige of emissaries from Rome. A passage in Tertullian shows that Christianity was taught in Britain before the end of the second century, and in the early part of the fourth century the British Church contributed to the noble army of martyrs in the Diocletian persecution.—A.D. 293.[4] Neander says, "That the peculiarity of the British Church is evidence against its origin from Rome, for in many ritual matters (of human device, and therefore not such as two independent bodies were likely to adopt from their own study of the sacred Scriptures), it departed from the usage of the Roman Church, and agreed much more nearly with the Churches of Asia Minor."[5] We are, therefore, warranted to believe that British Christianity retained the early form of the Christian Church.[6]

The mission of Ninian, usually called St. Ninian or Ringan, is noticed by Bede.[7] The early British Church held doctrines differing from those termed orthodox at Rome. This is plain, for Ninian,[8] a Briton

---

(1) *See* Sculp. Stones of Scot. Golspie Stone, plate 34.
(2) From Preface to the Liber Chartarum Prior. S. Andreæ—*Cosmo Innes.* The same author states that probably the Culdees most nearly resembled the order of the Canons Regular of S. Austin, the two orders living together under the same rule and discipline, and latterly the Austin Canons taking the place of the Culdees.
(3) John of Fordun states that the Priory of Abernethy was converted into a society of canons regular, before the close of the 13th century.—*Reeves*, part iii, sec. xi, p. 172.
(4) Gen. Ch. Hist. vol. i, p. 117.   (5) Early Scot. Church—*McLauchlan*, chap. v, p. 44.
(6) *Ibid*, p. 45.   (7) Bede Hist. Eccles., Bk. III, chap. iv.
(8) Early Scot. Ch.—*McLauchlan*, chap. vi, p. 65.

by birth, of Christian parents, born at Whithorn, about A.D. 360, or about 200 years before the time of Columba, having visited Rome, and conferred with the celebrated St. Martin, of Tours, was sent to bring his countrymen into accordance with the Roman Church. He returned to Britain, and fixed his abode and established a college on the primitive or Culdee model in the south-west of Valentia, on the northern shore of the Solway Firth, at a place called Leucophibia, or Rosnat, the white house of Saxon, and the Candida Casa of Latin history in Galloway.[1] Here the first tribe of the north Britons are recorded to have been converted to the belief in Christianity. So celebrated did this priory become that Margaret, wife of James III., in 1473, and James IV., made a pilgrimage to the sepulchre of St. Ninian, which was rich, and then contained numerous relics of the saint. According to Bede "The southern Picts, who dwelt on that side of the (Grampian) mountains, forsook the errors of idolatry, and embraced the truth, by the preaching of Nineas, or Ninian." The Britons were already Christians, but Ninian was the first emissary from Rome in the fourth century, hence he is called the first apostle to the Southern Picts. He is said to have been succeeded by his two disciples, *St. Serf* or *Servanus*, and *St. Ternan*, of whom nothing is known.

Kentigern was another saint and bishop who distinguished himself by his zeal, tempered with gentleness, devotion, and eloquence. He extolled the simple-minded and pure in heart, and denounced the hypocrite as the enemy of religion. His humble attire and bearing, the gravity of his deportment, and elegance of his tastes, exhibited his self-discipline and purity of character. He laboured chiefly in Glasgow, where he was known by the endearing name of Mungo.

The early Scottish saints who have left traces of their work and their names are as follows:

A.D. 361.—*Rule or Regulus*. A tower at St. Andrew's, said to be the oldest building in Scotland, is called by his name, and nothing more is known of him.

A.D. 404.—*Monan*. A church is dedicated to him at a small town still called St. Monance, on the coast of Fife.

Arrived in Ireland A.D. 431.—*Palladius*, the first missionary Bishop to the Scots, died at Fordun, in the Mearns.

A.D. 360—432.—*Ninian*, Bishop of the Southern Picts, built a church at Whithorn, in Galloway.

A.D. 443.—*Serf*, Bishop of the Orkney Isles.

A.D. 455.—*Ternan*, Bishop of the Picts, lived many years in the abbey of Culross, in Fife.

A.D. 521—563.—*Columba*, founded many monasteries in Scotland, especially that at Iona.

A.D. 514—578.—*Mungo* or *Kentigern*, Bishop of Glasgow, said to be the founder of that city.

In accordance with the religious usages of the time, the priests resorted to caves during Lent and at other times of penitential devotion, when by penance and prayers they purified their sinful nature. Such caves are found near each of the primitive churches. St. Ninian had one on the coast of the

---

(1) There are no remains but a ruined wall, which had formed a part of the abbey. From the history and position of Iona, the remains of the enlarged and beautiful church, with the graceful crosses and tombs of kings and great men, still remain.

NOTE.—The Breviary of Aberdeen, printed A.D. 1500, has a numerous list of the ancient Scottish Saints.

See Butler's Lives of the Saints, etc.

Solway Firth; St. Columba had his cave on the west coast at Killkerran, in Ayrshire; St. Ternan had his in Kintyre. There is the chapel cave of St. Medan on the west coast of Loch Luce; the cell of St. Genard at Kinneddar, in Moray; and the "ocean cave" of St. Rule, at St. Andrews. As the great poet sings—

> Good St. Rulé his holy lay,
> From midnight to the dawn of day,
> Sung to the billow's sound.

St. Serf had his cave of Dysart; and of St. Kentigern, his disciple, we read that his custom also was to retire to a cave during the term of Lent. In some of these caves crosses have been carved on the walls; and in the group of caves at East Wemyss and along the coast of Fife numerous crosses and other figures are still to be seen,[1] and some elephants and other symbols are found traced upon the wall. The cave of Ninian, the great saint of the district, and instructor of the Southern Picts, is on the rocky coast of Galloway, and is partially fallen in. It is near Whithorn—"the white church," called also Rosnat. Kentigern, who succeeded Ninian as the apostle of Strathclyde, and whom his biographer pictures at the mouth of the cave, and in the attitude of prayer, laboured in this district.

The island of Iona is three miles long, and not quite a mile broad. There are the remains of a church and of a monastery that was ruled by an abbot, who strictly enforced self-denial and asceticism. Between prayers, the priests were employed in reading and hearing the Scriptures, in the labour required for producing the necessaries of life by the cultivation of the land, and in fishing. Others copied books of the church service for use or for missions. Columba was proficient as a caligrapher. He died at the age of 77. After his death the island became a place of extraordinary sanctity, the chief seat of the Culdees.[2] Other seats of the Culdee Church are Abernethy, St. Andrews, Dunkeld, Dunblane, Brechin, and at other places. In the ninth century the Danes ravaged Iona. In the west St. Columba's great monastery of Hy exercised an influence felt in every quarter of Scotland. In the extreme north the Orkneys were rendered safe to the devout pilgrim by St. Columba; in the far south Melrose attained its greatest celebrity under Eata, one of St. Aidan's disciples; and, in the eastern extremity of Pictland, Drostan accompanied the indefatigable Columba when he founded the Church of Aberdour, perpetuating in Buchan the remembrance of fraternal attachment, in a church whose name of Deir, that is "tear," commemorated their parting, and whose after history, now preserved in the oldest known book of Scotland, is the sole relique of its early literature. Two establishments in the south-west were not of Columbite origin. Rosnat was founded by St. Ninian, prior to St. Columba's date, while in Glasgow St. Kentigern or Mungo, as he was familiarly called, was a Strathclyde Briton. The Céli-Dé, or Colidei in its Latinised form, had a fraternity in the church of Armagh from the commencement of the tenth century to the Reformation. Under the term "people of God," or, more technically, Céli-Dé, they would seem to have been the officiating attendants of the choir and altar. Much controversy has gathered round both the name and history of the Culdees, as they are usually termed. Their origin and influence has been variously estimated, but it can scarcely be doubted their tenets and practices resembled greatly the earlier and purer doctrines of the primitive and Eastern Church, until it was the powerful and advancing tide of the dominant Roman creed and ritual that succeeded in superseding and effacing these early pioneers of Christianity. But the story of their earnest lives and devotion remains enshrined in Britain, and we may well pay a merited tribute of respect to the very remarkable Celtic community, known as that of "The Culdees."

---

(1) Sir Jas. Lupton's account.
(2) *See* The Ancient Burial Places of the Early Christians, and The Early Christians in Rome, by Rev. J. Spencer Northcoat. M. A. Black. 1855.

APPENDIX.

At page 123 of this work I have explained the nature of the two ovals which I found on the lintel of a side-door of the entrance of a broch, with a meridian line proceeding from the ovals; and when completed, it explains the radii of two circles, the one representing the moon inside and the sun outside; or the sun revolving round the moon, which the able Greek astronomer Hipparchus proved was wrong, about the year *cir.* 150 B.C. The cup-dials near the Manse of Fodderty, in Cromarty, afforded another example of repeating the same observations to determine the age of the dial.[1]

As these markings on the broch are obviously of great antiquity—in all probability co-eval with the original erection itself—their correct interpretation must be regarded as of no small interest and importance.

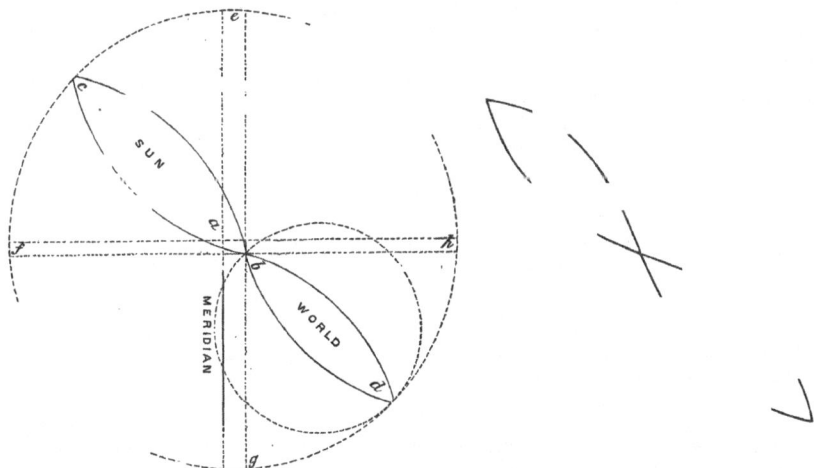

It was suggested by the Rev. Dr. Graham that the probable age of the broch might be obtained by taking angular and other measurements with finely graduated mathematical instruments, and thus afford one of the most satisfactory methods by which an approximation to the age (epoch) of these ancient buildings might be made. The latitude of the broch is 57° 59′ N., long. 3° 55′ W., and the door upon which the markings under consideration are inscribed looks directly south. The markings themselves consist of two ellipses joined together, and are the exact size here represented, whilst a deep, strong marking or line lies at an acute angle to a line passing through the longer axes of the ellipses. The deep, strong marking was found, after repeated experiments and testings with fine magnetic needles, to be exactly in the magnetic meridians, whilst the line uniting the longer axis

---

(1) It was the able, practical astronomer, the Rev. R. Graham, LL.D., who proposed the following observation, prepared accurate instruments, and accompanied me to Sutherland, where we carefully instituted experiments to determine the approximate ages of these two interesting antiquities.

LL

APPENDIX.

of the ellipses was found to lie at the points 318 and 38 of a great circle, in which the magnetic north is 0°. Believing that the ancient inhabitants of Caledonia were sun-worshippers, and that the rising and setting of the sun at particular periods of the year would be one of the principal means of determining their sacrifices and festal periods, we conceived the idea that the ellipses were employed to mark the direction of the solsticial point at the period when they were incised. As these points have, in the course of ages, moved, in consequence of the precession of the equinoxes; and as the rate of the precession is known, the lapse of time from their incision may be astronomically determined.

The problem is extremely interesting, and, to determine it, it is necessary to ascertain how much the line of the solsticial point at the present has departed from that inscribed upon the broch. As the simplest and the best method of finding the direction of the solsticial points is to ascertain the points on the horizon at which the sun rises or sets on the longest and shortest days in the year, and as the sun on the 21st June rises in lat. 57° 59', long. 3° 56' W., almost exactly in the N.N.E. point, the precession, allowing for the magnetic variation, will have amounted to 42°, or, in other words, the point of the sun's rising on the longest day has moved contra to the order of the signs 42°. The precession of the equinoxes is an exceedingly slow motion, requiring 25,868 years to complete an entire revolution. We have, consequently, only to ascertain the relation borne by 42° to 360°, of which 25,868 is the expression in time; as nearly as possible one degree is equivalent in time to 70 years, so that we have $42 \times 70 = 2,940$ years. The broch therefore, according to this method of computation, is nearly 3,000 years old. There can be little doubt that this method of computation is one in which a considerable amount of error may exist, since the small size of the ellipses makes it difficult to determine the precise point in the horizon to which the line of the apsides is directed; but, in the absence of any historical evidence, it cannot be regarded otherwise than suggestive.

It will be important to examine similar edifices of antiquity, with a view to ascertain if like markings exist upon them; as their presence or absence will determine the value of the above idea, and so prove whether, in this way, we can arrive approximately at the age of these interesting monuments of antiquity.

On our return from examining the Broch of Cairn Leath, we examined the cup-dial slab at the church of Fodderty (described at page 123 of this work), intending to institute the occurrence of the longest, and recurrence from it of the shortest, day of the year by the same angular method of computation of the broch. We found its age would be about 2500 years, and how far the one can be regarded as confirming the conclusions arrived at in regard to the other, must be determined by future discoveries.

HISTORY OF PAGANISM IN CALEDONIA.

INDEX.

INDEX.

	Page.
Abbotsford Cross	220
Aberdeenshire, Circles of Stones in	38
Aberfeldie, Sculptured Cups at	52
Aberlemno, Church of, 212; Cross at, 64, 177, 226, 232, 235, 236, 240; Sculptured Stones at, 170, 171, 175, 239	
Abernethy, Cross at, 222; Pillar Tower at ... 85, 211	
Abraham planted groves of Sacred Trees	192
Absalom's Burial	138
Abul Fazl	79, 150
Achan's Punishment	138
Ackerman, Mr., on British and Buddhist Horses on Coins	113
Adam's Peak, Ceylon	66, 67
Adder Stones	62
Ægis, a Buddhist Symbol, 242; found on Christian Crosses 238, 245	
Agârams, or Cromlechs	135
Aggle Stone, Purbeck	192
Aghaville, Round Tower of	209
Aghnacerribmas, Ireland, Sculptured Stone at	57
Agricola, a Roman General	200
Agriculture in Caledonia	17
Agni, Fire God	120
Ahriman, Devil of the Persians	97
Ahura-mazda, the Good Spirit	96
Air, as an object of Worship	104
Airlie, Cave in	11
Ajunta, Caves of, 109; Frescoes, 244; Temple	167
Aksholya	123
Alabaster, Mr., on Buddha's Footprint	66
Almora, India, Rocking Stone at	92
Altar, as a Celtic Symbol	176
Altar Stones	91
Altars, Primitive	247
Amad Stones	31
Ameraphoora, Temple of	194
Amiens, early Weapon and Bones	28
Amravati, Sculptures of	109
Anderson, Dr., on Age of Brochs	78
Andrew's, St., Cathedral, 229; Cross	236
Anglo-Norman Sepulchral Monuments	230
Angra-mainyus, the Bad Spirit	96
Animals on Crosses, 231, 233; used as Sacred Symbols, 185; derived from Buddhism	105

	Page.
Antiquarian Museum, Edinburgh	170
Anworth, Galloway, Buddhist Symbols at ... 155, 174, 175, 177	
Apollo, the Sun God	99
Apollonius Rhodens	91
Aran, Fort at	23
Arbuthnot, Lady	241
Architecture, Early Celtic	74
Ardmore, 182; Bell Tower, 85; Oghams, 71; Rocks at	65
Ardoilen, Incised Wheel at	207
Ark, The, on Mount Ararat	88
Armagh, Book of	252
Armour buried with the dead	129
Arran, Island of,	46
Artaxerxes Mnemon	97
Aryan Celts, their migrations	35
Ashdown, Victory of	113
Ash Tree, Symbolical use of	65
Asia, Monoliths in	28
Asoka	148, 150, 183
Auchtertyre, Roman Camp at	18
Anselm of Molle, on Land Boundaries	55
Avalokitesvara, a Hindu Deity	156
Avebury, 38, 42, 90, 108; Temple to the Moon, 94; Serpent Worship at	107
Avenues of Stones in various countries	47
Baal, Sun God, 98, 99; Temple to	98
Baalbec, Temple to the Sun	98
Baking Stones	19, 26
Balcallo, Monolith at	32
Ballutherie Stone	107
Ballymascoulan	137
Balmoral, Altar Stone at	57
Banshee	244
Banyan, a Sacred Tree	192
Barrows	138
Barry Hill Fort, 19, 24; Construction of	25, 26
Barth, M., on Religions of India, 117, 128	
Barter in Caledonia	17
Bass of Ury	41
Basins in Rocks	60
Baylanagra, Serpent Worship at	105
Beattie, the Poet	255
Bede, on the Races of Britain	69
Beehive Houses	10, 75
Beer of the Britons	19

	Page.
Beerboom, Sacred Tree at	194
Belief in the Holy Spirit by Orientals	242
Bell Towers are Modern	85
Belmont Castle, 20; Sculptured Cups at	51
Benares, centre of Brahminism, 159; Elephants Sculptured at	186
Bengal, Pillar Towers in	81
Benignus, St., at Arran	75
Beresov, Sacred Tree at	195
Betal, Stone Circles dedicated to	36
Bethluis Alphabet	71
Betrothal, Northern Custom of	65
Bhaugulpore, Tower at	80
Bhogilpore, Bengal, Footprints at	68
Bicker, a Drinking Cup	20
Birakala, or Cromlechs	135
Birch, W. Gray	83
Birds, Sacred	191
Blackmore, Mr., on Hole Stones	62
Block Buildings	74
Blyars, Pagodas of the	81, 180
Bo-tree, or Boddha-tree	194
Boadicea	17
Boar, The Sacred	105
Bodhisattva Vajruhhura	156
"Boduo," on British Coin	187
Boethius, Hector, on Christian Crosses	232
Bombay, Hole Stone at	63
Bos Bison	13
Bos Urus	13
Boulder Ornaments, 176; Boulder Monuments in Scotland, 215; Simple Erect Boulders, 115; Sacred Boulder Stones	243
Boundary Pillars, or Monoliths, 115; Crosses, 228; Stones	32
Brading, Swastica Cross at	118
Brahma, a Sun God, 98; among the Hindoos	120
Brahmins, 122, 144; Polytheism	119
Brash, on Architecture in Ireland	209
Brehons	8
Brechin, Bell Tower at	85
Bridget, St.	211
Britain, Buddhism in	81
Brittany, Cromlechs in, 137; Monoliths in	32
British Camps, 27; Carriages and Cars, 18; Fort near Stonehenge, 22; Early Crosses	221

INDEX.

Britons, Ancient, 1; their Agriculture, 18; Dress, 3; Dwellings, 11; Females' Dress, 4; Shoes, 4; Skulls of, 2; Tattooing, 3; Chiefs 3
Brochs, 77; at Caithness, 78; Orkney Isles 78
Brogar Ring of Orkney ... 65
Brucks, Mr., on Cromlechs 135
Bones found in Lake Dwellings ... 13
Buckland, Dr., on Stonehenge ...' 44
Buddha: as represented in Bengal, in Ceylon, in Ava, in Burmah, in China, 186; his Death and Ascension, 159; Foot-marks, 66, 160; Images of, 123, 167; as the Spirit of Wisdom 157
Buddhism, 144; Tenets of, 143, 150, 156, 180; Symbols of, 168; Eight Principles of, 158; derived from Religion of Bramah, 154; Missionary character of, 160; Modern, 149; Contact with Early Christianity, 160, 173, 201; and Catholic Ritual, 150; Decline of 147, 148
Buddhism in Africa, Europe, and British Isles, 81; in Caledonia, 154; in Ceylon, 201; in China, 149; in Ireland, 180; in Pictland, 168, 174; in Scotland and Ireland, 173, 187; in Thibet ... 201
Buddhist Missionaries, 233; Journeyed to the Setting Sun, 97; in the Caves of Fife, 179; in Pictland, 174; in Caledonia ... 249
Buddhist Symbols on Christian Monuments, 148, 204, 235, 242; on the Golspie Stone, 72; found only in Pictland ... 174
Buddhist Begging Pot, 153; Circles, 161; Monasteries, 180; Organic Symbols, 185; Prayer-wheels, 161; Priests, 151, 152; Priests as Physicians, 149; Ritual, 151; Symbols on Celtic Stones, 177, 201; Triratna, 156; Triad, 105, 156, 173; Trumpets, 181; Twelve Rules, 153; Use of Symbols instead of Language, 161; Wheels 161
Buddhists, Varieties of, 160; Hindoos and Arabs... ... 8
Bulgari, Round Tower at... 81
Bull, The Sacred, Symbolical... 105, 189
Burghead, Moray Firth, Bull at ... 190
Burmah, Buddhism in 160
Burmese, Burial Customs of 132
Burial among the Caledonians, 129; Position of Body 230
Burial places of the Celts 131
Busallor Mulfra... 10
Byrring's Chapel, Rocking Stone ... 92

Cæsar, Julius, 3, 7, 8, 11, 87; on Cremation, 130; on Language of the Gauls, 69; on origin of the Caledonians, 2; on the Tides of Britain, 101; on Valour of the Celts 19
Cairngorm Mountains, Well basins on 61
Cairns, 138, 139; the Earliest Form of Structure, 138; Development of, 139; as Boundaries, 32; as Legal Monuments, 90; at Hyderabad, 40; Leath Broch... 99, 124
Caithness, Caves in 13
Caldwell, Bishop, on the Tudas ... 31
Caledonia, Inhabitants of, their Social Character, 1; in the Megalithic age, 9; Druids Retreat there, 200; Sun Worship in 99
Caledonians, Dwelling-places of, 9, 10; their Hunting and Fishing, 15; Laziness, 2; Dress and Ornaments 3
Caligula 112
Callernish, 40, 46, 48, 137; Stone Circle 37
Carnac, Brittany 89, 107
Cambridge, Early MS. at... 250
Camden, on Names of Places... ... 69
Camel and Dromedary, Oriental Symbols, 191; Bactrian and Indian. 228
Canmore, Malcolm 6
Canna, Island of 218, 223
Canute, King 200
Caractacus, Camp of... . 27
Carew Bré Castle, Rock Basin at ... 60
Carnac, Mr. Rivett 57
Carriages and Cars of Britons... ... 18
Castledermot, Bell Tower at . . 85
Castle Hill, Roman Camp at, 18, 27; Sculptured Stones at... 177
Catacombs of Rome, 229, 230; Symbolical Carving in 233
Cathairs (Forts) 26
Catherthun, Celtic Fort at, 18, 23, 26, 107; Stones at, in the shape of a Serpent 24
Cat Stones, marking a place of battle 133
Caucasus, Round Towers in 81
Canoes and Coracles... 16
Caves as Dwelling-places, 10, 179; Cave-men, 10; Celtic, 12; used as Temples in India... 179
Celestine, Pope... ... ... 253, 254
Céli-Dé, The 259
Celtic Forts at various places... 18, 22, 27
Celtic Races, Origin of, 1; Patriarchal Religion, 87; Laws, 87; Legal Monuments, 90; Symbols on Christian Crosses, 64, 236; Similar in Europe and Asia, 48; Urns, 21, 140; Weapons... ... 21
Celts, Religion of, 21; Crosses with Buddhist Symbols, 226; Courts, 6; High Places, 88; Arms of, 22; War Chariots, 19; Social Grades, 4; The Tempster, 5; Slaves ... ...
Centaur, The Mythological, 188; on Stones in Scotland, 188; on British Coins 189
Cerberus 188
Ceylon, Buddhism in 160
Chalk Lines as Tallies 49
Charter and Coronation Stones, 32; at Girvan, 33; Inverness... ... 32
Charcoal Burners 11
Chatton Law, Sculptured Cups at ... 51
Chandwick, Cross at ... 236
Cheops, Pyramid of ... 132
Chieftain on Sculptured Stones ... 6
China, Buddhism introduced 149
Christian, Jas. 54
Christian Symbols cut on Pagan Monoliths 115, 231
Christians driven into Cornwall, Wales, and Pictavia 203
Christmas Eve, Festivities derived from Sun Worship 100
Christianity in Britain, 204; in Pictland, 201, 205, 206; not from Iona, 216; not derived from Buddhism, 160; use of Pagan Symbols 207
Church Island in Corraw 76
Churches, Primitive, 247; Mud, succeeded by Stone 209
Circars, Pagodas of 180
Circles of Stones, 35; as Memorials, Symbolism of, 37; Sacrifices within, 35, 38; as Sepulchres, 38; as a Triad, 169; Concentric, 116; Justice administered at, 37; Representing Deity, 116; in Asia, 38; at Callernish, 37; at Culna, 39; at Snago, Glendallock, the Hebrides, Penrith, Stennis, and Stonehenge 40
Circles of the Sun God, 161; Three represent the Triad, 169; Table of Measurements ... 171
Ciudad Maham, Africa, Hole Stone at 62
Civa, Lakshmana, Vishnu 67
Clachan Stones .. 174
Clack-an-tuil .. 65
Clach o' Leuchda Stones . 31
Clonmacnois .. 209
Clark, Sir James, Altar Stone on his Estate 57
Clava Tumuli, Cup-marks on ... 58
Clava, Valley of .. 47
Clickemin, Broch of ... 68
Clog-Almanacs .. 50
Clonmacnois, Round Tower of ... 249
Clonmáson, Christian Pillar Tower at 209
Cloyne, Church of, 85; Pillar Tower 182

INDEX.

Cluny, Forest of, Strathhardle ... 11
Cneph, Egyptian God 106
Coelfred, Abbot of Jarrow 211
Cœr-Craddock, Camp at 27
Cogue, a Drinking Cup 20
Coins of Early Britons were Buddhist 187
Cole, near Allyghur, Tower at ... 80
Colebrooke... 111
Collinsbury, Rev. J., on Landmarks 53
Colman, St. 182
Columba, St., 221, 236, 252, 258; used Coracles 16
Columbus' Discovery of America ... 97
Comyn, Earl of Buchan 250
Congresbury, Early Landmarks at... 53
Constantinople 252
Coronation Stones 32
Constantius 202
Constantine, Cornwall, Boulder at... 65
Coolrus Hill, Ireland 137
Copan, Central India, Sculptured Stones at 59
Coracles 16
Cormac's Chapel, Cashel 209
Council at Ariminium and at Arles... 203
Cornvealas or Cornwall, a Retreat of the Druids 200
Cornwall, Primitive Crosses in ... 221
Corgah, Grantown 178
Coronation of Maharajah of Tipperah 33
Cossins, Latin Cross at 218
Cow, Worship of, by Hindoos ... 189
Cran-leaca Stones 31
Crannoges 13, 14
Cremation, Pagan 130, 229
Crichie Circle 41
Crichton, The admirable 13
Cromlechs, Cup-marks on, 58 ; Coolrus Hill, 137 ; Orme's Head ... 136
Cross at Aberlemno, 240; Abernethy, 222 ; Dunfallandy, 244 ; Dunkeld. 222 ; Dupplin, 223 ; Eassie, 241 ; Fowles, 239 ; Golspie, 226 ; Hilton, 239; Hixhon, 223 ; Isle of Man, 221 ; Kirkmichael, 221 ; Meigle, with explanation of Symbols, 224, 225 ; Nigg, 226, 240; Ripon, 223 ; Somersby, 243 ; St. Vigean ... 240
Crosses, Primitive, 205, 221; Incised, 214 ; Bas-relief, 217 ; Celtic, Ornamented, 236 ; Pagan, 117, 223; with Symbols, 204; erected by Constantine, 205 ; by Spanish Navigators, 228 ; Greek and Latin, 214, 215, 221, 229, 250 ; on the Garments of Egyptian Priests, 118 ; Wooden, 223 ; over Doors, 210 ; Sick People bound upon, 223; as Instruments of Punishment, 215 ;

Weeping Cross, 223 ; Memorial, 229 ; with Nimbus, 218 ; Irish, 221 ; in Pictland ... .:. ... 222
Cruitnich, name for Lowlander ... 17
Crux, Ansata 117
Culdee Hermitages 76
Culdees, The 256, 259
Culna, Circle of Stones 39
Cumrington, Mr., Stonehenge... ...' 45
Cup-dial of the Celts 123
Cup-marks, Age of, 59 ; Primitive, 50 ; Celtic, 55 ; American, 57 ; Indian, 57 ; on Altars, 57 ; on Burial Stones, 58 ; as Records 50, 55
Currie, Mr., on Landmarks ... 55
Curw, a British Drink . 19
Cuvier, Baron, on Language 70
Cyclopean Buildings... 74
Cymrii, Battle with Britons ... 22
Cyril of Alexandria 144

Dalai-Lama of Thibet 122
Dalboquerque, Alfonso 83
Danes could not build Pillar Towers, 84 ; invade Ireland 248
Danish " Things " 90
Dant, name of maker of Crosses ... 221
Darancotta, City of, 40 ; Circles of Stones... 36
Dartmoor, Temples on 94
Daviot Stone 175
Deanside, Roman Camp at 18
Death, Celtic usages after, 128 ; Views of the Sun Worshippers upon 128
Deer, Book of, 8, 250; Monastery of, 256 ; Cross at Deer, Aberdeenshire, 217; Deer Stone 175
Deities, Sacred, 119 ; Two-Headed . 233
Delhi, Pillar of Victory at 183
Delvin, Roman Camp at 12, 18, 27
Demi-Dolmens 136
Denmark, Landmarks in, 52; Monoliths in... 33
Depaldinna, Temple of 39, 40
Deposits, Depth of Alluvial 208
Derricunniby, Rocking Stone ... 92
Devanampriya Preyadasin, King ... 184
Devenish Pillar Tower 182
Dharma, The 158
Dharmachakra 163
Dingle, Rock Basins at 61
Dingwall, Obelisk at... 56
Dinnacair, Church at... 248
Dinna-care Rock, Sculptured Stones 54
Diodorus 4, 10
Diodorus Siculus, on early Britons... 1

Ditmarshers, Landmarks of 52
Dodona, 195 ; Grove at 193
Dog, Mythological representations of, 188 ; on Obelisks 232
Dolar, Marchaud 137
Dolemoor, in Somersetshire 53
Dolman men-an-tol 61
Domitian, The Emperor 201
Doms, or Circle of Stones 90
Donaghmore Pillar Tower 210
Don, River, Sculptured Stones found in 42
Donsuho Tower. 85
Doonbey, Kerry, Stone Fort at ... 23
Dorge, The ... 165, 166, 170, 233, 234
Doter, a Landmark 53
Dowth, Rock basin at, 60; Mound at 89
Dr. Evans, on Mythological Horse.,, 187
Dr. Skene, on Crichie Circle 41
Dragon, The Emblematical 110
Dravidian Monuments 30
Drewsteignton Rocking Stone ... 92
Drinking Cups of Caledonians, 20 ; of Bone and Wood, 20 ; of Horn, 20 ; Stone and Pottery, 20 ; found in Cists 20
Drogheda, Symbolic Stone in... ... 183
Drostan, St. 255, 259
Druids, 7, 9, 143 ; Sacred Stones of, 31, 37 ; Christianity, 202 ; and Brahmins, 8, 87 ; Derivation of Name, 192 ; Knowledge of, 8 ; Use of Oghams, 71 ; Migration to Cornwall, Caledonia, and Ireland ... 200, 249, 250
Druidical Ceremonies at Midsummer 100
Drumcliff, Sligo, Pillar Towers ... 84
Drumnakelly, Tyrone, Cemetery at . 58
Drumobo, Door at 210
Dryden, Sir H., on Footprints ... 68
Ducks as Decoys 15
Duffryn, Wales 137
Dunfallandy, Cross at 234
Dunnoughmore Church 85
Dunannon Hill 10
Duncliffe, Pillar Tower at .. 181, 249
Duncinnan Hill 74
Dum Donnel, a Mound 89
Dunfallandy, Serpent at, 108 ; Cross at 236
Dunkeld, Cross at, 222 ; Bishop of... 13
Dunloe Rocking Stone 92
Dunmore, Cromlech at 137
Dunnoughmore 86
Dunoon, Celtic Fort at 18
Dunrobin Stone 175, 176
Duns (Forts) 26

INDEX.

	Page.
Dupplin Cross	223
Durga, The Goddess	163
Durnerdash, Tirhoot	183
Dyce, Aberdeenshire, Stone at	173, 237
Earth, Ancient Conception of	105
Earthern Forts, Ireland and England	22
Eassie, 196, 232; Cross at, 236, 241, 251	
Easter-day in Celtic Church is Eastern not Roman	240
Eastern Symbols on Celtic Stones	204
Eborius, Bishop	203
Ecclesgreig	256
Edward the Confessor, Tomb of	140
Edderton, Ross-shire, Holy Stone at	63, 219, 234
Effigies of Sacred Persons	123
Egilsay, Orkneys	249
Egypt, Obelisks and Pyramids of	34
Egyptian Hieroglyphics	237
Ephraim	144
Elagabalus, Sun God	98
Elements, Worship of	103
Elephant, The Celestial, 105, 185, 186, 227; Sculptured on Stones in Pictavia	186
Elephas Primigenius	22
Elliott, Sir W.	135
Ellora, Temple of	169
Embalming	131, 132
Emesa, Temple at	98
Entombing	131
Epiphanius, on Stone Circles	36
Ether, Anciènt Conception of	104
Etruscans, Burial of	132
Exchequer Tallies	49
Fa Hian, Chinese Traveller	79, 104
Falkirk, Cross at	236
Farnell Stone, Serpents carved on	107
Ferguson, Dr., 105, 140; on Pillar Tower at Delhi, 38; on Serpent Worship	109
Feroz Shah	38, 83, 183
Fiace's Hymn	248
Fichin, St., Church of	207
Ficus Indica	194
Finhaven, Celtic Fort at	18
Fire Worship in Cornwall, 100; in Britain	201
Firmorians, or African Pirates, Colonise Ireland	76
Fish, as a Sacred Symbol	191
Flag-stone Erections	75
Fleury, C. R. de, on the Cross	205
Flintstown, Cross at	223

	Page.
Florence Baptistry, Crucifix at	243
Foe Leou Sha's Tower to Buddha	80
Fodderty, Church of	123
Food and Drink of Caledonians	19
Footprints of Deity in various places, 68; on Stones	66
Forbes-Leslie, Major	45
Fordun, Church of	254
Fors, Incised Wheel at	207
Forthill, Fort at	18
Fortified Villages	22
Forts, Materials employed	24
Fowles, Cross of	239
Galgacus	17
Gallerus, Kerry, Oratory at	76
Galloway, Cups found in	51, 52
Galway, Rock basin of St. Patrick	60
Garlock, Maiden Stone at	217
Gautama, Buddha, 145, 194; Footprints of	68
Gayā, Temple of	67
Gibb, Andrew	54
Girvan Charter Stone	33
Glammis Castle, 113, 218; Manse	108
Glendallock	40
Glenesk, Church of	256
Glenesk, Forfarshire, Footmarks at	69
Glenfernis Obelisk	236
Glenfluren's Cross	220
Glen Urquhart, Argyleshire, Sculptured Cups at	58
Golspie Stone, Oghams on, 72; Buddhist Symbols on, 72; Cross, 226; Hole Stone	65
Gomor Rock	184
Goose, The Vehicle of Brahma	105, 191
Gordon's Itinerarium	208
Gorgon's Head	109
Gorucknuth, a name of Buddha	123
Gourdie, Perthshire	12
Govan, Tomb of, 222; Sculptured Stone	229
Grampian Mountains, 24; Battle on	17
Grange Barrow, Ireland, Cups at	56
Grand Lama	122
Grant, Major, Sculptured Stones on his farm	176
Graves, Bishop	59
Graves, Early British, 173; near Crosses	230
Graves, Rev. J., on Footprints, 69; Round Towers	209
Grecian origin of Irish Churches	247
Gregory, Dr.	172
Gregory, Pope, 234; on British Liturgy	251

	Page
Groves, Sacred	191, 192
Grugaich, Rock basins	61
Hag's Bed, Fermoy	137
Haliton Hill, Sculptured Cups at	51
Hanasa, or Goose	105
Hanway's Travels in Persia	81, 180
Harris, Island of, Cyclopean Buildings at	75
Hasta	53
Hecatæus	45
Hegenegorth, Cornwall	116
Heliogabalus, Sun God	98
Hengaston	112
Hengist and Horsa (stallion and mare)	112
Henry I.	23
Herodotus, 14; on the Foot of Hercules, 69; on Horse Sacrifice	111
Highlands, Feudal system in, 6; Sacred Trees	195
High Places considered Holy	88
Hill Forts in Scotland	23, 27
Hilton Cadbolt, Sculptured Stone at	239
Hindu Triad	169
Hindus Conquered Ceylon, 67; their Deities, 119; Sacrifices, 111; Cromlechs, 135; Cleanliness, 2; Cook within a Circle	36
Hindustan, Antiquities of, 30; Agriculture in, 17; Conversion to Buddhism, 147; Shell Worship, 59; Monuments	30
Hiouen-Thsang, Chinese Traveller, 79, 104	
Hipparchus	124
Hixhon, Crosses at	223
Hoare, Sir R. C., 23; on Incense Cups, 20; on Stonehenge	44
Hogan, Mr., on Tempul Fingin	209
Hole-Stones. 61; Prayers at, 62; used by Christians, 63; Development into Stone Crosses	63
Holm, Shetland	90
Homer alludes to Stone Circles	36
Hops not known in Britain until Henry VIII.	19
Horse Worship, 94, 111, 112; Developed from Sun Worship, 98; Sacrificed in India, 111; White Horse of Buddha, 105; Sacred to Wodin, 112; Depicted on British Coins, 113, 187; in Irish Mythology, 114; Bones at Lagon, 112; on Effington Downs, and in Hanover, 112; Places named after the Horse	112
Horse Shoe, an emblem used by Catholic Priests	175
Horsham	112
Horstead Keynes	112
Horsley	112
Hoxne	22

INDEX.

	Page
Huc, M.	166
Human Sacrifices	140
Hunter's Hill	229
Hunting Scenes on Crosses	240
Huntly-Tumulus	42
Hurley Pujah Festival in India	103
Huts of Caledonians, 9; and of Ireland	11
Hy, Monastery of	259
Iber, St.	253
Ibis, The Sacred	191
Image-maker in India	232
Innes, Cosmo	6
Incense Cups	20
Inch, Aberdeenshire, Picardy Stone at	107
Indian Museum, London, Horse Sculptured at	111
Indra, War God, 121; and Vitra	110
Inscriptions on Pillars	184
Inverness, Charter Stone at	33
Inverury, Aberdeenshire, Figure of Horse at	113
Inverussie, Argyleshire, Sculptured Cups at	56
Ireland, Pillar Towers in, 83, 180; Druids retreat to, 200; Consecration Stone	69
Irish Christians reject the Authority of the Pope	253
Irish Spoken at Aberdeen in Reign of Mary Stuart, 70; peculiarity of Irish Cross	221
Isla River	12
Isle of Man, Crosses in	221
Jacob's Monolith, 29, 32; his Pillar of Stone	90
Jervis, Mr., 170; on Footprints	69
Jewish Monoliths	29
Joass, Dr., 65, 56, 68; on Cairn Leath Broch	124
Jocelin	108
Jolly, Mr., Cup-marks discovered by	58
Jonah, a Type of the Resurrection	233
Josiah, King	207
Joss-houses	164
Jubelpore, India	14
Junagarth, Pillar at	183
Jura, Island of	69
Justice administered in Stone Circles	37
Kaimes Hill	126
Kali, Time-God	120
Kalorians, Monoliths of	30
Kashmir, Buddhism in	161
Katar, Arabia	83

	Page
Keilor Stone, The	172, 230
Keller, Dr. F.	13
Kells, Book of	223
Keneith, Pillar Tower at	182
Kenneth, IV.	212
Kennit	86
Kentigern, St.	258
Kent's Hole	22
Kent, White Horse of	112
Kerlescant, Brittany	65
Kerry, Drystone Forts at, 22; Oghams at, 71; Stone Cups at	52
Khasia Hills, Bengal, Pillar Stones	133
Khotubs at Delhi and Pubna	38
Kildare, Hole Stone at, 62; Pillar Tower	210
Kilhouslan, Hole Stone at	66
Killeany Village, Cyclopean Building at	75
Killiecrankie, 244; Pass, 216; Chapel	217
Killon of Cadboll, Cross at	236
Kilmakedar, Hole Stones at, 63; Circular Stone Houses at	248
Kilmalkedar, Kerry	248
Kincoldrum, Church of	220
Kinneller, Rock Basins at, 61; Stone Circle	169
Kintore, Castle Hill of	42
Kirk, origin of the word	174
Kirriemuir Rocking Stones	92
Kistvaens, or Stone Coffins	134
Kits Cotty House	136
Knockando, Morayshire	117
Knockfaril, Hill Fort at	27
Knock Farrel, Fort at	170
Krishna, The Man-God	121
Labacally, Ireland	137
Lagore, Lake of	13
Lackin, Circle at	43
Lake Dwellings	13
Lamas of Thibet	122, 163
Landmarks, common to many countries, 55; varieties	53
Language, as bearing on History of Migration	70
Lassa, Dorge carried to	166
Lâts, Inscriptions on	183
La Vendée, Pillar Stones at	207
Layard, on Egyptian Symbols	117
Lazarus, Raising of	233
Leader, Mr.	132
Leath Broch, Description of Cairn	124
Leucophibia	258
Lewis, Island of	46

	Page
Libarum, The	244
Lindores Stone, 117; Village	126
Lingard, Dr.	223
Lion, The Sacred	105, 190
Lises (Forts)	26
Loch-an-Eilan, Stathspey	13
Loch Muich, Inverness, Sculptured Cups at	58
Logan Stones	91
Logie Stone, Oghams on	72
Long Meg's Daughters	40
Looking-glass and Comb as Symbols	175
Lotus Flower	105, 196
Lough Curran, Fort at	23
Lough Fermanagh	76
Louis XVIII., Footmark of	69
Lowlands, Cultivation of the	17
Lucan, on Stone Forts	23
Lucian, on Britain	87
Luckea River	68
Lukes, Mr.	135
Lyons, Early Liturgy of	251
MacDara, St., Cyclopean Building at	76
Mackenzie, Colonel, on Monuments of Southern India	28
Maes Howe, Sepulchre at	47, 77
Mahadeva, Symbol of	183
Maharajah Runjeet Singh Cremated	131
Maharajah of Tipperah Cremated	130
Mahawelli-Ganga	66
Maiden Stone	217, 229, 236
Maido, Shield of St.	224
Major, John, Scotch Historian	70
Malcolm Canmore	6
Male and Female principle in various Religions	157
Maltese Cross, B.C. 880, a Sun Symbol	118
Man Cromlech, Orkney	137
Man of Hoy	65
Manx Runes	73
Marastin Stone, near Upsal	91
Marcellinus, Ammianus	1
Market Crosses	223
Mariaker Loch	137
Marsden Castle	27
Masimenus	202
Mason, on Rocking Stones	92
Mason marks in Round Towers	213
Mass-y-facroll	136
Max Müller, on Analogy of Languages	70
May-Day Festivals, 101; a survival of Sun Worship	99
McCarthy's Church	209

MM

INDEX.

	Page.
McSwin, Mr., on Oghams	72
Measures, Primitive	50
Meatæ had Husbandmen	17
Meigle, 113, 238; Cross at, 191, 222, 219, 224, 225, 226, 236; Burying Ground at, 229, 230; Sculptured Centaur, 189; Procession, 18, 242; Sidlaw Hills	172
Melitus, Abbot	234
Memorial Crosses	222, 229
Men-an-tol, Cornwall	65
Metempsychosis	130, 144
Metheglin	20
Merry Maiden's Circle, Stones at	62
Meru, Mount	42, 193
Mid-Summer Eve in the Highlands	101
Minar Monolith	32
Misger Round Tower	81
Mistletoe, The, 192; Qualities of	192
Mithra, the Sun	97
Mohammedan Tower of Victory	183
Mola mannaria and Molœ jumentoriœ	19
Mole-Arthur, Camp at	27
Monasterboice, Pillar Tower at, 210; Cross at	251
Monasteries in Thibet	180
Monkeys as Sacred Animals	185
Monoliths, Primitive, 28; Symbolical of Deity, 29, 31; used as Boundary Stones, 32; still Sacred in Hindustan, 31; Legal, 90; Sacred Stone among Druids, 31; Worship forbidden, 32; Christian, 207; in Arabia, 29; Asia, 28; Balcallo, 32; Bethel, 30; Brittany, 32; Minar, 32; Mizpeh, 30; Rath-na-Riogh, 33; Tudas	30
Monumental Stones at Delhi	38
Monuments, Common origin of the early	28
Moon Worship	94, 101
Morin, Banffshire, Horse at	114
Mortar for early Forts	24
Mountblow House, Cross at	236
Mount's Bay, Sun festival at	100
Mourning among the Celts	131
Mousa Broch	78
Mugdrum Cross of Lindores	228
Mummy of Joseph's wife	132
Mungo	258
Muts, Pyramidal Monuments	134
Mythology of the Sun and Moon	101
Nagpore, Serpent Worship at	105
Nahan, Rabbi	72
Naitan, King of the Picts	248
Na-Kie, a city of India	79
Narvia, Isle of Man	207

	Page.
Nature Worship	93
Nantes, Council of, on Monoliths	32
Neander	257
Neary, Rev. P., on Tempul Fingin	209
Nectan III., King of the Picts	211
Nennius, on Irish Belief	253
Nepaulese Tope	102
New Dailly, Ayrshire	33
New Grange, Mound at, 89, 138; Rock basin at	60
New South Wales, Ceremonies of Natives	47
Newton Stone, 110; Oghams on	72
Nicholson, Professor, on Landmarks	53
Nielgherry Hills, Monoliths	30
Nigg, Cross of	226, 236, 240
Ninian, St.	255, 258
Noah, a type of Christ	233
Norrie's Law, Fifeshire	4
Norwegians find Christian relics in Iceland	206
Novalis	104
Nubia, Sculptured Stones in	207
Oak Groves	192, 195
Obelisk, Symbol of rising Sun, 98; at Cadbole, 240; in Egypt, 34; in Pictland, 216; Grampians, 126; Rose Markie	220
Odin, Stones of	31, 65
O'Donoghue, Dr.	134
O'Donovan, Dr., on Coronation Stones	33
Œcumenical Council of Buddhists	160
Ogham writing, 69, 71, 72, 230; on Crosses, 204; at Golspie, 72, 226	
O'Halloran, on Ogham	72
Ohio. America, Fort in shape of a Serpent at	107
Olius Wormius	192
Olympus	88
Ormazd, good God of the Persians	97
Oratories in Ireland	76, 77
Ord, Old Man of the	65
Orientation of British Churches	248
Orkney	10
Orkneys, Cyclopean Buildings in	75
Orme's Head, 136; Rocking Stone	92
Ormuz	82
Osiris, a Sun-God	99
Osmond, Lord of Seez	23
Padie's Fair	255
Pagan Symbols of Deity, 207; allowed by Early Christians, 204, 238; Temples used as Churches	174
Palladius, 19, 205, 251, 254; his influence, 252; relics	255

	Page.
Pateræ, or Stone Cups	20
Patrick, St., 252, 253; often mistaken for Palladius	254
Pancha Pandawars, Stone Circles	36
Paxton, Early Landmarks at	53
"Peel," a Landmark	53
Pedrolallagalla Mountain	66
Persecution of British Christians	202
Persian Religious Creed	97
Petit Mont, Brittany, footprints	69
Petrie, Dr., 23, 86, 211, 224; on Footprints	69
Peumachin Churchyard	230
Pentecostal Fire	103
Phallus	120
Phœnicians, The, 2; in Britain, 202, 219; Rocking Stones	91
Phœnix Park, Cromlech at	136
Pictavia, Buddhism in, 154; the Celtic, Buddhist, and Christian periods	257
Pictish Language	69
Pictland, Buddhist Symbols in, 155; Serpent Worship in	107
Picts, Kingdom of the, 200; and Scots	203
Pict's House, Forfarshire	56
Pierre Martina Rocking Stone	91
Pierres-Trandlantes, in Brittany	91
Pillar Stones, 133, 207; Joshua's	133
Pillar Towers, 74, 82; Three sorts of, 210; on Coins, 181; not Christian, 86; Christian, 209; in Asia, 80; Britain, 79; Bengal, 81; Brechin, 212; Canada, 82; erected by Buddhists, 180; Ireland, 83, 180, 209; list of, in Scotland and Ireland, 210, 211; Duncliff	249
Piper Stone, Cornwall	62
Pliny, 3; on Rocking Stones	91
Pœonia, Roumelia	14
Pope, The early Irish Christians rejected authority of	253
Pottery before the use of the wheel, 20; at Stonehenge	45
Pratt, Mr.	250
Prayer Crosses, 222, 225; wheels, 161, 163	
Preaching Crosses	222
Priest-bards	0
Pritchard, on the Alliance of Languages	70
Prithri, Sun-God	98
Prolek Stone	137
Pyramids of Egypt, 34, 35; Sepulchral	134
Pythagoras	143
Quern, 19, n. 18; in India, 19; still used in Orkney Islands	19

INDEX.

	Page.
Quodam-Resúl, Footprint of	68
Ra, Egyptian Sun-God ...	97
Radegundis, St., Poictiers	69
Rahat, Hole Stone at ...	62
Raidrogg	135
Rajputan Sacrifice of the Horse, 111; Round Towers ...	
Rajmal Hill Tribes were Sun Worshippers	81
Rama, assisted by Sacred Animals...	116
Ramadhan Fast... ... ..., ...	185
Rath-na-Riogh, Obelisk at	125
Raths (Forts)	33
Reeves, Dr.	26
Refuse Heaps	257
Reignald's Tower, Waterford	14
Rhind, Mr....	78
Ripon, Boundary Crosses at	10
Rites of Early Churches like those of Abyssinia	223
Ritual of Ancient Churches	249
Rock Basins	.47
Rock Edicts ː..	60
Rocking Stones 91, 92	184
Roger, Bishop of Wilton	23
Romanesque Character	73
Romans in Britain, 3, 200, 203; in Gaul, 252; opposed by Druids	200
Roscian Tower, in Ireland	85
Rose-Markie Obelisk 220, 236	
Rosnat	259
Rossie Priory, Cross at, 219, 236; Procession on ..	242
Rostellan, 136; Altar Stones at ...	91
Rothienorman, Aberdeenshire... ...	170
Round Towers, 77; Clonmacnois, 249; Danish in Ireland, 78; Persia, 81; Ormuz	82
Runes, 69, 71, 73; on Crosses, 221, used for Landmarks, 53; at Upsal	73
Ruthven, Forfarshire...	12
Sacred Persons 121, 122	
Sacred Places and Monuments, Celtic and Buddhist	179
Sabæism, 94, 100; Sun Worship ...	41
Sakyamuni, 145, 194; compared with Solomon, 147; a Sacred Person...	123
Sánchi Buddhist Temple	45
Sánchi Tope 109, 175, 194	
Sancried, Church of	116
Sangha, The 159, 160	
Sanscrit cognate, with Western Languages 70, 199	

	Page.
Sarum, Battle at, 22; Camp at, 27; Early History of...	22, 23
Samanæi, Philosophy of ...	144
Samuel's Stone, called Ebenezer 133, 183	
Scandinavians, Dress of, 4; fear of Death	128
Scilly Isles, Hole Stones in ...	66
Score or Tally	49
Scotch Thane	6
Scouring of the White Horse	112
Scythians, 2; migrations	30
Searobyrus (Sarum) ...	22
Seeling, Galway, Towers at ...	84
Seneca, on Tree Worship	195
Serpent Worship, 94, 105, 106, 108; Sun Worship, 106; on Egyptian Monuments, 244; Serpent guarding Buddha, 105, 109; in Britain, 106; in Brittany, 208; in Pictland, 110; still prevalent in India	110
Sepulchral Monuments, 133; Monoliths	116
Severus	17
Seydes, Hindu Serpent ...	106
Sharjah, Round Tower at	83
Shandwick Stone ...	234
Shelgram, The 59, 60	
Shelldrake, a Sacred Bird	191
Shells, Sacred univalves	59
Siculus Diodorus ...	1, 9
Sidlaw, Celtic Fort at, 18; Sculpture at	172
Simpson, Sir J. Y., 58; on "Cups"	50
Sinai, Desert of, Stones in ...	52
Singar (Lion) the Sacred	105
Siva, Character of, 120; Dorge in Temple of, 166; Serpents on neck of, 109; Symbol of...	117
Skelligs, The	248
Sligo, Island of	64
Slings of the Caledonians..	22
Smith, Captain, on Round Towers...	80
Snago Altar Stones, 57; Circle ...	40
Snake Stones	62
Solsticial Points shown by Boulders	125
Somersby, Cross at ...	243
Sorberdunumburgh (Sarum) ...	23
Somme, Valley of the	22
Soul, Immortality of...	129
Sow and Boar Worship	190
Spalding Club, 54; List of Sculptured Stones	176
Spectacle Ornament, 161, 166, 170, 171, 218	
Spenser on Footprints	69
Sphinxes	47
Sri-pada Footprints	66

	Page.
Saint: Acheul, early Remains at. 22; Andrews Cathedral, 229, Cross, 236, Old Chapel, 220; Benignus in Arran, 75; Brendan, 97; Brière Saire, 108; Boniface, 112; Colman, 182; Colomb, Stone of, 69; Columba, 109, 236, Cross, 218; George and Dragon, 110, 106; John's Disciples in Caledonia, 201; Kelone, Round Tower, 209; Mac Dara, Cyclopean Building at, 76; Maido, 224; Mary's Island, Hole Stone at, 66; Michael, 109; Michael's Mount, 89; Orland, 218; Patrick, 69, 85, 205, Cross of, 64, Rock Basin, 60; Radegundis, 69; Serf, 258; Skeoch, 248; Suchnel, 253; Ternan, 256, 258; List of Early Scottish, 258; Vigean's Cross... ... ... 229, 240	
Stephens, Mr., on Cup Marks... ...	59
Stacy, Colonel	82
Stag, Emblematical of Resurrection	190
Stanley, Sir J., King of "Man" ...	89
Stars are the Souls of the Dead ...	128
Star Worship	102
Stennis, 40, 65; Circle of Stones 38, 47	
Stewart, Dr., on Sepulchral Stones...	38
Stone Coffins 134, 230	
Stone Forts...	23
Stone Sculptures, the Chronology of	249
Stonehenge, 37, 40, 43, 44, 45, 46; a Legal Monument	90
Strabo, 10, 11, 16, 19; on Early Britons	1
Strathardle Rocking Stone, 92; Circles, n.... ...	26
Strathmore, Roman Camps in... ...	18
Strathmore, Earl of	218
Strathpeffer Sculptured Stone... ...	170
Stukely, Dr., on Avebury... ...	108
Stump Crosses	223
Stuart, Dr.	130
Sulpicius Severus	203
Suetonius Paulinus	174
Sun Worship, 88, 94, 124. 125; in Caledonia, 123; on Christmas Eve, 100; still extant in Britain, 100; Nature and Cause, 96, 97; Symbols of, 37, 116; Degeneration of	98
Sneen Rocking Stone ...	92
Swan, Sacred	191
Swastika, a Mystic Cross... ... 50, 118	
Swiss Lake Dwellings	13
Sykes, Colonel	117
Tacitus, 2, 9, 11; mentions Horse Sacrifice, 111; on Early Britons	1
Tacoor, The God	116
Tartary, Buddhism in	149

INDEX.

	Page.
Tasse, a Drinking Cup	20
Tatooing, used by Britons	3
Tau, The Mystical	117, 118
Tempul Fingin	209
Tertullian, 204; on Crosses	223, 257
Tent Hill of the Celts	31
Tempster, The	5
Thales, Philosopher	104
Thane, The	6
Theodorius, Emperor	215
Thibet, Monasteries in	180
Thom, Mr., on the White Horse	112
Thomson, Alexander, of Braemar	54
Thoth, First Worshipper of the Serpent	106
Three-Rock Mountain, Cornwall, Rock-basins at	61
Thurman, Dr., on Stonehenge	45
Thurso Obelisk	176
Timahoe, Pillar Tower at	210
Ti-mohr, Representation of	59
Toledo, Council of	251
Tonsure, The, 252; of SS. John and Peter	251
Tot Hill of the Celts	31
Tottenhoe, a Fort in Bedfordshire	23
Towers of Silence, Exposure of Dead Bodies on	133
Towety, Cornwall, Hole Stone at	61
Trade between Gaul and Britain, 18; in Caledonia	17
Transmigration of Souls, 130; Six Grades of	165
Trees considered Sacred, 191; worshipped in France, 195; in Caledonia, 189; in Africa	195
Triad, The, 105, 161; in Buddhism, 156; Mundane, 175; Earth, Fire, and Water	98
Triangle Symbolical of Deity	243
Trimutri (see Triad)	98

	Page.
Trinity, Doctrine of the	158
Trusty Hill, Sculptured Stone on	177
Try-glyphs on Buddhist Coins	227
Tudas, Religion of, 31; Monoliths	30
Tull Stone	65
Tum, Egyptian God	98
Tumuli, 138, 139; at Westminster	140
Turmursery, Pillar Tower of	86
Turin, Forfarshire, Sculptured Cups at	51
Tynwald Hill, Isle of Man	89
Typhon	106
Tyres, River in Scythia	69
Urns, Varieties of, 140; Celtic	21
Upsal, Runes at	73
Vajrapani, or Indra	156
Valencia, Lord, on Pillar Towers	80
Vallancy, General	59
Vassariddi, Rajah, Stone Circles	36
Vesica Piscis	191
Vestments, Early Church	251
Vétal, an Indian Demon, 93; Stone Circles dedicated to	36
Vigean's, St., Cross of	229, 240
Vishnu-pad, 66; the Sun-God, 120; as a Fish, 191; Sacred Shell, 59; Lotus Flower, 196; Symbolical Boar	190
Vitrification of Stone Forts	24
Vitruvius	19
Wakeman, Mr., on a Pagan Cemetery	58
Wantage, Horse marked on the Chalk Downs	112
Ward, Mr.	111
Water, Ancient Conception of, 104; an Object of Worship	105
Watermills introduced by the Romans	19
Waterville in Kerry, Fort at	22

	Page.
Watt, Mr., Stones in his Garden	42
Wattle-work originated the Interlaced Ornaments	235
Wales, a Retreat for the Druids	200
Wayland Smith's Cave	113
Weapons, Celtic	21, 22
Weems, Dwelling-places	10
Westbury, Horse marked on Downs	112
Wharncliffe, Lord, and Keilor Stone	172
Wheel and Circle Symbolical of Divine Protection, 244; with Triad, 163; Wheel-Money, 244; of Transmigration, 161, 164; Buddhist, 162; Symbolic Meaning	117
White Bulls honoured by the Celts	189
White Horse of Kent	112
Wideford Hill, Cyclopean Building at	75
Widshanagra, Serpent Worship at	105
William the Lion	55
Williams, Rev. J., on Oghams	72
Wilde, Sir Wm.	13
Wilfrid, Anglo-Saxon Bishop	248
William I.	23
Wilson, Dr.	223
Wilton, Bishopric of	23
Wishart, George	255
Wittenham Hills, Camp at	27
Wodin, Feast Day of	112
"Woman's Stone," Cornwall	61
Writing Developed from Symbols	49
Vermon, or Lands of the Cross	228
Yoni as a Sacred Symbol	65
Yucatan	10
Yule, General, on Indian Monuments	28
Yule Log	100
Zoroaster	88, 99

BLADES, EAST AND BLADES, PRINTERS, 23, ABCHURCH LANE, LONDON, E.C.

CORRECTIONS AND ADDITIONS.

PREFACE.

In 1st par. l. 9, omit *the circles of.*
To Note (1) add *of the Magi in Western Europe.*

GENERAL INTRODUCTION.

Page vii, par. 2 l. 6, for *Burnoup* read *Burnouf.*
Page xvi, omit in Note (1) *Tacitus agrees,* 811.

BOOK I.

Page 38, l. 24, for *Gonnar* read *Gour.*
Chap. IV, p. 52, *Salagrama* (See also p. 60, l. 11, for same).
Chap. V, p 74, par. *(a)* l. 6, for *Duncinnan* read *Dunsinnan.*
Page 81, par. 2 l. 4, for *Guetris* read *Guebre.*
Page 84, par. 2 l. 1, for *pagan* read *Buddhist.*
Page 85, par. 2 l. 6, for *St. Paulimus* read *St. Paulinus.*
Page 112, par. 2 l. 5, for *Danes* read *Saxons.*
Chap. VIII, p. 118 l. 7, for *to* read *of.*
Page 122, par. 2 l. 2, read of a given spiritual *idea.*
Chap. IX, p. 136, par. 2, l. 1, *Llanduno* read *Llandudno.*

BOOK II.

Chap. I, p. 155, par. 2 l. 5, *Kineller* read *Kinellar.*
Page 176, in table, for *Inveravan* read *Inveravon,* and for *Eddeston* read *Edderton,* and for *Bulluthorn* read *Ballutheron,* and for *Criche* read *Crichie,* and for *Kineller* read *Kinellar.*
Chap. V, p. 186, par. 1 l. 2, for *lineal* read *linear.*
Page 187, par. 2 l. 9, *natural* read *natural than.*
Page 188 Note (2), add, *see Frontispiece to Chap. V p. 238.*
Page 192, par. 3 l. 1, for *Olius* read *Olaus.*
Page 192, Note (6), for *Monumentarium Dannorum,* read *Danica Monumenta.*

BOOK III.

Page 200, par. 1 l. 8, for *Cornvealas* read *Cornuailles.*
Page 201, par. 1 l. 6, for *Kashmcn* read *Kashmir.*
Page 201, Note (2), for *Lingaid's* read *Lingard's.*
Page 203, Note (1). for *with* read *into* Caledonia.

Chap. I, p. 207, par. 1 l. 5, for *St. Fichin's* read *St. Fichin.*
Page 209, par. 1 l. 1, for *Clonmason* read *Clonmacnois.*
Page 212, Note (5), for *Eusebuis'* read *Eusebius.*

Chap. II, p. 220, par. 3 l. 6, for *Glenfurness* read *Glenferness.*
Page 221, last par., for *Dant* read *Gaut.*
Page 223, l. 11, for *Hixhon* read *Hexham.*
Page 223, par. 2 l. 1, omit *Dupplin.*

Chap. IV, p. 235, par. 2 l. 11, for *Arcliffe* read *Aycliffe.*
Page 236, par. 2 l. 4, for *Killon* read *Hilton.*

Chap. V, p. 238, l. 1, for *Cadbolt* read *Cadboll.*
Page 240, par. 3 l. 1, for *Cadbole* read *Cadboll.*
Page 241, par. 1 l. 14, for *St. Vigean's* read *St. Vigeans,* and the same in following par.
Page 244, par. 3 l. 4, *Libarum* read *Labarum.*

Chap. VI, p. 251, par. 3 l. 5, for *St. Vigean's* read *St. Vigeans.*
Page 258, Note (1), read: *There are no remains but a ruined wall, which had formed part of the Abbey.* The remainder of the Note should be omitted.
Page 258, p. 9, to (A.D. 521–563), add: *The ruins of the enlarged and beautiful church of Iona, with the graceful crosses and tombs of kings and great men, still remain.*

INDEX.

Page xxxii, for *Clonmason* read *Clonmacnois.*
Page xxxiii, for *Cornvealas* read *Cornuailles;* for *Duplin* read *Canna;* for *Hixon* read *Hexham;* for *St. Vigean* read *St. Vigeans;* in the third column read *Dunsinnan.*
Page xxxiv, for *Dupplin* read *Canna;* for *Cadbolt* read *Cadboll.*
Page xxxv, for *Libarum* read *Labarum.*
Page xxxvi, for *Killon* read *Hilton.*

Made in the USA
Middletown, DE
13 November 2023